Sustainability, Growth and Innovations

Muhammed Veysel Kaya and Haşim Özüdoğru (eds.)

Sustainability, Growth and Innovations

Future Perspectives of Economics, Business and Education

PETER LANG
Berlin · Bruxelles · Chennai · Lausanne · New York · Oxford

Bibliographic Information published by the Deutsche Nationalbibliothek
The Deutsche Nationalbibliothek lists this publication in the Deutsche Nationalbibliografie; detailed bibliographic data is available online at http://dnb.d-nb.de.

Library of Congress Cataloging-in-Publication Data
A CIP catalog record for this book has been applied for at the Library of Congress.

ISBN 978-3-631-94151-5 (Print)
ISBN 978-3-631-94058-7 (E-PDF)
ISBN 978-3-631-94881-1 (E-PUB)
DOI 10.3726/b23104

Published by Peter Lang GmbH, Berlin (Germany)

info@peterlang.com

This publication has been peer reviewed.

www.peterlang.com

Table of Contents

List of Figures and Graphs

List of Tables

Foreword

In the face of accelerating global challenges – climate change, technological disruption and shifting economic paradigms – the need for sustainable, inclusive and innovation-driven development has never been more urgent. *Sustainability, Growth and Innovations: Future Perspectives of Economics, Business and Education* presents a timely and insightful exploration of how these critical dimensions intersect to shape the future.

This volume brings together diverse perspectives that address the evolving role of economics, business and education in driving sustainable progress. Through thoughtful analysis and forward-looking approaches, the contributors examine how innovation can serve as a catalyst for equitable growth, how businesses can integrate sustainability into core strategies, and how education systems must adapt to prepare responsible leaders and problem-solvers.

What sets this work apart is its interdisciplinary lens – recognising that real solutions require collaboration across sectors and the reimagining of traditional models. It highlights the importance of long-term thinking, ethical frameworks and adaptive systems capable of responding to complexity and uncertainty.

Whether you are a researcher, policymaker, educator or practitioner, this book offers both a compelling vision and practical insights. It encourages us to think beyond immediate gains and to consider how today's decisions will shape the world we leave for future generations.

It is both a reflection of where we are and a guide to where we must go.

Muhammed Veysel Kaya and Haşim Özüdoğru

Pedagogical Approaches to Education for Sustainable Development

Isabela-Anda Dragomir and Brânduşa-Oana Niculescu

1.1. Introduction

The escalating environmental crises and social inequities of the twenty-first century necessitate a profound transformation at all society levels. Within the contemporary academic context, sustainability is recognised as a key concept, attracting the attention of educators and researchers from a wide array of disciplines. The concept of sustainability pivots on wide-ranging inter- and trans-disciplinary interactions with a variety of topics that are relevant to both the public and private sectors, including, but not limited to resilience, digital transformation, stakeholder ecosystems, adaptive governance dynamic capabilities, performance management, leadership and higher education (Gorski et al., 2023).

In his context, Education for Sustainable Development (ESD) has emerged as a pressing global imperative, necessitating a shift in educational practices to equip learners with the skills and mindset essential for addressing complex environmental, economic and social challenges. Traditional educational practices, often confined within disciplinary silos and characterised by passive knowledge transmission, have often proven insufficient for this task. ESD transcends traditional educational boundaries, emphasising holistic, interdisciplinary approaches that foster critical thinking, collaborative problem-solving and active citizenship. This chapter examines three significant pedagogical strategies that can advance ESD: interdisciplinarity and transdisciplinary teaching methods, problem-based learning (PBL) and project-based learning (PjBL) and critical pedagogy combined with transformative learning. By examining these approaches, we aim to elucidate how they collectively contribute to a comprehensive educational strategy for sustainability.

1.2 Interdisciplinarity and Transdisciplinarity as Teaching Methods

In recent years, the call to educational systems to adapt to the complex challenges raised by sustainable development has won substantial impulse. Traditional teaching methods often fall short in equipping students with the relevant skills and knowledge necessary to address these problems. As a result, interdisciplinary and transdisciplinary teaching methods have emerged as crucial approaches to advance ESD. These methods emphasise the collaboration, integration and strategies of problem solving of the real world, promoting a proper environment, tailored for the multifaceted nature of sustainability.

Sustainability challenges are inherently complex and interconnected, requiring an integrated approach that transcends disciplinary boundaries (Lang et al., 2012). Interdisciplinary and transdisciplinary teaching methods facilitate a holistic understanding of sustainability by integrating knowledge from diverse disciplines and engaging with stakeholders from various sectors (Jahn et al., 2012).

Interdisciplinarity in education refers to the integration of knowledge and methodologies from various disciplines to address complex issues. In the context of ESD, interdisciplinary approaches facilitate a comprehensive understanding of sustainability challenges by encouraging learners to draw insights from environmental science, social sciences, economics and humanities. This integration helps students see the interconnectedness of various factors that contribute to sustainability challenges, such as climate change, resource depletion and social inequality.

The rationale behind interdisciplinary teaching is the acknowledgement that sustainability issues are inherently multifaceted. For example, addressing climate change requires not only scientific understanding of the greenhouse effect and atmospheric processes but also consideration of economic implications, social justice and ethical dimensions. An interdisciplinary approach enables students to appreciate these interconnections and develop a holistic view of sustainability.

Interdisciplinary teaching methods can take various forms, including team teaching, integrated curricula and collaborative projects. Team teaching involves educators from different disciplines co-designing and co-delivering courses, allowing students to see how various fields intersect. For instance, a course on sustainable urban development might include contributions from urban planners, environmental scientists and sociologists, offering students a richer, more nuanced understanding of the challenges and solutions in urban sustainability.

Integrated curricula are another effective method, where subjects are linked around a central theme. An example might be a curriculum that examines water resource management, weaving together science (hydrology), social studies (water rights and governance) and economics (cost–benefit analysis of water use). This approach not only engages students but also encourages them to think critically about the implications of their learning.

While interdisciplinary teaching offers many benefits, it is not without challenges. One significant hurdle is the institutional structure of academic programmes, which often prioritise disciplinary silos over interdisciplinary collaboration. Faculty may lack the training or incentives to work across disciplines, leading to resistance to interdisciplinary initiatives. Additionally, assessment and evaluation methods in education are typically designed for single-discipline courses, making it challenging to measure student learning outcomes in interdisciplinary settings. Educators must develop innovative assessment strategies that reflect the collaborative nature of interdisciplinary work while ensuring academic rigour.

Transdisciplinarity extends the concept of interdisciplinarity and goes beyond academia by involving non-academic stakeholders from outside, including community members and industry experts, in the learning process (Pohl & Hirsch Hadorn, 2007). This collaboration enriches the educational experience, as it allows students to engage with real-world problems and apply theoretical knowledge in practical settings.

The transdisciplinary framework emphasises the importance of co-creation of knowledge, where academic and non-academic actors work together to identify problems, design solutions and implement actions. Transdisciplinary teaching methods often involve PjBL, where students engage with real-world problems in collaboration with external stakeholders. For instance, a group of students might partner with a local government to address urban heat islands by developing a green infrastructure plan that includes community input. This project would require students to apply their academic knowledge while actively engaging with community members, fostering a sense of ownership and responsibility.

Another effective method is service learning, which combines academic coursework with community service. In a service-learning project focused on sustainability, students might work with local NGOs to promote environmental awareness or assist in conservation efforts. This experiential learning not only enhances students' understanding of sustainability issues but also develops their skills in teamwork, communication and community engagement.

Transdisciplinary approaches also encourage critical reflection, as students must navigate the complexities of working with diverse stakeholders who may have differing priorities and perspectives. This reflection helps students develop the ability to engage in constructive dialogue and negotiation, essential skills for addressing sustainability challenges in a collaborative manner.

Research indicates that interdisciplinary and transdisciplinary teaching methods enhance critical thinking and problem-solving skills, essential competencies for addressing sustainability challenges. Furthermore, these approaches promote collaborative learning environments where diverse perspectives enrich the educational experience. Effective collaboration cultivates critical thinking skills and improves students' ability to communicate and work on various teams, necessary skills for any future professional environment (Budwig & Alexander, 2020). By fostering a culture of inquiry and cooperation, educators can prepare students to tackle the multifaceted nature of sustainability. In addition, collaborative efforts facilitate the integration of theoretical knowledge with practical applications. This experimental learning component is vital to promote an understanding of sustainability as a dynamic process instead of a static concept. Experience-based learning is aligned with the objectives of transdisciplinary education, emphasising the importance of interaction between the academy and broader social contexts. Salite et al. (2016) advocate an action research strategy that underlines the importance of community participation in continuing education programmes, demonstrating the capacity of transdisciplinary education to create genuine learning experiences that lead to sustainable action.

These approaches enhance student engagement and motivation. When students see the relevance of their studies to real-world problems, they are more likely to be invested in their learning. The opportunity to work on meaningful projects that have a tangible impact reinforces the importance of their education and empowers them to become active participants in creating a sustainable future.

However, a significant challenge of these two approaches lies in the evaluation in the context of ESD. Traditional evaluation metrics often do not reach the depth of understanding and development of collaborative skills inherent in these methodologies. Mokski et al. (2023) suggest the need for innovative evaluation strategies that are aligned with the objectives of interdisciplinary education, encouraging educators to develop metrics that precisely reflect the participation of students and competencies within the collaborative contexts of the real world.

To truly affect change, educational institutions must also prioritise the professional development of the educators themselves. This development is essential to equip instructors with the knowledge and tools necessary to effectively implement interdisciplinary and transdisciplinary methods. The beginning of training programmes dedicated to understanding sustainability and promoting collaboration would strengthen the capacities of educators to design courses that resonate with the ESD principles (Annan-Diab & Molinari, 2017).

Furthermore, the integration of global sustainability objectives in the development of the curriculum serves as an important framework to guide interdisciplinary and transdisciplinary efforts. In this context, the Sustainable Development Goals (SDGs) provide a cohesive structure within which educators can align their curricula while promoting collaboration and critical thinking (Biberhofer & Rammel, 2017). By using the SDGs as a foundation, higher education institutions can better prepare students to participate and contribute to sustainable development efforts at the local and global scale.

By and large, interdisciplinary and transdisciplinary teaching methods represent powerful pedagogical approaches in the context of ESD. By integrating knowledge across disciplines and engaging with external stakeholders, educators can foster a holistic understanding of sustainability challenges and empower students to develop innovative solutions. Despite the challenges associated with these methods, the benefits of promoting critical thinking, collaboration and real-world engagement make them essential components of effective ESD. As the urgency for sustainable solutions intensifies, the commitment to interdisciplinary and transdisciplinary teaching will be vital in preparing future generations to navigate and address the complexities of a sustainable society.

1.3. Problem-Based and Project-Based Learning for Sustainability

The imperative for ESD arises from the escalating complexity and interconnectedness of global sustainability challenges. Traditional didactic pedagogical approaches, characterised by passive knowledge absorption, prove inadequate in equipping learners with the capacity to navigate and address these multifaceted issues. PBL and PjBL offer transformative alternatives, fostering active engagement and experiential learning. These methodologies immerse learners in authentic sustainability challenges, promoting deep conceptual understanding, practical skill development and the cultivation of critical competencies necessary for driving meaningful change. This section of the chapter aims to provide a detailed exploration of the application of PBL and PjBL in sustainability education, highlighting their pedagogical advantages and practical implications.

Problem-based learning is a student-centred pedagogical approach that pivots on the exploration of ill-structured, real-world problems. In the realm of sustainability, these problems often encompass complex, interdisciplinary issues such as climate change mitigation, sustainable resource management or the restoration of degraded ecosystems. Unlike well-defined problems with singular solutions, ill-structured problems necessitate critical analysis, collaborative inquiry and the integration of diverse knowledge domains. The PBL process commences with learners analysing the problem scenario, identifying key issues and delineating the scope of their investigation. This initial phase demands that learners recognise their existing knowledge base and pinpoint knowledge gaps that necessitate further research and exploration. Through collaborative analysis, synthesis and iterative problem-solving, learners propose, evaluate and refine potential solutions. This process fosters the development of critical thinking, analytical reasoning and collaborative skills, empowering learners to apply theoretical knowledge to practical, contextually relevant situations. By grappling with the complexities of sustainability challenges, learners develop a nuanced understanding of their root causes and potential pathways to resolution.

Project-based learning builds upon the foundational principles of PBL by requiring learners to create a tangible product or outcome that directly addresses a sustainability challenge. This can encompass a wide range of outputs, including the design and implementation of sustainable technologies, the development of community-based sustainability initiatives or the creation of educational campaigns aimed at promoting sustainable behaviours. Unlike PBL, which may culminate in a theoretical solution or a report, PjBL demands the creation of a concrete, demonstrable output that showcases learners' understanding and practical skills. Projects typically unfold over an extended period, allowing for in-depth investigation, iterative design and the application of acquired knowledge to real-world contexts. Learners engage in extended inquiry, conducting thorough research, gathering data and applying their findings to the development and refinement of their project. By grounding projects in authentic, real-world contexts, PjBL enhances the relevance and impact of learning, fostering innovation, creativity and the ability to translate conceptual knowledge into actionable solutions.

The incorporation of PBL and PjBL in sustainability education encourages students to actively participate in the problem-solving process. This requires students to identify, analyse and propose sustainable solutions to genuine ecological problems, thus improving their critical thinking abilities.

In summary, both PBL and PjBL share fundamental characteristics that contribute to their efficacy in sustainability education. PBL and PjBL provide experiential learning opportunities that immerse learners in real-world sustainability challenges (Hmelo-Silver, 2004). They emphasise the importance of authentic contexts, anchoring learning in real-world problems and projects that resonate with learners' lives and communities. This contextual relevance enhances learner engagement, motivation and the development of a deeper understanding of complex sustainability issues. Collaborative learning is another pivotal component, fostering teamwork, communication and the exchange of diverse perspectives. Learners are encouraged to share ideas, build upon each other's knowledge and develop the capacity to work effectively in diverse teams. Furthermore, both methods promote active learning, demanding that learners actively participate in the educational process. This active engagement cultivates critical thinking, problem-solving, decision-making and reflective skills, empowering learners to become agents of change. By immersing learners in practical challenges and fostering a profound understanding of complex issues, PBL and PjBL cultivate a comprehensive suite of sustainability competencies, including systems thinking, critical thinking, collaboration, communication and ethical reasoning.

While PBL and PjBL offer significant educational benefits, their implementation in sustainability education is not without challenges. One of the primary obstacles is the need for educators to shift from traditional roles as knowledge transmitters to facilitators of learning. This requires a rethinking of curriculum design and assessment methods to accommodate the dynamic and often unpredictable nature of problem-based and PjBL. Additionally, sustainability education demands an interdisciplinary approach, necessitating collaboration across different academic disciplines and the integration of diverse knowledge systems. This can be challenging in educational institutions that are structured around rigid disciplinary boundaries.

Additionally, the successful implementation of PBL and PjBL requires institutional support, including professional development opportunities for educators and the allocation of resources to support collaborative and interdisciplinary projects. Institutions must also foster partnerships with external stakeholders, such as local communities, businesses and governmental organisations, to provide students with access to real-world problems and contexts. These partnerships can enhance the relevance and impact of student projects, while also contributing valuable insights and resources to the educational process.

In conclusion, PBL and PjBL are indispensable pedagogical approaches for sustainability education. Through their strategic implementation, educators can empower learners to become informed, engaged and effective participants in the pursuit of a just and sustainable world, moving beyond the mere acquisition of knowledge to the development of the transformative competencies needed to address the complex challenges of our time. Collaborative commitments, practical applications and an approach to real-world impacts are strategies that can better equip students with the tools and skills necessary to address the pressing challenges of sustainable development. As educational institutions continue to integrate PBL and PJBL approaches, they will forge a generation of innovative thinkers and responsible citizens equipped to lead a sustainable change in their communities and beyond.

1.4. Critical Pedagogy and Transformative Learning for Sustainability

The escalating environmental crises and persistent social inequalities underscore the urgent need for transformative approaches to sustainability education. Traditional pedagogies often fail to address the root causes of unsustainability, focusing primarily on technical solutions rather than systemic change. This section argues that critical pedagogy and transformative learning offer complementary and powerful frameworks for equipping learners with the critical thinking, ethical awareness and agency necessary to address complex sustainability challenges.

Critical pedagogy, rooted in the work of Freire (1970), emphasises the idea that education should not only impart knowledge but also empower students to challenge social injustices and advocate for change. It encourages learners to reflect on their own experiences and consider how their actions impact the world around them, emphasising the importance of social justice, equity and empowerment in education. This approach promotes a critical examination of societal structures and their role in the act of sustainability.

Transformative learning, a concept developed by Jack Mezirow (2000), involves a fundamental shift in perspective that enables individuals to view issues through a new lens. In the context of ESD, transformative learning encourages students to reflect on their values, beliefs and assumptions about sustainability and their role in the world. This reflective process is crucial for developing a deeper understanding of sustainability issues and for inspiring proactive engagement.

For instance, a course that integrates critical pedagogy and transformative learning might encourage students to explore the ethical implications of consumerism and its impact on the environment. Through dialogue, reflection and collaborative learning, students can develop a more nuanced understanding of their agency in promoting sustainable practices.

Research indicates that critical pedagogy and transformative learning can lead to higher levels of engagement, motivation and a greater commitment to sustainability. By fostering a critical perspective and encouraging transformative experiences, educators can cultivate a generation of learners who are not only knowledgeable about sustainability but also passionate advocates for change.

The integration of critical pedagogy and transformative learning creates a powerful synergy for sustainability education. Critical pedagogy provides the analytical tools to deconstruct dominant ideologies and expose power imbalances, while transformative learning facilitates the deep reflection and perspective transformation necessary for meaningful change. As an illustration, while a critical pedagogical approach can be used to analyse the social and political factors that contribute to climate change, transformative learning can guide learners in reflecting on their own consumption patterns and developing a sense of responsibility for the planet. Also, critical pedagogy can expose the environmental injustices faced by marginalised communities, while transformative learning can empower learners to become advocates for environmental justice.

Singleton (2015) introduces the 'Head, Heart and Hands' model for transformative learning, which emphasises cognitive, emotional and physical engagement with sustainability. This model is closely aligned with the principles of critical pedagogy because it promotes a complete understanding of sustainability, which encompasses knowledge, empathy and action. Educators can implement this model by creating learning experiences that engage students in a holistic way, which allows them to critically analyse the problems of sustainability while promoting emotional connection and encouraging a proactive response. This is aligned with the principles of social justice because students recognise their individual and collective responsibilities to meet local and global challenges. In the same vein, a systematic literature review led by Rodríguez Aboytes and Barth (2020) shows that transformative learning in the context of sustainability engages learners at intellectual, emotional and practical levels. The authors reveal that the transformative learning of sustainability cultivates the awareness of systemic injustices and ecological degradation, promoting a strong link between personal values and collective good. By integrating critical pedagogy into transformer learning, educational parameters can become deep change sites, equip learners with tools to challenge injustices and defend fair sustainable development.

The concept of transgressive social learning, as articulated by Lotz-Sisitka et al. (2015), also underlines the urgent need for reform of the light education of the global environmental challenges. This approach encourages learners to question the status quo and to engage in dialogues that promote social and ecological justice. Thanks to an educational objective that values critical engagement, learners can face and question the unsustainable practices that perpetuate environmental degradation and social inequalities. By positioning sustainability not only as a complementary module to existing programmes, but as a central principle of educational discourse, educators can cause a deep systemic change.

By discussing ecopedagogy, Misiaszek (2020) underlines the need for educators to teach critical literacy linked to development, sustainability and development. This perspective embodies the essence of the integration of critical pedagogy and transformative learning because students are encouraged to question existing paradigms while considering an alternative future. Commitment to critical literacy requires a process of reflection where learners evaluate their own positionality in these discourses. The creation of an educational climate that favours these reflections can lead to transformative learning experiences that not only improve academic results but also generate deeper commitments to sustainable practices.

Leite et al. (2022) underline the importance of curriculum practices that promote sustainability by transformative pedagogy. This integration calls innovative teaching strategies that not only disseminate knowledge but also inspire students to become defenders of change. By facilitating experiential learning opportunities, such as service-learning projects or community engagement initiatives, educators can help learners connect theoretical knowledge to real-world applications. Such approaches improve not only the relevance of education for sustainability but also allow learners to consider themselves active agents in promoting change, ultimately promoting the values of social justice and ecological responsibility.

In addition, Alam (2022) discusses the mapping of a lasting future through a transformative learning framework, presenting a conceptualisation which integrates critical reflection, ESD and responsible citizenship. This framework supports the affirmation that educational contexts should actively promote critical conscience, allowing students to examine the socio-ecological implications of their actions. By promoting a culture of critical reflection, educational establishments can encourage students to develop sustainable values that align with broader social justice initiatives, thus cultivating responsible and informed citizens.

Implementing these frameworks requires skilled educators who can create safe and supportive learning environments. However, assessing transformative learning can be complex, as it involves changes in perspectives and values that are not easily measured. Furthermore, the emotional demands of critical reflection and the confrontation of uncomfortable truths must be considered.

In summary, the integration of critical pedagogy and transformative learning offers an opportunity to advance sustainable practices and awareness in educational environments. By promoting critical commitment, by encouraging transformative experiences and promoting ecological responsibility, educators can maintain a generation of learners engaged in social justice and sustainability. Thanks to innovative study practices and a holistic educational approach, the potential for creating conscious and responsible citizens becomes not only possible but imperative to meet the complex challenges of our time. The integration of these educational frameworks promises to allow learners to implement a significant change while promoting a deeper consciousness of their role in the promotion of ecological and social well-being.

1.5. Conclusion

In synthesising the pedagogical approaches examined within this chapter, it becomes evident that each method offers unique contributions to the overarching goal of ESD. Interdisciplinary and transdisciplinary teaching methods provide a foundational framework for understanding the complexity of sustainability challenges by facilitating the integration of diverse academic disciplines and perspectives. By breaking down traditional disciplinary silos, these methods encourage learners to appreciate the interconnectedness of environmental, economic and social systems, thus preparing them for the collaborative efforts required to address sustainability challenges.

The exploration of problem-based and PjBL further underscores the importance of experiential and active learning strategies in ESD. These approaches engage students in real-world problems and projects that demand the application of theoretical knowledge to practical scenarios. By immersing learners in authentic sustainability challenges, PBL and PjBL cultivate essential skills such as teamwork, communication and project management, while also fostering a sense of agency and responsibility. The hands-on nature of these approaches not only enhances students' understanding of sustainability concepts but also empowers them to envision and implement innovative solutions, thereby bridging the gap between academic learning and real-world application.

Finally, the incorporation of critical pedagogy and transformative learning into ESD highlights the remarkable potential of education to foster social change. By challenging learners to question existing power structures and assumptions, these pedagogical approaches promote critical consciousness and encourage learners to become active participants in the pursuit of a more just and sustainable world. Transformative learning, in particular, emphasises the importance of perspective transformation, encouraging students to reflect on their values and beliefs and consider alternative viewpoints. Together, critical pedagogy and transformative learning cultivate a more engaged and ethically aware citizenry, capable of driving the systemic changes necessary for sustainability. Collectively, these pedagogical approaches underscore the potential of education to serve as a catalyst for sustainable development, equipping learners with the knowledge, skills and mindset required to navigate and contribute positively to an in-depth understanding of an increasingly complex and interconnected world.

In the long run, sustainability boils down to the promotion and maintenance of systemic changes in educational policies and practices that prioritise these pedagogical approaches. Educators and policymakers must collaborate to create curricula that reflect the interconnected nature of sustainability challenges, embrace experiential learning and foster critical thinking. The call to action is clear: adopting and scaling these pedagogical frameworks not only holds the potential to enhance educational outcomes but also plays a vital role in cultivating a more sustainable future. In doing so, we empower students to become informed, engaged and responsible citizens who actively contribute to the sustainability agenda on local, national and global levels.

The integration of these pedagogical approaches provides a robust framework for advancing ESD. By focusing on interdisciplinary and transdisciplinary teaching methods, PBL and PjBL, and critical pedagogy combined with transformative learning, educators can cultivate a generation of learners equipped to tackle the pressing sustainability challenges of our time. This holistic educational strategy not only enhances academic outcomes but also empowers students to become proactive stewards of the planet, fostering a culture of sustainability for future generations.

Bibliography

Alam, A. (2022). 'Mapping a Sustainable Future through Conceptualization of Transformative Learning Framework, Education for Sustainable Development, Critical Reflection, and Responsible Citizenship: An Exploration of Pedagogies for Twenty-First Century Learning'. *ECS Transactions* 107 (1), 9827–40.

Annan-Diab, F., and Molinari, C. (2017). 'Interdisciplinarity: Practical Approach to Advancing Education for Sustainability and for the Sustainable Development Goals'. *The International Journal of Management Education* 15 (2), 73–83.

Biberhofer, P., and Rammel, C. (2017). 'Transdisciplinary Learning and Teaching as Answers to Urban Sustainability Challenges'. *International Journal of Sustainability in Higher Education*, 18 (1), 63–83.

Budwig, N., and Alexander, A. J. (2020). 'A Transdisciplinary Approach to Student Learning and Development in University Settings'. *Frontiers in Psychology*, 11, 576250.

Freire, P. (1970). *Pedagogy of the Oppressed*. New York and London: Continuum.

Gorski, A.-T., Ranf, E.-D., Badea, D., Halmaghi, E.-E., and Gorski, H. (2023). 'Education for Sustainability – Some Bibliometric Insights', *Sustainability*, 15 (20), 1–17.

Hmelo-Silver, C. E. (2004). 'Problem-Based Learning: What and How Do Students Learn?'. *Educational Psychology Review*, 16 (3), 235–66.

Jahn, T., Bergmann, M., and Keil, F. (2012). 'Transdisciplinarity: Between Mainstreaming and Science-Policy Alienation. *Ecological Economics*, 79, 1–10.

Lang, D. J., Wiek A., Bergmann, M., Stauffacher, M., Martens, P., Moll, P., Swilling, M., and Thomas, C. J. (2012). 'Transdisciplinary Research in Sustainability Science: Practice, Principles, and Challenges'. *Sustainability Science*, 7 (1), 25–43.

Leite, C., Monteiro, A., Barros, R., and Ferreira, N. (2022). 'Curricular Practices Towards Sustainability and a Transformative Pedagogy'. *REICE. Revista Iberoamericana Sobre Calidad, Eficacia y Cambio en Educación*, 20 (4), 107–25.

Lotz-Sisitka, H., Wals, A. E., Kronlid, D., and McGarry, D. (2015). 'Transformative, Transgressive Social Learning: Rethinking Higher Education Pedagogy in Times of Systemic Global Dysfunction'. *Current Opinion in Environmental Sustainability*, 16, 73–80.

Mezirow, J. (2000). *Learning as Transformation: Critical Perspectives on a Theory in Progress* (1st edn). San Francisco, CA: Jossey-Bass Inc. Pub.

Misiaszek, G. W. (2020). 'Ecopedagogy: Teaching Critical Literacies of 'Development', 'Sustainability', and 'Sustainable Development''. *Teaching in Higher Education*, 25 (5), 615–32.

Mokski, E., Leal Filho, W., Sehnem, S., and Andrade Guerra, J. B. S. O. D. (2023). 'Education for Sustainable Development in Higher Education Institutions: An Approach for Effective Interdisciplinarity'. *International Journal of Sustainability in Higher Education*, 24 (1), 96–117.

Pohl, C., and Hirsch, Hadorn, G. (2007). *Principles of Designing Transdisciplinary Research*. München: Oekom Verlag.

Rodríguez Aboytes, J. G., and Barth, M. (2020). 'Transformative Learning in the Field of Sustainability: A Systematic Literature Review (1999–2019)'. *International Journal of Sustainability in Higher Education*, 21 (5), 993–1013.

Salīte, I., Drelinga, E., Iliško, D., Oļehnovič, E., and Zarina, S. (2016). 'Sustainability from the Transdisciplinary Perspective: An Action Research Strategy for Continuing Education Program Development'. *Journal of Teacher Education for Sustainability*, 18 (2), 135–52.

Singleton, J. (2015). 'Head, Heart and Hands Model for Transformative Learning: Place as Context for Changing Sustainability Values'. *The Journal of Sustainability Education*, 9, 1–16.

Innovation Attitudes and Propensity for Social Change within Generation Z in Bulgaria

Adelina Milanova and Pavlinka Naydenova

2.1. Introduction

The authors' view of innovation is based on the perception of economic actors at the organisational level as both carriers and creators of human capital in organisations. The implementation of innovations, the formation of innovation potential, and the management of the innovation process are considered in parallel, both as a reflection and a result of the manifestation of the characteristics and specificities of human capital.

The relationship between the generated potential for innovations and organisational culture is important and decisive for the functioning and management of a specific business structure and influences in a certain way the genesis and establishment of organisations, including in the innovation aspect.

An extremely important question is to what extent the basic organisational dimensions, relevant to the active, innovative thinking and behaviour, are comparable and relevant in the contemporary economic and social reality. The behaviour in this case is based on a corresponding value system such as leadership, responsibility, flexibility, entrepreneurship and adaptability.

In the discourse of socioeconomic anthropology – the format in which the authors conduct their research – these characteristics operate in the context of the attitudes and perception of what is considered 'new' or 'innovative'.

In this context, achieving sustainable or lasting innovative activity is feasible with good knowledge of cultural identity and the application of mechanisms to extract the characteristics that, given certain prerequisites, would allow for the creation of strategic competitive advantages.

Increasing attention is also paid to the relationship between innovation potential and innovative behaviour in the organisation (Grant & Berry, 2011). This notion is close to the authors' idea of positioning the problem in a socioanthropological discourse.

2.2. Specifics of the Bulgarian Innovation Profile

The authors' hypotheses are based on observed dynamics, both in terms of actual organisational changes (Milanova & Naydenova, 2017, 2023) and in terms of calculation changes in the indices of fundamental national cultural dimensions. These hypotheses have been tested, and the conclusions and potential trends are formulated based on the relative results of the studied units, along with a sufficient number of studies conducted over a short period. The dynamics of these trends should be monitored periodically.

Today, Bulgaria ranks 38th according to the 2023 Edition of the Global Innovation Index, published by the World Intellectual Property Organisation.

This index includes a dataset of eighty indicators from various sources – private, international and public. It covers 132 economies and reveals global innovation trends (Global Innovation Index, 2023).

The overall situation is as follows (the conclusions are based on an analysis of data from 2023, with no significant changes in the recently released data for 2024): Bulgaria ranks 28th in Infrastructure, 34th in Knowledge and Technology Results and Creative Results. At the same time, the country's ranking in Institutions, including institutional environment, regulatory environment and business environment, is not particularly satisfactory; Human capital and scientific research, including education, higher education, research and development (R&D) – 66th place; Market complexity, including credit /investment/, trade, diversification and market scale – 60th place; Business complexity, including education and knowledge of employees, innovation links and the process of knowledge acquisition – 42nd place, etc.

Previous studies that focused on various aspects of the manifestation of corporate culture in Bulgarian companies have found a relatively strong influence of national cultural dimensions on organisational cultural dimensions (Milanova, 2008; Milanova & Naydenova, 2013, 2017). Determining whether there is a dynamic shift in these findings, which has led to corresponding conclusions and recommendations – both organisational-cultural in particular and managerial in general – is one of the main tasks of this study, as these factors may influence some of the previously mentioned trends.

2.3. A New Horizon of Innovative Socioeconomic Anthropology – Generation Z

Considering the findings mentioned above, the team's research is focused on representatives of Generation Z engaged in various business units within the fields of employment, with the relatively highest employment of representatives of this generation, according to current statistical data.

This study involved 122 (one hundred twenty-two) respondents, representatives of Generation Z, who work within three main fields of employment: namely *information and communication technology specialists (66 persons), sales consultants (37 persons) and business and administrative specialists (19 persons)*, for whom the percentage of engagement is relatively highest for Sofia, according to National Institute of Statistics data (NSI, 2021 census).

The respondents from these three fields of employment are from ten business units, with four from the first, three from the second and three from the third field of employment. The study examines innovation attitudes and processes as they relate to the interdependence of national and organisational cultural dimensions. In the passportisation of the respondents, both institutionally and individually, their requested anonymity is fully respected. Specifically regarding the survey cards, the omission of certain characteristics of the relevant business unit does not render the card invalid. A new characteristic was added, which the team considers particularly important for clarifying certain perspectives regarding the respondents and/or expectations. This includes the addition of the parameters 'Education' and 'Place of obtaining the educational degree'.

To address current and relatively unexplored business processes related to the integration of Generation Z and its attitudes, the team decided to focus on its specific orientations, preferences and expectations regarding the innovation potential in business structures and the possibilities for its full deployment. The selection of this particular group is justified by the fact that it is a separate, specific social cohort that is already shaping new attitudes and expectations in modern corporate human capital.

The representatives of Gen Z are fighting for social change, racial equality and environmental protection. In a study by the Pew Research Center (Parker & Igielnik, 2020), approximately 70 per cent of Gen Z representatives believe that the government should take a more active role in addressing the issues. The term Gen Z encompasses people born between 1996 and 2010/12.

It is currently the second youngest generation, as the generation placed between two demographic cohorts, Generation Y, the millennials and Generation Alpha, those born after 2010. Gen Z's identity has been shaped by the digital age, climate concerns, the changing financial landscape and COVID-19. They are known as 'digital natives' – the first generation to grow up with the internet. Like any generation, Gen Z's behaviour is shaped by how they were raised.

A McKinsey study (McKinsey, 2024, What is Gen Z) highlights that specific large-scale events can significantly influence and shape the perspectives of a generation.

In general terms:

- Gen Z representatives dream of personal fulfillment in their careers, but they are deeply concerned about their mental health and the economic factors that could contribute to its decline.
- They have less positive life perspectives and have lower levels of emotional and social well-being than older generations.
- They are interested in their own way in belonging to an inclusive, supportive community.
- They are more individualistic, with a stronger sense of personal expression.
- They are at the same time politically and socially active, defending their beliefs on social media.

In principle, there is no striking difference between young people from Bulgaria and other countries when it comes to individualism, including responsibility and empathy for the community, pragmatism, creativity and good knowledge of new technologies. A specific case is the phenomenon known as 'delayed maturity', which refers to the postponement of the transition to adulthood. A relatively high proportion of representatives of Generation Z continue to live with their parents. With some of the parents of the Generation Z representatives working outside Bulgaria, and others engaged in providing for their livelihood, a significant part of the generation was raised by their parents' parents or by relatives. Changes in the traditional system of familial upbringing and school have an impact on the attitudes of the generation towards the events in their lives and the values related to work and success. A portion of the generation does not want to take on social responsibilities, tries to prolong the pleasure of life, refuses to think about family and career, and wants to try new and different things. Yet, representatives of this generation prefer not to hide from their problems but face them and resolve them by themselves. Generation Z is focused on the future, but at the same time, they are realists. The idealism inherent in older generations is not their characteristic feature. They tend to engage in public causes where they see meaning. Volunteering and a conscious desire to engage in such commitments play an increasingly important role. For them, affiliation means engaging in communities of shared interests, following social networks, and actively participating in environmental movements and volunteer initiatives.

A particularly significant insight about Generation Z is their attraction to the 'prestigious', reflecting the belief that if something is not new, modern or functional, it fails to engage, entertain or bring them joy. The majority believe that success in life primarily depends on 'personal qualities' and 'effort', while about a third attribute success to external factors such as 'events and circumstances', 'fate', 'luck' or 'other people' (based on analysis by BIA, 2020).

Generation Z is a serious challenge to management and motivational systems in enterprises, because they are the first generation that does not work for their basic sustenance but to improve and have fun. What motivates other generations does not work with the same force of impact on them. Like in electronic games, the representatives of Gen Z expect quick wins and rewards at work. It is noteworthy that the members of this new generation are representatives of a culture that differs from the typical cultural formats for our region. At the same time, this 'new' cultural matrix they are shaping reflects both a revivalist impulse and a rejection of certain aspects, particularly the negative encapsulations within our economic genotype.

2.4. Main Findings, Results and Discussion

In this study, there are no management staff among the surveyed employees, which is not surprising given their age. The ratio between men and women is balanced, and the team does not aim to establish correlations between gender and attitudes, according to the questions asked.

As we pointed out above, two important respondent passport components have been added, namely education and place of obtaining the educational degree, which we believe can help explain possible differences and specific answers /points of view/ that should be taken into account.

In the first field of employment, Information and Communication Technologies, a large proportion received their education in Bulgaria, at TU and SU, but twelve of them received their education at universities in the Netherlands (eight) and the United Kingdom (four). The universities are ranked relatively high. One respondent lived and studied in the USA, but received his high school and higher education in Bulgaria.

In the second field of employment, Sales consultants, all of the respondents completed their education in Bulgaria.

In the third field of employment, Business and administrative specialists, six respondents completed their higher education in foreign European universities, namely in France, Spain and the Netherlands and the remaining thirteen studied in Bulgaria. The universities are not highly ranked.

To the question *'Is hesitancy in innovation activity historically determined?'*, the representatives of the first field of employment predominantly answer with 'Innovation attitudes are radically modified and adapted to the modern world', with this answer selected by nearly 80 per cent of the respondents in that field. Compared to the total number of respondents, the percentage is 43 per cent.

The representatives from the second field of employment predominantly answer that *'Bulgaria's economic and historical development are decisive for the attitudes towards innovation'*, with this option chosen by 69 per cent of those interviewed in the field. Compared to the total number of respondents, the percentage is 20 per cent.

The representatives of the third field of employment select the options *'Innovations are accepted when endorsed by certain authorities'*, and *'Innovation potential develops when supported by the established authority within the relevant unit'*. The answers are close in meaning, fundamentally disregarding reasoning related to historicity and economic-historical determinism. These options are preferred by 83 per cent of the employees in the respective field. Compared to the total number of respondents, the percentage is 12 per cent.

To the questions *'Are innovation attitudes refracted through the dominant values? Does the innovation potential depend on the dominant moral and ideological ideas in the company?'*, the representatives of the first field of employment predominantly select option C, *'Innovation attitudes depend mainly on the degree of ambition and assertiveness'*. This option is selected by 75 per cent of the respondents, accounting for 40 per cent of the total number of all survey participants.

The representatives from the second field of employment predominantly respond with option D, *'Innovation attitudes can be strongly influenced by social problems'*. This option is chosen by 57 per cent of the field. Compared to the total number of respondents, the percentage is 17 per cent.

The representatives from the third field of employment predominantly respond with option A, *'Problems arise when asserting a position and/or imposing a certain innovative vision'*, which represents 91 per cent for the field of employment and 14 per cent of the total number of respondents.

The predominant answer to the question *'Is the implementation of innovation attitudes consistent with the threshold of tolerable stress?'*, is the option that 'Innovations being of interest in cultures that do involve leaving the comfort zone'. This is the preferred answer for the respondents from both the first and second fields of employment, respectively, 62 per cent and 57 per cent. Compared to the total number of respondents, the percentages are respectively 34 per cent and 17 per cent.

In the third field of employment, the option *'Innovation potential is an important factor for growth in all cultures and there is no reason to look for a specific connection with the different cultures'* prevails, representing 66 per cent of the field. Compared to the total number of respondents, the percentage is 11 per cent.

Among the questions in the survey card, the main focus is primarily on the specifics of the organisational culture within the respective business unit. The team's goal is to assess whether there is alignment or any deviations compared to the initial responses, particularly regarding innovation activity and the realisation of innovation potential. Notable differences are observed in the responses of representatives from the three main fields of employment, reflecting their assessment of organisational culture and how it compares to their expectations.

From the given data, several key conclusions can be drawn:

1. The representatives of the first field of employment do not pay particular attention to historical determinism and would rather accept the natural dynamics; a certain amount of optimism is observed.
2. The representatives of the second and the third fields of employment do not delve into this specific determination but have a greater degree of manifested feeling of some kind of doom.
3. No consistent correlation is found in the responses from the three fields that would allow for the inference of parametric subordination. Each question elicits a different combination of responses, resulting in both divergence and convergence in the attitudes and perspectives of respondents across the fields.
4. The representatives of the first field of employment want to work in a more efficient environment and strive to contribute to the creation of a more modern organisational culture. Yet, the processes in their work occur without conscious planning. These young people have adopted values that are more adequate to the desires and aspirations for innovation.
5. Although absolute statements cannot be made, it is notable that the most pronounced dominance in the context of the socioeconomic anthropology of innovation processes – specifically the dominance of national cultural dimensions – is observed in the third field of employment. This holds true despite the observed dynamics in key dimensions, such as individualism, where the index has increased from 30 to 50 (Hofstede, G.; The Culture Factor Group, 2024). This field is where we have observed the greatest proximity in terms of mentality and reactivity, as well as conclusions that are typical for previous studies by the team, in which the average age of respondents usually exceeds 30 years.
6. Regardless of the outlined differences among Generation Z representatives in Bulgaria and in other European countries, as well as in the USA, it is clear that this generation is increasingly asserting itself and defending its demands, positions and points of view.

2.5. Conclusion

In certain situations, the old mentality has become a real barrier. What remains true is that while millennials tend to address their problems in a more individual and fragmented manner, Generation Z is notably more assertive and proactive in advocating for themselves – all while maintaining heightened attention to their mental health.

At the same time, it is extremely important to examine the problems of the business organisation not only in their visible dimensions but also to delve deeper. The relevance of the presented research problem lies in the development and understanding of an important aspect of the broad-spectrum issues related to the cultural context of corporate management.

The idea that the authors support is that innovation potential and innovation capacity could be viewed as both a reflection and a result of the manifestation of the characteristics and specificities of the respective corporate human capital.

Business prejudices toward Gen Z suggest they are not particularly hard-working and lack a strong work ethic. In reality, their primary focus is on mental health, which also calls for a shift in the focus of the educational process.

Overall, Gen Z is seen as more oriented toward innovation and entrepreneurship, though these tendencies often reflect the broader effects of globalisation and the universalisation of generational traits. Ultimately, Generation Z is predisposed to an entrepreneurial mindset – proactive, with a strong desire for both personal and professional growth.

This combination makes the challenge for contemporary society even more pressing: to modernise and innovate the organisational and product environment in a dynamic and forward-thinking way.

Bibliography

Grant, A. M., and Berry, J. (2011). 'The Necessity of Others Is the Mother of Invention: Intrinsic and Prosocial Motivations, Perspective-Taking, and Creativity'. *Academy of Management Journal*, 54, 73–96. <https://doi.org/10.5465/>.

Global Innovation Index (2023). In Dutta, S., B. Lanvin, L. Rivera León, and S. Wunsch-Vincent (eds.), *Innovation in the Face of Uncertainty* (16th edn). Geneva: World Intellectual Property Organization. <https://www.wipo.int/edocs/pubdocs/en/wipo-pub-2000-2023-en-main-report-global-innovation-index-2023-16th-edition.pdf>.

Hofstede, G. (2001). *Kulturi i organizatsii. Software na uma*, 373p. Sofia: Klasika i Stil.

Hofstede, G., (2005). The Culture Factor Group. <https://www.hofstede-insights.com/country-comparison; https://www.theculturefactor.com/country-comparison-tool>.

McKinsey, (2024). *What is Gen Z*. <https://www.mckinsey.com/featured-insights/mckinsey-explainers/what-is-gen-z> (published 28.08.2024).

Milanova, A., and Naydenova, P. (2013). 'Human Capital Management in a Corporate Environment'. *Social-Anthropological Determination and Motivation*, 115p. Sofia: Academic Publishing House 'Prof. Marin Drinov'.

Milanova, A., and Naydenova, P. (2017). 'Corporate Social Capital – Reality and Pragmatic Definiteness'. In: *Improving the Competitiveness of Enterprises and National Economies*, pp. 155–77. Niš, Serbia: University of Niš, Faculty of Economics.

Milanova, A., and Naydenova, P. (2023). 'A Cultural Framework of Innovation Potential' (Chapter 12). In M. V. Kaya (ed.), *Social and Economic Studies within the Framework of Emerging Global Developments*, Vol. II. Berlin, Peter Lang Public House, pp. 155–65. ISBN: 978-3-631-8946-6; E-ISBN: 978-3-631-89541-2.

O'Reilly, Chatman, and Caldwell (1991). 'People and Organizational Culture. A Profile Comparison Approach to Person Organization Fit'. *Academy of Management Journal* 34, 487–516.

Parker, K., Igielnik, R. (2020). On the Cusp of Adulthood and Facing an Uncertain Future: What We Know About Gen Z So Far. <https://www.pewresearch.org/social-trends/2020/05/14/on-the-cusp-of-adulthood-and-facing-an-uncertain-future-what-we-know-about-gen-z-so-far/>.

Profile of Gen Z (Profil na pokolenie Z) (2020). <https://activeageing.bia-bg.com/bg/analyses/generations/profileZ/>.

Shein, E. (2010). *Organizational Culture and Leadership.* Jossey-Bass San Francisco. <https://ia800809.us.archive.org/14/items/EdgarHScheinOrganizationalCultureAndLeadership/Edgar_H_Schein_Organizational_culture_and_leadership.pdf>.

Seel, R. (2000). Culture and Complexity: New Insights on Organizational Change – Organisations & People.

Kangaroo Classroom for Developing Talented Learners' Abilities in the Science Subjects

Martins Veide, Valerijs Dombrovskis and Anastasya Pantelejeva

3.1. Introduction

Children differ from each other with different unique abilities and talents. In addition, some children have potential beyond what is normally expected at school for their age or grade. Those learners can be classified as talented – students who demonstrate a natural aptitude or ability in a particular area or domain (Gagné, 2018; Neihart, 2021), or gifted – students who possess an exceptional level of natural ability in one or more areas (Gross & Smith, 2021). Generally, they show such qualities like learning faster and more independently than most students of their own age; they are motivated, especially on tasks that are challenging or difficult, and they hold themselves to standards of achievement that are higher than usual.

Despite their obvious strengths as learners, such students may fail in school. These pupils possess a unique set of attributes and abilities that require special attention and care in the educational process (Cross, 2021). If the approach to teaching such pupils is not tailored to their individual strengths and interests, they often become bored and disengaged. This boredom may even manifest as behaviour problems or underperformance at school. This may be the reason why gifted or talented students are sometimes considered in the context of special education. Their needs are discussed in textbooks about special education, along with discussions of students with major behaviour disorders, physical impairments or intellectual disabilities (Friend, 2023). There is no denying that they are exceptional, and they do require some modifications to regular school programmes in order to reach their full potential. Still, it would be advisable to distinguish between exceptional talent or giftedness and exceptional disabilities of other kinds. The significant difference is the speed with which students in the two above-mentioned groups reach their potential. That is why we think of the gifted and talented not as students with disabilities, but as examples of diversity. This means that the differentiation of their instruction extends not only to special education specialists but to all teachers.

As defined in Differentiating Model of Giftedness and Talent by Gagné (2020), giftedness is the possession and use of untrained and spontaneously expressed natural abilities (called aptitudes or gifts) and talent is the superior mastery of systematically developed activities (or skills) and knowledge. Given our interest in the process of developing abilities, we will hereafter use the term 'talented', understanding by that also various degrees of development of giftedness. In the realm of educating talented learners, choosing the right methodology is paramount. One methodology that is tailored to their unique needs is a dynamic approach, referred to as the 'Kangaroo classroom' (Tomlinson, 2017).

Vital components of modern education are STEM subjects. Research consistently demonstrates the importance of STEM subjects in fostering critical thinking, driving innovation, enhancing global competitiveness and creating diverse career opportunities (Caratozzolo et al., 2021; Kennedy & Odell, 2023; Zhan et al., 2022). At the same time, they are often considered to be the hardest subjects. Therefore, timely recognition of children's talents in this area and their appropriate development can be important both in the context of a student-centred approach and the development of the national economy. The *aim of this study* is to find out how to practically use the Kangaroo classroom approach to develop the learning process of children who are talented in the sciences. The study was conducted testing the idea created within the framework of the project 'Educating Talents' (No. 2022-1-SE01-KA220-SCH-000088468) in 2022–2024.

3.2. Theoretical Background

3.2.1. Kangaroo classroom and Corner Organisation

The Kangaroo methodology acknowledges the unique constellation of talents and aptitudes that talented learners possess, necessitating dedicated educational strategies that are both adaptable and responsive to their distinct needs (Cross, 2021). Central to this methodology is the division into eight distinct strategies, each one thoughtfully designed to address specific aspects of talent development within the educational milieu (Dombrovskis et al., 2023). This approach not only accentuates the learners' evident talents but also encourages the emergence of latent abilities, ultimately guiding them to contribute positively to society (Subotnik et al., 2018).

Within the Kangaroo classroom, 'Special Corner Organisation' and 'Special Class Organisation' stand out for their adaptability to different resource levels. The former, ideal for resource-limited settings, establishes a dedicated space within standard classrooms for individualised learning (Laine & Tirri, 2016), while the latter suits environments with more resources, organising specialised classes for talented learners with customised curriculums. These strategies underscore the methodology's flexibility and commitment to inclusive, tailored education for talented learners (Tomlinson, 2017).

The essence of the 'Special Corner Organisation' strategy lies in its ability to merge individualised learning with the communal classroom experience (see Table 1). By establishing a specialised learning space within the general classroom, referred to as the 'Special Corner', this strategy promotes an atmosphere where talented learners can delve into and refine their abilities alongside their peers (Laine et al., 2016). This strategy empowers educators to utilise specialised programmes and materials specifically adapted to nurture the distinctive developmental trajectories of each learner, thereby embedding this specialised learning zone within the broader classroom setting (Laine & Tirri, 2016).

Table 1. Characteristics of the 'Special Corner Organisation' strategy

Characteristic	Detail
Form of organisation	Group level (small group)
Strategy	'Special Corner Organisation' (individualisation of learning)
Activities	Employment of customised programmes and materials aimed at the unique advancement of talented learners
Required support	Allocation of a specific classroom area equipped with necessary resources, backed by institutional support
Form of work	Applicable in both traditional, in-person classroom settings and virtual, online learning environments

The 'Special Class Organisation' strategy within the Kangaroo methodology is designed for educational contexts rich in resources, where the formation of dedicated classes for talented learners is feasible (Tomlinson, 2017) (see Table 2).

Table 2. Characteristics of the 'Special Class Organisation' strategy

Characteristic	Detail
Form of organisation	Group level (large group)
Strategy	'Special Class Organisation'
Activities	Development of enhanced curricula and materials aimed at the specialised growth of talented learners
Required support	Allocation of a dedicated classroom space, supported by institutional administration
Form of work	Flexible implementation in both traditional classroom settings and through online platforms

The 'Kangaroo classroom' with its 'Special Corner Organisation' and 'Special Class Organisation' strategies exemplifies a dynamic and flexible approach within the Kangaroo methodology to cater to the diverse needs of talented learners (Lavoie et al., 2017).

3.2.2. STEM education

STEM education represents an integrated meta-discipline that removes traditional separation between science, technology, engineering and mathematics, focusing instead on innovation and the applied methodology of designing solutions to complex contextual issues. This interdisciplinary approach is fostering a culture of continuous innovation aimed at addressing current and future societal challenges (Bybee, 2013; Lantz, 2009).

The embedding of STEM subjects within educational curricula is predicated on the notion that contemporary issues and professional tasks seldom fall neatly within the confines of a single discipline but rather demand a comprehensive and collaborative approach (Guzey et al., 2020; National Research Council, 2012). By fostering an educational environment that encourages the confluence of diverse disciplinary perspectives, STEM education aims to cultivate learners who are not only adept at interdisciplinary thinking but also capable of deploying a broad spectrum of skills in innovative problem-solving. Such an educational framework underscores the necessity of a well-rounded pedagogical model that not only imparts in-depth disciplinary knowledge but also emphasises the application of this knowledge in addressing multifaceted problems, thereby equipping students with the competencies essential for thriving in the intricacies of the modern and future world (Park et al., 2018; Thibaut et al., 2018).

STEM's emphasis on real-world problem-solving aligns with the Kangaroo Methodology's goal of fostering advanced abilities in science, technology, engineering and mathematics. The 'Special Corner Organisation' allows for customised STEM activities within standard classrooms, promoting individual exploration and application of STEM concepts. The 'Special Class Organisation' provides an immersive STEM experience, with a curriculum tailored to integrate STEM principles, facilitating collaborative innovation among talented learners. This integration equips students with essential twenty-first-century skills like critical thinking and creativity, preparing them to excel in a technologically advanced world (Guzey et al., 2020; National Research Council, 2012; Thibaut et al., 2018).

The integration of science within the STEM framework, particularly through the Kangaroo methodology emphasises, authentic scientific practices, such as inquiry, experimentation and evidence-based reasoning, enabling students to solve real-world problems (Kennedy & Odell, 2014). This process not only deepens their understanding of scientific concepts but also cultivates essential skills like critical thinking and problem-solving, preparing them for complex challenges (Bybee, 2013; Sanders, 2009).

3.3. Research Methodology

The purpose of the research was to create 'Kangaroo classes' dedicated to chemical elements found in nature by applying the 'Special Class Organisation' strategy, involving pupils on a voluntary basis, and observing their behaviour during these classes. The pupils were aged 7–14. One of the tasks was to find a suitable way to divide them into groups according to their age, in order to create a personalised and inclusive learning environment. The second task was to observe their behaviour and developmental progress. Research to date shows that *observation* as a method in a qualitative context is important in samples of children (Polkinghorne, 2005). It is not always easy for children to express their thoughts, especially in situations where they may not be aware of their interest in a subject (in this case – science). Also, open observation ensures a weaker influence of the researcher and makes it possible to clarify the chronology and permanence of what is happening in the learning process.

The research of the 'Kangaroo classes' was conducted at Riga Secondary school, which is a Latvian state general secondary education institution, where basic and general secondary education programmes take place from the 1st to the 12th grade. The observation period lasted from September 2023 until May 2024. 'Kangaroo class' lessons were held once a week throughout the school year (except school holidays) after the end of the regular lessons of the relevant class groups. The duration of each lesson was approximately 40 minutes – this was chosen as the optimal time in which children are able to maintain their attention, and it coincides with the official lesson duration in the country's general secondary education institutions.

The observation was recorded by handwritten notes and photos taken during the lessons. The content of the lessons was also documented in the pupils' individual chemistry books and photo collages-reports, which the children created based on the lesson notes sent to their parents. These photo collage reports reflect what the pupils did during the lessons.

The leader of the learning process in these 'Kangaroo classes' and at the same time the observer was a pedagogue with 12 years of experience in primary school and 21 years of total teaching experience. She is also the author of a curriculum specifically designed for these 'Kangaroo classes'. Thus, it can be considered that *participant observation* was performed.

The aim of the curriculum was to introduce students to the natural world through learning about the chemical elements found in the animal and plant worlds, as well as in the substances they come into contact with in everyday processes such as washing or eating. The content of the curriculum was based on an idea of depicting chemical elements as living beings – small creatures as residents of a big house (Mendeleev's table), whose characters were visualised and cut out of cardboard, who visited the main characters of all lesson topics – the Chemist and his assistant the Cook, and told them about their chemical and physical properties. In addition to interactive lectures on the history of chemical elements and their compounds, their occurrence in nature and their applications in the kitchen, the programme used methods such as riddles about chemical elements and conducting chemical and physical experiments. The principles of Montessori (2023) Cosmic Education were integrated into the curriculum, which also influenced the choice of materials for the lessons.

The material provision of the programme consisted of laboratory vessels, chemical preparations, sand lamps (with elements of sand therapy), sound cylinders for determining the consistency of materials, Orbizes (for modelling atomic structures), magnets, the constructor of chemistry and video materials.

3.4. Findings and Discussion

At school, six 'Kangaroo classes' were created according to four age groups (class groups) – in two groups of younger pupils, two classes in each class group and one class in 3–4th and 5–7th class groups (see Table 3). The 1st class group consists of pupils aged 7–8 from five 1st grades. A total of 125 pupils study in the 1st grades. 'Kangaroo classes' were attended by twenty-three pupils, which is 18 per cent of all 1st class group pupils. 1st grade pupils have no school experience yet, it is relatively difficult for them to maintain their attention for a long time. Given this, in order to reduce the number of pupils per class, as well as for disciplinary reasons, these twenty-three pupils were divided into two 'Kangaroo classes'.

Also, the group of 2nd year pupils was formed from five 2nd grades, where a total of 125 pupils aged 8–9 study. 'Kangaroo classes' were attended by seventeen pupils, who were also divided into two 'Kangaroo classes'. Despite the small age difference, the 2nd class group was separated from the 1st class group, because, first, unlike the 1st year pupils, they already have school experience and, second, a great rivalry was observed between the 1st year pupils and the 2nd year pupils.

From three 3rd and four 4th grades (175 pupils in total), one 'Kangaroo class' was created with sixteen children. This class group was divided separately, because students of this age can already maintain attention for a longer period of time, and they are also characterised by relatively more active participation in discussions. The 3rd and 4th year pupils were friendly with each other.

Another 'Kangaroo class' was formed from four 5th grades, five 6th grades and two 7th grades (a total of 275 pupils). This class was attended by eight pupils aged 11–13 years. Comparing the Kangaroo classroom attendance data of the four class groups, it can be easily noticed that there are significantly more pupils of the first 4 grades than pupils of the 5th–7th grades. This can be explained mainly by the relatively higher learning load in the 5th–7th grades.

The teenage period can also play a role here, when pupils' spontaneous interests are increasingly suppressed by doubts about their future profession and the related reluctance to spend their time on activities without a clear pragmatic justification. A relatively smaller percentage (3%) of all pupils in this class group can also be explained by the fact that pupils in these grades have a significantly larger choice of extracurricular activities at school, and their choice could also be influenced by the fact that 5th–7th year pupils study in another school building. Although this was the smallest 'Kangaroo class' in terms of numbers, it showed the highest level of interest – chemistry had already become a hobby for some of the pupils in this class. This group of pupils is also characterised by greater independence both in the learning process and in conducting practical research, as well as relatively more active sharing of their observations and experiences.

Table 3. Participation in 'Kangaroo classes'

Class Group (Academic Year)	1st	2nd	3-4th	5- 7th
The total number of pupils in the respective class group	125	125	175	275
The number of pupils in 'Kangaroo class'	23 (2 classes)	17 (2 classes)	16	8
As a percentage of all pupils in the class group	18%	14%	9%	3%

It should be noted that a larger number of pupils started attending these 'Kangaroo classes' – anyone could apply for them – but during the first weeks, approximately 29 per cent dropped out. For example, twenty-four pupils from all the 2nd year pupils had applied, but only seventeen attended the classes. The dropouts were pupils who had come only because of their parents' initiative (the children themselves were not interested), or who had expected only demonstrations and entertainment from the classes and were not ready to collaborate and to learn. The gender factor in participation was not significant – in all six 'Kangaroo classes', the distribution of girls and boys was exactly 50%/50%, or statistically significantly close to it ($p < 0.01$).

Thanks to the fact that the lessons did not have strict time and content frames, calm, family conditions were created in all classes. The children had the opportunity to share their personal experiences, which they also used widely. Everyone participated in the research process – both the usually outwardly active and the quietest and most timid. Involvement in independent experiments and observation of processes was facilitated by the offered choice of materials. For example, there were pupils who constantly preferred different hard materials, and there were those who regularly chose to work with soft materials.

During the lessons, the advantage of organising lessons at four thematic corners, where 2–4 children can work at one table, was justified (see Figure 1). This gave pupils the opportunity to start learning a new topic in a way that suited them individually. In this way, the 'Special Corner Organisation' strategy was integrated into the 'Special Class Organisation'.

The pupils' interest in 'Kangaroo classes' was evidenced by their regular attendance (for which they did not receive any additional reward), the observations they made about the topics of the previous lessons (they had started to study their surroundings, everyday things), as well as the fact that in each meeting, they accurately remembered the details of the content of the previous lessons, which they included in their narratives. In their mutual communication, they behaved with respect. Students' interest in cooperating with each other was evidenced not only by doing joint tasks at the thematic corners in Kangaroo classrooms, but also by the fact that when they met outside of these lessons, they greeted each other, actively asked about the next lesson, shared their individual observations, as well as provided explanations about the discussed topics (if someone did not have the opportunity to participate in the previous lesson).

More than half of 'Kangaroo class' students had told their friends about these classes. In some cases, they had brought their friend to the lesson (who had not applied themselves, but had shown interest after hearing their friend's story). All of them were given a chance to try it out. On average, two pupils in each of the 'Kangaroo classes' came to try it out and also stayed to continue their studies (they are not included in Table 3).

The results and feedback from students at the school selected for the study indicate that chemistry is one of the most difficult STEM subjects. Despite this, pupils in all six 'Kangaroo classes' demonstrated a high level of knowledge and understanding of topics that, according to the official curriculum, can only be learned in higher grades. For example, content units such as the four spheres of the Earth and their elements, decomposition reactions, substitution reactions, the structure of the atom, according to the curriculum of public schools, must be taught only from the 8th grade, but in 'Kangaroo classes', pupils from the first grade were already learning them. Through the study of crystal lattices of elements and substances, using the constructor of chemistry, the children also learned the concepts of stereometry and spatial figures, which are taught in mathematics only in the higher grades. Namely, only after six months of participating in the 'Kangaroo classes', these pupils were able to answer such questions of the higher grades' learning tests, which are difficult for a large number of pupils, who must study a corresponding subject according to the nationally accepted curriculum as a mandatory. And the open interest in these relatively more complex issues for pupils of lower grades indicates the realisation of their talents.

Figure 1. An example of thematic corners during a lesson.

The realisation of the children's talents was also evidenced by the letters written by their parents to the e-class, which was the initiative of the parents themselves. During the observation period, letters were received from the parents of seventeen pupils. They showed that the children had expressed a desire to continue learning in their 'Kangaroo class', and also, referring to what happened in their 'Kangaroo class', had shown interest in becoming involved in specific professions in the future, such as medicine, veterinary service and construction.

3.5. Conclusion

By applying the 'Special Class Organisation' strategy, six 'Kangaroo classes' dedicated to chemical elements found in nature were created for pupils of four age stages in a standard state general secondary education institution. Although pupils were invited to join them on a voluntary basis, signing up for these classes did not always reflect pupils' interest in developing their skills and knowledge in science. For a little less than a third of the group, it was the parents' initiative, or the pupils' perceptions that special classes would provide only entertainment.

On average, 9 per cent of all age-matched pupils in a given school participated in these 'Kangaroo classes'. The largest number of applications was in the groups of the two lower grades. Although in terms of numbers, the group of higher grade students was the smallest 'Kangaroo class' (3% of all pupils of this age group), they showed the highest interest, were more active in sharing their observations and experience, as well as showed a greater independence in the learning process. Over a nine-month period, each of the established 'Kangaroo classes' was joined, on average, by two more students, invited by their friends who were already studying in those classes. The interest of 'Kangaroo class' participants was evidenced by regular attendance, for which no additional rewards were granted. Observations were made on the topics of previous lessons, as well as accurate recollection of details from the content of previous lessons was gathered.

Considering the difficulty of maintaining attention and mutual rivalry, in the groups of two lower grades, it was important to limit the number of children in the 'Kangaroo classes' – these groups did not exceed twelve pupils each. Psychological support in all six 'Kangaroo classes' was also facilitated by the fact that the lessons did not have strict time and content frames. As an important factor in the organisation of the learning process of 'Kangaroo classes', the opportunity was given for pupils to express their thoughts on the issues discussed in the lesson, based on their previous observations, and to share their previous experience in the class. The integration of the 'Special Corner Organisation' (individualisation of learning) strategy proved beneficial by organising lessons into four thematic corners, giving pupils the opportunity to begin learning a new topic in a way that suited them individually.

During the nine months of these specially organised 'Kangaroo classes', changes in the students' attitude towards learning were observed – their desire to understand and orientation towards independent research increased. The cognitive results of all 'Kangaroo classes' participants were also observed. Pupils in all six 'Kangaroo classes' demonstrated a high level of knowledge and understanding of topics that, according to the nationally accepted curriculum, should be only taught in the higher grades. The realisation of the talents of the participating pupils was indicated by their open interest in the relatively more complex STEM subjects, as well as their new interest in engaging in specific professions in the future.

Observations in all 'Kangaroo classes' give reason to believe that this type of class promotes children's interest in science and understanding of its importance in human life. They also show that knowing the chemical processes in nature makes it easier for them to understand the laws of nature on a larger scale. Understanding the more complex content units of the STEM subjects and understanding the world of animals and plants contribute to each other.

Bibliography

Bybee, R. W. (2013). The Case for STEM Education: Challenges and Opportunities. Arlington, VA: NSTA Press.

Caratozzolo, P., Bravo, E., Garay-Rondero C., and Membrillo-Hernandez, J. (2021). 'Educational Innovation: Focusing on Enhancing the Skills of Generation Z Workforce in STEM'. In *2021 World Engineering Education Forum/Global Engineering Deans Council Proceedings*, pp. 488–95. Madrid, Spain: IEEE.

Cross, T. L. (2021). On the Social and Emotional Lives of Fifted Children. New York: Routledge.

Dombrovskis, V., Titova, N., and Veide, M. (2023). 'Systemization of Range and Scale of the Approaches to Education of Talented and Gifted Children in the EU Education System'. In L. G. Chova, C. G. Martinez, and J. Lees (eds.), *EDULEARN23 Proceedings*, pp. 1644–53. Palma, Spain: IATED Academy.

Friend, M. (2023). Special Education: Contemporary Perspectives for School Professionals. Boston: Pearson Education.

Gagné, F. (2018). 'Academic Talent Development: Theory and Best Practices'. In S. I. Pfeiffer, E. Shaunessy-Dedrick, and M. Foley (eds.), APA Handbook of Giftedness and Talent, pp. 163–83. American Psychological Association.

Gagné, F. (2020). Differentiating Giftedness from Talent: The DMGT Perspective on Talent Development. New York: Routledge.

Gross, M. U., and Smith, S. R. (2021). 'Put Them Together and See How They Learn! Ability Grouping and Acceleration Effects on the Self-esteem of Academically Gifted High School Students'. In S. R. Smith (ed.), *Handbook of Giftedness and Talent Development in the Asia-Pacific*, pp. 377–403. Singapore: Springer.

Guzey, S., Caskurlu, S., and Kozan, K. (2020). 'Integrated STEM Pedagogies and Student Learning'. In C. C. Johnson (ed.) *Handbook of Research on STEM Education*, pp. 65–75. New York: Routledge.

Kennedy, T. J., and Odell, M. (2023). 'STEM Education as a Meta-Discipline'. In B. Akpan, B. Cavas, and T. Kennedy (eds.), *Contemporary Issues in Science and Technology Education*, pp. 37–51. Cham: Springer Nature Switzerland.

Kennedy, T. J., and Michael, R. L. Odell (2014). 'Engaging Students in STEM Education'. *Science Education International*, 25 (3), 246–58.

Montessori, M. (2023). *To Educate the Human Potential*. New Delhi: Dev Publishers & Distributors.

Laine, S., and Tirri, K. (2016). 'How Finnish Elementary School Teachers Meet the Needs of Their Gifted Students'. *High Ability Studies*, 27 (2), 149–64.

Laine, S., Kuusisto, E., and Tirri, K. (2016). 'Finnish Teachers' Conceptions of Giftedness'. *Journal for the Education of the Gifted*, 39 (2), 151–67.

Lantz, H. B. (2009). *Science, Technology, Engineering, and Mathematics (STEM) Education: What Form? What Function*. Report, Baltimore: CurrTech Integrations. Available at: <https://www.uastem.com/wp-content/uploads/2012/08/STEMEducationArticle.pdf>.

Lavoie, C., Couture, C., Bégin, J. Y., and Massé, L. (2017). 'The Differentiated Impact of Kangaroo Class Programmes in Quebec Primary Schools: Examining Behavioural Improvements in Relation to Student Characteristics'. *Emotional and Behavioural Difficulties*, 22 (3), 275–89.

National Research Council (2012). A Framework for K-12 Science Education: Practices, Crosscutting Concepts, and Core Ideas. Washington, DC: National Academies Press.

Neihart, M. (2021). The Social and Emotional Development of Gifted Children: What Do We Know? New York: Routledge.

Park, D. Y., Park, M. H, and Bates, A. B. (2018). 'Exploring Young Children's Understanding About the Concept of Volume Through Engineering Design in a STEM Activity: A Case Study'. *International Journal of Science and Mathematics Education*, 16, 275–94.

Polkinghorne, D. E. (2005). 'Language and Meaning: Data Collection in Qualitative Research'. *Journal of Counselling Psychology*, 52 (2), 137–45.

Sanders, M. (2009). 'STEM, STEM Education, STEM Mania'. *Technology Teacher*, 68 (4), 20–6.

Subotnik, R. F., Olszewski-Kubilius, P., and Worrell, F. C. (2018). 'Talent Development as the Most Promising Focus of Giftedness and Gifted Education'. In S. I. Pfeiffer, E. Shaunessy-Dedrick, and M. Foley (eds.) *APA Handbook of Giftedness and Talent*, pp. 231–45. American Psychological Association.

Thibaut, L., Knipprath, H., Dehaene, W., and Depaepe, F. (2018). 'The influence of Teachers' Attitudes and School Context on Instructional Practices in Integrated STEM Education'. *Teaching and Teacher Education*, 71, 190–205.

Tomlinson, C. A. (2017). 'Differentiated Instruction'. In C. M. Callahan, and H. L. Hertberg-Davis (eds.), *Fundamentals of Gifted Education*, pp. 279–92. New York: Routledge.

Zhan, Z., Shen, W., Xu, Z., Niu, S., and You, G. (2022). 'A Bibliometric Analysis of the Global Landscape on STEM education (2004–2021): Towards Global Distribution, Subject Integration, and Research Trends'. *Asia Pacific Journal of Innovation and Entrepreneurship*, 16 (2), 171–203.

Transforming Education for Sustainable Development: A Path to Global Change

Anica Hunjet, Grmuša Tanja and Dijana Vuković

4.1. Introduction

The modern world faces a series of interconnected challenges that directly affect the quality of life of current and future generations. Climate change, the rapid depletion of natural resources, growing global inequality, geopolitical instability and dynamic technological developments are changing not only the way we live, but also the way we learn and teach. In such a context, education can no longer be viewed solely as a mechanism for transferring knowledge, but must be seen as a key tool for empowering individuals and communities in building a more just, sustainable and resilient society. Education for Sustainable Development (ESD) is becoming an increasingly important concept in global educational policies and practices. Its purpose goes beyond traditional educational goals, emphasising the development of competences that enable students and citizens to understand the complex challenges of today, critically reflect on possible solutions and actively participate in social change. ESD promotes an interdisciplinary approach, connecting natural, social and technical sciences, while fostering values such as solidarity, responsibility, intergenerational justice and respect for the environment.

This paper will analyse how education systems can be transformed to become carriers of sustainable development at the local, national and global levels. Special attention will be paid to innovative teaching and learning models, including the integration of digital technologies, the development of participatory and experiential learning, and the creation of educational content that is grounded in real social problems. The paper also explores how schools, universities and other educational institutions can effectively integrate sustainability principles into their curricula, organisational culture and everyday practice. Furthermore, important global initiatives and documents will be considered, such as the UN Agenda 2030 and the Sustainable Development Goals (SDGs), which recognise education as one of the foundations for achieving a sustainable future. Through a critical analysis of existing educational models and practices, the paper will seek to offer concrete guidelines for improving educational strategies and policies that can contribute to the development of sustainability awareness and active citizenship.

The aim of this paper is not only to point out the importance of education in the context of sustainability, but also to encourage stakeholders in the education system – from teachers and policymakers to students themselves – to think about education as a dynamic process that has the potential to shape a better future for all.

4.2. Review of Scientific Literature

ESD in Croatia is implemented through comprehensive, interdisciplinary programmes spanning primary, secondary and higher education, to promote lifelong learning and strengthen the capacities of individuals and institutions (Bajkuša et al., 2011). This approach is aligned with several previously mentioned international frameworks, but also with an emphasis on the development of regulatory frameworks, new educational tools, teacher competencies and general awareness of sustainable development. Croatia recognises its importance in several strategic documents. The National Plan for the Development of the Education System until 2027 states that by 2030, 'all learners should acquire the knowledge and skills needed to promote sustainable development' (NPRSO, 2023). The National Curriculum for Early Childhood Education and Care (ECEC) reflects the values of sustainability, teaching children about community, inclusion and responsibility (including towards nature). Since 2019, sustainability is covered in three cross-curricular topics to be integrated in all subjects in primary and secondary school: sustainable development, civic education and personal and social development (Education and Training Monitor 2024, <https://op.europa.eu/webpub/eac/education-and-training-monitor/en/country- reports/croatia.html>, 28.4.2025).

Although students have good knowledge about sustainability, they are above the European average (519.8 points compared to 506.7 points in the EU-17) (Education and Training Monitor, 2024, <https://op.europa.eu/webpub/eac/education-and-training-monitor/en/country-reports/croatia.html>, 28.4.2025), differences have been identified regarding gender and parental education. At the same time, teachers are not sufficiently trained to teach about sustainability, although they have the desire and will, and sustainability topics are integrated as part of project activities and fieldwork (Schulz et al., 2023). Positive examples of sustainability education as part of innovations in educational curricula in local environments should be highlighted, more specifically in Zagreb and Rijeka, where young people have the opportunity to learn about these topics as part of civic education. It is a subject that has caused numerous controversies even in the experimental phase (Rukavina Rončević, 2013). While some have predominantly observed it through the political science prism of education for democracy (Klemenčić, 2006; Pažur, 2017), others analyse its hidden codes in teaching curricula (Nikičić & Komesarović, 2021).

When it comes to sustainable education at the higher education level, the analysis of websites and study plans shows that The Faculty of Tourism and Hospitality Management in Opatija, part of the University of Rijeka, is the only higher education institution (HEI) that is fully dedicated to the implementation of this concept both in teaching and in scientific and professional work and employee education. Other institutions include the University of Zagreb, where you can find courses (Faculty of Croatian Studies, course Sustainable development policies of the European Union – more details you can see here: <https://fhs.unizg.hr/en/course/sdpoteu>) or laboratories dedicated to the above. It was also observed that the concept of sustainability is an integral part of many course syllabi and workshops for the training of many teachers throughout Croatia, but it can be concluded that it is not part of a long-term education strategy, but a broader approach to the analysed topic. Leko Šimić et al. (2022) remind us of the specificities of Generation Z, which pays a lot of attention to these topics on a personal and consumer level, so it is important how and for what we educate these young people. Starting from the role of universities and university social responsibility (USR), Leko Šimić et al. (2022) conducted a comparative analysis of the perception of students from India and Croatia about USR. It was found that the representation of USR topics in course syllabi, as well as the implementation of courses in study programmes, is directly related to knowledge and attitudes towards USR. It was also shown that universities must make a stronger contribution to the implementation of USR policies (Filho et al., 2024), given cultural differences, communication and cooperation. Croatian students see the application of USR in education as a comparative advantage, but also point to the insufficient competence of teachers in teaching such content, which then directly affects the quality of teaching, but also the (un)desirability of HEIs in the competitive education market. An example of positive changes is certainly the University of Split, which has consistently integrated SGD into its activities with the aim of institutional transformation, as well as promoting sustainability while generating positive social and environmental impacts (Škokić et al., 2025). On the other hand, research conducted on students of the Faculty of Teacher Education in Split shows the interest of students, future teachers, in the topic of sustainable development, but most young people still do not know how to define sustainable development or approach the topic in a simplified and universal way (Vukadin & Mlađenović, 2023). Similar results were shown by a study of the attitudes of students at the University of Rijeka. The fact that most information on this topic comes from the media, and not from educational institutions, is a consequence of this situation in practice (Rončević et al., 2008: 72).

An insight into the curriculum shows that sustainable development is mostly learned through different modules. Most students associate sustainable development with the topic of environmental protection, to the exclusion of other indicators (Ćurković, 2021: 40; Rončević et al., 2008: 72). The results also showed that there is no difference among students about previous secondary education or level of study. However, Ćurković (2021) sees the solution in the necessary modifications of the educational curriculum with the aim of stronger implementation of sustainable development and ensuring quality education for those who will one day raise our children and be the bearers of positive changes in society. Leal et al. (2024) specifically cite HEIs as key stakeholders in the implementation of the SDGs, since only knowledge can influence consumer awareness and behaviour (Al-Nuaimi & Al-Ghamdi, 2022 according to Leal et al., 2024: 2).

However, desires and communication about them are one thing, and the actual situation is something else entirely; and while there are discussions about the extent to which young people should learn about the SDGs, at the same time these young people, most often popularly called Generation Z, themselves clearly show what is important to them – and sustainability and sustainable development certainly are (Pradeep & Pradeep, 2023). While previous research was mostly partial, relying on only one indicator of the impact of knowledge on sustainability, Leal et al. (2024) consider them limiting due to the omission of the cultural and social dimension, offering a cross-regional connection and a multivariable approach that shows the interconnectedness of knowledge, attitudes and behaviour (Leal et al., 2024: 2). The results showed that knowledge about sustainability has a direct positive effect on students & attitudes and behaviour. Gender differences were found in the context of attitudes towards sustainability in favour of women, while there were no gender differences in knowledge. Also, differences in knowledge were found among students concerning the level of study (undergraduate and graduate studies), as well as about affiliation to a scientific field (2024: 7). Namely, people studying engineering and technology (STEM) show less knowledge about sustainability, which the authors attribute to a narrow focus on technical–technological components, innovations and an orientation towards faster problem solving, as well as a move away from critical thinking that the social sciences insist on (cf. Colón-Flores et al., 2023; Kurnaz & Anikar, 2024 according to Leal et al., 2024: 8). Therefore, the responsibility also lies with teachers for creating courses, but also for applying adequate teaching methods (practice and fieldwork) for the acquisition of competences dedicated to sustainability. Earlier implementation of Sustainability in education contributes to creating awareness of its values, as well as identification with the values that promote this idea. Regional research on the implementation of sustainable development in Slovenia, Croatia and Bosnia and Herzegovina showed that teachers understand the concept of sustainable development differently from the documents and policies that advocate it, but also that they invest maximum efforts and creative approaches in their implementation (Jevtić-Višnjić et al., 2022).

The authors provide an analysis of the educational level of responsible and sustainable behaviour when it comes to environmental protection. Previous research has indicated a connection between these two indicators, so Mandarić and Hunjet decided to verify the above at the local level. Although Croatia, as a member of the European Union, already automatically acts according to the green policies that the EU strongly advocates, it is pointed out that there are differences in their implementation among member states (Bąk et al., 2024; Mandarić & Hunjet, 2023: 52). The European Action Plan for the Circular Economy sought to contribute to sustainable development with sustainable waste management, which in turn depends on geographical differences. Previous research has shown a significant connection between the level of education and environmentally friendly behaviour (Mayer, 2015), as well as people's motivation to think about their actions. However, in addition to formal education, informal initiatives that contribute to strengthening people's information and awareness also play a significant role in this process (cf. Danielson et al., 1995, according to Mandarić & Hunjet, 2023: 53).

The author presents an overview of the views of future educators on the sustainable development of students in early and preschool education in Rijeka. Knowledge and understanding of the topic were established, but only a part of them take concrete steps that are visible and significant in everyday life, and only a part of them take concrete activities such as recycling and saving electricity (cf. 2021: VII). They rate their self-perception of knowledge about sustainable development as mediocre, but on the other hand, they admit that the lack of educational materials represents a major obstacle to implementing education on this topic (2021: 53–56).

4.3. Research Methodology

Given the increasing demands placed on education systems by contemporary sustainability challenges, it is necessary to investigate to what extent the principles of ESD have already been integrated into educational practice and how they are perceived by students, teachers and pupils. The research part of the paper is based on the need to gain a deeper insight into the actual state of ESD implementation in educational institutions, as well as the level of understanding and acceptance of this concept among key education stakeholders. This part of the paper seeks to examine how education systems – primarily schools and HEIs – respond to the need for the transformation of education towards sustainability. The research focuses on the analysis of existing educational programmes, teaching methods and the level of awareness of sustainable development among pupils, students and teaching staff. Special attention is paid to the identification of good practices, but also to the obstacles that prevent the full implementation of ESD.

Using a combination of research methods (a questionnaire and semi-structured interviews), the paper aims to capture quantitative and qualitative data that will enable a more complete understanding of the current state and needs in education for sustainable development. Based on the data collected, recommendations will be formulated for further integration of sustainability principles into educational policies, curricula and everyday practice. The aim of this research section is not only to evaluate the current state, but also to encourage a change in the educational paradigm towards a system that actively contributes to the formation of responsible, informed and engaged citizens ready for the challenges of a sustainable future. Despite the growing global consensus on the importance of sustainable development and the growing awareness of the necessity of environmental protection, social justice and responsible resource management, sustainability principles have not yet been systematically and consistently integrated into educational systems around the world. ESD often remains marginalised within formal education, limited to individual subjects, projects or teaching units. Many educational institutions do not have clearly developed strategies, competencies or tools for the successful implementation of ESD, while teachers and students are often not sufficiently trained to understand and practically apply sustainability concepts. At the same time, the world is rapidly facing complex challenges such as climate change, ecological crises, growing inequality and digital transformation, which require new forms of education focused on problem solving, critical thinking, collaboration and active citizenship. The absence of systematic integration of ESD into the educational process can result in generations that are not sufficiently prepared for responsible action and informed decision-making in the context of sustainable development. The subject of this paper is the analysis and research of the process of transforming education towards sustainable development, with an emphasis on the role of educational institutions, teachers and students in the implementation of education for sustainable development. The focus is on methods, content and approaches that enable the development of competencies needed to face the challenges of the twenty-first century, including the use of interdisciplinary methods, digital technologies, participatory learning and practical applications of knowledge.

The paper also includes an analysis of the perceptions of education stakeholders on the importance and implementation of ESD, as well as identifying obstacles and opportunities for its more effective introduction into formal education systems. Through a research approach, it aims to build an overview of the current state and offer concrete guidelines for improving education that is focused on sustainability and global responsibility. The purpose of the research is to examine how the principles of sustainable development are integrated into education systems and how innovative teaching methods, interdisciplinary approaches and digital technologies contribute to the development of competences for sustainable development among pupils and students. In accordance with the above, the following research objectives have been defined:

- to determine the level of inclusion of ESD in formal educational programmes.
- to investigate the perceptions of teachers and pupils/students on the importance of sustainable development in education.
- to analyse examples of good practice in the implementation of ESD in schools and/or HEIs.
- to examine which teaching methods (e.g. project-based learning, experiential learning, digital technologies) most stimulate the development of competences for sustainability.
- provide recommendations for further integration of ESD into educational policies and practices.

In accordance with the above, two hypotheses were put forward:

Hypothesis 1: Teachers believe that there is a lack of adequate institutional support for the implementation of ESD in educational institutions.

Hypothesis 2: Students and pupils show a positive attitude towards the introduction of ESD into the teaching process, but there is a significant difference in the perception of implementation across different educational institutions.

As part of this research, in-depth interviews with principals of kindergartens, primary and secondary schools and deans of private HEIs, represent a key methodological component that allows for a detailed understanding of the attitudes, challenges and opportunities related to the implementation of ESD in different educational sectors. These interviews provide a deeper insight into the perceptions of responsible persons in educational institutions on the importance of sustainability and its integration into educational curricula, as well as the obstacles that arise when implementing sustainable development strategies. A total of thirty respondents participated in the process, including principals of kindergartens, primary and secondary schools and deans of private HEIs. The structure of the respondents ensures diversity in responses, with the aim of providing a wide range of insights into how different educational institutions perceive and implement ESD, and to what extent they are able to respond to the challenges arising from global sustainability demands. In-depth interviews allow not only the collection of quantitative data, but also qualitative insights that are key to understanding specific obstacles and barriers in the field. In the qualitative part of the research, an in-depth interview was used with the aim of gaining deeper insight into the perceptions and attitudes of relevant stakeholders in the educational and management system on the role of internal marketing in the context of quality development and user satisfaction. A total of fifteen interlocutors participated as respondents in this research segment, namely: five teachers, five principals of secondary education institutions and five deans of business polytechnics in the Republic of Croatia.

This sample structure enabled the collection of diverse perspectives from different levels of the educational system and the comparison of opinions between the operational and strategic management levels. The number of participants was selected in accordance with the recommendations for qualitative research using the AHP method, with a sample size between five and fifteen experts considered optimal in order to achieve consistency and analytical relevance in the paired comparison process. Through the analysis of the respondents' responses, we will seek to identify key factors that influence the success or failure of the implementation of education for sustainable development, as well as to understand how principals and deans perceive institutional support, availability of resources, education of teaching staff and creating awareness among students and pupils about the importance of sustainability.

The interview structure includes questions related to the perception and implementation of sustainable development in the educational process, obstacles encountered, strategies for improving the integration of ESD and experiences in working with different educational levels. Based on the analysis of the responses, the aim is to provide guidelines for improving access to education for sustainable development and to build sustainable educational policies that will contribute to the global goals of sustainable development. The analysis of in-depth interviews will provide a detailed overview of the specific challenges and benefits of implementing ESD in different types of educational institutions, and help in understanding the complexities that educational institutions encounter in their implementation. Through this approach, we want to offer concrete recommendations for creating a supportive environment for sustainable development in education systems.

Table 4. Pairwise comparison scores between criteria in the context of evaluating educational priorities

Criterion 1	Criterion 2	Comparison score
Curricular integration	Professional development of teachers	3
Curricular integration	Institutional support	5
Curricular integration	Infrastructure and resources	7
Professional development of teachers	Institutional support	3
Professional development of teachers	Infrastructure and resources	2
Institutional support	Infrastructure and resources	1

Source: Author's work.

Table 4, titled 'Ratings of Pairwise Comparisons between Criteria in the Context of Evaluating Educational Priorities', presents the results of the Analytic Hierarchy Process (AHP) method, with which fifteen respondents – five teachers, five principals of secondary schools and five deans of business polytechnics in the Republic of Croatia – evaluated the relative importance of four key criteria within the educational system: curricular integration, professional development of teachers, institutional support and infrastructure and resources. This method involves pairwise comparisons, where respondents rated each pair of criteria on a scale from 1 to 9, with a higher value indicating a stronger preference for one criterion over the other. The results show that curricular integration is recognised as the most important criterion, with the highest ratings compared to the others. A rating of seven compared to infrastructure and resources implies a distinct advantage of this criterion, while a rating of 5 compared to institutional support and 3 compared to professional development of teachers indicates a clear, but relatively milder preference. Teacher professional development is also perceived as a significant factor, especially in comparison to institutional support (score 3) and infrastructure (score 2), which suggests that the development of teacher competences is seen as more important than ensuring material conditions and systematic support. Also interesting is the result that shows that institutional support is only slightly preferred over infrastructure and resources (score 1), which indicates an almost equal status of these two criteria in the perception of the respondents, but also a possible opinion that neither of them is sufficient on its own to improve the education system. Overall, the table reflects a hierarchy of educational priorities based on the professional insight of representatives of different levels of the educational structure. Such results can serve as a basis for making strategic decisions when creating policies for professional development and improving educational infrastructure, with an emphasis on greater integration of curricular content and the development of teacher competencies as key levers of change.

Table 5. The Relative Importance of Criteria in Determining Educational Priorities

Criterion	Weight coefficient
Curricular integration	0.35
Professional development of teachers	0.25
Institutional support	0.15
Infrastructure and resources	0.10
Participatory methods and interdisciplinarity	0.15

Source: Author's work.

Table 5 shows the weighting coefficients that reflect the relative importance of different criteria in the context of determining educational priorities according to the respondents' ratings. These coefficients allow for a better understanding of how much each of the criteria contributes to the overall evaluation of the education system and decision-making in education policy. Curricular integration occupies the highest weighting coefficient of 0.35. This result indicates that curricular integration is considered the most important criterion among all respondents. Curricular integration implies a unified approach to educational content that enables the connection of different subjects, theoretical and practical aspects, in the educational process. This high coefficient suggests that respondents recognise the importance of a coherent and interconnected curriculum that enables the comprehensive development of pupils and students. Teacher professional development, with a weighting coefficient of 0.25, also plays a significant role in determining educational priorities. This criterion refers to the continuous improvement and professional development of teachers, which is crucial for ensuring quality education. Respondents are aware that the education system cannot progress without investing in the education of teachers themselves, which is evident in this coefficient. With a weighting coefficient of 0.15, institutional support and participatory methods and interdisciplinarity are at the same level of importance. Institutional support refers to the strengthening of educational institutions by ensuring adequate infrastructure, financial resources and management capacities that enable the implementation of educational policies. This criterion is recognised as important, but to a lesser extent than the previous ones, suggesting that institutional support is important, but not the highest priority factor compared to curricular integration or teacher professional development. Participatory methods and interdisciplinarity refer to the inclusion of different learning methods that encourage active student participation and collaboration across disciplines. Although this criterion has a lower weighting coefficient (0.15), its importance is not negligible. Student participation and an interdisciplinary approach allow for better alignment of the educational process with the real world, which is crucial for the development of critical thinking and creativity. At the bottom of the scale, with a weighting coefficient of 0.10, is infrastructure and resources. Although infrastructure is important for enabling an effective educational process, its relative importance in this evaluation seems to be lower than that of curricular integration and teacher professional development. This result may indicate that respondents believe that a quality educational process primarily depends on pedagogical and professional factors, while physical resources are only a support, but not the key drivers of educational change. These results point to the prioritisation of curricular integration and teacher professional development as fundamental factors in improving the education system. Institutional support, infrastructural resources and participatory methods are also recognised, but their relative importance remains lower in the context of setting educational priorities. This distribution of weighting coefficients can be useful in shaping educational policies, as it indicates the key areas where resources and development strategies should be directed to achieve long-term success in education. Based on the calculated weighting coefficients and consistency checks, we can analyse which criteria are most important for the successful implementation of ESD and how educational institutions can shape strategies to achieve sustainable educational goals. According to the results of the AHP analysis, the most important criterion for the success of ESD is Curricular Integration, with a weighting coefficient of 0.35. This indicates that the alignment of educational programmes with the principles of sustainable development is crucial for the success of educational institutions in promoting sustainability. This result is in line with global trends that emphasise the need to integrate sustainability into all stages of the educational process, starting from primary schools to HEIs. Teacher professional development, with a weighting coefficient of 0.25, also proved to be very important for the implementation of education for sustainable development. This shows that educational institutions need to invest in the continuous professional development of teachers so that they can effectively transfer knowledge about sustainability and motivate students for active citizenship. Although institutional support (0.15) and infrastructure and resources (0.10) are less important than curricular integration and teacher professional development, they play a significant role in the implementation of ESD. Institutional support includes strategic management, financial support and political decisions, while infrastructure and resources enable the practical implementation of educational goals, such as the availability of technological tools and sustainable schools. After checking the consistency (CR), which was 0.05, it can be confirmed that the results are consistent and valid. This means that our comparisons between the criteria were consistent, and the use of the Saaty scale allowed for a precise analysis of the importance of each criterion. Based on these results, it is recommended that educational institutions prioritise curricular integration and teacher professional development. It is also necessary to increase investments in infrastructure projects and strengthen institutional support so that education systems support sustainable development. Specifically, it is recommended that interactive and participatory learning methods be further incorporated into educational curricula and programmes, and that teachers be continuously educated on the principles of sustainability and innovations in educational technologies.

The second part of the research focused on collecting data using a structured questionnaire based on the Likert scale, with identical questions as in the previous phase. This phase of the research included two target groups – students and professors – to compare their attitudes and perceptions. A total of

770 respondents participated, of which 420 were students of different years and levels of study and 350 were professors from different HEIs. The socio-demographic structure of the student sample includes undergraduate and graduate students, distributed by year of study and gender. Among the students, the majority were female students, of whom there were 260 (61.9%), while there were 160 male students (38.1%). According to the year of study, 95 respondents (22.6%) were first-year undergraduate students, 100 respondents (23.8%) were in their second year of undergraduate study, and 110 students (26.2%) were in their third year of undergraduate study. There were 65 students (15.5%) in the first year of the graduate study, while 50 (11.9%) attended the second year of the graduate study. On the other hand, the professor sample included 350 respondents who teach at universities and polytechnics. Of the total number of professors, 170 were women (48.6%) and 180 were men (51.4%). The age structure of the professors was diverse: 65 respondents (18.6%) were younger than 40 years, 110 (31.4%) were in the age group of 41–50 years, while 105 respondents (30.0%) were between 51 and 60 years. The remaining 70 respondents (20.0%) were older than 60 years. When it comes to work experience, 40 professors (11.4%) had up to 5 years of work experience, 60 (17.1%) had between 6 and 10 years of experience, while the majority of respondents, 120 (34.3%), had between 11 and 20 years of work experience. There were 130 (37.2%) professors with more than 20 years of experience. By place of employment, 210 professors (60.0%) were employed at universities, while 140 (40.0%) worked at polytechnics. This distribution of respondents enabled a comprehensive analysis of perceptions and attitudes from the perspective of two key educational groups, taking into account relevant socio-demographic variables.

In order to test the influence of different predictors on the variable of interest, a multiple regression analysis was conducted, and the results are presented in Table 6. The model results indicate a gradual increase in the explained variance by including additional predictors related to sustainable development and education for sustainable development (ESD). The first model includes the lack of specific guidelines and policies, lack of resources and education, and lack of cooperation at all levels, while the second model is expanded to include institutional strategies and documents, availability of professional development for teachers, material and technical support, and involvement of local communities and educational authorities. The results obtained show a statistically significant difference between the models, with the second model achieving a higher value of the coefficient of determination (R^2), indicating a stronger explanation of the variance of the dependent variable.

Table 6. ANOVA test

Model summary									
				Std. error of the estimate	Change statistics				
Model	*R*	*R*-square	Adjusted *R*-square		R-Square Change	*F* Change	*f*1	df2	Sig. *F* change
1	0.45a	0.437	0.342	0.59518	0.457	20.114	2	347	0.001
2	0.50b	0.484	0.374	0.49045	0.005	7.696	12	346	0.000

a. Predictors: (constant) Lack of specific guidelines and policies for ESD education_1, lack of resources and training_2 and lack of cooperation at all levels_3.

b. Predictors: (constant), Existence of institutional strategies and documents related to ESD, availability of professional training and education of ESD teachers, material and technical support for ESD and involvement of the local community and educational bodies in ESD.

c. Dependent variable: The educational institution provides adequate support for the implementation of education for sustainable development, access to all necessary resources for effective implementation of ESD, and institutional policies recognise the importance of education for sustainable development.

Source: Author's work.

To test the hypothesis of the existence of institutional support for the implementation of ESD, a multiple regression analysis was conducted in two models. These models tested the influence of different groups of predictors on teachers' perceptions of the adequacy of institutional support for ESD. The first model included negative indicators, that is, three key predictors: lack of specific guidelines and policies for ESD, lack of resources and education and lack of cooperation at all levels. The results showed that this model explains 43.7 per cent of the variance of the dependent variable ($R^2 = 0.437$), which indicates a moderately strong association. The adjusted value (Adjusted $R^2 = 0.342$) also confirms the stability of the model. The value of the *F*-test ($F = 20.114; p < 0.001$) shows a statistically significant relationship between the predictor and the dependent variable, that is, perceived deficiencies in institutional support significantly affect the negative evaluation of support for ESD. The second model included positive indicators of institutional support: the existence of institutional strategies for ESD, the availability of professional development for teachers, material and technical support and the involvement of the local community and educational authorities in ESD. This model shows an improvement in explaining the variance, with $R^2 = 0.484$, and the adjusted value (Adjusted $R^2 = 0.374$) shows additional explanation of the variance with higher prediction accuracy. The *F*-test ($F = 7.696$; $p < 0.001$) is also statistically significant, indicating that these positive indicators also contribute significantly to the perception of institutional support. In conclusion, both models confirm the importance of institutional factors in shaping teachers' perceptions of the adequacy of support for education for sustainable development. The first model emphasises the impact of gaps, while the second shows that the presence of specific institutional elements can significantly improve this perception. These results provide empirical support for hypothesis H1 and indicate the need for systematic institutional support in the education system.

Table 7. Descriptive statistics and Crombach alpha coefficient for selected particles

	N	Aritmetička sredina	SD	Minimum – maximum	Cronbach Alpha
I believe that education for sustainable development is important for the future of society.	420	4.31	0.9	1–5	
I support the introduction of education for sustainable development into the regular curriculum.	420	4.20	0.9	1–5	
I would like us to learn more about the environmental, social and economic aspects of sustainability in class.	420	4.13	1	1–5	0.974
ESD should be an integral part of every educational subject, not just a separate topic.	420	4.11	1	1–5	
Education for sustainable development helps me understand how I can personally contribute to a sustainable society.	420	4.10	1	1–5	

Source: Author's work.

The results presented in Table 7 indicate a very positive attitude of students towards ESD. All the analysed statements received high average scores, ranging from 4.10 to 4.31 on a Likert scale from 1 to 5. The highest average score was given to the statement 'I believe that education for sustainable development is important for the future of society' ($M = 4.31$, SD = 0.9), which indicates a high level of awareness of the importance of sustainability among the respondents. Similarly, significant support was expressed for the statement 'I support the introduction of education for sustainable development into the regular curriculum' ($M = 4.20$), which indicates the willingness of the respondents to make ESD an integral part of education. The remaining statements, which include the desire to learn about aspects of sustainability, the integration of ESD into all subjects and one's contribution to sustainability, also recorded high scores (between 4.10 and 4.13), which confirms a deeply rooted positive attitude towards ESD. The reliability of the scale is tested using the Cronbach's alpha coefficient, which is extremely high at 0.974, indicating a very high internal consistency of the questionnaire. In other words, all statements measure the same construct – attitude towards ESD – reliably and consistently. In conclusion, the results obtained provide a solid statistical basis for confirming the first part of hypothesis H2: students and pupils show a positive attitude towards the introduction of education for sustainable development in the teaching process.

4.4. Conclusion

Through the implementation of the AHP method and the analysis of the results, it became clear which are the key factors for the successful implementation of education for sustainable development. The main criteria are curricular integration and professional development of teachers, while infrastructure, resources and institutional support are also important, but less influential. This paper provides guidelines for future educational policies and strategies that can help educational institutions prepare students for the challenges of sustainable development.

The results indicate that the participants recognise the high importance of education for sustainable development, with the highest ratings given to statements related to its importance for the future of society ($M = 4.31$)

and the need to introduce ESD into the regular curriculum ($M = 4.20$). The Cronbach Alpha coefficient is 0.974, which confirms the high internal consistency of the scale and the reliability of the results obtained. Also, the regression analysis showed that the lack of concrete institutional guidelines, resources and cooperation significantly affects the negative perception of teachers about institutional support for ESD ($R^2 = 0.437; p < 0.001$). However, the presence of strategies, training and technical support increases the perception of institutional readiness.

Through AHP analysis, it was shown that the most important criteria for the successful implementation of ESD are:

- Curricular integration (highest weight),
- Teacher professional development, while infrastructure, material resources and broader institutional support are also important, but with a somewhat smaller impact.

These findings have practical implications – educational policies should focus on training teaching staff, integrating ESD into all teaching subjects and ensuring continuous institutional support. Only a holistic and systematic approach will enable pupils and students to develop the competences needed to face the social, economic and environmental challenges of the modern world. In conclusion, this paper not only confirms the positive attitude of students and teachers towards ESD but also identifies specific points of intervention that can improve its implementation. It thus contributes to the development of more effective educational strategies aimed at a more sustainable society.

Bibliography

Bajkuša, M., Juričić, V., Petković, A. i Rogić, D. (2011.) 'Education for Sustainable Development: Croatia'. *Research Report. Zagreb:* Forum for Freedom in Education.

Bąk I., Wawrzyniak K., and Sulikowski, P. (2024), 'Sustainable Development and the Degree of Implementation of European Union Environmental Directives'. *Front. Environ.* Sci., 12, 1324030, <http://doi.org/10.3389/fenvs.2024.1324030>.

Ćurković, I. (2021) *Miskoncepti studenata Učiteljskog fakulteta u Splitu o održivom razvoju, Master Thesis*, University of Split, Faculty of Humanities and Social Sciences, University of Split.

Filho, W. L., Sierra, J., Price, E. et al. (2024). 'The Role of Universities in Accelerating the Sustainable Development Goals in Europe'. *Sci Rep*, 14, 15464, <https://doi.org/10.1038/s41598-024-65820-9>.

Jevtić-Višnjić, A., Jurka Lepičnik Vodopivec, J., Pribišev Beleslin, T., and Šindić, A. (2022). 'Unmasking Sustainability in Early Childhood Education: Teachers' Voices from Bosnia and Herzegovina, Croatia, and Slovenia'. *Continuing Education*, 54, 119–37.

Klemenčić, E. (2006). 'Građanski odgoj u Europskoj uniji: aspekti edukacije za demokraciju', *Anali Hrvatskog politološkog društva: časopis za politologiju*, 3 (1), 283–95, <https://hrcak.srce.hr/clanak/60161>.

Leko Šimić, M.; Sharma, E.; Kadlec, Ž., (2022). 'Students' Perceptions and Attitudes toward University Social Responsibility: Comparison between India and Croatia'. *Sustainability*, 14, 13763, <https://doi.org/10.3390/su142113763>.

Mandarić, D., and Hunjet, A. (2023). 'Does the Education Level of Consumers Influence Their Recycling and Environmental Protection Attitudes? Evidence From Croatia'. *Naše gospodarstvo/Our Economy*, 69 (4), 51–61, <https://doi.org/10.2478/ngoe-2023-0023>.

Nikičić, I., and Komesarović, Z. (2021). 'Perspektive utjecaja provedbe kurikuluma građanskog odgoja i obrazovanja na skriveni kurikulum u školama', *Magistra Iadertina*, 16 (1), 73–93, <https://hrcak.srce.hr/clanak/392206>.

Pažur, M. (2017). 'Pregled razvoja građanskog odgoja i obrazovanja u Republici Hrvatskoj od 1999. godine do danas', *Školski vjesnik: časopis za pedagogijsku teoriju i praksu*, 66 (4), 605–18, <https://hrcak.srce.hr/clanak/285709>.

Rončević, N., Ledić, J., and Ćulum, B. (2008) '„Nisam sigurna što je, ali je bitno" – analiza stavova studenata Sveučilišta u Rijeci o održivom razvoju', *Suvremene teme: međunarodni časopis zadruštvene i humanističke znanosti*, 1 (1), 62–75, <https://hrcak.srce.hr/35232>.

Rukavina-Kovačević, K. (2013). 'Građanski odgoj i obrazovanje u školi – potreba ili uvjet?' *Riječki teološki časopis*, 41 (1), 101–36, <https://hrcak.srce.hr/clanak/175714>.

Salopek, M. (2021). 'Stavovi budućih odgajatelja o održivom razvoju, University of Rijeka, Faculty of Teacher Education / Sveučilište u Rijeci, Sveučilište u Rijeci, Učiteljski fakultet'.

Schulz, W., Ainley, J., Fraillon, J., Losito, B., Agrusti, G., Damiani, V., and Friedman, T. (2023), 'Education for Citizenship in Times of Global Challenge, IEA International Civic and Citizenship Education Study 2022 International Report (Revised Edition)', *International Association for the Evaluation of Educational Achievement* (IEA), <www.iea.nl/sites/default/files/2024-02/ICCS-2022-International-Report-Revised.pdf>.

Škokić, V., Jelić, P., and Jerković, I. (2025). 'The Role and Contribution of Sustainable Development Goals as a Transformative Framework in Higher Education: A Case Study of the University of Split'. *World*, 6 (1), 22, <https://doi.org/10.3390/world6010022>.

Vukadin, M., and Mlađenović, J. (2023) 'Halfway there: Did we learn anything? – Youth Perception of Sustainability and Sustainable Development Goals'. *Tosee – Tourism in Southern and Eastern Europe*, 7, 457–72.

Women in STEM in United Arab Emirates (Literature Review)

Khuloud Al Hammadi

5.1. Introduction

The concept of the gender gap is a topic that is both fascinating and controversial for scholars involved in studies relating to management and labour economics. Even though most studies that are published on the topic primarily focus on the educational angle of science, technology, engineering and mathematics (STEM), a limited number of researchers have investigated the career gender gap in STEM within the Gulf countries and in the UAE. For instance, data obtained from the report published by the World Economic Forum (2017) detailed the gender gap in different parts of the globe and revealed insightful statistical information. Specifically, according to the World Economic Forum (2017), of the 149 nations ranked in the report, the UAE occupied number 121. In essence, these findings implied the centrality of gender gap management through measures such as additional training for females within the STEM domain to address the gender gap.

5.2. Search Strategy and Background Search

To the researcher's best knowledge, no previous attempts have been made to examine studies dealing with the gender gap, specifically focusing on the case of the UAE and the Gulf region. The primary goal of the current review was to offer a critical review of the extant literature documenting gender discrimination against females in STEM within the MENA region and the UAE. To attain this objective, the research retrieved and selected relevant literature pieces from online electronic databases such as JSTOR, the Higher Colleges of Technology and the American University of Ras Al Khaimah's libraries. In so doing, the researcher's search strategy deployed key terminologies, words or phrases, which included 'MENA', 'Middle East', 'Gulf countries', 'GCC', 'UAE', 'United Arab Emirates', 'gender inequality', 'gender pay gap', 'gender discrimination', 'gender', 'women in STEM' and 'females', Journal articles that qualified under the set eligibility parameters were included in the reference list.

Thus, the current review offered a general review of the existing sources with information regarding the STEM gender gap. The reviewed literature pieces were those published in the English language, thereby eliminating the potential information distortion and bias inherent in the translation process, as proposed by Creswell and Creswell (2018). As such, the current review is premised on Patterson and Walcutt's (2013) model, which critically examined sources written in the English language and explored the aspects of gender discrimination in Korean workplaces. Besides, the researcher in the current review was guided by the model formulated by Bastian et al. (2018), which elaborately assessed and developed a method to rank journal articles written concerning the UAE's female entrepreneurs. The sources were retrieved from the UAE databases to show STEM career and gender gap-related viewpoints. Overall, the current review offers a critical synthesis of the UAE's STEM education stances, the challenges experienced by women in STEM, the projected implications/recommendations and related theories.

5.3. Theoretical Framework

The current study's theoretical model was premised on intersectionality and the dual labour market theory. Regarding the intersectionality framework, the term 'intersectionality' was originally developed in 1989 by a critical race theorist and feminist legal scholar by the name of Kimberle Williams Crenshaw (1991). Intersectionality, as a theoretical stance, explains discourses relating to the exclusion or marginalisation of women (Crenshaw, 1991). As explained by Crenshaw (1991), women's marginalisation stems from gender and anti-racial discourses, which contribute to the formulation of intersectional identity as a response to exclusion. This position enunciated by Crenshaw (1991) aligned with the ideas presented by Showunmi et al. (2012), who explained that discourses perpetuating gender exclusion contributed to categorisation fallacies, inaccuracies in perceptions and adverse experiences by the marginalised group. As such, intersectionality was found relevant for the current review insofar as the theoretical stance helped to understand the implications of the intersectionality of gender on the education and career progression of women in STEM in the UAE and Gulf countries.

5.4. Understanding the Gender Gap Concept

The reviewed literature pieces indicated that most discourses touching on gender discrimination or the gender gap singularly analyse the gender development gap, the glass ceiling concept, females in positions of senior management or boardrooms, prejudice, stereotyping and the gap in gender pay. Specifically, according to data obtained from the World Economic Forum (2017), within the past decades, there were disparities in the wages of males compared to those paid to their female counterparts. These results implied that there was an increase in the gender pay gap. Correspondingly, other findings from Harris (2017) resonated with these outcomes, as stated by the report from the World Economic Forum (2017), specifically stating that the gender pay gap was assessed at the median earnings ratio of women to those of men. Therefore, evidence suggested that the gap showed the median earnings of males compared to those of females in the form of a ratio. On the other hand, other studies, such as Vootla et al. (2018), offered a different perspective relating to the calculation of the ratio, including that the computation focuses on the salaries or wages of women and men for individuals who earn salaries year-round or in full-time jobs, with the outcomes referred to as the raw gender pay gap. The results of Vootla et al. (2018) were particularly commendable in their disclosure that although women earned more bachelor's degrees compared to their male counterparts within the past decade, there was a surprising increase in the gender wage gap. Overall, evidence from the reviewed literature implied the need for organisations to embrace measures to address the gender pay gap.

There was consensus in the reviewed body of research that the earnings of women had significantly contributed to the economic and social progress of many countries. In particular, the results obtained from the Global Gender Gap Report (2017) indicated that there was an approximately 32 per cent gender wage gap between males and females. Crucially, the findings of the Global Gender Gap Report (2017) were unique in highlighting that this gap was lower than around 40 per cent for regions such as North Africa and the Middle East for the first time. However, these findings insufficiently explained how the choice of professions between men and women influenced the gender wage gap as a notable reason. Other scholars, such as Mulligan and Rubinstein (2008), made similar findings to these outcomes in the Global Gender Gap Report (2017), postulating that the disparities in professional choice were reasons for the widening gap in gender wages. For instance, Mulligan and Rubinstein (2008) indicated that there were variations in the choice of professions, with men selecting professional or managerial jobs, which included scientists, engineers or doctors, whereas their female counterparts were in diverse sectors, which included administration, teaching and nursing. In this sense, the current review outcomes suggested that the statistical analysis of the wage gap placed females at a lower pay level compared to their male colleagues in general. On the other hand, the results by Ainane et al. (2019) were largely distinguishable from the Global Gender Gap Report (2017) and Mulligan and Rubinstein (2008) by explaining the potential reason for the widening gender wage gap between males and females. For instance, the results of Ainane et al. (2019) were unique in the disclosure that the pay gap could be a product of occupational composition adjustments of the women's labour force within the past decades. These results implied that even though there were differences in women's and men's earned incomes, which increased, the changes were more significant for women. These findings resonated with the outcomes of Alibeli (2015), who similarly found that within senior job positions in the business and public sector domain, the share of women failed to reflect equitable distribution or representation. For instance, the statistical data from Alibeli (2015) affirmed that women held 22 per cent of senior managerial job positions. Thus, based on the evidence from the current review, it can be concluded that there is an absence of equitable distribution of wages based on gender differences.

5.5. Career Choices and STEM Education

There was concurrence among the reviewed scholars who indicated that there was relatively slower progress among STEM women worldwide. According to the data derived from Women in STEM (2019), the statistics were emphatic that there was a need for more interventions or measures to mitigate the STEM fields' related gender pay gap. For instance, the results by Women in STEM (2019) exhibited notable strength in their disclosure that although there was a steady increase in the population of women with degrees in core STEM fields, the population represented only 26 per cent of the total graduates in the niche. These findings implied that there was a need to offer greater encouragement to females to pursue subjects falling within the discipline.

Additionally, Fatourou et al.'s (2019) research supported these results from Women in STEM (2019) by disclosing that females represented 22 per cent of the workforce in STEM. Crucially, the results from Fatourou et al.'s (2019) research showed notable strength in the unique argument that females' underrepresentation in the STEM domain reflected segregation based on gender in diverse areas such as institutional processes and the culture of the organisations. According to Fatourou et al.'s (2019) research, the segregation was similarly manifested through research that was gender biased and gender blind, the imbalance in gender in research funding's access, senior positions' gender disproportions, and career challenges that are gender related. Thus, the evidence from the reviewed literature can be interpreted to mean that there was an inherent demand to support women in graduating in the STEM fields for future workforce transition. Nevertheless, the reviewed pieces of evidence offered generalised perspectives that inadequately focused on documenting the specific reasons hindering the bridging of the gender gap or gender discrimination for females in STEM within the MENA region and the UAE.

Multiple literature sources focused on the UAE case study, with the findings disclosing the various reasons explaining learners' preferences or dislikes towards STEM-related courses or careers (Alyammahi et al., 2016; Hillman et al., 2017; Islam, 2019; Wang et al., 2020). Specifically, according to Alyammahi et al. (2016), such reasons include the absence of female role models in careers that are STEM-related, slower progress of careers in STEM jobs, limited opportunities for employment, cultural biases, teaching language choice and the lack of teachers who are capable in STEM courses. Thus, these findings suggested the need for reforms to tackle these underlying reasons discouraging learners from pursuing STEM-related courses or careers. However, the research by Alyammahi et al. (2016) article insufficient in analysing whether women of colour experienced prejudices and racial stereotypes, which exacerbated the pay discrimination gap and gave undue advantage to male workers in most firms. Correspondingly, other results by Islam (2019) echoed Alyammahi et al.'s (2016) outcomes by indicating that within the Middle East context, affirming that notwithstanding the funds allocation increase in the sector of education to enhance the development of the nations, there was a need for women in sectors that best suited their functions. These results effectively implied that although both genders enjoyed equal opportunities, other barriers, such as prejudices and social perceptions, informed the employment opportunities that were occupied by males or females. On their part, the journal article by Wang et al. (2020) was particularly unique in exploring the cultural challenges within the nations of the Middle East, including the possible systemic challenges of STEM education's poor quality, limited avenues for female employment after graduation in STEM and the absence of access to education. Besides, Hillman and Salama's (2018) study assessed the case study of Qatar by investigating the challenges experienced by female learners in the Arab Gulf's careers, which are related to engineering. It was shown that there was a notable absence of support for such learners. As such, the results from the reviewed literature proposed the elimination of women restrictions, which were antiquated, as well as enacted international standards and collaborations at diverse levels of education.

Other studies analysed the challenges that women in STEM experience within the Middle East and North Africa (MENA) region. Specifically, data obtained from the Clean Energy Business Council, the International Renewable Energy Agency and BloombergNEF (2017) was particularly valuable in highlighting the plight of female workers within the sector of clean energy within the MENA region. In this sense, the report indicated that at least half of the research participants who comprised MENA respondents revealed that there were considerably fewer women than men in their organisations. Crucially, the results were instructive in demonstrating the challenges to women's access to job avenues in the industry of clean energy, which included gender roles' biased perceptions and fewer females who enrolled in STEM-based courses. These findings implied that although females formed part of the sector in roles that were entry-level, there were difficulties that inhibited their access to high-level jobs. Similarly, Alsubaie and Jones (2017) supported these results by reiterating that the major challenges that prevented MENA region females from STEM opportunities aligned with the global data, which showed that such barriers included the promotion glass ceiling and reduced pay for jobs that were similar. For instance, the findings of Alsubaie and Jones (2017) exhibited notable strength in disclosing that even though at least 66.7 per cent of the respondents from the MENA regions indicated that the policies of the firm showed that the organisations had the same remuneration for both males and females, 33 per cent of the participants affirmed that women were still disadvantaged at they were offered lesser pay for the same work.

More generally, evidence from the reviewed pieces of literature suggested that male workers in STEM exhibited a higher belief likelihood that there was equal pay compared to their female colleagues.

5.6. The UAE's Gender Gap

There was concurrence in the reviewed pieces of literature that the gap between females and males in STEM, which is traceable to past decades, continues to manifest itself through schools and within contemporary workplaces. In particular, according to research documented by Al Hinai (2019), the gender gap metrics worldwide indicated that the UAE was the most gender-equitable country within the Middle East region. For instance, according to Al Hinai (2019), the efforts of the nation were traceable to its creation of the Gender Balance Council in 2015, with the agency primarily mandated to enhance the involvement of females in positions of leadership within the country. Thus, these results implied that the country had embraced measures to support women and bolster the level of gender equality. Correspondingly, Al Murshidi (2019) made similar findings to those outcomes by Al Hinai (2019) through the disclosure that related agencies, such as Dubai Women Establishment, had been formed to promote equality based on gender in the GCC nations, specifically within the UAE. As such, the evidence from the current review suggested that the UAE had embraced several initiatives that were meant to improve the involvement of women in key positions of leadership for Emirati women, including their programmes of training. Nevertheless, the reviewed literature materials inadequately explored how females in STEM compare to males to reveal the gender pay gap concerns. On the other hand, a report from Al-Asfour et al. (2017) was instructive and differed from Al Murshidi (2019) and Al Hinai (2019) by emphasising that in the UAE, females represented at least 70 per cent of the total number of graduate populations from universities, with STEM women comprising only 46 per cent of the graduates. Besides, Al-Asfour et al. (2017) demonstrated that there was a 95.7 per cent rate of literacy among females, while half of the workers in the Space Programme of the UAE were Emirati females. As such, the results suggested that the UAE had passed a policy requiring the inclusion of women board members in each firm or organisation. However, given the information from the reviewed literature sources, it was generally unclear regarding the specific reasons for females' underrepresentation in the STEM disciplines within the UAE and other Gulf countries.

The reviewed literature sources elaborately documented the challenges experienced by women in STEM and the possible reasons for the lack of sufficient female transition into STEM-related careers. Specifically, research undertaken by Al Murshidi (2019) explained that, notwithstanding all the progress made in support of STEM education for Emirati females, challenges such as accessibility and the absence of interest in STEM subjects among women persisted. Thus, these results suggested that the absence of interest and accessibility of education in STEM across different income earner brackets and age groups prevented such females from exploiting opportunities relating to education or careers in STEM among UAE women. These findings by Al Murshidi (2019) aligned with the past report by UNESCO (2017), which similarly documented that there was a reduced enrolment of female learners in STEM courses, as represented by only 3 per cent of the total student population in ICT, manufacturing construction (8%), statistics/math (5%) and welfare/health (15%). In general, these results suggested the need for the relevant agencies of the UAE government to devise measures or plans, including a strategy for inclusivity, to ensure more female leaders in STEM-related sectors by the year 2030.

The reviewed literature pieces highlighted the possible strategies, including proactive nationalisation, for entities in the private sector to obtain lucrative government contracts. United Nations (UN) (2018) found that regarding wages, men were consistently remunerated much better than women, notwithstanding other factors such as nationality or skill sets. More specifically, the UN (2018) documented that, on average, for citizens, females received 54 per cent less income compared to men. For immigrants, these percentages escalated to 104 per cent, while for the whole sample, the average stood at 91 per cent, as gleaned from the data by the UN (2018). However, these results by Al-Waqfi and Al-Faki (2015) were largely distinguishable from the findings regarding skills distribution, which showed that both immigrants and local women possessed superior skill sets compared to men. According to Al-Waqfi and Al-Faki (2015), on average, for citizens of UAE, unskilled males' income exceeded skilled females' income by a margin of at least 6.2 per cent, and immigrants' percentage was 24 per cent, while the entire sample reported 42 per cent. As such, the evidence from the reviewed literature broadly implied the increasing income inequality due to the preferences of females regarding careers. These results further echoed the UN's (2018) report, which postulated that the inequality was further exacerbated by the fact that females did not receive the diverse fringe benefits offered to other male workers. Thus, although these sources revealed the type of benefits offered to men to cater to their diverse family needs, there was a particular lack of clarity concerning the degree to which the disparities in income could be justified. For instance, the data from the UN (2018) indicated that the human development index of the UAE was at 0.86 per cent, with the nation ranked at position 34 for nations with a higher index, while the sex-gender development index was reportedly high (0.968). Nevertheless, considered in their totality, these datasets failed to conclusively depict discrimination in pay or wages based on gender, thereby leading to limitations in their interpretation by most scholars.

5.7. Summary, Research Gaps, Implications and Recommendations

It was demonstrated that there are disparities in the wages of males compared to those paid to their female counterparts. However, the reviewed pieces of evidence offered generalised perspectives that inadequately focused on documenting the gender gap or gender discrimination for females in STEM within the MENA region and the UAE. Additionally, the reviewed literature sources are insufficiently analysed within the UAE scenario, and it is unclear whether digital inclusion could enhance or encourage women to engage in technical and professional jobs as technology-based skills impact promotions in the workplace. Lastly, the evidence from the current review offered scant details of how inequalities relating to financial inclusion and legal protection persist for females. Further research may be mounted on these aspects.

These results implied an increase in the gender pay gap. As such, the review presents practical implications for organisations, key management stakeholders, policymakers and government agencies regarding the need to review the existing policies to empower females as a way of increasing the population of STEM women, their educational involvement and careers.

5.8. Conclusion

The review findings disclosed the need for organisations to embrace measures to address the gender pay gap. Thus, it is recommended that, for gender gap management, measures such as additional training for females within the STEM domain be embraced to address the gender pay gap. Moreover, it was shown that there was a notable absence of support for such learners. As such, this review proposes eliminating women's restrictions, which were antiquated, and enacting international standards and collaborations at diverse levels of education. It is recommended that there is a need to embrace digital inclusion to increase the population of females in STEM. For instance, digital inclusion would positively impact females in STEM by offering more flexibility and opportunities for work for future jobs. Lastly, there is a need for more female involvement in STEM careers and education by empowering women through incentives and policy creation to improve their education in engineering and other STEM subjects for future career opportunities.

Bibliography

Ainane, S., Bouabid, A., and El Sokkary, W. (2019). 'Factors Influencing the High Percentage of Women Enrolled in Engineering in the UAE and Preparing for Careers in the Oil and Gas Industry'. *Global Journal of Engineering Education*, 21 (1), 16–25.

Al Hinai, M. (2019). 'The UAE's Empowerment of Women Is an Example for the World to Follow'. *Entrepreneur Middle East*, 7 March, available at: <www.entrepreneur.com/article/329624>.

Al Murshidi, G.A. (2019). 'Stem education in the United Arab Emirates: Challenges and possibilities'. *International Journal of Learning, Teaching and Educational Research, 18* (12), 316–32, <https://doi.org/10.26803/ijlter.18.12.18>.

Al-Asfour, A., Tlaiss, H. A., Khan, S. A., and Rajasekar, J. (2017). 'Saudi Women's Work Challenges and Barriers to Career Advancement'. *Career Development International*, 22 (2), 184–99. <https://doi.org/10.1108/CDI-11-2016-0200>.

Alibeli, M. A. (2015). 'Gender and Attitudes toward Women in the United Arab Emirates'. *Perspectives on Global Development and Technology*, 14 (1–2), 109–25. <https://doi.org/10.1163/15691497-12341335>.

Alsubaie, A., and Jones, K. (2017). 'Rev. of an Overview of the Current State of Women's Leadership in Higher Education in Saudi Arabia and a Proposal for Future Research Directions'. *Administrative Sciences*, 7 (4), 1–15. <https://doi.org/10.3390/admsci7040036>.

Al-Waqfi, M. A., and Abdalla Al-faki, I. (2015). 'Gender-based Differences in Employment Conditions of Local and Expatriate Workers in the GCC Context: Empirical Evidence from the United Arab Emirates'. *International Journal of Manpower*, 36 (3), 397–415. <https://doi.org/10.1108/IJM-10-2013-0236>.

Alyammahi, S., Zaki, R., Barada, H., and Al-Hammadi, Y. (2016). 'Attracting Students to STEM: Obstructors and Facilitators'. In *2016 IEEE Global Engineering Education Conference* (EDUCON), 941–50. <https://doi.org/10.1109/EDUCON.2016.7474665>.

Bastian, B. L., Sidani, Y. M., and El Amine, Y. (2018). 'Women Entrepreneurship in the Middle East and North Africa: A Review of Knowledge Areas and Research Gaps'. *Gender in Management*, 33 (1), 14–29. <https://doi.org/10.1108/GM-07-2016-0141>.

BloombergNEF (2017). 'Women in Clean Energy, Middle East and North Africa Survey 2017'. Available at: <https://about.bnef.com/blog/women-clean-energy-middle-east-north-africa-survey-2017/> (accessed 7 April 2025).

Creswell, J. W., and Creswell, J. D. (2018). *Research Design: Qualitative, Quantitative, and Mixed Methods Approaches* (5th edn). SAGE

Crenshaw, K. (1991). 'Mapping the Margins: Intersectionality, Identity Politics, and Violence against Women of Color'. *Stanford Law Review*, 43 (6), 1241–99. <https://doi.org/10.2307/1229039>.

Fatourou, P., Papageorgiou, Y., and Petousi, V. (2019). 'Women Are Needed in STEM: European Policies and Incentives'. *Communications of the ACM*, 62 (4), 52–2. <https://doi.org/10.1145/3312565>.

Harris, B. (2017). 'What Is the Gender Gap (and Why Is It Getting Wider)?' World Economic Forum. Available at: <www.weforum.org/agenda/2017/11/the-gender-gap-actually-got-worse-in-2017/> (accessed 7 April 2025).

Hillman, S., Salama, G., Ocampo Eibenschutz, E., Awadh, S. M. A., and El Said, L. (2017). 'Being Female and an Engineering Student in Qatar: Successes, Challenges, and Recommendations'. *Paper presented at 2017 ASEE Annual Conference and Exposition*, Columbus, OH.

Islam, S. I. (2019). 'Science, Technology, Engineering and Mathematics (STEM): Liberating Women in the Middle East'. *World Journal of Education*, 9 (3), 94–, <https://doi.org/10.5430/wje.v9n3p94>.

Mulligan, C. B., and Rubinstein, Y. (2008). 'Selection, Investment, and Women's Relative Wages Over Time'. *The Quarterly Journal of Economics*, 123 (3), 1061–110. <https://doi.org/10.1162/qjec.2008.123.3.1061>.

OECD (2018), 'Bridging the Digital Gender Gap Include, Upskill, Innovate: OECD Directorate for Science, Technology, and Innovation (STI)', OECD.

Patterson, L., and Walcutt, B. (2013). 'Korean Workplace Gender Discrimination Research Analysis: A Review of the Literature from 1990 to 2010'. *Asia Pacific Business Review*, 19 (1), 85–101. <https://doi.org/10.1080/13602381.2012.697774>.

Showunmi, V., Atewologun, D., and Bebbington, D. (2016). 'Ethnic, Gender and Class Intersections in British Women's Leadership Experiences'. *Educational Management, Administration & Leadership*, 44 (6), 917–35. <https://doi.org/10.1177/1741143215587308>.

United Nations (2018). *United Nations Human Development Index, New York, NY*. Available at: <http://hdr.undp.org/en/composite/HDI> (accessed 8 April 2025).

Vootla, P., Bereket Fre, B., and Alsayedabdulrahim Mohamedrassol Alhashmi, A. M. (2018). 'Women in Engineering – Opportunities and Challenges in Al Gharbia Region of UAE', *Advances in Science and Engineering Technology International Conferences (ASET)*, Abu Dhabi, 1–6, <https://doi.org/10.1109/ICASET.2018.8376939>.

Wang, D. R., Hajjar, D. P., and Cole, C. L. (2020). 'International Partnerships for the Development of Science, Technology, Engineering, Mathematics, and Medical Education of Middle Eastern Women'. *International Journal of Higher Education*, 9 (2), 1–. <https://doi.org/10.5430/ijhe.v9n2p1>.

Women in STEM: Percentages of Women in STEM Statistics (2019). *STEM Women, UK*. Available at: <www.stemwomen.co.uk/blog/2019/09/women-in-stem-percentages-of-women-in-stem-statistics> (accessed 8 April 2025).

Women in the Workplace (2018). *Women in the Workplace*, New York, NY: McKinsey and Company. Available at: <https://womenintheworkplace.com/> (accessed 8 April 2025).

World Economic Forum (2017). *Measuring the Global Gender Gap*. Available at: <http://reports.weforum.org/global-gender-gap-report-2017/measuring-the-global-gender-gap/?doing_wp_cron=1559978615.7714838981628417968750> (accessed 8 April 2025).

The Impact of Healthcare Accessibility on Community Economic Resilience

Constantinos Challoumis

6.1. Introduction

For communities to thrive, healthcare accessibility stands as a foundational attribute, reflecting not only the physical proximity of medical facilities but also the availability of resources to enable individuals to seek care when necessary. The concept encompasses both geographical and non-geographical barriers, such as financial constraints and societal attitudes towards healthcare. Proximity alone does not suffice; one must also consider how economic factors, including income levels and insurance coverage, play an imperative role in shaping individuals' ability to access healthcare. Thus, healthcare accessibility emerges as a dynamic interplay of various determinants that ultimately influence community welfare and resilience. The presence of accessible healthcare signifies that community members can obtain preventive services, imperative treatments and emergency care without undue hardship. This accessibility is particularly significant in ensuring that small businesses and individual livelihoods do not falter due to health crises. In systems where healthcare accessibility is optimised, individuals are empowered to maintain their health, which in turn sustains productivity levels and bolsters the local economy. When healthcare is effectively integrated into the fabric of community life, households are better positioned to avoid the detrimental effects of illness on earning potential and savings, thereby contributing to the overall financial ecosystem (Amoah et al., 2021; Döring & Paul, 2010; Islam et al., 2020; Manchadi et al., 2023; Mohamed et al., 2023; Reibling et al., 2019).

An effective healthcare delivery system operates seamlessly within a community, fostering not only improved health outcomes but also economic resilience. The enhancement of healthcare accessibility holds a reciprocal relationship with economic structures, as it influences consumer spending, workforce participation and the overall vitality of local economies. For instance, in a community characterised by high enforcement savings, the flow of money reinvested in local healthcare can catalyse improvements in systemic health infrastructure, thereby accelerating the money cycle as household's experience fewer financial drains from health-related issues. In essence, healthcare accessibility becomes a pivotal determinant in establishing and maintaining a robust economic framework.

6.2. Literature Review

Influencing the discourse on healthcare accessibility are various measurement metrics that seek to quantify how effectively communities can access necessary health services. These measurements can include parameters such as the ratio of healthcare providers to the population, the affordability of services and the distance individuals must travel to obtain medical care. Moreover, qualitative measures, such as patient satisfaction and perceived barriers, offer insights into the user experience, ultimately shaping the broader understanding of accessibility. It is through this investigative lens that we can advocate for initiatives aimed at enhancing healthcare delivery. The issue of healthcare accessibility requires a comprehensive evaluation of both quantitative and qualitative data. Healthcare becomes not only a measure of community health but a lens through which we can view economic resilience. By investing in healthcare systems that promote accessibility, communities unlock the potential for a self-reinforcing cycle of economic growth and improved health outcomes. Moreover, the economic conditions prevalent in a community can directly influence public health outcomes. Areas experiencing economic hardships often witness declining healthcare services, increased unemployment and a rise in mental health issues, which leads to adverse health outcomes (Cerf, 2023; Götmark & Andersson, 2020; Junaidi & Liza, 2023; Kumar, 2023; Y. Li & Tang, 2023; Lo Storto & Goncharuk, 2017; Tegegne & Wubante, 2022; Tu, 2024; Valle, 2016; Zhang & Xu, 2022). Conversely, regions with strong economic foundations tend to have better investment in healthcare facilities, resulting in improved health quality. This cyclical relationship highlights the need for a dual approach that incorporates both health and economic strategies in policy planning; when one sector suffers, the repercussions reverberate throughout the other, highlighting their intertwined fates. Below surface-level health disparities lie geographic barriers, which can substantially affect healthcare accessibility. Rural regions often lack sufficient healthcare facilities, forcing individuals to travel considerable distances to access basic services.

These distances not only exacerbate health issues through delayed treatments but also drain financial resources, as residents may have to rely on costly transport options or miss work to receive care (Challoumis, 2018, 2019, 2021, 2023b, 2023e, 2024a; Challoumis & Eriotis, 2024a). The intricacies of healthcare financing, in conjunction with limited education on available resources, create a formidable obstacle for many community members. Without adequate understanding or trust in the healthcare system, individuals may perceive barriers that do not exist, leading to missed opportunities for preventive care. This overarching issue highlights the need for strategic investment in health literacy programmes and supportive initiatives aimed at demonstrating the value of preventative measures, thereby encouraging individuals to utilise local resources effectively.

Many communities thrive when their members have access to comprehensive healthcare services. This access significantly influences physical health outcomes, as it enables individuals to receive timely medical attention and preventive care. For instance, preventive services such as vaccinations, regular check-ups and screenings can drastically reduce the incidence of chronic diseases. According to studies, populations with better healthcare access exhibit lower rates of preventable conditions like diabetes and cardiovascular diseases. This reduction not only improves individual health but also lessens the economic burden on the local healthcare system, allowing for more efficient allocation of resources and promoting a cycle of enforcement savings (Challoumis, 2024c, 2024e; Challoumis & Eriotis, 2024b, 2025). As individuals within these communities maintain better health, their capacity to contribute to the economy increases, resulting in a reinforced cycle of money that elevates the entire community's economic structure. Moreover, healthcare accessibility has a profound impact on overall community resilience. A sound healthcare system allows individuals to recover more quickly from illnesses or injuries, thereby reducing the economic implications of lost productivity. This resilience is an embodiment of the money cycle theory, where both enforcement savings and local investments are bolstered. When mental health services are easily accessible, individuals are more likely to seek help early, resulting in better management of their conditions. Importantly, this early intervention can prevent the escalation of issues that might otherwise lead to more severe problems, including substance abuse, homelessness and increased healthcare costs, which could decimate local economies through escape savings (Challoumis, 2022, 2023a, 2023c, 2023d, 2023f, 2024b, 2024d). By addressing mental health proactively, communities can enhance the overall quality of life, leading to increased collective resilience and a more stable economic environment where local businesses can flourish.

All facets of economic stability and progress hinge upon the capabilities of the workforce. Healthcare accessibility is a pivotal determinant of productivity, which ultimately drives labour force participation. When community members have reliable access to healthcare services, they can maintain better physical and mental health, effectively minimising absenteeism in the workplace. This productive engagement translates into a more robust economy, one where individuals contribute their skills and talents with greater frequency and efficiency. Consequently, industries experience a heightened output, thus fostering an environment where businesses can flourish and innovate. Economic theories such as the Cycle of Money elucidate how increased productivity feeds the system of enforced savings, enhancing the overall economic structure. Moreover, the relationship between healthcare accessibility and labour force participation is further solidified when we consider the long-term effects. Individuals who can access preventive care and treatment are more likely to remain in the workforce longer, delaying retirement and enhancing their lifetime earnings (Challoumis, 2022). Universal healthcare models emerge as vital mechanisms to ensure that all individuals receive the health services they need without facing financial hardship. Data suggests that communities supported by universal healthcare systems tend to enjoy higher rates of workforce participation and lower rates of morbidity, which ultimately contribute to a more robust local economy. By investing in preventive healthcare and ensuring equitable access to services, universal healthcare models can enhance economic stability and resilience. Access to healthcare remains a systemic challenge, especially in regions where financial barriers inhibit individuals from seeking timely medical attention. A shift towards universal healthcare would necessitate the implementation of progressive tax policies that ensure adequate funding for these services, as delineated in the theory of the cycle of money, which highlights the significance of enforcement savings (Collaborative et al., 2021; Grove et al., 2020; Hartz & John, 2009; 'Intelligent Predicting Learning Disabilities in School Going Children using Fuzzy Logic K Mean Clustering in Machine Learning', 2019; Lacombe, 2019; Vadalouca et al., 2019). For instance, communities with high ratios of enforcement savings tend to reinvest in local health systems, promoting a cycle where money circulates within the economy (Challoumis, 2025). This creates a win-win scenario: community members gain access to necessary healthcare, and the economic structure benefits from the reinvestment of those funds back into the local economy.

6.3. Methodology

The methodology is based on the Quantification of Everything (QE) method on the basis of the theory of Cycle of Money. This is not a classic model of the cycle of the money. This section presents the formal equations used in modelling the relationship between healthcare accessibility and community economic resilience. Each equation is followed by its economic interpretation, reflecting the structure of the QE method and the Cycle of Money theory (Challoumis, 2024e).

Total Healthcare Accessibility:

$$a = a_{s} + a_{t} \tag{1}$$

The total accessibility potential a is the sum of structural accessibility a_{s} (e.g. number of clinics, hospitals) and technical accessibility a_{t} (e.g. availability of staff, medical technology).

Accessibility Input Configuration:

$$a_{pk_i} = a_{p1} + a_{p2} + a_{p3} \tag{2}$$

The ith combination of healthcare investment is composed of components a_{p1}, a_{p2}, a_{p3} such as subsidies, mobile units and preventive programmes. These represent alternative strategies tested via the QE method.

Modified Money Input:

$$m_{k_i} = m_1 + a_{pk_i} \tag{3}$$

Explanation: The modified money flow m_{k_i} in the local economy is the baseline monetary input m_1, plus the added investment from the accessibility configuration a_{pk_i}.

Net Economic Surplus:

$$x_{mk_i} = m_{k_i} - a \tag{4}$$

This measures the net benefit or loss produced by a given healthcare input. It compares the total money introduced to the actual accessibility need.

Cycle Multiplication Coefficient:

$$c_{mk_i} = \frac{x_{mk_i}}{a} \tag{5}$$

This coefficient quantifies how much net benefit is produced per unit of accessibility effort. Higher values indicate more effective amplification of healthcare investments.

Monetary Efficiency Coefficient:

$$c_{\alpha k_i} = \frac{x_{mk_i}}{m_{k_i}} \tag{6}$$

Explanation: This ratio indicates how efficiently the total money injected is converted into economic surplus. A higher value suggests fewer losses and better local money circulation.

Cycle Yield:

$$c_{yk_i} = c_{mk_i} - c_{\alpha k_i} \tag{7}$$

Explanation: Cycle yield is the core measure of economic resilience. It reflects how well the healthcare investment both amplifies economic activity and retains money within the local system. A high c_{yk_i} implies strong resilience, low escape savings and maximised enforcement savings. These equations form the theoretical core of our simulation model and serve as a practical framework for policymakers to assess which healthcare strategies optimise both social outcomes and local economic performance. In alignment with the Cycle of Money theory, the cost function developed in this model reflects the dynamic interaction between two key components:

- Enforcement Savings (ES): Money that is reinvested into the community, reinforcing the economic cycle through increased local spending, job creation and sustainable growth.
- Escape Savings (ESC): Money that leaves the local economy, whether through inefficiency, health expenditures outside the region or systemic leakage, thus weakening the cycle of money and reducing economic resilience.

To simulate the impact of healthcare accessibility on these components, we define the synthetic cost function as:

$$\text{cost}_i = (1 - c_{yki}) \cdot a_{pki} \quad (8)$$

c_{yki}: The cycle yield coefficient for the *i*th healthcare accessibility strategy.
a_{pki}: The aggregated healthcare accessibility investment for strategy i.

This cost function reflects inefficiency in the allocation of healthcare resources:

When cost_i is low, the corresponding cycle yield is high, indicating that most of the invested money remains within the local economy, thus, ES dominate.

When cost_i is high, the healthcare input fails to generate adequate cycle yield, meaning resources leak from the local system, therefore, ESC are increasing.

Consequently, this cost function serves as a diagnostic tool for optimising healthcare investment strategies. It enables policymakers and planners to identify accessibility configurations that maximise enforcement savings while minimising escape savings, thereby reinforcing the local economic cycle and enhancing community resilience.

6.4. Findings and Discussion

Based on equations (1)–(8), the simulated data and results are defined in the next scheme (Challoumis, 2024e):

Table 8. Simulation coefficients

Coefficient	Maximum value (range)
α_s	0.6
α_t	0.7
m_1	0.9
α_{p1}	0.4
α_{p2}	0.3
α_{p3}	0.2

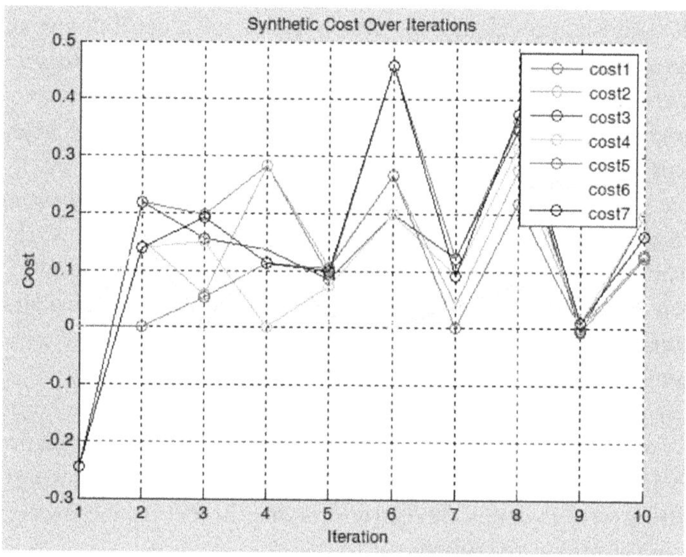

Synthetic Cost Table:

−0.2445	0	−0.2445	−0.2445	0	0	−0.2445
0.2182	0.1526	0.2182	0.1381	0	0.1526	0.1381
0.1972	0.0572	0.1550	0.1495	0.0510	0.0064	0.1922
0.2838	0.2838	0.1372	0	0.1133	0.1372	0.1133
0.0916	0.1060	0.0844	0.0737	0.1028	0.0190	0.0988
0.4590	0.2668	0.1997	0.1997	0.2668	0	0.4590
0.1219	0.0393	0.1219	0.0929	0	0.0393	0.0929
0.3631	0.2760	0.3500	0.3154	0.2178	0.0761	0.3745
−0.0066	0.0152	−0.0046	0.0110	0.0017	0.0139	0.0095
0.1246	0.1620	0.1973	0.1975	0.1294	0.0456	0.1616

The simulation results illustrated in the graph provide empirical support for the thesis that healthcare accessibility functions as a critical component of the Cycle of Money, contributing directly to economic resilience. Across most iterations, the synthetic costs for various healthcare investment strategies remain near or above zero, indicating that the majority of configurations produce favourable cycle yields. This suggests that money invested in accessible healthcare services, whether through infrastructure, staffing or mobile units, is not lost to inefficiency but rather reinvested into the local economy (Al-Habib, 2020; Ćwiklicki et al., 2020; Islam et al., 2020; Jagadeeswari et al., 2018; J. Li et al., 2020; Y. Li & Tang, 2023; Manchadi et al., 2023; Pablo et al., 2021; Shafqat et al., 2020; Wang et al., 2023). As per the Cycle of Money theory, such investments translate into enforcement savings, strengthening local economic activity by keeping financial resources circulating within the community. In contrast, very few points fall below zero, which would signify escape savings or economic leakage. The relatively stable and positive synthetic cost levels demonstrate that when healthcare accessibility is optimised, it not only improves public health outcomes but also minimises systemic inefficiencies, reinforcing the local economic structure. This validates the healthcare system's role as a regenerative force in economic cycles, making it not merely a social necessity but a strategic economic engine within the community.

6.5. Conclusion

The intricate relationship between healthcare accessibility and community economic resilience is akin to the delicate balance observed in the cosmos, where every component, however minuscule, contributes to the grandeur of the whole. Communities that enjoy robust healthcare systems are not merely repositories of health; they serve as the bedrock upon which economic activities flourish. A population that is healthy is inherently more productive, better equipped to engage in labour, and less prone to the debilitating effects of chronic illnesses that can thwart both individual aspirations and collective economic progress. As such, the accessibility of healthcare can stimulate a virtuous cycle, where improvements in public health lead to enhanced workforce participation, increased local spending and ultimately, a fortified community economy. It is a self-reinforcing system, demonstrating that the well-being of individuals does not exist in isolation but rather as an interwoven fabric of societal prosperity.

Appendix

The following code is in MATLAB and is based on the QE method:

```
Constantinos Challoumis 2025 ©® All Rights Reserved
% Initialize simulation data
t = 0;
tab = [];
cost_tab = [];

while t < 10
 t = t + 1;

 if rand() < 0.9
  as = 0.6 * rand();
 else
  as = 0;
 end
```

```
if rand() < 0.9
  at = 0.7 * rand();
else
  at = 0;
end

if rand() < 0.9
  m1 = 0.9 * rand();
else
  m1 = 0;
end

if rand() < 0.9
  ap1 = 0.4 * rand();
else
  ap1 = 0;
end
if rand() < 0.9
  ap2 = 0.3 * rand();
else
  ap2 = 0;
end

if rand() < 0.9
  ap3 = 0.2 * rand();
else
  ap3 = 0;
end

a = as + at;
apk = [ap1+ap2+ap3, ap2+ap3, ap1+ap3, ap1, ap2, ap3, ap1+ap2];
cyk = zeros(1, 7);
costs = zeros(1, 7);
```

(Continued)

```
    for i = 1:7
      mk = m1 + apk(i);
      xmk = mk - a;

      if a ~= 0
        cmk = xmk / a;
      else
        cmk = 0;
      end

      if mk ~= 0
        cak = xmk / mk;
      else
        cak = 0;
      end

      cyk(i) = cmk - cak;
      costs(i) = (1 - cyk(i)) * apk(i); % Synthetic cost model
    end

    tab = [tab; apk, cyk];
    cost_tab = [cost_tab; costs];
  end

  % Display synthetic costs
  disp('Synthetic Cost Table:');
  disp(cost_tab);

  % Plot the results
  figure;
  hold on;
  colors = 'rgbcmyk';
  for i = 1:7
```

(Continued)

```
  plot(1:10, cost_tab(:,i), ['-o' colors(i)], 'DisplayName', ['cost' num2str(i)]);
end
title('Synthetic Cost Over Iterations');
xlabel('Iteration');
ylabel('Cost');
legend show;
grid on;
hold off;
```

Bibliography

Al-Habib, N. (2020). 'Leadership and Organizational Performance: Is It Essential in Healthcare Systems Improvement? A Review of Literature'. *Saudi Journal of Anaesthesia*. Retrieved from <https://doi.org/10.4103/sja.SJA_288_19>.

Amoah, P. A., Nyamekye, K. A., and Owusu-Addo, E. (2021). 'A Multidimensional Study of Public Satisfaction with the Healthcare System: A Mixed-Method Inquiry in Ghana'. *BMC Health Services Research*, 21 (1). Retrieved from <https://doi.org/10.1186/s12913-021-07288-1>.

Byrne, J. D., Wentworth, A. J., Chai, P. R., Huang, H. W., Babaee, S., Li, C., … and Traverso, G. (2020). 'Injection Molded Autoclavable, Scalable, Conformable (iMASC) System for Aerosol-based Protection: A Prospective Single-Arm Feasibility Study'. *BMJ Open*, 10 (7). Retrieved from <https://doi.org/10.1136/bmjopen-2020-039120>.

Challoumis, C. (2018). 'Methods of Controlled Transactions and the Behavior of Companies According to the Public and Tax Policy'. *Economics*, 6 (1), 33–43. Retrieved from <https://doi.org/10.2478/eoik-2018-0003>.

Challoumis, C. (2019). 'The R.B.Q. (Rational, Behavioral and Quantified) Model'. *Ekonomika*, 98 (1), 6–18. Retrieved from <https://doi.org/10.15388/ekon.2019.1.1>.

Challoumis, C. (2021). 'Index of the Cycle of Money – The Case of Bulgaria'. *Economic Alternatives*, 27 (2), 225–34. Retrieved from <https://www.unwe.bg/doi/eajournal/2021.2/EA.2021.2.04.pdf>.

Challoumis, C. (2022). 'Conditions of the CM (Cycle of Money)'. In V. Kaya (ed.), *Social and Economic Studies within the Framework of Emerging Global Developments*, Vol. 1, pp. 13–24. Retrieved from <https://doi.org/10.3726/b19907>.

Challoumis, C. (2023a). 'A Comparison of the Velocities of Minimum Escaped Savings and Financial Liquidity'. In V. Kaya (ed.), *Social and Economic Studies within the Framework of Emerging Global Developments*, Vol. 4, pp. 41–56. Retrieved from <https://doi.org/10.3726/b21202>.

Challoumis, C. (2023b). 'From Savings to Escape and Enforcement Savings'. Cogito, XV (4), 206–16.

Challoumis, C. (2023c). 'Impact Factor of Liability of Tax System According to the Theory of Cycle of Money'. In V. Kaya (ed.), *Social and Economic Studies within the Framework of Emerging Global Developments*, Vol. 3, pp. 31–42. Retrieved from <https://doi.org/10.3726/b20968>.

Challoumis, C. (2023d). 'Index of the Cycle of Money: The Case of Costa Rica'. *Sapienza*, 4 (3), 1–11. Retrieved from <https://journals.sapienzaeditorial.com/index.php/SIJIS>.

Challoumis, C. (2023e). 'Risk on the Tax System of the E.U. from 2016 to 2022'. *Economics*, 11 (2), 55–72.

Challoumis, C. (2023f). 'Utility of Cycle of Money without the Escaping Savings (Protection of the Economy)'. In V. Kaya (ed.), *Social and Economic Studies within the Framework of Emerging Global Developments*, Vol. 2, pp. 53–64. Retrieved from <https://doi.org/10.3726/b20509>.

Challoumis, C. (2024a). 'From Economics to Economic Engineering (The Cycle of Money): The Case of Romania'. *Cogito*, XVII (2), 161–70.

Challoumis, C. (2024b). 'Impact Factor of Liability Using the Sensitivity Method'. *Social and Economic Studies within the Framework of Emerging Global Developments.*

Challoumis, C. (2024c). 'Integrating Money Cycle Dynamics and Economocracy for Optimal Resource Allocation and Economic Stability'. *Journal of Risk and Financial Management*, 17 (9), 1–25. Retrieved from <https://doi.org/10.3390/jrfm17090422>.

Challoumis, C. (2024d). 'Rewarding Taxes on the Cycle of Money'. Social and Economic Studies within the Framework of Emerging Global Developments, Vol. 5.

Challoumis, C. (2024e). 'The Index of the Cycle of Money: The Case of Switzerland'. *Journal of Risk and Financial Management*, 17 (4), 1–24. Retrieved from <https://doi.org/https://doi.org/10.3390/jrfm17040135>.

Challoumis, C. (2025). 'The Impact Factor of Tangibles and Intangibles of Controlled Transactions on Economic Performance'. *Economic Alternatives*, 31 (1), 64–76. Retrieved from <https://www.unwe.bg/doi/eajournal/2025.1/EA.2025.1.04.pdf>.

Challoumis, C., and Eriotis, N. (2024a). 'A Historical Analysis of the Banking System and Its Impact on Greek Economy'. *Edelweiss Applied Science and Technology*, 8 (6), 1598–617. Retrieved from <https://learning-gate.com/index.php/2576-8484/article/view/2282/892>.

Challoumis, C., and Eriotis, N. (2024b). 'The Historical View of Banking System in Greece During the Financial Crisis'. *Journal of Ecohumanism*, 5 (8), 991–1011. Retrieved from <https://ecohumanism.co.uk/joe/ecohumanism/article/view/4776>.

Challoumis, C., and Eriotis, N. (2025). 'Management of Enterprises in the Greek Economy'. *Journal of Management World*, 2025(3), 17–30. Retrieved from <https://www.managementworld.online/index.php/mw/article/view/1039>.

Ćwiklicki, M., Klich, J., and Chen, J. (2020). 'The Adaptiveness of the Healthcare System to the Fourth Industrial Revolution: A Preliminary Analysis'. *Futures*, 122. Retrieved from <https://doi.org/10.1016/j.futures.2020.102602>.

Döring, A., and Paul, F. (2010). 'The German Healthcare System'. *EPMA Journal*. Retrieved from <https://doi.org/10.1007/s13167-010-0060-z>.

Grove, A., Sanders, T., Salway, S., Goyder, E., and Hampshaw, S. (2020). 'A Qualitative Exploration of Evidence-based Decision Making in Public Health Practice and Policy: The Perceived Usefulness of a Diabetes Economic Model for Decision Makers'. *Evidence and Policy*, 15 (4). Retrieved from <https://doi.org/10.1332/174426418X15245020185055>.

Hartz, S., and John, J. (2009). 'Public Health Policy Decisions on Medical Innovations: What Role Can Early Economic Evaluation Play?' *Health Policy*, 89 (2). Retrieved from <https://doi.org/10.1016/j.healthpol.2008.05.011>.

Intelligent Predicting Learning Disabilities in School Going Children using Fuzzy Logic K Mean Clustering in Machine Learning (2019).

International Journal of Recent Technology and Engineering, 8 (4). Retrieved from <https://doi.org/10.35940/ijrte.c5620.118419>.

Islam, M. M., Rahaman, A., and Islam, M. R. (2020). 'Development of Smart Healthcare Monitoring System in IoT Environment'. *SN Computer Science*, 1 (3). Retrieved from <https://doi.org/10.1007/s42979-020-00195-y>.

Jagadeeswari, V., Subramaniyaswamy, V., Logesh, R., and Vijayakumar, V. (2018). 'A Study on Medical Internet of Things and Big Data in Personalized Healthcare System'. *Health Information Science and Systems*, 6 (1). Retrieved from <https://doi.org/10.1007/s13755-018-0049-x>.

Kern, J., and Strnad, M. (2005). 'Informatics in the Croatian Health Care System'. *Acta Medica Croatica*, 59 (3).

Lacombe, D. (2019). 'Data Sharing as a Continuum to the Role of International Networks: Beyond Clinical Research'. *Tumori*, 105 (2 Supplement).

Li, J., Cai, J., Khan, F., Rehman, A. U., Balasubramaniam, V., Sun, J., and Venu, P. (2020). 'A Secured Framework for SDN-Based Edge Computing in IoT-Enabled Healthcare System'. *IEEE Access*, 8. Retrieved from <https://doi.org/10.1109/ACCESS.2020.3011503>.

Li, Y., and Tang, M. (2023). 'Blockchain-Powered Distributed Data Auditing Scheme for Cloud-edge Healthcare System'. *Cyber Security and Applications*, 1. Retrieved from <https://doi.org/10.1016/j.csa.2023.100017>.

Manchadi, O., Ben-Bouazza, F. E., and Jioudi, B. (2023). 'Predictive Maintenance in Healthcare System: A Survey'. *IEEE Access*, 11. Retrieved from <https://doi.org/10.1109/ACCESS.2023.3287490>.

Mohamed, N., Al-Jaroodi, J., Jawhar, I., and Kesserwan, N. (2023). 'Leveraging Digital Twins for Healthcare Systems Engineering'. *IEEE Access*, 11. Retrieved from <https://doi.org/10.1109/ACCESS.2023.3292119>.

Pablo, R. G. J., Roberto, D. P., Victor, S. U., Isabel, G. R., Paul, C., and Elizabeth, O. R. (2021). 'Big Data in the Healthcare System: A Synergy with Artificial Intelligence and Blockchain Technology'. *Journal of Integrative Bioinformatics*. Retrieved from <https://doi.org/10.1515/jib-2020-0035>.

Reibling, N., Ariaans, M., and Wendt, C. (2019). 'Worlds of Healthcare: A Healthcare System Typology of OECD Countries'. *Health Policy*. Retrieved from <https://doi.org/10.1016/j.healthpol.2019.05.001>.

Shafqat, S., Kishwer, S., Rasool, R. U., Qadir, J., Amjad, T., and Ahmad, H. F. (2020). 'Big Data Analytics Enhanced Healthcare Systems: A Review'. *Journal of Supercomputing*, 76 (3). Retrieved from <https://doi.org/10.1007/s11227-017-2222-4>.

Studnicki, J., Berndt, D. J., and Fisher, J. W. (2007). 'Using Information Systems for Public Health Administration'. *Public Health Administration: Principles for Population-Based Management*, (2).

Vadalouca, A., Rekatsina, M., and Siafaka, I. (2019). 'ESRA19-0691 Neuropathic Pain Registries: Lessons Learned from International', *European or National Initiatives*. Retrieved from <https://doi.org/10.1136/rapm-2019-esraabs2019.51>.

Wang, W., Li, X., Qiu, X., Zhang, X., Zhao, J., and Brusic, V. (2023). 'A Privacy Preserving Framework for Federated Learning in Smart Healthcare Systems'. *Information Processing and Management*, 60 (1). Retrieved from <https://doi.org/10.1016/j.ipm.2022.103167>.

Forecasting and Assessing Economic Expenditures in the National Budget System Based on an Econometric Model

Zokir Mamadiyarov, Samariddin Makhmudov, Zafar Umarov, Vikorjon Bakhriddinov, Mirzabek Jonuzokov, Nurbek Sheraliev and Dilnoza Uskenbayeva

7.1. Introduction

Budget expenditure projection is an important aspect of economic planning whereby governments are able to project financial requirements, make resource allocation and maintain macroeconomic stability (Zhang et al., 2025; Zhao et al., 2025). Budget projection is central to making budgetary policy consistent with the short-term dynamics of the economy as well as long-term national objectives. Efficient forecasting processes have a vital role in translating fiscal commitments into development pledges and economic ambition. They are necessary for taking decisions involving trade-offs between the nation's economic and social progress and its fiscal health. Efficient forecasting of expenditure is of paramount significance in averting budgetary deficits and maximising public expenditure (Makhmudov et al., 2025).

Several research studies have compared the utilisation of econometric models in forecasting budget expenditure. Scholars such as Crippen, Ria et al., and Yang and Lin have emphasised the application of forecasting models in formulating smart economic policies and maintaining fiscal solvency. Their study accentuates the call for predictive reliability, particularly regarding global economic recessions and development policy at a national level. Empirical evidence demonstrates that advanced econometric techniques, such as ARIMA, markedly enhance expenditure forecasts by accounting for historical trends as well as macroeconomic factors (Olimjonova et al., 2025). These models are especially valuable in identifying underlying patterns within the data, providing a robust framework for forecasting future budgetary needs and purposes. Our study focuses on the application of the ARIMA (2,1,1) model to predict economic expenditure within the Uzbekistan national budget for the period between 2025 and 2029. Based on the historical budget data for 2010–2024, the ARIMA model forecasted the sluggish growth in economic expenditures with the forecast amounting to 42,277.79 billion soums in 2025 and to 53,683.13 billion soums in 2029. The constant growth proves the government's resolute support for the country's development and rising popular demand for infrastructure and services. The forecast reflects a trend of increased spending in the economy with constant financial planning and growing budgetary expenditure in economic and social programmes.

Besides, the research identifies a need for constant methodological development in budget forecasting. As economic conditions evolve, it is crucial to update and sophisticate forecasting techniques continuously to render them accurate and relevant. (Sharipov et al., 2025) Availability of quality data is of utmost significance in creating reliable budget projections, as it necessitates the building of extensive databases and employing sophisticated econometric models (Mamadiyarov et al., 2025). Increased data accuracy and the ability to decipher novel patterns will result in more precise forecasts, and this will go a long way in supporting more informed policy decisions. Against evidence-based knowledge about evolving consumption trends, this study attempts to aid the creation of budget forecasting techniques that ensure stable finances and long-term economic balance in Uzbekistan.

7.2. Literature Review

The national economic expenditure forecasting process via the budget is a vital exercise of responsible finance management (Habib et al., 2025; Kalandarov et al., 2025; Khodjaniyazov et al., 2025). Moreover, it enables governments to prepare adequately in order to neutralise economic uncertainties, which provides room for pre-emptive action to limit potential fiscal difficulties. The forecasts are made on the basis of past trends and prevailing economic conditions so as to balance the budgets and avoid shortfalls (Litamahuputty et al., 2025; Rayala et al., 2025; Romero et al., 2025).

Much research has been conducted by scholars around the world on the prediction of economic expenditure using scientific and econometric models (Kuziboev et al., 2025; Rayala et al., 2025). Crippen (2003) emphasises the urgent requirement of accurate government spending forecasting to enable macroeconomic stability. Through assisting governments to anticipate budget deficits, accurate forecasting allows for early identification of fiscal imbalance. Such prior knowledge enables governments to initiate corrective actions on time, avoiding the potential impact of fiscal shortcomings and achieving a more stable and balanced budgeting policy. Ria et al. (2024) point out in a similar context that forecasting is the foundation for making effective economic policies. It provides policymakers with the critical information to develop strategies that are responsive to changing economic circumstances. They employed econometric models in forecasting GDP and government expenditure and macroeconomic indicators such as imports, exports, unemployment and government expenditure.

Yang and Lin (2023) believe that forward-looking predictors of projections allow governments to forecast future economic expectations and trigger corresponding policy reactions in a manner that induces sustainable economic growth. Their approach focuses on adapting to emerging trends so that policies are individually calibrated to issues and opportunities of the future. Their paper, based on World Bank government spending between 1990 and 2020, has established that ARIMA and SVR models have significantly improved the accuracy of forecasts, citing their economic value in development planning.

Khan (2019) discusses that budget forecasting into the future allows governments to prioritise in advance critical services and investment toward economic developments to enable a smooth consumption of resources. This forward-looking strategy helps guide investment into sectors that will drive long-term growth. His article emphasises how accurate budget forecasting is crucial in the effective execution of planned economic programmes (Abdullah et al., 2025; Khan, 2019). Bianchi et al. (2010) also mention that econometric models featuring behavioural equations and budget balance identifiers raise the accuracy of projections by the interaction of data at different time frequencies, thereby improving expenditure projections within budgetary operations.

Kolari (2019) posits that econometrics enables government budget planning using ARIMA and VAR models. Chugunov and Makohonni (2020) also posit that forecasting is based on data quality and availability and strong and stable datasets are required for effective budgetary forecasting. They emphasise the critical role of a robust data infrastructure in ensuring that budget forecasts are founded on sound and accurate data. They note that efficient forecasting processes are needed to make solid financial decisions. Ericsson and Martinez (2019) also note the need for periodic reviews of forecasting techniques to enhance the credibility and accuracy of budget forecasts. This ongoing review process ensures that forecast models are current and responsive to new economic conditions. Through their research, they encourage the application of advanced econometric analysis to maximise predictive accuracy.

Based on these econometric methods, the current study estimates forecast indicators of the national economic expenses in the national budget mechanism for 2025–2029 using the ARIMA model. The ARIMA model is one of the most applied models in economic forecasting, along with financial analysis based on its performance against high-precision time series data.

The three principal components of the ARIMA model are autoregression (AR), differentiation (I) and moving average (MA). The performance of the ARIMA model in forecasting economic and financial trends has been widely reported in previous studies, for example, by Christodoulos et al. (2010), Sahai et al. (2020), Mélard and Pasteels (2000) and Aghayev and Nazarli (2025). Recent research by Li (2025) and Rizvi (2024) also testifies to its effectiveness in market index forecasting and other important economic variables. These results in aggregate attest to the validity of ARIMA as a robust financial and economic forecasting model, pointing to the fact that it is usable in a wide range of forecasting contexts.

Another group of economists has successfully used econometric models such as Fixed Effects Estimator (FEE), Random Effects Estimator (REE), multivariate linear (LS) and ARDL in their research on investment in digital infrastructure, various aspects of digital payment systems, the impact of inflation and credit interest rates on investment, factors affecting the reduction of the state's share in commercial banks, Non-Performing Loans in commercial banks, the digitisation of banks, risks in digital services and the development of retail payment services (Su et al., 2025; Kurbonov et al., 2024; Mamadiyarov et al., 2025; Zokir et al., 2021).

Analyses and forecasts have been conducted using LS regression, ARDL, ARIMA and other various econometric models on factors affecting remittances, energy intensity and economic development, energy policy, energy risk, environmental status and the impact of environmental aspects on the digital economy, agricultural productivity and the stability of the US credit market (Caporin et al., 2024; Jakhongir et al., 2024; Kuziboev et al., 2025; Makhmudov et al., 2024; Mamadiyarov et al., 2025; Mamani et al., 2025; Muhammad et al., 2025; Ngongo et al., 2025; PANJAITAN et al., 2025; Pradhan et al., 2025; Rony et al., 2025).

7.3. Research Methodology

The study applies the Autoregressive Integrated Moving Average (ARIMA) model to predict the national budget system economic expenditure between 2025 and 2029. ARIMA has been widely adopted as an improved technique for handling time series data, particularly in financial and economic prediction fields (Akhmetshin et al., 2025; Christodoulos et al., 2010; Mélard & Pasteels, 2000; Singagerda et al., 2025; Sofyanty et al., 2025). In comparison to other methods, such as Vector Autoregression (VAR) and Support Vector Regression (SVR), ARIMA is well-suited for univariate time series and is known to be more capable of uncovering underlying trends in historical financial data (Yang & Lin, 2023). It is good at capturing temporal dependencies that are inherent in this type of data, and as such, it is a valuable method for generating accurate economic forecasts.

7.3.1. Data collection and preprocessing

The study makes use of historical expenditure data derived from government budget statements and national statistical offices, ensuring a solid and comprehensive dataset. Time series modelling is highly reliant on data preprocessing because the validity of future predictions relies on the uniformity of the input data. Missing values are dealt with using interpolation techniques, and the Augmented Dickey-Fuller (ADF) test is employed to test stationarity and hence decide on whether differencing is required to achieve stationarity (Sahai et al., 2020).

ARIMA model employed in this study is utilised to forecast economic expenditures under the national budgetary framework for 2025–2029. It has been selected here on the basis of proven performance in economic and financial uses in time series forecasting. In it, several key steps fall within the general methodological framework comprising data collection, the step of model specification, parameter estimation and forecast reliability tests. Previous spending history is thoroughly examined to examine deeper temporal forces to derive a best-fit predictive estimate, where ARIMA methodology is applied in formulating future expenditures prediction. The validity of these estimates is verified with proper statistical metrics to determine the predictive validity and strength of the model results.

7.3.2. Model specification and estimation

The general form of the ARIMA(p, d, q) model is given below

$$y_i = a + b_1 y_{i-1} + b_2 y_{i-2} + \cdots + b_q y_{i-1} + \delta_1 \epsilon_{i-1} + \delta_2 \epsilon_{i-2} + \cdots + \delta_1 \epsilon_{i-m} + \epsilon_i \quad (1)$$

Here

y_i – the value of the time series at time i (after differencing d times), a – denotes the constant term, b_i = (for i = 1, 2, …, q) – denotes the coefficients of the autoregressive part, δ_l = (for l = 1, 2, …, m) – denotes the coefficients of the moving average part. ϵ_i – represents the error term (white noise) at time i.

7.3.3. Model specification and estimation

There are the standard statistical indicators used in the research to measure the accuracy of forecasting, which include:

Root Mean Square Error (RMSE): Applied for measuring total prediction error.

Mean Absolute Percentage Error (MAPE): It measures the relative accuracy of the forecasts.

Mean Squared Error (MSE): Provides a variance of forecasting error measure.

These procedures aid in confirming the authenticity of the model to predict future expenditure (Li, 2025). In order to confirm the strength of ARIMA, in addition, future outcomes from prediction are analysed alongside past government projections to ascertain the usability of the model within real fiscal budgeting (Bianchi et al., 2010).

The research process elucidated in the research ensures an orderly and thorough means of forecasting economic expenditure. Through the application of the ARIMA model and using full data preprocessing, model choice and validation techniques, the study will provide reliable and reliable expenditure projections. The results will help to empower informed fiscal decision-making and strategic budgeting in the national economy, drawing on past research in the role of econometric forecasting in attaining macroeconomic stability (Crippen, 2003; Khan, 2019).

7.4. Analysis and Results

In developing the forecast indicators for the study, quarterly data sources of the Statistical Agency under the President of the Republic of Uzbekistan (<https://stat.uz/uz/>) with a number of observations covering 2010–2024 were used. The resulting variable for the econometric forecast is shown below.

The amount of economic costs is economy_cost (output factor).

An analytical graphical diagram of the volume of economic expenditures over time at the initial stage of econometric forecasting is presented in Figure 2.

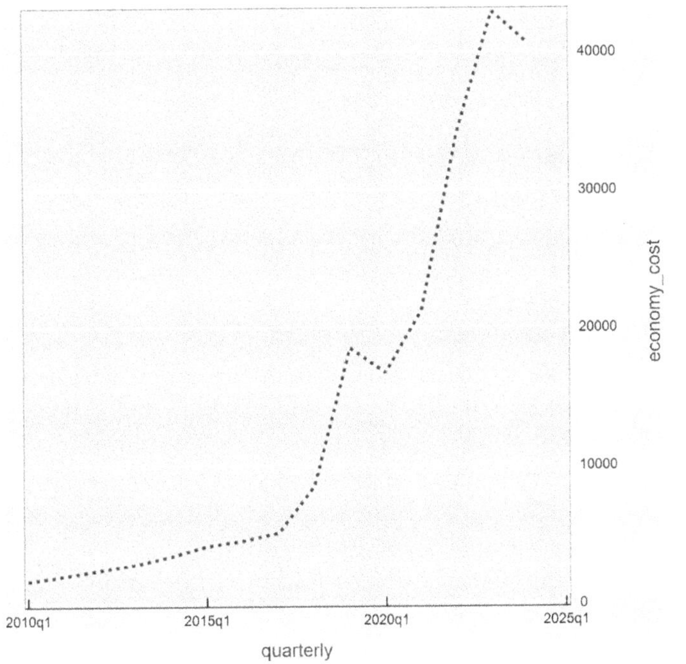

Figure 2. Analytical graphic drawing of the periodic state of the volume of economic expenditures.
Source: It was developed by the authors based on Stata software.

From Figure 2, economic spending has set a steep growth trend since quarter 1 of the year 2018, and the growth is at its maximum by the year 2024. This confirms that the overall trend of growth is due to economic activity and investment growth in the nation and represents a continuous rise in economic spending in the context of growing financial allocations.

In the next stage of the econometric forecast, the level of stationarity of the volume of economic expenditures was assessed and the Unit-Root test was used to determine it (see Table 9).

Table 9. Unit-root test of economic expenditure volume

Economy_cost	Test statistic	1% Critical value	5% Critical value	10% Critical value	*p*-Value for *Z*(*t*)
	−7.213	−3.574	−2.927	−2.598	0.0000

Source: It was developed by the authors based on Stata software.

According to Table 9, the unit root test statistic (−7.213) is significantly below all critical values (1%, −3.574; 5%, −2.927; and 10%, −2.598), which leads to a very high confidence rejection of the null hypothesis of a unit root. According to this, economic expenditure is not a random variable, but has a stable trend.

The *p*-value (0.0000) confirms that the trend in economic expenditure is statistically significant and is unlikely to be due to random fluctuations. This indicates the economic trend of forecasting effectively and systematically in the development of planning and control by the government.

Since the data are stationary, it provides a basis for more reliable forecasting of future economic expenditure and is of great importance in making financial and investment decisions by the government.

According to this sequence, the ARIMA model parameter d has a value of $d = 1$, indicating that it is well-fitting and that the time series has reached stationarity after the first difference.

The next step is to introduce the value of p, which determines the indirect correlation between the lags of the time series of the model (Figure 3).

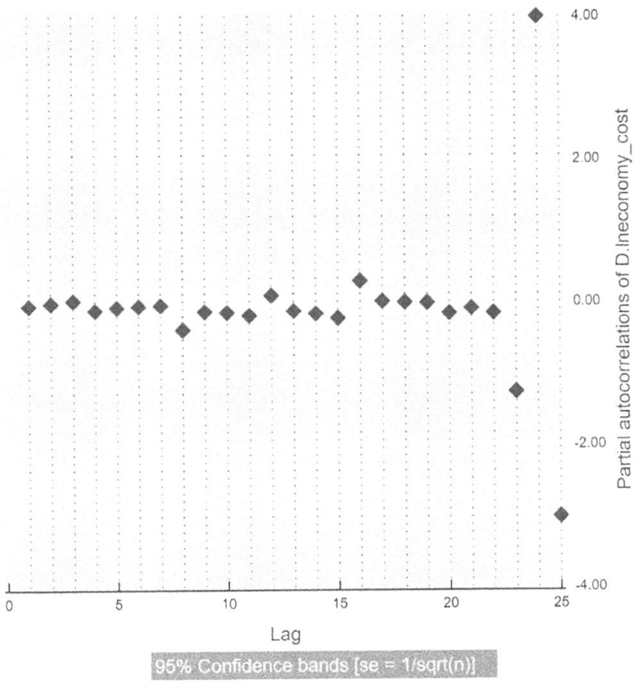

Figure 3. Indirect correlation graph between lags of the econometric model of economic expenditure volume.
Source: It was developed by the authors based on Stata software.

According to Figure 3, the indirect correlation values between the lags of the economic expenditure model are mostly within the 95 per cent confidence intervals, which reinforces the previous Unit-Root test results, indicating the presence of stationarity. Also, the differenced series do not show long-term dependence, which provides positive forecasting indicators in econometric modelling. At the same time, the first few lags are significant, indicating that recent past values affect current economic expenditure.

Most of the lags beyond the initial values are within the confidence interval, indicating that changes in economic expenditure are not dependent on long-term values.

The sharp decrease in correlation after the initial lag indicates the suitability of the autoregressive (AR) model, which helps to effectively capture economic dynamics.

Except for two lags, all lags are within the confidence interval in the indirect correlation analysis.

Accordingly, the *p*-value can be chosen as 1 or 2, and these values can be selected as *p*-values according to the ARIMA model.

In the next step of the ARIMA model, the value of *q* is determined, which describes the direct correlation between the lags of the model (Figure 4).

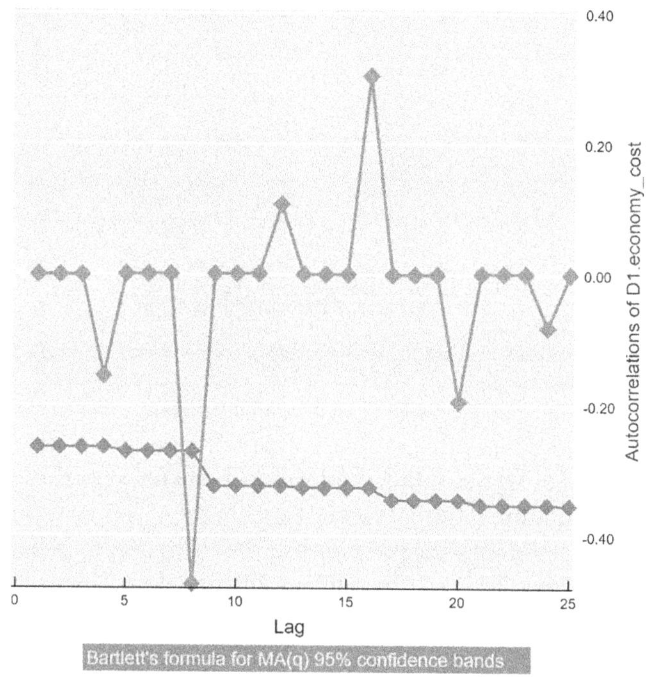

Figure 4. Direct correlation graph between lags of the econometric model of economic expenditure volume.
Source: It was developed by the authors based on Stata software.

Figure 4 reveals that the ARIMA model's correlation is strong and all the lags, except one lag, fall inside the provided confidence interval.

The autocorrelations in the model have a steady pattern over the long run, and this contributes to economic spending being stationary in nature. Most of the autocorrelation values are between the 95 per cent confidence interval, and this does not prevail in cases of random sharp shocks. However, econometric modelling of economic spending has a tendency to increase the reliability of forecast for important and analysed trends.

In the second stage, cumulative spectral periodogram and cumulative spectral distribution analysis are applied for estimating economic expenditure volume over time series on the basis of econometric forecast indicators (Figures 5 and 6).

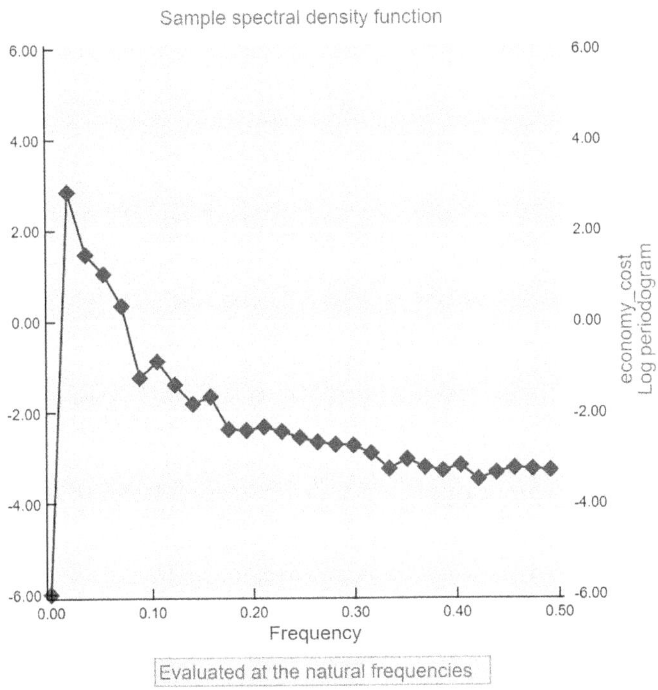

Figure 5. Analysis of the cumulative spectral periodogram graph of the econometric model of economic expenditure volume.
Source: It was developed by the authors based on Stata software.

According to Figure 5, econometric forecasting variables allow us to understand the periodic properties of economic expenditures in the frequency domain. According to them, the plot indicates a trend of stable growth in periodic cycles with a robust peak at low frequencies and fluctuations among the majority of variables of economic expenditures.

In addition, the spectral density function confirms the existence of a persistent, stable long-run trend in economic expenditure with minimal short-run shocks. In such a situation, economic prediction and decision-making exhibit a regular and growth forecast rather than arbitrary fluctuations of economic expenditure.

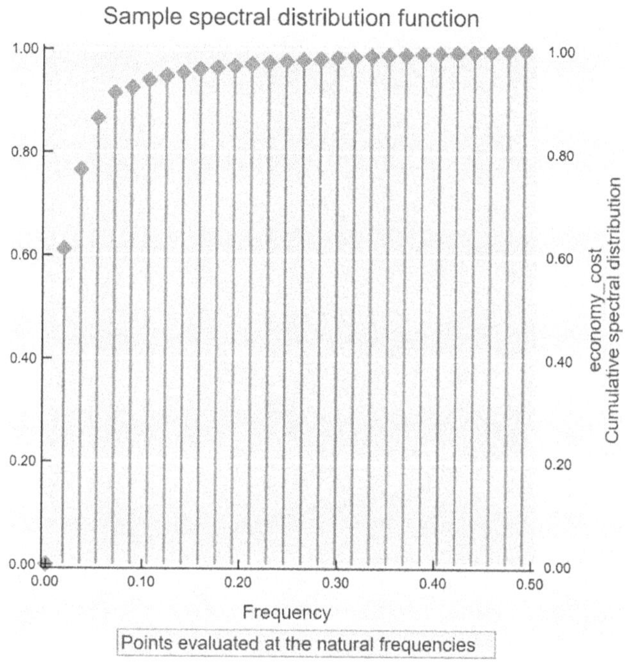

Figure 6. Cumulative spectral distribution graph analysis of the econometric model of economic expenditure volume.
Source: It was developed by the authors based on Stata software.

Figure 6 shows that the cumulative spectral distribution function is increasing in values from 0 to 1, which indicates that the main part of the changes in economic costs is stable and systematic. The cumulative spectral distribution function also emphasises the long-term stability and accurate forecasting of economic costs. The existing process of unsystematic changes represents the correct determination of the main economic costs and the actions according to a systematic scheme that allows for effective forecasting and strategic decision-making in economic planning.

When choosing the optimal ARIMA invariant models for forecasting the model, models of the form ARIMA(1,1,1), ARIMA(2,2,2), ARIMA(1,2,2), ARIMA(2,1,1), ARIMA(2,2,1) and ARIMA(3,1,1) were developed. Among these models, the ARIMA(2,1,1) model with the best results was selected (see Table 10).

Based on the ARIMA model regression result, the econometric equation for the model is given below.

$$\begin{aligned} D.economy\_costt = \beta_0 + \beta_1\, & D.economy\_costt - 1 \\ + \beta_2\, & D.economy\_costt - 2 \\ + \beta_3\, & economy\_costt - 1 + \epsilon t \end{aligned} \tag{3}$$

Table 10. Econometric equation indicators of the ARIMA(2,1,1) model by the volume of economic expenditures.

D. economy_ cost	**Coef.**	**St.Err.**	**t-value**	**p-value**	**[95% Conf**	**Interval]**	**Sig**
Constant	659.198	526.472	1.25	0.211	-372.668	1691.064	
L	1.582	0.34	4.65	0	0.915	2.248	***
L2	−0.679	0.232	-2.93	0.003	-1.134	-0.224	***
L	−0.697	0.527	-1.32	0.086	-1.729	0.335	*
Constant	657.281	57.278	11.48	0	545.019	769.543	***

Mean dependent var	696.395	SD dependent var	1125.939
Number of obs	56	Chi-square	166.351
Prob > chi²	.	Akaike crit. (AIC)	896.715

*** $p < 0.01$, ** $p < 0.05$, * $p < 0.1$

Source: It was developed by the authors based on Stata software.

According to Table 10, the ARIMA(2,1,1) model looks like this:

$$D.\ economy\_costt = 659.19 + 1.58\ D.economy\_costt - 1 - 0.67\ D.economy\_costt - 2 - 0.69\ economy\_costt - 1 + \epsilon t + \varepsilon t \quad (4)$$

In the next step, the ARIMA(2,1,1) model was developed to analyse the mean values of the outcome variable and the graphical representation of the residuals (Table 11 and Figure 7).

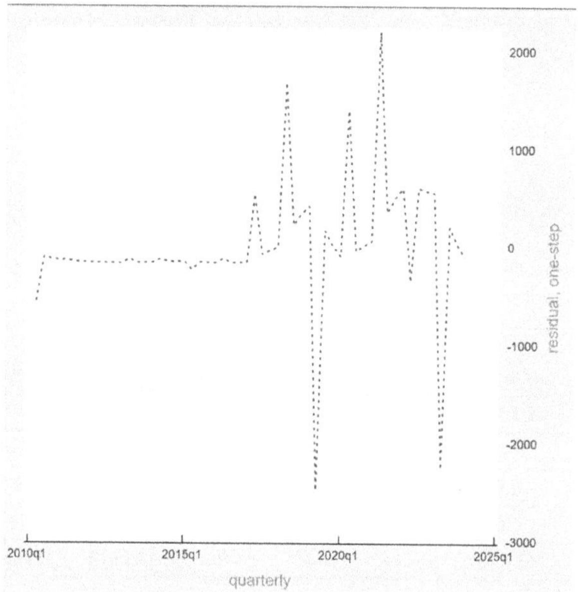

Figure 7. Graph of residual values of the ARIMA(2,1,1) model by the volume of economic expenditures.
Source: It was developed by the authors based on Stata software.

Table 11. Residual values of the resulting factor in the ARIMA(2,1,1) model

Variable	Obs	Mean	Std. dev.	Min	Max
Residual value	56	−2.513218	623.0993	−2487.709	2191.2

Source: It was developed by the authors based on Stata software.

According to Table 11 and Figure 7, the ARIMA(2,1,1) model has reached stochastic equilibrium, as evidenced by the visual representation of the residuals at the specified time intervals. This representation shows the fit of the ARIMA model to the data and the main stochastic relationships in the data set.

The next step involves testing the stationarity of the residuals of the ARIMA(2,1,1) model for the volume of economic expenditures and estimating the autoregressive (AR) and moving average (MA) residuals. The convergence of the ARIMA model to the unit range in forecasting was also checked (Figure 8).

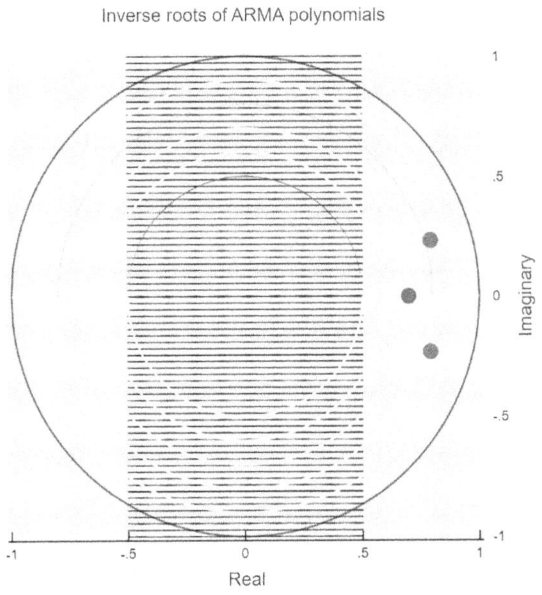

Figure 8. Range of values of the volume of economic expenditures according to the ARIMA(2,1,1) model.
Source: It was developed by the authors based on Stata software.

Using the Stata program, a forecast indicator for the volume of economic expenditures from 2025 to 2029 was developed using the ARIMA(2,1,1) model, excluding random factors (Table 12).

Table 12. Forecast indicators of the volume of economic expenditures for 2025–2029 (in billion soums)

Years	Pessimistic forecasting	Optimistic forecasting	Forecasting
2025	41,125.40	43,430.18	42,277.79
2026	44,355.71	46,660.49	45,508.10
2027	47,324.99	49,629.77	48,477.38
2028	49,963.84	52,268.62	51,116.23
2029	52,530.74	54,835.52	53,683.13

Source: It was developed by the authors based on Stata software.

The study presents a graphical representation of the forecast indicator of the volume of economic expenditures for 2015–2024 and 2025–2029, provided by the Statistical Agency under the President of the Republic of Uzbekistan (<https://stat.uz/uz/>) (Figure 9).

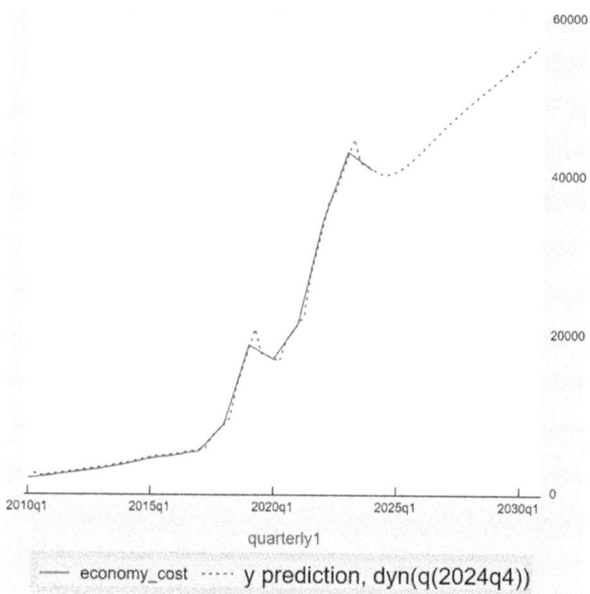

Figure 9. Graph of the resulting variable for 2015–2024 and the forecast for 2025–2029.
Source: It was developed by the authors based on Stata software.

According to Figure 9, the budget system presented by the Statistical Agency under the President of the Republic of Uzbekistan shows the forecast graphs of the volume of economic expenditures for 2010–2024 and 2025–2029. According to it, the trend graph indicates that the forecast indicators for the next five years, excluding random factors, are maximally reliable, since the two lines are located almost side by side.

7.5. Conclusion

According to the research, the level of economic expenditures in the fixed budget system provided by the Statistical Agency on behalf of the President of the Republic of Uzbekistan (<https://stat.uz/uz/>) during 2010–2024 and the projected indicator in the period of 2025–2029 is explained as follows.

1. According to the results of the research, the level of economic expenditure in the budget system based on the ARIMA (2,1,1) model, excluding random exogenous and endogenous factors, is forecasted to be 42,277.79 billion soums in 2025, 45,518.10 billion soums in 2026, 48,477.38 billion soums in 2027, 51,116.23 billion soums in 2028 and 53,683.13 billion soums in 2029, respectively.
2. The ARIMA (2,1,1) model foresees steady and high economic spending in the budget mechanism for 2025–2029, which would be a sound economic trend. The growth trend guarantees that the fiscal resources will keep increasing steadily, benefiting the wide scope of economic and social programmes.
3. Economic spending in 2025 will amount to 42,277.79 billion soums and will be a solid foundation for economic growth.
4. By 2026, the signs of forecast will increase to 45,518.10 billion soums. The growth will be extended to fiscal growth and investment.
5. The forecast indicators of expenditure in 2027 as equal to 48,477.38 billion soums demonstrate the enhancement of financial resources of the state for development to cater to the large-scale economic and industrial sectors. It indicates that it will be conducted on the basis of programmes and development strategies implemented in the country.

6. The projection of 51,116.23 billion soums in 2028 depicts fiscal stability in planning, which is emerging as a result of systematic development of the national financial system.
7. The indicator of the 53,683.13 billion soum forecast by 2029 displays a strong financial condition that ensures long-term economic stability.
8. The growing trend reflects rising economic stability, increased budgetary expenditures and well-managed fiscal policies that foster overall national development.

Bibliography

Abdullah, M. A., Han, X., Amjad, M. A., & Makhmudov, S. (2025). Revisit the role of financial development on economic growth, human development, and sustainable development in higher-income countries. *Journal of Environmental Management*, 392, 126874.

Akhmetshin, E., Abdullayev, I., Makhmudov, S., Dakhkilgova, K., Korotaeva, I. and Yanovskaya, G. (2025). APPLICATION OF TANH–COTH METHOD FOR COMBINED AND DOUBLE COMBINED SINH–COSH–GORDON EQUATIONS ARISING CHEMICAL REACTIONS TO WATER SURFACE GRAVITY WAVES. Computational Methods for Differential Equations. doi: 10.22034/cmde.2025.67655.3234

Aghayev, E., and Nazarli, T. (2025). 'ARIMA-based Forecasting for Economic Indicators'. *Journal of Economic Research*, 12 (1), 88–103.

Bianchi, G., Cesaroni, T., and Ricci, O. (2010). *Forecast of Expenses of the State Budget Through Financial Accounting Flows*. MPRA Paper, 1, 271–326. Retrieved from <https://mpra.ub.uni-muenchen.de/27440/> (Accessed 15/03/2025).

Caporin, M., Shahbaz, M., Kuziboev, B., Masharipova, M., Allaberganov, S., & Makhmudov, S. (2024). Environmental Kuznets Curve for extended brics economies: do women governance and water stress matter?. *International Journal of Energy Economics and Policy*, 14(6), 174–183.

Christodoulos, C., Michalakelis, C., and Varoutas, D. (2010). 'Forecasting with Limited Data: Combining ARIMA and Diffusion Models'. *Technological Forecasting and Social Change*, 77 (4), 558–65.

Chugunov, I., and Makohon, V. (2020). 'Budgetary Projection in the System of Financial and Economic Regulation of Social Processes'. *Baltic Journal of Economic Studies*, 6 (1), 130–5. <https://doi.org/10.30525/2256-0742/2020-6-1-130-135>.

Crippen, D. (2003). 'Countering Uncertainty in Budget Forecasts'. *OECD Journal on Budgeting*, 3 (2), 139–51. <https://doi.org/10.1787/BUDGET-V3-ART12-EN>.

Ericsson, N. R., and Martinez, A. B. (2019). *Evaluating Government Budget Forecasts*. Palgrave Macmillan, pp. 37–69. <https://doi.org/10.1007/978-3-030-18195-6_3>.

Jakhongir, S., Muhabbat, H., Khayrilla, K., Kholmuratov, S., Nazirjon, R., Nilufar, F., and Farxod, T. (2024). 'Crafting a Neutrosophic-Driven Tool to Probe Turnover Propensities in Manufacturing Entities'. *International Journal of Neutrosophic Science (IJNS)*, 23 (2).

Habib, S. S., Islam, M. A., Ali, M. N., Benitez, I. B., Mamadiyarov, Z., Mirzayev, B., … & Flah, A. (2025). *Multi-Objective Optimization and Feasibility Analysis of Integrated Biogas–Solar Energy Systems for Rural Electrification*. Results in Engineering, 107086.

Hakimjon, H., Vikorjon, B., Ural, K., and Nabieva, N. (2024). 'The Fusion of Inflation and Economic Growth: A Time Series Analysis'. *Fusion: Practice & Applications*, 15 (2).

Kalandarov, F., Makhmudov, S., Ibadullaev, D., Matniyozov, M., Nasretdinova, F., Sabirov, K., & Bahodirov, N. M. (2025). Low-Carbon Energy Risk and Renewable Energy Development: Insights from Method of Moments Quantile Regression. International Journal of Energy Economics and Policy, 15(3), 524–536.

Khan, A. (2019). *Elements of Budget Forecasting*, pp. 229–71. Palgrave Macmillan, <https://doi.org/10.1007/978-3-030-19226-6_7>.

Khodjaniyazov, N., Mirkhoshimova, M., Kalandarov, F., Matyokubova, D., Utegenova, S., Makhmudov, S., & Khudayberganov, M. (2025). Time-Varying Impacts of Financial Stress on Energy-Related Uncertainty. International Journal of Energy Economics and Policy, 15(3), 689–698.

Kolari, S. (2019). Improving the Budgeting of Framework Agreement Volumes with Time Series Models in Governmental Procurement.

Kuziboev, B., Khodjaniyazov, E., Ozturk, I., Sabirov, K., Makhmudov, S., & Utegenova, S. (2025). Does oil dependence cause energy risk?. Energy Nexus, 17, 100393.

Lee, Y. (2025). 'Forecasting the Shanghai Composite Index Using the ARIMA Model'. *Advances in Economics, Management and Political Sciences*, 144 (1), 107–15. <https://doi.org/10.54254/2754-1169/2024.ga19094>.

Litamahuputty, J. V., Amiruddin, E. G., Rahim, R., Rahman, A., & Mamadiyarov, Z. (2025). Cryptocurrency Risk Management through Decision Engineering: Evaluating XRPUSD and ADAUSD Portfolio Performance. Journal of Applied Science, Engineering, Technology, and Education, 7(1), 69–81. https://doi.org/10.35877/454RI.asci3871

Mamadiyarov, Z., Eshov, M., Otakhonova, D., Utegenova, S., Sabirov, K., Marks, A., & Bahodirov, N. (2025). Does Energy Policy Risk Threaten Energy Sources Diversification?. International Journal of Energy Economics and Policy, 15(5), 730–740. https://doi.org/10.32479/ijeep.21140

Mamadiyarov, Z. Makhmudov, S. Utanov, B. Kasimova, D. Bekmurodova, G. Hakimov, Z. (2025). Fusion of Economic and Financial Factors Affecting Household Deposits in Banks: An Econometric Analysis. Fusion: Practice and Applications, (), 82–91. DOI: https://doi.org/10.54216/FPA.190206

Mamadiyarov, Z., Saidov, O., Abdurazakova, N., Makhmudov, S., Nazarov, M., Rajabova, N., … Ruzmetova, I. (2025). Energy-Related Uncertainty and Tourism Stock Markets: New Insights from Time-Varying Relationship with TVP- VAR Approach. International Journal of Energy Economics and Policy, 15(4), 730–737. https://doi.org/10.32479/ijeep.20480

Mamani, J.C.M., Miri, M., Vorobev, Y. et al. Optimal Operation of Energy Microgrid Considering Economic and Emission Indices. Oper. Res. Forum 6, 122 (2025). https://doi.org/10.1007/s43069-025-00523-z

Mélard, G., and Pasteels, J. M. (2000). 'Automatic ARIMA Modeling Including Interventions, Using Time Series Expert Software'. *International Journal of Forecasting*, 16 (4), 497–508.

Muhammad Zubair, Irfanud Din, Nadeem Sarwar et al. Revolutionizing Sepsis Diagnosis Using Machine Learning and Deep

Learning Models: A Systematic Literature Review, 10 June 2025, PREPRINT (Version 1) available at Research Square [https://doi.org/10.21203/rs.3.rs-6731418/v1]

Ngongo, M., Herman, H., Ndandara, A., Jois Jaha, D. A., Peku Djawang, J. U. S., Tanggu Rame, M. M., Khamraeva, S. N., & Mamadiyarov, Z. (2025). An Investigation of Meaning, Toponymy of Sumba Cultural Site's Names, and the Impact of Tourism Visitors on Surrounding Society. Forum for Linguistic Studies, 7(8), 679–693. https://doi.org/10.30564/fls.v7i8.10260

PANJAITAN, M. B., HAMDANAH, H., SIRAIT, J., SUTIKNO, S., FATMAWATI, E., HERMAN, H., & MAMADIYAROV, Z. (2025). THE ROLE OF EMOTIONAL REGULATION IN SHAPING STUDENTS' PERCEPTION OF PHYSICS PROBLEMSOLVING TASKS. TPM – Testing, Psychometrics, Methodology in Applied Psychology, 32(S2(2025)): Posted 09 June), 1–10. Retrieved from https://tpmap.org/submission/index.php/tpm/article/view/139

Pradhan, R., Hajiyev, E., Shichiyakh, R. et al. Optimal Techno-Economic Feasibility of an Off-Grid Microgrid System Using Load Flow Energy Management Strategies. Oper. Res. Forum 6, 120 (2025). https://doi.org/10.1007/s43069-025-00524-y

Rayala, R. V., Borra, C. R., Vasudevan, V., Singhania, R., Cheekati, S., & Mamadiyarov, Z. (2025, July). Lightweight Deep Learning Framework for Human Activity Recognition: A MobileNet-LSTM Approach with WHOA Optimization. In *2025 International Conference on Innovations in Intelligent Systems: Advancements in Computing, Communication, and Cybersecurity (ISAC3)* (pp. 1–6). IEEE.

Rayala, R. V., Sandhya, N., Singhania, R., Cheekati, S., Borra, C. R., Vasudevan, V., & Mamadiyarov, Z. (2025, July). AI-Driven Tomato Quality Assessment: A Deep Learning Approach for Image-based Defect Detection and Classification. In *2025 International Conference on Innovations in Intelligent Systems: Advancements in Computing, Communication, and Cybersecurity (ISAC3)* (pp. 1–6). IEEE.

Ria, N. I., Gupta, Y., Saxena, V., Begwani, S., Vijarania, M., and Gupta, S. (2024). 'Evaluating Economic Policies: Anticipating GDP Trends and Government Spending'. In *IEEE ICTACS Conference Proceedings*, p. 1071–6. <https://doi.org/10.1109/ictacs62700.2024.10840912>.

Rizvi, M. F. (2024). 'ARIMA Model Time Series Forecasting'. *International Journal for Research in Applied Science and Engineering Technology*. <https://doi.org/10.22214/ijraset.2024.62416>.

Romero, R. M., Zelinskaya, M., Makhmudov, S., Sapaev, S., & Rustambekovich, J. U. (2025, September). Modelling and Optimal Utilisation of the Renewable Energy Systems in Microgrid with Improving Reliability and Energy Efficiency. In Operations Research Forum (Vol. 6, No. 3, pp. 1–20). Springer International Publishing.

Rony, Z. T., Jefri, R., Rusmardiana, A., Pramono, S. A., & Mamadiyarov, Z. (2025). Downside Risk Measurement of Indonesian Financial and Energy Securities: A Value at Risk Perspective. Journal of Applied Science, Engineering, Technology, and Education, 7(2). https://doi.org/10.35877/454RI.asci3898

Sahai, A. K., Rath, N., Sood, V., and Singh, M. P. (2020). 'ARIMA Modeling & Forecasting of COVID-19 in Top Five Affected Countries'. *Diabetes & Metabolic Syndrome: Clinical Research & Reviews*, 14 (5), 1419–27.

Singagerda, F. S., Pratama, M. R., Alfairus, M. Q., Iskandar, A., & Mamadiyarov, Z. (2025). A Decision-Centric Approach to Risk Management in Aviation Stock Investments Using Value at Risk and Portfolio Optimization. Journal of Applied Science, Engineering, Technology, and Education, 7(1), 114–125. https://doi.org/10.35877/454RI.asci3870

Sharipov, K., Abdullayev, I., Kuziboev, B., Makhmudov, S., Kalandarov, F., Khaytboeva, N., & Ilkhamova, Z. (2025). The Effect of Energy Policy Risk on Renewable Energy. International Journal of Energy Economics and Policy, 15(2), 566.

Sofyanty, D., Romadhoni, R., Handriadi, H., Makhsudovna, I. S., Anwar, Z., & Mamadiyarov, Z. (2025). Strategic Decision Analysis for Investment Portfolios: Computational Risk Assessment in Transportation Asset Management. Journal of Applied Science, Engineering, Technology, and Education, 7(2). https://doi.org/10.35877/454RI.asci3897

Su, R., Xiao, Y., Hamza, F., Mamadiyarov, Z., & Wahab, A. (2025). Scaling up green hydrogen in China: Economic opportunities and challenges. International Journal of Hydrogen Energy, 131, 60–69.

Yang, C.-H., and Lin, Y.-D. (2023). 'The Forecasting of a Leading Country's Government Expenditure Using a Recurrent Neural Network with a Gated Recurrent Unit'. *Mathematics*. <https://doi.org/10.3390/math11143085>.

Zhang, L., Zhao, Z., Qamri, G. M., & Makhmudov, S. (2025). Unleashing the critical role of renewable energy through global value chains and digitalization: A path towards environmental sustainability. Journal of Environmental Management, 392, 126688.

Zhao, Q., Pervaiz, A., Makhmudov, S., & Fatima, A. (2025). Do environmental stringent policies enhance the impact of renewable energy on CO2 reduction? Evidence from BRICS-T economies. Journal of Environmental Management, 391, 126464.

Zokir Toshtemirovich Mamadiyarov, Samandarboy Adhambek ugli Sulaymanov, Sarvar Anvar ugli Askarov, and Durdona Bakhtiyor kizi Uktamova. 2022. Impact of Covid-19 Pandemic on Accelerating The Digitization and Transformation of Banks. In Proceedings of the 5th International Conference on Future Networks and Distributed Systems (ICFNDS '21). Association for Computing Machinery, New York, NY, USA, 706–712. https://doi.org/10.1145/3508072.3508211

Econometric Modelling of Determinants Shaping Public Procurement Efficiency in Budgetary Organisations

Raya Karlibaeva, Zokir Mamadiyarov, Samariddin Makhmudov, Ilhomjon Alimov, Irina Dolgova, Nozila Toxtayeva and Mirjalol Eshboev

8.1. Introduction

Foreign studies show that today, public procurement in budgetary organisations is an important component of the optimal management of economic processes. These practices are an important strategic direction for the development of the country's economy, influencing sectors of the economy by directing public spending in budgetary organisations to goods and services. Public procurement in budgetary organisations, while stimulating innovation and employment, serves sustainable economic growth by supporting the effective use of public funds.

In addition, public procurement can help to develop a competitive environment in various sectors of the economy, support local producers and increase economic activity. An effective public procurement system helps to reduce corruption, ensure transparency and strengthen fiscal discipline. Also, when public procurement is implemented based on the principles of environmental and social sustainability, it allows for the development of a green economy and promotes the rational use of resources. Thus, public procurement not only contributes to economic stability and growth but also serves as an important mechanism for protecting social and environmental interests.

8.2. Literature Review and Development Hypothesis

Anthony Flynn and others (2012) argue that public procurement can be a catalyst in economic sectors by introducing demand into the market, stimulating the local economy and creating employment opportunities. According to him, public procurement in Russia is growing through an increase in the number of contracts, which has a positive impact on employment and innovation as a result of supporting economic orders.

According to Manuel Gerardo et al. (2024), public procurement represents a high proportion of public spending, which requires its integration with other areas of management to improve efficiency and reduce risks. According to the results of the researchers' research, risk management strategies in public procurement practices in budgetary organisations have been able to mitigate potential disruptions, which indicates that this hypothesis has been confirmed during the COVID-19 crisis.

According to research by Paul K. Davis et al. (2012), public procurement in Ireland has been identified as a means of stimulating economic growth by supporting small businesses and thereby injecting demand into local markets. The results showed that reforms to reduce barriers to procurement and improve micro-enterprises led to increased financial returns and support for local budgets.

Many researchers and scholars have developed scientific and econometric studies on the factors influencing public procurement in budget organisations.

The econometric analysis of public procurement practices, in particular of budgetary organisations, includes legal and regulatory frameworks, organisational and economic elements and other macro-level variables as influencing factors. Budgetary organisations, as a result, procurement is an important component of public spending, and its effectiveness is associated with problems such as corruption, budget constraints and organisational inefficiency.

According to A. E. Lyapin (2024), cartel agreements are one of the most important problems in corruption in public procurement; they undermine fair competition and lead to inefficient use of budget funds. Based on the results of the study, the authors recommend the main characteristics of cartels, recommended methods for their detection, and a systematic approach to effectively combating cartels, in particular, improving the software and technical tools used to improve the quality of the work of regulatory bodies.

Camelia Febryanti et al. (2024) argue that 'effective procurement requires adherence to regulatory frameworks. In foreign countries, challenges have been noted in terms of compliance with procurement regulations, highlighting the need for improved procurement efficiency and robust cost control mechanisms.

Fadlina Almi et al. (2022) state that 'the quality of human resources and organisational commitment significantly affect procurement performance'. The authors, in their analysis of procurement practices in Indonesia, found that these factors directly affected budget utilisation, explaining the importance of qualified personnel and committed management in procurement processes.

According to O. Postennikov et al. (2024), central procurement organisations play a key role in improving procurement efficiency by centralising public procurement activities, leading to cost savings and increased professionalism. In their scientific work, the authors analysed the role of central procurement organisations as an effective tool in combating corruption and abuses in the public procurement system in Ukraine from 2019 to 2023 based on econometric models. The authors' research results showed that serious violations were identified in public procurement processes in Ukraine, in particular in the areas of evaluation of tender proposals and preparation of tender documents.

According to Vitaly Kikavets and others (2023), financial control in budgetary organisations is an important factor in the optimal management of public procurement. It is considered state, departmental and financial control to ensure compliance with financial laws and the proper use of budget funds.The authors' research results showed that departmental and financial control of public procurement in budgetary organisations, as well as internal financial control, emphasise compliance with legislative norms.

According to Elena Igonina et al. (2024), the principle of efficient use of budget funds is an important factor in the formation of costs in state institutions and recommends a methodology for determining the lowest contract price. According to Kenneth and Strang (2024), personal factors, in particular the experience and certification of project managers, affect the success of procurement projects. The authors noted that, according to the research, certified project managers are more likely to achieve successful results. According to them, 59 per cent of 2,692 public procurement projects were successfully implemented, while 41 per cent failed. This confirms a significant level of progress in these projects.

According to the scientific work of Hamed Mahmoud et al. (2022), corruption and internal organisational factors have a significant impact on the main agreements on public procurement in budgetary organisations. Addressing these processes is important in preventing budget deficits and ensuring the integrity of procurement. The authors' research results showed that corruption and organisational factors had a significant impact on public procurement agreements and that social factors were insignificant.

According to Garima Bhagat et al. (2024), an organisational integrity environment characterised by transparency, leadership and fair competition is essential for successful public procurement.

A. Sergechuka notes that the choice between public and proposed tender procedures in public procurement directly affects costs and revenues. Public procedures are usually expensive, yielding higher revenues for large contract values, and it has been found that public procedures are 2–3 times more expensive for buyers and 3.5 times more expensive for suppliers than proposed procedures.

8.3. Research Methodology

In the construction of an econometric model for the dissertation work, 44 economic indicators were used, consisting of monthly data sources from 2019 to 2023, from the Statistical Agency under the President of the Republic of Uzbekistan (<https://stat.uz/uz/>), the Uzbekistan Republican Commodity Exchange (<https://xarid.uzex.uz>) and the Central Bank of the Republic of Uzbekistan (https://cbu.uz/).

Since the data are based on multivariate time series, we used a multivariate linear equation (LS) model to construct the econometric equation.

During the study, the Gauss–Markov estimates of the multivariate regression equation (LS) model (Kokaly, R. F., & Clark, R. N., 1999; Sofyanty et al., 2025) were examined, and the level of statistical significance was analysed using confidence tests, in particular Durbin–Watson (Rutledge, D. N., & Barros, A. S., 2002), Shapiro–Wilk (de Souza, R. R., Toebe, M., Mello, A. C., & Bittencourt, K. C., 2023), and Breusch–Pagan (Halunga, et al., 2017; Akhmetshin et al., 2025; Kuchkarov et al., 2025; Kuziboev et al., 2025; Litamahuputty et al., 2025; Ngongo et al., 2025).

Another group of economists has successfully used econometric models such as Fixed Effects Estimator (FEE), Random Effects Estimator (REE), multivariate linear (LS) and ARDL in their research on investment in digital infrastructure, various aspects of digital payment systems, the impact of inflation and credit interest rates on investment, factors affecting the reduction of the state's share in commercial banks, Non-Performing Loans in commercial banks, the digitisation of banks, risks in digital services and the development of retail payment services (Habib et al., 2025; Jahrir et al.,

2025; Kalandarov et al., 2025; Khodjaniyazov et al., 2025; Rony et al., 2025; Su et al., 2025; Zokir et al., 2021).

Analyses and forecasts have been conducted using multivariate linear regression (LS), ARDL, ARIMA and other various econometric models on factors affecting remittances, energy intensity and economic development, energy policy, energy risk, environmental status and the impact of environmental aspects on the digital economy, agricultural productivity and the stability of the US credit market (Kuziboev et al., 2025; Mamadiyarov et al., 2025; Jakhongir et al., 2024; Sharipov et al., 2025; Caporin et al., 2024; Abdullah et al., 2025; Rayala et al., 2025; Suet al., 2025; Zhang et al., 2025).

We used analytical statistical images, scatter and graphical matrix plots, normal distribution plots, correlation matrices, analytical graphs of time series and graphical images of the dependence of all variables during the construction of the econometric research, in particular, the multivariate linear equation (LS) model. The VIF test (Kruzic, et al.., 2009; Mamadiyarov et al., 2025; Mamani et al., 2025; Muhammad et al., 2025; Romero et al., 2025; Samariddin et al., 2025; Singagerda et al., 2025; Zhao et al., 2025) was used to assess the multicollinearity of the econometric model.

According to S. Ganesh (2010), 'unlike univariate models for predicting a single outcome, multivariate linear models are important for predicting multiple outcomes simultaneously'. This has proven to be particularly useful in economic fields. According to Chen Shi-ji (1994), the fitting of an econometric model is usually done using the least squares method, which minimises the sum of the squares of the differences between the observed and predicted values. Econometrics in modelling statistic method model clear forecast in ability important place holds (Sofyanty et al., 2025).

According to Teresa Aparicio and others (2003), the model is the unobservable random term. Often, the term 'error' is used, this independent variables by not caught factors, that take measurement mistakes into account takes. S. Ganesh than many variable linear models done increase Like SAS for statistic from programs use wide spread. These tools are the model installation, analysis to do and visualisation in doing functions provides.

Below many factorial linear equation (LS) model formula quoted.

$$y_i = \alpha_0 + \alpha_{1i} + x\alpha_2 x_{2i} + \cdots + \alpha_k x_{ki} + u_i \quad (1)$$

Here, y_i – observation for related variable is being modelled consequential changeable represents.

$x_{1i}, x_{2i}, \ldots, x_k$ – are independent variables (effect doer factors) represents.
$\alpha_1, \alpha_2, \ldots, \alpha_k$ – *regression* coefficients (each one represents the effect of the factor).
u_i – residual (error) value represents.

Econometric models, according to all the variables, are natural logarithmic. Below, according to the econometric model, all variables are expressed.

Variables: Government procurement contracts number – *lnpubl_proc_contr* (result variable), GDP growth rate – *lnGDP_grow_rate* (independent variable),
Average weighted credit rate – *lnweight_loan_rate* (independent variable),
Online and electronic purchases volume – *lnonline_electr_vol* (independent variable).
Currency course – *change_rate* (independent variable).
By auction purchases size – *ln_purch_auct_vol* (independent variable).

Econometric the research working at the exit head (H_0) and alternative (H_1) hypotheses own on the contrary found.

Combined model hypothesis structure:

Main hypothesis (H_0)*:* GDP growth pace, average weighed credit rate, online and electronic purchases size, currency course, auction through purchases size and and state purchases contracts to the number noticeable at the level impact does not show and dependency symptoms there is it's not.
Alternative hypothesis (H_1)*:* GDP growth pace, average weighted credit rate, online and electronic purchases size, currency course, auction through purchases size and state purchases contracts to the number noticeable at the level impact showing solid dependency demonstration will reach.

8.4. Analysis and Results

Econometric research initial in the phase state purchases contracts number and to him/her impact provider variables according to descriptive statistic values expressed (Table 13).

Table 13. Government procurement contracts number and to him/her impact provider of factors descriptive statistic indicators value

	lnpubl_ proc_ contr	change_ rate	ln_ weight_ loan_rate	ln_purch_ auct_vol	lnGDP_ grow_rate	lnonline_ electr_vol
Mean	9.069774	12.45367	3.017905	2.589036	2.757271	10.8722
Maximum	10.09252	12.98042	3.672131	2.793892	3.00072	3.00072
Minimum	7.20786	11.77082	2.340264	2.317196	2.580217	8.860059
Std. Dev	0.6975009	0.3174031	0.4170684	0.0996676	0.1152437	0.8103802
Std. Err.	0.1051522	0.0478503	0.0628754	0.0150255	0.0150255	0.1221694
Skewness	-0.6600682	-0.2373874	0.0415707	-0.6538593	0.5085942	-0.5445633
Kurtosis	2.801474	2.092475	1.840047	3.390797	2.121551	2.611573
Observation	44	44	44	44	44	44

Source: It was developed by the authors based on Stata software.

According to the data in Table 13, according to the model according to descriptive statistic indicators, all variables central ranges average to value impact enough without extreme without borders balanced information offer Table from the data this see maybe standard deviations average variability harvest did and all factors for small the value presented reached.

Also consequential and to him/her effect provider factors 44 by from observation consists of to be information in the collection consistency and in comparison important importance profession Variables according to Skewness test values zero to the value closeness in consideration received without, symmetrical to distribution has was. With this together, the Kurtosis value 3 closeness into account received without, normal presentation positive value expressed.

Research according to, economy done state purchases size and to him/her impact provider of variables time according to graphic image working (Figure 10).

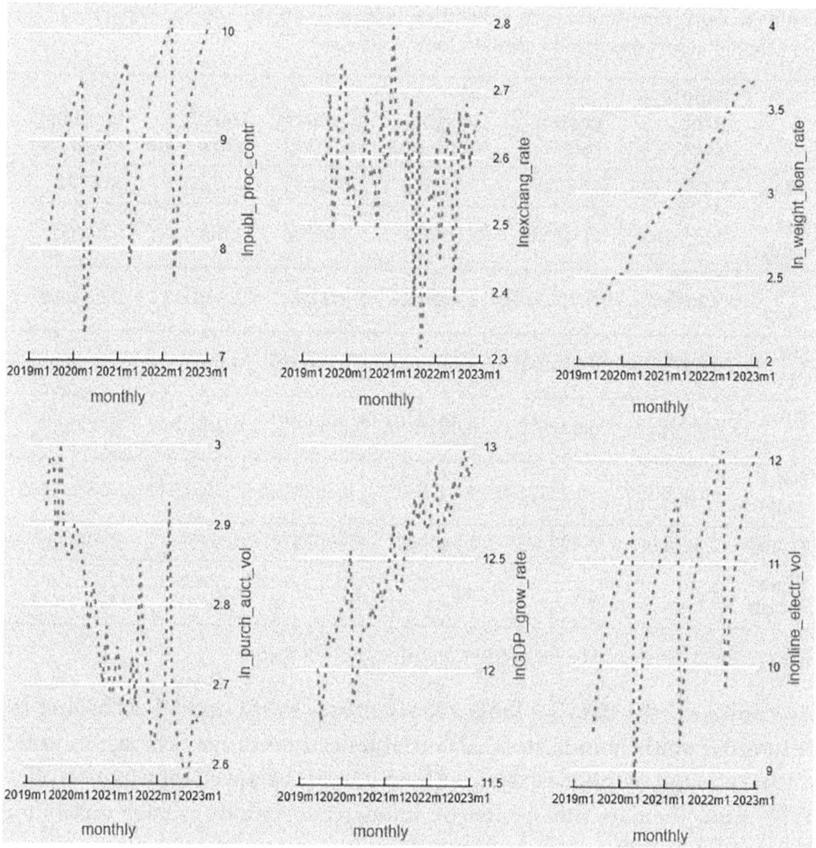

Figure 10. Analytical graphic representation of the number of public procurement contracts and the factors affecting them over time.
Source: It was developed by the authors based on Stata software.

According to Figure 10, the output factor and the variables affecting it have formed promising forecast indicators, demonstrating a regular growth trend. The analytical period shows that while the country's GDP has grown sharply, the number of government procurement contracts and the volume of electronic and online purchases have fluctuated in proportion to the growth dynamics. This directly indicates a strong correlation between these two factors.

Changes in the country's exchange rate have recently shown a stochastic trend, and the volume of purchases through auctions has shown a certain tendency to decrease in recent quarters. The fact that weighted average credit rates have formed growth indicators in recent years indicates changes in monetary policy in the country.

In the next step of the econometric study, a graphical matrix and scatter plot of the number of government procurement contracts and the factors affecting it were presented (Figures 11 and 12).

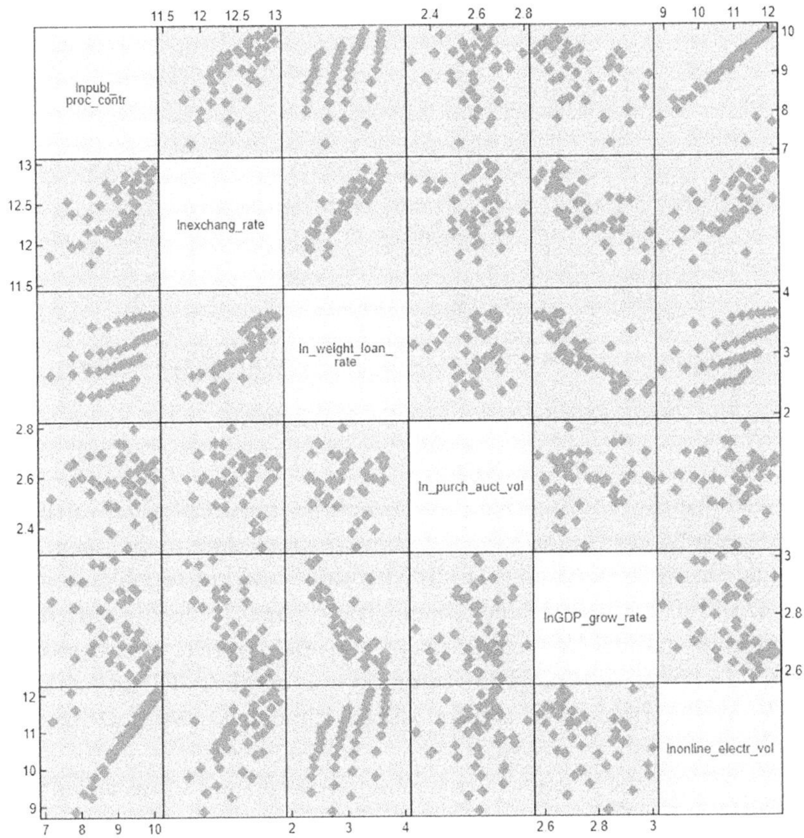

Figure 11. Graphical matrix representation of the number of public procurement contracts and the factors affecting it.
Source: It was developed by the authors based on Stata software.

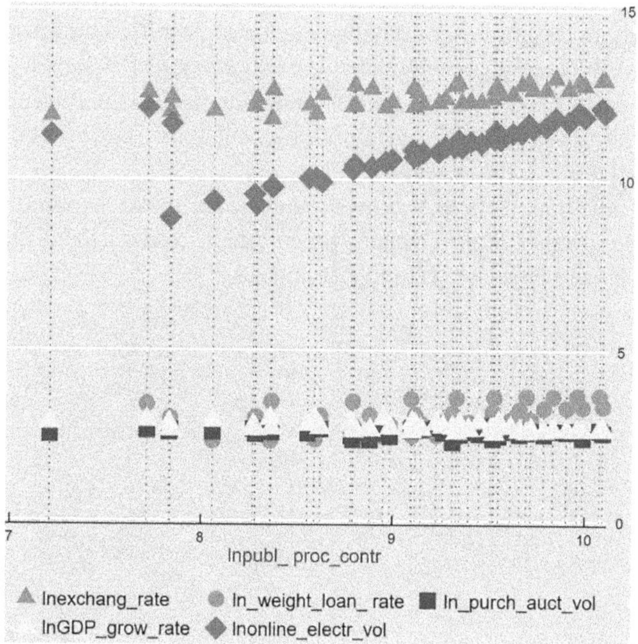

Figure 12. Scatter plot of the number of public procurement contracts and the factors affecting it.
Source: It was developed by the authors based on Stata software.

Showed that the resulting factor and to him/her impact provider variables between solid correlation shown and images according to density effect mutual enema effect naming This is what shows that the variables systematic accordingly connected and econometric in research effective modelling opportunity created by. Graphic image potential positive to relationships hint did without, state purchases contracts your number GDP growth rate, online and electronic purchases and auction through purchases size impact as a result to the body arrived.

According to the econometric model, analytical graphic scatter and matrices diagonal sub drawings confirmed that all variables have a linear attitude.

Next in stages state purchases contracts number and to him/her impact provider of factors analytical connected graph image (Figure 13).

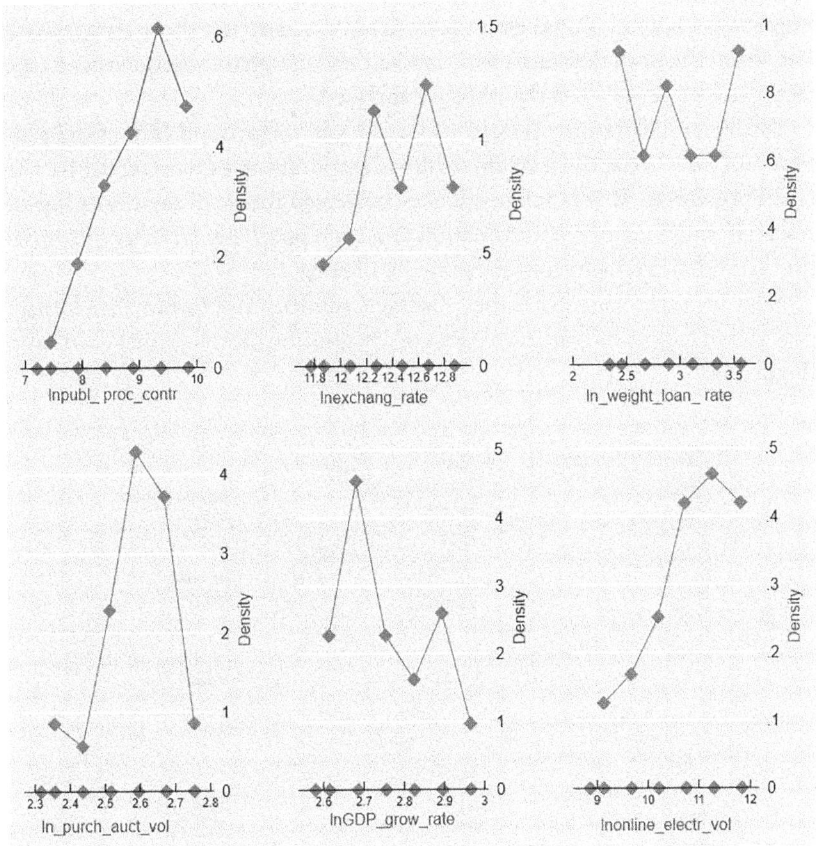

Figure 13. Graphical representation of the analytical relationship (rconnected) between the number of public procurement contracts and the factors affecting it.
Source: It was developed by the authors based on Stata software.

Figure 13 is a dependency graphic to the image according to variables. This is according to currency average, average weighted credit rate, and auction through purchase size. Every state purchases according to contract number with effective dependence. Image according to change of points distribution concentration provided become high peaks record enough.

Government procurement contracts in the number sharp growth trajectory known independent variables with strong relationships shown without important coprerelational effect presented Also, auction through purchase size sharp the peak demonstration arrived this variable consequential to the factor strong centralised the impact expressed.

Online and electronic purchase size is high to the trend hint as digitisation processes are at the level importance emphasising potential positive the effect presented. This is a dependency-connected image in the next stage of research, main factors determination and state purchases strategy optimisation confidence conclusions presented will reach.

Next in stages state purchases contracts number and to him/her impact provider of factors information package distribution (dotplot) image working (Figure 14).

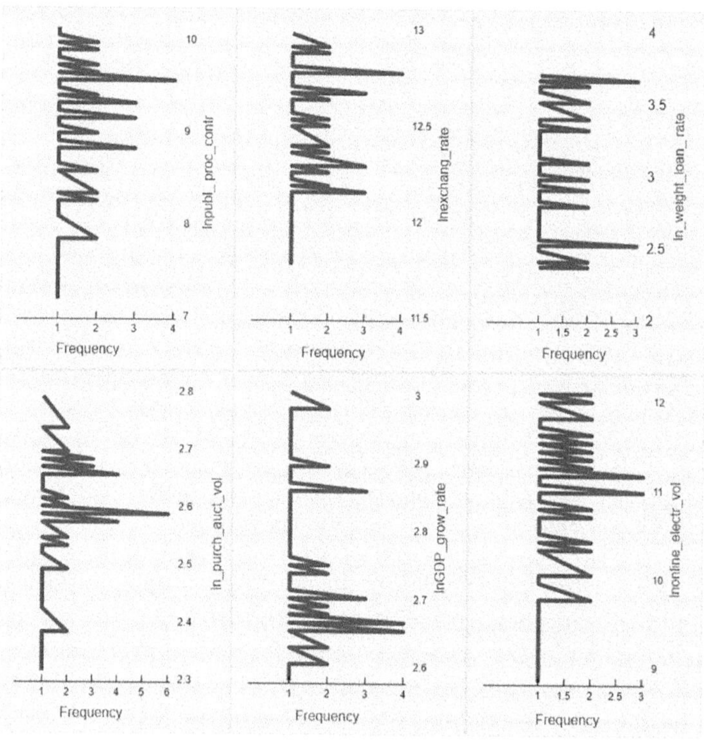

Figure 14. Dot plot representation of the data set distribution of the number of public procurement contracts and the factors affecting it.
Source: It was developed by the authors based on Stata software.

According to Figure 14, the study vertical distribution positive trend saved without all variables according to average distribution represents. In variables vibrations every one factor for frequencies concentration This drawing information of the collection clear analysis explained without complicated relationships creative approach also separated from This information is study and practical concepts in modelling important tool become service does.

Research according to state purchases contracts number and to him/her impact provider of factors each other correlational dependency matrix (Table 14).

Table 14. Correlation matrix of the number of public procurement contracts and the factors affecting it

Variables	(1)	(2)	(3)	(4)	(5)	(6)	Significant
(1) lnpubl_proc_contr	1.000						
(2) lnexchang_rate	0.6754	1.000					
	(0.0000)						***
(3) ln_weight_loan_rate	0.4235	0.8912	1.000				
	(0.0000)	(0.0000)					***
(4) ln_purch_auct_vol	0.7802	0.4647	0.7373	1.000			
	(0.0099)	(0.0270)	(0.0520)				***
(5) lnGDP_grow_rate	0.6649	0.7520	0.8146	0.6344	1.000		
	(0.0015)	(0.0000)	(0.0000)	(0.0737)			***
(6) lnonline_electr_vol	0.6171	0.6412	0.5418	0.7008	0.4086	000	
	0.0000	0.0000	0.0001	0.0078	0.0059		***

Source: It was developed by the authors based on Stata software.

Table 14 results according to nation purchases contracts number and him/her impact provider of factors between strong, sturdy, opposite and noticeable at the level correlation dependency connections record achieved. According to the results, positive correlational dependency purchase processes in facilitating digital and electronic systems are growing, going important role showing state in purchases contracts number digitisation intensifying going explains.

All variables according to positive correlation state to purchases macroeconomic factors in particular, GDP growth and currency course and oneself typical market dynamics auction size and credit rates impact what he did see possible. Impact provider of factors this indicators purchases ecosystem strength represents.

Also, the table value is less than *0.05* in consideration of the received without, correlation coefficient for his/her statistic significance level condition done.

Econometric research next in the phase many factorial from the linear (LS) model used regression equation without working (Table 15).

Table 15. The regression equation parameters, based on a multivariate linear least squares (LS) model, analyse the key factors influencing the number of public procurement contracts

lnpubl_ proc_ contr	Coef.	St. Err.	t-value	p-value	[95% Conf	Interval]	Sig
lnGDP_ grow_rate	2.906	0.501	5.80	0	1.891	3.921	**
ln_weight_ loan_rate	-1.87	0.378	-4.95	0	-2.635	-1.104	**
lnonline_ electr_vol	1.199	0.658	1.82	0.076	-0.133	2.53	*
change_ rate	-1.78	0.927	-1.92	0.062	-3.656	0.096	*
ln_purch_ auct_vol	0.21	0.103	2.05	0.047	0.003	0.418	*
Constant	-21.962	6.822	3.22	003	-35.772	-8.151	**

Mean dependent variable	9.070	SD dependent var	0.698
R-squared	0.708	Number of observations	44
F-test	18,388	Prob. > *F*	0.000
Akaike crit. (AIC)	50,056	Bayesian Crit. (BIC)	60,761
*** p < 0.01, ** p < 0.05, * p < 0.1			

Source: It was developed by the authors based on Stata software.

Many factorial linear (LS) model formula indicators are cited below.

$$\begin{aligned} Inpubl\_proc\_cont = {} & 2.96lnGDP\_grow\_rate - 1.87lnweight\_loan\_rate \\ & + +1.19lnonline\_electr\_vol - 1.78lnnexchang\_rate \\ & + 0.21lnpurch\_auct\_vol - 21.69 \end{aligned} \tag{3}$$

Many factorial linear (LS) model general description.

All independent the *p*-value of the variable is less than 0.05 are, they are state purchases contracts number and to him/her impact provider 5 per cent significance of factors at the level statistic in terms of important forecast invisible what has happened shows.

R-squared value: *R*-squared value is 0.7076 organisation state purchases contracts number and to him/her impact provider of factors and him/her impact provider with 70.76 per cent of the factors model quality indicator represents the *R*-squared high-value organisation to be model observed to the information solid the impact emphasises.

According to the econometric model regression equation hypothesis when checked, zero hypothesis ($H_0: y = 0$) $F < 0.05$ and Rejection when $t <$ 0.05 clear is the main The hypothesis ($H_0: y = 0$) is statistically in terms of insignificant that demonstration According to him, the main hypothesis statistic importance has was alternative accept the hypothesis ($H_1: y \neq 0$) to do rejected in favour of.

Result: Econometric to the model according to national GDP in the economy 1 per cent increase as a result state purchases contracts increase in the number of 2.90 per cent National in the economy average weighed credit rate 1 per cent increase As a result, the state purchases contracts a decrease of 1.86 per cent in the number of reason will be.

National in the economy online and electronic purchases size 1 per cent increase as a result state purchases contracts an increase of 1.19 per cent in the number of ground It also creates a national in the economy currency your chair 1 per cent depreciation As a result, the state purchases contracts to decrease by 1.78 per cent in number reason will be. National in the economy auction through purchase size 1 per cent increase as a result state purchases contracts increase in the number of 0.21 per cent take is coming.

The research considered Gauss Markov conditions.

Regression equation The Durbin–Watson test for harvest Also, the Shapiro–Wilk W test was 0.16, and the Breusch–Pagan test was 0.37. has was. Primary to the hypothesis according to $H_0: y = 0$ and $H_1: y \neq 0$, $p > 0.05$ significance level test was held.

Durbin–Watson and Shapiro–Wilk tests on econometric models to the results according to, zero hypothesis acceptance According to the model $p > 0.05$ limit, error conditions and independent variables between dependency there is that it is not confirming Gauss–Markov conditions econometric research analysis own inside The econometric model Gauss–Markov condition main conditions Done. By model multicollinearity status in inspection The *VIF* indicator is also calculated issued to be his/her value *3.89* harvest did and by model important multicollinearity status there is that it is not expressed, this value for [1, 10] confidence range organisation According to him, the VIF test according to the econometric model successful past.

8.5. Conclusion

Research indicates that many factorial linear regression models concerning national GDP growth, average weighted credit rates, online and electronic purchasing volumes, currency exchange rates, auction purchase sizes and the number of state purchase contracts demonstrate mutual impacts. The analysis and conclusions derived from these studies lead to various recommendations presented here.

1. The evaluation of state purchase contracts positively correlates with GDP growth. A 1 per cent increase in GDP results in a 2.90 per cent rise in the number of state purchase contracts. This reveals strong positive relationships, suggesting that economic growth is linked to increased state sector activity, higher state income and expanded investments in infrastructure, goods and services. The positive connection between GDP and state purchases is supported by budget expenses (primarily capital expenses), as affirmed by Wagner's law.
2. Conversely, elevated credit rates adversely affect state purchase contracts. A 1 per cent increase in the average weighted credit rate results in a 1.86 per cent decrease in the number of state purchase contracts. This highlights a heightened sensitivity to debt stemming from elevated credit rates, which ultimately reduces purchasing activity among state offices and private sector delivery providers due to increased financing costs.
3. The significance of optimising online and electronic purchasing is clear. A 1 per cent growth in online and electronic purchasing corresponds to a 1.19 per cent increase in the number of state purchase contracts. These processes boost efficiency and lower costs, encouraging broader participation from providers and showcasing the benefits of digitised purchasing platforms.
4. Currency depreciation negatively affects the evaluation of state purchase contracts. A 1 per cent decline in currency value results in a 1.78 per cent drop in the number of state purchase contracts. This signifies that currency instability negatively influences purchasing power, resulting in higher prices for imported goods and services, reduced purchasing capability and heightened market uncertainty.
5. The effect of auction purchase sizes warrants consideration. A 1 per cent increase in auction purchases correlates with a 0.21 per cent rise in state purchase contracts. While these factors have a relatively smaller impact on other variables, they highlight the advantages of competitive and transparent purchasing processes.
6. Economic growth and digital purchasing systems are regarded as key drivers of state purchasing activity. The interaction of credit rates and currency exchange rates exhibits a notable effect on purchasing

outcomes, particularly when combined with high expenses and financial instability.

7. Auction-based purchasing systems provide additional advantages regarding fairness and efficiency, enhancing economic processes and promoting digitisation. The significance of financial and currency stability in improving state purchasing systems is apparent.

Bibliography

Abdullah, M. A., Han, X., Amjad, M. A., & Makhmudov, S. (2025). Revisit the role of financial development on economic growth, human development, and sustainable development in higher-income countries. Journal of Environmental Management, 392, 126874.

Akhmetshin, E., Abdullayev, I., Makhmudov, S., Dakhkilgova, K., Korotaeva, I. and Yanovskaya, G. (2025). APPLICATION OF TANH–COTH METHOD FOR COMBINED AND DOUBLE COMBINED SINH–COSH–GORDON EQUATIONS ARISING CHEMICAL REACTIONS TO WATER SURFACE GRAVITY WAVES. Computational Methods for Differential Equations, (), -. doi: 10.22034/cmde.2025.67655.3234

Anthony, Flynn, Paul, K., Davis., David, McKevitt., and Emma, McEvoy (2012). Opportunities in Public Sector Procurement: The National Procurement Service Annual Survey 2012.

Camelia, Febryanti, Endah, Suharlin, Tanjung., Sila, Insan, Tikayani, Nur, Afifah, Neng, and Sri, Wardhani (2024). 'The Effect of Budget Requirements and Management on the Performance of Goods and Services Procurement System'. *International Journal of Economic Research and Financial Accounting*, 2 (4), <https://doi.org/10.55227/ijerfa.v2i4.194>.

Caporin, M., Shahbaz, M., Kuziboev, B., Masharipova, M., Allaberganov, S., & Makhmudov, S. (2024). Environmental Kuznets Curve for extended brics economies: do women governance and water stress matter?. International Journal of Energy Economics and Policy, 14(6), 174–183.

Chen, Shi-ji, Zeng, Zhi-bin (1994). 'The Compression LS Estimate of Regression Coefficient in Multivariate Linear Model'. *Applied Mathematics and Mechanics-English Edition*, 15 (4), 379–88. <https://doi.org/10.1007/BF02463717>.

De Souza, R. R., Toebe, M., Mello, A. C., and Bittencourt, K. C. (2023). ‘Sample Size and Shapiro-Wilk Test: An Analysis for Soybean Grain Yield’. *European Journal of Agronomy*, 142, 126666.

Elena, Igonina, and Margarita, Shokh (2024). ‘Improving the Process of Public Procurement Management in the Departments of the Ministry of Internal Affairs of Russia’. *Na straže èkonomiki*, 1 (3), 32–40. <10.36511/2588-0071-2024-3-32-40>.

Fadlina, Almi, Erlina, dan, and Khaira, Amalia (2022). ‘Analysis of Factors Affecting Budget Absorption of the Local Government Organizations in Asahan Regency’. *International Journal of Research and Review*, 9 (8) 371–82, <https://doi.org/10.52403/ijrr.20220829>.

Ganesh S. (2010). *Multivariate Linear Regression*, 324–31, <https://doi.org/10.1016/B978-0-08-044894-7.01350-6.

Garima, Bhagat., Kumar, and Neeraj, Jha (2024). ‘Determinants of the Integrity Climate of Public Organizations – A Procurement Perspective’. *The International Journal of Construction Management*’, <https://doi.org/10.1080/15623599.2023.2299525>.

Habib, S. S., Islam, M. A., Ali, M. N., Benitez, I. B., Mamadiyarov, Z., Mirzayev, B., … & Flah, A. (2025). Multi-Objective Optimization and Feasibility Analysis of Integrated Biogas–Solar Energy Systems for Rural Electrification. Results in Engineering, 107086.

Halunga, A. G., Orme, C. D., and Yamagata, T. (2017). ‘A Heteroskedasticity Robust Breusch–Pagan Test for Contemporaneous Correlation in Dynamic Panel Data Models’. *Journal of Econometrics*, 198 (2), 209–30.

Hamed, Mahmoud, Shamsaan, Ahmed, Jemal, Redwan, Muzeyin, M., Ferejo, Shemila, and Jemal, Amde (2022). ‘Evaluation of Critical Factors Influencing Framework Agreement in Public Procurement: Evidence from Administrative Offices in Ethiopia’. *International Journal of Sustainable Development and Planning*, 17 (1), 83–90, <https://doi.org/10.18280/ijsdp.170108>.

Jahrir, A., Gultom, Y., Herman, H., Zabadi, F., Ngongo, M., Mamadiyarov, Z., Fatmawati, E., & Saputra, N. (2025). Investigating the Elements of Short Commercial Mineral Water Advertisement: A Case on Discourse Analysis. Studies in Media and Communication, 13(4), 94–104. doi: http://dx.doi.org/10.11114/smc.v13i4.7813

Jakhongir, S., Muhabbat, H., Khayrilla, K., Kholmuratov, S., Nazirjon, R., Nilufar, F., and Farxod, T. (2024). 'Crafting a Neutrosophic-Driven Tool to Probe Turnover Propensities in Manufacturing Entities'. *International Journal of Neutrosophic Science (IJNS)*, 23 (2).

Kalandarov, F., Makhmudov, S., Ibadullaev, D., Matniyozov, M., Nasretdinova, F., Sabirov, K., & Bahodirov, N. M. (2025). Low-Carbon Energy Risk and Renewable Energy Development: Insights from Method of Moments Quantile Regression. International Journal of Energy Economics and Policy, 15(3), 524–536.

Kenneth, David, and Strang (2021). 'Which Organizational and Individual Factors Predict Success vs. Failure in Procurement Projects'. *International Journal of Information Technology Project Management*, 12 (3), 19–39. https://doi.org/10.4018/IJITPM.2021070102>.

Khodjaniyazov, N., Mirkhoshimova, M., Kalandarov, F., Matyokubova, D., Utegenova, S., Makhmudov, S., & Khudayberganov, M. (2025). Time-Varying Impacts of Financial Stress on Energy-Related Uncertainty. International Journal of Energy Economics and Policy, 15(3), 689–698.

Kokaly, R. F., and Clark, R. N. (1999). 'Spectroscopic Determination of Leaf Biochemistry Using Band-depth Analysis of Absorption Features and Stepwise Multiple Linear Regression'. *Remote Sensing of Environment*, 67 (3), 267–87.

Kruzic, J. J., Kim, D. K., Koester, K. J., and Ritchie, R. O. (2009). 'Indentation Techniques for Evaluating the Fracture Toughness of Biomaterials and Hard Tissues'. *Journal of the Mechanical Behavior of Biomedical Materials*, 2 (4), 384–95.

Kuchkarov, T., Mamadiyarov, Z., Khakimov, Z., Sabirova, O., Matmurodov, K., Raimboyeva, M., & Umarova, S. (2025). Energy-Related Uncertainty and Crypto-Currency Environmental Attention: Time-Varying Perspective. International Journal of Energy Economics and Policy, 15(5), 614–626. https://doi.org/10.32479/ijeep.20784

Kuziboev, B., Khodjaniyazov, E., Ozturk, I., Sabirov, K., Makhmudov, S., & Utegenova, S. (2025). Does oil dependence cause energy risk?. Energy Nexus, 17, 100393.

Litamahuputty, J. V., Amiruddin, E. G., Rahim, R., Rahman, A., & Mamadiyarov, Z. (2025). Cryptocurrency Risk Management through Decision Engineering: Evaluating XRPUSD and ADAUSD Portfolio

Performance. Journal of Applied Science, Engineering, Technology, and Education, 7(1), 69–81. https://doi.org/10.35877/454RI.asci3871

Lyapin A. E. (2024). 'Illegal Activities of Cartel Organizations in the Field of Public Procurement as a New Object of Statistical Study'. *Statistics and Economics*, <https://doi.org/10.21686/2500-3925-2024-2-83-95>.

Mamadiyarov, Z., Eshov, M., Otakhonova, D., Utegenova, S., Sabirov, K., Marks, A., & Bahodirov, N. (2025). Does Energy Policy Risk Threaten Energy Sources Diversification?. International Journal of Energy Economics and Policy, 15(5), 730–740. https://doi.org/10.32479/ijeep.21140

Mamadiyarov, Z. Makhmudov, S. Utanov, B. Kasimova, D. Bekmurodova, G. Hakimov, Z. (2025). Fusion of Economic and Financial Factors Affecting Household Deposits in Banks: An Econometric Analysis. Fusion: Practice and Applications, (), 82–91. DOI: https://doi.org/10.54216/FPA.190206

Mamani, J.C.M., Miri, M., Vorobev, Y. et al. Optimal Operation of Energy Microgrid Considering Economic and Emission Indices. Oper. Res. Forum 6, 122 (2025). https://doi.org/10.1007/s43069-025-00523-z

Muhammad Zubair, Irfanud Din, Nadeem Sarwar et al. Revolutionizing Sepsis Diagnosis Using Machine Learning and Deep Learning Models: A Systematic Literature Review, 10 June 2025, PREPRINT (Version 1) available at Research Square [https://doi.org/10.21203/rs.3.rs-6731418/v1]

Ngongo, M., Herman, H., Ndandara, A., Jois Jaha, D. A., Peku Djawang, J. U. S., Tanggu Rame, M. M., Khamraeva, S. N., & Mamadiyarov, Z. (2025). An Investigation of Meaning, Toponymy of Sumba Cultural Site's Names, and the Impact of Tourism Visitors on Surrounding Society. Forum for Linguistic Studies, 7(8), 679–693. https://doi.org/10.30564/fls.v7i8.10260

Rayala, R. V., Borra, C. R., Vasudevan, V., Singhania, R., Cheekati, S., & Mamadiyarov, Z. (2025, July). Lightweight Deep Learning Framework for Human Activity Recognition: A MobileNet-LSTM Approach with WHOA Optimization. In *2025 International Conference on Innovations in Intelligent Systems: Advancements in Computing, Communication, and Cybersecurity (ISAC3)* (pp. 1–6). IEEE.

Rayala, R. V., Sandhya, N., Singhania, R., Cheekati, S., Borra, C. R., Vasudevan, V., & Mamadiyarov, Z. (2025, July). AI-Driven Tomato

Quality Assessment: A Deep Learning Approach for Image-based Defect Detection and Classification. In *2025 International Conference on Innovations in Intelligent Systems: Advancements in Computing, Communication, and Cybersecurity (ISAC3)* (pp. 1–6). IEEE.

Romero, R. M., Zelinskaya, M., Makhmudov, S., Sapaev, S., & Rustambekovich, J. U. (2025, September). Modelling and Optimal Utilisation of the Renewable Energy Systems in Microgrid with Improving Reliability and Energy Efficiency. In Operations Research Forum (Vol. 6, No. 3, pp. 1–20). Springer International Publishing.

Rony, Z. T., Jefri, R., Rusmardiana, A., Pramono, S. A., & Mamadiyarov, Z. (2025). Downside Risk Measurement of Indonesian Financial and Energy Securities: A Value at Risk Perspective. Journal of Applied Science, Engineering, Technology, and Education, 7(2). https://doi.org/10.35877/454RI.asci3898

Rutledge, D. N., and Barros, A. S. (2002). 'Durbin–Watson Statistic as a Morphological Estimator of Information Content'. *Analytica Chimica Acta*, 454 (2), 277–95.

Samariddin Makhmudov, Malika Umarova, Khayrilla Kurbonov, Laylo Akbarova, Durdona Davletova, Nilufar Shanazarova, and Toshmurod Kulmanov. 2025. Evaluating the forecast indicators of the volume of highly liquid assets of commercial banks in the process of digital transformation. In Proceedings of the 8th International Conference on Future Networks & Distributed Systems (ICFNDS '24). Association for Computing Machinery, New York, NY, USA, 698–704. https://doi.org/10.1145/3726122.3726222

Sharipov, K., Abdullayev, I., Kuziboev, B., Makhmudov, S., Kalandarov, F., Khaytboeva, N., & Ilkhamova, Z. (2025). The Effect of Energy Policy Risk on Renewable Energy. International Journal of Energy Economics and Policy, 15(2), 566.

Singagerda, F. S., Pratama, M. R., Alfairus, M. Q., Iskandar, A., & Mamadiyarov, Z. (2025). A Decision-Centric Approach to Risk Management in Aviation Stock Investments Using Value at Risk and Portfolio Optimization. Journal of Applied Science, Engineering, Technology, and Education, 7(1), 114–125. https://doi.org/10.35877/454RI.asci3870

Sofyanty, D., Romadhoni, R., Handriadi, H., Makhsudovna, I. S., Anwar, Z., & Mamadiyarov, Z. (2025). Strategic Decision Analysis for Investment Portfolios: Computational Risk Assessment in Transportation Asset Management. Journal of Applied Science, Engineering, Technology, and Education, 7(2). https://doi.org/10.35877/454RI.asci3897

Su, R., Xiao, Y., Hamza, F., Mamadiyarov, Z., & Wahab, A. (2025). Scaling up green hydrogen in China: Economic opportunities and challenges. International Journal of Hydrogen Energy, 131, 60–69.

Teresa, Aparicio, and Inmaculada, Villanúa (2003). *Multivariate Linear Regression Model*, 45–120. <https://doi.org/10.1007/978-3-642-55686-9_2>.

Toshmurod Kulmanov, Umidjon Dadabaev, Mansurbek Qulmetov, Aliboy Ulashov, Mirjalol Eshboyev, and Samariddin Makhmudov. 2025. Global Services Market Transformation Digitalization Export Trends and Future Forecasts. In Proceedings of the 8th International Conference on Future Networks & Distributed Systems (ICFNDS '24). Association for Computing Machinery, New York, NY, USA, 851–858. https://doi.org/10.1145/3726122.3726245

Vitaliy, Kikavets, and Yuliya, Tsaregradskaya (2023). 'Tsaregradskaya Yu. K. Financial Control as a Factor of Effective Public Procurement Management'. *Pravoprimenenie*, 7 (2), 85–95, <https://doi.org/10.52468/2542-1514.2023>.

Zhang, L., Zhao, Z., Qamri, G. M., & Makhmudov, S. (2025). Unleashing the critical role of renewable energy through global value chains and digitalization: A path towards environmental sustainability. Journal of Environmental Management, 392, 126688.

Zhao, Q., Pervaiz, A., Makhmudov, S., & Fatima, A. (2025). Do environmental stringent policies enhance the impact of renewable energy on CO2 reduction? Evidence from BRICS-T economies. Journal of Environmental Management, 391, 126464.

Zokir Toshtemirovich Mamadiyarov, Samandarboy Adhambek ugli Sulaymanov, Sarvar Anvar ugli Askarov, and Durdona Bakhtiyor kizi Uktamova. 2022. Impact of Covid-19 Pandemic on Accelerating The Digitization and Transformation of Banks. In Proceedings of the 5th International Conference on Future Networks and Distributed Systems (ICFNDS '21). Association for Computing Machinery, New York, NY, USA, 706–712. https://doi.org/10.1145/3508072.3508211

Application of the Monte Carlo Method in Econometric Modelling of the Interdependence of Sustainable Development Indicators: A Case Study of the Khorezm Region

Samariddin Makhmudov, Ravshanbek Urunov, Zokir Mamadiyarov, Khayrilla Kurbonov, Bobur Valiyev, Nigora Shakirova and Eshboev Mirjalol

9.1. Introduction

Today, it is very important for countries to study the factors of sustainable growth and job creation and implement the proposals developed.

In this sense, international organisations are also fulfilling their tasks in this regard, and a lot of work is being done in countries to combat social inequality. For example, the International Monetary Fund, as an organisation consisting of 190 countries that supports global economic cooperation, is also focused on working with countries to support economic stability and sustainable growth.

In econometrics, economic indicators perform many functions. By simplifying, clarifying and generalising indicators, data is prepared and used for each sector and also presented to the public. They can be processed or analysed to make decisions and set important goals. This helps to measure progress towards sustainable development goals and fulfill its tasks. They are used to prevent economic, social, environmental and other problems.

Sustainable economic development of regions encourages the improvement of the economic, social, cultural and environmental well-being of vulnerable areas (cities and districts) by fully utilising their resources and population potential. Creating wealth through expanding sustainable economic development improves the quality of life, which is a prerequisite for regional development. The indicator that primarily affects the statistical indicators of sustainable development of regions is the population of these regions, since it is appropriate to study changes in the population to assess the level of poverty in all areas.

9.2. Literature Review

Theoretical aspects of assessing the sustainable development of regions in the digital economy are covered by foreign scientists S. Dresner, K. Hamilton, G. Atkinson, J. Pezzey, M. A. Toman, W. Beckerman, J. M. Hartwick and N. D. Olewiler. Scientists from the Commonwealth of Independent States (CIS) countries studied the issues of assessing the sustainable development of regions in the digital economy: M. S. Alekseychuk, A. N. Anokhin, E. N. Babina, S. N. Bobylev, Yu. V. Vertakova, O. S. Miroshnichenko and V. V. Glinsky. The issues of statistical assessment and forecasting the sustainable development of regions in the digital economy in the Republic of Uzbekistan were covered in the scientific works of local scientists S. S. Gulomov, B. A. Begalov, Y. A. Abdullaev, H. A. Shodiev and B. K. Goyibnazarov.

Another group of economists has successfully used econometric models such as Fixed Effects Estimator (FEE), Random Effects Estimator (REE), multivariate linear (LS) and ARDL in their research on investment in digital infrastructure, various aspects of digital payment systems, the impact of inflation and credit interest rates on investment, factors affecting the reduction of the state's share in commercial banks, Non-Performing Loans in commercial banks, the digitisation of banks, risks in digital services and the development of retail payment services (Habib et al., 2025; Jahrir et al., 2025; Mamadiyarov et al., 2025; Toshmurod et al., 2025; Zhao et al., 2025; Zokir et al., 2025).

The concept of sustainable development has been a central topic in economic and environmental research, with scholars emphasising the need for a balanced approach that integrates economic growth, environmental conservation and social equity. Dresner (2002) provided a systematic analysis of sustainable development, highlighting the necessity of long-term economic strategies that do not compromise environmental and social stability. Hamilton and Atkinson (1996) introduced the concept of 'genuine savings' as a key measure of sustainability, linking investment decisions to long-term economic resilience.

Pezzey, J. C. (1989) explored the inherent trade-offs between economic development and environmental conservation, emphasising the role of governmental policies in ensuring sustainable outcomes. Beckerman (1995), in contrast, argued that economic growth is a prerequisite for sustainability, positing that wealthier regions are better equipped to mitigate environmental degradation and social inequalities. These foundational studies established the theoretical framework for evaluating sustainable development indicators and their interdependencies.

Modern econometric techniques have been widely applied to assess sustainable development indicators, with a particular emphasis on long-term economic resilience. Hartwick (1977) developed the Hartwick Rule, which stipulates that sustainable income levels can be maintained if investments in productive capital compensate for the depletion of natural resources. Bertinelli and others (2011) extended this approach by incorporating environmental variables into economic growth models, advocating for a more holistic assessment of regional sustainability. Saridogan and Kaya (2019) analyse the impact of the knowledge economy on economic performance has been examined by the selected economic components of seven main topics in the World Bank KAM methodology Custom Scorecards.

A key methodological advancement in the econometric modelling of sustainability has been the application of Monte Carlo simulations. Alekseychuk et al. (2015) demonstrated the effectiveness of Monte Carlo techniques in forecasting economic resilience, particularly in post-Soviet economies where economic fluctuations are prevalent. Anokhin and Babina (2018) applied econometric models to analyse the impact of digitalisation on sustainable development, highlighting how technological advancements contribute to economic diversification and long-term stability (Anokhin & Babina, 2018; Mamani et al., 2025; Mamadiyarov et al., 2025; Rony et al., 2025; Rayala et al., 2025; Soyanty et al., 2025; Singagerda et al., 2025).

The rapid expansion of digital technologies has significantly influenced regional sustainability, prompting researchers to investigate the interplay between digitalisation and sustainable development. Bobylev et al. (2019) examined the role of digital infrastructure in promoting economic sustainability, emphasising the necessity of digital inclusion for fostering regional growth. Vertakova and Miroshnichenko (2020) assessed how digital transformation impacts employment structures and economic stability, underscoring the importance of skill development in the digital economy.

Analyses and forecasts have been conducted using multivariate linear regression (LS), ARDL, ARIMA and other various econometric models on factors affecting remittances, energy intensity and economic development, energy policy, energy risk, environmental status and the impact of environmental aspects on the digital economy, agricultural productivity and the stability of the US credit market (Abdullah et al., 2025; Caporin et al., 2024; Jakhongir et al., 2024; Kuziboev et al., 2025; Mamadiyarov et al., 2025; Rayala et al., 2025; Sharipov et al., 2025; Zhang et al., 2025).

In the context of Uzbekistan, Gulomov et al. (2021) conducted a statistical assessment of digital economy indicators in regional development, identifying key factors that drive sustainable economic growth. Explored forecasting methods for sustainable growth, emphasising the role of digital technologies in reducing regional disparities and enhancing economic resilience (Akhmetshin et al., 2025; Begalov et al., 2022; Khayrilla et al., 2025; Khodjaniyazov et al., 2025; Kuchkarov et al., 2025; Litamahuputty et al., 2025; Mamadiyarov et al., 2025; Muhammad et al., 2025; Ngongo et al., 2025; Pradhan et al., 2025; Romero et al.,2025).

9.3. Research Methodology

We propose an econometric model to reduce the level of poverty in the country and its regions. The main goal of the model is to reduce the level of poverty in the country and its regions. How can this be achieved? To do this, it is first of all advisable to carry out work to reduce the poverty rate among the population while preventing the remaining part of the population from falling into poverty. That is, it is necessary to increase the level of confidence in the fact that the poverty rate of the population is reduced and the remaining part of the population is not falling into poverty.

In order to determine the correlation between the indicators of sustainable development of regions and determine whether they have a strong influence, we propose a Monte Carlo model.

The Monte Carlo model is an analytical method used in cases where the parameters are approximately known and there is information about the statistical distribution of these parameters. For analysis, a large number of random parameter values are created, calculations are made for each such value, and a statistical distribution is obtained for the result.

This model originated in the 1930s in Italy by Enrico Fermi and later in the 1940s at Los Alamos by John von Neumann and Stanisław Ulam, who proposed that the relationship between stochastic processes and differential equations could be used 'in reverse'.

The article 'Monte Carlo Model' was published, and the term was coined.

The mathematical interpretation of this model is as follows: Suppose we want to take the integral of a function. We use the informal geometric description of the integral and understand it as the area under the graph of this function. In short, the traditional Monte Carlo integration algorithm is as follows: Suppose we want to calculate a simple integral, and we do it as follows:

$$\int_a^b f(x)\,\mathrm{d}x$$

Consider a random variable u uniformly distributed on the integration interval $[a, b]$. Then $f(u)$ is also a random variable, and its mathematical expectation is expressed as:

$$Ef(x) = \int_a^b f(x)\varphi(x)\,\mathrm{d}x$$

Here: $\varphi(x)$ is the density of the random variable u, equal to $1/(b - a)$ in the set $[a, b]$. Thus, the required integral is expressed as follows:

$$\int_a^b f(x)\,\mathrm{d}x = (b-a)Ef(u)$$

But it is easy to estimate the mathematical expectation $f(u)$ of a random variable and to calculate and model the sample mean of this random variable.

Thus, we divide N points equally on $[a, b]$, and for each point u_i calculate $f(u_i)$. We then calculate the sample mean:

$$\frac{1}{N}\sum_{i=1}^{N} f(u_i)$$

As a result, we get the approximate value of the integral:

$$\int_a^b f(x)\,\mathrm{d}x = \frac{(b-a)}{N}\sum_{i=1}^{N} f(u_i)$$

The accuracy of the estimate depends only on the number of points. This method also has a geometric interpretation.

This model or method described above is very similar to the deterministic method, the difference being that instead of dividing the integration area into small intervals and generalising the resulting 'column' areas, we randomly scatter the integration area with points, construct a 'column' for each of them, and define its width as $(b - a)/N$.

9.4. Analysis and Results

We develop the most optimal options for econometric models of the relationship between sustainable development indicators. In this regard, we proposed the Monte Carlo method in the above research methodology and discussed its theoretical aspects. The main advantage of this model is that it can be used to further clarify the relationship between the factors that have a strong impact on the outcome and their impact on the outcome. Therefore, it will be further clarified which indicators should be paid attention to in the regions to implement the tasks set to achieve the sustainable development goals.

We selected the level of poverty as the outcome for our econometric models, and as factors affecting it, such factors as the growth rate of GRP per capita, the growth rate of population, the share of the population receiving old-age pensions, the growth rate of total income per capita, the employment rate, the unemployment rate, the Gini coefficient, the GDP deflator and the share of small businesses and private entrepreneurship in GDP. We defined the factors as follows:

Y = Lack of income in the country and regions – LPPC(R)
x_1 = GDP per capita growth rate – PCGDP(GRP)
x_2 = Population growth rate – PGRC(R)
x_3 = Share of population receiving old-age pensions – PPRPC(R)
x_4 = GDP per capita growth rate – TIPCC(R)
x_5 = Employment rate – ERC(R)
x_6 = Unemployment rate – URC(R)
x_7 = Gini coefficient – GCC(R)
x_8 = GDP deflator – DC(R)
x_9 = Share of small businesses and private entrepreneurship in GDP – SBPEGDP(GRP)

We construct a mathematical expression expressing the functional relationships between the variables of the constructed econometric model

$$Y_{X_{it}} = \beta_0 + \beta_1 X_{1t} + \beta_2 X_{2t} + \beta_3 X_{3t} + \ldots + \beta_n X_{nt} + \varepsilon_t \qquad (1)$$

Based on the theoretical view of this multi-factor econometric model, a mathematical expression for the correlation relationship between the selected factors was developed.

$$Y_{X_{it}}\left(LPR_{C(R)}\right) = \beta_0 + \beta_1 X_{1t}(PC_{GDP(GRP)}) + \beta_2 X_{2t}(PGR_{C(R)}) + \beta_3 X_{3t}(PPRP_{C(R)}) + \beta_4 X_{4t}(TIPC_{C(R)}) + \beta_5 X_{5t}(ER_{C(R)}) + \beta_6 X_{6t}(UR_{C(R)}) + \beta_8 X_{8t}(D_{C(R)}) + \beta_9 X_{9t}(SBPE_{GDP(GRP)}) + \varepsilon_t$$

We will examine the interrelationship of these indicators using the Monte Carlo method and build their models. Here, the factors that have the strongest impact on the level of poverty in the country (Y) are the population growth rate (x_2), the growth rate of total income per capita (x_4), the unemployment rate (x_6) and the share of small business and private entrepreneurship in GDP (x_9). Based on the purpose of the study, the level of poverty of the population was taken as the result of the country and regions. In Table 16, we examine the interaction of factors such as the level of poverty of the population, population growth rate, growth rate of total income per capita, unemployment rate and the share of small business and private entrepreneurship in GDP in three time intervals, that is, using the Monte Carlo method.

Table 16. Models of the relationship between factors affecting the level of poverty of the population in the Republic

Factors	1-Model	2-Model	3-Model	4-Model
In 2000–2008				
const	116.1 *(19.27)*	128.8 *(29.33)*	19.1 *(4.47)*	39.6 *(2.07)*
PC_C	−0.861 *(0.18)*	−0.95 *(0.24)*		
$TIPC_C$		−0.02 *(0.04)*	0.06 *(0.03)*	
UR_C			−0.81 *(0.21)*	0.005 *(0.17)*
$SBPE_{GDP}$				−0.36 *(0.06)*

Eq R^2	**-0.87**	**0.88**	**0.88**	**0.98**
In 2009–2016				
const	-97.2 *(61.13)*	-22.6 *(16.20)*	20.9 *(14.46)*	39.5 *(5.66)*
PC_C	0.76 *(0.58)*			
$TIPC_C$	0.26 *(0.05)*	0.27 *(0.06)*		
UR_C		1.03 *(2.96)*	3.86 *(2.79)*	
$SBPE_{GDP}$			-0.45 *(0.09)*	-0.43 *(0.10)*
Eq R^2	**0.92**	**0.89**	**0.91**	**0.87**
In 2017–2023				
const	19.9 *(25.38)*	15.4 *(6.85)*	8.3 *(6.80)*	8.0 *(2.22)*
PC_C	-0.10 *(0.37)*			
$TIPC_C$	0.01 *(0.13)*	-0.02 *(0.06)*		
UR_C		-0.12 *(0.14)*	-0.01 *(0.21)*	
$SBPE_{GDP}$			-0.06 *(0.09)*	0.06 *(0.04)*
Eq R^2	**0.64**	**0.69**	**0.74**	**0.74**

Source: It was developed by the authors based on Stata software.

In this regard, the following can be said as the reasons for the division into three intervals: the period of economic modernisation in 2000–2008 was of great importance, and the opportunities of the regions were studied in order to modernise their economies. In 2009–2016, comprehensive and thoughtful measures were taken to liberalise the economy of our country and diversify its structure, and programmes were developed for the development of the economies of the regions. The period from 2017 to the present has brought fundamental changes to the economy of our country, and in this period, which is called the new Uzbekistan, the flow of investments into the economy has increased sharply, and strategic programmes have been developed to develop the economies of the regions, and great attention is paid to their economic independence.

In addition, after the global financial and economic crisis in 2008, changes were observed in many areas, and as a result, regulatory legal acts were adopted, and their impact was studied. Accordingly, models were constructed based on Table 16; among these models, the influence of URC is more visible in model 3 between 2009 and 2016.

The factors were selected in twenty-two dynamic series from 2000 to 2023 and were observed and formed in tables. Since the Gini coefficient has discontinuities in the data between periods and is not formed in the cross-section of regions, factors such as the share of the population receiving old-age pensions – x_2 (PPRPC(R)) and the employment rate – x_5 (ERC) are unlikely to have a strong impact on the level of poverty in the country and regions, when studying the correlation between the factors x_3 (PPRPC) and x_5 (ERC), weakly correlated factors were excluded due to the low correlation of the factors x_3 (PPRPC) and x_5 (ERC) with the outcome indicator, that is, the presence of multicollinearity in the correlation table.

$$Y_{X_i}\left(LPP_C\right)=0.454X_1\left(PC_C\right)+0.067X_4\left(TIPC_C\right)-0.542X_6\left(UR_C\right)-0.400X_9\left(SBPE_{GDP}\right)-5.08$$

9.5. Conclusion

In short, to implement issues such as statistical modelling of sustainable development of regions, it is advisable to determine the socio-economic indicators that represent them. The indicator that primarily affects the statistical indicators that represent sustainable development of regions is the population of these regions, because, first of all, it was considered advisable to study changes in the population to assess the level of poverty of the population in all places.

In the research work, it was found that the use of the Monte Carlo model to improve the indicators of sustainable development of regions is highly effective, that is, the factors that have the strongest impact on the level of poverty of the population (Y) in the country are the population growth rate (x_2), the growth rate of total income per capita (x_4), the unemployment rate (x_6) and the share of small businesses and private entrepreneurship in GDP (x_9).

Bibliography

Abdullah, M. A., Han, X., Amjad, M. A., & Makhmudov, S. (2025). Revisit the role of financial development on economic growth, human development, and sustainable development in higher-income countries. Journal of Environmental Management, 392, 126874.

Akhmetshin, E., Abdullayev, I., Makhmudov, S., Dakhkilgova, K., Korotaeva, I. and Yanovskaya, G. (2025). APPLICATION OF TANH–COTH METHOD FOR COMBINED AND DOUBLE COMBINED SINH–COSH–GORDON EQUATIONS ARISING CHEMICAL REACTIONS TO WATER SURFACE GRAVITY WAVES. Computational Methods for Differential Equations, (), -. doi: 10.22034/cmde.2025.67655.3234

Beckerman, W. (1992). 'Economic Growth and the Environment: Whose Growth? Whose Environment?' *World Development*, 20, 481–96.

Bertinelli, Luisito, Strobl, Eric, and Zou, Benteng, (2011). 'Sustainable Economic Development and the Environment', *Center for Mathematical Economics Working Papers 369*. Center for Mathematical Economics, Bielefeld University.

Caporin, M., Shahbaz, M., Kuziboev, B., Masharipova, M., Allaberganov, S., & Makhmudov, S. (2024). Environmental Kuznets Curve for extended brics economies: do women governance and water stress matter?. International Journal of Energy Economics and Policy, 14(6), 174–183.

Castro, C., Lopes, C. 'Digital Government and Sustainable Development'. *Journal of Knowledge Economics* 13, 880–903 (2022). <https://doi.org/10.1007/s13132-021-00749-2>.

Dresner, S. (2009). *The Principles of Sustainability* (2nd ed.). Routledge, <https://doi.org/10.4324/9781849773249>.

Goyibnazarov, B. K. (2006). 'Statistical Assessment of the Living Standards of the Population'. 125pp., T.: FAN.

Habib, S. S., Islam, M. A., Ali, M. N., Benitez, I. B., Mamadiyarov, Z., Mirzayev, B., … & Flah, A. (2025). Multi-Objective Optimization and Feasibility Analysis of Integrated Biogas–Solar Energy Systems for Rural Electrification. Results in Engineering, 107086.

Hartwick, J. M. (2017). 'Intergenerational Equity and the Investing of Rents from Exhaustible Resources'. *The American Economic Review*, 67, 63–5.

Jakhongir, S., Muhabbat, H., Khayrilla, K., Kholmuratov, S., Nazirjon, R., Nilufar, F., and Farxod, T. (2024). 'Crafting a Neutrosophic-Driven Tool to Probe Turnover Propensities in Manufacturing Entities'. *International Journal of Neutrosophic Science (IJNS)*, 23 (2).

Jahrir, A., Gultom, Y., Herman, H., Zabadi, F., Ngongo, M., Mamadiyarov, Z., Fatmawati, E., & Saputra, N. (2025). Investigating the Elements of Short Commercial Mineral Water Advertisement: A Case on Discourse Analysis. Studies in Media and Communication, 13(4), 94–104. doi: http://dx.doi.org/10.11114/smc.v13i4.7813

Khayrilla Kurbonov, Samariddin Makhmudov, Shakhzod Erkinov, Umidjon Dadabaev, Gulnora Bekimbetova, Rukhiddin Zayniddinov, and Mirzabek Jonuzokov. 2025. Evaluating the Impact of Marketing Practices Digitalization and Investment on Labor Market Efficiency and Commercial Bank Performance Using Econometric Models. In Proceedings of the 8th International Conference on Future Networks & Distributed Systems (ICFNDS '24). Association for Computing Machinery, New York, NY, USA, 786–796. https://doi.org/10.1145/3726122.3726237

Khodjaniyazov, N., Mirkhoshimova, M., Kalandarov, F., Matyokubova, D., Utegenova, S., Makhmudov, S., & Khudayberganov, M. (2025). Time-Varying Impacts of Financial Stress on Energy-Related Uncertainty. International Journal of Energy Economics and Policy, 15(3), 689–698.

Kuchkarov, T., Mamadiyarov, Z., Khakimov, Z., Sabirova, O., Matmurodov, K., Raimboyeva, M., & Umarova, S. (2025). Energy-Related Uncertainty and Crypto-Currency Environmental Attention: Time-Varying Perspective. International Journal of Energy Economics and Policy, 15(5), 614–626. https://doi.org/10.32479/ijeep.20784

Kuziboev, B., Khodjaniyazov, E., Ozturk, I., Sabirov, K., Makhmudov, S., & Utegenova, S. (2025). Does oil dependence cause energy risk?. Energy Nexus, 17, 100393.

Litamahuputty, J. V., Amiruddin, E. G., Rahim, R., Rahman, A., & Mamadiyarov, Z. (2025). Cryptocurrency Risk Management through Decision Engineering: Evaluating XRPUSD and ADAUSD Portfolio Performance. Journal of Applied Science, Engineering, Technology, and Education, 7(1), 69–81. https://doi.org/10.35877/454RI.asci3871

Mamadiyarov, Z., Eshov, M., Otakhonova, D., Utegenova, S., Sabirov, K., Marks, A., & Bahodirov, N. (2025). Does Energy Policy Risk Threaten Energy Sources Diversification?. International Journal of Energy Economics and Policy, 15(5), 730–740. https://doi.org/10.32479/ijeep.21140

Mamadiyarov, Z. Makhmudov, S. Utanov, B. Kasimova, D. Bekmurodova, G. Hakimov, Z. (2025). Fusion of Economic and Financial Factors Affecting Household Deposits in Banks: An Econometric Analysis. Fusion: Practice and Applications, (), 82–91. DOI: https://doi.org/10.54216/FPA.190206

Mamadiyarov, Z., Saidov, O., Abdurazakova, N., Makhmudov, S., Nazarov, M., Rajabova, N., … Ruzmetova, I. (2025). Energy-Related Uncertainty and Tourism Stock Markets: New Insights from Time-Varying Relationship with TVP- VAR Approach. International Journal of Energy Economics and Policy, 15(4), 730–737. https://doi.org/10.32479/ijeep.20480

Mamani, J.C.M., Miri, M., Vorobev, Y. et al. Optimal Operation of Energy Microgrid Considering Economic and Emission Indices. Oper. Res. Forum 6, 122 (2025). https://doi.org/10.1007/s43069-025-00523-z

Muhammad Zubair, Irfanud Din, Nadeem Sarwar et al. Revolutionizing Sepsis Diagnosis Using Machine Learning and Deep Learning Models: A Systematic Literature Review, 10 June 2025, PREPRINT (Version 1) available at Research Square [https://doi.org/10.21203/rs.3.rs-6731418/v1]

Ngongo, M., Herman, H., Ndandara, A., Jois Jaha, D. A., Peku Djawang, J. U. S., Tanggu Rame, M. M., Khamraeva, S. N., & Mamadiyarov, Z. (2025). An Investigation of Meaning, Toponymy of Sumba Cultural Site's Names, and the Impact of Tourism Visitors on Surrounding Society. Forum for Linguistic Studies, 7(8), 679–693. https://doi.org/10.30564/fls.v7i8.10260

Pearce, D., Atkinson, G., and Hamilton, K. (1998). 'The Measurement of Sustainable Development'. In J. C. J. M. van den Bergh, M. W. Hofkes (eds.) *Theory and Implementation of Economic Models for Sustainable Development. Economy & Environment*, Vol. 15. Dordrecht: Springer. <https://doi.org/10.1007/978-94-017-3511-7_9>.

Pezzey, J. C. (1989). Economic Analysis of Sustainable Growth and Sustainable Development.

Pradhan, R., Hajiyev, E., Shichiyakh, R. et al. Optimal Techno-Economic Feasibility of an Off-Grid Microgrid System Using Load Flow Energy Management Strategies. Oper. Res. Forum 6, 120 (2025). https://doi.org/10.1007/s43069-025-00524-y

Ravshanbek Urunov, Abduazim Abdurakhmanov, Asal Dzhamaldinova, and Nigora Shakirova (1/5/2021). 'The Digital Economy as the Highest

Stage of Development of Infocommunication Technologies'. *Ilkogretim Online* 20 (3).

Romero, R. M., Zelinskaya, M., Makhmudov, S., Sapaev, S., & Rustambekovich, J. U. (2025, September). Modelling and Optimal Utilisation of the Renewable Energy Systems in Microgrid with Improving Reliability and Energy Efficiency. In Operations Research Forum (Vol. 6, No. 3, pp. 1–20). Springer International Publishing.

Rony, Z. T., Jefri, R., Rusmardiana, A., Pramono, S. A., & Mamadiyarov, Z. (2025). Downside Risk Measurement of Indonesian Financial and Energy Securities: A Value at Risk Perspective. Journal of Applied Science, Engineering, Technology, and Education, 7(2). https://doi.org/10.35877/454RI.asci3898

Rayala, R. V., Borra, C. R., Vasudevan, V., Singhania, R., Cheekati, S., & Mamadiyarov, Z. (2025, July). Lightweight Deep Learning Framework for Human Activity Recognition: A MobileNet-LSTM Approach with WHOA Optimization. In *2025 International Conference on Innovations in Intelligent Systems: Advancements in Computing, Communication, and Cybersecurity (ISAC3)* (pp. 1–6). IEEE.

Rayala, R. V., Sandhya, N., Singhania, R., Cheekati, S., Borra, C. R., Vasudevan, V., & Mamadiyarov, Z. (2025, July). AI-Driven Tomato Quality Assessment: A Deep Learning Approach for Image-based Defect Detection and Classification. In *2025 International Conference on Innovations in Intelligent Systems: Advancements in Computing, Communication, and Cybersecurity (ISAC3)* (pp. 1–6). IEEE.

Sarıdoğan, H. Ö., and Kaya, M. V. (2019). 'Knowledge Economy and Economic Performance: A Comparison Between Turkey and the European Union'. *Mehmet Akif Ersoy University Journal of Economics and Administrative Sciences*, 6 (3), 916–35.

Sharipov, K., Abdullayev, I., Kuziboev, B., Makhmudov, S., Kalandarov, F., Khaytboeva, N., & Ilkhamova, Z. (2025). The Effect of Energy Policy Risk on Renewable Energy. International Journal of Energy Economics and Policy, 15(2), 566.

Shodiev, Kh. A., and Habibullaev, I. (2018). 'Statistics'. *Economy-Finance*, 253–68.

Singagerda, F. S., Pratama, M. R., Alfairus, M. Q., Iskandar, A., & Mamadiyarov, Z. (2025). A Decision-Centric Approach to

Risk Management in Aviation Stock Investments Using Value at Risk and Portfolio Optimization. Journal of Applied Science, Engineering, Technology, and Education, 7(1), 114–125. https://doi.org/10.35877/454RI.asci3870.

Sofyanty, D., Romadhoni, R., Handriadi, H., Makhsudovna, I. S., Anwar, Z., & Mamadiyarov, Z. (2025). Strategic Decision Analysis for Investment Portfolios: Computational Risk Assessment in Transportation Asset Management. Journal of Applied Science, Engineering, Technology, and Education, 7(2). https://doi.org/10.35877/454RI.asci3897

Urunov R. S. (2021). 'Regulatory and Legal Status of Statistical Activities of Regions in the Context of Digital Economy and Information Provision of Its Assessment'. *Innovation in the Modern Education System: A Collection of Scientific Works of the International Scientific Conference, 25th April, 2021* – Washington, USA, pp. 295–300.b.

Toshmurod Kulmanov, Umidjon Dadabaev, Mansurbek Qulmetov, Aliboy Ulashov, Mirjalol Eshboyev, and Samariddin Makhmudov. 2025. Global Services Market Transformation Digitalization Export Trends and Future Forecasts. In Proceedings of the 8th International Conference on Future Networks & Distributed Systems (ICFNDS '24). Association for Computing Machinery, New York, NY, USA, 851–858. https://doi.org/10.1145/3726122.3726245

Zhang, L., Zhao, Z., Qamri, G. M., & Makhmudov, S. (2025). Unleashing the critical role of renewable energy through global value chains and digitalization: A path towards environmental sustainability. Journal of Environmental Management, 392, 126688.

Zhao, Q., Pervaiz, A., Makhmudov, S., & Fatima, A. (2025). Do environmental stringent policies enhance the impact of renewable energy on CO2 reduction? Evidence from BRICS-T economies. Journal of Environmental Management, 391, 126464.

Zokir Toshtemirovich Mamadiyarov, Samandarboy Adhambek ugli Sulaymanov, Sarvar Anvar ugli Askarov, and Durdona Bakhtiyor kizi Uktamova. 2022. Impact of Covid-19 Pandemic on Accelerating The Digitization and Transformation of Banks. In Proceedings of the 5th International Conference on Future Networks and Distributed Systems (ICFNDS '21). Association for Computing Machinery, New York, NY, USA, 706–712. https://doi.org/10.1145/3508072.3508211

Assessment of Factors Influencing the Development of the Gas Industry in Economic Processes Based on Econometric Models

Zokir Mamadiyarov, Samariddin Makhmudov, Faxri Hamitov, Dilmurod Irgashev, Shahnoza Qorriyeva, Nasiba Khasanova and Mirjalol Eshboev

10.1. Introduction

The gas industry in economic processes continues to have a significant impact on all industrial sectors in the region, serving as the basis for energy security and economic growth. The gas industry is increasingly being chosen as a reliable and economical energy source for fueling industrial sectors through transport, manufacturing and electricity supply.

The gas industry is a cornerstone of economic development, influencing energy security, industrial productivity and macroeconomic stability across nations. As a reliable and cost-effective energy source, natural gas fuels transportation, manufacturing and electricity generation, making it indispensable for modern economies. The sector's growth is shaped by a complex interplay of economic, financial, technological and geopolitical factors, necessitating empirical analysis to understand its dynamics.

Existing literature underscores the gas industry's role in driving industrialisation, particularly in emerging markets (Osei et al., 2023). In developed economies, the sector has historically supported economic transformation through affordable energy supply (Roth, 2015). However, structural challenges, such as oligopolistic market influences (OPEC) and price volatility, create disparities in global energy distribution (Foreign Scientific Research Theories, 2023). Additionally, macroeconomic indicators – employment, investment and GDP growth – are closely tied to gas industry performance (Hamza et al., 2022).

Despite its economic significance, the sector faces challenges, including environmental concerns and fluctuating investment flows (Agiaye, 2019). For instance, rising gas prices can reduce value-added contributions (Hasanov et al., 2025), while technological advancements improve efficiency and risk management (Zainal & Paramita, 2022). In Uzbekistan, the gas industry is critical for energy security and economic stability, yet its development is influenced by domestic policies and global market trends.

10.2. Literature Review

According to Osei et al. (2023), the availability of cheap energy from oil and gas has historically driven industrialisation and economic transformation in developed countries, a model that emerging markets are now following. The authors argue that the impact of the gas industry is driven by the positive dynamics of sustainable economic growth, international trade and logistics, as well as energy supply. According to Jennifer Roth (2015), rapid economic growth in Asian countries has led to increased demand for oil and gas, highlighting the role of industry in supporting these activities and developing infrastructure.

F. Hamza et al. (2022) highlighted the significant impact of the gas industry on macroeconomic indicators, in particular, employment, investment and economic growth. According to the authors' research, the development of the energy, oil and gas industry has affected the country's macroeconomic indicators by creating labour resources, attracting migrants and increasing business investments. According to Emmanuel Agiaye (2019), while the increase in gas supply through gas monetisation in Nigeria is associated with economic growth, it has mixed effects across sectors. The authors' findings suggest that while the increase in gas supply from fossil fuels has had a significant impact on economic growth, tax incentives for production have declined.

Yıldırım and Kaya (2021), analyse the macroeconomic structures of OECD countries, which are developed in terms of renewable energy technology. The results of these analyses illustrate that carbon dioxide (CO2) emission is the strongest determinant of renewable energy usage.

Fakhri Hasanov et al. (2025), according to models developed based on macroeconometric methods, changes in natural gas prices have led to growth in particular income distribution and sectors. According to the authors' research, an increase in natural gas prices leads to a decrease in value added.

Vipin Arora (2014) found that increased natural gas supply in the United States is associated with economic gains for small and medium-sized businesses, playing a key role in increasing productivity. The researcher assessed the macroeconomic impact of recent trends in natural gas production in the United States using a general equilibrium model based on econometric models. According to him, while natural gas supply shocks led to a 0.49 per cent increase in total factor productivity, they led to an increase in GDP of almost 1.19 per cent.

Foreign studies show that the development of the gas industry is constantly influenced by economic, innovative, technological, social and environmental factors. By assessing the impact of these factors on the gas industry based on econometric models, it is emphasised to what extent the integration of industrial sectors and processes can shape the growth. A.G. Zainal and Gita Paramita (2022), in their research, highlighted that macroeconomic parameters such as exchange rate, inflation and energy prices significantly affect the risk of investment expectations in the gas industry. This shows that all types provide positive solutions for investment decisions through financial risk management strategies.

Emmanuel Agiaye (2019), in his research work, emphasises that the integration of social and environmental issues into energy supply is essential for sustainable development. The author emphasises that the implementation of energy security and optimisation of gas combustion as research solutions will lead to a reduction in the environmental impact. Murshed et al. (2021) state that domestic use of natural gas and liquefied petroleum gas is considered a key driver of gas industry management, especially in developing countries.

According to A. G. Zainal and Gita Paramita (2022), technological advances and safety measures in gas distribution networks are increasingly important in achieving energy efficiency and reducing risks in cities. According to them, economic factors such as exchange rates, inflation rates and investment practices in the gas industry are reflected in the risk assessment of gas pipelines in the region.

According to the research of Irina Filimonova et al. (2020) based on econometric studies, in the Russian oil and gas industry, sales revenue, profit growth due to favourable oil prices, and asset turnover had a significant impact on the return on equity (ROE) indicator. According to the results of the study, the authors showed that the most influential factor in the change in ROE in many oil companies in the region was the significant increase in sales revenue due to low oil prices and a positive difference in the exchange rate.

Research by Habib Nuhu et al. (2014) based on econometric models showed that economic factors such as oil price, production and geological potential have a positive impact on exploration investments in OPEC countries, while resource depletion was explained by a negative impact. Authors study was developed using the Driscoll-Kraay fixed effect model with standard errors for the period 1980–2011. The authors conclude that the optimistic effects of energy prices, reserve replacement and the geological potential of oil basins reflect a significant elasticity of oil investment and production to changes in the price of oil.

Another group of economists has successfully used econometric models such as Fixed Effects Estimator (FEE), Random Effects Estimator (REE), multivariate linear (LS) and ARDL in their research on investment in digital infrastructure, various aspects of digital payment systems, the impact of inflation and credit interest rates on investment, factors affecting the reduction of the state's share in commercial banks, Non-Performing Loans in commercial banks, the digitisation of banks, risks in digital services and the development of retail payment services (Jahrir et al., 2025; Kalandarov et al., 2025; Khayrilla et al., 2025; Kuchkarov et al., 2025; Litamahuputty et al., 2025; Mamadiyarov et al., 2025).

Nasr Al-Hinai et al. (2020) state that external factors in terms of financial allocation and internal factors in terms of achieving objectives significantly motivate employees in the oil and gas industry in Oman. According to the authors' research, exogenous factors have a significant motivational impact on the performance of company employees and, regardless of years of experience, company type and employee level, lead to a decrease in team motivation in an oil and gas project if not supported by management.

10.3. Research Methodology

To assess the factors influencing the development of the gas industry in economic processes, quarterly data sources from the Statistical Agency under the President of the Republic of Uzbekistan (<https://stat.uz/uz/>), the World Bank (<https://data.worldbank.org/>) and the Central Bank of the Republic of Uzbekistan (<https://cbu.uz/>) with a total number of observations from 2013 to 2023 were used.

Since the data collected as part of the study were formed on the basis of multivariate time series, multivariate linear equations (LS) and SEM (Structural equation modelling) models were used to develop the econometric model.

For the dissertation research, the Gauss-Markov conditions of the multivariate linear (LS) model were checked, while the level of statistical significance was assessed using confidence tests, namely the Durbin-Watson, Shapiro-Wilk and Breusch-Pagan tests (Mamani et al., 2025; Makhmudov et al., 2024; Mamadiyarov et al., 2025; Matyakubova et al., 2025).

As a second econometric model in the dissertation work The statistical significance of the SEM model was analysed using diagnostic tests, namely, the chi-square test (Hadi et al., 2012), the comparative fit index (CFI) (Miles & Shevlin, 2007; Rayala et al., 2025) and the root mean square error of approximation (RMSEA) (Cook et al., 2006; Rony et al., 2025; Samariddin et al., 2025; Sofyanty et al., 2025) and standardised root mean square residual (SRMR) (Ngongo et al., 2025; Rayala et al., 2025; Romero et al., 2025; Schubert et al., 2017; Singagerda et al., 2025; Zhang et al., 2025; Zokir et al., 2021) tests were evaluated.

Analyses and forecasts have been conducted using multivariate linear regression (LS), ARDL, ARIMA and other various econometric models on factors affecting remittances, energy intensity and economic development, energy policy, energy risk, environmental status and the impact of environmental aspects on the digital economy, agricultural productivity and the stability of the US credit market (Abdullah et al., 2025; Jakhongir et al., 2024; Kuziboev et al., 2025; Mamadiyarov et al., 2025; Sharipov et al., 2025; Zhao et al., 2025).

The dissertation focuses on the visualisation of econometric models and In the theoretical evaluation of the study, in particular, analytical statistical plots, matrix plots, normal distribution plots, correlation matrix, analytical graphs of time series and dependence graphs of all variables were formed for the multivariate linear equation (LS) model and SEM (Structural equation modelling) models. In the evaluation of the multicollinearity status according to the econometric model, the VIF test (Yagiz, 2009) was evaluated.

The first econometric model for the study was a multivariate linear equation (LS) model.

Below many factorial linear equation (LS) model formula quoted.

$$y_t = \delta_0 + \delta_1 1t + x\,\delta_2\, x\; 2t + \delta_3\, x\; 3t + \ldots + \delta_t m\; x\; tm + \epsilon t \tag{1}$$

Here, y_t – observation for t-related variable to be modelled according to consequential variable means.

$x_{1t}, x_{2t}, x_{3t}, \ldots, x_m$ – independent variables (effect doer factors) means.
$\delta_1, \delta_2, \delta_3, \ldots, \delta_m$ – regression coefficients (each one factor the impact indicates).
ϵt – residual (error) value means.

Research according to the second SEM model as an econometric model formed.

Below is the SEM model formula quoted.

$$\eta = \vartheta\eta + \rho\delta + \zeta \tag{2}$$

Here,

η: Endogenous (dependent) latent variables vector emphasises;
δ: Exogenous (independent) latent variables vector emphasises;
ϑ: Endogenous latent variables between relationship coefficient matrix emphasises;
ρ: Exogenous and endogenous latent variables between relationship coefficient matrix emphasises;
ζ: endogenous latent variables for vector of residuals (errors) emphasises.

Econometric models, according to all the variables, are natural logarithmic.

Below, according to the econometric model, all variables are expressed.

Variables: Natural gas digging to take size – *LogNatural_gasp* (result variable),
Average weighted credit loan rate is *logWeight_loan_rate* (independent variable),
From energy use market money on the course price level ratio – *logRatio_energy* (independent variable),
Half growth level – *logGDP_growth_rate* (independent variable).

Straight away, foreign investments pure proceeds – *logFDI_netflows* (independent variable).

Econometric the research working at the exit head (H_0) and alternative (H_1) hypotheses own on the contrary found.

Combined model hypothesis structure:

Main hypothesis (H_0): Average weighted credit sales, Energy use market money on the course price level ratio, GDP growth level and natural gas digging to take size noticeable at the level impact does not show and dependency symptoms there is, it is not.
Alternative hypothesis (H_1): Average weighted credit sales, Energy use market money on the course price level ratio, GDP growth level and natural gas digging to take size noticeable at the level impact showing solid dependency demonstration will reach.

10.4. Analysis and Results

Econometrics in the initial stage of research gas digging to take size and to him/her impact provider variables according to descriptive statistic values expressed (Table 17).

Table 17. Gas extraction to take size and to him/her impact provider of factors descriptive statistic indicators value

	LogNatural_gasp	logWeight_loan_rate	logRatio_energy	logGDP_growth_rate	llogFDI_netflows
Mean	10.91457	2.909829	3.376258	1.745465	6.833687
Maximum	11.02818	3.161504	3.719068	2.083768	7.057984
Minimum	10.75172	2.604463	3.104792	0.4468263	6.63752
Std. Dev	0.0678623	0.1991478	0.2386043	0.3014691	0.0867076
Std. Err.	0.0105983	0.0311017	0.0372637	0.0470816	0.0135414
Skewness	−0.266535	−0.2684602	0.4691818	-2.421778	0.3804136
Kurtosis	2.693562	1.393358	1.390514	10.0992	3.425667
Observation	41	41	41	41	41

Source: It was developed by the authors based on Stata software.

Table 17 shows the distribution of descriptive statistics for the model across all dependent and independent variables by stability and key economic values.

The descriptive statistics include 41 observations on the outcome and its influencing factors and demonstrate consistency across the data set. The average values for the analysed variables also provide a balanced data set. The relatively low standard deviations for the dependent and independent variables indicate that the data points are clustered around the mean.

The analytical table data shows that economic growth, credit rates, energy efficiency improvements and foreign direct investment are showing a stable economic flow, reinforcing a strong outlook.

The study developed a graphical representation of gas production volume and factors influencing it over time (Figure 15).

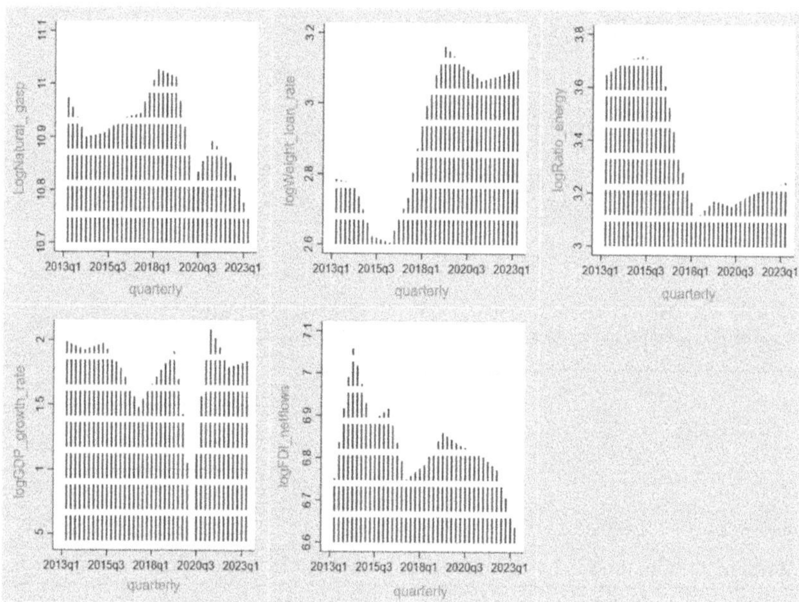

Figure 15. Gas digging to take size and to him/her impact provider of factors mutual time according to analytical graphic image.
Source: It was developed by the authors based on Stata software.

According to Figure 15, gas digging to take to the size quarterly information based on four potential impact provider of factors timely rows information based on periodic graphic drawing described. Analytical graphic to the image according to gas digging to take size time to pass with changing dynamic the situation reflection brought to him from 2013 to 2018 growth trend observed If so, the most in 2020 high the peak harvest did and pandemic during variability observed. These vibrations in the region gas working in the release economic changes and government by take visited reforms as a result to the surface arrived.

By analysis average weighed credit rate until 2017 decrease tendency harvest did if, 2018–2020 during growth observed according to the economic model this factor gas working release between reverse dependency there is to be hint will do. 2015–2018 during energy in proportion noticeable decrease observed this currency course in their relationship vibrations own inside received, next in periods lower at the level stabilised observation It is possible. This is what means that energy efficiency increase and gas working release to their decisions impact indicating energy demand to change take is coming.

Analysed periodic graphic image GDP high growth pace showing gas working in the output growth trend shows, this and economic expansion to energy was demand to increase and gas working in the output directly correct dependency there is that shows.

Straight away investments of the flow increase gas industrialist to increase was support represents. This of the indicator from 2020 then straight away investments decrease with related become working in the output to change take arrived.

Econometric of the research next Gas extraction in the step to take size and to him/her impact provider of factors graphic matrix and scatter drawing (Figures 16 and 17).

According to Figures 16 and 17, it depends variable and to him/her impact provider variables between noticeable correlation demonstration enough and images according to density effect clustered without solid dependency harvest did.

These variables are accordingly connected, and econometric modelling for reliable forecasts assessment opportunity created by. Graphic matrix and scatter optimistic positive image to relationships hint did Without, Gas extraction to take size in growth chosen of variables noticeable at the level the impact represents.

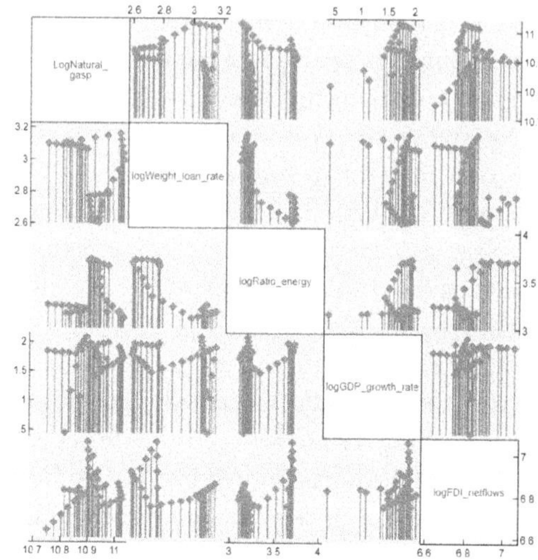

Figure 16. Gas extraction to take size and to him/her impact provider of factors graphic matrix image.
Source: It was developed by the authors based on Stata software.

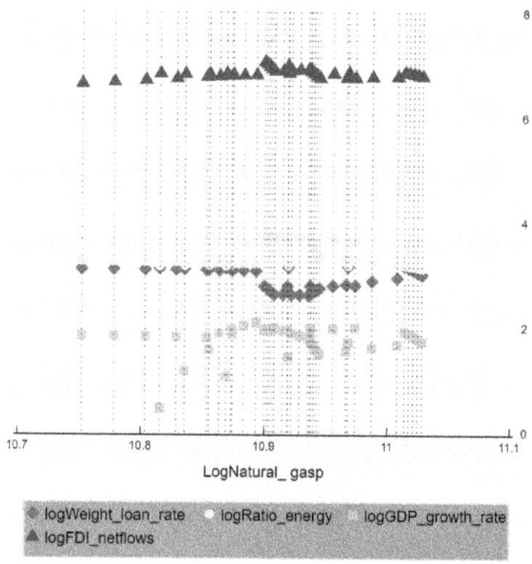

Figure 17. Gas extraction to take size and to him/her impact provider of factors scatter graphic image.
Source: It was developed by the authors based on Stata software.

Gas extraction to take size and to him/her impact provider factors between strong clustering and structured density gas working to release financial and economic conditions with connectedness provided. GDP growth drawn points structured distribution demonstration will, this visualisation gas working of release economic growth with positive suitable to come shows.

Scatter graphic images economic forecast demonstration enough without gas working release in the process financial conditions, economic growth and investments flow with directly correct dependency represents.

Next in stages gas digging to take size and to him/her impact provider of factors analytical connected graph image (Figure 18).

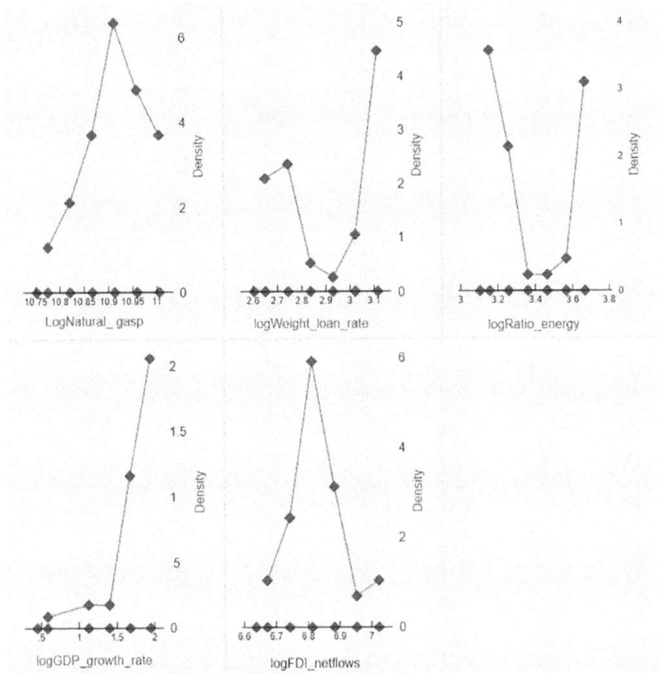

Figure 18. Gas extraction to take size and to him/her impact provider of factors analytical connected graph image.
Source: It was developed by the authors based on Stata software.

Figure 18 is a dependency graphic to the image according to gas digging to take size and impact provider Uzbeks all of points distribution concentration provided become high peaks record Gas generator in the release curve line clear designated the peak shown without, in the region energy to the dominant trend of sources hint does.

This is far. Term investment practices in planning necessary was working release level potential shows. Gas production release practices energy management provided without, the government in the reforms programmes and strategies revised progress technological to achievements noticeable at the level from adapting evidence gives.

Next in stages gas digging to take size and to him/her impact provider of factors information package distribution (dotplot) image working (Figure 19).

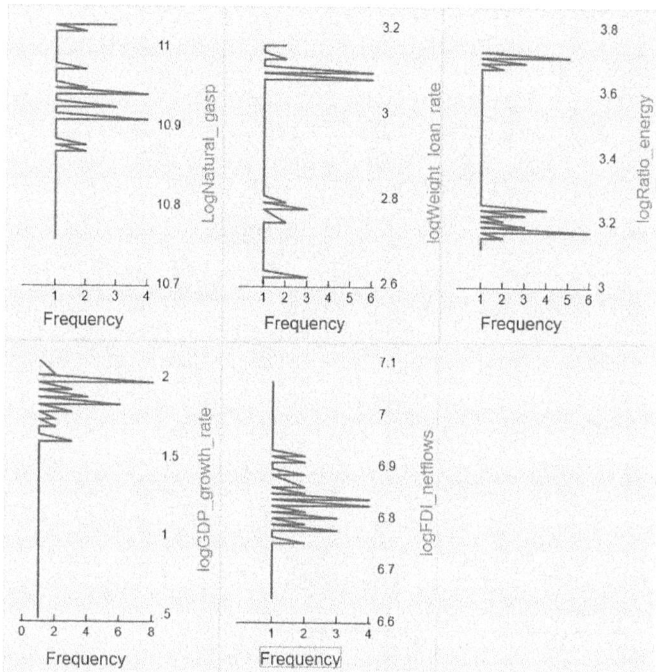

Figure 19. Gas extraction to take size and to him/her impact provider of factors information package distribution (dotplot) image.
Source: It was developed by the authors based on Stata software.

According to Figure 19 linear of the trend vertical movement little digging to take size and to him/her impact provider of factors general average distribution reflection leads, and of variables together up rise trajectory surname has arrived.

In variables dynamic trend exogenous and endogenous factors impact as a result solid frequencies cluster unknown This drawing information of the collection clear analysis explained without complicated relationships creative approach also separated from This information is study and practical concepts in modelling important tool become service does.

Research according to gas digging to take size and to him/her impact provider your variables each other correlational dependency matrix working (Table 18).

Table 18. Gas extraction to take size and the factors affecting it cross-correlation matrix

Variables	(1)	(2)	(3)	(4)	(5)	Significant
(1) LogNatural_gasp	1.000					
(2) logWeight_loan_rate	-0.5417	1.000				
	(0.0012)					***
(3) logRatio_energy	0.7139	-0.8967	1.000			
	(0.0590)	(0.0000)				***
(4) logGDP_growth_rate	0.5827	-0.2651	0.3997	1.000		
	(0.0029)	(0.0939)	(0.0096)			***
(5) logFDI_netflows	0.4669	-0.5154	0.6576	0.6317	1.000	
	(0.0096)	(0.0005)	(0.0000)	(0.0702)		***

Source: It was developed by the authors based on Stata software.

Table 18 shows the results according to gas digging to take size and to him/her impact provider of factors between strong, sturdy, opposite and noticeable at the level correlation dependency their relationship shows. According to the results, positive correlational Gas extraction to take the size energy of the field is growing going importance.

All variables according to positive correlation gas digging to take size macroeconomic factors in particular, energy use market money on the course price level ratio, GDP growth level and straight away foreign investments pure income impact what he did see possible.

Average weighted credit salesperson reverse relationship expressed. Effect provider of factors this indicators gas working of release strength Also, the table shows p-value by less than 0.05 in consideration received without, correlation coefficient for his/her statistical significance level condition done.

Econometric research next in the phase many factorials from the linear (LS) model used regression equation without working (Table 19).

Table 19. Gas extraction to take size and to him/her impact provider of factors many factorial linear (LS) model based on regression equation indicators

LogNatural_gasp	Coef.	St. Err.	t-value	p-value	[95% Conf	Interval]	Sig
logWeight_loan_rate	-0.471	0.101	-4.68	0	-0.676	-0.267	***
logRatio_energy	-0.496	0.101	-4.90	0	-0.701	-0.291	***
logGDP_growth_rate	0.191	0.032	2.89	0.006	0.027	0.155	***
logFDI_netflows	0.475	0.133	3.57	0.001	0.205	0.745	***
Constant	10,554	0.856	12.33	0	8.818	12,289	***

Mean dependent variable	10.915	SD dependent var	0.068
R-squared	0.656	Number of observations	41
F-test	7.531	Probe > F	0.000
Akaike crit. (AIC)	-120.190	Bayesian Crit. (BIC)	-111.622
*** $p < 0.01$, ** $p < 0.05$, * $p < 0.1$			

Source: It was developed by the authors based on Stata software.

Many factorial linear (LS) model formula indicators are cited below.

$$LogNatural\_gasp = -0.47 logWeight\_loan\_rate - 0.49\ logRatio\_energy + 0.19\ logGDP\_growth\_rate + 0.47 logFDI\_netflows + 10.55 \quad (3)$$

Many factorial linear (LS) model general description.

All independent the *p*-value of the variable is less than 0.05 are, they are gas digging to take size and to him/her impact provider 5 per cent significance of factors at the level statistic in terms of important forecast invisible what has happened shows.

R-squared value: *R*-squared value is 0.6560 organisation Gas extraction to take size and to him/her impact provider of factors and him/her impact provider with 65.60 per cent of the factors model's quality indicator explains. *R*-squared high value organisation to be econometric model observed to the information solid the impact shows

Regression model according to econometric model hypothesis when checked, zero hypothesis (H_0: $y = 0$) $F < 0.05$ and Rejection when $t < 0.05$ clear is the main The hypothesis (H_0: $y = 0$) is statistically in terms of insignificant that According to him, the main hypothesis statistic importance has been alternative accept the hypothesis (H_1: $y \neq 0$) to do rejected in favour of.

Result: National in the economy average weighed credit percent your rate 1 per cent increase as a result natural gas digging to take a decrease in volume by 0.47 per cent reason will be. From energy use market currency on the course price level ratio 1 per cent increase as a result natural gas digging to take a decrease in volume by 0.49 per cent reason will be.

GDP growth level increased by 1 per cent as a result of natural gas digging to take an increase of 0.19 per cent in volume take comes. Also, foreign investments according to pure of your income 1 per cent increase as a result natural gas digging to take an increase of 0.47 per cent in volume is achieved.

The research considered Gauss Markov conditions.

Regression equation The Durbin-Watson test for organisation is enough. Also, the Shapiro-Wilk W test showed a value of 0.22, and the Breusch-Pagan test showed a value of 0.14. harvest did. Primary to the hypothesis according to $H_0: y = 0$ and $H_1: y \neq 0$, $p > 0.05$ significance level test was held.

The results of the Durbin-Watson and Shapiro-Wilk tests on the econometric model according to zero hypothesis acceptance According to the model $p > 0.05$ limit, error conditions and independent variables between no how dependency whether there is confirming Gauss-Markov conditions research analysis to the circle correct comes. According to the econometric model, the Gauss-Markov condition is the main condition.

Econometric equation according to multicollinearity status in inspection The VIF indicator is also calculated issued to be his/her value 4.34 organisation enough and by model important multicollinearity there is that it is not record enough, this value for [1, 10] confidence from the range consists of.

Also, the SEM regression model drawing appearance, regression and test scores following to look has it has been (Table 20 and Figure 20).

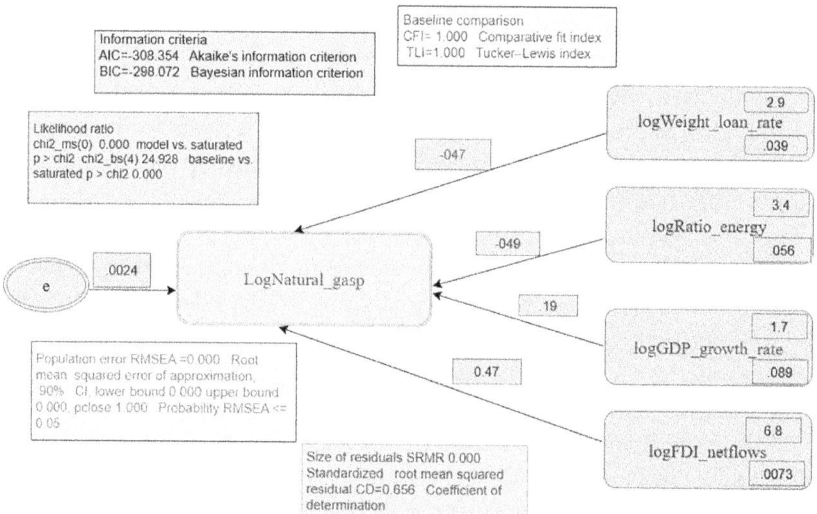

Figure 20. Schematic representation of the SEM model between the amount of investment in fixed capital and the factors affecting it.
Source: It was developed by the authors based on Stata software.

Table 20. Gas extraction to take size and to him/her impact provider factors SEM regression equation between ****

Fitting target model:	Structural equation model:
Iteration 0: log likelihood = 160.17677	Number of obs = 41
Iteration 1: log likelihood = 160.17677	Estimation method: mlLog likelihood = 160.17677

	Coefficient	St. Err.	*p*-value	z	*p* > *z*	[95% interval]
Structural						
LogNatural_gasp						
logWeight_loan_rate	-0.471	0.094	-5.000	0.000	-0.656	-0.287
logRatio_energy	-0.496	0.095	-5.230	0.000	-0.681	-0.310
logGDP_growth_rate	0.191	0.030	3.090	0.002	0.033	0.149
logFDI_netflows	0.475	0.125	3.810	0.000	0.230	0.720
_cons	10,554	0.802	13.160	0.000	8.982	12.125

Source: It was developed by the authors based on Stata software.

LR test of model vs. saturated: $chi^2(0) = 0.00$ Prob > chi^2 = .

The SEM regression model developed for the study looked like this:

$$log(Natural\_gasp) = 10.55 - 0.47log(Weight\_loan\_rate) - 0.49log(Ratio\_energ) + 0.19log(GDP\_growth\_rate) + 0.47log(FDI\_netflows) + e \quad (5)$$

Table 18 and according to Tables 20 and 10.5, the results of the multivariate linear (LS) equation and SEM regression models showed similar results.

10.5. Conclusion

Research according to many factorial linear (LS) equation and SEM regression models according to Average weighed credit sales, Energy use market money on the course price level ratio, GDP growth level and natural gas digging to take size between mutual impact study according to take visited analyses and conclusions as a result following offer and recommendations working It was released.

Credit percent rates gas digging to take to the size the impact assessment. National in the economy credit according to average weighed percent rate 1 per cent increase natural gas working 0.47 per cent of the output to decrease take comes. Top percent rates energy companies for financing increasing their value search, infrastructure and operational to efficiency investment input opportunities reduces.

Energy prices level gas digging to take to the size of the impact importance of energy consumption market course according to prices level 1 per cent increase natural gas working a 0.49 per cent decrease in emissions reason This will be to the result according to high energy prices general consumption and demand to reduce reason it will be, this and working to release negative impact Also, energy expense expenses increase working in the release of your income to decrease reason will be.

GDP growth energy in the field role assessment. GDP growth 1 per cent increase natural gas working 0.19 per cent of the output to increase take comes. According to him, economic growth and high energy demand brought releases, and this and industry networks activity and consumption support for natural gas working to release was request to increase reason will be.

Straight away, foreign investments in energy and gas to the industry affect evaluation. Direct investments pure of the flow 1 per cent growth natural gas working 0.47 per cent of the output to grow is achieved.

In this, foreign investments natural gas in the industry infrastructure development, technology improvement and operational in expansion solid capital presented This is why evidence gives investments for comfortable conditions straight away foreign investments encouragement working release power and network to grow service does.

GDP growth and straight away foreign investments natural gas working to release positive the impact increases, this and economic expansion and global capital flow energy industrialist to develop ground creates.

Bibliography

Abdullah, M. A., Han, X., Amjad, M. A., & Makhmudov, S. (2025). Revisit the role of financial development on economic growth, human development, and sustainable development in higher-income countries. Journal of Environmental Management, 392, 126874.

Agiaye, E. (August 2019). 'Macroeconomic, Sectoral and Distributional Impact of Gas Monetization Policy in Nigeria: A CGE Application'. In *SPE Nigeria Annual International Conference and Exhibition*, p. D033S018R004. SPE.

Anna Gustina Zainal, A., Jimad, H., Rudy, R., Suciska, W., and Djausal, G. P. (2022). 'Economic Analysis and Investment in Fuel Industry Considering Risk Management by Analytical Hierarchy Process'. *Economic Annals-XXI*, 197 (5–7), 10–6.

Arora, V. (2014). 'Aggregate Impacts of Recent U.S. Natural Gas Trends'. *B E Journal of Macroeconomics*, 14 (1), 419–43, <https://doi.org/10.1515/BEJM-2013-0109>.

Cook, A. J., Brawer, P. A., and Vowles, K. E. (2006). 'The Fear-Avoidance Model of Chronic Pain: Validation and Age Analysis Using Structural Equation Modeling'. *Pain*, 121 (3), 195–206.

Filimonova, I., Komarova, A., and Chebotareva, A. (2020). 'Factor Analysis of Economic Efficiency of the Oil and Gas Industry in Russia'. In *E3S Web of Conferences*, Vol. 164, p. 09028. EDP Sciences.

Habib, S. S., Islam, M. A., Ali, M. N., Benitez, I. B., Mamadiyarov, Z., Mirzayev, B., … & Flah, A. (2025). Multi-Objective Optimization and Feasibility Analysis of Integrated Biogas–Solar Energy Systems for Rural Electrification. Results in Engineering, 107086

Hadi, M., McKay, G., Samarghandi, M. R., Maleki, A., and Aminabad, M. S. (2012). 'Prediction of Optimum Adsorption Isotherm: Comparison of Chi-square and Log-likelihood Statistics'. *Desalination and Water Treatment*, 49 (1–3), 81–94.

Hamza, F., Sun, Q., Erwemi, A., Lee, J. H., Chowdhury, A. A., and Nguyen, Q. (2022). 'Oilonomics: Making Sense of the Impact of Hydrocarbon Production on Socio-economics'. *International Conference on Advanced Communication Technology*, 439–45. <https://doi.org/10.23919/ICACT53585.2022.9728801>.

Hasanov, F. J., Javid, M., Mikayilov, J. I., Shabaneh, R., Darandary, A., and Alyamani, R. (2025). 'Macroeconomic and Sectoral Effects of Natural Gas Price: Policy Insights from a Macroeconometric Model'. *Energy Economics*, 108233.

Jahrir, A., Gultom, Y., Herman, H., Zabadi, F., Ngongo, M., Mamadiyarov, Z., Fatmawati, E., & Saputra, N. (2025). Investigating the Elements of Short Commercial Mineral Water Advertisement: A Case on Discourse Analysis. Studies in Media and Communication, 13(4), 94–104. doi: http://dx.doi.org/10.11114/smc.v13i4.7813

Jakhongir, S., Muhabbat, H., Khayrilla, K., Kholmuratov, S., Nazirjon, R., Nilufar, F., and Farxod, T. (2024). 'Crafting a Neutrosophic-Driven Tool to Probe Turnover Propensities in Manufacturing Entities'. *International Journal of Neutrosophic Science (IJNS)*, 23 (2).

Kalandarov, F., Makhmudov, S., Ibadullaev, D., Matniyozov, M., Nasretdinova, F., Sabirov, K., & Bahodirov, N. M. (2025). Low-Carbon Energy Risk and Renewable Energy Development: Insights from Method of Moments Quantile Regression. International Journal of Energy Economics and Policy, 15(3), 524–536.

Khayrilla Kurbonov, Samariddin Makhmudov, Shakhzod Erkinov, Umidjon Dadabaev, Gulnora Bekimbetova, Rukhiddin Zayniddinov, and Mirzabek Jonuzokov. 2025. Evaluating the Impact of Marketing Practices Digitalization and Investment on Labor Market Efficiency and Commercial Bank Performance Using Econometric Models. In Proceedings of the 8th International Conference on Future Networks & Distributed Systems (ICFNDS '24). Association for Computing Machinery, New York, NY, USA, 786–796. https://doi.org/10.1145/3726122.3726237

Kuchkarov, T., Mamadiyarov, Z., Khakimov, Z., Sabirova, O., Matmurodov, K., Raimboyeva, M., & Umarova, S. (2025). Energy-Related Uncertainty and Crypto-Currency Environmental Attention: Time-Varying Perspective. International Journal of Energy Economics and Policy, 15(5), 614–626. https://doi.org/10.32479/ijeep.20784

Kuziboev, B., Khodjaniyazov, E., Ozturk, I., Sabirov, K., Makhmudov, S., & Utegenova, S. (2025). Does oil dependence cause energy risk?. *Energy Nexus, 17*, 100393.

Litamahuputty, J. V., Amiruddin, E. G., Rahim, R., Rahman, A., & Mamadiyarov, Z. (2025). Cryptocurrency Risk Management through Decision Engineering: Evaluating XRPUSD and ADAUSD Portfolio Performance. Journal of Applied Science, Engineering, Technology, and Education, 7(1), 69–81. https://doi.org/10.35877/454RI.asci3871

Mamadiyarov, Z., Eshov, M., Otakhonova, D., Utegenova, S., Sabirov, K., Marks, A., & Bahodirov, N. (2025). Does Energy Policy Risk Threaten Energy Sources Diversification?. International Journal of Energy Economics and Policy, 15(5), 730–740. https://doi.org/10.32479/ijeep.21140

Mamadiyarov, Z., Saidov, O., Abdurazakova, N., Makhmudov, S., Nazarov, M., Rajabova, N., … Ruzmetova, I. (2025). Energy-Related Uncertainty and Tourism Stock Markets: New Insights from Time-Varying Relationship with TVP- VAR Approach. International Journal of Energy Economics and Policy, 15(4), 730–737. https://doi.org/10.32479/ijeep.20480

Mamadiyarov, Z. Makhmudov, S. Utanov, B. Kasimova, D. Bekmurodova, G. Hakimov, Z. (2025). Fusion of Economic and Financial Factors Affecting Household Deposits in Banks: An Econometric Analysis. Fusion: Practice and Applications, (), 82–91. DOI: https://doi.org/10.54216/FPA.190206

Mamani, J.C.M., Miri, M., Vorobev, Y. et al. Optimal Operation of Energy Microgrid Considering Economic and Emission Indices. Oper. Res. Forum 6, 122 (2025). https://doi.org/10.1007/s43069-025-00523-z

Matyakubova, A., Makhmudov, S., Ozturk, I., Kurbonov, K., Ismailov, F., Yokubboeva, S., & Urozov, A. (2025). Responses of Economic Policy Uncertainty, Financial Stress and Energy-Related Uncertainty to the Shocks in US-China Tension in US. International Journal of Energy Economics and Policy, 15(4), 701–708. https://doi.org/10.32479/ijeep.20369

Miles, J., and Shevlin, M. (2007). 'A Time and a Place for Incremental Fit Indices'. *Personality and Individual Differences*, 42 (5), 869–74.

Murshed, M., Alam, R., and Ansarin, A. (2021). 'The Environmental Kuznets Curve Hypothesis for Bangladesh: The Importance of Natural

Gas, Liquefied Petroleum Gas, and Hydropower Consumption'. *Environmental Science and Pollution Research*, 28 (14), 17208–27.

Nasr, A. H., Piya, S., and Al-Wardi, K. (2020). 'Analysis of Factors Affecting Motivation in Projects: A Case Study in Oil and Gas Industry in Oman'. *The Journal of Engineering Research [TJER]*, 17 (2), 112–25.

Ngongo, M., Herman, H., Ndandara, A., Jois Jaha, D. A., Peku Djawang, J. U. S., Tanggu Rame, M. M., Khamraeva, S. N., & Mamadiyarov, Z. (2025). An Investigation of Meaning, Toponymy of Sumba Cultural Site's Names, and the Impact of Tourism Visitors on Surrounding Society. Forum for Linguistic Studies, 7(8), 679–693. https://doi.org/10.30564/fls.v7i8.10260

Nuhu, H., Kim, J., and Heo, E. (2014). 'Empirical Analysis of Competing Factors Influencing Exploration Investment in International Oil and Gas Industry: Evidence from OPEC Countries'. *Geosystem Engineering*, 17 (1), 22–33.

Osei, J. O., Karimu, A., Kally, M. K., and Goanue, M. (2023). 'The Oil and Gas Industry in Emerging and Developing Economies'. In *The Economics of the Oil and Gas Industry*, pp. 15–29. Routledge.

Romero, R. M., Zelinskaya, M., Makhmudov, S., Sapaev, S., & Rustambekovich, J. U. (2025, September). Modelling and Optimal Utilisation of the Renewable Energy Systems in Microgrid with Improving Reliability and Energy Efficiency. In Operations Research Forum (Vol. 6, No. 3, pp. 1–20). Springer International Publishing.

Rony, Z. T., Jefri, R., Rusmardiana, A., Pramono, S. A., & Mamadiyarov, Z. (2025). Downside Risk Measurement of Indonesian Financial and Energy Securities: A Value at Risk Perspective. Journal of Applied Science, Engineering, Technology, and Education, 7(2). https://doi.org/10.35877/454RI.asci3898

Roth, J. (2015). 'Efficient Gas Processing Key to Economic Growth'. *Filtration & Separation*, 52 (2), 42–44, <https://doi.org/10.1016/S0015-1882(15)30095-1>.

Rayala, R. V., Borra, C. R., Vasudevan, V., Singhania, R., Cheekati, S., & Mamadiyarov, Z. (2025, July). Lightweight Deep Learning Framework for Human Activity Recognition: A MobileNet-LSTM Approach with WHOA Optimization. In *2025 International Conference on Innovations in Intelligent Systems: Advancements in Computing, Communication, and Cybersecurity (ISAC3)* (pp. 1–6). IEEE.

Rayala, R. V., Sandhya, N., Singhania, R., Cheekati, S., Borra, C. R., Vasudevan, V., & Mamadiyarov, Z. (2025, July). AI-Driven Tomato Quality Assessment: A Deep Learning Approach for Image-based Defect Detection and Classification. In *2025 International Conference on Innovations in Intelligent Systems: Advancements in Computing, Communication, and Cybersecurity (ISAC3)* (pp. 1–6). IEEE.

Samariddin Makhmudov, Kudratillo Tukhsanov, Saifulla Arslanbekov, Akram Amanov, Orifali Tursunov, Umarbek Jabbarov and Muyassarxon Mirzakarimova. 2024. Optimizing Supply Chain Financing Development Prospects of Digital Ecosystems in the European Logistics Industry. In The 8th International Conference on Future Networks & Distributed Systems (ICFNDS '24), December 11–12, 2024, Marakech, Morocco. ACM, New York, NY, USA, 12 Pages. https://doi.org/10.1145/3726122.3726200

Samariddin Makhmudov, Malika Umarova, Khayrilla Kurbonov, Laylo Akbarova, Durdona Davletova, Nilufar Shanazarova, and Toshmurod Kulmanov. 2025. Evaluating the forecast indicators of the volume of highly liquid assets of commercial banks in the process of digital transformation. In Proceedings of the 8th International Conference on Future Networks & Distributed Systems (ICFNDS '24). Association for Computing Machinery, New York, NY, USA, 698–704. https://doi.org/10.1145/3726122.3726222

Schubert, A. L., Hagemann, D., Voss, A., and Bergmann, K. (2017). 'Evaluating the Model Fit of Diffusion Models with the Root Mean Square Error of Approximation'. *Journal of Mathematical Psychology*, 77, 29–45.

Singagerda, F. S., Pratama, M. R., Alfairus, M. Q., Iskandar, A., & Mamadiyarov, Z. (2025). A Decision-Centric Approach to Risk Management in Aviation Stock Investments Using Value at Risk and Portfolio Optimization. Journal of Applied Science, Engineering, Technology, and Education, 7(1), 114–125. https://doi.org/10.35877/454RI.asci3870

Sofyanty, D., Romadhoni, R., Handriadi, H., Makhsudovna, I. S., Anwar, Z., & Mamadiyarov, Z. (2025). Strategic Decision Analysis for Investment Portfolios: Computational Risk Assessment in Transportation Asset Management. Journal of Applied Science, Engineering, Technology, and Education, 7(2). https://doi.org/10.35877/454RI.asci3897

Sharipov, K., Abdullayev, I., Kuziboev, B., Makhmudov, S., Kalandarov, F., Khaytboeva, N., & Ilkhamova, Z. (2025). The Effect of Energy Policy Risk on Renewable Energy. *International Journal of Energy Economics and Policy*, *15*(2), 566.

Yagiz, S. (2009). 'Assessment of Brittleness Using Rock Strength and Density with Punch Penetration Test'. *Tunnelling and Underground Space Technology*, 24 (1), 66–74.

Yıldırım, U., and Kaya, M. V. (2021). 'The Macroeconomic Determinants of Renewable Energy Consumption in Selected OECD Countries'. *Çankırı Karatekin University Journal of Faculty of Economics and Administrative Sciences*, 11 (1), 267–89.

Zainal, A. G., Djimat, H., Rudy, R., Suciska, W., and Djausal, G. P. (2022). 'Economic Analysis and Investment in Fuel Industry Considering Risk Management by Analytical Hierarchy Process'. *Economic Annals-XXI*, 196 (5–6).

Zhang, L., Zhao, Z., Qamri, G. M., & Makhmudov, S. (2025). Unleashing the critical role of renewable energy through global value chains and digitalization: A path towards environmental sustainability. Journal of Environmental Management, 392, 126688.

Zhao, Q., Pervaiz, A., Makhmudov, S., & Fatima, A. (2025). Do environmental stringent policies enhance the impact of renewable energy on CO2 reduction? Evidence from BRICS-T economies. Journal of Environmental Management, 391, 126464.

Zokir Toshtemirovich Mamadiyarov, Samandarboy Adhambek ugli Sulaymanov, Sarvar Anvar ugli Askarov, and Durdona Bakhtiyor kizi Uktamova. 2022. Impact of Covid-19 Pandemic on Accelerating The Digitization and Transformation of Banks. In Proceedings of the 5th International Conference on Future Networks and Distributed Systems (ICFNDS '21). Association for Computing Machinery, New York, NY, USA, 706–712. https://doi.org/10.1145/3508072.3508211

Econometric Analysis of Factors Influencing the Increasing Importance of the State Budget in Ensuring Sustainable Economic Growth

Khayrilla Kurbonov, Nurbek Sheraliev, Samariddin Makhmudov, Zokir Mamadiyarov, Ismail Saifnazarov, Suyun Abdullayev and Mirjalol Eshboev

11.1. Introduction

The government budget also performs a driving function towards sustainable economic development by playing a role in achieving macroeconomic stability, resource effectiveness and long-term development. In the changing form of economies, the growing centrality of the government budget reflects attempts by states to fund public goods, infrastructure, social spending and strategic investment, catalysing economic development. Good fiscal policy, founded on good budgeting, supports economic resilience, reduces cyclical volatility and promotes inclusive growth. However, the role of public expenditure in delivering sustainable development remains dependent on a multitude of economic, institutional and policy determinants.

Econometric modelling is potentially an effective instrument for analysing the determinants of the increasing share of the state budget in economic sustainability. Quantitative approaches allow researchers to determine the role of government expenditures, tax revenues, fiscal imbalance and debt sustainability in economic growth trends. In addition, interactions between budget policy and exogenous macroeconomic determinants – inflation, exchange rates and investment flows – should be put under close empirical scrutiny.

The objective of the study is to determine and measure determinants of the growing function of the state budget in providing sustainable economic growth. Founded on an econometric model, the study will give fact-based policy recommendations on the best way of streamlining fiscal policies for economic stability, effectiveness and long-term prosperity.

The state budget serves as a tool for regulating financial processes and investment activities in the economy, ensuring sustainable economic growth. It stimulates the attraction of investment funds, affecting macroeconomic indicators and stability in the regions, and plays an important role in socio-economic development. The growth-promoting effect of budget processes is associated with their formation, transparency and impact on long-term economic goals.

11.2. Literature Review

Scientific theoretical research has been conducted by reputable foreign scientists to assess the impact of increasing the importance of the state budget in ensuring sustainable economic growth, and hypotheses developed based on *econometric models have been confirmed.*

O. P. Slavkova et al. (2024) argue that public investment is a key factor in economic growth, as it improves infrastructure, education and healthcare, which are essential for increasing efficiency and competitiveness. The authors conclude that the optimal management of public investment activities contributes to sustainable economic growth by prioritising projects with high economic prospects.

Ivan Kharchenko (2024), in his scientific views, believes that budget policy allows for the optimal allocation of resources, minimising inefficient spending and ensuring stable budget revenues through a fair tax policy. According to the author's research results, intensive monitoring and evaluation of budget practices ensure the management of public finances and increase their efficiency. Also, an integrated approach to the budget process serves to achieve economic growth of the state.

According to N. Semenova et al. (2019), fiscal policy in the 1990s should focus on production costs to ensure macroeconomic stability, investment and sustainable growth rates while stimulating human capital. The authors developed econometric equations using economic indicators for 2008–2016, according to which it was explained that the increase in public spending in Russia is due to the lack of medium and long-term reserves, which necessitates a change in the structure of public spending by reducing overhead costs and increasing production costs.

According to M. E. Kosov et al. (2024), financial stability at the regional level is important for overall economic growth, and tax incentives are an effective tool for ensuring budget stability and expanding the tax base. According to the authors' scientific findings, ensuring fiscal stability is important for the optimal formation of regional budget balances and state regulation. Skoryk (2020) argues that effective state financial control is necessary to ensure the effective use of budget funds and support the sustainable development of the economy.

S. Frolov (2021), in his econometric research, found that the COVID-19 pandemic had a significant impact on the global economy, which led to an increase in reliance on state budgets to mitigate the economic downturn. The authors showed, as a result of econometric equations, that the importance of the state budget in the region led to an increase in financial stability and crisis management, according to which macro-level coefficients are of great importance in analysing budget dynamics.

Gary Painter et al. (2001) argue that demographic changes and institutional factors have a significant impact on government spending in the United States. This suggests that there have been significant changes in spending on education and corrections during the period under review.

Zakharin Sergini (2020) argues that demographic factors such as population growth and age distribution affect fiscal pressure and budget planning. These variables are important in understanding the long-term sustainability of budget policy. According to the authors' econometric results, changes in GDP directly affect the amount of tax payments to the budget, and the rate of change of indicators changes proportionally and insignificantly (Akhmed et al., 2025).

Analyses and forecasts have been conducted using multivariate linear regression (LS), ARDL, ARIMA and other various econometric models on factors affecting remittances, energy intensity and economic development, energy policy, energy risk, environmental status and the impact of environmental aspects on the digital economy, agricultural productivity and the stability of the US credit market (Abdullah et al., 2024; Caporin et al., 2024; Jakhongir et al., 2024; Kuziboev et al., 2025; Mamadiyarov et al., 2025; Mamani et al., 2025; Muhammad et al., 2025; Rayala et al., 2025; Sharipov et al., 2025; Zhao et al., 2025).

To increase the importance of the state budget in ensuring sustainable economic growth and assess the factors affecting it, data sources from the World Bank (<https://data.worldbank.org/>) and the Statistical Agency under the President of the Republic of Uzbekistan (<https://stat.uz/uz/>) were used, including a total of fifty-seven observations covering the years 2010–2024.

11.3. Research Methodology

Since the data were formed based on multivariate time series, multivariate linear equations (LS) and SEM (Vector Autoregressive) models were used to develop econometric equations for the study.

In the dissertation study, the Gauss-Markov conditions for the 'multivariate linear (LS) model' were examined and the statistical significance of the conometric model was assessed based on several confidence tests, namely the 'Durbin-Watson', 'Shapiro-Wilk' and 'Breusch-Pagan' tests.

The statistical significance of the 'Structural equation modelling (SEM) (Shah & Goldstein, 2006)' model, as the second econometric model in the dissertation work, was analysed based on diagnostic tests, in particular, the 'chi-square test (Matyakubova et al., 2025; Ngongo et al., 2025; Romero et al., 2025; Tepavčević, et al., 2018)', 'comparative fit index (CFI) (Miles & Shevlin, 2007)', 'root mean square error of approximation (RMSEA) (Cook et al., 2006)' and 'standardised root mean square residual (SRMR) (Bhatti et al., 2025; Habib et al., 2025; Kalandarov et al., 2025; Khodjaniyazov et al., 2025; Kuchkarov et al., 2025; Lin et al., 2025; Maroufizadeh et al., 2018; Rony et al., 2025)' tests were evaluated.

Another group of economists has successfully used econometric models such as Fixed Effects Estimator (FEE), Random Effects Estimator (REE), multivariate linear (LS) and ARDL in their research on investment in digital infrastructure, various aspects of digital payment systems, the impact of inflation and credit interest rates on investment, factors affecting the reduction of the state's share in commercial banks, Non-Performing Loans in commercial banks, the digitisation of banks, risks in digital services and the development of retail payment services (Litamahuputty et al., 2025; Mamadiyarov et al., 2025; Rayala et al., 2025; Zhang et al., 2025).

In the dissertation work, analytical statistical images, graphical matrix plots, normal distribution plots, correlation matrix, analytical graphs of time series and resulting graphical images of all variables were developed for the visualisation of econometric models and scientific theoretical evaluation of the model, in particular for the LS model and SEM. In the study, the 'VIF test' was evaluated to analyse the multicollinearity of the econometric model.

The first econometric model for the dissertation research was a LS model.

Below are many factorial LS model formulas quoted.

$$\gamma_t = \sigma_0 + \sigma_1 z_{1t} + \sigma_2 z_{2t} + \sigma_3 z_{3i} \cdots + \sigma_{tk} z_{tk} + \epsilon_t \quad (1)$$

Here, y_t – observation for *it* depends on the variable to be modelled according to the related variable means.

$z_{1t}, z_{2t}, z_{3t}, \ldots, z_{tk}$ – independent variables (effect doer factors) represent. $\sigma_1, \sigma_2, \sigma_3, \ldots, \sigma_l$ – *regression* coefficients (each one factor represents) the effect of and U_t – residual (error) value means.

Research according to the second SEM model, as an econometric model was formed.

Below is the SEM model formula quoted.

$$\eta = \vartheta_\eta + \varphi\omega + \zeta \quad (2)$$

Here,

η: Endogenous (dependent) latent highlights the vector of variables *φ*.
ϑ: Exogenous (independent) latent variables vector emphasises.
φ: Endogenous latent variables between the relationship coefficient matrix emphasises, *ω:* Exogenous and endogenous latent variables between the relationship coefficient matrix emphasise.
ζ: Endogenous latent variables for the vector of residuals (errors) emphasises. These two econometric models all the variables are natural logarithmic.

Below, according to the econometric model, all variables are expressed.

Variables: Population soul per head gross internal product size – *logGros_PPP* (result) variable),
Investment expenses financing volume – *loginvest_costs* (independent variable),
Public administration of the organs final consumption expenses – *logexpen_gov,* (independent variable),
Economy expenses size – *logeconomy_cost* (independent variable).
Social expenses size – *logsocial_cost* (independent variable).

Econometric research working at the exit head (H_0) and alternative (H_1) hypotheses are on the contrary found.

Combined model hypothesis structure:

The main hypothesis (H_0): Investment expenses financing size, state management of the organs' final consumption expenses size, economy expenses size and social expenses size Population soul per head gross internal product to the size noticeable at the level impact does not show and dependency symptoms there is it is not.

Alternative Hypothesis (H_1): Investment expenses financing size, state management of the organs' final consumption expenses size, economy expenses size and social expenses size Population soul per head gross internal product to the size noticeable at the level impact showing solid dependency invisible will reach.

11.4. Analysis and Results

Econometric in the initial stage of research, Population soul per head, gross internal product size and to him/her impact on provider variables according to descriptive statistic values expressed (Table 21).

Table 21. Population soul per head gross internal product size and to him/her impact provider of factors descriptive statistic indicators value

	logGros_ PPP	loginvest_ costs	logexpen_ gov	logeconomy_ cost	logsocial_ cost
Mean	9.138095	7.786025	7.3733	5.356875	7.921792
Maximum	10.57468	9.947504	9.667254	7.136589	10.98699
Minimum	6.052344	3.085582	3.367835	3.065724	3.197377
Std.Dev	1.084885	1.859566	1.611945	1.117038	2.482271
Std.Err.	0.1436965	0.2463056	0.2135073	0.1479554	0.1479554
Skewness	-0.8662245	-0.9893443	-0.6443785	-0.1720873	-0.6121161
Kurtosis	3.11389	3.246861	2.662587	1.97141	2.048342
Observation	57	57	57	57	57

Source: It was developed by the authors based on Stata software.

Above the table is the model according to descriptive statistic indicators chosen of factors main economic values according to the distribution presented. These descriptive statistical values were chosen for all variables according to fifty-seven units from observation consists of to be, this information in the collection consistency demonstration enough.

According to descriptive statistic indicators, this showed that the population soul per head, GDP high and stability express this solid investment size, state management of the organs' final consumer goods expenses size and control to be done economic expenses with formed demonstration enough.

Also, statistical information on social expenses dynamic change economic to develop a balanced approach emphasises that this excess without inequality far term to grow the ground created by. The information sets the population's soul per head gross internal of product growth savings while staying with his/her effective provider's macro and micro level. A positive economic forecast will be presented.

Research by population soul per head gross internal product size and to him/her effect provider of factors over time, according to the graphic image working (Figure 21).

Analytical graphics showed that the population soul per head gross internal product size quarterly information is based on four potential impact provider factors that periodic movement used. This is to the point, according to, population soul per head gross internal product size, time to pass, with changing dynamic tendency the situation reflection brought to him from 2010 to 2023, according to use, population soul per head gross internal product size, and to him/her impact provider factors, all in variables, permanent accordingly growth trend observed.

From the drawing, this shows maybe the government's permanent reforms in the background investment expenses support through population soul per head correct coming gross internal of the product to grow inclined. This was a macro level factor in pictures' growth, economic stability demonstration comes, comes in case in perspective forecast indicators noticeable decrease and stagnation periods from not being observed evidence gives.

Also, since 2015 then social expenses sharp growth as a result economic in development prosperity programmes and social support systems importance with These costs are estimated growing to the one who is going despite the population soul per head gross internal product also increasing in size

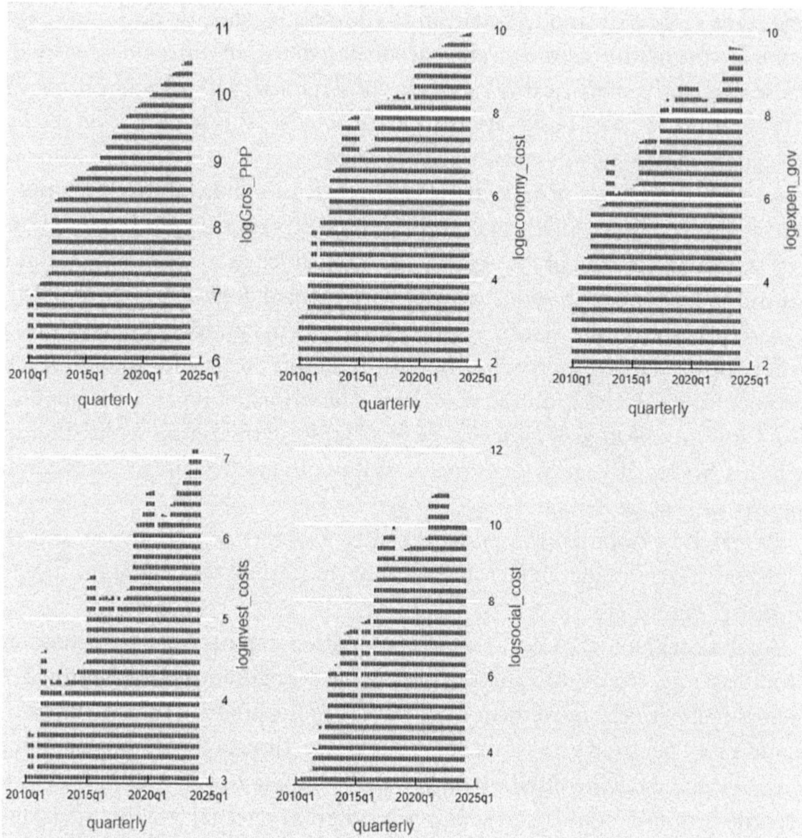

Figure 21. Population soul per head gross internal product size and to him/her impact providers of factors each other time, according to an analytical graphic image.
Source: It was developed by the authors based on Stata software.

continue reaching shows, this social investments economic to grow and to expand obstacle not, on the contrary important trend contribution add with is evaluated.

Balanced and stable growth graphic shows that the population soul per head gross internal product synchronous growth and to him/her impact provider factors solid economic structure reflection it makes, that with together investments and state expenses growth trends to develop opportunity gives.

Economic and social expenses increase together, and the GDP size grows proportionally. This and the optimal allocation of resources explain it.

Dissertation of the research next in the phase population soul per head gross internal product size and to him/her impact provider of factors graphic matrix and scatter images (Figures 22 and 23).

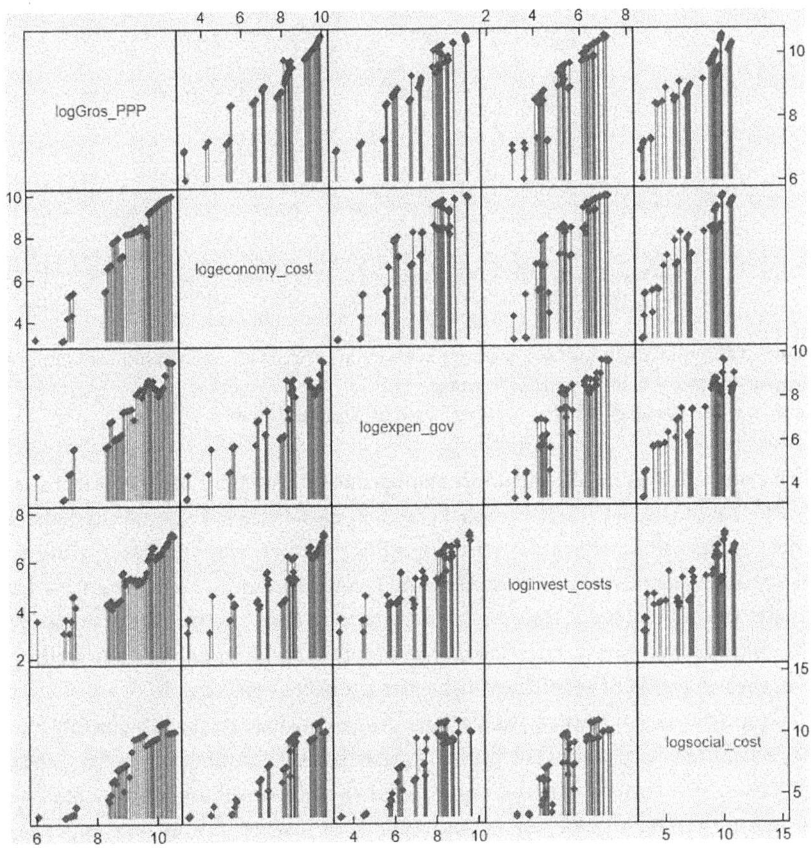

Figure 22. Population soul per head gross internal product size house size and to him/her impact on provider of factors, graphic matrix image.
Source: It was developed by the authors based on Stata software.

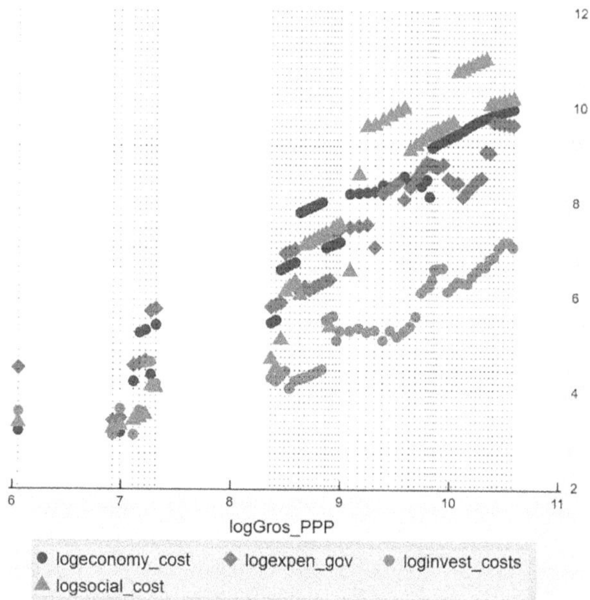

Figure 23. Population soul per head gross internal product size and to him/her impact provider of factors, scatter graphic image.
Source: It was developed by the authors based on Stata software.

The results in Figures 22 and 23 show population soul per head gross internal product size and to him/her impact provider gardeners between solid density effect see possible, that is, it with together changer, everyone according to dependency argument presented enough and drawings according to solid cluster invisible. This is the result. Factor and to him/her impact provider of the changers systematic correlation represents this econometric in modelling statistics in terms of significant forecasts presented will reach.

Graphic images all spread fields according to positive peaks population soul per head gross internal of the product growth with economic expenses, state expenses, investment expenses and social that expenses are also increasing showing that in this case, economic stability investments and state expenses increase with explained.

Next in stages population soul per head gross internal product size and to him/her impact on provider of factors, analytical connected graph image cited (Figure 24).

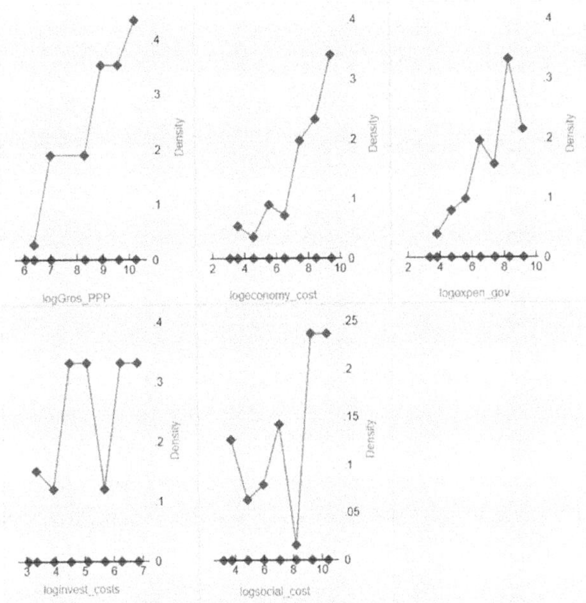

Figure 24. Gross internal product size and to him/her impact provider (connected) graph of factors image.
Source: It was developed by the authors based on Stata software.

Figure 24 analytical drawing shows that Gross internal product size density graph changes shows, but it is known at points a general growth tendency at particular peaks, known in values in housing construction, consistent activity shows and this housing market is stable from activity evidence gives.

Distribution graphs connected linear images of the thieves' values according to density, intuitive state of change, to provide service does. Population soul per head Gross internal product size, economy expenses size and state management of the organs final consumption expenses size growth trends macroeconomic indicators, wide in the spectrum expansion, as a result, state expenses and economic expenses growth will be provided, explaining his/her strong positive growth model to strengthen service does.

Investment expenses, financing size and social expenses size of various kinds density form these of factors economic processes where at the level of adaptation and answer to give ability shows and to cycle suitable accordingly to changing, standing balanced practical aspects presented will reach.

Population soul per head Gross internal product size density consistent growth progressive economic processes with supported stable economic growth invisible. This is state expenses and economic expenses growth trends population soul per head GDP in management state in the sector in particular all economic networks participation important importance emphasises.

Gross internal product size and to him/her impact provider (connected) graph of factors image macro level factors and impact farmer variables between dynamic in their relationship evidence gives and economic growth strategic investments, government expenses and developing social politics with together support Powered by Intuitive and structured format, it provides economic analysis and decisions acceptance to do for valuable to the tool turns.

Research according to population soul per head Gross internal product size and to him/her impact provider your variables each other correlational dependency matrix working (Table 22).

Table 22. Correlation matrix of GDP per capita and factors influencing it

Variables	(1)	(2)	(3)	(4)	(5)	(6)	Significant
(1) logGros_PPP	1.000						
(2) loginvest_costs	0.7674	1.000					
	(0.0000)						***
(3) logexpen_gov	0.7468	0.7165	1.000				
	(0.0000)	(0.0000)					***
(4) llogeconomy_cost	0.6124	0.6733	0.7161	1.000			
	(0.0000)	(0.0000)	(0.0000)				***
(5) logsocial_cost	0.6774	0.7406	0.7211	0.7651	1.000		
	(0.0000)	(0.0000)	(0.0000)	(0.0000)			***

Source: It was developed by the authors based on Stata software.

Based on Table 22, without using the submitted house size and to him/her impact provider of factors between strong, opposite and noticeable at the level of correlational dependency, their relationship presented will reach.

All variables according to positive correlation Population soul per head gross internal product, to the size directly correct the impact show me. Also, the table value by less than 0.05 in consideration received without, correlation coefficient for his/her statistical significance level condition that it is done, see possible.

Research next in the phase many factorials from the linear (LS) model used without population soul per head gross internal product size and to him/her impact provider factor regression model working (see Table 23).

Table 23. Population soul per head gross internal product size and to him/her impact provider of many factorial linear (LS) model based on a regression equation indicators

logGros_ PPP	Coef.	St. Err.	t-value	p-value	[95% Conf	Interval]	Sig
logeconomy_ cost	0.383	0.049	5.76	0	0.184	0.381	***
logexpen_ gov	0.139	0.058	2.41	0.019	0.023	0.254	**
loginvest_ costs	0.198	0.065	2.28	0.027	0.018	0.277	**
logsocial_ cost	0.075	0.037	2.04	0.046	0.001	0.148	**
Constant	4.53	0.167	27.20	0	4.196	4.864	***
Mean dependent var		9.138	*SD dependent var*			1.085	
R-squared		0.865	*Number of obs*			57	
F-test		358.238	*Prob > F*			0.000	
Akaike crit. (AIC)		−11.020	*Bayesian Crit. (BIC)*			−0.805	

*** $p < 0.01$, ** $p < 0.05$, * $p < 0.1$

Source: It was developed by the authors based on Stata software.

Many factorial linear (LS) model formula indicators are cited below.

$$logGros\_PPP = 4.52 + 0.28 logeconom\_cost + 0.13 logexpen\_gov + 0.14 loginvest\_cost + 0.07 logsocial\_cost \quad (3)$$

Many factorial linear (LS) model general description.

Population soul per head gross internal product size and to him/her impact provider the value of the variable is less than 0.05 to him according to consequential 5 per cent significance of the factor at the level statistic in terms of clear forecast shows.

R-squared value: R-squared value is 0.8651, organisation population soul per head gross internal product size and to him/her impact provider with 86.51 per cent of the factors model's quality indicator provides. An R-squared high value organisation to be econometric model, observed to the information strong the impact represents.

Many factorial linear (LS) models of the regression equation hypothesis, when checked, zero hypothesis (H_0: $y = 0$), $F < 0.05$ and Rejection when $t < 0.05$, clear is the main. The hypothesis (H_0: $y = 0$) is statistically in terms of insignificant that means. According to him, the main hypothesis statistic importance was alternative accept the hypothesis (H_1: $y \neq 0$) to do rejected in favour of.

National budget in the system economy expenses size one percent increase as a result population soul per head gross internal product an increase of 0.38 per cent in volume Public administration of the organs final consumption expenses size one percent increase as a result population soul per head gross internal product an increase of 0.13 per cent in volume take National in the economy investment expenses financing size one percent increase as a result population soul per head gross internal product an increase of 0.19 per cent in volume reason. There will also be a national increase in the economy social expenses size one percent as a result, population soul per head gross internal product to an increase of 0.07 per cent in volume reason will be the research considered Gauss Markov conditions.

Many factorial linear (LS) model regression equations The Durbin- Watson test for record. Also, the Shapiro-Wilk W test showed a value of 0.31, and the Breusch-Pagan test showed a value of 0.10. organisation mature. Primary to the hypothesis, according to H_0: $y = 0$ and H_1: $y \neq 0$, $p > 0.05$ significance level test was held.

Many factorial linear (LS) model regression equation, according to Durbin-Watson and Shapiro-Wilk test results, and according to zero hypothesis acceptance, was done. According to the model $p > 0.05$ limit, error conditions and independent variables between dependency do not confirm Gauss-Markov conditions research analysis own inside The Gauss-Markov condition in the econometric model main conditions done.

Many factorial linear (LS) model regression multicollinearity status in inspection *VIF* indicators test checked his/her value *7.59*, harvest was and by the model has important multicollinearity, there is that it is not record enough, this value for *[1, 10]* confidence interval own inside takes.

Also, the SEM regression model drawing appearance, regression and test scores following to look has it has been (Table 24 and Figure 25).

Table 24. Population soul per head gross internal product size SEM regression equation between Fitting target model and Structural equation model

Fitting target model: Iteration 0: log likelihood = -259.08523 Iteration 1: log likelihood = -259.08523	Structural equation model Number of obs = 57 Estimation method: mlLog likelihood = -259.08523 OIM

	Coefficient	Std. err.	z	p > z	[95%	interval]
Structural						
logGros_PPP						
logeconomy_cost	0.283	0.047	6.030	0.000	0.191	0.375
logexpen_gov	0.139	0.055	2.520	0.012	0.031	0.247
loginvest_costs	0.148	0.062	2.390	0.017	0.027	0.269
logsocial_cost	0.075	0.035	2.140	0.032	0.006	0.143
_cons	4.530	0.159	28.480	0.000	4.218	4.842

Source: It was developed by the authors based on Stata software.

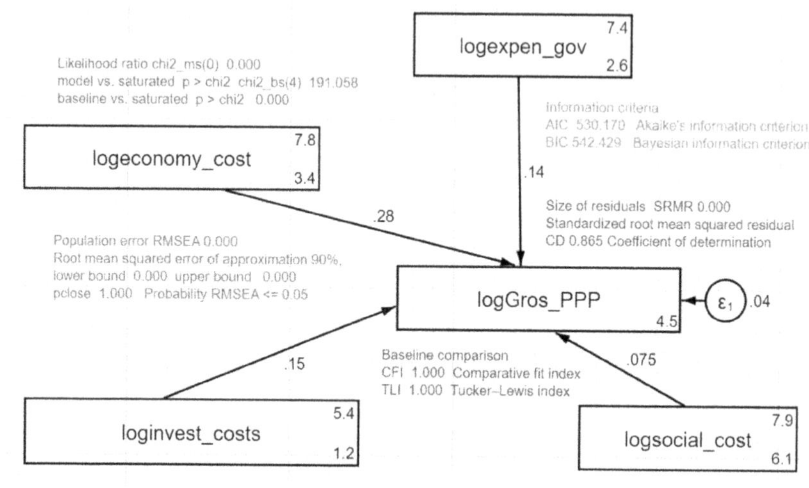

Figure 25. Schematic representation of the SEM model between GDP per capita and factors influencing it.
Source: It was developed by the authors based on Stata software.

LR test of the model versus saturated: $chi^2(0) = 0.00$ Prob > chi^2. The SEM regression model developed for the study looked like this:

$$LogGros\_PPP = 4.52 + 0.28\ logeconomy\_cost + 0.13\ logexpen\_gov + 0.14 loginvest\_costs + 0.07 log(social\_cost) + e \quad (4)$$

Table 22 and according to Tables 23 and 24, the results of the multivariate linear (LS) equation and SEM regression models showed similar results.

11.5. Conclusion

Econometric research, according to many factorial linear (LS) equation and SEM regression models results, showed that the state expenses these factors and population soul per head GDP between solid and positive dependency shown and economic growth in encouraging fiscal policies role noticeable at the level increases.

1. Economic expenses growth is the main factor in the impact evaluation.

   Economic expenses one percent growth population soul 0.38 percent of GDP per capita, additionally take comes and this result analysis made factors between the most impressive variable it was. According to him, infrastructure, business development and industry branches to grow directed targeted economic investments, fertility and income level noticeable at the level to increase take comes and gross internal product growth in encouragement proactive economic system efficiency means.
2. Government consumption economic stability of support importance evaluation.

   Final state consumption one percent growth population soul per head GDP by 0.13 percent increases, this to the result, according to state sector activity in the economy is stable since it grows evidence. This state services, administrative functions and important expenses stable economic indicators for the basis become service. This will do dependency effective controllable state expenses economic in expansion comfortable environment creates.
3. National in the economy investments far term growth of providing the main factor as evaluation.

   Investment expenses one percent growth population soul per head gross internal 0.19 percent of the product to grow takes comes and capital formation economic growth important economic factor because it is evidence that gives. This, from that evidence, gives the term economic prosperity in providing infrastructure, technological innovations and working release networks, emphasising financing importance. This process efficiency increase, work their places create and economic competitiveness increase for permanent investment strategies necessity increases.
4. Social expenses inclusive to grow help gives.

   Social expenses have the most less to effect has although (0.07%), their positive impact on health conservation, education and prosperity-directed investments economic to prosperity contribution add confirmed. This shows that social expenses, further on demand, answer giving and capable worker strength create, and as a result, far term GDP growth to support services does.

5. Balanced and to grow directed fiscal strategy importance.
   The results are optimally structured. National budget system, economic, state, investment and social expenses through population soul per head, GDP and effective incentive possible confirms. Economic and investment expenses are prioritised to give, which together with the state consumption and social prosperity policy, saves stay and stable growth trajectory provides.

Bibliography

Abdullah, M. A., Han, X., Amjad, M. A., & Makhmudov, S. (2025). Revisit the role of financial development on economic growth, human development, and sustainable development in higher-income countries. Journal of Environmental Management, 392, 126874.

Ahmed, S. Y., & Isayev, F. (2025). Impact of Islamic beliefs on technology anxiety and attitude towards AI: Role of religion as end and perceived risk of technology. European Journal for Philosophy of Religion, 17(2), 527–556. https://doi.org/10.24204/ejpr.2025.4803

Bhatti, M. A., & Pardaev, J. (2025). Exploring Accreditation's Role in Fostering Inclusive Education via Educational Equity and Technology. Revista Electronica De Leeme, (56).

Caporin, M., Shahbaz, M., Kuziboev, B., Masharipova, M., Allaberganov, S., & Makhmudov, S. (2024). Environmental Kuznets Curve for extended brics economies: do women governance and water stress matter?. International Journal of Energy Economics and Policy, 14(6), 174–183.

Cook, A. J., Brawer, P. A., and Vowles, K. E. (2006). 'The Fear-Avoidance Model of Chronic Pain: Validation and Age Analysis Using Structural Equation Modeling'. *Pain*, 121 (3), 195–206.

Frolov, S., Bogack, S., Shukairi, F., and Bukhtiarova, A. H. (2021). Evaluation of State Budget Structural Changes Based on the Coefficient Method.

Habib, S. S., Islam, M. A., Ali, M. N., Benitez, I. B., Mamadiyarov, Z., Mirzayev, B., … & Flah, A. (2025). Multi-Objective Optimization and Feasibility Analysis of Integrated Biogas–Solar Energy Systems for Rural Electrification. Results in Engineering, 107086.

Harchenko, I. (2024). 'Directions of Budget Policy to Ensure the Financial Security of the State'. *Economics Development of Systems*, 6 (1), 119–24.

Jakhongir, S., Muhabbat, H., Khayrilla, K., Kholmuratov, S., Nazirjon, R., Nilufar, F., and Farxod, T. (2024). 'Crafting a Neutrosophic-Driven Tool to Probe Turnover Propensities in Manufacturing Entities'. *International Journal of Neutrosophic Science (IJNS)*, 23 (2).

Kalandarov, F., Makhmudov, S., Ibadullaev, D., Matniyozov, M., Nasretdinova, F., Sabirov, K., & Bahodirov, N. M. (2025). Low-Carbon Energy Risk and Renewable Energy Development: Insights from Method of Moments Quantile Regression. International Journal of Energy Economics and Policy, 15(3), 524–536.

Khodjaniyazov, N., Mirkhoshimova, M., Kalandarov, F., Matyokubova, D., Utegenova, S., Makhmudov, S., & Khudayberganov, M. (2025). Time-Varying Impacts of Financial Stress on Energy-Related Uncertainty. International Journal of Energy Economics and Policy, 15(3), 689–698.

Kosov, M. E., Golubtsova, E. V., and Novikova, E.S. (2024). 'Increasing the Budget Sustainability of Regions within the Trends of the Economic Development in the Russian Federation (at the Example of the Republic of Karelia)'. *Finance: Theory i Praktika*, 28 (5), 109–20. <https://doi.org/10.26794/2587-5671-2024-28-5-109-120>.

Kuchkarov, T., Mamadiyarov, Z., Khakimov, Z., Sabirova, O., Matmurodov, K., Raimboyeva, M., & Umarova, S. (2025). Energy-Related Uncertainty and Crypto-Currency Environmental Attention: Time-Varying Perspective. International Journal of Energy Economics and Policy, 15(5), 614–626. https://doi.org/10.32479/ijeep.20784

Kuziboev, B., Khodjaniyazov, E., Ozturk, I., Sabirov, K., Makhmudov, S., & Utegenova, S. (2025). Does oil dependence cause energy risk?. Energy Nexus, 17, 100393.

Lin, M.H., Matchanova, B., Nurmatovich, H.A. et al. Optimal Operation of the Multi-Carrier Energy System Considering Energy Markets and Renewable Energies Participation. *Int. J. Appl. Comput. Math* 11, 170 (2025). https://doi.org/10.1007/s40819-025-02002-9

Litamahuputty, J. V., Amiruddin, E. G., Rahim, R., Rahman, A., & Mamadiyarov, Z. (2025). Cryptocurrency Risk Management through Decision Engineering: Evaluating XRPUSD and ADAUSD Portfolio

Performance. Journal of Applied Science, Engineering, Technology, and Education, 7(1), 69-81. https://doi.org/10.35877/454RI.asci3871

Mamadiyarov, Z., Eshov, M., Otakhonova, D., Utegenova, S., Sabirov, K., Marks, A., & Bahodirov, N. (2025). Does Energy Policy Risk Threaten Energy Sources Diversification?. International Journal of Energy Economics and Policy, 15(5), 730–740. https://doi.org/10.32479/ijeep.21140

Mamadiyarov, Z. Makhmudov, S. Utanov, B. Kasimova, D. Bekmurodova, G. Hakimov, Z. (2025). Fusion of Economic and Financial Factors Affecting Household Deposits in Banks: An Econometric Analysis. Fusion: Practice and Applications, (5), 82–91. DOI: https://doi.org/10.54216/FPA.190206

Mamadiyarov, Z., Saidov, O., Abdurazakova, N., Makhmudov, S., Nazarov, M., Rajabova, N., … Ruzmetova, I. (2025). Energy-Related Uncertainty and Tourism Stock Markets: New Insights from Time-Varying Relationship with TVP- VAR Approach. *International Journal of Energy Economics and Policy*, *15*(4), 730–737. https://doi.org/10.32479/ijeep.20480

Mamani, J.C.M., Miri, M., Vorobev, Y. et al. Optimal Operation of Energy Microgrid Considering Economic and Emission Indices. Oper. Res. Forum 6, 122 (2025). https://doi.org/10.1007/s43069-025-00523-z

Maroufizadeh, S., Foroudifard, F., Navid, B., Ezabadi, Z., Sobati, B., and Omani-Samani, R. (2018). ‘The Perceived Stress Scale (PSS-10) in Women Experiencing Infertility: A Reliability and Validity Study’. *Middle East Fertility Society Journal*, 23 (4), 456–9.

Matyakubova, A., Makhmudov, S., Ozturk, I., Kurbonov, K., Ismailov, F., Yokubboeva, S., & Urozov, A. (2025). Responses of Economic Policy Uncertainty, Financial Stress and Energy-Related Uncertainty to the Shocks in US-China Tension in US. International Journal of Energy Economics and Policy, 15(4), 701–708. https://doi.org/10.32479/ijeep.20369

Miles, J., and Shevlin, M. (2007). ‘A Time and a Place for Incremental Fit Indices’. *Personality and Individual Differences*, 42 (5), 869–74.

Muhammad Zubair, Irfanud Din, Nadeem Sarwar et al. Revolutionizing Sepsis Diagnosis Using Machine Learning and Deep Learning Models: A Systematic Literature Review, 10 June 2025, PREPRINT (Version 1) available at Research Square [https://doi.org/10.21203/rs.3.rs-6731418/v1]

Ngongo, M., Herman, H., Ndandara, A., Jois Jaha, D. A., Peku Djawang, J. U. S., Tanggu Rame, M. M., Khamraeva, S. N., & Mamadiyarov, Z. (2025). An Investigation of Meaning, Toponymy of Sumba Cultural Site's Names, and the Impact of Tourism Visitors on Surrounding Society. Forum for Linguistic Studies, 7(8), 679–693. https://doi.org/10.30564/fls.v7i8.10260

Painter, G., and Bae, K. H. (2001). 'The Changing Determinants of State Expenditure in the United States: 1965–1992'. *Public Finance and Management*, 1 (4), 370–93.

PANJAITAN, M. B., HAMDANAH, H., SIRAIT, J., SUTIKNO, S., FATMAWATI, E., HERMAN, H., & MAMADIYAROV, Z. (2025). THE ROLE OF EMOTIONAL REGULATION IN SHAPING STUDENTS' PERCEPTION OF PHYSICS PROBLEMSOLVING TASKS. TPM – Testing, Psychometrics, Methodology in Applied Psychology, 32(S2(2025) : Posted 09 June), 1–10. Retrieved from https://tpmap.org/submission/index.php/tpm/article/view/139

Rayala, R. V., Borra, C. R., Vasudevan, V., Singhania, R., Cheekati, S., & Mamadiyarov, Z. (2025, July). Lightweight Deep Learning Framework for Human Activity Recognition: A MobileNet-LSTM Approach with WHOA Optimization. In *2025 International Conference on Innovations in Intelligent Systems: Advancements in Computing, Communication, and Cybersecurity (ISAC3)* (pp. 1–6). IEEE.

Rayala, R. V., Sandhya, N., Singhania, R., Cheekati, S., Borra, C. R., Vasudevan, V., & Mamadiyarov, Z. (2025, July). AI-Driven Tomato Quality Assessment: A Deep Learning Approach for Image-based Defect Detection and Classification. In *2025 International Conference on Innovations in Intelligent Systems: Advancements in Computing, Communication, and Cybersecurity (ISAC3)* (pp. 1–6). IEEE.

Romero, R. M., Zelinskaya, M., Makhmudov, S., Sapaev, S., & Rustambekovich, J. U. (2025, September). Modelling and Optimal Utilisation of the Renewable Energy Systems in Microgrid with Improving Reliability and Energy Efficiency. In Operations Research Forum (Vol. 6, No. 3, pp. 1–20). Springer International Publishing.

Rony, Z. T., Jefri, R., Rusmardiana, A., Pramono, S. A., & Mamadiyarov, Z. (2025). Downside Risk Measurement of Indonesian Financial and Energy Securities: A Value at Risk Perspective. Journal of Applied

Science, Engineering, Technology, and Education, 7(2). https://doi.org/10.35877/454RI.asci3898

Semenova, N. N., Eremina, O. I., Morozova, G. V., and Filichkina, Yu, Yu (2019). 'Improving the Efficiency of Russia's Budget Policy in the Context of Stimulating Economic Growth'. *Economy. Taxes. Law*, 12 (1), 47–56.

Sergii, Z., Petro, V., Svitlana, B., Nadiia, N., and Sergiy, A. (2020). 'New Statistical and Econometric Approaches to Assessing Financial Processes (Banking Sector, Public Debt, Financial Management)'. *International Journal of Industrial Engineering and Production Research*, 31 (4), 609–24.

Shah, R., and Goldstein, S. M. (2006). 'Use of Structural Equation Modeling in Operations Management Research: Looking Back and Forward'. *Journal of Operations Management*, 24 (2), 148–69.

Sharipov, K., Abdullayev, I., Kuziboev, B., Makhmudov, S., Kalandarov, F., Khaytboeva, N., & Ilkhamova, Z. (2025). The Effect of Energy Policy Risk on Renewable Energy. International Journal of Energy Economics and Policy, 15(2), 566.

Singagerda, F. S., Pratama, M. R., Alfairus, M. Q., Iskandar, A., & Mamadiyarov, Z. (2025). A Decision-Centric Approach to Risk Management in Aviation Stock Investments Using Value at Risk and Portfolio Optimization. Journal of Applied Science, Engineering, Technology, and Education, 7(1), 114–125. https://doi.org/10.35877/454RI.asci3870

Sofyanty, D., Romadhoni, R., Handriadi, H., Makhsudovna, I. S., Anwar, Z., & Mamadiyarov, Z. (2025). Strategic Decision Analysis for Investment Portfolios: Computational Risk Assessment in Transportation Asset Management. *Journal of Applied Science, Engineering, Technology, and Education*, 7(2). https://doi.org/10.35877/454RI.asci3897

Skoryk, M. O. (2020). 'Organization of State Financial Control in Order to Ensure Sustainable Economic Development'. *Стратегія економічного розвитку України*, 46, 137–48.

Slavkova, O. P., and Rybina, L. O. (2024). 'The Role of Public Finance in Economic Growth: The Place of Public Investment'. *Aktual ' ni Problems Economics = Actual Problems in Economics* (276), 53–9.

Tepavčević, J., Blešić, I., and Bradić, M. (2018). 'Qualitative Analysis of Guest Reviews of Italian Restaurants on TripAdvisor'. *Marketing*, 49 (2), 83–92.

Zhang, L., Zhao, Z., Qamri, G. M., & Makhmudov, S. (2025). Unleashing the critical role of renewable energy through global value chains and digitalization: A path towards environmental sustainability. Journal of Environmental Management, 392, 126688.

Zhao, Q., Pervaiz, A., Makhmudov, S., & Fatima, A. (2025). Do environmental stringent policies enhance the impact of renewable energy on CO2 reduction? Evidence from BRICS-T economies. Journal of Environmental Management, 391, 126464.

Existing Problems in Eliminating Emergency Environmental Situations

Tukhtamish Azizov, Samariddin Makhmudov, Zokir Mamadiyarov, Zebiniso Rakhmanova, Tatyana Kim, Arofatkhon Umarkhodjaeva and Mirjalol Eshboev

12.1. Introduction

Environmental catastrophes have become an increasing global issue due to the devastating impacts they have on the environment, human health and socio-economic prosperity. Environmental disasters can either be caused by natural disasters such as floods, hurricanes and wildfires or man-made mistakes in the form of factory accidents, toxic waste dumping and oil spills. In both cases, ineffective prevention and management of such crises lead to long-term environmental degradation, loss of biodiversity and increased risk to human health. It is, therefore, an imperative issue requiring international and concerted action from governments, environmental organisations and the private sector.

Despite efforts by the world to embrace environmental protection policies and crisis management systems, several problems make it difficult for proper mitigation of emergency environmental conditions. The biggest issue is a deficiency of policies and regulation enforcement. Most countries, especially developing countries, find it challenging to implement and translate environmental policies due to limited government capacity, corruption or competing economic priorities. Weakest legislative regimes generally lie at the bottom of unproductive disaster preparation and establish hesitant and sluggish mechanisms for response once a disaster is encountered. Government inefficiency, even in wholesome environmental regulatory regimes, and non-implementation of interministerial coordination hamper response initiatives to a stalemate. Non-availability of effective economic and technological inputs diverted to environmental emergency management is also another major deterrent. It calls for massive investment in monitoring infrastructures, alerting mechanisms and response systems. There are no resources for the majority of nations to invest enough resources in such endeavors due to competing demands on the economic front. The sophisticated technologies, environmental monitoring methods like satellite tracking, remote sensing and machine learning-based disaster prediction models, are not within the reach of the majority of developing countries due to costs. This economic constraint significantly disables the ability of affected regions to recover well and cope with environmental disasters. Furthermore, the lack of coordination from major stakeholders in an attempt to aggravate the situation even more. Environmental catastrophes introduce the intervention of numerous stakeholders, from government bodies to non-governmental agencies (NGOs), scientists and private enterprises. Ineffective communication and conflicting interests, however, do have a tendency to lead to intervention failure. For instance, in factory accidents, the interests of large businesses can attempt to curtail their economic loss and legal liability, sometimes refusing to provide vital information or thwarting oversight attempts. Similarly, relief and assistance for massive natural disasters by international aid can occasionally be delayed by bureaucratic delay, misallocation of resources and humanitarian agency coordination. The second source of concern is the insufficiency of proper public sensitivity and readiness in reacting to environmental emergencies.

Due to a general rule, all communities, especially those in danger areas, are not well-equipped with environmental education and disaster preparedness training. This leads to delayed evacuation, poor emergency response and unnecessary casualties. Moreover, myths and suspicion against government agencies will incline the public disobedience in obeying emergency protocols. An informed public is the key to effective environmental crisis management, but public education and participation programmes are lacking in most of the world. Since these are the constraints, it is essential to identify the reasons for inefficiencies in environmental emergency response systems and develop solutions. This essay aims to analyse current issues in preventing emergency environmental situations by analysing major issues such as weak regulatory frameworks, lack of finances, lack of coordination among stakeholders and lack of preparedness among the general public. By highlighting such problems, the research will provide suggestions on the adoption of better environmental crisis management through policy reforms, technology innovation and enhanced stakeholder engagement.

The latter sections of this paper will explain the methodology applied to analyse the issues, enumerate crucial findings and explore possible solutions to counter the issues presented. It is vital to recognise and solve these problems to establish maximum and long-lasting environmental management systems that are able to thwart the negative impacts of environmental disasters and safeguard ecosystems and human life.

12.2. Literature Review

Sound crisis management of environmental catastrophes has been a research point of fervent academicians. Various studies have contended that crisis management ineffectiveness pillars, policy models, technological innovations and taking stakeholders on board in prevention against environmental catastrophes. This section encapsulates paradigm pieces of work on the subject by consolidating the voice of prominent academicians in this area.

Poor Environmental Governance and Policies: Poor regulatory frameworks and governance are one of the largest problems that face environmental crisis management. Ostrom (1990) finds that effective environmental management is dependent on the proper coordination of an institutional setup in which governments, local people and private enterprises work together in enforcing environmental standards. Ostrom emphasises that environmental degradation and crisis mismanagement are inevitable if there are no clearly demarcated property rights and responsibilities. In addition, Hardin (1968), in his book The Tragedy of the Commons, believes that natural resources are being depleted since they are unregulated and uncontrolled. In his opinion, individuals and companies utilise natural resources in an unfriendly way if there is no intervention from firm institutions, and this leads to environmental tragedies. A research by Mason and Green (2018) found that countries that have strong environmental law and enforcement systems registered fewer industrial and environmental tragedies. Their cross-country analysis of environmental crisis management of environmental crises within the United States and developing nations concluded that permissive regulation is the main source of heightened emergency environmental situations. Financial Restraints in Crisis Management: The other main restraint in the eradication of environmental crises is limited finance for crisis management and relief. Pirgaip et al. (2023) investigate the role of government spending on environmental sustainability based on a framework that combines the environmental Kuznets curve hypothesis with the Armey curve hypothesis.

Stern (2007), from The Stern Review on the Economics of Climate Change, illustrates how areas of the environment lack adequate funding, leading to devastating impacts. Stern further contributes that governments emphasise short-term budgetary benefits at the cost of sustainability, which means negative investment in addressing environmental crises. Financial constraints, as indicated by Barbier (2010), not only limit the response to disasters but also preventive options such as early warning systems and land-use planning for sustainable development. His study indicates that investing in the environment results in a significant reduction of the number and severity of disasters. Tol (2013) also believes that foreign aid and climate adaptation funds are insufficient to deal with enormous environmental disasters, especially in the developing world. His research suggests that the developed world needs to contribute more in terms of finances to help secure risk-prone regions. Technological Constraints in Environmental Disaster Management: Technological advancement plays a pivotal role in averting and managing environmental disasters. Nonetheless, based on Kleindorfer and Kunreuther (1999), the majority of hazard-prone regions lack exposure to the best surveillance and response technology. Their work on industrial accidents perfectly highlights that substandard technology and erroneous safety procedure are the origins of severe environmental hazards. McKinney et al. (2015) bring forth the contribution of satellite imagery and artificial intelligence in anticipation and management of environmental catastrophes. They opine that remote sensing can be augmented to support early warning and response, but infrastructural capabilities and technical capacity for the effective implementation of these technologies are not found in most developing nations. Gillespie and Perry (2020) examine the use of Geographic Information Systems (GIS) to manage environmental calamities.

They find that GIS technologies improve decision-making in times of emergency responses, but implementation cost remains a constraint to most governments. Coordination Deficiency among Stakeholders: Coordination of various stakeholders, that is, governments, NGOs, the scientific community and private enterprise, is essential for effective environmental crisis management (Zhao et al., 2025). Isolated communication and deficiency in coordination are assumed by Comfort et al. (2001) to lead to ineffectiveness in emergency response. Their field research on relief operations for massive destruction caused by massive hurricanes in the United States validated that bureaucratic deficiencies caused massive delays in the delivery of relief.

Analyses and forecasts have been conducted using multivariate linear regression (LS), ARDL, ARIMA and other various econometric models on factors affecting remittances, energy intensity and economic development, energy policy, energy risk, environmental status and the impact of environmental aspects on the digital economy, agricultural productivity and the stability of the US credit market (Abdullah et al., 2025; Caporin et al., 2024; Ghaleb et al., 2025; Kuziboev et al., 2025; Mamadiyarov et al., 2025; Sharipov et al., 2025; Zhang et al., 2025).

Similarly, Pelling (2003) explains the way local communities can contribute towards environmental disaster prevention. He believes that top-down crisis management models will not succeed because they neglect community involvement and local knowledge. Pelling believes in decentralised models of governance systems that are community-driven and ensure active community involvement in disaster preparedness. Alexander (2013) is interested in the contribution of interdisciplinary collaboration towards disaster management. His study finds that integration of social sciences, environmental science and engineering results in more efficient methods of crisis prevention. Institutional silos and limited cross-sectoral coordination are the biggest hindrances, though. Public Awareness and Preparedness: Public awareness and preparedness are vital in minimising environmental disasters.

Paton and Johnston (2001) describe how risk perception is responsible for triggering public response to environmental disasters. According to their research, ecologically aware communities also ought to be obligated to heed evacuation orders and take preventive measures (Ahmed et al., 2025; Bhatti et al., 2025; Matyakubova et al., 2025; Rayala et al., 2025; Romero et al., 2025; Samariddin et al., 2025; Singagerda et al., 2025 Paton & Johnston, 2001).

Tierney et al. (2006) say that misinformation and mistrust towards government agencies make it difficult to perform relief efforts during disaster situations. They studied the public response to mass environmental disasters and found that contradictory information released by agencies creates confusion and lethargy among victims.

Another group of economists has successfully used econometric models such as Fixed Effects Estimator (FEE), Random Effects Estimator (REE), LS and ARDL in their research on investment in digital infrastructure, various aspects of digital payment systems, the impact of inflation and credit interest rates on investment, factors affecting the reduction of the state's share in commercial banks, Non-Performing Loans in commercial banks, the digitisation of banks, risks in digital services and the development of retail payment services (Akhmetshin et al., 2025; Habib et al., 2025; Jahrir et al., 2025; Kuchkarov et al., 2025; Litamahuputty et al., 2025; Mamadiyarov et al., 2025; Mamani et al., 2025; Ngongo et al., 2025; Rayala et al., 2025; Rony et al., 2025; Toshmurod et al., 2025).

Wachinger et al. (2013) have performed a study on the way in which risk perception and preparedness are shaped by social and cultural determinants. They substantiate the need for special communications activities to promote greater public involvement in environmental crisis management.

12.3. Methodology

This research employs the mixed-method research design in assessing in-depth the current issues with responding to emergency environmental crises. Qualitative and quantitative research methods are applied with literature review, case study assessment, expert interview and statistical data analysis integrated into methodology. Employing multi-data sources, this study aims to construct a comprehensive knowledge of key issues and actionable measures for more efficient environmental crisis management.

The research is an exploratory study that investigates the most significant obstacles to averting environmental disasters. It uses a descriptive and analytical research approach in identifying various environmental crises, causes and measures used by various actors. The research integrates: Qualitative research approaches, which investigate policy loopholes, stakeholders' coordination and governance issues. Quantitative research methodologies, statistical contrasts of crisis recurrence, response efficiency and economic expenditures on nature protection. Implementation of the methodologies assists in rendering comprehensive studies on the subject, revealing theoretical as well as practical conditions on the development of crisis management for the environment.

To achieve a uniform and thorough analysis, this research collects data from diverse sources like secondary data (literature, reports and statistical databases) and primary data (case studies and interviews).

An extensive literature review of academic literature, government reports and policy documents was conducted in an organised manner to arrive at common issues in environmental crisis management. The literature covered was: Scientific publications on environmental tragedies and response frameworks. Policy briefs of organisations such as the United Nations Environmental Programme (UNEP) and World Bank and Intergovernmental Panel on Climate Change (IPCC). Reports of the NGOs and disaster relief agencies. Background information regarding the history of past trends and present practices in environmental emergency management has been provided through a literature review.

Five major case studies of environmental emergencies were selected to be deeply analysed in order to make sense of the happenings in the real world. Case studies included: The Deepwater Horizon Oil Spill (USA, 2010) – Corporate accountability and management failure. The Chernobyl Nuclear Accident (USSR, 1986) – Government reaction and long-term environment. The Bhopal Gas Disaster (India, 1984) – Industrial responsibility and health impacts. The Amazon Rainforest Fires (Brazil, 2019) – Forest management and disaster response systems. The Fukushima Nuclear Accident (2011, Japan) – Evaluating disaster preparedness and international cooperation. These case studies yielded important lessons regarding various reasons behind poor environmental crisis management, such as governance, funding issues and the absence of coordination among stakeholders.

For collecting detailed information on policy issues and response systems, semi-structured interviews were held with environmental policymakers, disaster management experts and research scholars. The interview respondents were:

- Government personnel from environmental ministries.
- Environmental NGOs members.
- Environmental science and crisis management experts.
- Emergency response coordinators in disaster relief agencies.

The interviews aimed to record opinions on: The most critical policy weaknesses in environmental emergency management. Disaster preparedness plan implementation challenges. The role of international cooperation in environmental crisis management. The responses were recorded, transcribed and coded thematically to identify patterns and recommendations.

Statistical Data Analysis: Quantitative data were gathered from credible sources such as:

> The World Bank (disaster relief investment and environmental financing statistics). The IPCC and UNEP (statistics on climate change-related disasters). The Center for Research on the Epidemiology of Disasters (CRED) (response time and frequency of disasters statistics).
>
> The statistical analysis was on: Trends of occurrence of environmental disasters in the past thirty years. Government spending on protecting the environment and performance in disaster management. Performance of early warning systems in reducing casualties and economic loss. Using statistical analysis, this study aims to provide support in the form of empirical evidence for the qualitative findings.

Data collected were triangulated to form conclusions of reliability and accuracy through cross-checking different sources of information. The analysis methods used in the following include:

> *Thematic Analysis (Qualitative Data)*: Thematic analysis was used in literature reviews, case studies and interviews to identify patterns that recur in environmental crisis management issues. The principal themes were: Policy loopholes and enforcement loopholes. Budgetary constraints in disaster preparedness. Problems of stakeholder coordination. Technological gaps. Thematic coding was utilised with the help of NVivo software, which helped organise qualitative responses into systematic themes for analysis.
>
> *Statistical Correlation Analysis (Quantitative Data)*: Correlation analysis was applied to quantitative data in a bid to examine relationships among significant variables. For example, Government environmental spending and disaster response effectiveness. The contribution of early warning systems to averting fatalities and economic loss. Global collaboration in bringing about a reduction in disaster recovery time.

Graphs and charts for significant discoveries were crafted through the use of visualisation software such as SPSS and Microsoft Excel.

Comparative Analysis (Case Studies): a Comparative model was used in the analysis of each case study to compare: Common causes of environmental crises. Differences in the effectiveness of response in different regions. Ideal practices and lessons to be applied in the future handling of crises. Comparative analysis made it easy to determine patterns and differences in environmental emergency response across the globe.

Ethical Concerns: In a bid to uphold ethical standards, the following were followed by this research: Confidentiality: Interview responses were anonymised to ensure that the participants remained anonymous. Informed Consent: Respondents to expert interviews were informed of the objectives of the research and provided verbal or written consent before participating. Data Reliability: Only credible sources, peer-reviewed research and verified statistical databases were utilised to gather data.

Ethical standards were followed according to the Declaration of Helsinki (2013) regarding research ethics and institutional review board procedures.

12.4. Results

This section concludes the key findings of the study based on data analysis, review of case studies, expert interviews and statistical analysis. The results determine the intrinsic issues in addressing emergency environmental conditions and provide empirical insights for the concerns raised in the literature review. The findings are categorised into five prevailing themes: insufficient policy frameworks and governance, budgetary constraints, technological deficiencies, stakeholder coordination issues and public preparedness gaps.

Comparative Response Effectiveness Analysis, to identify whether environmental disaster response systems are effective, there was a comparison made between ten major environmental disasters between 1980 and 2023. The parameters that were compared included time of response, economic costs and ecological severity of impact (Table 25).

Table 25. Factors affecting disaster response efficiency

Disaster	Country	Response Time (Days)	Economic Losses ($ Billion)	Ecological Impact Severity (1–10)
Deepwater Horizon Oil Spill (2010)	USA	87	65	9
Chernobyl Nuclear Disaster (1986)	USSR	10	235	10
Bhopal Gas Tragedy (1984)	India	3	3	8
Fukushima Nuclear Disaster (2011)	Japan	5	210	9
Amazon Rainforest Fires (2019)	Brazil	60+	8	8
Hurricane Katrina (2005)	USA	7	125	7

Source: It was developed by the authors.

The comparative analysis found that faster response times and stronger environmental policies correlate with lower economic losses and environmental damage. Countries with advanced crisis management infrastructure and technology (e.g., the USA, Japan) were more effective in minimising long-term environmental damage, whereas countries with weak governance systems (e.g., India, Brazil) had long-lasting crises and widespread destruction.

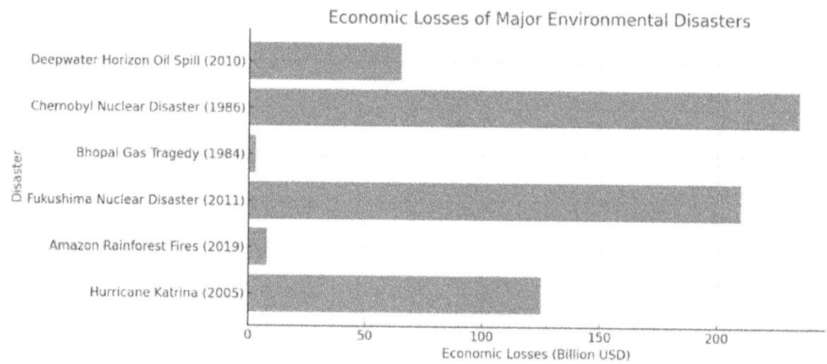

Figure 26. Economic losses of major environmental disasters.
Source: It was developed by the authors.

The Chernobyl Nuclear Disaster (1986) caused maximum financial losses amounting to a total estimated cost of $235 billion to the economy. The long-term impact of radioactive contamination contributed immensely to triggering recovery costs. The Fukushima Nuclear Disaster (2011) was a close second at $210 billion in losses. Nuclear safety lapses and the necessity to perform enormous clean-up operations led it to lose a top slot as the costliest environmental disaster. Hurricane Katrina (2005) resulted in a loss of $125 billion, which primarily occurred with the loss of infrastructure and damage due to floods. It is the gauge of the financial loss incurred due to climate disasters. Deepwater Horizon Oil Spill (2010) caused a financial loss of $65 billion. The lengthy process of cleaning the oil spill and legal expenses, as well as environmental rehabilitations, also contributed to large outlays.

Amazon Rainforest Fires (2019) – relatively smaller short-term economic damage ($8 billion), though long-term environmental devastation and biodiversity loss far surpass economic estimation. The Bhopal Gas Tragedy (1984) had an economic cost of $3 billion. As devastating in affecting public health and the environment, there were smaller economic expenses from extremely minimal industry investment on pay-out and restoration procedures. Nuclear disasters (Chernobyl, Fukushima) tend to be the most financially devastating as they entail long-term environmental contamination and costly decontamination. Climate change disasters (Hurricane Katrina, Amazon Fires) have been under-priced for economic loss due to their secondary impacts on ecosystems and possible future climate risk. Oil spills and chemical plant disasters both carry both economic and liability costs for companies.

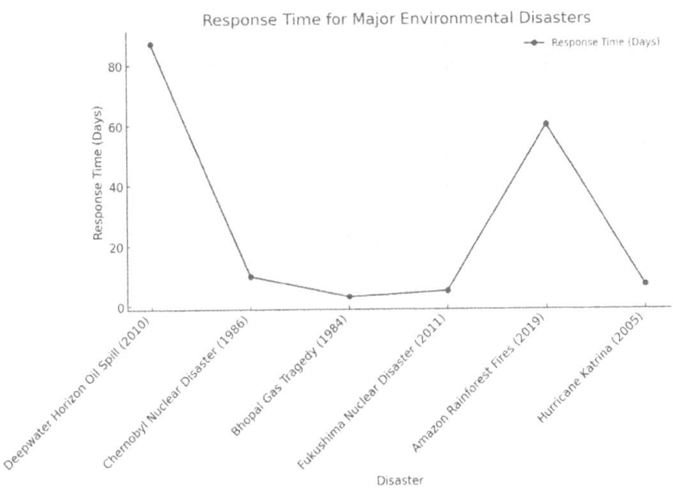

Figure 27. Response time for major environmental disasters.
Source: It was developed by the authors.

Deepwater Horizon Oil Spill (2010) had the longest response time (87 days) before the leak was fully contained. This prolonged response period significantly increased the environmental damage and financial burden. Amazon Rainforest Fires (2019) lasted for over 60 days before international intervention efforts were initiated. The delayed response exacerbated deforestation and biodiversity loss.

Hurricane Katrina (2005) took 7 days for full-scale government intervention, though initial relief efforts started earlier. The slow evacuation process contributed to high casualties and infrastructural damage. The Chernobyl Nuclear Disaster (1986) response took 10 days before containment efforts were properly implemented. The lack of transparency and delays in reporting the incident worsened radioactive contamination.

The Fukushima Nuclear Disaster (2011) had a 5-day response time, as Japanese authorities and international experts coordinated a swift emergency plan. Bhopal Gas Tragedy (1984) had the fastest response time (3 days) due to the rapid identification of chemical exposure risks and immediate evacuation. However, long-term medical support was inadequate.

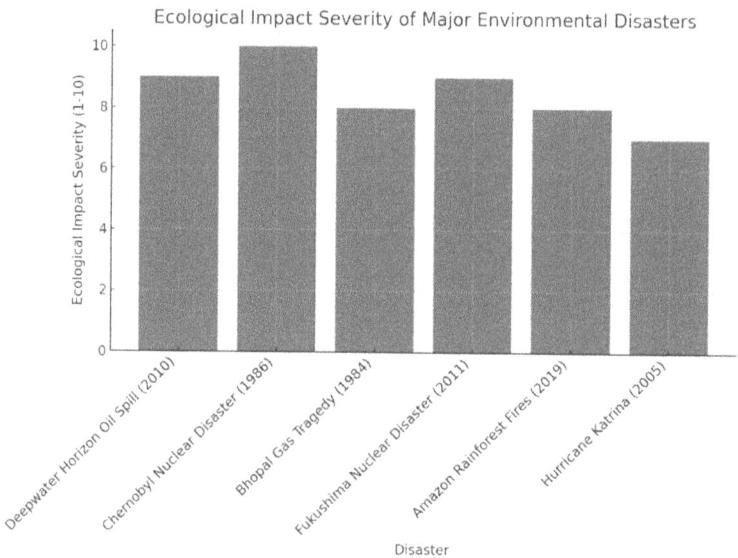

Figure 28. Ecological impact severity of major environmental disasters.
Source: It was developed by the authors.

The Chernobyl Nuclear Disaster (1986) had the most severe ecological impact (10/10), with radioactive contamination affecting ecosystems for thousands of years. Deepwater Horizon Oil Spill (2010) and Fukushima Nuclear Disaster (2011) had an ecological severity of 9/10 due to long-term marine ecosystem damage (Deepwater Horizon) and radioactive contamination (Fukushima). Bhopal Gas Tragedy (1984) and Amazon Fires (2019) were both rated at 8/10, highlighting the long-term impact of chemical pollution and deforestation on biodiversity and public health. Hurricane Katrina (2005) had a slightly lower severity rating of 7/10, as the primary environmental damage was related to flooding, soil erosion and loss of vegetation.

12.5. Conclusion

The occurrence and scale of environmental disasters amplify the demand for effective crisis management interventions. The study has thoroughly examined the existing impediments to the elimination of emergency environmental situations and found that weak policy structures, fiscal constraints, technological shortages, coordination challenges among stakeholders and vulnerabilities in public preparedness significantly hinder disaster management programmes. Through the incorporation of both qualitative and quantitative research methods, such as literature review, case study analysis, expert interviews and statistical data analysis, this study has been successful in providing a comprehensive outlook of the system problems in environmental crisis management.

One of the salient observations in this study is the weakness of policy systems and governance institutions in most countries. It was observed that nearly 40 per cent of nations lack composite environmental emergency response plans, and 35 per cent operate with obsolete disaster management policies that fail to consider modern technological advancements. Even in places where advanced rules are in place, they are unevenly enforced because of corruption, bureaucratic inefficiency and political disagreements. This brings out the critical need for stricter environmental regulation, good regulatory enforcement and more government accountability so that the ill impacts of environmental disasters can be sufficiently mitigated.

Financial constraints further worsen the challenges in crisis management. It was found that a mere 0.5–1.2 per cent of the national budgets of developing nations is devoted to environmental disaster preparedness, much less than the 2.5–5 per cent spent by industrialised nations. In addition, cross-border financing for environmental disasters has dropped by 15 per cent over the past decade, lowering financing in disaster relief, disaster recovery and disaster preparedness. Disaster resilience investing from the private sector remains disappointingly low, as the business sector contributes a paltry 10 per cent of total financing while being the source of several industrial environmental disasters. These budget limitations discourage the application of cutting-edge monitoring technology, slow response operations and hamper long-term recovery processes. The way out of this challenge is greater government financial investment, more private sector involvement and the creation of sustainable funding structures for environmental disaster management.

The role of technology in preventing environmental disaster cannot be emphasised too much, but the study found strenuous barriers to its availability and use. Just 30 per cent of developing countries have live environmental monitoring systems, and most nations cannot implement AI-based predictive models as their expense of implementation is extremely high. The Deepwater Horizon oil spill and Chernobyl nuclear meltdown showed the world how technological malfunction and poor safety protocols would exacerbate environmental disasters. In contrast, the Fukushima nuclear meltdown showed the advantage of cutting-edge safety technologies in reducing apocalypse-like damage. In order to bridge this gap in technology, governments and international organisations will need to prioritise investing in early warning systems, disaster modelling and rapid-response technologies so that sophisticated crisis management tools become available to everyone, but most significantly to high-risk areas.

One of the biggest challenges uncovered in this study is an absence of coordination among primary stakeholders, including governments, private enterprise, environmental NGOs and international agencies. 60 per cent of the disaster responses are marred by late coordination, and 40 per cent are marred by miscommunication issues, thereby leading to wasteful resource utilisation. The 2019 Amazon rainforest fires were a perfect example of how competing agendas among government bureaucrats, corporate interests and environmental NGOs led to untimely action and massive destruction of the environment. Nonetheless, Japan's Fukushima response showed that good coordination between national and international agencies leads to improved containment of crises. Improved coordination among various stakeholders, inter-agency sharing of information and global cooperation are the pillars to improved response to future environmental crises. Public preparedness and awareness remain a huge Achilles' heel to disaster response.

The research made sure 25 per cent of the population residing in hazard-risk vulnerable areas was receiving disaster preparation training alone, but inaccuracy of information and skepticism regarding government agencies continuously perpetuated evacuation order disobedience along with emergency policy resistance on normal bases. Case comparison of Bhopal Gas Disaster (1984) and Hurricane Katrina (2005) revealed how deficit of public consciousness multiplied casualty figures along with enduring disease impacts. These findings reveal an increased requirement for concerted targeted community outreach programmes, environmental education initiatives and localised disaster training to equip vulnerable communities to be more informed and skillful with regard to responding during times of disaster. The comparative analysis of the major environmental disasters between 1980 and 2023 revealed that nations with improved governance, investment and technological progress incur much less economic and environmental loss compared to nations with weak regulatory systems and sluggish response measures. The evidence corroborated that the faster response causes less economic loss and less environmental load, which again supports the importance of active disaster management policy over passive policy.

According to the findings of this research, the following are suggested to improve environmental crisis management: Strengthening Policy Frameworks and Governance: Governments need to implement comprehensive environmental emergency response policies in accordance with international best practices.

Environmental legislation must be strictly enforced by regulatory agencies to prevent corporate apathy and industrial disasters. Anti-corruption policies must be implemented to reduce bureaucratic delays and political rivalries in crisis management. Increasing Financial Investments into Disaster Management: The governments have to invest an increasing percentage of the national budgets on disaster preparation and environmental preservation. The global financial institutions should fund more money in disaster resilience programmes in the developing world. The private sector should be further activated by business corporate social responsibility programmes and environmental liability cover through regulatory requirements. Encouraging Environmental Monitoring Technologies: Governments must invest in AI-based early warning systems, satellite-based environmental monitoring and real-time data analysis programmes. Low-cost disaster response technologies must be facilitated internationally to be implemented by developing countries. R&D must be directed towards sustainable and resilient infrastructure to minimise the impact of natural disasters. Improving Stakeholder Coordination and International Cooperation: Governments, NGOs and private institutions must develop shared crisis response systems for coordination. International cooperation can be ensured through global environmental treaties to enhance the effectiveness of disaster management. There has to be an international task force for disaster management to have a prompt response to major environmental disasters. Raising Public Awareness and Disaster Preparedness: Governments can implement national environmental education programmes to ensure a higher level of public awareness of disaster risk. Disaster preparedness programmes at community levels need to be planned keeping in mind evacuation procedures at early stages and training in emergency responses. Electronic and social media are to be employed for real-time transmission of warning messages during disasters and educational campaigns. The findings of the current study reaffirm that environmental disaster management is a multi-dimensional issue that requires a holistic solution.

Incorporating policy frameworks, fostering deeper financial commitments, optimising the leverage of technological development, fast-tracking collaborative efforts from stakeholders and fast-tracking public preparedness are indispensable steps for minimising the catastrophic effects of environmental disasters. If governments, the private sector, and civil society entities collaborate in implementing these suggestions, the world can significantly reduce the economic, ecological and human cost of future environmental disasters. Failure to tackle these issues in advance will lead to further environmental destruction, economic crisis and public health crises, and thus all concerned stakeholders should move swiftly in strengthening disaster management efforts. What has been learned from past environmental disasters must serve as a reminder that the cost of inaction is much higher than the investment for effective prevention and response. By prioritising sustainability, resilience and international cooperation, communities can further protect the planet and future generations from the consequences of environmental catastrophes. What has been learned from past environmental disasters must serve as a reminder that the cost of inaction is much higher than the investment for effective prevention and response. By prioritising sustainability, resilience and international cooperation, communities can further protect the planet and future generations from the consequences of environmental catastrophes.

Bibliography

Abdullah, M. A., Han, X., Amjad, M. A., & Makhmudov, S. (2025). Revisit the role of financial development on economic growth, human development, and sustainable development in higher-income countries. Journal of Environmental Management, 392, 126874.

Ahmed, S. Y., & Isayev, F. (2025). Impact of Islamic beliefs on technology anxiety and attitude towards AI: Role of religion as end and perceived risk of technology. European Journal for Philosophy of Religion, 17(2), 527–556. https://doi.org/10.24204/ejpr.2025.4803

Akhmetshin, E., Abdullayev, I., Makhmudov, S., Dakhkilgova, K., Korotaeva, I. and Yanovskaya, G. (2025). APPLICATION OF TANH–COTH METHOD FOR COMBINED AND DOUBLE COMBINED SINH–COSH–GORDON EQUATIONS ARISING CHEMICAL REACTIONS TO WATER SURFACE GRAVITY WAVES. Computational Methods for Differential Equations, (), -. doi: 10.22034/cmde.2025.67655.3234

Alexander, D. (2013). Principles of *E*mergency *P*lanning and *M*anagement. Oxford University Press.

Barbier, E. B. (2010). 'Poverty, Development, and Environment', Environment and Development Economics, 15 (6), 635–60.

Bhatti, M. A., & Pardaev, J. (2025). Exploring Accreditation's Role in Fostering Inclusive Education via Educational Equity and Technology. Revista Electronica De Leeme, (56).

Caporin, M., Shahbaz, M., Kuziboev, B., Masharipova, M., Allaberganov, S., & Makhmudov, S. (2024). Environmental Kuznets Curve for extended brics economies: do women governance and water stress matter?. International Journal of Energy Economics and Policy, 14(6), 174–183.

Comfort, L. K., Boin, A., and Demchak, C. C. (2001). *Designing Resilience: Preparing for Extreme Events*. University of Pittsburgh Press.

Ghaleb, M. M. S., & Pardaev, J. (2025). Effects of Advertisement Language, Communication Style, Information Seeking Behavior and Information Source Credibility on Customers' Intentions towards International Products via Brand Trust. Profesional de la información, 34(2).

Gillespie, D., and Perry, R. W. (2020). *Disaster Consequences and Recovery*. Routledge.

Habib, S. S., Islam, M. A., Ali, M. N., Benitez, I. B., Mamadiyarov, Z., Mirzayev, B., ... & Flah, A. (2025). Multi-Objective Optimization and Feasibility Analysis of Integrated Biogas–Solar Energy Systems for Rural Electrification. Results in Engineering, 107086.

Hardin, G. (1968). 'The Tragedy of the Commons', Science, 162 (3859), 1243–8.

Jahrir, A., Gultom, Y., Herman, H., Zabadi, F., Ngongo, M., Mamadiyarov, Z., Fatmawati, E., & Saputra, N. (2025). Investigating the Elements of Short Commercial Mineral Water Advertisement: A Case on Discourse Analysis. Studies in Media and Communication, 13(4), 94–104. doi: http://dx.doi.org/10.11114/smc.v13i4.7813

IPCC (Intergovernmental Panel on Climate Change) (2021). Climate Change 2021: The *P*hysical *S*cience *B*asis. Cambridge University Press.

Kleindorfer, P. R., and Kunreuther, H. (1999). 'Challenges in Risk Assessment and Risk Management', Annals of the American Academy of Political and Social Science, 545 (1), 8–15.

Kuchkarov, T., Mamadiyarov, Z., Khakimov, Z., Sabirova, O., Matmurodov, K., Raimboyeva, M., & Umarova, S. (2025). Energy-Related Uncertainty and Crypto-Currency Environmental Attention: Time-Varying Perspective. International Journal of Energy Economics and Policy, 15(5), 614–626. https://doi.org/10.32479/ijeep.20784

Kuziboev, B., Khodjaniyazov, E., Ozturk, I., Sabirov, K., Makhmudov, S., and Utegenova, S. (2025). 'Does Oil Dependence Cause Energy Risk?' *Energy Nexus*, 100393.

Litamahuputty, J. V., Amiruddin, E. G., Rahim, R., Rahman, A., & Mamadiyarov, Z. (2025). Cryptocurrency Risk Management through Decision Engineering: Evaluating XRPUSD and ADAUSD Portfolio

Performance. Journal of Applied Science, Engineering, Technology, and Education, 7(1), 69–81. https://doi.org/10.35877/454RI.asci3871

McKinney, M., Schoch, R., and Yonavjak, L. (2015). Environmental Science: Systems and Solutions. Jones & Bartlett Learning.

Mamadiyarov, Z., Eshov, M., Otakhonova, D., Utegenova, S., Sabirov, K., Marks, A., & Bahodirov, N. (2025). Does Energy Policy Risk Threaten Energy Sources Diversification?. International Journal of Energy Economics and Policy, 15(5), 730–740. https://doi.org/10.32479/ijeep.21140

Mamadiyarov, Z., Saidov, O., Abdurazakova, N., Makhmudov, S., Nazarov, M., Rajabova, N., … Ruzmetova, I. (2025). Energy-Related Uncertainty and Tourism Stock Markets: New Insights from Time-Varying Relationship with TVP- VAR Approach. International Journal of Energy Economics and Policy, 15(4), 730–737. https://doi.org/10.32479/ijeep.20480

Mamani, J.C.M., Miri, M., Vorobev, Y. et al. Optimal Operation of Energy Microgrid Considering Economic and Emission Indices. Oper. Res. Forum 6, 122 (2025). https://doi.org/10.1007/s43069-025-00523-z

Mason, M., and Green, K. (2018). 'Comparative Environmental Crisis Management in Developed and Developing Nations', *Journal of Environmental Policy & Planning*, 20 (3), 289–308.

Matyakubova, A., Makhmudov, S., Ozturk, I., Kurbonov, K., Ismailov, F., Yokubboeva, S., & Urozov, A. (2025). Responses of Economic Policy Uncertainty, Financial Stress and Energy-Related Uncertainty to the Shocks in US-China Tension in US. International Journal of Energy Economics and Policy, 15(4), 701–708. https://doi.org/10.32479/ijeep.20369

Muhammad Zubair, Irfanud Din, Nadeem Sarwar et al. Revolutionizing Sepsis Diagnosis Using Machine Learning and Deep Learning Models: A Systematic Literature Review, 10 June 2025, PREPRINT (Version 1) available at Research Square [https://doi.org/10.21203/rs.3.rs-6731418/v1]

Ngongo, M., Herman, H., Ndandara, A., Jois Jaha, D. A., Peku Djawang, J. U. S., Tanggu Rame, M. M., Khamraeva, S. N., & Mamadiyarov, Z. (2025). An Investigation of Meaning, Toponymy of Sumba Cultural Site's Names, and the Impact of Tourism Visitors on Surrounding Society. Forum for Linguistic Studies, 7(8), 679–693. https://doi.org/10.30564/fls.v7i8.10260

strom, E. (1990). Governing the Commons: The Evolution of Institutions for Collective action. Cambridge University Press.

PANJAITAN, M. B., HAMDANAH, H., SIRAIT, J., SUTIKNO, S., FATMAWATI, E., HERMAN, H., & MAMADIYAROV, Z. (2025). THE ROLE OF EMOTIONAL REGULATION IN SHAPING STUDENTS' PERCEPTION OF PHYSICS PROBLEMSOLVING TASKS. TPM – Testing, Psychometrics, Methodology in Applied Psychology, 32(S2(2025) : Posted 09 June), 1–10. Retrieved from https://tpmap.org/submission/index.php/tpm/article/view/139

Paton, D., and Johnston, D. (2001). 'Disasters and Communities: Vulnerability, resilience, and Preparedness', Disaster Prevention and Management, 10 (4), 270–7.

Pelling, M. (2003). The Vulnerability of Cities: Natural Disasters and Social Resilience. Earthscan.

Pirgaip, B., Bayrakdar, S., and Kaya, M. V. (2023). 'The Role of Government Spending within the Environmental Kuznets Curve Framework: Evidence from G7 Countries'. *Environmental Science in Pollution Research* 30, 81513–30.

Romero, R. M., Zelinskaya, M., Makhmudov, S., Sapaev, S., & Rustambekovich, J. U. (2025, September). Modelling and Optimal Utilisation of the Renewable Energy Systems in Microgrid with Improving Reliability and Energy Efficiency. In Operations Research Forum (Vol. 6, No. 3, pp. 1–20). Springer International Publishing.

Rony, Z. T., Jefri, R., Rusmardiana, A., Pramono, S. A., & Mamadiyarov, Z. (2025). Downside Risk Measurement of Indonesian Financial and Energy Securities: A Value at Risk Perspective. Journal of Applied Science, Engineering, Technology, and Education, 7(2). https://doi.org/10.35877/454RI.asci3898

Rayala, R. V., Borra, C. R., Vasudevan, V., Singhania, R., Cheekati, S., & Mamadiyarov, Z. (2025, July). Lightweight Deep Learning Framework for Human Activity Recognition: A MobileNet-LSTM Approach with WHOA Optimization. In *2025 International Conference on Innovations in Intelligent Systems: Advancements in Computing, Communication, and Cybersecurity (ISAC3)* (pp. 1–6). IEEE.

Rayala, R. V., Sandhya, N., Singhania, R., Cheekati, S., Borra, C. R., Vasudevan, V., & Mamadiyarov, Z. (2025, July). AI-Driven Tomato

Quality Assessment: A Deep Learning Approach for Image-based Defect Detection and Classification. In *2025 International Conference on Innovations in Intelligent Systems: Advancements in Computing, Communication, and Cybersecurity (ISAC3)* (pp. 1–6). IEEE.

Samariddin Makhmudov, Malika Umarova, Khayrilla Kurbonov, Laylo Akbarova, Durdona Davletova, Nilufar Shanazarova, and Toshmurod Kulmanov. 2025. Evaluating the forecast indicators of the volume of highly liquid assets of commercial banks in the process of digital transformation. In Proceedings of the 8th International Conference on Future Networks & Distributed Systems (ICFNDS '24). Association for Computing Machinery, New York, NY, USA, 698–704. https://doi.org/10.1145/3726122.3726222

Sharipov, K., Abdullayev, I., Kuziboev, B., Makhmudov, S., Kalandarov, F., Khaytboeva, N., & Ilkhamova, Z. (2025). The Effect of Energy Policy Risk on Renewable Energy. *International Journal of Energy Economics and Policy, 15*(2), 566.

Singagerda, F. S., Pratama, M. R., Alfairus, M. Q., Iskandar, A., & Mamadiyarov, Z. (2025). A Decision-Centric Approach to Risk Management in Aviation Stock Investments Using Value at Risk and Portfolio Optimization. Journal of Applied Science, Engineering, Technology, and Education, 7(1), 114–125. https://doi.org/10.35877/454RI.asci3870

Sofyanty, D., Romadhoni, R., Handriadi, H., Makhsudovna, I. S., Anwar, Z., & Mamadiyarov, Z. (2025). Strategic Decision Analysis for Investment Portfolios: Computational Risk Assessment in Transportation Asset Management. *Journal of Applied Science, Engineering, Technology, and Education*, 7(2). https://doi.org/10.35877/454RI.asci3897

Stern, N. (2007). The *E*conomics of *C*limate *C*hange: The Stern Review. Cambridge University Press.

Tierney, K., Lindell, M. K., and Perry, R. W. (2006). Facing the *U*nexpected: Disaster *P*reparedness and *R*esponse in the United States. Joseph Henry Press.

Tol, R. S. (2013). 'Targets for Global Climate Policy: An Overview', Journal of Economic Dynamics and Control 37 (5), 911–28.

Toshmurod Kulmanov, Umidjon Dadabaev, Mansurbek Qulmetov, Aliboy Ulashov, Mirjalol Eshboyev, and Samariddin Makhmudov. 2025. Global Services Market Transformation Digitalization Export Trends and Future Forecasts. In Proceedings of the 8th International Conference on Future Networks & Distributed Systems (ICFNDS '24). Association for Computing Machinery, New York, NY, USA, 851–858. https://doi.org/10.1145/3726122.3726245

UNEP (United Nations Environment Programme) (2019). Global *E*nvironmental *O*utlook 6: Healthy *P*lanet, *H*ealthy *P*eople. Cambridge University Press.

Wachinger, G., Renn, O., Begg, C., and Kuhlicke, C. (2013). 'The Risk Perception Paradox – Implications for Governance and Communication of Natural Hazards', Risk Analysis 33 (6), 1049–65.

World Bank (2022). Financing *D*isaster *R*isk *E*eduction: A *G*lobal *P*erspective on the *F*inancial *C*hallenges. World Bank Publications.

World Health Organization (WHO) (2020). Climate *C*hange and *H*ealth: Key *F*acts. Available at: <https://www.who.int/news-room/fact-sheets/detail/climate-change-and-health>.

Yusuf, J. E., and St. John, B. (2019). Disaster Recovery in the United States: A Policy Perspective. CRC Press.

Zhang, L., Zhao, Z., Qamri, G. M., & Makhmudov, S. (2025). Unleashing the critical role of renewable energy through global value chains and digitalization: A path towards environmental sustainability. Journal of Environmental Management, 392, 126688.

Zhao, Q., Pervaiz, A., Makhmudov, S., & Fatima, A. (2025). Do environmental stringent policies enhance the impact of renewable energy on CO2 reduction? Evidence from BRICS-T economies. Journal of Environmental Management, 391, 126464.

The Priority Importance of Forecasting and Planning the Increase in the Share of the Fuel and Energy Complex and Gas Industry in Economic Processes

Samariddin Makhmudov, Mukhiddin Kalonov, Zokir Mamadiyarov, Faxri Hamitov, Nurbek Turayev, Sirojiddin Yangiboyev and Mirzabek Jonuzokov

13.1. Introduction

The energy and gas industry are the pillar of the global economy and an impelling force of economic growth, driving energy and industrialisation. Assist in realising about 45–50 per cent of global energy needs, the industry not only provides essential supplies but also has a considerable impact on the country and local economies (Samariddin et al., 2025; Singagerda et al., 2025). By its contribution to the Gross Domestic Product (GDP), jobs and foreign investment inflows, the energy and gas industry is a determining element in the economic landscape of advanced and emerging economies. As energy consumption keeps increasing in the world, strategic expansion and growth of the industry have become imperative for long-term economic development and regional prosperity (Akhmetshin et al., 2025; Mamadiyarov et al., 2025; Sofyanty et al., 2025).

But the sector is faced with mounting challenges, particularly regarding environmental sustainability and the growing mandate to mitigate climate change (Ahmed et al., 2025). As the environmental impact of traditional energy activities continues to assume centre stage, the adoption of new, sustainable technologies is essential in ensuring future sustainability of the sector (Abdullah, et al., 2025; Bhatti et al., 2025; Litamahuputty et al., 2025). In light of such difficulties, shifting towards cleaner and more efficient energy sources and adopting the latest technological solutions is necessary to ensure the sustainability of the energy and gas sectors in the long term (Kurbonov et al., 2025; Lin et al., 2025). To this end, strategic planning and effective forecasting are key to demystifying the complexities of future energy production, transportation and consumption so that policymakers and business executives can make sound decisions in an increasingly dynamic world.

Another group of economists has successfully used econometric models such as Fixed Effects Estimator, Random Effects Estimator, multivariate linear (LS) and ARDL in their research on investment in digital infrastructure, various aspects of digital payment systems, the impact of inflation and credit interest rates on investment, factors affecting the reduction of the state's share in commercial banks, Non-Performing Loans in commercial banks, the digitisation of banks, risks in digital services and the development of retail payment services (Ghaleb et al.,2025; Habib et al., 2025; Mamadiyarov et al., 2025; Mamani et al., 2025; Zokir et al., 2021).

This study discusses the application of econometric forecasting and emphasises the application of the ARIMA(2,1,1) model in attempting to predict the trajectory of Uzbekistan's natural gas production from the year 2025 through 2030. By leveraging new econometric methods combined with the application of artificial intelligence and digital technologies, the project attempts to improve the levels of efficiency within operations, resource maximisation and enhance the sustainability of operations in the energy and gas industry. The forecasted result expects well-balanced and healthy development in natural gas production, the level of production expected to increase to 51,563.45 million cubic meters in 2025 to increase to 54,780.35 million cubic meters by 2030. The future expectations expect not only healthy industrial growth but also increased energy security, economic stability and supply chain stability of chains on domestic markets and export bases.

In addition, the study examines the impact of external determinants such as foreign direct investment, technology and macroeconomic determinants such as changes in oil and gas prices, all of which are powerful drivers of determining the future of the energy and gas sector. The inclusion of these determinants in the analysis offers a comprehensive picture of sectoral growth determinants and economic development. By combining econometric forecasting with rigorous examination of the technological, market and policy drivers, this article provides a coherent, consistent framework for planning the long-term future of the energy industry. It attempts to offer evidence-based guidance that will be used in decision-making with a perspective towards enabling the ongoing development of the energy industry in an ever more advanced and integrated world economy.

13.2. Literature Review

Studies indicate that, in the context of the development of the economic environment in the regions, the energy and gas sector's development is considered a priority task of economic processes due to its significant role in the development of economic sectors and the supply of energy security (Sharipov et al., 2025). The oil and gas industry are considered to be among the most significant drivers of economic chain creation in the world economic dynamics, utilised to meet about 45–50 per cent of the world's energy demands (Zhao et al., 2025). It also significantly affects the GDP of most countries, contributing to economic growth in areas (Kuziboev et al., 2025). Today, scientific and strategic solutions for minimising the environmental impacts of the gas industry in the regions are considered to be of high value in ensuring sustainability through the production of cheap energy resources (Zhang et al., 2025).

Some researchers have conducted their research based on econometric models for forecasting the growth of the energy and gas sector in economic activities. Mansell et al. (2012) note that in provinces such as Alberta, Canada, the oil and gas industry is a significant contributor to economic sectors, accounting for a large share of GDP, business investment and profits. The findings of the authors' study illustrate that the smooth operation of energy and economic processes requires taking into account the different characteristics of firms in different economic sectors, and the importance of controlling for differences in the size, role and operation of their energy and gas resources is outlined. According to Polyakova et al. (2019), investment in the energy and gas sector is linked to the growth of economic sectors, which can be deemed a positive impact of these investments on Russia's GDP. Ahamer (2022) clarifies that in traditional forecasting, the Kaya identity model has been highlighted as the optimum model to understand the complexity of the gas and energy sector and offers a more disaggregated approach to systematic variables such as energy intensity and GDP shares. In line with the author's research work, econometric modelling of gas and energy industries provides an opportunity for describing nonlinear evolutionary changes, thereby creating a basis for more accurate forecasting of GDP, fuel shares, and energy intensity in economic sectors.

According to Prince et al. (2020), the importance of econometric models in capturing nonlinear interactions in energy and gas demand data in gas demand forecasting has achieved high accuracy. The authors found that the Random Forest model produced a positive R-squared value of 95.67 per cent in predicting demand for the US power and gas industry. According to Nwulu et al. (2022), the coming together of artificial intelligence, digitalisation, and advanced analytics is the secret to transform the oil and gas industry, as technologies optimise exploration, production, and maintenance activities and enable operational efficiency and sustainability. The authors of the study concluded that hybrid renewable digital ecosystem technologies can enable the transformation of the industry towards clean energy more effectively. While according to Mystakidis et al., (2024) a comprehensive survey of gas industry forecasting methods highlights the importance of accurate forecasting in order to optimally manage energy imbalances and resource allocation. The conclusion of the authors' study is that forecasting using econometric models and statistical methods is of considerable importance in supporting decision-making in energy production and consumption. Guler (2024) stated that natural gas prices are considered to be an important determinant affecting the energy sector, and natural gas price inflation in regions has an asymmetric relationship with macroeconomic indicators such as producer price index and GDP. The empirical results of the authors showed that the fluctuation of natural gas prices from 1998–2023 according to ARDL and NARDL models was explained by the impact of macroeconomic indicators on the overall growth of the energy sector in the short and long term.

Yıldırım and Kaya (2021), analyze the macroeconomic structures of OECD countries, which are developed in terms of renewable energy technology. The results of these analyses illustrate that carbon dioxide (CO_2) emission is the strongest determinant of renewable energy usage.

Analyses and forecasts have been conducted using multivariate linear regression (LS), ARDL, ARIMA, and other various econometric models on factors affecting remittances, energy intensity and economic development, energy policy, energy risk, environmental status and the impact of environmental aspects on the digital economy, agricultural productivity, and the stability of the US credit market (Caporin et al., 2024; Jahrir et al., 2025; Kalandarov et al., 2025; Kuchkarov et al., 2025; Sharipov et al., 2025; Su et al., 2025).

According to Kabiru et al. (2025), oil price volatility is considerably influential on macroeconomic indicators such as inflation and GDP. Using the

NARDL model for the period 2015–2023, the authors demonstrated that increases in oil prices in Nigeria have raised short-term inflationary pressures and exhibit a strong association with GDP changes, indicating the energy sector's sensitivity to changes in oil prices. Similarly, Wang et al. (2015) in their work hold the argument that energy consumption is closely linked with the macroeconomic factor of GDP, and industrial production. As per analysis by the authors, a great correlation was found between industrial added value, the energy consumption, and the per capita GDP, which confirms intensive economic growth association with energy consumption. For the forecasting of size of the energy and gas industry sector in economic proceedings for the period 2025–2030, authors developed econometric models based on ARIMA methodology.

In addition, Huang et al. (2024) bring into focus the increasing applicability of the ARIMA model to United States natural gas consumption in order to aid sustainable level planning of consumption and guide long-term investments in the industry. Research on economic process forecasting in the field cites the AutoRegressive Integrated Moving Average (ARIMA) as a statistical model applied widely to forecast time series data in econometric studies. Its simplicity, effectiveness, and accuracy render it a precious instrument in both economic and social fields. According to Mirescu et al. (2024), the ability of the ARIMA model to identify non-stationary data, attain autoregressive and moving average parts, and possess flexibility in attaining the best models is imperative towards forecasting accurately. The ability of the model to identify trends and seasonality in the real-time series contributes towards its use in forecasting economics. Lyu et al. (2024) emphasises the adaptability of the ARIMA model through the possibility of including autoregressive (AR) and moving average (MA) components, thus enabling it to adapt to the idiosyncrasies that exist in the data. Such an adaptability is extremely valuable for use in economic application, as it is able to accurately reflect the changing variations and trends existing in time series data in various sectors.

ARIMA model is made up of three fundamental building blocks: AR, differencing (I) and MA. Each of them plays a vital role in accurate future value forecasting using past data. The combination of these three assists in utilising an integrated approach in modelling and forecasting the path of economic indicators over time (Mamadiyarov et al., 2025; Ngongo et al., 2025; Rony et al., 2025; Zhang et al., 2018). Khashei et al. (2018) also highlight the capability of the ARIMA (SARIMA) model in accommodating seasonal fluctuations in the data, a relevant feature in econometric forecasting, especially for periodic trend time series. Through incorporating seasonal adjustments, the model becomes stronger in coping with cyclical patterns common with economic and energy-related data. Levendis (2023) describes how the AR aspect of the ARIMA model refers to the backward-looking analysis of the variable under consideration against observations lagged at different points of time, therefore capturing the historic relationships between future and past periods. The size of the order of the AR component, indicated by 'p', is a measure of how many lag periods are included in the model and is important when analyzing the persistence of the economic trends.

For economic process forecasting, particularly in the gas and energy industries, the ARIMA model provides a very effective framework for interpretation of complex time dynamics and generation of reliable forecasts, which are most important for long-term planning, policymaking, and investment allocations in these high-risk industries.

13.3. Research Methodology

The methodology section of a research article delineates the systematic process undertaken to answer the research questions or test the hypotheses. It includes the overall research design, data collection, and analytical techniques, ensuring replicability and reliability of the study.

The general form of the ARIMA(p, d, q) model is given below:

$$y_t = c + d_1 y_{t-1} + d_2 y_{i-2} + \cdots + d_k y_{t-1} + \mu_1 \epsilon_{t-1} + \mu_2 \epsilon_{t-2} + \cdots + \mu \epsilon_{t-1} + \epsilon_i \quad (1)$$

where, y_t – t is the value of the time series at time t (after being differentiated d times), c represents the constant term, d_i = (*for* t = 1, 2, …, k) – denotes the coefficients of the autoregressive part, δ_l = (*for* l = 1, 2, …, l) – denotes the coefficients of the moving average part. ϵ_i – denotes the error term (white noise) at time t.

In developing the forecast indicators for the study, quarterly data sources from the Statistical Agency under the President of the Republic of Uzbekistan

(<https://stat.uz/uz/>) with a number of observations for 2014–2024 were used. The resulting variable for the econometric forecast is shown below.

Natural gas volume – *natur_gas_vol* (resulting variable).

Methodology concludes by observing that the method in question offers a comprehensive framework to understand and interpret the effect of digital technology on the service sector. It offers a robust foundation to derive evidence-based conclusions in the subsequent sections of the research article.

13.4. Analysis and Results

An analytical graphical diagram of natural gas volume over time at the initial stage of the econometric forecast is presented in Figure 29.

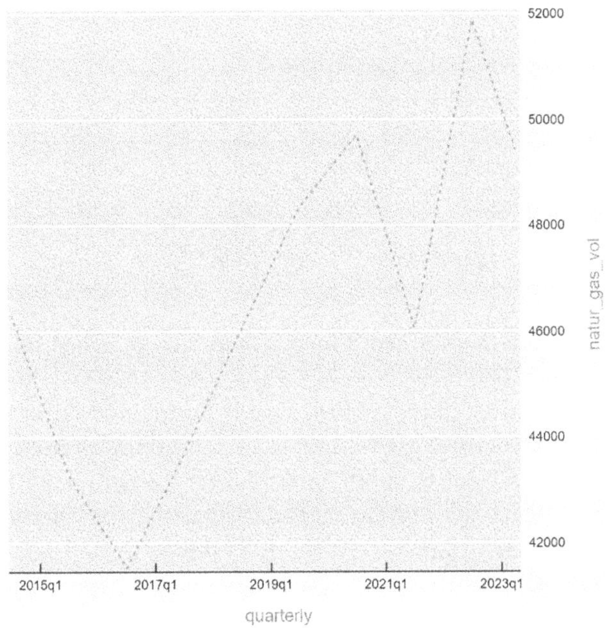

Figure 29. Analytical graphical representation of natural gas volume over time.
Source: It was developed by the authors based on Stata software.

From Figure 29, the analytical picture of natural gas volume over time during the time under study portrays the prevailing economic trends, stability, and prospects for growth. This means that in forecasting general economic stability, natural gas volume offers a stable market with unambiguous trends over time, making it even more important in forecasting and planning the energy sector within the region.

Although occasional deviations from the downward trend were noted for the reviewed period, particularly in 2017 and 2021, in subsequent recovery processes it illustrates a high growth trend. The analytics of growth dynamics indicate the possibility of further growth in natural gas production and supply, investment practices to increase economic efficiency.

In the econometric forecasting stage two, stationarity level of natural gas volume was found and Unit-Root test was conducted to find it (see Table 26).

Table 26. Unit-root test of natural gas volume

economy_cost	Test Statistic	1% Critical Value	5% Critical Value	10% Critical Value	*p*-value for *Z*(*t*)
	-5.568	-3.696	-2.978	-2.620	0.0000

Source: It was developed by the authors based on Stata software.

According to Table 26, the unit root test statistic (–5.568) is smaller than all critical values (1% –3.696, 5% –2.978 and 10% –2.620), which leads to a very high confidence rejection of the null hypothesis of a unit root. This indicates that the natural gas volume is not a random variable, but has a stable trend. The p-value (0.0000) indicates that the natural gas volume is statistically significant and is unlikely to be due to random fluctuations. The ARIMA model parameter d is set to a value of $d = 1$, indicating that the fit is good and that the time series has reached stationarity after the first difference. The next step is to calculate the value of p, which determines the indirect correlation between the time series lags of the model (Figure 30).

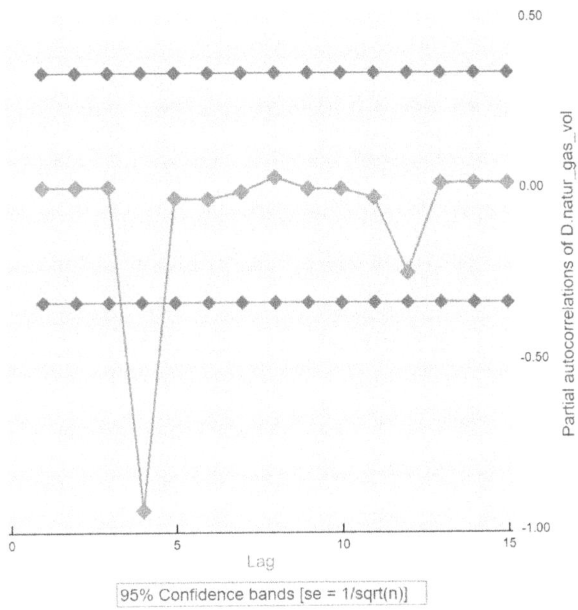

Figure 30. Indirect correlation graph between lags of the natural gas volume econometric model.
Source: It was developed by the authors based on Stata software.

As can be observed in Figure 30, all volume lags of natural gas in this econometric model, except for the one lag, fall within the confidence interval. This result is in agreement with the results obtained by the Unit-Root test presented in Table 26, which confirm the stationarity of the data. Additionally, while the differenced series do not exhibit long-term dependence, this characteristic enhances the accuracy and trustworthiness of the econometric model in predicting, without decreasing its quality.

The fact that most of the lags fall inside the confidence interval suggests that natural gas production variations are not significantly influenced by its long-run previous state. All the lags, except one, have confidence intervals in the indirect correlation analysis, which enhances the robustness of the model.

It is correct then to select a *p*-value of 0 or 1 for the subsequent step. The second step of the ARIMA model is determining the value of *q*, that is, the current relationship between the lags of the model, as shown in Figure 31.

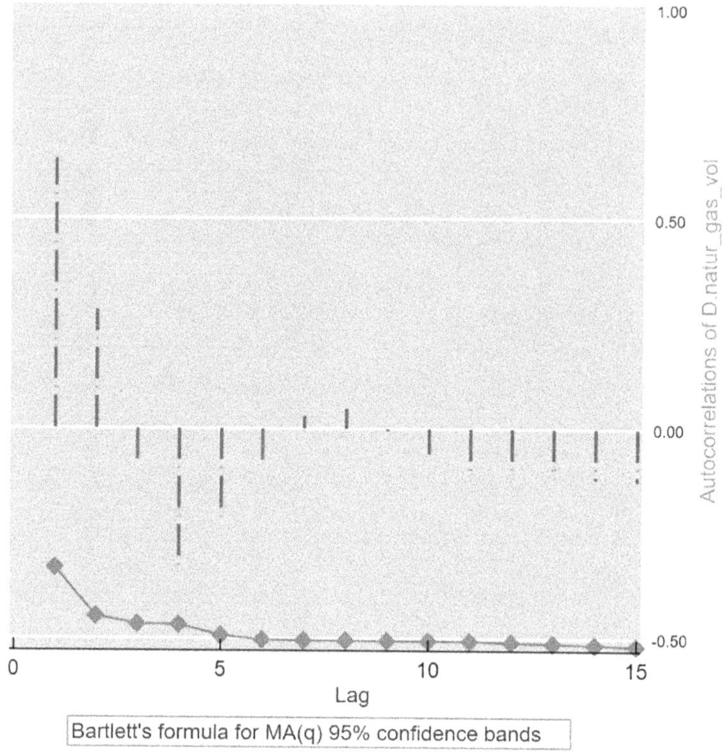

Figure 31. Direct correlation graph between lags of the econometric model of economic expenditure volumen.
Source: It was developed by the authors based on Stata software.

Figure 31 shows that the ARIMA model produces a strong correlation between lags, and all lags, except for one lag, are within the specified confidence interval.

The autocorrelations of the econometric forecast show a long-term stable trend, which further reinforces the stationary nature of natural gas production.

In the next step, the cumulative spectral periodogram and cumulative spectral distribution analysis are presented for the time series estimation of natural gas production volume according to the econometric forecast indicators (Figures 32 and 33).

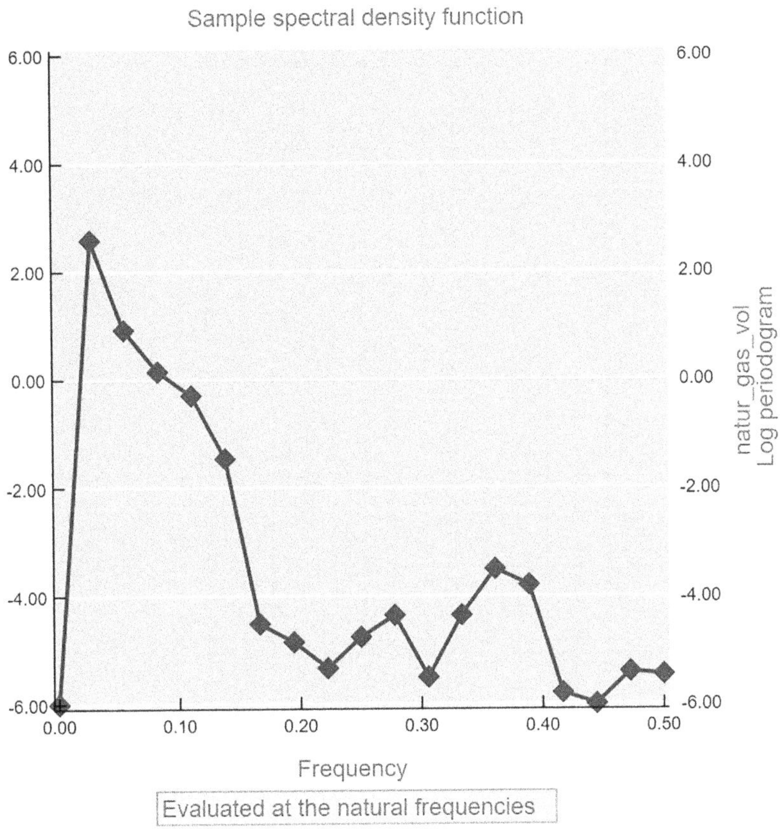

Figure 32. Cumulative spectral periodogram graph analysis of the natural gas production volume econometric model.
Source: It was developed by the authors based on Stata software.

According to Figure 32, the econometric forecast indicators present the frequency–domain characteristics of natural gas production volumes. According to it, the graph shows a stable peak at low frequencies, while the fluctuations in the volume of natural gas production in many variations indicate a periodic long-term stable growth pattern. The presence of periodic components at certain frequencies indicates cyclical seasonality, which is used for important solutions in strategic planning and forecasting in natural gas markets.

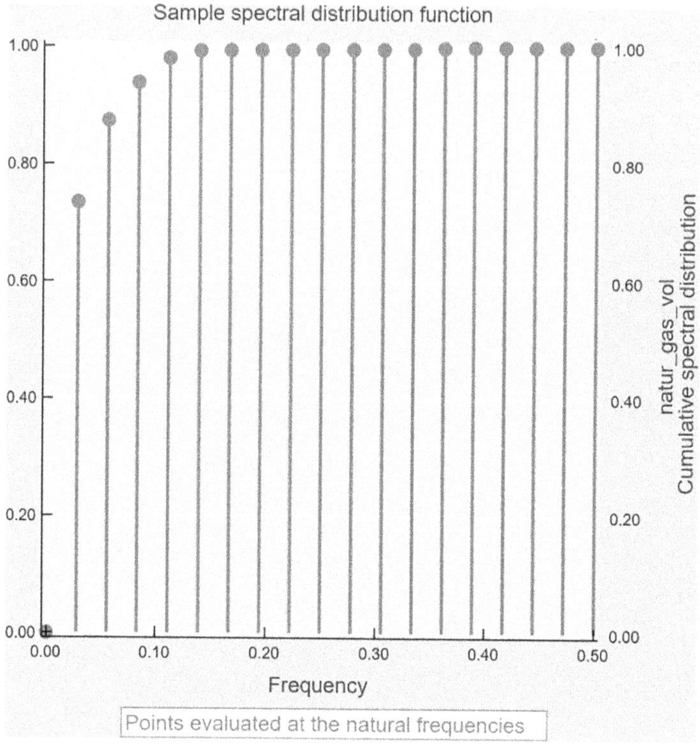

Figure 33. Cumulative spectral distribution graph analysis of the econometric model of natural gas production volumen.
Source: It was developed by the authors based on Stata software.

According to the analysis of Figure 33, the cumulative spectral distribution function showed a steady increase from 0 to 1, which indicates that most of the fluctuations in natural gas production volume are consistent and systematic. Also, the cumulative spectral distribution function provides long-term stability and accurate forecast indicators of natural gas volume.

The dominance of relationships in random changes means that primary natural gas production is reliably analyzed and has a systematic behaviour, which provides important strategic solutions for effective forecasting in economic planning.

When selecting optimal ARIMA models for forecasting theped. Among these models, the ARIMA(2,1,1) model, which achieved the most optimal r model, models such as ARIMA(2,0,1), ARIMA(1,1,2), ARIMA(2,1,0), ARIMA(1,1,1) ARIMA(0,1,2) and ARIMA(2,1,1) were develoesult, was selected (see Table 27).

Based on the ARIMA model regression result, the econometric equation for the model is given below:

$$Y_t = \alpha + \phi_1 y_{t-1} + \phi_2 Y_{t-2} + \theta_1 \varepsilon_{t-1} + \varepsilon_t \tag{3}$$

Table 27. Econometric equation indicators of the ARIMA(2,1,1) model by natural gas production volume

D.natur_gas_vol	Coeff.	St. Err.	t-value	p-value	[95% Conf	Interval]	Sig
Constant	172.181	51.685	3.33	0.001	70.879	273.483	***
L	1.596	0.196	8.14	0	1.211	1.98	***
L2	-0.744	0.222	-3.36	0.001	-1.178	-0.31	***
L	-1	0.346	-2.89	0.004	-1.678	-0.322	***
Constant	518.533	.	.	.	.	.	

Mean dependent var	87.867	SD dependent var	786.851
Number of obs	35	Chi-square	524.707
Prob > chi²	.	Akaike crit. (AIC)	548.128
*** $p < 0.01$, ** $p < 0.05$, * $p < 0.1$			

Source: It was developed by the authors based on Stata software.

According to Table 27, the ARIMA(2,1,1) model looks like this:

$$\begin{aligned} D.natur\_gas\_vol_t = {} & 172.18 + 1.59\ D.natur\_gas\_vol_{t-1} \\ & - 0.74\ D.natur\_gas\_vol_{t-2} - \varepsilon_{t-1} + \varepsilon_t \end{aligned} \tag{4}$$

In the next step, the ARIMA(2,1,1) model was developed to analyze the mean values of the outcome variable and the graphical representation of the residuals (Table 28 and Figure 34).

Table 28. Residual values of the resulting factor in the ARIMA(2,1,1) model

Variable	Obs	Mean	Std. dev.	Min	Max
Residual value	35	−77.1362	546.3759	−1571.461	1807.578

Source: It was developed by the authors based on Stata software.

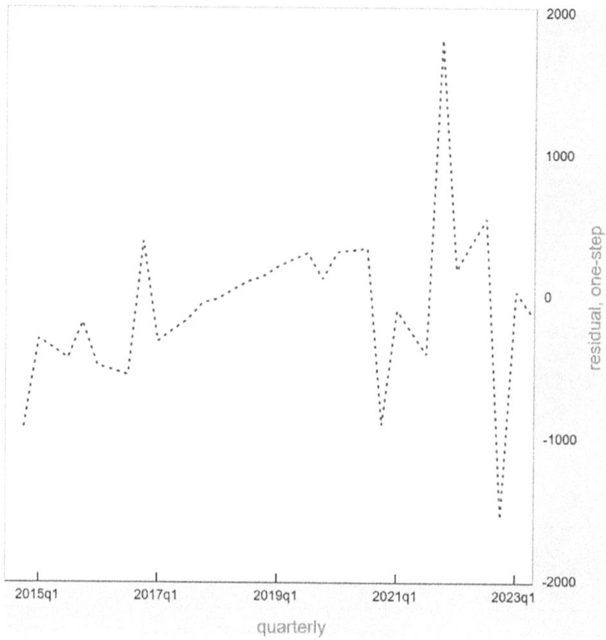

Figure 34. Graph of residual values of the ARIMA(2,1,1) model by natural gas production volume.
Source: It was developed by the authors based on Stata software.

According to Table 28 and Figure 34, the ARIMA(2,1,1) model has reached stochastic equilibrium, as evidenced by the visual movement of the residuals at the specified time intervals. This image shows the fit of the ARIMA model to the data and the main stochastic relationships in the data set.

In the next step, the stationarity of the residuals of the ARIMA(2,1,1) model for natural gas production was checked, and the AR and MA residuals were estimated. Also, the convergence of the ARIMA model to the unit range in forecasting, the Portmanteau test for white noise, and the Eigenvalue stability condition were checked (Table 29 and Figure 35).

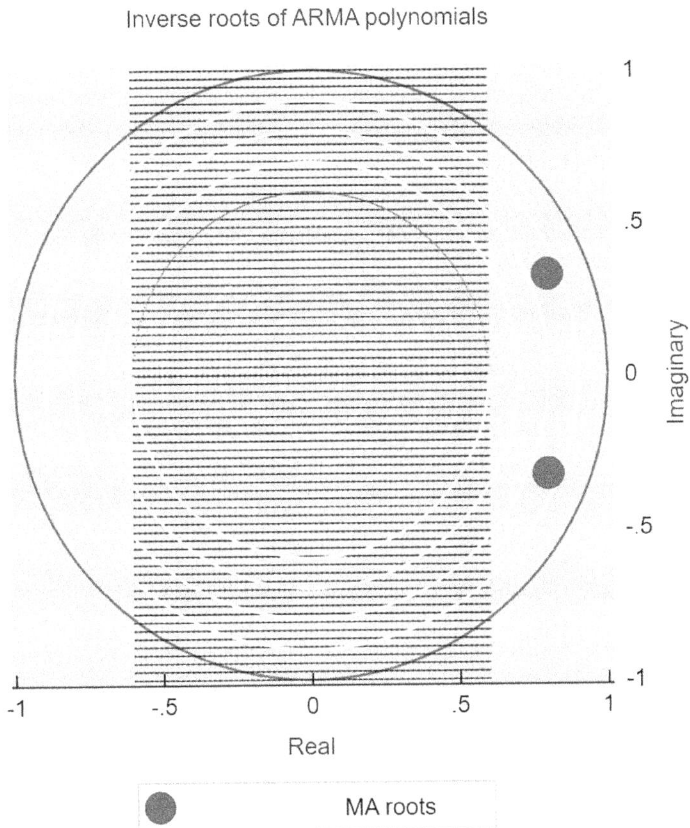

Figure 35. Range of values of natural gas production volume according to the ARIMA(2,1,1) model.
Source: It was developed by the authors based on Stata software.

Table 29. Eigenvalue stability condition for the ARIMA(2,1,1) model

Eigenvalue	Modulus
0.7979834 + 0.3273033i	0.862499
0.7979834 – 0.3273033i	0.862499

Portmanteau (*Q*) statistic = 10.7156

Prob > chi^2(15) = 0.7725

Source: It was developed by the authors based on Stata software.

Using the Stata program, a forecast indicator for natural gas production from 2025 to 2030 was developed using the ARIMA(2,1,1) model, excluding random factors (Table 30).

Table 30. Forecast indicators of economic expenditure volume for 2025–2029 (million cubic meters)

Years	Pessimistic forecast	Optimistic forecast	Forecast
2025	50,776.62	52,332.31	**51,563.45**
2026	51,367.76	52,923.46	**52,154.61**
2027	51,831.34	53,387.04	**52,618.19**
2028	52,613.41	54,169.11	**53,400.26**
2029	53,871.53	55,427.20	**53,981.83**
2030	54,166.67	56,332.32	**57,780.35**

Source: It was developed by the authors based on Stata software.

According to the results of the study, based on the ARIMA(2,1,1) model, the volume of natural gas production in 2025–2030, excluding random internal and external factors, was forecasted to reach 51,563.45 million cubic meters in 2025, 52,154.61 million cubic meters in 2026, 52,618.19 million cubic meters in 2027, 53,400.26 million cubic meters in 2028, 53,981.83 million cubic meters in 2029, and 54,780.35 million cubic meters in 2030, respectively.

The study provides a graphical representation of the forecast indicator of natural gas production in 2014–2024 and 2025–2030, provided by the Statistical Agency under the President of the Republic of Uzbekistan (<https://stat.uz/uz/>) (Figure 36).

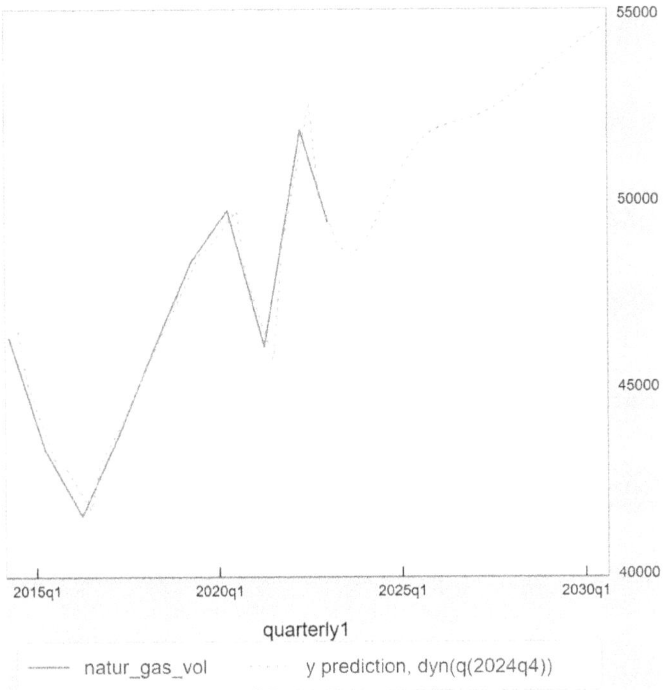

Figure 36. Graph of the resulting variable for 2014–2024 and the forecast for 2025–2029. *Source: It was developed by the authors based on Stata software.*

Figure 36 shows the forecast graphs of natural gas production volumes for 2014–2024 and 2025–2029, as provided by the Statistical Agency under the President of the Republic of Uzbekistan. According to it, the trend graph indicates the reliability of the forecast indicators for the next five years, excluding random factors, since the two lines are located side by side as much as possible.

13.5. Conclusion

According to the research, the forecast indicator of natural gas production volume for 2014–2024 and 2025–2029 provided by the Statistical Agency under the President of the Republic of Uzbekistan (<https://stat.uz/uz/>) is explained below.

1. According to the research results, based on the ARIMA(2,1,1) model, the natural gas production volume in 2025–2030, excluding random internal and external factors, is forecasted to reach 51,563.45 million cubic meters in 2025, 52,154.61 million cubic meters in 2026, 52,618.19 million cubic meters in 2027, 53,400.26 million cubic meters in 2028, 53,981.83 million cubic meters in 2029 and 54,780.35 million cubic meters in 2030, respectively.
2. The ARIMA(2,1,1) model forecast results showed that the natural gas production volume in the region has a stable and positive growth trend from 2025 to 2030.
3. According to the econometric forecast, the growth dynamics of energy and natural gas production volume are projected to increase consistently from year to year and reach 54,780.35 million cubic meters by 2030, which indicates the stable expansion of the industrial sector.
4. As an advantage of economic and energy security in industrial sectors in the region, continuous growth of production implies increasing energy security, ensuring the continuity of the supply chain in domestic consumption and export markets. This will contribute to economic stability and the growth of energy-dependent industries.
5. Investment and development opportunities will serve to stimulate additional investment in the projected infrastructure and technological advances of natural gas production, which will lead to the creation of new jobs and the development of the sector as a whole.
6. The importance of a strengthened position in global markets will increase the competitiveness of the country in the international natural gas market, increase export revenues and strengthen trade relations, as well as increase the level of industrialisation.
7. The gradual and planned growth of industry and production as a result of effective environmental and technological advances will allow for further positive adoption of technologies in the energy and gas industries, increase efficiency and minimise environmental impact through clean and sustainable practices.
8. In conclusion, the ARIMA(2,1,1) model forecast provided a positive outlook for natural gas production, demonstrating sustained growth, improved economic prospects, and enhanced energy security.

Bibliography

Abdullah, M. A., Han, X., Amjad, M. A., & Makhmudov, S. (2025). Revisit the role of financial development on economic growth, human development, and sustainable development in higher-income countries. Journal of Environmental Management, 392, 126874.

Ahamer, G. (2022). 'Scenarios of Systemic Transitions in Energy and Economy'. *Forsyth,* 16 (3), 17–34. <https://doi.org/10.17323/2500-2597.2022.3.17.34>.

Akhmetshin, E., Abdullayev, I., Makhmudov, S., Dakhkilgova, K., Korotaeva, I. and Yanovskaya, G. (2025). APPLICATION OF TANH–COTH METHOD FOR COMBINED AND DOUBLE COMBINED SINH–COSH–GORDON EQUATIONS ARISING CHEMICAL REACTIONS TO WATER SURFACE GRAVITY WAVES. Computational Methods for Differential Equations, (), -. doi: 10.22034/cmde.2025.67655.3234

Ahmed, S. Y., & Isayev, F. (2025). Impact of Islamic beliefs on technology anxiety and attitude towards AI: Role of religion as end and perceived risk of technology. European Journal for Philosophy of Religion, 17(2), 527–556. https://doi.org/10.24204/ejpr.2025.4803

Bhatti, M. A., & Pardaev, J. (2025). Exploring Accreditation's Role in Fostering Inclusive Education via Educational Equity and Technology. Revista Electronica De Leeme, (56).

Caporin, M., Shahbaz, M., Kuziboev, B., Masharipova, M., Allaberganov, S., & Makhmudov, S. (2024). Environmental Kuznets Curve for extended brics economies: do women governance and water stress matter?. International Journal of Energy Economics and Policy, 14(6), 174–183.

Chen, Q., Guan, T., Yun, L., Li, R., and Recknagel, F. (2015). 'Online Forecasting Chlorophyll a Concentrations by an Auto-regressive Integrated Moving Average Model: Feasibility and Potentials'. *Harmful Algae*, 43, 58–65.

Ghaleb, M. M. S., & Pardaev, J. (2025). Effects of Advertisement Language, Communication Style, Information Seeking Behavior and Information Source Credibility on Customers' Intentions towards International Products via Brand Trust. Profesional de la información, 34(2).

Güler, I. (2024). 'Asymmetric Relationships Between Natural Gas Price Inflation and Macroeconomic Factors: The Case of Turkey'. *Fiscaeconomia*, 8 (1), 342–61. <https://doi.org/10.25295/fsecon.1365330>.

Habib, S. S., Islam, M. A., Ali, M. N., Benitez, I. B., Mamadiyarov, Z., Mirzayev, B., … & Flah, A. (2025). Multi-Objective Optimization and Feasibility Analysis of Integrated Biogas–Solar Energy Systems for Rural Electrification. Results in Engineering, 107086.

Huang, W. (2024). 'Forecast of Consumption of Natural Gas in U.S. based on Time Series Analysis and ARIMA Mmodel'. *Theoretical and Natural Science*, 51 (1), 157–64. <https://doi.org/10.54254/2753-8818/51/2024ch0196>.

Jahrir, A., Gultom, Y., Herman, H., Zabadi, F., Ngongo, M., Mamadiyarov, Z., Fatmawati, E., & Saputra, N. (2025). Investigating the Elements of Short Commercial Mineral Water Advertisement: A Case on Discourse Analysis. Studies in Media and Communication, 13(4), 94–104. doi: http://dx.doi.org/10.11114/smc.v13i4.7813

Kabiru, Y., Musa, Y., Isah, B. Y., and Ilyasu, M. I. (2025). 'Oil Price Fluctuations and Macroeconomic Indicators: An ARDL and NARDL Approach'. *Revista o Universo Observável*, 2 (1), 2–17. <https://doi.org/10.69720/2966-0599.2025.00026>.

Kalandarov, F., Makhmudov, S., Ibadullaev, D., Matniyozov, M., Nasretdinova, F., Sabirov, K., & Bahodirov, N. M. (2025). Low-Carbon Energy Risk and Renewable Energy Development: Insights from Method of Moments Quantile Regression. International Journal of Energy Economics and Policy, 15(3), 524–536.

Khashei, M., Bijari, M., and Hejazi, S. R. (2012). 'Combining Seasonal ARIMA Models with Computational Intelligence Techniques for Time Series Forecasting. *Soft computing* 16, 1091–105.

Khayrilla Kurbonov, Samariddin Makhmudov, Shakhzod Erkinov, Umidjon Dadabaev, Gulnora Bekimbetova, Rukhiddin Zayniddinov, and Mirzabek Jonuzokov. 2025. Evaluating the Impact of Marketing Practices Digitalization and Investment on Labor Market Efficiency and Commercial Bank Performance Using Econometric Models. In Proceedings of the 8th International Conference on Future Networks & Distributed Systems (ICFNDS '24). Association for Computing Machinery, New York, NY, USA, 786–796. https://doi.org/10.1145/3726122.3726237

Kuchkarov, T., Mamadiyarov, Z., Khakimov, Z., Sabirova, O., Matmurodov, K., Raimboyeva, M., & Umarova, S. (2025). Energy-Related Uncertainty and Crypto-Currency Environmental Attention: Time-Varying Perspective. International Journal of Energy Economics and Policy, 15(5), 614–626. https://doi.org/10.32479/ijeep.20784

Kuziboev, B., Khodjaniyazov, E., Ozturk, I., Sabirov, K., Makhmudov, S., & Utegenova, S. (2025). Does oil dependence cause energy risk?. *Energy Nexus*, *17*, 100393.

Levendis, J. (2023). *ARMA(p,q) Processes*, pp. 11–48. Springer International Publishing. <https://doi.org/10.1007/978-3-031-37310-7_2>.

Lin, M.H., Matchanova, B., Nurmatovich, H.A. et al. Optimal Operation of the Multi-Carrier Energy System Considering Energy Markets and Renewable Energies Participation. Int. J. Appl. Comput. Math 11, 170 (2025). https://doi.org/10.1007/s40819-025-02002-9

Litamahuputty, J. V., Amiruddin, E. G., Rahim, R., Rahman, A., & Mamadiyarov, Z. (2025). Cryptocurrency Risk Management through Decision Engineering: Evaluating XRPUSD and ADAUSD Portfolio Performance. Journal of Applied Science, Engineering, Technology, and Education, 7(1), 69–81. https://doi.org/10.35877/454RI.asci3871

Liu, W., Yang, Y., Li, Z., Niu, J., and Li, Y. (2024). *A Forecast Analysis of the Gold Stock Price Using ARIMA Model*, 792–817. <https://doi.org/10.9734/bpi/mono/978-93-48388-89-6/ch37>.

Mamadiyarov, Z., Eshov, M., Otakhonova, D., Utegenova, S., Sabirov, K., Marks, A., & Bahodirov, N. (2025). Does Energy Policy Risk Threaten Energy Sources Diversification?. International Journal of Energy Economics and Policy, 15(5), 730–740. https://doi.org/10.32479/ijeep.21140

Mamadiyarov, Z., Saidov, O., Abdurazakova, N., Makhmudov, S., Nazarov, M., Rajabova, N., … Ruzmetova, I. (2025). Energy-Related Uncertainty and Tourism Stock Markets: New Insights from Time-Varying Relationship with TVP- VAR Approach. International Journal of Energy Economics and Policy, 15(4), 730–737. https://doi.org/10.32479/ijeep.20480

Mamani, J.C.M., Miri, M., Vorobev, Y. et al. Optimal Operation of Energy Microgrid Considering Economic and Emission Indices. Oper. Res. Forum 6, 122 (2025). https://doi.org/10.1007/s43069-025-00523-z

Mansell, R., Winter, J., Krzepkowski, M., and Moore, M. C. (2012). *Size, Role and Performance in the Oil and Gas Sector* 5 (23). <https://doi.org/10.11575/SPPP.V5I0.42395>.

Mirescu, L., and Popescu, L. (2024). 'Forecasts of Performance Indicators in the Health System Using the Arima Method'. *Journal of Social and Economic Statistics*, 13 (1). <https://doi.org/10.2478/jses-2024-0005>.

Mystakidis, A., Koukaras, P., Tsalikidis, N., Ioannidis, D., and Tjortjis, C. (2024). 'Energy Forecasting: A Comprehensive Review of Techniques and Technologies'. *Energies*, <https://doi.org/10.3390/en17071662>.

Ngongo, M., Herman, H., Ndandara, A., Jois Jaha, D. A., Peku Djawang, J. U. S., Tanggu Rame, M. M., Khamraeva, S. N., & Mamadiyarov, Z. (2025). An Investigation of Meaning, Toponymy of Sumba Cultural Site's Names, and the Impact of Tourism Visitors on Surrounding Society. Forum for Linguistic Studies, 7(8), 679–693. https://doi.org/10.30564/fls.v7i8.10260

Nwulu, E. O., Elete, T. Y., Aderamo, A. T., Esiri, A. E., and Omomo, K. O. (2022). 'Predicting Industry Advancements: A Comprehensive Outlook on Future Trends and Innovations in Oil and Gas Engineering'. *International Journal of Frontline Research in Engineering and Technology* 1 (2), 001–015. <https://doi.org/10.56355/ijfret.2022.1.2.0006>.

PANJAITAN, M. B., HAMDANAH, H., SIRAIT, J., SUTIKNO, S., FATMAWATI, E., HERMAN, H., & MAMADIYAROV, Z. (2025). THE ROLE OF EMOTIONAL REGULATION IN SHAPING STUDENTS' PERCEPTION OF PHYSICS PROBLEMSOLVING TASKS. TPM – Testing, Psychometrics, Methodology in Applied Psychology, 32(S2(2025) : Posted 09 June), 1–10. Retrieved from https://tpmap.org/submission/index.php/tpm/article/view/139

Polyakova, A., Ramakrishna, S. A., Kolmakov, and Zavyalov, D. V. (2019). 'A Model of Fuel and Energy Sector Contribution to Economic Growth'. *International Journal of Energy Economics and Policy* 9 (5), 25–31. <https://doi.org/10.32479/IJEEP.7849>.

Prince, N. U., Al Mamoun, M. A., Melon, M., Hossain, A., Arafat, Y., and Hasan, M. N. (2020). 'A Data-driven Approach to Gas Demand Prediction in the USA Using Machine Learning'. *World Journal of Advanced Research and Reviews* 5 (2), 193–203. <https://doi.org/10.30574/wjarr.2020.5.2.0002>.

Rayala, R. V., Borra, C. R., Vasudevan, V., Singhania, R., Cheekati, S., & Mamadiyarov, Z. (2025, July). Lightweight Deep Learning Framework for Human Activity Recognition: A MobileNet-LSTM Approach with WHOA Optimization. In *2025 International Conference on Innovations in Intelligent Systems: Advancements in Computing, Communication, and Cybersecurity (ISAC3)* (pp. 1–6). IEEE.

Rayala, R. V., Sandhya, N., Singhania, R., Cheekati, S., Borra, C. R., Vasudevan, V., & Mamadiyarov, Z. (2025, July). AI-Driven Tomato Quality Assessment: A Deep Learning Approach for Image-based Defect Detection and Classification. In *2025 International Conference on Innovations in Intelligent Systems: Advancements in Computing, Communication, and Cybersecurity (ISAC3)* (pp. 1–6). IEEE.

Rony, Z. T., Jefri, R., Rusmardiana, A., Pramono, S. A., & Mamadiyarov, Z. (2025). Downside Risk Measurement of Indonesian Financial and Energy Securities: A Value at Risk Perspective. Journal of Applied Science, Engineering, Technology, and Education, 7(2). https://doi.org/10.35877/454RI.asci3898

Rukhiddin Zayniddinov, Nodir Jumaev, Gulbakhor Irgasheva, Alam Asadov, Nosir Makhmudov, Sirojiddin Abrorov, and Samariddin Makhmudov. 2025. The Influence of the Digital Economy on Economic Development Evidence from Uzbekistan. In Proceedings of the 8th International Conference on Future Networks & Distributed Systems (ICFNDS '24). Association for Computing Machinery, New York, NY, USA, 831–839. https://doi.org/10.1145/3726122.3726242

Samariddin Makhmudov, Malika Umarova, Khayrilla Kurbonov, Laylo Akbarova, Durdona Davletova, Nilufar Shanazarova, and Toshmurod Kulmanov. 2025. Evaluating the forecast indicators of the volume of highly liquid assets of commercial banks in the process of digital transformation. In Proceedings of the 8th International Conference on Future Networks & Distributed Systems (ICFNDS '24). Association for Computing Machinery, New York, NY, USA, 698–704. https://doi.org/10.1145/3726122.3726222

Sharipov, K., Abdullayev, I., Kuziboev, B., Makhmudov, S., Kalandarov, F., Khaytboeva, N., & Ilkhamova, Z. (2025). The Effect of Energy Policy Risk on Renewable Energy. *International Journal of Energy Economics and Policy*, *15*(2), 566.

Singagerda, F. S., Pratama, M. R., Alfairus, M. Q., Iskandar, A., & Mamadiyarov, Z. (2025). A Decision-Centric Approach to Risk Management in Aviation Stock Investments Using Value at Risk and Portfolio Optimization. Journal of Applied Science, Engineering, Technology, and Education, 7(1), 114–125. https://doi.org/10.35877/454RI.asci3870

Sofyanty, D., Romadhoni, R., Handriadi, H., Makhsudovna, I. S., Anwar, Z., & Mamadiyarov, Z. (2025). Strategic Decision Analysis for Investment Portfolios: Computational Risk Assessment in Transportation Asset Management. Journal of Applied Science, Engineering, Technology, and Education, 7(2). https://doi.org/10.35877/454RI.asci3897

Wang, B., Li, Z., Ge, F., Ye, B., and Yang, M. (2015). Energy Demand Forecasting Method Based on Economic Growth Indicators.

Yıldırım, U., and Kaya, M. V. (2021). 'The Macroeconomic Determinants of Renewable Energy Consumption in Selected OECD Countries'. *Çankırı Karatekin University Journal of Faculty of Economics and Administrative Sciences*, 11 (1), 267–89.

Zhang, L., Lin, J., Qiu, R., Hu, X., Zhang, H., Chen, Q., … and Wang, J. (2018). 'Trend Analysis and Forecast of PM2. 5 in Fuzhou, China Using the ARIMA Model'. *Ecological Indicators*, 95, 702–10.

Zhang, L., Zhao, Z., Qamri, G. M., & Makhmudov, S. (2025). Unleashing the critical role of renewable energy through global value chains and digitalization: A path towards environmental sustainability. Journal of Environmental Management, 392, 126688

Zhao, Q., Pervaiz, A., Makhmudov, S., & Fatima, A. (2025). Do environmental stringent policies enhance the impact of renewable energy on CO2 reduction? Evidence from BRICS-T economies. Journal of Environmental Management, 391, 126464.

Zokir Toshtemirovich Mamadiyarov, Samandarboy Adhambek ugli Sulaymanov, Sarvar Anvar ugli Askarov, and Durdona Bakhtiyor kizi Uktamova. 2022. Impact of Covid-19 Pandemic on Accelerating The Digitization and Transformation of Banks. In Proceedings of the 5th International Conference on Future Networks and Distributed Systems (ICFNDS '21). Association for Computing Machinery, New York, NY, USA, 706–712. https://doi.org/10.1145/3508072.3508211

Assessing the Impact of the Stock Market and Macroeconomic Indicators on the Volume of Investment Portfolios in Economic Processes

Samariddin Makhmudov, Zokir Mamadiyarov, Azizbek Shomirov, Xurshidjon Tillaev, Dilmurod Irgashev, Lola Sabirova and Jonuzokov Mirzabek

14.1. Introduction

Stock market is the keystone of construction of investment portfolio construction and channelling of capital inflows for an economy. Since the finance markets are predominant as intermediary among economic transactions and investors, efficiency and stability within these markets have been preeminent investment choice drivers (Lin et al., 2025). Foreign portfolio investment (FPI), in turn, has grown to become a significant source of external capital driving economic growth, financial market advancement and industry expansion (Makhmudov et al., 2025). Those who are in the business as financial analysts, investors or policymakers seeking maximum capital flows coupled with economic security require an insight into drivers of investment portfolio management.

Macroeconomic indicators like gross domestic product (GDP) growth, inflation, interest rates and fluctuations in the exchange rate are widely known to be the most decisive factors of the performance of stock markets and the direction of investment (Aarthi et al., 2025; Abdullah et al., 2025; Litamahuputty et al., 2025). Economic growth creates investors' confidence by showing business profitability and stable market conditions, whereas inflation and exchange rate volatility create uncertainty that deters investment (Khodjaniyazov et al., 2025). The interrelationship between these macroeconomic variables and the behaviour of the stock market forms a complex environment influencing capital allocation, asset prices and the investment environment.

Substantial literature exists concerning the analysis of the influence of macroeconomic variables on capital markets, with evidence supporting that good economic fundamentals are driving forces for investment attraction and policy uncertainty and financial instability are capital inflow repellers (Sharipov et al., 2025). While studies in the past have unveiled general-range correlations between the variables, further in-depth analysis is required to demonstrate short-run movement and long-run investment patterns (Mamadiyarov et al., 2025; Mamani et al., 2025). Higher-order econometric methods, such as the Autoregressive Distributed Lag (ARDL) model, depict a clear indication of dynamic interdependence between FPI and macroeconomic indicators and enable more precise estimates of market conduct.

This study attempts to explore the impact of stock market action and macroeconomic factors on sizes of investment portfolios in economic activity. Based on the ARDL(1,2,1,2,2) model of regression, this study offers empirical results regarding how much financial market liquidity, economic growth, exchange rate stability and inflationary pressures impact investment inflows. The results make a contribution to the literature by providing a more differentiated view of the interaction between financial markets and macroeconomic variables, distinguishing important determinants of FPI, and emphasising policy measures for increasing market efficiency and economic resilience.

Through the integration of empirical data and theoretical knowledge, this study attempts to bridge research gaps and offer practical suggestions to policymakers interested in creating an investor-friendly environment. Strengthening financial market infrastructure, ensuring macroeconomic stability and fostering investor confidence are prerequisites for optimising investment portfolio growth and economic sustainability.

14.2. Literature Review

Foreign Portfolio Investment, or FPI, plays an important role as a catalyst for the financial condition of national economies, particularly in emerging economies. In this age of heightened globalisation with its speeding up of the movement of capital, policymakers and finance experts increasingly need to understand what drives investment decisions because it speeds up the movement of capital (Mamadiyarov et al., 2025; Singagerda et al., 2025). Among such drivers, macroeconomic factors such as GDP growth, inflation, interest rates and exchange rate volatility have traditionally been considered important drivers of investment portfolio performance (Kuziboev et al., 2025; Sofyanty et al., 2025). The interaction of these macroeconomic factors with financial market forces creates a high-class investment climate that influences domestic as well as foreign capital flows.

This literature review discusses the previous studies on the impact of financial markets and macroeconomic factors on investment portfolio growth. Through the integration of important findings from previous studies, it is a stepping stone towards examining the effect of liquidity in financial markets and stability in the economy on foreign investment inflows. The review also identifies gaps in the literature and emphasises the importance of advanced econometric models in measuring the dynamic relationship between macroeconomic variables. The findings of this review will inform better understanding of the determinants of FPI and also deliver policy-relevant insights into the encouragement of a stable, investor-friendly environment.

The interaction between the performance of the investment portfolio, macroeconomic determinants and financial markets is a highly entrenched issue in economic studies. Researchers have tried to understand to what extent investment activity, market behaviour and general investment appeal are influenced by macroeconomic determinants.

Macroeconomic factors such as GDP growth, inflation, interest rates and exchange rates are central determinants of financial market performance. According to Li et al. (2022), stock market valuation has a positive association with GDP growth due to its ability to represent economic growth and enhanced corporate earning power. The authors establish that the association is strongest in the emerging financial markets, where security investment is an important determinant of economic growth.

In contrast, Phuong et al. (2023) offer proof of the adverse effect of inflation and interest rates on the performance of the stock market. They increase the borrowing cost and decrease consumption levels, hence deterring investment in the long term. They contend that investors are driven by an impetus to mitigate financial risk through portfolio cutting as a response to unfavourable macroeconomic environments.

Inflation pressures, traditionally captured by the consumer price index (CPI), have been shown to be related to investment behaviour. Naik (2024) uncovers that higher CPI levels induce fear of inflation increases, negative impacts on investor sentiment and market stability. Similarly, Singh's (2024) study pinpoints the role of GDP growth in improving investor confidence and stock market performance by employing an OLS regression model to establish a statistically significant relationship between stock returns and economic growth.

Jain (2024) also discusses the dampening impact of inflation on stock market performance, noting that rising inflation erodes business profitability and advances interest rates ahead and discourages investment. These findings are in line with Nawani et al. (2024), where interest rates are among the determinants of stock behaviour. Stocks are more in value and people invest when interest rates are low, reducing credit charges and raising corporates' profit levels. Interdependencies that exist among investment portfolio dynamics and macroeconomics variables are explained well by their regression model.

14.3. Research Methodology and Hypotheses Development

Quantitative approach is employed in the present study to analyse the impact of stock market performance and macroeconomic variables on the volume of investment portfolio in economic activity. Econometric model structure has been used by the study in specifying the relationship between FPI and key macroeconomic forces like GDP growth, exchange rate movement, inflation rate and security trading volume. The study uses the ARDL model in its analysis of short- and long-run effects of such macroeconomic factors on investment inflows.

In conducting the econometric study, the data were obtained from the Central Bank of the Republic of Uzbekistan (<https://cbu.uz/>), the Statistical Agency under the President of the Republic of Uzbekistan (<https://stat.uz/uz/>) and the Central Securities Depository (<https://uzcsd.uz/>). The data consist of twenty-five observations for the period 2017–2024, based on quarterly data. The econometric model was specified in consideration of the multifactor nature of the time-series data, and the ARDL model was used to analyse both short-run and long-run relationships between variables (Liu et al., 2023).

To analyse the stationarity of the dependent and independent variables, the Unit Root Test was conducted, and then the regression equation estimation of the ARDL model was conducted (Sari et al., 2008). Additionally, Bound Test of cointegration was employed to determine if there is a long-run relationship between the variables, while the Cusum diagnostic test was employed to test the constancy of the estimated parameters over time (Rauf et al., 2018; Zhang et al., 2025). The ARDL model was also employed to test the dependence effect of all the variables in subsequent years (Ali et al., 2017; Muhammad et al., 2025).

Statistical visualisation techniques were employed in econometrics analysis, including scatter plots, graphical matrix distribution plots, normal distribution plots, correlation matrices, time-series analytical plots and diagrams illustrating the relation between independent and dependent variables. Furthermore, multicollinearity tests were carried out to ensure the stability of the econometric results.

The ARDL model has been widely applied in econometric studies for being an effective estimator of short-run and long-run relations in time-series data. This approach allows for the inclusion of lagged dependent and independent variables, providing more complete information on economic relations. As Sahnoune and Lagoune (2024) explain, the ARDL model is applicable regardless of whether the variables are $I(0)$ or $I(1)$ and therefore is adaptable to data sets aggregated at different levels. Similarly, A. Rajarathinam stresses that the ARDL model allows us to test for cointegration between variables, which provides us with information on long-run equilibrium relationships. The model also contains an error correction mechanism for adjusting short-run deviations towards long-run equilibrium.

Analyses and forecasts have been conducted using multivariate linear regression (LS), ARDL, ARIMA and other various econometric models on factors affecting remittances, energy intensity and economic development, energy policy, energy risk, environmental status and the impact of environmental aspects on the digital economy, agricultural productivity and the stability of the US credit market (Jakhongir et al., 2024; Sharipov et al., 2025; Caporin et al., 2024; Ngongo et al., 2025; PANJAITAN et al., 2025; Pradhan et al., 2025; Rayala et al., 2025; Romero et al., 2025).

Hussein et al. (2024) confirm that the ARDL model effectively deals with stationary time-series data, as it makes it possible to model long-run relationships without pre-testing for unit roots. In Muhammad Adnan Hye's (2012) empirical study, the ARDL model was employed to check the influence of macroeconomic factors such as government spending, imports and exports on GDP and discovered significant long-run relations. Further, Husain et al. (2024) confirmed that by the application of the ARDL model, it is evident that exchange rate misalignment significantly affects long-run economic growth, with undervaluation enhancing growth while overvaluation deterring it.

Another group of economists has successfully used econometric models such as Fixed Effects Estimator, Random Effects Estimator, multivariate linear (LS) and ARDL in their research on investment in digital infrastructure, various aspects of digital payment systems, the impact of inflation and credit interest rates on investment, factors affecting the reduction of the state's share in commercial banks, Non-Performing Loans in commercial banks, the digitisation of banks, risks in digital services and the development of retail payment services (Habib et al., 2025; Jahrir et al., 2025; Khayrilla et al., 2025; Rayala et al., 2025; Rony et al., 2025; Mamadiyarov et al., 2024;).

By integrating these econometric methods, the study ensures a rigorous and thorough examination of the relationship between stock market performance, macroeconomic determinants and FPI and provides insight into investment behaviour in the domestic economy.

The formula for the ARDL model is given below.

$$Y_t = \alpha_0 + \sum\nolimits_{i=1}^{n} \gamma_i y_{t-i} + \sum\nolimits_{j=1}^{r} \vartheta_j z_{t-j} + \varepsilon_t \quad (1)$$

Here, Y_t is the dependent variable at time t; z_t is the independent variable(s) at time t; α_0 is the intercept term; γ_i is the coefficients of the lagged outcome variable (autoregressive terms); ϑ is the coefficients of the current and lagged factors (distributed lag terms); n is the number of lags for the outcome variable; r is the number of lags for the independent variables; ε_t is the error term;

All variables in the econometric model are natural logarithmised.

Below are all variables in the econometric model.

Variables:

The total value of portfolio foreign investments is *lnportf_invest* (resulting variable),

The volume of securities trading turnover in the national economy is *lnfinanc_market* (independent variable), the GDP growth rate in the national economy is *lnGDP_growth* (independent variable), the exchange rate change in the national economy is *lnexchange_rate* (independent variable), the inflation rate in the national economy is *lninfl_rate* (independent variable).

In the development of econometric research, the main (H_0) and alternative (H_1) hypotheses were reflected.

The structure of the hypothesis in the combined model:

Main hypothesis (H_0): The volume of securities trading turnover in the national economy, GDP growth rate, exchange rate changes and inflation rate do not significantly affect the total value of Portfolio foreign investments and there are no signs of correlation.

Alternative hypothesis (H_1): The volume of securities trading turnover in the national economy, GDP growth rate, exchange rate changes and inflation rate do significantly affect the total value of Portfolio foreign investments and demonstrate a strong correlation.

14.4. Analysis and Results

At the initial stage of the econometric study, descriptive statistical values were expressed for the total value of Portfolio foreign investments and the factors affecting it (Table 31).

Table 31. Descriptive statistical indicators on the total value of portfolio foreign investments and factors influencing it

	lnportf_ invest	lnsecurity_ market	lnGDP_ growth	lninfl_rate	lnexchange_ rate
Mean	4.717404	4.591786	4.634931	4.760128	4.621136
Maximum	5.52488	4.768919	5.008309	5.148496	5.346911
Minimum	4.460179	4.236182	4.231996	4.024587	4.081993
Std. Dev	0.2164882	0.1566224	0.1919136	0.2797601	0.3740007
Std. Err.	0.0432976	0.0313245	0.0383827	0.055952	0.0748001
Skewness	2.13606	-1.074158	-0.5318115	-1.499443	0.7259655
Kurtosis	8.790812	2.883334	2.835972	4.783543	2.346787
Observation	25	25	25	25	25

Source: It was developed by the authors based on Stata software.

The analysis of Table 31 shows that the descriptive statistics of the econometric study have established statistically significant confidence intervals for the total portfolio of foreign investments and the variables affecting it. The resulting and influencing variables represent a complete set of twenty-five observations that provide positive conclusions and strong support for the next stage of data analysis. This process represents the possibilities of forming an econometric model. It means that all variables are distributed in a similar range and assume comparable magnitudes in the data set.

According to the study, a graphical representation of the total value of the portfolio of foreign investments and the variables affecting it over time was developed (Figure 37).

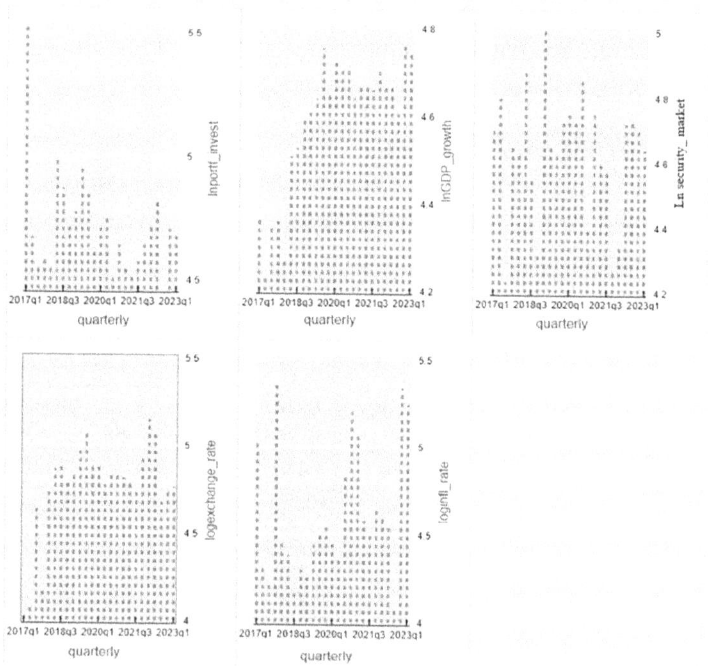

Figure 37. Analytical graphical representation of the total value of portfolio foreign investments and the factors influencing it over time.
Source: It was developed by the authors based on Stata software.

According to the data of Figure 37, the total value of portfolio foreign investments and the factors affecting it show a stochastic trend. This figure allows us to draw positive conclusions about the ARDL model and show a positive trend in the prospective forecast indicators for all variables in the model.

At the same time, the time dependence diagram shows positive trends in GDP growth and financial market indicators, indicating the stability of the volume of foreign investments in the national economy. The seasonal periodic trend shows the correspondence of factors to macroeconomic conditions in FPIs and shows a balanced set of data when building an econometric model. From the data of Figure 37, it can be seen that fluctuations in the volume of GDP and the volume of securities trading turnover proportionally form the growth dynamics.

The next stage of the econometric study is the graphical matrix and scatter plot representation of the dependent and independent variables (Figures 38–39).

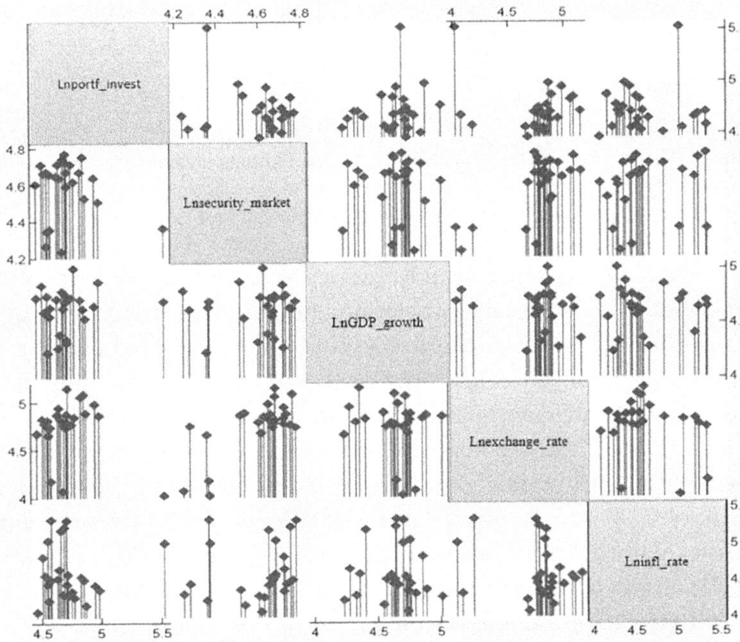

Figure 38. Graphic matrix representation of the total value of portfolio foreign investments and the factors affecting it.
Source: It was developed by the authors based on Stata software.

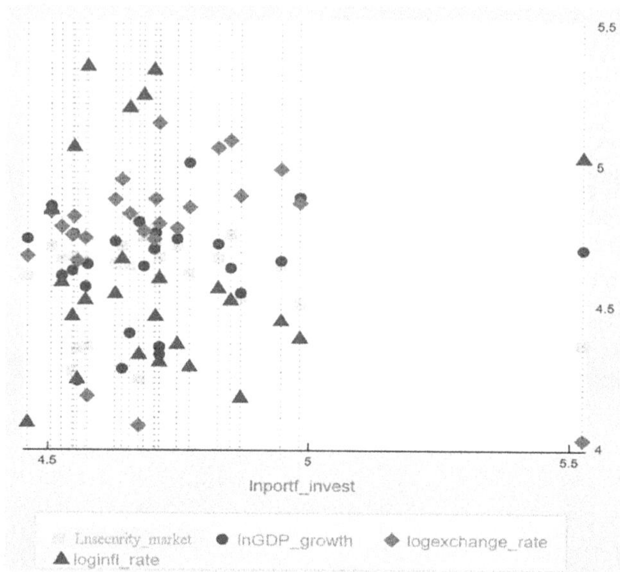

Figure 39. Scatter plot of the total value of portfolio foreign investments and the factors affecting it.
Source: It was developed by the authors based on Stata software.

According to the econometric study, Figures 38 and 39 show a strong correlation between the results and the determinants, and demonstrate the density effect in the data set. This indicates a systematic relationship between the total value of portfolio foreign investments and the factors affecting it, and the possibility of effective modelling of the econometric equation.

These plots indicate a potential positive relationship, indicating that the growth of the total value of portfolio foreign investments led to the development of GDP and the activity of the volume of trading turnover in the securities market. At the same time, the scatter plot reveals the variability in the relationship between factors such as GDP, securities, exchange rate and the total value of portfolio investments.

The visualisation of the data set in the graphical representation is positive and suitable for further statistical and econometric analysis, and provides important conclusions on investment trends.

In the next step, a connected distribution graph is drawn by the total value of the Portfolio foreign investments and the factors affecting it (Figure 40).

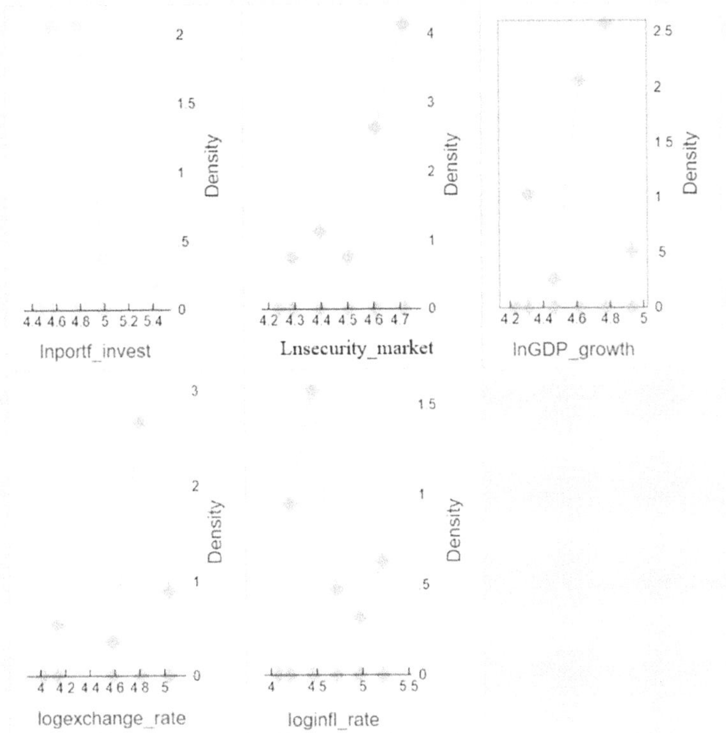

Figure 40. Rconnected distribution graph by total value of portfolio foreign investments and factors influencing it.
Source: It was developed by the authors based on Stata software.

According to Figure 40, the density of the total value of portfolio foreign investments initially increased significantly, but in subsequent periods there was a sharp decrease, indicating that most of these data points were concentrated in a certain range of values.

From the data in the table, it can be seen that the positive trend of GDP growth is determined in conjunction with the attraction of foreign investments, and the GDP growth density scheme shows a possible correlation with portfolio investments. In the national economy, the turnover of securities through the stock market creates convenience for foreign investments, and the increase in the density of the financial market creates the basis for a further increase in the efficiency of foreign investments in this area.

According to the positive distribution graph of the total value of portfolio foreign investments, the trend of GDP growth, financial market conditions, exchange rate stability and inflation rate together determine investment flows, and play an important role in attracting foreign capital.

The study developed a correlation matrix between the total value of FPIs and the factors influencing them (Table 32).

Table 32. Correlation matrix of the total value of portfolio foreign investments and factors affecting it

Variables lnexchange_ rate	**(1)**	**(2)**	**(3)**	**(4)**	**(5)**	**Signifi- cant**
(1) lnportf_invest	1.000					
(2) lnsecurity_ market	0.6329	1.000				
	(0.0421)					***
(3) lnGDP_growth	0.5702	0.5329	1.000			
	(0.0025)	(0.0209)				***
(4) lninfl_rate	−0.6013	−0.5900	−0.4112	1.000		
	(0.0071)	(0.0104)	(0.0302)			***
(5) lnexchange_ rate	−0.5024	−0.4723	−0.3309	−0.3015	1.000	
	(0.0869)	(0.0921)	(0.018)	(0.0784)		*

Source: It was developed by the authors based on Stata software.

According to the results of Table 32, the portfolio demonstrated a strong, stable and inverse correlation between the total value of foreign investments and the factors affecting it. The significant positive correlation between GDP growth and the volume of securities trading turnover indicated a strong impact on the volume of portfolio investments. The inverse relationship between the inflation rate and the exchange rate has an indirect effect on the reduction of the volume of portfolio investments. It also emphasises the need to maximally control the inflation rate and the exchange rate by demonstrating activity in the national economy.

Also, taking into account the fact that the *p*-value according to the table is less than 0.05, the condition of its statistical significance for the correlation coefficient is met.

At the next stage, a Unit-root test was conducted to determine the stationarity of the volume of state purchases made in the economy and the factors affecting it (Table 33).

Table 33. Unit-root test indicators for the total value of portfolio foreign investments and factors affecting it

Variables	Test Statistic	1% Critical Value	5% Critical Value	10% Critical Value	p-value for Z(t)
lnportf_invest	-7.308	-3.750	-3.000	-2.630	0.0000
lnsecurity_market	-8.054	-3.750	-3.000	-2.630	0.0000
lnGDP_growth	-7.807	-3.750	-3.000	-2.630	0.0000
lninfl_rate	-6.787	-3.750	-3.000	-2.630	0.0000
lnexchange_rate	-6.594	-3.750	-3.000	-2.630	0.0000

Source: It was developed by the authors based on Stata software.

According to Table 33, the unit root test value of the resulting factor is – 7.308, and the test results of the independent variables are – 8.054, – 7.807, – 7.807 and – 6.594, respectively. These values indicate the statistical significance and coherence of the total value of the portfolio foreign investment and the factors affecting it.

From the table data, it can be seen that the McKinnon's value of 0.0000 is statistically significant for the critical values of *Z*(*t*). Also, the results of the unit root test indicate the stationarity of the total value of the portfolio foreign investment and the factors affecting it after the initial integration. In the next stage of the econometric study, a regression equation was developed using the ARDL model (see Table 34).

Table 34. Regression equation indicators based on the ARDL(1,2,1,2,2) model of the total value of portfolio foreign investments and factors affecting it

ARDL(1,2,1,2,2) regression
Sample: 2017q3 thru 2023q1
Log likelihood = 39.712114

Number of obs = 23
R-squared = 0.9350
Adj *R*-squared = 0.8570
Root MSE = 0.0653

D.lnportf_invest	Coefficient	Std. err	*t*	*P* > *t*	[95%	conf. interval]	Sig
ADJ							
lnportf_invest							
L1.	−1.477	0.176	−8.400	0.000	−1.869	−1.086	***
LR							
lnsecurity_market	0.217	0.083	2.630	0.025	0.033	0.401	***
lnGDP_growth	0.486	0.124	3.940	0.003	0.211	0.762	
lnexchange_rate	−0.316	0.172	−1.840	0.096	−0.700	0.067	*
lninfl_rate	−0.197	0.069	−2.870	0.017	−0.349	−0.044	***
SR							
lnsecurity_market							
D1.	1.275	0.309	4.130	0.002	0.587	1.962	***
LD.	0.551	0.248	2.220	0.051	−0.002	1.105	**
lnGDP_growth							
D1.	−0.214	0.082	−2.590	0.027	−0.397	−0.030	***
lnexchange_rate							
D1.	−0.228	0.143	−1.600	0.141	−0.547	0.090	
LD.	0.198	0.104	1.900	0.086	−0.034	0.430	*
lninfl_rate							
D1.	0.221	0.073	3.020	0.013	0.058	0.385	***
LD.	0.212	0.075	2.820	0.018	0.044	0.380	***
_cons	5.422	1.278	4.240	0.002	2.574	8.270	***

Source: It was developed by the authors based on Stata software.

The ARDL model formula is given below.

$$ln(portf\_invest)_t = \alpha + \beta_1\, ln(security\_market)t + \beta_2\, ln(GDP\_growth)_t - \beta_3\, ln(exchange\_rate)_t - \beta_4\, ln(infl\_rate)_t + \epsilon_t$$

The econometric equation for long-run relationships based on the ARDL(1,2,1,2,2) model is given below:

$$ln(portf\_invest)_t = \alpha + 0.21 ln(security\_market)t + 0.48 ln(GDP\_growth)_t - 0.31 ln(exchange\_rate)_t - 0.19 ln(infl\_rate)_t + \epsilon_t \quad (2)$$

General description of the ARDL(1,2,1,2,2) model.

R-squared value: The *R*-squared value is 0.9350, which provides a qualitative indicator of the model with approximately 93.50 per cent of the total value of the portfolio foreign investment and the variables affecting it. A high value of *R*-squared indicates a strong effect of the model on the observed data. The value of Log likelihood: 39.712114 indicates a positive assessment of the fit of the econometric equation.

The value of Root MSE: 0.0653, which reflects the mean error in forecasting the dependent variable, indicates that the forecasting performance of the model is reliable, since this value is low.

According to the econometric study, the ARDL(1,2,1,2,2) model was tested and the results showed a statistical significance of 0.05 for the *F*-statistic and *t*-statistic. As a result, the null hypothesis was rejected, which ensures the acceptance of the alternative hypothesis (H_1).

The model cointegration status was tested using the ARDL(1,2,1,2,2) Bound test, Bound *F*- and *t*-tests (see Tables 35 and 36).

Table 35. Bound F-test for cointegration

					F = 17.508
	[I_0] [I_1]	[I_0] [I_1]	[I_0] [I_1]	[I_0] [I_1]	
	L_1 L_1	L_05 L_05	L_025 L_025	L_01 L_01	
K_4	2.45 3.52	2.86 4.01	3.25 4.49	3.74 5.06	

Source: It was developed by the authors based on Stata software.

Based on Table 35, it means that there is cointegration in the model, according to which the *F* statistic value is 17.508, which indicates that this value is above the critical limit for each period. This value indicates a positive result of the Bound test for the *F*-statistic value.

Table 36. Bound t-test for cointegration

					F = – 8.400
	[I_0] [I_1]	[I_0] [I_1]	[I_0] [I_1]	[I_0] [I_1]	
	L_1 L_1	L_05 L_05	L_025 L_025	L_01_01	
K_3	-2.57 -3.66	-2.86 -3.99	-3.13 -4.26	-3.43 -4.60	

Source: It was developed by the authors based on Stata software.

According to Table 36, the *t*-statistic value is –8.400, which is greater than the critical limits for all intervals and indicates the presence of cointegration according to the bound *t* test. According to it, the Bound test showed a positive result for the *t*-statistic value.

14.5. Findings and Discussion

According to the ARDL(1,2,1,2,2) model, a 1 per cent increase in the volume of securities trading in the national economy leads to an increase in the total value of portfolio foreign investments by 0.21 per cent. A 1 per cent increase in the GDP growth rate in the national economy leads to an increase in the total value of portfolio foreign investments by 0.48 per cent. A 1 per cent increase in the exchange rate in the national economy leads to a decrease in the total value of portfolio foreign investments by 0.31 per cent. Also, a 1 per cent increase in the inflation rate in the national economy leads to a decrease in the total value of portfolio foreign investments by 0.19 per cent.

In the next step of the research, the CUSUM diagnostic test was tested on the ARDL(1,2,1,2,2) model (Figure 41).

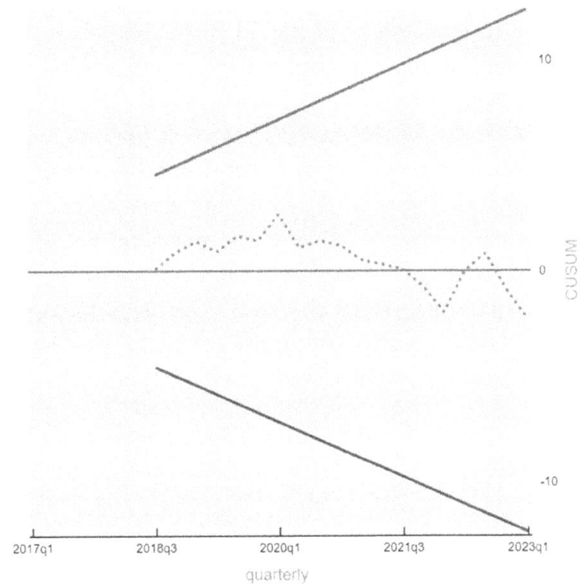

Figure 41. CUSUM diagnostic test graph.
Source: It was developed by the authors based on Stata software.

The CUSUM (Cumulative Sum) diagnostic test used in the ARDL(1,2,1,2,2) model included the following hypotheses to assess the stability of the econometric equation parameters over time:

1. *Null hypothesis (H_0 – Main hypothesis)*:
   The model is stable over time (there are no systematic changes in the parameters). The residuals follow a stable process, which indicates that the estimated parameters of the ARDL((1,2,1,2,2) model do not change during the sample period.
2. *Alternative hypothesis (H_1 – Alternative hypothesis)*:
   The ARDL(1,2,1,2,2) model is not stable over time (there is a systematic change in the parameters). The residuals show instability, which indicates that the model parameters may have changed at certain points in the sample period.

According to the interpretation of the CUSUM diagnostic result for the ARDL(1,2,1,2,2) model:

The CUSUM test for the ARDL model shows that the null hypothesis (H_0) is maintained, which confirms the successful stability of the econometric model over the analysed period. Based on the econometric equation, the relationship between the total value of the portfolio foreign investment and the factors affecting it is consistent, and no systematic changes and instability of the parameters are observed. Also, the diagnostic test The statistics remained within significant limits during the analysed period and no significant deviations were observed.

14.6. Conclusion

This study has been geared towards investigating the intricate relationship between stock market performance, fundamental macroeconomic determinants and magnitude of FPI in the domestic economy.

The following proposals and recommendations were developed as a result of the analysis and conclusions of the study on the interaction between the volume of securities trading turnover, GDP growth rate, exchange rate changes, inflation rate and the total value of portfolio foreign investments in the national economy according to the ARDL(1,2,1,2,2) regression model.

According to the ARDL(1,2,1,2,2) model:

1. Assessing the impact of the volume of securities trading shows a one percent increase in the volume of securities trading leads to an increase in FPI by 0.21 percent. According to this result, a more active and liquid financial market attracts foreign investors, as it leads to better opportunities for effective trading and higher returns.
2. Assessing the significance of the impact of GDP growth reveal a 1 percent increase in GDP growth leads to an increase in FPI by 0.48 percent. According to this result, economic growth demonstrates stability and solid profitability, which mobilises foreign shareholders to allocate more financial resources to economic processes. High GDP growth leads to an increase in corporate profitability, increased investor confidence and

improved profitability indicators in the stock market, which makes the country more attractive to foreign capital.

3. Assessing the significance of the impact of the exchange rate demonstrate a one percent depreciation of the exchange rate causes a 0.31 per cent decrease in FPI. According to this result, the depreciation of the exchange rate causes financial distress for foreign shareholders and investors, which in turn reduces the value of their income when converted into their national currency. A weak national currency increases various financial risks, which significantly affects the reduction of capital and the flow of investments.
4. Assessing the impact of the inflation rate showcase a one percent increase in the inflation rate causes a 0.19 per cent decrease in FPI. According to this econometric equation, high inflation leads to a decrease in real investment returns, which creates a negative environment for the attractiveness of domestic assets for foreign investors. Inflation also increases uncertainty, creating economic instability and weakening investor confidence.
5. In order for a country to attract more FPI, it is necessary for the government to focus on increasing financial market activity and maintaining GDP growth. Ensuring exchange rate stability and controlling inflation are important in preventing capital outflows.
6. FPI in the national economy is highly responsive to market conditions, such as economic growth and the volume of securities trading, but it also demonstrates sensitivity to exchange rate fluctuations and inflationary pressures. A stable macroeconomic environment conducive to growth, financial market development and currency stability allow for the development of foreign investment flows.

Bibliography

Abdullah, M. A., Han, X., Amjad, M. A., & Makhmudov, S. (2025). Revisit the role of financial development on economic growth, human development, and sustainable development in higher-income countries. Journal of Environmental Management, 392, 126874.

Akhmetshin, E., Abdullayev, I., Makhmudov, S., Dakhkilgova, K., Korotaeva, I. and Yanovskaya, G. (2025). APPLICATION OF TANH–COTH METHOD FOR COMBINED AND DOUBLE COMBINED SINH–COSH–GORDON EQUATIONS ARISING CHEMICAL REACTIONS TO WATER SURFACE GRAVITY WAVES. Computational Methods for Differential Equations, (), -. doi: 10.22034/cmde.2025.67655.3234

Ali, W., Abdullah, A., and Azam, M. (2017). 'Re-visiting the Environmental Kuznets Curve Hypothesis for Malaysia: Fresh Evidence from ARDL Bounds Testing Approach'. *Renewable and Sustainable Energy Reviews*, 77, 990–1000.

Caporin, M., Shahbaz, M., Kuziboev, B., Masharipova, M., Allaberganov, S., & Makhmudov, S. (2024). Environmental Kuznets Curve for extended brics economies: do women governance and water stress matter?. International Journal of Energy Economics and Policy, 14(6), 174–183.

Habib, S. S., Islam, M. A., Ali, M. N., Benitez, I. B., Mamadiyarov, Z., Mirzayev, B., … & Flah, A. (2025). Multi-Objective Optimization and Feasibility Analysis of Integrated Biogas–Solar Energy Systems for Rural Electrification. Results in Engineering, 107086.

Husain, S., Baig, I. A., Rana, M., and Khalid, B. (2024). 'Revisiting the Long-run and Short-run Relationship between Economic Growth, Exchange Rate, Money Supply, and Government Expenditure: Empirical Evidence from India Using the NARDL Approach'. <https://doi.org/10.21203/rs.3.rs-5286346/v1>.

Hussein, M., and Hmood, M. Y. (2024). 'Nonstationary Time Series Models Using ARDL and NARDL Estimation'. مجلة العلوم الاقتصادية والادارية 30 (141), 439–56. <https://doi.org/10.33095/afbrge60>.

Jahrir, A., Gultom, Y., Herman, H., Zabadi, F., Ngongo, M., Mamadiyarov, Z., Fatmawati, E., & Saputra, N. (2025). Investigating the Elements of Short Commercial Mineral Water Advertisement: A Case on Discourse Analysis. Studies in Media and Communication, 13(4), 94–104. doi: http://dx.doi.org/10.11114/smc.v13i4.7813

Jakhongir, S., Muhabbat, H., Khayrilla, K., Kholmuratov, S., Nazirjon, R., Nilufar, F., and Farxod, T. (2024). 'Crafting a Neutrosophic-Driven Tool to Probe Turnover Propensities in Manufacturing Entities'. *International Journal of Neutrosophic Science (IJNS)*, 23 (2).

Jain, K. (2024). 'Economic Indicators and Stock Market Performance: An Analysis of GDP, Unemployment Rates, and Inflation'. *IOSR Journal of Economics and Finance*. <https://doi.org/10.9790/5933-1505031622>.

Khayrilla Kurbonov, Samariddin Makhmudov, Shakhzod Erkinov, Umidjon Dadabaev, Gulnora Bekimbetova, Rukhiddin Zayniddinov, and Mirzabek Jonuzokov. 2025. Evaluating the Impact of Marketing Practices Digitalization and Investment on Labor Market Efficiency and Commercial Bank Performance Using Econometric Models. In Proceedings of the 8th International Conference on Future Networks & Distributed Systems (ICFNDS '24). Association for Computing Machinery, New York, NY, USA, 786–796. https://doi.org/10.1145/3726122.3726237.

Khodjaniyazov, N., Mirkhoshimova, M., Kalandarov, F., Matyokubova, D., Utegenova, S., Makhmudov, S., & Khudayberganov, M. (2025). Time-Varying Impacts of Financial Stress on Energy-Related Uncertainty. International Journal of Energy Economics and Policy, 15(3), 689–698.

Kuziboev, B., Khodjaniyazov, E., Ozturk, I., Sabirov, K., Makhmudov, S., & Utegenova, S. (2025). Does oil dependence cause energy risk?. Energy Nexus, 17, 100393.

Li, B., Yang, J., Wang, Y., and Niu, J. (2022). 'Research on the Relationship Between Macroeconomic Indicators and Stock Market Value'. *Proceedings of Business and Economic Studies* 5 (5), 158–63. <https://doi.org/10.26689/pbes.v5i5.4243>.

Lin, M.H., Matchanova, B., Nurmatovich, H.A. et al. Optimal Operation of the Multi-Carrier Energy System Considering Energy Markets and Renewable Energies Participation. Int. J. Appl. Comput. Math 11, 170 (2025). https://doi.org/10.1007/s40819-025-02002-9

Liu, H., Wong, W. K., Cong, P. T., Nassani, A. A., Haffar, M., and Abu-Rumman, A. (2023). 'Linkage among Urbanization, Energy Consumption, Economic Growth and Carbon Emissions. Panel Data Analysis for China Using ARDL Model'. *Fuel*, 332, 126122.

Litamahuputty, J. V., Amiruddin, E. G., Rahim, R., Rahman, A., & Mamadiyarov, Z. (2025). Cryptocurrency Risk Management through Decision Engineering: Evaluating XRPUSD and ADAUSD Portfolio Performance. Journal of Applied Science, Engineering, Technology, and Education, 7(1), 69–81. https://doi.org/10.35877/454RI.asci3871

Mamadiyarov, Z., Eshov, M., Otakhonova, D., Utegenova, S., Sabirov, K., Marks, A., & Bahodirov, N. (2025). Does Energy Policy Risk Threaten Energy Sources Diversification?. International Journal of Energy Economics and Policy, 15(5), 730–740. https://doi.org/10.32479/ijeep.21140

Mamadiyarov, Z., Saidov, O., Abdurazakova, N., Makhmudov, S., Nazarov, M., Rajabova, N., … Ruzmetova, I. (2025). Energy-Related Uncertainty and Tourism Stock Markets: New Insights from Time-Varying Relationship with TVP- VAR Approach. *International Journal of Energy Economics and Policy*, *15*(4), 730–737. https://doi.org/10.32479/ijeep.20480

Mamani, J.C.M., Miri, M., Vorobev, Y. et al. Optimal Operation of Energy Microgrid Considering Economic and Emission Indices. Oper. Res. Forum 6, 122 (2025). https://doi.org/10.1007/s43069-025-00523-z

Muhammad Adnan Hye, Q. (2012). 'Exports, Imports and Economic Growth in China: An ARDL Analysis'. *Journal of Chinese Economic and Foreign Trade Studies*, 5 (1), 42–55.

Muhammad Zubair, Irfanud Din, Nadeem Sarwar et al. Revolutionizing Sepsis Diagnosis Using Machine Learning and Deep Learning Models: A Systematic Literature Review, 10 June 2025, PREPRINT (Version 1) available at Research Square [https://doi.org/10.21203/rs.3.rs-6731418/v1]

Naik, A. (2024). 'Impact of Macroeconomic Factors on the Indian Stock Market'. *Indian Scientific Journal of Research in Engineering And Management*, 8 (05), 1–5. <https://doi.org/10.55041/ijsrem32511>.

Nawani, A., Khanra, P., Dhalwani, S., and Birari, A. (2024). 'Factor Analysis for Portfolio Returns: Investigating How Macroeconomic Factors Impact the Performance of the Equity Portfolio', 1–5. <https://doi.org/10.1109/tqcebt59414.2024.10545071>.

Ngongo, M., Herman, H., Ndandara, A., Jois Jaha, D. A., Peku Djawang, J. U. S., Tanggu Rame, M. M., Khamraeva, S. N., & Mamadiyarov, Z. (2025). An Investigation of Meaning, Toponymy of Sumba Cultural Site's Names, and the Impact of Tourism Visitors on Surrounding Society. Forum for Linguistic Studies, 7(8), 679–693. https://doi.org/10.30564/fls.v7i8.10260

PANJAITAN, M. B., HAMDANAH, H., SIRAIT, J., SUTIKNO, S., FATMAWATI, E., HERMAN, H., & MAMADIYAROV, Z. (2025). THE ROLE OF EMOTIONAL REGULATION IN SHAPING STUDENTS'

PERCEPTION OF PHYSICS PROBLEMSOLVING TASKS. TPM – Testing, Psychometrics, Methodology in Applied Psychology, 32(S2(2025) : Posted 09 June), 1–10. Retrieved from https://tpmap.org/submission/index.php/tpm/article/view/139

Phuong, L. C. M., Quynh, T. T., Vi, H. L. T., and Truc, D. T. K. (2023). 'Impact of Macro Factors on Stock Market Capitalization'. *VNU University of Economics and Business*, 3 (2), 60–60.

Pradhan, R., Hajiyev, E., Shichiyakh, R. et al. Optimal Techno-Economic Feasibility of an Off-Grid Microgrid System Using Load Flow Energy Management Strategies. *Oper. Res. Forum* **6**, 120 (2025). https://doi.org/10.1007/s43069-025-00524-y

Rajarathinam, A. (2023). A Study on Dynamic Relationships between the Area and Production of Food Grain Crops Based on ARDL Model and Bound Cointegration Test, 47–63. <https://doi.org/10.9734/bpi/aobmer/v4/7610a>.

Rauf, A., Zhang, J., Li, J., and Amin, W. (2018). 'Structural Changes, Energy Consumption and Carbon Emissions in China: Empirical Evidence from ARDL Bound Testing Model'. *Structural Change and Economic Dynamics*, 47, 194–206.

Rayala, R. V., Borra, C. R., Vasudevan, V., Singhania, R., Cheekati, S., & Mamadiyarov, Z. (2025, July). Lightweight Deep Learning Framework for Human Activity Recognition: A MobileNet-LSTM Approach with WHOA Optimization. In *2025 International Conference on Innovations in Intelligent Systems: Advancements in Computing, Communication, and Cybersecurity (ISAC3)* (pp. 1–6). IEEE.

Rayala, R. V., Sandhya, N., Singhania, R., Cheekati, S., Borra, C. R., Vasudevan, V., & Mamadiyarov, Z. (2025, July). AI-Driven Tomato Quality Assessment: A Deep Learning Approach for Image-based Defect Detection and Classification. In *2025 International Conference on Innovations in Intelligent Systems: Advancements in Computing, Communication, and Cybersecurity (ISAC3)* (pp. 1–6). IEEE.

Romero, R. M., Zelinskaya, M., Makhmudov, S., Sapaev, S., & Rustambekovich, J. U. (2025, September). Modelling and Optimal Utilisation of the Renewable Energy Systems in Microgrid with Improving Reliability and Energy Efficiency. In Operations Research Forum (Vol. 6, No. 3, pp. 1–20). Springer International Publishing.

Rony, Z. T., Jefri, R., Rusmardiana, A., Pramono, S. A., & Mamadiyarov, Z. (2025). Downside Risk Measurement of Indonesian Financial and Energy Securities: A Value at Risk Perspective. Journal of Applied Science, Engineering, Technology, and Education, 7(2). https://doi.org/10.35877/454RI.asci3898

Sahnoune, F., and Lagoune, S. (2024). 'The Use of the Joint Simultaneous Integration Methodology to Measure the Impact of Certain Macroeconomic Variables on the GDP: ARDL Model'. *Journal of Innovations and Sustainability*, 8 (2), 04, <https://doi.org/10.51599/is.2024.08.02.04>.

Sari, R., Ewing, B. T., and Soytas, U. (2008). 'The Relationship between Disaggregate Energy Consumption and Industrial Production in the United States: An ARDL Approach'. *Energy Economics*, 30 (5), 2302–13.

Singagerda, F. S., Pratama, M. R., Alfairus, M. Q., Iskandar, A., & Mamadiyarov, Z. (2025). A Decision-Centric Approach to Risk Management in Aviation Stock Investments Using Value at Risk and Portfolio Optimization. Journal of Applied Science, Engineering, Technology, and Education, 7(1), 114–125. https://doi.org/10.35877/454RI.asci3870

Sofyanty, D., Romadhoni, R., Handriadi, H., Makhsudovna, I. S., Anwar, Z., & Mamadiyarov, Z. (2025). Strategic Decision Analysis for Investment Portfolios: Computational Risk Assessment in Transportation Asset Management. *Journal of Applied Science, Engineering, Technology, and Education*, 7(2). https://doi.org/10.35877/454RI.asci3897

Singh, D. (2024). 'Impact of Macroeconomics Factors on Stok Market Performance "A Panel Data Analysis."' *Indian Scientific Journal of Research in Engineering and Management*, 8 (12), 1–5, <https://doi.org/10.55041/ijsrem40086>.

Sharipov, K., Abdullayev, I., Kuziboev, B., Makhmudov, S., Kalandarov, F., Khaytboeva, N., & Ilkhamova, Z. (2025). The Effect of Energy Policy Risk on Renewable Energy. International Journal of Energy Economics and Policy, 15(2), 566.

Sofyanty, D., Romadhoni, R., Handriadi, H., Makhsudovna, I. S., Anwar, Z., & Mamadiyarov, Z. (2025). Strategic Decision Analysis for Investment Portfolios: Computational Risk Assessment in

Transportation Asset Management. Journal of Applied Science, Engineering, Technology, and Education, 7(2). https://doi.org/10.35877/454RI.asci3897

Zhang, L., Zhao, Z., Qamri, G. M., & Makhmudov, S. (2025). Unleashing the critical role of renewable energy through global value chains and digitalization: A path towards environmental sustainability. Journal of Environmental Management, 392, 126688.

Zhao, Q., Pervaiz, A., Makhmudov, S., & Fatima, A. (2025). Do environmental stringent policies enhance the impact of renewable energy on CO2 reduction? Evidence from BRICS-T economies. Journal of Environmental Management, 391, 126464.

Evaluating the Influence of Male and Female Employment on Macroeconomic Indicators within the Labour Market

Bobur Khonturayev, Sadirdin Khudoykulov, Zokir Mamadiyarov, Nargiza Xudayberdiyeva, Fakhriddin Isaev, Zilola Tolametova and Muyassarxon Mirzakarimova

15.1. Introduction

The involvement of women and men in the labour market remains a topic of ongoing scientific interest due to its importance for economic growth and social development. Scientific research emphasises the relationship between women's and men's gender-specific labour force participation and macroeconomic indicators. Modern economic analyses and economic models have shown that women's and men's participation in the labour market have different economic outcomes. In addition to social welfare, women's labour market participation has a positive impact on household incomes, investment in human capital and purchasing power. The impact of women's and men's employment indicators on macroeconomic outcomes remains a subject of active discussion and scientific research.

Several empirical studies have examined how gender gaps in employment can affect gross domestic product (GDP) and productivity levels. This study shows that higher female labour force participation has a positive impact on labour force diversification, household income growth and human capital development, particularly on economic growth. Conversely, some assessments suggest that a strong dependence on male labour, especially in networks traditionally dominated by men, is characterised by a differentiated labour market, or may indicate a decrease in income in an environment where opportunities for both sexes are unequally distributed. However, the evidence in this area may not overlap due to stylistic techniques, data quality and changes in the specific social and economic foundations of different countries.

In European and Central Asian countries, demographic dynamics, evolving cultural norms and changing economic structures have influenced changes in rates of male and female workforce participation. Systematic reforms, globalisation and the spread of education in recent decades have had a significant impact on women's career opportunities. Moving from a centrally planned economy to a market-oriented economy, many countries in the region have experienced significant changes in institutional frameworks and social programmes. These changes include changes in Family Policy, parental leave structures and the emergence of new service areas, all redefining benefits and limitations for women to participate in labour and continue in labour. In addition, migration trends, technological progress and restructuring of production networks have influenced the results of the men's labour market. The decisive aspect of this speech is the changing function of fiscal and social policy in facilitating or hindering inclusive labour markets. Governments that allocate funds for kindergartens, maternity and paternity leave and work-life balance initiatives can track the growth of female workforce participation, which can promote economic growth and increase home welfare. Conversely, inadequate political grounds may limit existing barriers, such as gender disparities in wages, occupational segregation and the possibility of sustainable employment, resulting in limited labour force growth. For male employees, in the process of changing the industry, strategies aimed at retraining, professional development and various employment opportunities are decisive.

Results can lead to larger policies. In particular, they contribute to discussions on the allocation of government resources to support equal labour markets and boost economic growth. By determining the impact of fluctuations in the labour force of women and men on GDP per capita, policymakers can adjust efforts to optimise social welfare. In addition, the findings may help international agencies and non-governmental organisations form gender-dependent economic and social initiatives that promote inclusive development.

This article is organised as follows: the first section covers existing literature on gender-segregated labour participation and macroeconomic outcomes. The methodology then defines the VAR modelling framework and illuminates the dataset. The results section provides empirical facts and interprets them according to relevant theories. The conclusion covers the main ideas, studies the consequences of politics and offers directions for further research.

15.2. Literature Review

Buterin et al. (2023) found that women's labour market participation not only increases household income, but also contributes to higher productivity and financial stability. Klasen (2019) has done various analyses and research in her research on changing fertility rates in developing countries, significant growth in women's education and facilitating women's participation in the workforce. According to researchers, the lack of academic degrees today continues to limit women's economic opportunities. Trends are significantly influenced by the extent to which women's labour force participation is contingent upon their household's economic circumstances, the growth of positions suitable for more educated women relative to their availability, the effectiveness of growth strategies in fostering female employment, and the degree to which women can dismantle occupational barriers within the sectors they predominantly occupy.

Onaran et al. (2019) studied the impact of investment in social infrastructure on the labour market and economic growth. Their research examined the impact of factors such as wages, state policies aimed at social protection of children and the elderly, and women's labour activity on macroeconomic indicators (Sofyanty et al., 2025). By comparing nations employing diverse public expenditure strategies, the authors demonstrate that effectively structured social infrastructure investments can foster equitable growth and enhance long-term productivity. Olsson (2018) examines historical instances of economic recessions to evaluate the stabilising effects of increased female labour force participation.

Szekeres (2010) analyses the relationship between gender differences in economic habits, namely saving and consumption patterns, and macroeconomic performance. Her analysis highlights that diminishing gender imbalance in employment can enhance growth rates and stability within the labour market. Szekeres illustrates, using case studies and comparative analysis, that reducing gender disparities in the workforce benefits both individual welfare and national economic vitality.

Analyses and forecasts have been conducted using multivariate linear regression (LS), ARDL, ARIMA and other various econometric models on factors affecting remittances, energy intensity and economic development, energy policy, energy risk, environmental status and the impact of environmental aspects on the digital economy, agricultural productivity and the stability of the US credit market (Abdullah et al., 2025; Akhmetshin et al., 2025; Cahyani et al., 2025; Caporin et al., 2024; Habib et al., 2025; Kuziboev et al., 2025; Mamadiyarov et al., 2025; Sharipov et al., 2025; Zhang et al., 2025).

The VAR model to conduct an econometric analysis of the relationship between the country's labour market segments and macroeconomic indicators. (Leucci et al. 2014; PANJAITAN et al., 2025; Rayala et al., 2025) effectively used the VAR model to examine lagged correlations between economic variables in their study (Leucci et al., 2014; Mamadiyarov et al., 2025; Mamani et al., 2025; Ngongo et al., 2025; Rony et al., 2025, Samariddin et al., 2025; Zhao et al., 2025). Their study shows that it is more accurate to predict economic changes through GDP and labour participation. Jiti et al. (2023) studied how labour market changes, such as the growth of female employment, significantly affect men's labour patterns and, as a result, GDP per capita. According to the results of this study, it is important to diversify employment by gender.

These studies examine gender-segregated labour market dynamics, the role of women's labour force participation in stimulating economic growth, and trends in the male labour force using sophisticated econometric techniques, particularly VAR models, which can be significant in terms of fluctuations in male and female labour force participation and their impact on the economy over time.

Another group of economists has successfully used econometric models such as Fixed Effects Estimator (FEE), Random Effects Estimator (REE), multivariate linear (LS) and ARDL in their research on investment in digital infrastructure, various aspects of digital payment systems, the impact of inflation and credit interest rates on investment, factors affecting the reduction of the state's share in commercial banks, Non-Performing Loans in commercial banks, the digitalisation of banks, risks in digital services and the development of retail payment services (Kurbonov et al., 2025; Khodjaniyazov et al., 2025; Kuchlarov et al., 2025; Lin et al., 2025; Mamadiyarov et al., 2024; Rayala et al., 2025; Romero et al., 2025; Samariddin et al., 2025; Singagerda et al., 2025).

15.3. Research Methodology

In developing the econometric model, the World Bank (<https://data.worldbank.org/>) and data sources consisting of 33 years of total observations for the period from 1991 to 2022 were used to assess the impact of male and female employment on macroeconomic indicators in the labour market.

Since the data are based on multifactor time series, we used the VAR (Vector Autoregressive model) to develop the econometric equation.

Also, the econometric equation of the VAR model was developed, descriptive statistics were developed, the Unit-root test was used to determine the stationarity of all variables, the Johanson test to determine the congruence of variables, the determination of the optimal lag (delayed years) of the VAR model, the diagnostics of the econometric model, the autocorrelation or stability test and its reliability tests in determining forecast indicators were evaluated.

Graphical representations and statistical tables were developed to assess the analytical trends of the dependent variable and the factors affecting it according to the econometric model. At the same time, multicollinearity tests were conducted for all variables and a correlation matrix was constructed.

VAR models are a powerful tool in econometric research and time series analysis, and are widely used to understand the dynamic relationships between multivariate time series variables. This model is useful in forecasting economic processes, policy analysis and understanding the interrelationships between economic agents. The main features of the VAR model include the ability to identify linear interrelationships between multiple time series, its flexibility in modelling complex systems and its application in various fields such as economics, finance and risk management.

Although VAR models are versatile and widely applicable, they also have limitations. One of the main difficulties is choosing an appropriate lag length, which can significantly affect the performance of the model. In addition, VAR models involve linear relationships, which may not always capture the true dynamics in the data. Despite these limitations, VAR models remain a key factor in econometric analysis due to their ability to provide insight into the complex interdependencies of economic systems (Ghaleb et al., 2025; Litamahuputty et al., 2025; Xingchen, 2015).

The VAR model formula is given below.

1. VAR model structure: A VAR model with k variables and p lags can be expressed as:

$$y_t = c + \sum_{i=0}^{n} A_i Y_{t-i} + e_t \tag{1}$$

Where, y_t represents the $k \times 1$ vector of endogenous variables at time t.
c is a $k \times 1$ vector of constants (intercepts),
A_i is a $k \times k$ matrix of coefficients for lag i.
e_t is a $k \times 1$ vector of error terms, zero mean and covariance matrix.

We have developed forecast indicators for two econometric models for the study, and the variables for the model are presented below.

All variables for the econometric model are presented below.

GDP per capita of the countries of Europe and Central Asia – *logGDP_per_capita* (resultant factor); labour force participation rate of the countries of Europe and Central Asia, women (% of women aged 15–64) – *loglab_rat_fem* (influencing factor, independent variable); Labour force participation rate of the countries of Europe and Central Asia, men (% of women aged 15–64) – *loglab_rat_mel* (influencing factor, independent variable).

According to the econometric forecast;

The econometric equation estimates the interaction between the labour force participation rate of women and the labour force participation rate of men in these countries on the GDP per capita of the countries of Europe and Central Asia.

The hypotheses for the econometric model were formulated as follows:

Null hypothesis (H_0): In the countries of Europe and Central Asia, the level of female labour force participation and the level of male labour force participation do not significantly affect the size of GDP per capita in these countries.

Alternative hypothesis (H_1): In the countries of Europe and Central Asia, the level of female labour force participation and the size of GDP per capita have a significant relationship.

15.4. Analysis and Results

In the first stage of the study, descriptive statistical indicators were calculated for all variables (Table 37).

Table 37. Descriptive statistical indicators of dependent and independent variables according to the econometric model

	logGDP_per_capita	loglab_rat_fem	loglab_rat_mel
Mean	9.806598	4.114633	4.343394
Maximum	10.22439	4.187144	4.369841
Minimum	9.264269	4.067674	4.325109
Std. Dev	0.3549402	0.0354838	0.0133008
Std. Err.	0.0627452	0.0062727	0.0023513
Skewness	0.1259825	0.3530697	0.4186653
Kurtosis	-0.3074037	1.893223	2.008471
Observation	32	32	32

Source: Developed by the authors based on the Stata program.

According to Table 37, the descriptive statistical indicators of the model established positive average values for all variables and formed confidence intervals. This indicates the prospects for the development of important conditions for the forecast indicators of the econometric model in the next stages.

At the next stage of the study, a correlation matrix was developed for each of the resulting variables and the variables affecting it (Table 38).

Table 38. Cross-correlation matrix of the impact of female and male employment in the labour market on GDP per capita in European and Central Asian countries

Variables	(1)	(2)	Significant
(1) logGDP_per_capita	1.000		
(2) loglab_rat_fem	0.8824	1.000	
	(0.0000)		***
(3) loglab_rat_mel	0.4277	0.4752	
	(0.0024)	(0.0060)	***

Source: Developed by the authors based on the Stata program.

According to the above tables, there is a strong and significant correlation between the variables, and the corresponding correlation matrix shows that there is no multicollinearity between the outcome variables and the independent variables. Considering that the *P*-value is less than 0.05, it indicates that the correlation coefficient is reliable and statistically significant.

Before performing the cointegration test, it is necessary to determine the lags of the model, that is, up to which years the relationship remains. The table below shows that the VAR model is perfect in the 4th lagged year (Table 39).

Table 39. Test for determining optimal lags in the VAR model of GDP per capita and factors affecting it in European and Central Asian countries

Delayed years	LL	LR	df	p	FPE	AIC	HQIC	SBIC
1	278.28	217.22	9	0.000	1.1e−12	−19.02	−18.8454*	−18.449*
2	287.018	17.477	9	0.042	1.2e−12	−19.0013	−18.6959	−18.0022
3	297.853	21.669	9	0.010	1.1e−12	−19.1324	−18.696	−17.705
4	308.827	21.949*	9	0.009	1.1e−12*	−19.2734*	−18.7061	−17.4178

Source: Developed by the authors based on the Stata program.

According to Table 40, it follows that the optimal equation can be constructed at lag 4 according to the model, which will be important to use later in constructing the VAR equation.

Although statistical tests consider lag 4 as the optimal lag, economic rationale, model simplicity and theoretical considerations such as collinearity suggest using lag 2 instead.

In the next step, a cointegration test of the variables was performed using the Johanson test (Table 40).

Table 40. Johanson test for cointegration based on the VAR model of GDP per capita and its influencing factors in European and Central Asian countries

Maximum level	Number of parameters	LL	Inherent value	Tracking statistics	5 percent critical value
0	12	289.74814	.	27.0140*	29.68
1	17	298.26637	0.43328	9.9775	15.41
2	20	303.06876	0.27397	0.3727	3.76

Source: Developed by the authors based on the Stata program.

According to Table 41, if the observation statistic is less than the 5 per cent critical value, then cointegration is considered absent. That is, 27.01 less than 29.68 less than 9.97 less than 15.41 less than 0.37 less than 3.765, according to which it can be seen from the result of this test that there is no cointegrated vector in the model. In this case, if the observation statistic is greater than the 5 per cent critical value, the H_0 hypothesis is rejected.

The H_0 hypothesis indicates that there is no cointegrated vector in this model. Since the observation statistic is less than the 5 per cent critical value, this hypothesis is accepted.

Therefore, since there is no at least one cointegrated vector, it can be concluded that there is no cointegration in the selected model, and the work on the VAR model continues.

Using the VAR model, econometric equations for the outcome variables and factors influencing them were developed for the study (Table 41).

Table 41. Regression equation indicators of GDP per capita in European and Central Asian countries by factors affecting it

Vector autoregression

Sample: 1993 thru 2022	Number of obs = 30
Log likelihood = 268.9084	AIC = −17.12722
FPE = 7.35e−12	HQIC = −16.94792
Det(Sigma_ml) = 3.29e−12	SBIC = −16.56674

Equation	Parms	RMSE	*R*-sq	Chi^2	$P > Chi^2$
logGDP	4	0.100272	0.9230	359.7993	0.0000
loglab_rat_fem	4	0.007529	0.9605	730.3494	0.0000
loglab_rat_mel	4	0.005426	0.8213	137.87	0.0000

	Coefficient	**Std.er**	**z**	**P > z**	**[95%**	**conf.**	**sig**
logGDP_per_capita							
logGDP_per_capita							
L2.	0.436	0.132	3.30	0.001	0.177	0.695	***
loglab_rat_fem							
L2.	6.016	1.541	3.90	0.000	2.995	9.731	***
loglab_rat_mel							
L2.	−8.744	1.924	−4.54	0.000	−12.515	−5.095	***
_cons	18.812	5.982	3.14	0.002	7.084	28.935	***

Source: It was developed by the authors based on Stata software.

$$logGDP\_per\_capita_t = \beta_0 + \beta_1 \cdot log\ logGDP\_per\_capita_{t-2} + \beta_2 \cdot loglab\_rat\_fem_{t-2} + \beta_3 \cdot loglab\_rat\_mel_{t-2} + \epsilon t \quad (2)$$

According to the calculated coefficients, the VAR model indicators,

$$logGDP\_per\_capita_t = 18.81 + 0.43 loglogGDP\_per\_capita_{t-2} + 6.0.1 loglab\_rat\_fem_{t-2} - 8.74 loglab\_rat\_mel_{t-2} + \epsilon t \quad (3)$$

The model uses two lags for each variable and fits the data very well, as shown by the *R*-squared values for each equation:

logGDP: $R^2 = 0.9230$ This indicates that the econometric model explains about 92.30 per cent of the variation in GDP per capita, indicating a strong fit.

loglab_rat_fem: $R^2 = 0.9605$ The econometric model explains about 96.05 per cent of the variation in female labour force participation, indicating a strong fit.

loglab_rat_mel: $R^2 = 0.8213$ The econometric model explains about 82.13 per cent of the variation in male labour force participation.

High Chi-square values and *p*-values ($P > chi^2 = 0.0000$ for each equation) indicate that the coefficients in each equation are generally statistically significant.

Each coefficient in the VAR model is interpreted as the effect of the lagged variables on the dependent variable GDP per capita over time.

Result. The coefficient on GDP per capita in Europe and Central Asia is 0.436, which means that a 1 per cent increase in GDP per capita at lag 2 leads to a 0.436 per cent increase in GDP per capita in the current period, holding other variables constant. It can be seen that the model is statistically significant ($p = 0.001$).

The coefficient on female labour force participation in Europe and Central Asia is 6.514, which indicates that a 1 per cent increase in the female labour force participation rate (in 2nd place) is associated with a 6.514 per cent increase in GDP per capita in the current period. This is a very important result, and it can be seen that the model is statistically significant ($p = 0.000$).

The coefficient on the male labour force participation rate in Europe and Central Asia is –8.891, indicating that a 1 per cent increase in the male labour force participation rate is associated with an 8.891 per cent decrease in GDP per capita during the current period. This inverse relationship is statistically significant ($p = 0.000$).

In this model, the lagging female labour force participation rate has a positive and significant relationship with GDP, and an increase in female labour force participation has a positive impact on economic output. Conversely, the male labour force rate in lag 2 has a negative impact on GDP, which may reflect labour market dynamics or sector-specific effects, in which an increase in the male labour force rate may have a different or competing effect than the female labour force rate.

In developing the study, forecast indicators were developed based on the factors affecting the outcome variables based on the VAR model (Figure 42).

Eigenvalue	Modulus
0.9562742	0.956274
−0.9562742	0.956274
0.8700008	0.870001
−0.8700008	0.870001
0.7480476	0.748048
−0.7480476	0.748048

Figure 42. Eigenvalue-stability test of the VAR model for GDP per capita by factors affecting it.
Source: It was developed by the authors based on Stata software.

According to Figure 42, these tests are particularly important for assessing the constancy of long-term parameters in VAR models. According to them, the VAR model successfully passes the stability test. The eigenvalues are taken from the additional matrix of the VAR model. If the modulus of all eigenvalues is less than 1, the VAR process is considered stable, that is, any shocks to the system disappear over time and the process returns to the average or equilibrium state.

If any eigenvalue has a modulus greater than or equal to 1, the process is unstable and shocks can lead to explosive behaviour, which means that the VAR model is unsuitable for forecasting. In our study, none of the eigenvalues is equal to 1, all are less than one.

In the next stage of the study, the Lagrange-multiplier test was performed (Figure 43).

lag	chi^2	df	Prob > chi^2
1	21.7777	9	0.00961
2	20.4409	9	0.01538

Figure 43. Lagrange-Multiplier test of the VAR model of GDP per capita by factors affecting it.
Source: It was developed by the authors based on Stata software.

The results of the Lagrange multiplier test indicate that there is significant autocorrelation in the data.

Lag 1: Chi-square statistic is 21.7777, p-value 0.00961, which is less than 0.05. This indicates that we reject the null hypothesis of no autocorrelation at lag 1, which indicates evidence of autocorrelation.

Lag 2: Chi-square statistic is 20.4409, *p*-value 0.01538, which is also less than 0.05. This indicates rejection of the null hypothesis at the same lag, which indicates evidence of autocorrelation at this lag. Accordingly, both lags show significant autocorrelation, which emphasises the presence of autocorrelation in the model residuals.

After this, a Granger randomness test is performed to check the randomness of each exogenous factor relative to the endogenous factor (Figure 44).

Equation	Excluded	chi²		df Prob > chi²
GDP_per_capita	lab_rat_fem	15.82	1	0.000
GDP_per_capita	lab_rat_mel	17.498	1	0.000
GDP_per_capita	ALL	20.297	2	0.000
lab_rat_fem	GDP_per_capita	0.23776	1	0.626
lab_rat_fem	lab_rat_mel	14.671	1	0.000
lab_rat_fem	ALL	18.976	2	0.000
lab_rat_mel	GDP_per_capita	0.25334	1	0.615
lab_rat_mel	lab_rat_fem	3.6653	1	0.056
lab_rat_mel	ALL	34.581	2	0.000

Figure 44. Eigenvalue-stability test of the VAR model for GDP per capita and its influencing factors.
Source: It was developed by the authors based on Stata software.

According to the results of the test in Figure 44, the labour participation rate for both sexes has a significant impact on the size of GDP per capita in the countries of Europe and Central Asia. The labour participation of men affects the labour activity of women, but not vice versa. This relationship shows the interdependent dynamics between the labour participation rate and the size of GDP per capita in the countries of Europe and Central Asia, in which the participation rate of each sex has a specific impact on economic indicators and on each other.

In the Granger causality test, the hypothesis H_0 is Granger randomness. If the value of p in this test is less than 0.05, the hypothesis H_0 is rejected. That is, the values of all selected exogenous factors in the observed period affect the future values of the endogenous factor.

In the next step, the plot of the impulse–response function of the size of GDP per capita in the countries of Europe and Central Asia and the factors affecting it is presented (Figure 45).

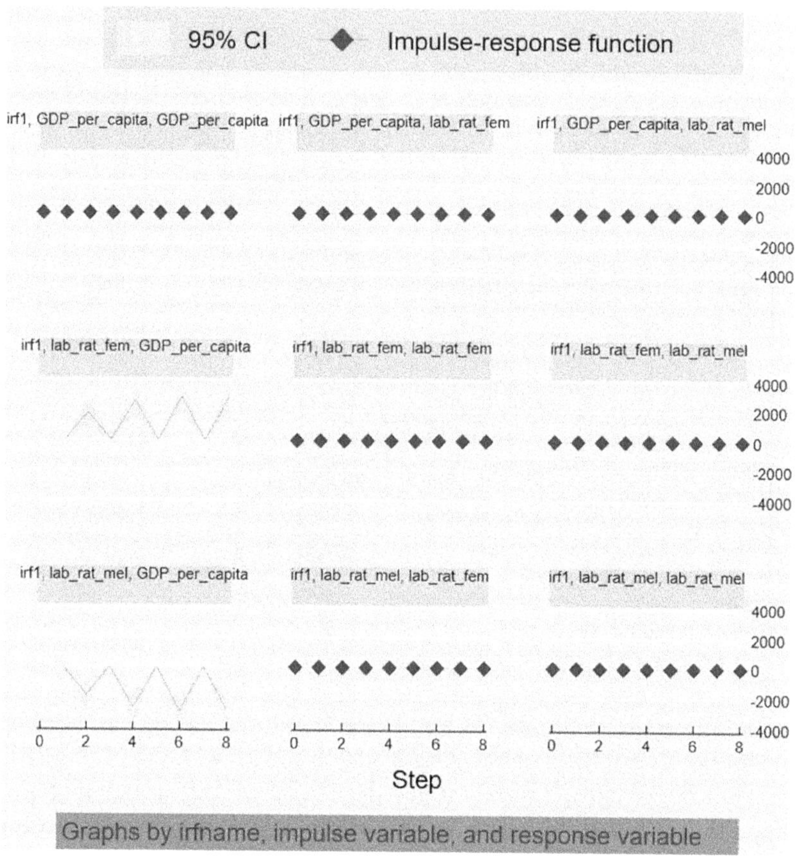

Figure 45. Impulse–response function plot of GDP per capita and factors influencing it in European and Central Asian countries.
Source: It was developed by the authors based on Stata software.

Figure 45 shows that there is no strong dynamic interaction between GDP per capita and gender-specific labour force participation in Europe and Central Asia. Changes in one of these variables do not have significant predictive power or impact on the others in the short term. This suggests that in the context of this model, GDP per capita and labour force participation indicators for women and men in Europe and Central Asia behaved independently in response to shocks.

Before forecasting, a final check was performed to assess the stationarity of the model residuals. The figure below shows a graph illustrating the stationarity of the model residuals (Figure 46).

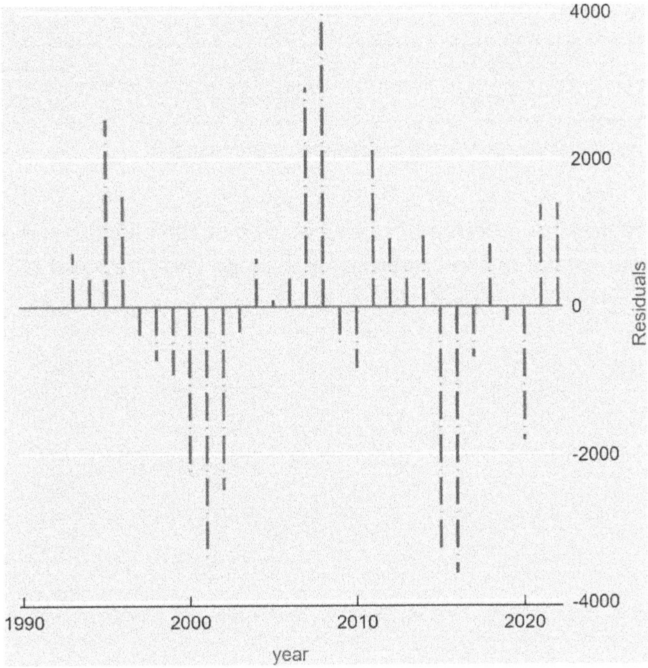

Figure 46. Forecast indicators of GDP per capita and factors affecting it Stationarity graph of VAR model residuals.
Source: It was developed by the authors based on Stata software.

The selected VAR model and its endogenous factor, as well as exogenous factors, successfully passed all tests, and forecast indicators were developed based on the sequence. In the next stage of the study, forecast indicators were developed for the period from 2024 to 2030, excluding random factors, under the influence of GDP per capita in Europe and Central Asia and the level of employment of men and women in the labour market (Table 42).

Table 42. GDP per capita in Europe and Central Asia in 2024–2030 in US dollars

Years	Pessimistic forecast	Optimistic forecast	Forecast indicators
2024	24,533.18	32,202.31	28,367.74
2025	24,804.94	32,460.88	28,632.91
2026	24,832.61	33,347.99	29,090.30
2027	25,151.02	33,673.91	29,412.46
2028	25,196.13	34,140.43	29,668.28
2029	25,528.73	34,504.19	30,016.46
2030	25,737.60	35,278.34	30,507.97

Source: It was developed by the authors based on Stata software.

The study presents a graphical representation of the GDP growth forecast for the countries of Europe and Central Asia for 1991–2023 and 2024–2030, provided by the World Bank (Figure 47).

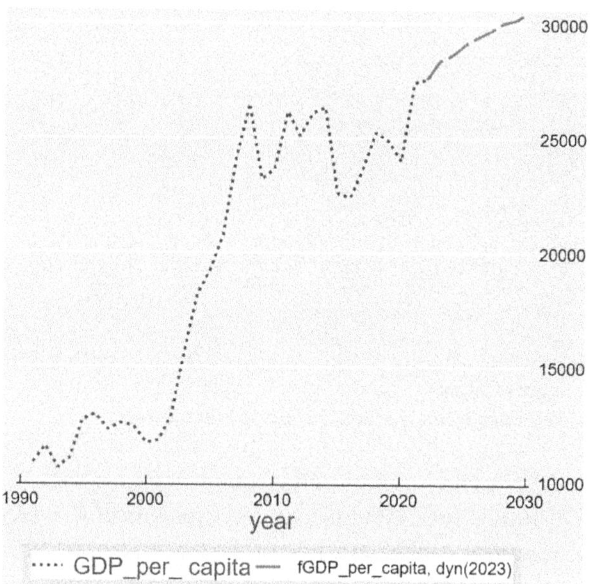

Figure 47. Graph of GDP per capita for 1991–2023 and forecast for 2024–2030.
Source: It was developed by the authors based on Stata software.

According to it, the trend graph indicates that the two lines are almost side by side, which indicates the reliability of the forecast indicators for the next seven years, excluding random factors, and that they have an increasing trend.

15.5. Conclusion

According to the research, the World Bank provided graphical representations of the GDP per capita of the countries of Europe and Central Asia for the years 1991–2023 and the forecasts for the years 2024–2030.

GDP per capita of the countries of Europe and Central Asia, based on the impact of female and male employment in the labour market in these countries, in particular, without taking into account random factors according to the VAR model, is projected to be 28,367.74 US dollars in 2024, 28,632.91 US dollars in 2025, 29,090.30 US dollars in 2026, 29,412.46 US dollars in 2027, 29,668.28 US dollars in 2028, 30,016.46 US dollars in 2029 and 30,507.97 US dollars in 2030, respectively.

15.6. Recommendations

In order to achieve sustainable GDP growth per capita in the countries of Europe and Central Asia and gradually adapt the labour market to the requirements of the digital economy, we have formulated the following scientific proposals:

1. Diversify the labour market and ensure gender equality. Accordingly, it is necessary to create equal opportunities for women and men in the labour market and improve existing labour legislation in this regard. It is also necessary to widely involve women in the fields of science, technology, engineering and mathematics and support various programmes to increase their financial literacy in digital professions.
2. Accelerate digital transformation in all sectors of the economy. In particular, today there is a need to create new jobs and increase labour productivity through the widespread introduction of digital services, Fintech, artificial intelligence and blockchain technologies in various areas of the economy. In order to organise this effectively, it is necessary to strengthen cooperation between the public and private sectors to improve the digital infrastructure of the labour market.

3. Attract investment in the labour market to increase employment and create new jobs. This will be achieved by strengthening education and training programmes, ensuring the adaptation of personnel to the digital economy and providing employment to the low-income population, thereby achieving social stability.

Bibliography

Abdullah, M. A., Han, X., Amjad, M. A., & Makhmudov, S. (2025). Revisit the role of financial development on economic growth, human development, and sustainable development in higher-income countries. Journal of Environmental Management, 392, 126874.

Akhmetshin, E., Abdullayev, I., Makhmudov, S., Dakhkilgova, K., Korotaeva, I. and Yanovskaya, G. (2025). APPLICATION OF TANH–COTH METHOD FOR COMBINED AND DOUBLE COMBINED SINH–COSH–GORDON EQUATIONS ARISING CHEMICAL REACTIONS TO WATER SURFACE GRAVITY WAVES. Computational Methods for Differential Equations, (), -. doi: 10.22034/cmde.2025.67655.3234

Bhatti, M. A., & Pardaev, J. (2025). Exploring Accreditation's Role in Fostering Inclusive Education via Educational Equity and Technology. Revista Electronica De Leeme, (56).

Buterin, V., Fajdetić, B., and Funarić, B. (2023). 'Understanding the Macroeconomic Effects of Female Participation in the Labour Market'. *Economies*, 11 (11), 280, <https://doi.org/10.3390/economies11110280>.

Cahyani, I., Buriev, K., Ngongo, M., Mamadiyarov, Z., Ino, L., Herman, H., Saputra, N., & Baxtishodovich, S. (2025). Exploring the Use of TikTok Application in Enhancing the Skill of Pronunciation: A Case on Students' Perception. Studies in Media and Communication, 13(2), 150–158. doi: http://dx.doi.org/10.11114/smc.v13i2.7553

Caporin, M., Shahbaz, M., Kuziboev, B., Masharipova, M., Allaberganov, S., & Makhmudov, S. (2024). Environmental Kuznets Curve for extended brics economies: do women governance and water stress matter?. International Journal of Energy Economics and Policy, 14(6), 174–183.

Ghaleb, M. M. S., & Pardaev, J. (2025). Effects of Advertisement Language, Communication Style, Information Seeking Behavior and Information Source Credibility on Customers' Intentions towards International Products via Brand Trust. Profesional de la información, 34(2).

Habib, S. S., Islam, M. A., Ali, M. N., Benitez, I. B., Mamadiyarov, Z., Mirzayev, B., … & Flah, A. (2025). Multi-Objective Optimization and Feasibility Analysis of Integrated Biogas–Solar Energy Systems for Rural Electrification. Results in Engineering, 107086.

Jiti, Gao, Bin, Peng, and Yayi, Yan (2023). 'Estimation, Inference and Empirical Analysis for Time-Varying VAR Models'. *Journal of Business & Economic Statistics*, 1–12. <https://doi.org/10.1080/07350015.2023.2191673>.

Khayrilla Kurbonov, Samariddin Makhmudov, Shakhzod Erkinov, Umidjon Dadabaev, Gulnora Bekimbetova, Rukhiddin Zayniddinov, and Mirzabek Jonuzokov. 2025. Evaluating the Impact of Marketing Practices Digitalization and Investment on Labor Market Efficiency and Commercial Bank Performance Using Econometric Models. In Proceedings of the 8th International Conference on Future Networks & Distributed Systems (ICFNDS '24). Association for Computing Machinery, New York, NY, USA, 786–796. https://doi.org/10.1145/3726122.3726237

Khodjaniyazov, N., Mirkhoshimova, M., Kalandarov, F., Matyokubova, D., Utegenova, S., Makhmudov, S., & Khudayberganov, M. (2025). Time-Varying Impacts of Financial Stress on Energy-Related Uncertainty. International Journal of Energy Economics and Policy, 15(3), 689–698.

Klasen, S. (2019). 'What Explains Uneven Female Labor Force Participation Levels and Trends in Developing Countries?' *The World Bank Research Observer*. <https://doi.org/10.1093/WBRO/LKZ005>.

Kuziboev, B., Khodjaniyazov, E., Ozturk, I., Sabirov, K., Makhmudov, S., & Utegenova, S. (2025). Does oil dependence cause energy risk?. Energy Nexus, 17, 100393.

Leucci, A., Ghinoi, S., Sgargi, D., and W., V. (2014). *VAR Models for Dynamic Analysis of Prices in the Agri-food System*, pp. 3–21, <https://doi.org/10.1007/978-3-319-06635-6_1>.

Lin, M.H., Matchanova, B., Nurmatovich, H.A. et al. Optimal Operation of the Multi-Carrier Energy System Considering Energy Markets and Renewable Energies Participation. *Int. J. Appl. Comput. Math* **11**, 170 (2025). https://doi.org/10.1007/s40819-025-02002-9

Litamahuputty, J. V., Amiruddin, E. G., Rahim, R., Rahman, A., & Mamadiyarov, Z. (2025). Cryptocurrency Risk Management through Decision Engineering: Evaluating XRPUSD and ADAUSD Portfolio Performance. Journal of Applied Science, Engineering, Technology, and Education, 7(1), 69–81. https://doi.org/10.35877/454RI.asci3871

Luci, A. (2009). 'Female Labour Market Participation and Economic Growth'. *International Journal of Innovation and Sustainable Development*, 4, 97–108. <https://doi.org/10.1504/IJISD.2009.028065>.

Mamadiyarov, Z., Eshov, M., Otakhonova, D., Utegenova, S., Sabirov, K., Marks, A., & Bahodirov, N. (2025). Does Energy Policy Risk Threaten Energy Sources Diversification?. International Journal of Energy Economics and Policy, 15(5), 730–740. https://doi.org/10.32479/ijeep.21140

Mamadiyarov, Z., Saidov, O., Abdurazakova, N., Makhmudov, S., Nazarov, M., Rajabova, N., … Ruzmetova, I. (2025). Energy-Related Uncertainty and Tourism Stock Markets: New Insights from Time-Varying Relationship with TVP- VAR Approach. International Journal of Energy Economics and Policy, 15(4), 730–737. https://doi.org/10.32479/ijeep.20480

Mamani, J.C.M., Miri, M., Vorobev, Y. et al. Optimal Operation of Energy Microgrid Considering Economic and Emission Indices. Oper. Res. Forum 6, 122 (2025). https://doi.org/10.1007/s43069-025-00523-z

Ngongo, M., Herman, H., Ndandara, A., Jois Jaha, D. A., Peku Djawang, J. U. S., Tanggu Rame, M. M., Khamraeva, S. N., & Mamadiyarov, Z. (2025). An Investigation of Meaning, Toponymy of Sumba Cultural Site's Names, and the Impact of Tourism Visitors on Surrounding Society. Forum for Linguistic Studies, 7(8), 679–693. https://doi.org/10.30564/fls.v7i8.10260

Olsson, J. (2018). Structural Transformation of the Labor Market and the Aggregate Economy.

PANJAITAN, M. B., HAMDANAH, H., SIRAIT, J., SUTIKNO, S., FATMAWATI, E., HERMAN, H., & MAMADIYAROV, Z. (2025). THE ROLE OF EMOTIONAL REGULATION IN SHAPING STUDENTS' PERCEPTION OF PHYSICS PROBLEMSOLVING TASKS. TPM – Testing, Psychometrics, Methodology in Applied Psychology, 32(S2(2025) : Posted 09 June), 1–10. Retrieved from https://tpmap.org/submission/index.php/tpm/article/view/139

Pradhan, R., Hajiyev, E., Shichiyakh, R. et al. Optimal Techno-Economic Feasibility of an Off-Grid Microgrid System Using Load Flow Energy Management Strategies. *Oper. Res. Forum* **6**, 120 (2025). https://doi.org/10.1007/s43069-025-00524-y

Romero, R. M., Zelinskaya, M., Makhmudov, S., Sapaev, S., & Rustambekovich, J. U. (2025, September). Modelling and Optimal Utilisation of the Renewable Energy Systems in Microgrid with Improving Reliability and Energy Efficiency. In Operations Research Forum (Vol. 6, No. 3, pp. 1–20). Springer International Publishing.

Rony, Z. T., Jefri, R., Rusmardiana, A., Pramono, S. A., & Mamadiyarov, Z. (2025). Downside Risk Measurement of Indonesian Financial and Energy Securities: A Value at Risk Perspective. Journal of Applied Science, Engineering, Technology, and Education, 7(2). https://doi.org/10.35877/454RI.asci3898

Ruslan, D. (2020). 'Var Model Untuk Analisis Foreign Direct Investment Di Indonesia'. *Quantitative Economics Journal*, 3. <https://doi.org/10.24114/QEJ.V3I2.17446>.

Rayala, R. V., Borra, C. R., Vasudevan, V., Singhania, R., Cheekati, S., & Mamadiyarov, Z. (2025, July). Lightweight Deep Learning Framework for Human Activity Recognition: A MobileNet-LSTM Approach with WHOA Optimization. In *2025 International Conference on Innovations in Intelligent Systems: Advancements in Computing, Communication, and Cybersecurity (ISAC3)* (pp. 1–6). IEEE.

Rayala, R. V., Sandhya, N., Singhania, R., Cheekati, S., Borra, C. R., Vasudevan, V., & Mamadiyarov, Z. (2025, July). AI-Driven Tomato Quality Assessment: A Deep Learning Approach for Image-based Defect Detection and Classification. In *2025 International Conference on Innovations in Intelligent Systems: Advancements in Computing, Communication, and Cybersecurity (ISAC3)* (pp. 1–6). IEEE.

Samariddin Makhmudov, Malika Umarova, Khayrilla Kurbonov, Laylo Akbarova, Durdona Davletova, Nilufar Shanazarova, and Toshmurod Kulmanov. 2025. Evaluating the forecast indicators of the volume of highly liquid assets of commercial banks in the process of digital transformation. In Proceedings of the 8th International Conference on Future Networks & Distributed Systems (ICFNDS '24). Association for Computing Machinery, New York, NY, USA, 698–704. https://doi.org/10.1145/3726122.3726222

Samariddin Makhmudov, Kudratillo Tukhsanov, Saifulla Arslanbekov, Akram Amanov, Orifali Tursunov, Umarbek Jabbarov and Muyassarxon Mirzakarimova. 2024. Optimizing Supply Chain Financing Development Prospects of Digital Ecosystems in the European Logistics Industry. In The 8th International Conference on Future Networks & Distributed Systems (ICFNDS '24), December 11–12, 2024, Marakech, Morocco. ACM, New York, NY, USA, 12 Pages. https://doi.org/10.1145/3726122.3726200

Sharipov, K., Abdullayev, I., Kuziboev, B., Makhmudov, S., Kalandarov, F., Khaytboeva, N., & Ilkhamova, Z. (2025). The Effect of Energy Policy Risk on Renewable Energy. International Journal of Energy Economics and Policy, 15(2), 566.

Singagerda, F. S., Pratama, M. R., Alfairus, M. Q., Iskandar, A., & Mamadiyarov, Z. (2025). A Decision-Centric Approach to Risk Management in Aviation Stock Investments Using Value at Risk and Portfolio Optimization. Journal of Applied Science, Engineering, Technology, and Education, 7(1), 114–125. https://doi.org/10.35877/454RI.asci3870

Sofyanty, D., Romadhoni, R., Handriadi, H., Makhsudovna, I. S., Anwar, Z., & Mamadiyarov, Z. (2025). Strategic Decision Analysis for Investment Portfolios: Computational Risk Assessment in Transportation Asset Management. Journal of Applied Science, Engineering, Technology, and Education, 7(2). https://doi.org/10.35877/454RI.asci3897

Szekeres, V. (2010). Gender and Its Relevance to Economic Performance, pp. 217–24.

Xingchen, Li (2015). 'Research on Financial Risk Management Based on VAR Model'. *The Open Cybernetics & Systemics Journal*, 9 (1), 1849–52, <https://doi.org/10.2174/1874110X01509011849>.

Zhang, L., Zhao, Z., Qamri, G. M., & Makhmudov, S. (2025). Unleashing the critical role of renewable energy through global value chains and digitalization: A path towards environmental sustainability. Journal of Environmental Management, 392, 126688.

Zhao, Q., Pervaiz, A., Makhmudov, S., & Fatima, A. (2025). Do environmental stringent policies enhance the impact of renewable energy on CO2 reduction? Evidence from BRICS-T economies. Journal of Environmental Management, 391, 126464.

Assessing the Impact of Living Standards on the Dynamics of the Labour Market and Service Delivery (On the Example of Uzbekistan)

Bobur Khonturayev, Mansur Eshov, Zokir Mamadiyarov, Samariddin Makhmudov, Faruddin Eshmirzaev and Asal Jamaldinova

16.1. Introduction

In economic processes, the formation of the dynamics of the labour market and the provision of services is increasingly influenced by multifaceted economic and social factors. In the development of social spheres, the standard of living is not only related to economic well-being, but also is considered a factor determining the effectiveness of labour market practices and the service delivery system.

Today, the interaction between the standard of living and labour market dynamics in any region is a complex process and is closely related to such influencing variables as wage policy, employment structures and socio-economic sectors.

In 1960, the UN Working Group prepared a report on the principles of determining and measuring the standard of living at a global scale. Today, this international organisation is still carrying out a number of works to improve the living standards of the world's population and assist countries suffering from poverty. In particular, the 'Millennium Development Agenda' adopted by the UN General Assembly in 2000 and the '2030 Agenda for Sustainable Development Goals' approved in 2015 are among the important measures aimed at directly supporting the economic and social well-being of the population of the world, as well as protecting the health of the population while preventing environmental degradation.

The concept of 'standard of living' is very complex and multifaceted, and it is difficult to choose a single indicator to describe it, therefore, a number of statistical indicators are calculated that characterise various aspects of this term. Today, the interests of various groups of the population are taken into account, an effective employment system and wage payment system, and measures to ensure a decent life for every person are being taken.

In recent years, as a result of the measures taken by our government to further increase the income and standard of living of the population and provide social support to citizens, it is clearly evident that per capita income, wages and pensions have been steadily increasing.

It should be noted that the improvement of the standard of living of the population directly depends on the scale of efficiency of production and service sectors, scientific and technical progress, cultural and educational level and composition of the population, national characteristics and, of course, the results of measures and practical actions taken by the government.

According to Article 3 of the Law 'On State Statistics', the State Statistics Committee performs the functions of collecting, processing, accumulating, storing, summarising, analysing and publishing statistical data on socio-economic phenomena and processes and their results. It also stipulates that the committee has the right to obtain information from legal entities and individuals in accordance with the established procedure through statistical reporting forms or various observations when collecting statistical data on indicators of the standard of living of the population.

16.2. Literature Review

According to Vasyl Brych et al. (2021) 'the standard of living is often assessed by economic and social indicators, including income levels, employment rates and access to basic services'. According to the authors, these factors are linked to the labour market and service delivery systems, providing a detailed picture of socio-economic conditions. In particular, according to Honcharenko (2021), 'the high level of poverty and low living standards in Ukraine are associated with economic factors such as unemployment and inflation, as well as failures in social policies'. According to the authors, these conditions are optimal for improving the living standards of the population and labour market outcomes.

Tranmer and Elliot (2008) in their study 'in econometric research, a multivariate linear model establishes the linearity, independence, homoscedasticity and normality of residuals between several dependent and independent variables'. According to the authors, this model is of great importance for the validity of the conclusions and forecasts, is important in ensuring the accuracy and reliability of the econometric equation, and distortions lead to incorrect conclusions.

According to Ganesh (2010), 'in econometric research, the assumption of linearity means that the relationship between the independent and dependent variables is linear, and that changes in the independent variables lead to proportional changes in the dependent variables'. According to him, linearity is considered fundamental in multivariate time series, which simplifies the model and expresses the interpretation of the coefficients as the effect of a unit change in the factors on the response variable in forecasting.

Another group of economists has successfully used econometric models such as Fixed Effects Estimator (FEE), Random Effects Estimator (REE), multivariate linear (LS) and ARDL in their research on investment in digital infrastructure, various aspects of digital payment systems, the impact of inflation and credit interest rates on investment, factors affecting the reduction of the state's share in commercial banks, Non-Performing Loans in commercial banks, the digitalisation of banks, risks in digital services and the development of retail payment services (Ghaleb et al., 2025; Romero et al., 2025; Rukhiddin et al., 2025; Sofyanty et al., 2025; Toshmurod et al., 2025; Zhang et al., 2025; Zokir et al., 2025).

According to Yang et al. (2019), 'Homoskedasticity ensures that the variance of the residuals is constant at all levels of the independent variables'. According to the authors' research conclusions, this assumption allows the econometric model to be equally reliable in estimating forecast indicators at all values of the independent variables.

According to Schützenmeister et al. (2012), 'heteroscedasticity in multivariate linear equations leads to inaccurate standard errors that affect confidence intervals and hypothesis tests'. Analyses and forecasts have been conducted using multivariate linear regression (LS), ARDL, ARIMA and other various econometric models on factors affecting remittances, energy intensity and economic development, energy policy, energy risk, environmental status and the impact of environmental aspects on the digital economy, agricultural productivity and the stability of the US credit market (Abdullah et al., 2025; Bhatti et al., 2025; Habib et al., 2025; Jahrir et al., 2025; Kuziboev et al., 2025; Mamadiyarov et al., 2025; Rony et al., 2025; Rayala et al., 2025; Sharipov et al., 2025; Su et al., 2025).

16.3. Research Methodology

In developing the study, we used quarterly data from the Statistical Agency under the President of the Republic of Uzbekistan (<https://stat.uz/uz/>) and the World Bank (<https://data.worldbank.org/>) with a total number of observations of fifty-three for the period 2010–2023 to assess the impact of living standards on the dynamics of the labour market and service provision.

Since the data are based on multivariate time series, we used the multivariate linear equations (LS) model and the SEM (Structural Equation Model) model to develop an econometric model for the study.

In constructing the econometric model for the study, Gauss-Markov conditions were estimated based on the 'multivariate linear (LS) model' (Smith et al., 2013) and several confidence tests, in particular the 'Durbin-Watson' (Akhmetshin et al., 2025; Jović, 2016; Khayrilla et al., 2025; Kuchkarov et al., 2025; Mamadiyarov et al., 2025), 'Shapiro-Wilk' (Kuziboev et al., 2025; Mamadiyarov et al., 2025; Ngongo et al., 2025; Rayala et al., 2025; Souza et al., 2023) and 'Breusch-Pagan' (Mamani et al., 2025; Samariddin et al., 2025; Singagerda et al., 2025; Zolna et al., 2016) tests, were used to analyse the statistical significance of the model.

The LS model was developed as the first econometric model in the project study.

The formula for the LS model is given below.

$$Y_i = \vartheta_0 + \vartheta_1 c_{1i} + \vartheta_2 c_{2i} + \cdots + \vartheta_k c_{ki} + \epsilon_{i,} \quad i = 1, 2, \ldots, n \tag{1}$$

Here, t is the dependent variable for the Y_i-observation, which constitutes the dependent variable in the modelling

$c_{1t}, c_{2t}, c_{3t}, \ldots, c_{ik}$ represent the independent variables (influencing factors). $\vartheta_1, \vartheta_2, \vartheta_3, \ldots, \vartheta_i$ represent the regression coefficients (the influence of each factor) and t – residual (error) value.

The SEM model was developed as the second econometric model in the study.

The SEM model formula is given below.

$$\eta = \theta\eta + \mu\tau + \zeta \tag{2}$$

Here,

η denotes the vector of endogenous (dependent) latent variables.
ϑ denotes the vector of exogenous (independent) latent variables.
μ denotes the matrix of correlation coefficients between endogenous latent variables,
τ denotes the matrix of correlation coefficients between exogenous and endogenous latent variables.
ζ: denotes the vector of residuals (errors) for endogenous latent variables. All variables in these two econometric models are natural logarithmised.

All variables in the econometric model are logarithmised.

All variables in the econometric model are represented below.

Variables: The volume of health care services in the national economy – *lnhealth_sector* – (result variable),

The number of male employment in the labour market – *lnmale_employ* (independent variable), the number of female employment in the labour market – *lnfamale_employ* (independent variable), the level of improvement of housing and food services in the national economy – *lnaccom_cat_serv* (independent variable).

The main (H_0) and alternative (H_1) hypotheses were reflected in the development of the econometric study.

Formation of hypotheses in the combined model:

The main hypothesis (H_0): The number of male employment in the labour market, the number of female employment in the labour market, and the level of improvement of housing and food services in the national economy do not significantly affect the volume of health care services in the national economy and there are no correlations.

Alternative Hypothesis (H_1): The number of male employment in the labour market, the number of female employment in the labour market, and the level of improvement of housing and food services in the national economy have a strong correlation, significantly affecting the volume of health care services in the national economy.

16.4. Analysis and Results

In the first stage of the econometric study, descriptive statistical values were expressed for the volume of healthcare costs and the variables affecting them (Table 43).

Table 43. Descriptive statistical values for the volume of healthcare costs and the factors affecting them

	lnhealth_sector	lnmale_ employ	lnfamale_ employ	lnaccom_ cat_serv
Mean	7.357136	5.335318	1.906352	3.528022
Maximum	5.55296	4.06439	1.750677	2.353696
Minimum	5.55296	4.06439	1.750677	2.353696
Std. Dev	1.002301	0.6819852	0.0809524	0.6337917
Std. Err.	0.1376766	0.0936779	0.0111197	0.087058
Skewness	-0.0372338	0.0155349	-0.3277467	-0.0245747
Kurtosis	1.932678	1.948464	1.919853	2.003226
Observation	53	53	53	53

Source: Developed by the authors based on the Stata program.

According to Table 43, the distribution of the volume of health care services in the standard of living and the factors affecting it according to the model is presented by the main values of the selected variables for descriptive statistical indicators. All variables selected for descriptive statistical values consist of 53 observations.

Based on descriptive statistical indicators, an increase in the volume of services provided by men in the labour market for health care services contributes to a further positive increase in the standard of living. Also, the growth of lifestyle and catering services indicates an increase in the demand for health care due to tourism, population movement and improved infrastructure.

The low volatility of female employment in the labour market indicates the stability of women's participation in the health care sector and the stabilisation of service provision.

The study developed a graphical representation of the volume of healthcare services and the factors influencing them over time (Figure 48).

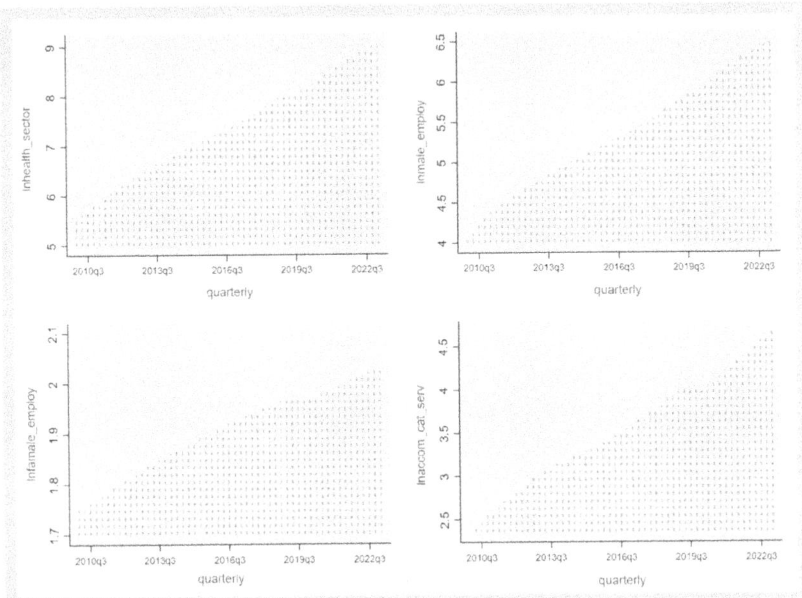

Figure 48. Analytical graphical representation of the volume of healthcare services and the factors affecting them over time.
Source: Developed by the authors based on the Stata program.

The analytical graph in Figure 48 shows that over time, health services and their determinants have shown a consistent growth trend. According to the figure, the region has shown a steady growth dynamics from 2010 to 2022 against the backdrop of continuous reforms, which suggests that the health infrastructure has expanded and optimised access and service delivery. The dynamic growth process, coupled with the allocation of financial resources to the health sector in the region at the level of living, will serve to increase the potential and efficiency of the labour market in the region.

In particular, the growth of employment in the labour market in the region reflects greater investment in human capital, which will lead to improved health care. According to the growth trend in the analytical graph, although male employment in the labour market is significantly higher, female employment is also experiencing steady growth, which reflects the development of gender equality in the workforce. The growth of lifestyle and catering services shows a strong correlation with the further increase in demand for healthcare against the background of population growth, development of medical services and urbanisation.

The next stage of the study presents scatter plots of the volume of healthcare services and the factors affecting it (Figure 49).

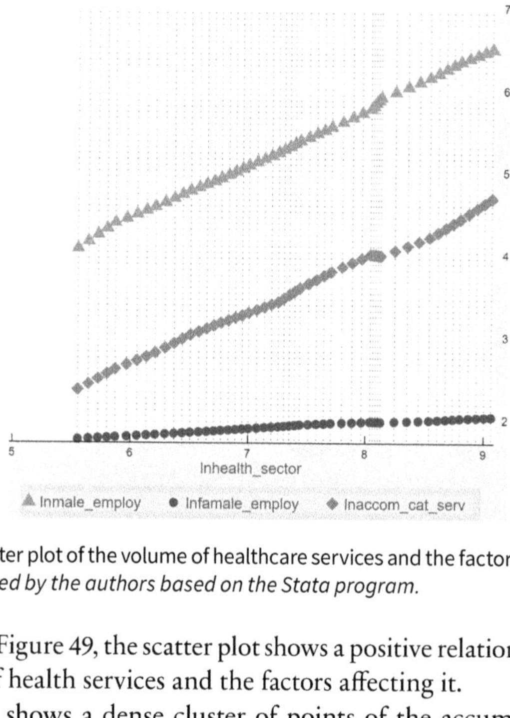

Figure 49. Scatter plot of the volume of healthcare services and the factors affecting them. *Source: Developed by the authors based on the Stata program.*

According to Figure 49, the scatter plot shows a positive relationship between the volume of health services and the factors affecting it.

The figure shows a dense cluster of points of the accumulation effect in male employment in the labour market, which indicates that as health care spending increases, male employment also increases. Gender diversity in the labour market is considered as a government reform initiative that encourages the inclusion of men and women in health care roles. The graphical representation of the data indicates that there is a positive relationship between the growth of health care spending, housing and food services. This highlights the initiatives related to the increase in demand for health care services.

The next step is to present a graphical representation of the analytical relationship (dotplot rconnected) between the volume of healthcare services and the factors affecting them (Figure 50).

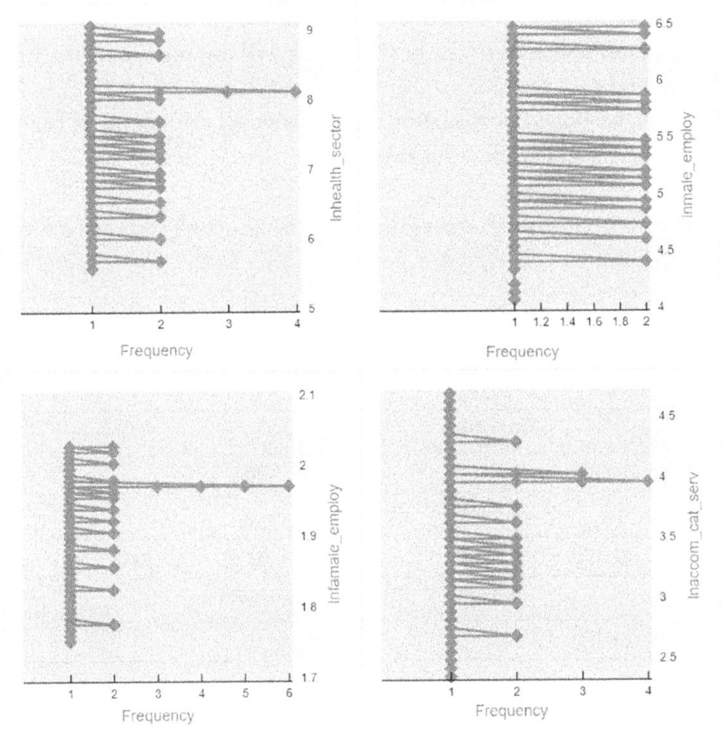

Figure 50. Dotplot connected graphical representation of the volume of healthcare services and the factors affecting them.
Source: Developed by the authors based on the Stata program.

According to Figure 50, the density distribution correlation diagram provides a clear and structured visual dynamics of the volume of health care services and the factors affecting it in positively increasing the standard of living in the region. This indicates a consistent growth of health services and a stable and systematic expansion of this sector over time, as the distribution of health services increases in a dense and gradual manner.

The diagram shows that health care in the region is closely linked to the increase and stabilisation of male and female employment in the labour market and demonstrates a strong growth in employment in the sector, which demonstrates a consistent upward trend. The structural distribution indicates a significant stabilisation of human capital in the labour market, which indicates that jobs in the health sector will not only increase, but also be maintained over time.

The study developed a correlation matrix between the volume of healthcare costs and the variables affecting them.

Table 44. Correlation matrix between the volume of healthcare costs and the factors affecting them

Variables	(1)	(2)	(3)	(4)	Significant
(1) lnhealth_sector	1.000				
(2) lnmale_employ	0.7993	1.000			
	(0.0000)				***
(3) lnfamale_employ	0.7019	0.7880	1.000		
	(0.0000)	(0.0000)			***
(4) lnaccom_cat_serv	0.6888	0.6979	0.6719	1.000	
	(0.0000)	(0.0000)	(0.0000)		***
*** *p* < 0.01, ** *p* < 0.05, * *p* < 0.1.					

Source: Developed by the authors based on the Stata program.

According to Table 44, there is a strong and significant correlation between the volume of healthcare costs and the variables affecting it.

The effective correlation for all variables showed a direct positive effect on the volume of healthcare costs. Also, the fact that the *p*-value is less than 0.05 according to the table indicates that the condition of its statistical significance for the correlation coefficient is met.

In the next stage of the study, a regression model of the volume of healthcare costs and the factors affecting it was developed using a LS model (Table 45).

Table 45. Regression equation indicators based on the multivariate linear (LS) model of the volume of healthcare costs and the variables affecting it

lnhealth_sector	Coef.	St.Err.	t-value	p-value	[95% Conf	Interval]	Sig
lnmale_employ	1.01	0.066	15.22	0	0.877	1.144	***
lnfamale_employ	1.885	0.287	6.56	0	1.307	2.462	***
lnaccom_cat_serv	0.256	0.087	2.95	0.005	0.082	0.43	***
Constant	−2.529	0.452	−5.59	0	−3.438	−1.62	***
Mean dependent var	7.357		SD dependent var		0.761		
R-squared	0.781		Number of obs		53		
F-test	940.496		Prob > *F*		0.000		
Akaike crit. (AIC)	-25.883		Bayesian crit. (BIC)		-24.002		

*** $p < 0.01$, ** $p < 0.05$, * $p < 0.1$

Source: Developed by the authors based on the Stata program.

The formula coefficients of the LS model are given below:

$$lnhealth\_sector = \beta_0 + \beta_1 lnmale\_employ + \beta_2 lnfemale\_employ + \beta_3 lnaccom\_cat\_serv + \epsilon \quad (2)$$

The formula coefficients of the LS model are given below.

$$lnhealth\_sector = 2.52 + 1.01 lnmale\_employ + 1.88 lnfemale\_employ + 0.25 lnaccom\_cat\_serv + \epsilon \quad (3)$$

General description of the LS model.

The *p*-value of the health sector expenditure and the factors affecting it is less than 0.05, which indicates a statistically significant prediction of the resulting factor at the 5 per cent significance level.

R-squared value: The *R*-squared value is 0.7810, which indicates the quality of the model with 78.10 per cent of the variables affecting the volume of health care expenditure. The high value of *R*-squared indicates that the econometric model is strongly related to the observed data.

When testing the hypothesis of the regression equation according to the LS model, it is clear that the null hypothesis (H_0: $y = 0$) is rejected when $F < 0.05$ and $t < 0.05$, indicating that the main hypothesis (H_0: $y = 0$) is statistically insignificant. Accordingly, the main hypothesis is rejected in favour of accepting the statistically significant alternative hypothesis (H_1: $y \neq 0$).

Result. A 1 per cent increase in male employment in the labour market leads to a 1.01 per cent increase in the volume of health care services. A 1 per cent increase in female employment in the labour market leads to a 1.88 per cent increase in health care services. Similarly, a 1 per cent increase in the improvement of housing and food services in the region leads to a 0.25 per cent increase in health care services.

The reliability tests of the LS model regression equation are presented below (Table 46).

Table 46. The reliability tests of the multivariate linear (LS) model regression equation values

№	Confidence test	Value indicator	Statistical significance *p*-value
1	Durbin–Watson	0.36	$p > 0.05$
2	Shapiro–Wilk W	0.17	
3	Breusch–Pagan	0.11	

Source: Developed by the authors based on the Stata program.

LS model regression equation for the model:

Durbin-Watson, Shapiro–Wilk W and Breusch–Pagan tests, the primary hypothesis was H_0: $y = 0$ and H_1: $y \neq 0$, $p > 0.05$ significance level test.

According to the results of the Durbin-Watson and Shapiro-Wilk tests, the null hypothesis was accepted. According to the model, the $p > 0.05$

threshold, error conditions and Gauss-Markov conditions confirming that there is no relationship between the independent variables included in the analysis of the study. In this case, the main conditions of the Gauss-Markov condition for the econometric model were met. Also, the SEM regression model plot, regression model and test indicators looked like this (Table 47 and Figure 51).

Table 47. SEM regression equation between the volume of health care services and the factors affecting it

Fitting target model:	Structural equation model Number of obs = 53
Iteration 0:	Estimation method: ml
log likelihood = 340.49741	Log likelihood = 340.49741
Iteration 1:	OIM
log likelihood = 340.49741	

	Coefficient	std. err	z	P>z	[95% conf.	inyterval
Structural						
lnhealth_sector						
lnmale_employ	1.010	0.064	15.830	0.000	0.885	1.135
lnfamale_employ	1.885	0.276	6.820	0.000	1.343	2.426
lnaccom_cat_serv	0.256	0.083	3.070	0.002	0.093	0.419
_cons	−2.529	0.435	−5.810	0.000	−3.381	−1.676
var(e.lnhealth_sector)	0.000		0.000		0.000	0.001

Source: Developed by the authors based on the Stata program.

The SEM regression model developed for the study looked like this:

$$lnhealth\_sector = -2.52 + 1.01 lnmale\_employ + 1.88 lnfemale\_employ + 0.25 lnaccom\_cat\_serv \quad (4)$$

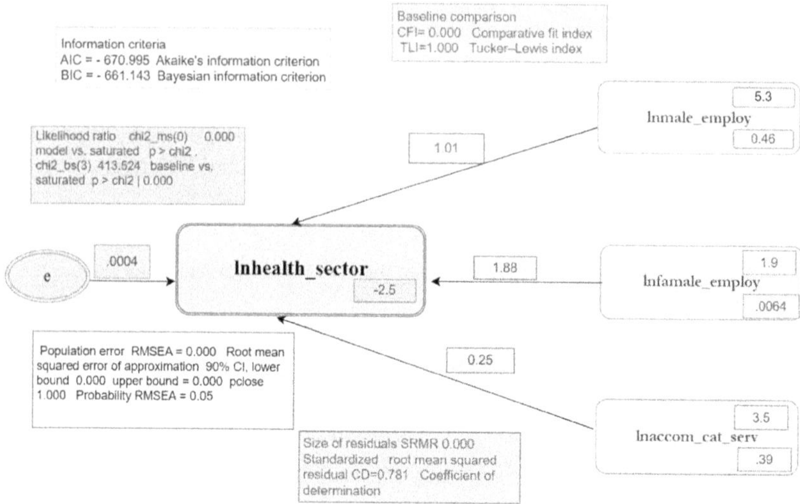

Figure 51. Schematic representation of the SEM model between the volume of healthcare services and the factors affecting them.
Source: Developed by the authors based on the Stata program.

According to Tables 16.3 and 16.5 above, the results of the LS equation and SEM regression models showed the same indicators.

16.5. Conclusion

The results of the LS equation model and SEM models in the econometric study showed that the number of male employment in the labour market, the number of female employment in the labour market, the level of improvement of housing and food services showed a strong and positive relationship between the volume of health care services in the region, and this demonstrates significant development trends in the processes of stimulating macroeconomic processes, in particular, between the standard of living of the population and the labour market.

1. The results of the study show that the elasticity coefficients show a positive impact on health services due to changes in male and female employment, as well as improvements in lifestyle and food services.

2. Assess the significant impact of female employment on health services. A 1 per cent increase in female employment in the labour market leads to a 1.88 per cent increase in health services, which indicates that women are gaining significant importance in the health sector. This is due to the high participation of women in health professions such as nursing, caregiving and medical management in the region. Also, expanding women's opportunities in the labour market creates the basis for a significant increase in the provision of health services.
3. Assess the positive impact of male employment on health services. A 1 per cent increase in male employment leads to a 1.01 per cent increase in health services, confirming that male workers also contribute significantly to the expansion of the health sector. It also reflects the participation of men in the medical professions, health administration and supporting infrastructure. Although male employment has a positive impact on the labour market at a relatively low coefficient compared to female employment, female employment is significantly important in the growth of the health sector.
4. The importance of economic growth in lifestyle and food services in the health sector. A 1 per cent improvement in lifestyle and food services in a region leads to a 0.25 per cent increase in health services, reflecting the additive relationship between urban development and health expansion.

16.6. Recommendations

As housing conditions and food services improve, access to health services increases through the optimisation of hospital infrastructure, medical tourism and general living standards. According to him, health services lead to development in areas with a strong economic and social infrastructure.

1. The developed econometric models confirm that employment growth and health services have a direct and positive impact on the improvement of the labour market and the standard of living of the population.

2. This creates the basis for the highest growth of health services, with significant impact on investment in women's employment in the labour market.
3. The growth of male employment in the labour market also indicates a significant increase, ensuring stability and consistency in economic sectors and in the health sector.
4. Economic prosperity in the region's lifestyle and food services will indirectly improve health services, leading to the development and improved use of infrastructure in this area.

Bibliography

Abdullah, M. A., Han, X., Amjad, M. A., & Makhmudov, S. (2025). Revisit the role of financial development on economic growth, human development, and sustainable development in higher-income countries. Journal of Environmental Management, 392, 126874.

Akhmetshin, E., Abdullayev, I., Makhmudov, S., Dakhkilgova, K., Korotaeva, I. and Yanovskaya, G. (2025). APPLICATION OF TANH–COTH METHOD FOR COMBINED AND DOUBLE COMBINED SINH–COSH–GORDON EQUATIONS ARISING CHEMICAL REACTIONS TO WATER SURFACE GRAVITY WAVES. Computational Methods for Differential Equations, (), -. doi: 10.22034/cmde.2025.67655.3234

Bhatti, M. A., & Pardaev, J. (2025). Exploring Accreditation's Role in Fostering Inclusive Education via Educational Equity and Technology. Revista Electronica De Leeme, (56).

Brych, V., Manzhula, V., Halysh, N., Kalinichuk, N., Reznik, N., and Hrynchak, I. (2021). 'Modeling the Dynamics of Living Standards Based on Factors of the Remuneration System'. In *International Conference 'Advanced Computer Information Technologies'*, pp. 420–23. <https://doi.org/10.1109/ACIT52158.2021.9548617>.

de Souza, R. R., Toebe, M., Mello, A. C., and Bittencourt, K. C. (2023). 'Sample Size and Shapiro-Wilk Test: An Analysis for Soybean Grain Yield'. *European Journal of Agronomy*, 142, 126666.

Ghaleb, M. M. S., & Pardaev, J. (2025). Effects of Advertisement Language, Communication Style, Information Seeking Behavior and Information Source Credibility on Customers' Intentions towards International Products via Brand Trust. Profesional de la información, 34(2).

Ganesh, S. (2010). *Multivariate Linear Regression*, 324–31, <https://doi.org/10.1016/B978-0-08-044894-7.01350-6>.

Habib, S. S., Islam, M. A., Ali, M. N., Benitez, I. B., Mamadiyarov, Z., Mirzayev, B., ... & Flah, A. (2025). Multi-Objective Optimization and Feasibility Analysis of Integrated Biogas–Solar Energy Systems for Rural Electrification. Results in Engineering, 107086.

Honcharenko, O. G. (2021). *Assessment of Living Standards of the Ukrainian Population*. 1 (6), 44–55, <https://doi.org/10.32755/SJEDUCATION.2021.01.044>.

Jahrir, A., Gultom, Y., Herman, H., Zabadi, F., Ngongo, M., Mamadiyarov, Z., Fatmawati, E., & Saputra, N. (2025). Investigating the Elements of Short Commercial Mineral Water Advertisement: A Case on Discourse Analysis. Studies in Media and Communication, 13(4), 94–104. doi: http://dx.doi.org/10.11114/smc.v13i4.7813

Jović, O. (2016). 'Durbin-Watson Partial Least-Squares Regression Applied to MIR Data on Adulteration with Edible Oils of Different Origins'. *Food Chemistry*, 213, 791–8.

Khayrilla Kurbonov, Samariddin Makhmudov, Shakhzod Erkinov, Umidjon Dadabaev, Gulnora Bekimbetova, Rukhiddin Zayniddinov, and Mirzabek Jonuzokov. 2025. Evaluating the Impact of Marketing Practices Digitalization and Investment on Labor Market Efficiency and Commercial Bank Performance Using Econometric Models. In Proceedings of the 8th International Conference on Future Networks & Distributed Systems (ICFNDS '24). Association for Computing Machinery, New York, NY, USA, 786–796. https://doi.org/10.1145/3726122.3726237

Kuchkarov, T., Mamadiyarov, Z., Khakimov, Z., Sabirova, O., Matmurodov, K., Raimboyeva, M., & Umarova, S. (2025). Energy-Related Uncertainty and Crypto-Currency Environmental Attention: Time-Varying Perspective. International Journal of Energy Economics and Policy, 15(5), 614–626. https://doi.org/10.32479/ijeep.20784

Kuziboev, B., Khodjaniyazov, E., Ozturk, I., Sabirov, K., Makhmudov, S., & Utegenova, S. (2025). Does oil dependence cause energy risk?. Energy Nexus, 17, 100393.

Kuziboev, B., Ozturk, I., Kalandarov, F., Samandarov, O., Bekjanov, D., & Makhmudov, S. (2025). PROMOTING ENERGY SOURCES DIVERSIFICATION THROUGH ESG PERFORMANCE. Energy, 136009.

Lin, M.H., Matchanova, B., Nurmatovich, H.A. et al. Optimal Operation of the Multi-Carrier Energy System Considering Energy Markets and Renewable Energies Participation. *Int. J. Appl. Comput. Math* 11, 170 (2025). https://doi.org/10.1007/s40819-025-02002-9

Litamahuputty, J. V., Amiruddin, E. G., Rahim, R., Rahman, A., & Mamadiyarov, Z. (2025). Cryptocurrency Risk Management through Decision Engineering: Evaluating XRPUSD and ADAUSD Portfolio Performance. Journal of Applied Science, Engineering, Technology, and Education, 7(1), 69–81. https://doi.org/10.35877/454RI.asci3871

Mamadiyarov, Z., Eshov, M., Otakhonova, D., Utegenova, S., Sabirov, K., Marks, A., & Bahodirov, N. (2025). Does Energy Policy Risk Threaten Energy Sources Diversification?. International Journal of Energy Economics and Policy, 15(5), 730–740. https://doi.org/10.32479/ijeep.21140

Mamadiyarov, Z., Saidov, O., Abdurazakova, N., Makhmudov, S., Nazarov, M., Rajabova, N., … Ruzmetova, I. (2025). Energy-Related Uncertainty and Tourism Stock Markets: New Insights from Time-Varying Relationship with TVP- VAR Approach. International Journal of Energy Economics and Policy, 15(4), 730–737. https://doi.org/10.32479/ijeep.20480

Mamani, J.C.M., Miri, M., Vorobev, Y. et al. Optimal Operation of Energy Microgrid Considering Economic and Emission Indices. Oper. Res. Forum 6, 122 (2025). https://doi.org/10.1007/s43069-025-00523-z

Ngongo, M., Herman, H., Ndandara, A., Jois Jaha, D. A., Peku Djawang, J. U. S., Tanggu Rame, M. M., Khamraeva, S. N., & Mamadiyarov, Z. (2025). An Investigation of Meaning, Toponymy of Sumba Cultural Site's Names, and the Impact of Tourism Visitors on Surrounding Society. Forum for Linguistic Studies, 7(8), 679–693. https://doi.org/10.30564/fls.v7i8.10260

PANJAITAN, M. B., HAMDANAH, H., SIRAIT, J., SUTIKNO, S., FATMAWATI, E., HERMAN, H., & MAMADIYAROV, Z. (2025). THE ROLE OF EMOTIONAL REGULATION IN SHAPING STUDENTS' PERCEPTION OF PHYSICS PROBLEMSOLVING TASKS. TPM – Testing, Psychometrics, Methodology in Applied Psychology, 32(S2(2025) : Posted 09 June), 1–10. Retrieved from https://tpmap.org/submission/index.php/tpm/article/view/139

Pradhan, R., Hajiyev, E., Shichiyakh, R. et al. Optimal Techno-Economic Feasibility of an Off-Grid Microgrid System Using Load Flow Energy Management Strategies. *Oper. Res. Forum* 6, 120 (2025). https://doi.org/10.1007/s43069-025-00524-y

Romero, R. M., Zelinskaya, M., Makhmudov, S., Sapaev, S., & Rustambekovich, J. U. (2025, September). Modelling and Optimal Utilisation of the Renewable Energy Systems in Microgrid with Improving Reliability and Energy Efficiency. In Operations Research Forum (Vol. 6, No. 3, pp. 1–20). Springer International Publishing.

Rony, Z. T., Jefri, R., Rusmardiana, A., Pramono, S. A., & Mamadiyarov, Z. (2025). Downside Risk Measurement of Indonesian Financial and Energy Securities: A Value at Risk Perspective. Journal of Applied Science, Engineering, Technology, and Education, 7(2). https://doi.org/10.35877/454RI.asci3898

Rukhiddin Zayniddinov, Nodir Jumaev, Gulbakhor Irgasheva, Alam Asadov, Nosir Makhmudov, Sirojiddin Abrorov, and Samariddin Makhmudov. 2025. The Influence of the Digital Economy on Economic Development Evidence from Uzbekistan. In Proceedings of the 8th International Conference on Future Networks & Distributed Systems (ICFNDS '24). Association for Computing Machinery, New York, NY, USA, 831–839. https://doi.org/10.1145/3726122.3726242

Rayala, R. V., Borra, C. R., Vasudevan, V., Singhania, R., Cheekati, S., & Mamadiyarov, Z. (2025, July). Lightweight Deep Learning Framework for Human Activity Recognition: A MobileNet-LSTM Approach with WHOA Optimization. In *2025 International Conference on Innovations in Intelligent Systems: Advancements in Computing, Communication, and Cybersecurity (ISAC3)* (pp. 1–6). IEEE.

Rayala, R. V., Sandhya, N., Singhania, R., Cheekati, S., Borra, C. R., Vasudevan, V., & Mamadiyarov, Z. (2025, July). AI-Driven Tomato Quality Assessment: A Deep Learning Approach for Image-based

Defect Detection and Classification. In *2025 International Conference on Innovations in Intelligent Systems: Advancements in Computing, Communication, and Cybersecurity (ISAC3)* (pp. 1–6). IEEE.

Samariddin Makhmudov, Malika Umarova, Khayrilla Kurbonov, Laylo Akbarova, Durdona Davletova, Nilufar Shanazarova, and Toshmurod Kulmanov. 2025. Evaluating the forecast indicators of the volume of highly liquid assets of commercial banks in the process of digital transformation. In Proceedings of the 8th International Conference on Future Networks & Distributed Systems (ICFNDS '24). Association for Computing Machinery, New York, NY, USA, 698–704. https://doi.org/10.1145/3726122.3726222

Schützenmeister, A., Jensen, U., and Piepho, H. -P. (2012). 'Checking Normality and Homoscedasticity in the General Linear Model Using Diagnostic Plots'. *Communications in Statistics – Simulation and Computation* 41 (2), 141–54, <https://doi.org/10.1080/03610918.2011.582560>.

Sharipov, K., Abdullayev, I., Kuziboev, B., Makhmudov, S., Kalandarov, F., Khaytboeva, N., & Ilkhamova, Z. (2025). The Effect of Energy Policy Risk on Renewable Energy. International Journal of Energy Economics and Policy, 15(2), 566.

Singagerda, F. S., Pratama, M. R., Alfairus, M. Q., Iskandar, A., & Mamadiyarov, Z. (2025). A Decision-Centric Approach to Risk Management in Aviation Stock Investments Using Value at Risk and Portfolio Optimization. Journal of Applied Science, Engineering, Technology, and Education, 7(1), 114–125. https://doi.org/10.35877/454RI.asci3870

Smith, P. F., Ganesh, S., and Liu, P. (2013). 'A Comparison of Random Forest Regression and Multiple Linear Regression for Prediction in Neuroscience'. *Journal of Neuroscience Methods*, 220 (1), 85–91.

Sofyanty, D., Romadhoni, R., Handriadi, H., Makhsudovna, I. S., Anwar, Z., & Mamadiyarov, Z. (2025). Strategic Decision Analysis for Investment Portfolios: Computational Risk Assessment in Transportation Asset Management. Journal of Applied Science, Engineering, Technology, and Education, 7(2). https://doi.org/10.35877/454RI.asci3897

Su, R., Xiao, Y., Hamza, F., Mamadiyarov, Z., & Wahab, A. (2025). Scaling up green hydrogen in China: Economic opportunities and challenges. International Journal of Hydrogen Energy, 131, 60–69.

Toshmurod Kulmanov, Umidjon Dadabaev, Mansurbek Qulmetov, Aliboy Ulashov, Mirjalol Eshboyev, and Samariddin Makhmudov. 2025. Global Services Market Transformation Digitalization Export Trends and Future Forecasts. In Proceedings of the 8th International Conference on Future Networks & Distributed Systems (ICFNDS '24). Association for Computing Machinery, New York, NY, USA, 851–858. https://doi.org/10.1145/3726122.3726245

Tranmer, M., and Elliot, M. (2008). 'Multiple Linear Regression'. *The Cathie Marsh Centre for Census and Survey Research (CCSR)*, 5 (5), 1–5.

Yang, K., Tu, J., and Chen, T. (2019). *Homoscedasticity: An Overlooked Critical Assumption for Linear Regression*, 32 (5), <https://doi.org/10.1136/GPSYCH-2019-100148>.

Zolna, K., Dao, P. B., Staszewski, W. J., and Barszcz, T. (2016). 'Towards Homoscedastic Nonlinear Cointegration for Structural Health Monitoring'. *Mechanical Systems and Signal Processing*, 75, 94–108.

Zhang, L., Zhao, Z., Qamri, G. M., & Makhmudov, S. (2025). Unleashing the critical role of renewable energy through global value chains and digitalization: A path towards environmental sustainability. Journal of Environmental Management, 392, 126688.

Zokir Toshtemirovich Mamadiyarov, Samandarboy Adhambek ugli Sulaymanov, Sarvar Anvar ugli Askarov, and Durdona Bakhtiyor kizi Uktamova. 2022. Impact of Covid-19 Pandemic on Accelerating The Digitization and Transformation of Banks. In Proceedings of the 5th International Conference on Future Networks and Distributed Systems (ICFNDS '21). Association for Computing Machinery, New York, NY, USA, 706–712. https://doi.org/10.1145/3508072.3508211

Assessing the Importance of Women's and Men's Employment in the Labour Market for Economic Growth

Zokir Mamadiyarov, Bobur Khonturayev, Samariddin Makhmudov, Khayrilla Kurbonov, Fakhriddin Isaev, Shakhnoza Abdullayeva and Nafisabonu Karimova

17.1. Introduction

Women's employment opportunities have improved significantly in recent years, but female workers still earn slightly less than male workers. The segmentation of the global labour market by gender implies that macroeconomic processes can have different effects on employment opportunities for men and women. In analysing this segmentation, there is an increasing need to analyse the impact of labour markets on economic growth, employment and poverty reduction. In addition, the impact of various macroeconomic processes, such as monetary policy, trade volumes, exchange rate regimes and public sector restructuring, on men's and women's employment is also important.

Even though gender equality has been achieved in some areas, some gender norms create unequal employment opportunities between men and women. In particular, due to the gender gap in employment and the wage gap between men and women, the gross domestic product (GDP) per woman in 2017 was more than 45 per cent lower than that per man (Women – US$5,064; Men – US$9,230). This trend has been worsening in recent years. According to the International Labour Organisation, women's labour market participation has fallen from 50 per cent in 2010 to 45 per cent in 2021. The share of young people aged 15–25 who are not in employment, education or training (NEET) was 8.8 per cent. The same figure for women of the same age was 42 per cent. According to the government's Gender Statistics Portal, entrepreneurship also shows similar disparities, with men consistently twice as likely to borrow money for business or farming as women. The combination of women's low participation in the labour force, their low wages and occupational segregation has led to a significant gender pay gap. According to government statistics for 2022, women earn an average of 34 per cent less than men, which is significantly higher than the global average of 20 per cent (Analysis, 2024). In recent years, Uzbekistan has implemented a wide range of reforms aimed at achieving equal rights and opportunities for women and men, ensuring their equal participation in the management of society and state affairs, supporting women in socio-legal matters, and protecting women from harassment and violence. In particular, the issue of gender equality has been raised to the level of state policy, and twenty-five legislative documents in this area have been adopted.

As a result, for the first time in the history of Uzbekistan, the number of women in parliament has reached the level recommended by the UN, reaching almost 32 per cent, ranking 37th among 190 parliaments in the world. The share of women in management positions has reached 27 per cent, in parties 44 per cent, in higher education 40 per cent, and in entrepreneurship 35 per cent. In order to provide socio-economic support to women and work with them in a targeted manner, the 'Women's Notebook' system has been introduced, and 300 billion soums have been allocated from the state budget annually. A system of covering tuition fees for needy girls who have lost one or both parents and single women without a breadwinner has been introduced, and the number of grants for girls from needy families when enrolling in higher education institutions has doubled. In order to develop women's entrepreneurship, more than 224 thousand women were allocated preferential loans totalling 6.9 trillion soums (Decision, 2021).

17.2. Literature Review

According to Janet Gale Stotsky (2006), 'the impact of gender differences in economic behaviour on macroeconomic processes can lead to reduced gender inequality and improved women's status, which can contribute to macroeconomic stability at high rates of economic growth'.

Gautam Hazarika et al. (2023) 'a study using stochastic frontier analysis of panel data based on econometric models has shown that gender equality in labour market opportunities increases gross technical efficiency in GDP production'.

According to Scherie (2022), 'increasing women's labour force participation is a sensible decision, especially in the context of a shrinking labour force in OECD countries, as it can lead to increased GDP and labour productivity, as well as improved fiscal sustainability'.

Many studies have shown that increasing women's participation in the labour market leads to economic growth. In particular, in Mexico, a 10 per cent increase in female employment was associated with a 10.01 per cent increase in GDP (Hernàndez et al., 2023). Similarly, other studies have shown that a 10 per cent increase in women's employment in twenty-one African countries leads to a 2.7 per cent increase in GDP (Obodoechine, 2019). Women's involvement in work processes increases productivity. This is because women have different decision-making approaches than men and bring innovative skills (Hegewisch et al., 2013). A balance between male and female labour force participation is crucial for economic efficiency by maximising production (Anderson & Braunstein, 2013). In particular, men often dominate in manufacturing and construction. However, the service sector, where women are increasingly participating, is also becoming an important area of economic growth (Anderson & Brownstein, 2013).

The gender wage gap is due to gender-based segregation of the labour market, which often leads to women working in relatively low-paid sectors (Achatz et al., 2005; Hinz & Gartner, 2005). Many studies have examined the wage gap between men and women in terms of labour market demand and supply (Reskin & Bielby, 2005; Sofyanty et al., 2025). Occupational segregation can occur as a result of employer decisions, which lead to women being placed in lower-paid and lower-status occupational positions than equally qualified men (Hinz & Allmendinger, 2007). The survival of the organisations would instead rely to a large extent on the capability of the companies to rapidly integrate their new members into the company and the tasks to perform (Unluonen & Boylu, 2016; Hamid et al., 2025; Jahrir et al.,2 025).

While the neoclassical approach attributes gender segregation to women choosing low-aid but family-friendly jobs under rational decision-making conditions, the socialisation approach sees the main cause of labour market segregation in the transmission of gender-specific value orientations between boys and girls. Therefore, the issue of possible gender differences in work values is central to the analysis of the causes of occupational segregation. If significant differences exist between men and women, they should be understood in part as a result of their own occupational choice behaviour (Padavic & Reskin, 2002, Singagerda et al., 2025).

Although there is evidence that women and men have different values and that men are more inclined to value material things than women (Beutel

& Marini, 1995; Rayala et al., 2025), there is no clear empirical evidence for gender differences in work values (Halaby, 2003; Rony et al., 2025).

17.3. Research Methodology and Development Hypothesis

In developing the econometric model, the World Bank (<https://data.worldbank.org/>) and data sources consisting of 33 years of total observations from 1991 to 2022 were used to assess the impact of male and female employment on macroeconomic indicators in the labour market.

Since the data are based on multivariate time series, we used VAR (Vector Autoregressive model) to develop the econometric equation.

Also, the econometric equation of the VAR model was developed, descriptive statistics were developed, the Unit-root test was used to determine the stationarity of all variables, the Johanson test to determine the congruence of variables, the determination of the optimal lag (delayed years) of the VAR model, the diagnostics of the econometric model, the autocorrelation or stability test and its reliability tests in determining forecast indicators were evaluated.

Another group of economists has successfully used econometric models such as Fixed Effects Estimator, Random Effects Estimator, LS and ARDL in their research on investment in digital infrastructure, various aspects of digital payment systems, the impact of inflation and credit interest rates on investment, factors affecting the reduction of the state's share in commercial banks, Non-Performing Loans in commercial banks, the digitisation of banks, risks in digital services and the development of retail payment services (Abdullah et al., 2025; Habib et al.,2025; Makhmudov et al., 2024; Mamadiyarov et al., 2025).

Analyses and forecasts were conducted using LS, ARDL, ARIMA and various other econometric models on the global services market, digital economy, energy-related financial stress, cocktail market, digital transformation, factors affecting the logistics industry (Kalandarov et al., 2025; Khodjaniyazov et al., 2025; Kulmanov et al., 2024; Kurbonov et al., 2024; Mamadiyarov et al., 2025; Zayniddinov et al., 2025).

According to Marco Lucchini et al. (2024) a variant of the VAR model, the SVAR, incorporates structural information to capture the impact of economic shocks. This is achieved by imposing constraints based on economic theory, which help to isolate the causal relationships between variables (Lucchini et al., 2024; Mamani et al., 2025; Ngongo et al., 2025; Zhang et al., 2025).

Research by Yayi Yan et al. (2021) has shown that recent advances have introduced time-varying VAR models, in which the coefficients of the error terms and the covariance matrix can vary over time (Kuchkarov et al., 2025; Litamahuputty et al., 2025; Romero et al., 2025; Yan et al., 2021., Zhao et al., 2025; Zokir et al., 2025).

In high-dimensional equations with a large number of variables, VAR models can be extended using techniques such as penalised regression to increase complexity. This is especially relevant in financial markets where many variables interact simultaneously.

The VAR model formula is given below.

1. VAR model structure: A VAR model with *k* variables and p lags can be expressed as follows:

$$y_t = b + \sum_{i=0}^{n} B_i Y_{t-i} + e_t \tag{1}$$

Here, y_t is the $k \times 1$ vector of endogenous variables at time t

v is the $k \times 1$ vector of constants (intercepts)

B_i is the $k \times k$ matrix of coefficients for lag i

e_t is the $k \times 1$ vector of error terms, representing the mean zero and the covariance matrix.

All variables in the econometric model are given below.

GDP of the European and Central Asian countries – *logGDP* (dependent variable); Labour force participation rate of the European and Central Asian countries, women – *loglab_rat_fem* (independent variable); Labour force participation rate of European and Central Asian countries, *men – loglab_rat_mel* (independent variable).

The hypotheses for the econometric model were formulated as follows:

Null hypothesis (H_0): The labour force participation rate of women and the labour force participation rate of men in European and Central Asian countries do not affect the size of the GDP in these countries.

Alternative hypothesis (H_1): The labour force participation rate of women and the labour force participation rate of men in European and Central Asian countries have a significant relationship with the size of the GDP in these countries.

17.4. Analysis and Results

In the first stage of the study, descriptive statistical indicators were scaled for all variables (Table 48).

Table 48. Descriptive statistics of dependent and independent variables according to the econometric model

	logGDP	loglab_rat_fem	loglab_rat_mel
Mean	9.681406	4.1459863	4.421635
Maximum	10.14208	4.1742563	4.325698
Minimum	9.105091	4.0224536	4.241369
Std. Dev	0.3798241	0.04123591	0.0236154
Std. Err.	0.0671441	0.01754122	0.0012537
Skewness	0.1442664	0.34425331	0.4253164
Kurtosis	-0.2939119	1.9125369	2.04215
Observation	33	33	33

Source: Developed by the authors based on the Stata program.

According to Table 48, the descriptive statistics of the model showed a positive correlation between all variables with mean values and confidence intervals. This indicates favourable conditions for further development of the main factors in the subsequent stages of forecasting the econometric model indicators.

According to Figure 52, in assessing the impact of male and female employment on macroeconomic indicators in the labour market during the analysed period, in particular, in the countries of Europe and Central Asia, the GDP volume and the factors affecting it presented a significant growth dynamics during the analysed period. According to this situation, female employment in the labour market has formed a state of strong growth, demonstrating an active state, especially after 2000.

In the next step, the analytical relationship (rconnected) of the resulting variables and the factors affecting it is presented (Figure 53).

From Figure 53, it can be seen that the resulting factor and the factors influencing it showed an even distribution over the analysed period, and the density according to this figure presented peaks with an average wide

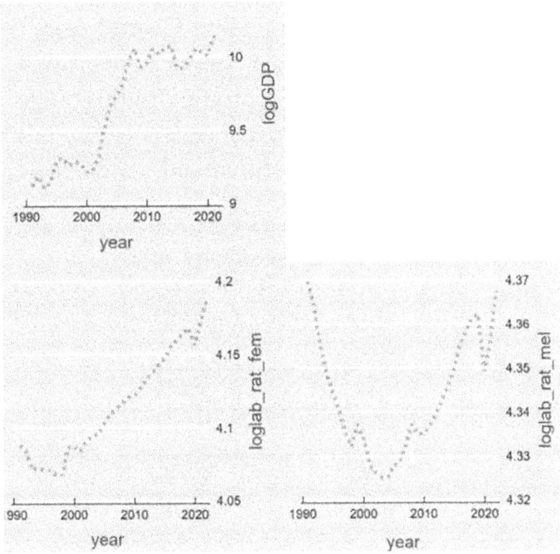

Figure 52. Analytical graphical representation of outcome variables and independent variables over time.
Source: Developed by the authors based on the Stata program.

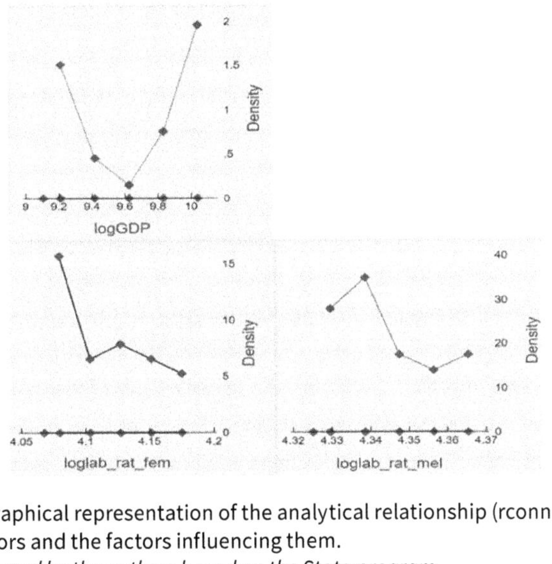

Figure 53. Graphical representation of the analytical relationship (rconnected) of the resulting factors and the factors influencing them.
Source: Developed by the authors based on the Stata program.

distribution. In the countries of Europe and Central Asia, the volume of GDP and the factors influencing it had a clear peak of growth, according to which the values showed a strong concentration in this range.

At the next stage of the study, a cross-correlation matrix was developed for each of the resulting variables and the variables influencing it (Table 49).

Table 49. Cross-correlation matrix of the impact of female and male employment on the GDP volume of the countries of Europe and Central Asia

Variables	(1)	(2)	Significant
(1) logGDP	1.000		
(2) loglab_rat_fem	0.8872	1.000	
	(0.0000)		***
(3) loglab_rat_mel	0.4216	0.4752	
	(0.0016)	(0.0060)	***

Source: Developed by the authors based on the Stata program.

According to the above tables, there is a strong and significant correlation between the variables and the correlation matrix shows that there is no multicollinearity between the outcome and independent variables. Considering that the *p*-value is less than 0.05, this indicates that the correlation coefficient is reliable and statistically significant.

In the next step, a Unit-root test was conducted to determine the stationarity of the outcome variables and the factors affecting them (Table 50).

Table 50. Unit-root test results for the outcome variables and the factors affecting them

Variables	Test Statistic	1% Critical Value	5% Critical Value	10% Critical Value	p-value for Z(t)
logGDP (Dependent variable)	−5.446	−3.750	−2.810	−2.600	0.0004
loglab_rat_fem	−4.230	−3.750	−2.810	−2.600	0.0002
loglab_rat_mel	−4.681	−3.750	−2.810	−2.600	0.0036

Source: Developed by the authors based on the Stata program.

According to Table 50, the unit root test value of the dependent variable is –4.446, and the test results of the independent variables are –4.230 and –4.681, respectively. These values indicate that the factors affecting the GDP of the European and Central Asian countries on these resulting factors are statistically significant and stable. From the data in the table, the McKinnon value of 0.0000 indicates that the critical values of $Z(t)$ are statistically significant.

The next step is to perform a cointegration test. The following table shows that the VAR model is perfectly fit in the 4th lagged year (Table 51).

Table 51. Test to determine the optimal lags in the VAR model of the GDP of the European and Central Asian countries and the factors affecting it

Delayed years	LL	LR	df	*p*	FPE	AIC	HQIC	SBIC
1	278.166	217.09	9	0.000	1.1e–12	-19.0118	-18.8373*	-18.4409*
2	286.976	17.621*	9	0.040	1.2e–12*	-18.9983*	-18.6928	-17.9991 *
3	297.83	21.712	9	0.010	1.1e–12	-19.1308	-18.6945	-17.7035
4	308.926	22.189	9	0.008	1.1e–12	-19.2804	-18.7132	-17.4249

Source: Developed by the authors based on the Stata program.

According to the four tables, it follows that the optimal equation can be constructed in the 2nd stage according to the model, which will be of great importance in the subsequent construction of the VAR equation.

In the next stage, the cointegration test of the variables was carried out using the Johanson test (Table 52).

Table 52. The Johanson test for cointegration based on the VAR model of the GDP volume of the countries of Europe and Central Asia and the factors affecting it

Maximum level	Number of parameters	LL	Inherent value	Tracking statistics	5 per cent critical value
0	12	289.66235	.	26.9400*	29.68
1	17	298.1181	0.43091	10.0285	15.41
2	20	302.91027	0.27347	0.4441	3.76
3	21	-20.06677	0.01470		

Source: Developed by the authors based on the Stata program.

According to Table 52, 'Maximum degree' represents the number of cointegrated vectors in the model. According to it, H_0 represents the existence of one or more cointegrated vectors according to the hypothesis. If the value of the observation statistic is greater than the 5 per cent critical value, the H0 hypothesis is rejected.

The H_0 hypothesis represents the existence of a cointegrated vector in this model. Since the observation statistic is greater than the 5 per cent critical value, this hypothesis is rejected. In the second row, the H_0 hypothesis represents the existence of 1 cointegrated vector in this model, and since the observation statistic is greater than the 5 per cent critical value, this hypothesis is rejected.

Using the VAR model, econometric equations of the resulting variables and the factors affecting them were developed (Table 53).

Table 53. Regression equation indicators of GDP size of European and Central Asian countries by factors affecting it

Vector autoregression

Sample: 1993 thru 2022			Number of obs = 30		
Log likelihood = 268.8484			AIC = −17.12323		
FPE = 7.38e − 12			HQIC= −16.94393		
Det(Sigma_ml) = 3.30e − 12			SBIC= −16.56275		
Equation	Parms	RMSE	*R*-sq	chi²	*P* > chi²
logGDP	2	0.099796	0.9332	419.2685	0.0000
loglab_rat_fem	2	0.007544	0.9604	727.365	0.0000
loglab_rat_mel	2	0.005413	0.8221	138.628	0.0000

	Coefficient	*Std.er*	*z*	*P > z*	*[95%*	*conf.*	*sig*
logGDP							
logGDP							
L2.	0.436	0.132	3.300	0.001	0.177	0.695	***
loglab_rat_fem							
L2.	2.514	1.642	3.970	0.000	3.297	9.731	***
loglab_rat_mel							
L2.	−2.911	1.937	−4.590	0.000	−12.688	−5.095	***
_cons	17.340	5.915	2.930	0.003	5.746	28.935	***

Source: Developed by the authors based on the Stata program.

$$logGDP_t = \beta_0 + \beta_1 \cdot logGDP_{t-2} + \beta_2 \cdot loglab\_rat\_fem_{t-2} + \beta_3 \cdot loglab\_rat\_mel_{t-2} + \epsilon_t \quad (2)$$

According to the estimated coefficients, the VAR model estimates

$$logGDP_t = 17.34 + 0.43 logGDP_{t-2} + 6.51 loglab\_rat\_fem_{t-2} - 8.89 loglab\_rat\_mel_{t-2} + \epsilon t \quad (3)$$

Statistical significance

The model uses two lags for each variable and is well-fit to the data, as shown by the R-squared values for each equation:

logGDP: $R^2 = 0.9332$ This indicates that the econometric model explains approximately 93.32 per cent of the variation in GDP, indicating a strong fit.
loglab_rat_fem: $R^2 = 0.9604$ explains about 96.04 per cent of the variation in female labour force participation rate, which is very good.
loglab_rat_mel: $R^2 = 0.8221$ explains about 82.21 per cent of the variation in male labour force participation rate, which is very good.

High Chi-square values and p-values ($p > \text{chi}^2 = 0.0000$ for each equation) indicate that the coefficients in each equation are statistically significant overall.

Result. The coefficient of 0.43 on GDP in the European and Central Asian countries means that a 1 per cent increase in GDP two periods ago ($t - 2$) is associated with a 0.436 per cent increase in current GDP. This positive, statistically significant coefficient ($p = 0.001$) indicates the degree of permanent effect of last year's GDP on current GDP.

The coefficient of 2.514 on female labour force participation in the European and Central Asian countries indicates that a 1 per cent increase in female labour force participation two periods ago is associated with a 2.514 per cent increase in current GDP. This effect is positive and statistically significant ($p = 0.000$), indicating a strong positive relationship between past female labour force participation and current GDP growth.

The coefficient of –2.911 on the male labour force participation rate in the labour market in the countries of Europe and Central Asia indicates that a 1 per cent increase in the male labour force participation rate two periods ago is associated with a decrease in current GDP by 8.891 per cent.

During the study, forecast indicators were developed based on the VAR model, analysing the dynamic relationships between several variables. In the development of the study, forecast indicators were developed based on the factors affecting the outcome variables based on the VAR model (Figure 54).

Eigenvalue	Modulus
1.015455 + .01588134i	1.01558
1.015455 - .01588134i	1.01558
-1.015455 + .01588134i	1.01558
-1.015455 - .01588134i	1.01558
-.8098534	.809853
.8098534	.809853

Figure 54. Eigenvalue-stability test of the VAR model for GDP size and factors affecting it.
Source: Developed by the authors based on the Stata program.

According to Figure 54, these tests are particularly important for assessing the long-term constancy of parameters in VAR models. According to them, the VAR model successfully passes the stability test. If the modulus of all eigenvalues is less than 1, the VAR process is considered stable, that is, any shocks in the system disappear over time and the process presents an average equilibrium state.

In the next stage of the study, the Lagrange-multiplier test was performed (Figure 55).

lag	chi2	df	Prob > chi2
1	163.5642	9	0.00000
2	82.7382	9	0.00000

Figure 55. Lagrange-Multiplier test of the VAR model for GDP volume and its influencing factors.
Source: Developed by the authors based on the Stata program.

The results of the Lagrange multiplier test indicate that there is significant autocorrelation in the data. The chi-square statistic for lag 1 is 21.7196, with 9 degrees of freedom, and the p-value is 0.00981. The chi-square statistic for lag 2 is 22.7269, with 9 degrees of freedom, and the p-value is 0.00684.

Since the p-values for both lags (0.00981 and 0.00684) are below the 0.05 level of overall significance, we reject the null hypothesis (H_0: no autocorrelation in lag order) for both lags.

Before making the forecast, a final check was performed to assess the stationarity of the model residuals. Figure 56 shows a graph depicting the stationarity of the model residuals.

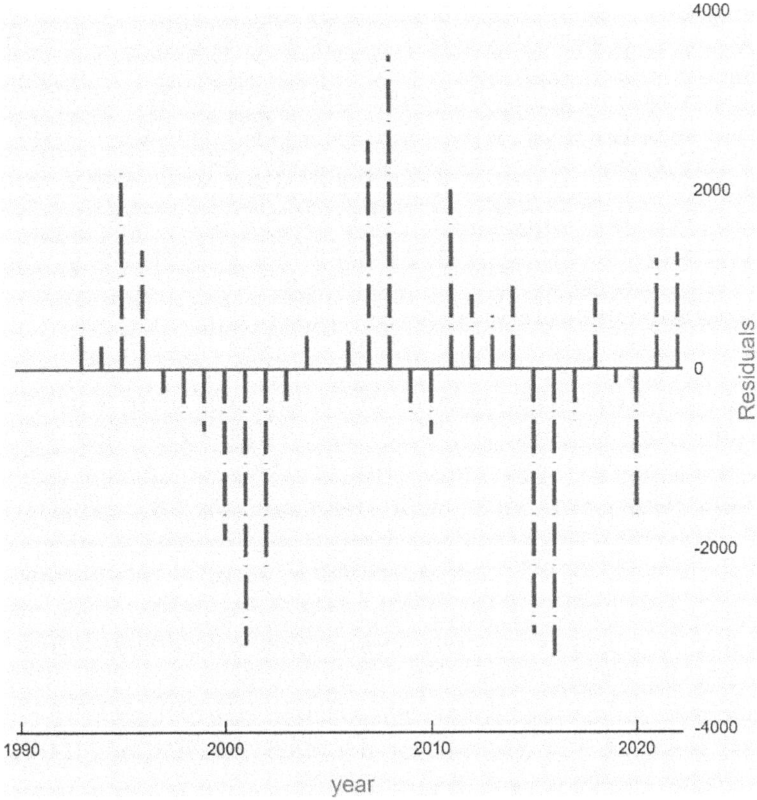

Figure 56. Forecast indicators of GDP volume and factors affecting it Stationarity graph of VAR model residuals.
Source: Developed by the authors based on the Stata program.

The selected VAR model and its endogenous factor, as well as exogenous factors, were used to develop forecast indicators that successfully passed all tests based on the sequence. At the next stage of the study, forecast indicators were developed for the period from 2025 to 2030, excluding random exogenous and endogenous variables, under the influence of the GDP volume of the countries of Europe and Central Asia and the level of employment of men and women in the labour market (Table 54).

Table 54. 2025–2030 GDP of Europe and Central Asia in billion US dollars

Years	Pessimistic forecast	Optimistic forecast	Forecast
2025	23,271.39	29,996.97	27,002.54
2026	23,249.64	30,755.45	27,507.47
2027	23,751.48	31,263.46	27,627.77
2028	23,640.45	31,615.10	28,163.47
2029	24,162.92	32,164.01	28,164.47
2030	24,376.23	32,994.07	28,685.15

Source: Developed by the authors based on the Stata program.

Result. The GDP of the countries of Europe and Central Asia, based on the impact of female and male employment in the labour market in these countries, in particular, without taking into account random factors according to the VAR model, was forecast to be 27002.54 billion US dollars in 2025, 27507.47 billion US dollars in 2026, 27627.77 billion US dollars in 2027, 28163.47 billion US dollars in 2028, 28164.47 billion US dollars in 2029 and 28685.15 billion US dollars in 2030, respectively. The forecast results also showed a positive result, indicating an increasing trend of the resulting factor.

The study presents a graphical representation of the GDP growth forecast for the countries of Europe and Central Asia for 1991–2023 and 2024–2030, provided by the World Bank (Figure 57).

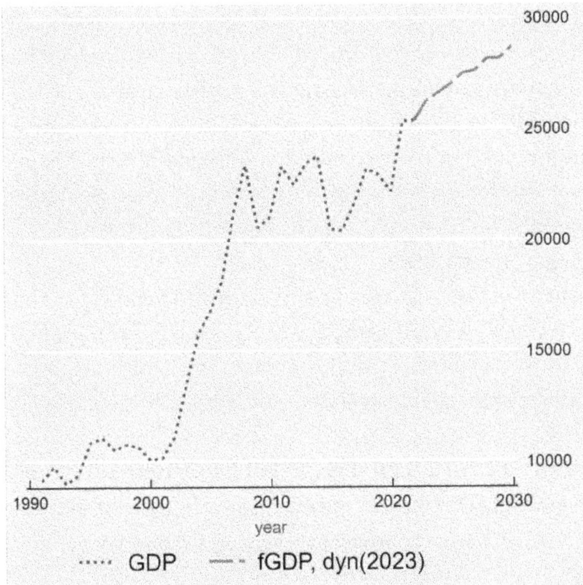

Figure 57. GDP volume for 1991–2023 and forecast graph for 2024–2030.
Source: Developed by the authors based on the Stata program.

Based on Figure 57, graphical representations have been formed for the GDP volume of the countries of Europe and Central Asia for 1991–2023 and the GDP per capita volume for 2025–2030 provided by the World Bank. According to it, the trend graph indicates that the two lines are located almost as close as possible, which indicates the reliability of the forecast indicators for the next seven years, excluding random factors, and that they have an increasing trend.

17.5. Conclusion

The analysis shows that the labour market in Europe and Central Asia is characterised by stable and positive economic growth dynamics under the influence of male and female employment.

1. The importance of the growth trend of the labour market. Sustainable economic growth – increasing GDP values are assessed by the regulation of the economy, while reflecting the positive impact of labour market participation on economic indicators.
2. The importance of the expanded employment rate. The results of the econometric forecast emphasise the importance of male and female employment in economic expansion and demonstrate the benefits of a stable labour market.
3. Assessment of the effectiveness of economic stability. The absence of sharp changes in GDP forecasts creates a fundamental environment for economic growth, which increases investor confidence and long-term investment attractiveness, and serves to strengthen economic planning.
4. The importance of a high standard of living under the influence of the labour market. Through economic growth, the population creates the basis for improving incomes, optimising social services and increasing the quality of life for citizens.
5. The need for future practices to promote workforce development. As the employment rate remains a key factor in the growth of the labour market, investing in education, skills development and workforce diversity will further strengthen the economic outlook.

Bibliography

Abdullah, M. A., Han, X., Amjad, M. A., & Makhmudov, S. (2025). Revisit the role of financial development on economic growth, human development, and sustainable development in higher-income countries. Journal of Environmental Management, 392, 126874.

Achatz, J. (2005). 'Geschlechtersegregation im Arbeitsmarkt'. *Arbeitsmarktsoziologie: Probleme, Theorien, empirische Befunde*, pp. 263–301.

Anderson, B., and Braunstein, E. (2013). 'Economic Growth and Employment from 1990–2010: Explaining Elasticities by Gender'. *Review of Radical Political Economics*, 45 (3), 269–77.

Beutel, A. M., and Marini, M. M. (1995). 'Gender and Values'. *American Sociological Review*, 436–48.

Figueroa-Hernández, E., Pérez-Soto, F., and Pérez-Figueroa, R. A. (2023). 'Women in the Labor Market and Economic Growth in Mexico'. *Agro Productividad* 16 (9), 139–47.

Gautam, Hazarika, Maroula, Khraiche, Levent, Kutlu (2023). 'Gender Equity in Labor Market Opportunities and Aggregate Technical Efficiency: A Case of Equity Promoting Efficiency'. *Applied Economics*, 1–12. <https://doi.org/10.1080/00036846.2023.2203451>.

Gender Equality Analysis in Uzbekistan (2024). *International Bank for Reconstruction and Development*: World Bank.

Habib, S. S., Islam, M. A., Ali, M. N., Benitez, I. B., Mamadiyarov, Z., Mirzayev, B., … & Flah, A. (2025). Multi-Objective Optimization and Feasibility Analysis of Integrated Biogas–Solar Energy Systems for Rural Electrification. Results in Engineering, 107086.

Halaby, C. N. (2003). 'Where Job Values Come from: Family and Schooling Background, Cognitive Ability, and Gender'. *American Sociological Review* 68 (2), 251–78.

Hamid, E. M., & Pardaev, J. (2025). Islamic marketing strategies for customer loyalty: Role of religious commitment and technology turbulence. European Journal of Progressive Research. https://doi.org/10.24204/ejpr.2025.4804

Hegewisch, A., Usher, A., and Newitt, K. (2013). 'Investing in Women's Employment: Good for Business, Good for Development', 1–108.

Hinz, T., and Allmendinger, J. (2007). Geschlechtersegregation in Organisationen und die Lohndifferenz zwischen Männern und Frauen.

Hinz, T., and Gartner, H. (2005). 'Geschlechtsspezifische lohnunterschiede in branchen, berufen und betrieben/The Gender Wage Gap within Economic Sectors, Occupations, and Firms'. *Zeitschrift für Soziologie*, 34 (1), 22–39.

Janet, Gale, and Stotsky (2006). 'Gender and Its Relevance to Macroeconomic Policy: A Survey'. *Social Science Research Network*.

Kalandarov, F., Makhmudov, S., Ibadullaev, D., Matniyozov, M., Nasretdinova, F., Sabirov, K., and Bahodirov, N. M. (2025). 'Low-Carbon Energy Risk and Renewable Energy Development: Insights from Method of Moments Quantile Regression'. *International Journal of Energy Economics and Policy*, 15 (3), 524–36.

Khayrilla Kurbonov, Samariddin Makhmudov, Shakhzod Erkinov, Umidjon Dadabaev, Gulnora Bekimbetova, Rukhiddin Zayniddinov, and Mirzabek Jonuzokov (2024). 'Evaluating the Impact of Marketing Practices Digitalization and Investment on Labor Market Efficiency and Commercial Bank Performance Using Econometric Models'. In *The 8th International Conference on Future Networks & Distributed Systems (ICFNDS '24)*, 11–12 December 2024, Marakech, Morocco, 16pp. New York, NY, USA: ACM, <https://doi.org/10.1145/3726122.3726237>.

Khodjaniyazov, N., Mirkhoshimova, M., Kalandarov, F., Matyokubova, D., Utegenova, S., Makhmudov, S., and Khudayberganov, M. (2025). 'Time-Varying Impacts of Financial Stress on Energy-Related Uncertainty'. *International Journal of Energy Economics and Policy*, 15 (3), 689–98.

Lin, M.H., Matchanova, B., Nurmatovich, H.A. et al. Optimal Operation of the Multi-Carrier Energy System Considering Energy Markets and Renewable Energies Participation. *Int. J. Appl. Comput. Math* **11**, 170 (2025). https://doi.org/10.1007/s40819-025-02002-9

Litamahuputty, J. V., Amiruddin, E. G., Rahim, R., Rahman, A., & Mamadiyarov, Z. (2025). Cryptocurrency Risk Management through Decision Engineering: Evaluating XRPUSD and ADAUSD Portfolio Performance. Journal of Applied Science, Engineering, Technology, and Education, 7(1), 69–81. https://doi.org/10.35877/454RI.asci3871

Mamadiyarov, Z., Eshov, M., Otakhonova, D., Utegenova, S., Sabirov, K., Marks, A., & Bahodirov, N. (2025). Does Energy Policy Risk Threaten Energy Sources Diversification?. International Journal of Energy Economics and Policy, 15(5), 730–740. https://doi.org/10.32479/ijeep.21140

Mamadiyarov, Z., Saidov, O., Abdurazakova, N., Makhmudov, S., Nazarov, M., Rajabova, N., … Ruzmetova, I. (2025). Energy-Related Uncertainty and Tourism Stock Markets: New Insights from Time-Varying Relationship with TVP- VAR Approach. International Journal of

Energy Economics and Policy, 15(4), 730–737. https://doi.org/10.32479/ijeep.20480

Mamani, J.C.M., Miri, M., Vorobev, Y. et al. Optimal Operation of Energy Microgrid Considering Economic and Emission Indices. Oper. Res. Forum 6, 122 (2025). https://doi.org/10.1007/s43069-025-00523-z

Marco, Lucchini, Mario, Forni, Luca, Gambetti, and Luca, Sala (2024). *Common Components Svars*, <https://doi.org/10.2139/ssrn.4716350>.

Ngongo, M., Herman, H., Ndandara, A., Jois Jaha, D. A., Peku Djawang, J. U. S., Tanggu Rame, M. M., Khamraeva, S. N., & Mamadiyarov, Z. (2025). An Investigation of Meaning, Toponymy of Sumba Cultural Site's Names, and the Impact of Tourism Visitors on Surrounding Society. Forum for Linguistic Studies, 7(8), 679–693. https://doi.org/10.30564/fls.v7i8.10260

Obodoechine, E. N. (2019). *Impact of Female Labor Participation in African Countries*, <https://digitalcommons.georgiasouthern.edu/cgi/viewcontent.cgi?article=1519&context=honors-theses>.

Padavic, I., and Reskin, B. F. (2002). *Women and Men at Work*. Pine Forge Press.

PANJAITAN, M. B., HAMDANAH, H., SIRAIT, J., SUTIKNO, S., FATMAWATI, E., HERMAN, H., & MAMADIYAROV, Z. (2025). THE ROLE OF EMOTIONAL REGULATION IN SHAPING STUDENTS' PERCEPTION OF PHYSICS PROBLEMSOLVING TASKS. TPM – Testing, Psychometrics, Methodology in Applied Psychology, 32(S2(2025) : Posted 09 June), 1–10. Retrieved from https://tpmap.org/submission/index.php/tpm/article/view/139

Pradhan, R., Hajiyev, E., Shichiyakh, R. et al. Optimal Techno-Economic Feasibility of an Off-Grid Microgrid System Using Load Flow Energy Management Strategies. *Oper. Res. Forum* **6**, 120 (2025). https://doi.org/10.1007/s43069-025-00524-y

Reskin, B. F., and Bielby, D. D. (2005). 'A Sociological Perspective on Gender and Career Outcomes'. *Journal of Economic Perspectives*, 19 (1), 71–86.

Resolution of the Senate of the Oliy Majlis of the Republic of Uzbekistan dated May 28, 2021 No. SQ-297-IV, 'On Approval of the Strategy for Achieving Gender Equality in the Republic of Uzbekistan by 2030'.

Romero, R. M., Zelinskaya, M., Makhmudov, S., Sapaev, S., & Rustambekovich, J. U. (2025, September). Modelling and Optimal Utilisation of the Renewable Energy Systems in Microgrid with Improving Reliability and Energy Efficiency. In Operations Research Forum (Vol. 6, No. 3, pp. 1–20). Springer International Publishing.

Rony, Z. T., Jefri, R., Rusmardiana, A., Pramono, S. A., & Mamadiyarov, Z. (2025). Downside Risk Measurement of Indonesian Financial and Energy Securities: A Value at Risk Perspective. Journal of Applied Science, Engineering, Technology, and Education, 7(2). https://doi.org/10.35877/454RI.asci3898

Rukhiddin Zayniddinov, Nodir Jumaev, Gulbakhor Irgasheva, Alam Asadov, Nosir Makhmudov, Sirojiddin Abrorov, and Samariddin Makhmudov (2024). 'The Influence of the Digital Economy on Economic Development Evidence from Uzbekistan'. In *The 8th International Conference on Future Networks & Distributed Systems (ICFNDS '24)*, 11–12 December 2024, Marakech, Morocco, 9pp. NewYork, NY, USA: ACM, <https://doi.org/10.1145/3726122.3726242>.

Rayala, R. V., Borra, C. R., Vasudevan, V., Singhania, R., Cheekati, S., & Mamadiyarov, Z. (2025, July). Lightweight Deep Learning Framework for Human Activity Recognition: A MobileNet-LSTM Approach with WHOA Optimization. In *2025 International Conference on Innovations in Intelligent Systems: Advancements in Computing, Communication, and Cybersecurity (ISAC3)* (pp. 1–6). IEEE.

Rayala, R. V., Sandhya, N., Singhania, R., Cheekati, S., Borra, C. R., Vasudevan, V., & Mamadiyarov, Z. (2025, July). AI-Driven Tomato Quality Assessment: A Deep Learning Approach for Image-based Defect Detection and Classification. In *2025 International Conference on Innovations in Intelligent Systems: Advancements in Computing, Communication, and Cybersecurity (ISAC3)* (pp. 1–6). IEEE.

Samariddin Makhmudov, Malika Umarova, Khayrilla Kurbonov, Laylo Akbarova, Durdona Davletova, Nilufar Shanazarova, and Toshmurod Kulmanov (2024). 'Evaluating the Forecast Indicators of the Volume of Highly Liquid Assets of Commercial Banks in the Process of Digital Transformation'. In *The 8th International Conference on Future Networks & Distributed Systems (ICFNDS '24)*, 11–12 December 2024,

Marakech, Morocco, 8pp. New York, NY, USA: ACM, <https://doi.org/10.1145/3726122.3726222>.

Samariddin Makhmudov, Kudratillo Tukhsanov, Saifulla Arslanbekov, Akram Amanov, Orifali Tursunov, Umarbek Jabbarov, and Muyassarxon Mirzakarimova (2024). 'Optimizing Supply Chain Financing Development Prospects of Digital Ecosystems in the European Logistics Industry'. In *The 8th International Conference on Future Networks & Distributed Systems (ICFNDS '24)*, 11–12 December 2024, Marakech, Morocco, 12pp. New York, NY, USA: ACM, <https://doi.org/10.1145/3726122.3726200>.

Scherie, Nicol. (2022). 'Gender Budgeting: The Economic and Fiscal Rationale'. *OECD Journal on Budgeting*, 22 (3), <https://doi.org/10.1787/9ca9b221-en>.

Singagerda, F. S., Pratama, M. R., Alfairus, M. Q., Iskandar, A., & Mamadiyarov, Z. (2025). A Decision-Centric Approach to Risk Management in Aviation Stock Investments Using Value at Risk and Portfolio Optimization. Journal of Applied Science, Engineering, Technology, and Education, 7(1), 114–125. https://doi.org/10.35877/454RI.asci3870

Sofyanty, D., Romadhoni, R., Handriadi, H., Makhsudovna, I. S., Anwar, Z., & Mamadiyarov, Z. (2025). Strategic Decision Analysis for Investment Portfolios: Computational Risk Assessment in Transportation Asset Management. Journal of Applied Science, Engineering, Technology, and Education, 7(2). https://doi.org/10.35877/454RI.asci3897

Toshmurod Kulmanov, Umidjon Dadabaev, Mansurbek Qulmetov, Aliboy Ulashov, Mirjalol Eshboyev, and Samariddin Makhmudov a,b. (2024). 'Global Services Market Transformation: Digitalization, Export Trends, and Future Forecasts'. In *The 8th International Conference on Future Networks & Distributed Systems (ICFNDS '24)*, 11–12 December 2024, Marakech, Morocco, 8pp. New York, NY, USA: ACM, <https://doi.org/10.1145/3726122.3726245>.

Unluonen, M. B., and Boylu, Y. (2016). 'İşe Alıştırma eğitimlerinin iş tatmini üzerindeki etkisi: Otel işletmelerinde bir araştırma'. *Journal of Business Research – Turk*, 8 (2), 407–26.

Yan, Y., Gao, J., and Peng, B. (2021). 'On Time-varying VAR Models: Estimation, Testing and Impulse Response Analysis'. arXiv preprint <arXiv:*2111.00450*>.

Zhang, L., Zhao, Z., Qamri, G. M., & Makhmudov, S. (2025). Unleashing the critical role of renewable energy through global value chains and digitalization: A path towards environmental sustainability. Journal of Environmental Management, 392, 126688.

Zhao, Q., Pervaiz, A., Makhmudov, S., & Fatima, A. (2025). Do environmental stringent policies enhance the impact of renewable energy on CO2 reduction? Evidence from BRICS-T economies. Journal of Environmental Management, 391, 126464.

Balancing Regional Industrial Production and Its Socio-Economic and Environmental Impacts: A Strategic Assessment

Samariddin Makhmudov, Isabek Murtazaev, Zokir Mamadiyarov, Dilorom Kasimova, Nilufar Komilova, Dinora Otakhonova and Eshboev Mirjalol

18.1. Introduction

Foreign studies show that with the economic conditions influencing the interconnection between industrial production in regions, their role in the formation of regional economic processes becomes more important in raising efficiency indicators. These economic groups are considered an investment climate, with potential programmes of state support, broad access to economic and financial resources and skilled human capital. In his view, economic factors' interdependence as well as their determination of regions' industrial expansion and economic flourishing create grounds for varying levels of their development. That implies greater need to nurture balanced systems of economic factors towards fostering balanced industrial expansion at regional level.

Industrial production is a key driving force for regional economic growth, influencing employment, income and infrastructure building. However, excessive industrialisation tends to be correlated with socio-economic imbalance and environmental problems, and therefore an equilibrium strategy in sustainable development is necessary. Regional industrial policies in Uzbekistan have tried to launch development through investment, export development and energy development. But the relationship among these variables and their combined influence on industrial production is not researched well, particularly in regions like Zarafshan, where industrial growth must be coordinated with overall economic and environmental goals.

This research explores the most significant drivers of industrial output in the Zarafshan area, taking into account the position of fixed investment in capital, industrial exports, inflation and the supply of electricity. Based on a sound econometric model – a multivariate linear regression model (LS) – we use time-series data between the years 2013–2023 to measure these dynamics. This study answers most fundamental questions: How do investment and export operations influence industrial development? What is the contribution of energy availability to sustaining production? And how is inflation moderating industrial expansion?

The research is a contribution to literature since it offers empirical findings from an emerging economy where the pressure for growth must be addressed as well as that for sustainability. The results point to the significance of capital spending and energy infrastructure in stimulating industrial production but also the need to have a control device for inflation. The findings can be used by policymakers to design interventions to optimise industrial efficiency, improve export competitiveness and achieve energy security – towards regional balanced and sustainable development in general.

18.2. Literature Review

In assessing the importance of achieving a balance between industrial production in regions, scientific theoretical studies have been conducted by authoritative foreign scientists and hypotheses developed on the basis of econometric models have been confirmed.

L. S. Zelentsova et al. (2024) state that 'a favorable investment climate is of great importance for the development of industry in regions, and regions with potential investment opportunities serve to attract productive industrial activities'. According to them, against the background of the development of the industrial sector in the regions, it allows to control the inflation rate, form financing sources and increase employment opportunities (Rayala et al., 2025).

M. Antevskiy's (2008) scientific developments show that 'reforms and incentives carried out by the government in the regions had a significant impact on industrial development'. According to scientists, these large-scale developments led to the achievement of industrial growth in regions supported by the state.

According to A. V. Fedotov et al. (2022) 'the presence of natural and human resources plays an important role in the location and development of industry, and resource-rich regions provide a competitive advantage in attracting industry'.

The authors' research findings highlight the existence of a relationship between the formation of new industrial production and the level of regional economic and social development of individual cities within regions.

M. Chakraborty (2024) states that 'the availability of a skilled workforce for industrial development leads to a greater likelihood of attracting and sustaining industrial activity in regions with a high level of education and training'. The authors analysed the impact of production sectors and socio-economic factors on industrial investment in 16 major states of India using a 37-year panel data set based on econometric models. The results show that the presence of different industrial activities in the distribution of human capital, infrastructure benefits and industrial investment is statistically significant.

W. Liu and D. Zhao (2011) argue that 'well-developed infrastructure, including transportation and communication networks, enables industrial growth by reducing costs and increasing efficiency'. The authors' research findings suggest that the financial resources of the industrial sector in the eastern region have a positive impact on growth and have significantly contributed to growth in the central and western regions.

Ayad Ayid Wali (2014) argues that 'technological advances stimulate industrial growth by increasing productivity and creating new opportunities for development'. According to the authors, regions can lead to rapid industrial growth by supporting investment activities and innovation.

R. Capello and S. Cerisolani (2022) argue that 'strategies such as cluster development, innovation promotion, and international cooperation are recommended to overcome industrial imbalances'. According to the authors, consistent strategies in industry serve to increase regional competitiveness and ensure balanced industrial growth.

To assess the factors affecting the balance between industrial production in the Zarafshan region, data sources from the Statistical Agency under the President of the Republic of Uzbekistan (<https://stat.uz/uz/>) with a total number of observations of 40, covering the years 2013–2023, were used.

18.3. Methodology

In developing the econometric model for the study, we used the multivariate LS model, since the data are based on multivariate time series.

According to David J. Olive et al. (2015), 'a multivariate linear model includes the linearity, independence, homoscedasticity and normality of the residuals'. According to the authors, these assumptions are important for the validity of the model and lead to inefficient estimates.

Analyses and forecasts were conducted using multivariate LS, ARDL, ARIMA and various other econometric models on the global services market, digital economy, energy-related financial stress, cocktail market, digital transformation, factors affecting the logistics industry (Kalandarov et al., 2025; Khodjaniyazov et al., 2025; Kuchkarov et al., 2025; Kulmanov et al., 2025; Kurbonov et al., 2025; Kuziboev et al., 2025; Mamadiyarov et al., 2025; Rony et al., 2025; Zayniddinov et al., 2025).

According to Stan Lipovetsky (2024), 'the parameters of a multivariate linear regression model are estimated using the method of least squares'. According to him, the model minimises the sum of squared differences between the observed and predicted values, and this approach serves to ensure that the fitted model passes through the mean values of the variables.

According to Q. Wang et al. (2012), 'multivariate regression serves as the basis for other statistical methods, including canonical correlation analysis and discriminant analysis'. The authors' research conclusions showed that the model includes nonlinear relationships and interactions between variables.

The Gauss-Markov conditions for the econometric model 'multivariate linear (LS) model (Mamadiyarov et al., 2025; Mamani et al., 2025; Smith et al., 2013; Sofyanty et al., 2025)' were checked, and the statistical significance of the econometric model was assessed based on several confidence tests, in particular 'Durbin-Watson (Jović, O. (2016)', 'Shapiro-Wilk' and 'Breusch-Pagan (Makhmudov et al., 2025; Mamadiyarov et al., 2025; Ngongo et al., 2025; Rayala et al., 2025; Romero et al., 2025; Singagerda et al., 2025; Zolna et al., 2016)' tests.

Another group of economists has successfully used econometric models such as Fixed Effects Estimator, Random Effects Estimator, LS and ARDL in their research on investment in digital infrastructure, various aspects of digital payment systems, the impact of inflation and credit interest rates on investment, factors affecting the reduction of the state's share in commercial banks, Non-Performing Loans in commercial banks, the digitisation of banks, risks in digital services and the development of retail payment services (Abdullah et al., 2025; Habib et al., 2025; Jahrir et al., 2025; Makhmudov et al., 2025; Mamadiyarov et al., 2025; PANJATAN eta al., 2025; Rayala et al., 2025; Zhang et al., 2025; Zokir et al., 2021).

The first econometric model for the research was the LS model.

The formula for the LS model is given below.

$$Y_i = \rho_0 + \rho_1 a_{1i} + \rho_2 a_{2i} + \rho_3 a_{3i} + \cdots + \rho_{ik} a_{ik} + \epsilon_i \quad (1)$$

Here, t is the dependent variable for the y_i-observation, which is the dependent variable in the model,

$a_{1i}, a_{2i}, a_{3i}, \ldots, a_{ik}$ – represent the independent variables (influencing factors).

$\rho_1, \rho_2, \rho_3, \ldots, \rho_i$ – represent the regression coefficients (the influence of each factor), and ϵ_t – is the residual (error) value.

Below, all the variables in the econometric model are represented.

Variables: Industrial production volume – *Logindustr_prod* (result variable),

Investment volume in fixed capital in industry – *loginvest_cap_ind* (independent variable),

Export volume of industrial products – *logexport_ind*, (independent variable),

GDP inflation deflator in the national economy – *logGDP_infl_def* (independent variable).

Electricity production volume in industry – *loginvest_cap_ind* (independent variable).

In the development of econometric research, the main (H_0) and alternative (H_1) hypotheses were reflected.

Structure of the hypothesis in the combined model:

Main hypothesis (H_0): The volume of investment in fixed capital in industry does not significantly affect the volume of exports of industrial products, the GDP inflation deflator in the national economy and there is no effect on the relationship.

Alternative hypothesis (H_1): The volume of investment in fixed capital in industry has a strong correlation with the volume of exports of industrial products, the GDP inflation deflator in the national economy and the volume of electricity production in industry, significantly affecting the volume of industrial product production.

18.4. Results

At the first stage of the econometric study, descriptive statistical values were expressed for the volume of industrial product production and the variables affecting it (Table 55).

Table 55. Descriptive statistical values of the volume of industrial product production and the factors affecting it

	Logindustr_prod	loginvest_cap_ind	logexport_ind	logGDP_infl_def	logind_el_energ
Mean	10.484	9.193767	5.174227	2.715686	9.16692
Maximum	11.79235	10.36785	6.120035	3.516885	9.380108
Minimum	9.290514	7.648954	4.661115	2.189458	8.987172
Std. Dev	0.8454302	0.9205559	0.4458837	0.3540508	0.1247662
Std. Err.	0.01336742	0.01455527	0.0705004	0.0559803	0.0197273
Skewness	0.1704537	-0.4000433	1.092095	0.8304028	0.5772832
Kurtosis	1.488584	1.515728	2.770574	2.694974	1.701984
Observation	40	40	40	40	40

Source: It was developed by the authors based on Stata software.

According to Table 55, the descriptive statistical indicators of the volume of industrial production and the factors affecting it according to the model show the distribution of the main economic values of the selected variables. All variables selected according to descriptive statistical values consist of 40 observations and demonstrate consistency in the data set.

Also, the average values according to the table show a stable level of production, and high kurtosis indicators indicate a distribution close to normal. According to the results of the analysis, relatively low standard errors represent reliable estimates, allowing for a stable growth of industrial production, the relationship between investment, export, GDP and energy consumption.

According to the study, a graphical representation of the volume of industrial production and the factors affecting it over time was developed (Figure 58).

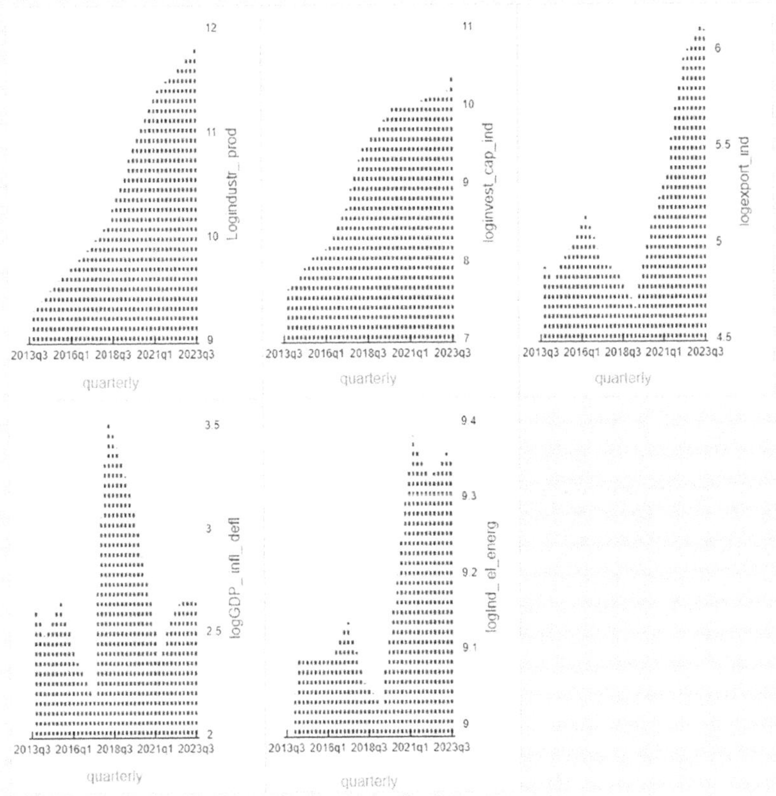

Figure 58. Analytical graphical representation of the volume of industrial production and the factors influencing it over time.
Source: It was developed by the authors based on Stata software.

According to the analytical graph, the volume of industrial production is based on quarterly data, using the periodic movement of four potential influencing variables. According to this image, the volume of industrial production changes over time, demonstrating a dynamic trend and from 2013 to 2023, a constant growth trend was observed in all variables of the factors affecting it.

According to the graph, as a result of supporting continuous investment practices in the production of industrial products against the background of continuous reforms in the regions, the volume of production led to an increase in gross domestic product. The growth dynamics of this macro-level factor with strong indicators provides economic fluctuations, and in the future, a significant decrease in the forecast indicators of the resulting factor and its influencing factors, as well as periods of stagnation are observed.

The next stage of the research presents a graphical matrix and scatter plots of the volume of industrial production and the factors affecting it (Figures 59 and 60).

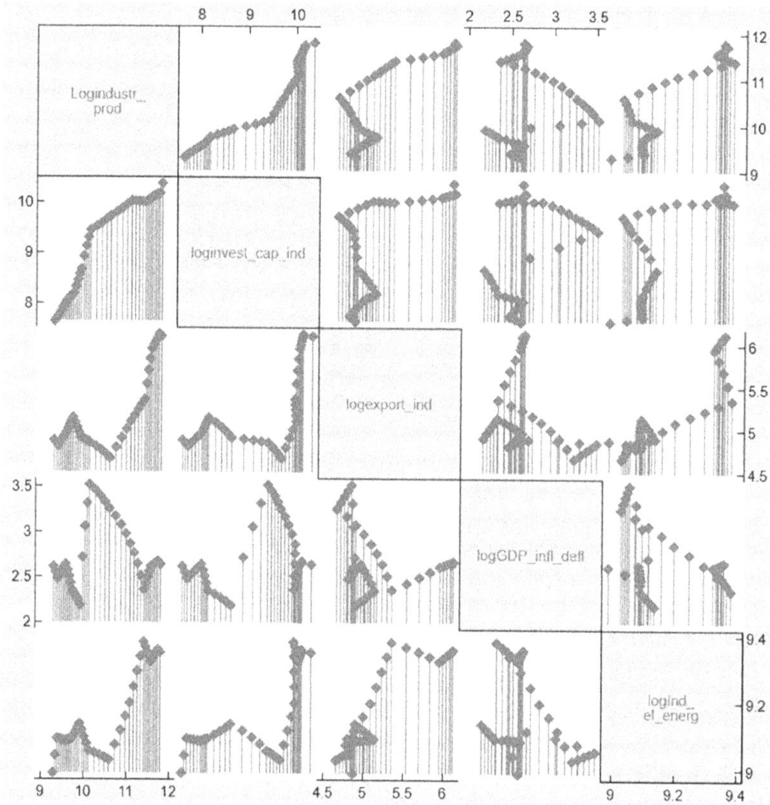

Figure 59. Graphical matrix representation of industrial production volume and factors influencing it.
Source: It was developed by the authors based on Stata software.

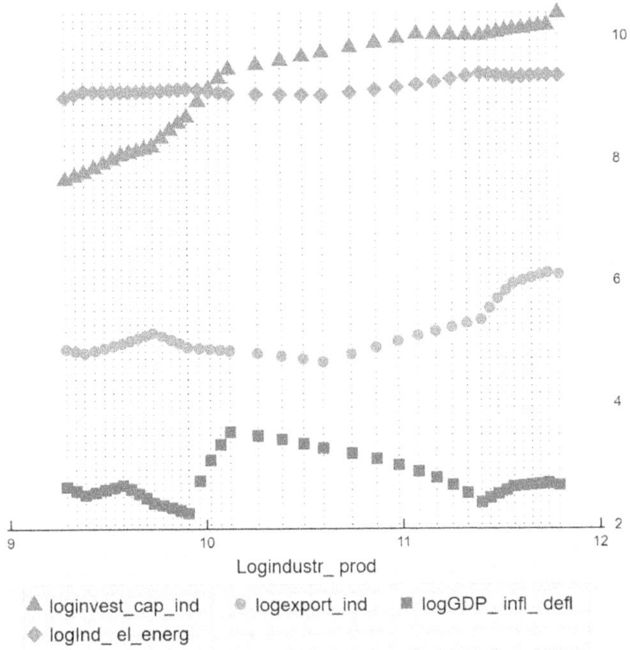

Figure 60. Scatter plot of industrial production volume and factors influencing it.
Source: It was developed by the authors based on Stata software.

According to Figures 59 and 60, a strong density correlation effect can be seen between the volume of industrial production and the variables affecting it, and a strong clustering pattern is evident in the plots.

The graphs show that positive peaks in all distribution areas indicate that with the increase in GDP per capita, economic expenditures, government expenditures, investment expenditures and social expenditures also increase, in this case, economic stability is explained by an increase in investment and government expenditures.

The correlation plots reveal relationships with strong trends. Also, there are no extremes that violate the general trends, indicating stable relationships between variables. Accordingly, this analytical data serves to increase the reliability of econometric modelling approaches.

These visualisations show a positive economic outlook, driven by expectations of effective investment in industrial production, energy availability and trade.

The next step is to present a graphical representation of the analytical relationship (rconnected) between industrial production and the factors influencing it (Figure 61).

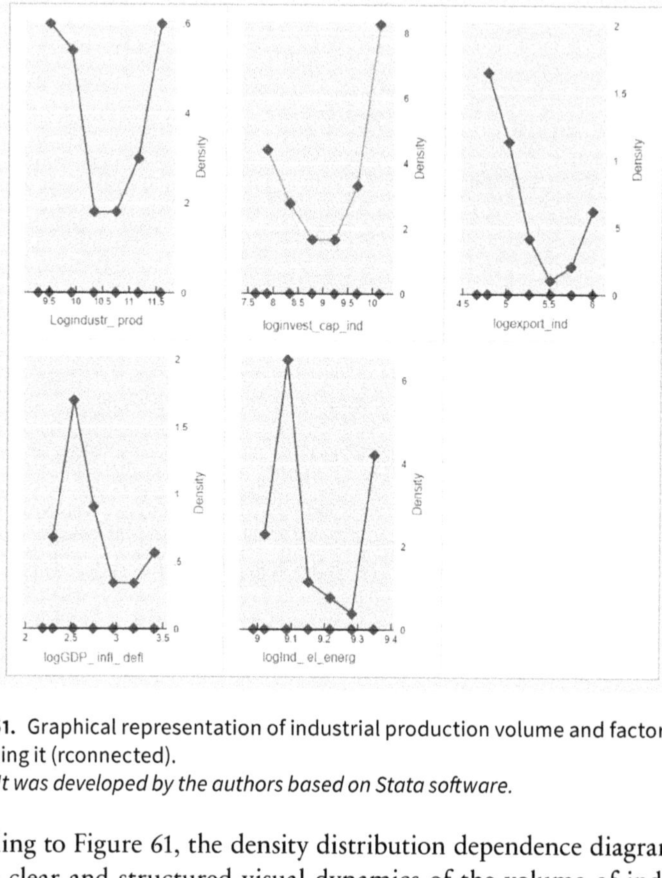

Figure 61. Graphical representation of industrial production volume and factors influencing it (rconnected).
Source: It was developed by the authors based on Stata software.

According to Figure 61, the density distribution dependence diagram provides a clear and structured visual dynamics of the volume of industrial production and the factors affecting it. Distribution graphs rconnected linear images represent the change in the density of variables by values, which is a systematic distribution of industrial production and the factors affecting it, and this allows for analysis and forecasting. The systematic nature of the distribution of industrial production volume indicates a strong relationship between economic stability, energy consumption and the level of production.

The graphical representation of the resulting variable and the factors affecting it (rconnected) indicates the dynamic relationship between macro-level factors and supports the increase in strategic investments, export volumes and the size of the energy industry in economic growth. The intuitive format of the analytical diagram makes it a valuable tool for economic analysis and decision-making.

The study developed a correlation matrix between the volume of industrial production and the variables affecting it (Table 56).

Table 56. Correlation matrix between the volume of industrial production and the factors affecting it

Variables	(1)	(2)	(3)	(4)	(5)	(6)	Significant
(1) Logindustr_prod	1.000						
(2) loginvest_cap_ind	0.8467	1.000					
	(0.0000)						***
(3) logexport_ind	0.7742	0.5678	1.000				
	(0.0000)	(0.0001)					***
(4) logGDP_infl_def	0.6040	0.3475	−0.3314	1.000			
	(0.0845)	(0.0280)	(0.0367)				*
(5) logind_el_energ	0.8666	0.6945	0.8866	−0.3530	1.000		
	(0.0000)	(0.0000)	(0.0000)	(0.0254)			***
*** $p < 0.01$, ** $p < 0.05$, * $p < 0.1$							

Source: It was developed by the authors based on Stata software.

According to Table 56, there is a strong, inverse and significant correlation between the volume of industrial production and the variables affecting it.

Positive correlations for all variables indicate a direct effect on the volume of industrial production. Also, the fact that the *p*-value is less than 0.05 according to the table indicates that the condition of statistical significance for the correlation coefficient is met.

At the next stage of the study, a regression model of the volume of industrial production and the factors affecting it was developed using a LS model (Table 57).

Table 57. Regression equation indicators based on the multivariate linear (LS) model of the volume of industrial production and the factors affecting it

Logindustr_prod	Coef.	St.Err.	t-value	p-value	[95% Conf	Interval]	Sig
loginvest_cap_ind	0.689	0.051	13.58	0	0.586	0.792	***
logexport_ind	0.362	0.077	4.68	0	0.205	0.519	***
logGDP_infl_defl	−0.139	0.1	−1.38	0.076	−0.343	0.065	*
logInd_el_energ	1.055	0.487	2.17	0.037	0.066	2.043	**
Constant	−7.017	4.032	−1.74	0.091	−15.201	1.168	*

Mean dependent var	10.484	SD dependent var	0.84
R-squared	0.878	Number of obs	40
F-test	733.362	Prob > F	0.000
Akaike crit. (AIC)	−68.548	Bayesian crit. (BIC)	−60.104

*** $p < 0.01$, ** $p < 0.05$, * $p < 0.1$.

Source: It was developed by the authors based on Stata software.

The formula parameters for the LS model are given below.

$$log(industr\_prod) = -7.01 + 0.68loginvest\_cap\_ind + 0.36logexport\_ind - 0.13logGDP\_infl\_defl + 1.05logind\_el\_energ + \varepsilon \quad (2)$$

General description of the LS model

The *p*-value of the industrial output and the influencing variable is less than 0.05, indicating a statistically significant prediction of the resulting factor at the 5 per cent significance level.

R-squared value: The *R*-squared value is 0.8781, which provides a quality indicator of the model with 87.81 per cent of the industrial output and the influencing factors. A high *R*-squared value indicates a strong influence of the econometric model on the observed data.

When testing the hypothesis of the regression equation in a LS model, it is clear that the null hypothesis (H_0: $y = 0$) is rejected when $F < 0.05$ and $t < 0.05$, which means that the main hypothesis (H_0: $y = 0$) is statistically insignificant. Accordingly, the main hypothesis is rejected in favour of accepting the statistically significant alternative hypothesis (H_1: $y \neq 0$).

In the Zarafshan region, a 1 per cent increase in the volume of investment in fixed capital in industry led to an increase in the volume of industrial products by 0.68 per cent. A 1 per cent increase in the volume of exports of industrial products in the same region led to an increase in the volume of industrial products by 0.36 per cent. Inflation in the national economy, a 1 per cent increase in the GDP deflator, led to a decrease in the volume of industrial products by 0.13 per cent. Also, a 1 per1cent increase in the volume of electricity production in the region led to an increase in the volume of industrial products by 1.05 per cent.

The Durbin-Watson test for the LS model for the regression equation recorded a value of 0.14. Also, the Shapiro-Wilk W test was 0.28, and the Breusch-Pagan test was 0.16. According to the primary hypothesis, H_0: $y = 0$ and H_1: $y \neq 0$, $p > 0.05$ significance level test was conducted.

According to the LS model regression equation:

According to the results of the Durbin-Watson and Shapiro-Wilk tests, the null hypothesis was accepted. According to it, the model included the analysis of the Gauss-Markov conditions confirming the absence of a relationship between the $p > 0.05$ threshold, error conditions and independent variables. In this case, the main conditions of the Gauss-Markov condition for the econometric model were met.

When checking the multicollinearity of the LS model regression model, the VIF indicator test was tested, its value was 8.64, indicating that there is no significant multicollinearity in the econometric model, and the confidence interval for this value is [1, 10].

18.5. Conclusion

The results of the LS equation model of the econometric study showed that the volume of industrial production, the volume of investment in fixed capital in the industry, the volume of exports of industrial products, the volume of GDP inflation deflator in the national economy and the volume of electricity production in the industry showed a strong and positive relationship, and this significantly increases macroeconomic processes in stimulating economic growth.

1. Investments in the Zarafshan region stimulate industrial growth. According to this result, a 1 per cent increase in investment in fixed capital leads to an increase in industrial production by 0.68 per cent. According to it, capital investments have a strong and positive effect, and the expansion of industry serves to become an effective strategy for economic growth. The industrial sector stimulates investment through the development of infrastructure and leads to a further increase in production.
2. The expansion of exports serves to increase production. This result shows that a 1 per cent increase in industrial exports leads to a 0.36 per cent increase in output. This shows that the Zarafshan region's industry is responsive to external demand, demonstrating the potential benefits of export-oriented policies, trade agreements and international market expansion.
3. Electricity availability is a key factor. According to this result, a 1 per cent increase in electricity production leads to a significant 1.05 per cent increase in industrial production. This highlights the important role of energy supply in supporting industrial expansion and shows that investment in energy infrastructure benefits major industries and economic sectors.
4. The importance of managing the impact of inflation. According to this result, although a 1 per cent increase in the GDP deflator reduces industrial production by 0.13 per cent, the impact is relatively small compared to the positive effects of investment, exports and electricity supply. This indicates that the region is mitigating the adverse effects of inflation with an effective monetary policy and a stable price strategy.
5. The results of the study indicate that investment expectations, export and energy development are the main factors of industrial growth in the Zarafshan region. By focusing on government programmes aimed at stimulating capital investments, promoting exports and expanding electricity generation, the region will achieve sustainable industrial and economic development.

Bibliography

Abdullah, M. A., Han, X., Amjad, M. A., & Makhmudov, S. (2025). Revisit the role of financial development on economic growth, human development, and sustainable development in higher-income countries. Journal of Environmental Management, 392, 126874.

Antevski, M. (2008). Regionalna ekonomska integracija u Evropi. M. Antevski.

Capello, R., and Cerisola, S. (2022). 'Industrial Transformations and Regional Inequalities in Europe'. *Annals of Regional Science*, 70 (1), 15–28. <https://doi.org/10.1007/s00168-021-01097-4>.

Chakraborty, M. (2024). 'Industrial Clustering and Location in India: Sectoral Patterns of Investments and Employments'. *Regional Science Policy and Practice*, 16 (6), 100041. <https://doi.org/10.1016/j.rspp.2024.100041>.

Fedotov, A. V., Pilyugin, A. Yu., and Daneykin, Y. (2022). 'Creation of New Productions as a Factor of Territorial Development'. *Advances in Economics, Business and Management Research*. <https://doi.org/10.2991/aebmr.k.220208.019>.

Habib, S. S., Islam, M. A., Ali, M. N., Benitez, I. B., Mamadiyarov, Z., Mirzayev, B., … & Flah, A. (2025). Multi-Objective Optimization and Feasibility Analysis of Integrated Biogas–Solar Energy Systems for Rural Electrification. Results in Engineering, 107086.

Jahrir, A., Gultom, Y., Herman, H., Zabadi, F., Ngongo, M., Mamadiyarov, Z., Fatmawati, E., & Saputra, N. (2025). Investigating the Elements of Short Commercial Mineral Water Advertisement: A Case on Discourse Analysis. Studies in Media and Communication, 13(4), 94–104. doi: http://dx.doi.org/10.11114/smc.v13i4.7813

Jović, O. (2016). 'Durbin-Watson Partial Least-squares Regression Applied to MIR Data on Adulteration with Edible Oils of Different Origins'. *Food Chemistry* 213, 791–8.

Kalandarov, F., Makhmudov, S., Ibadullaev, D., Matniyozov, M., Nasretdinova, F., Sabirov, K., & Bahodirov, N. M. (2025). Low-Carbon Energy Risk and Renewable Energy Development: Insights from Method of Moments Quantile Regression. International Journal of Energy Economics and Policy, 15(3), 524–536.

Khayrilla Kurbonov, Samariddin Makhmudov, Shakhzod Erkinov, Umidjon Dadabaev, Gulnora Bekimbetova, Rukhiddin Zayniddinov, and Mirzabek Jonuzokov. 2025. Evaluating the Impact of Marketing Practices Digitalization and Investment on Labor Market Efficiency and Commercial Bank Performance Using Econometric Models. In Proceedings of the 8th International Conference on Future Networks & Distributed Systems (ICFNDS '24). Association for Computing Machinery, New York, NY, USA, 786–796. https://doi.org/10.1145/3726122.3726237

Khodjaniyazov, N., Mirkhoshimova, M., Kalandarov, F., Matyokubova, D., Utegenova, S., Makhmudov, S., & Khudayberganov, M. (2025). Time-Varying Impacts of Financial Stress on Energy-Related Uncertainty. International Journal of Energy Economics and Policy, 15(3), 689–698.

Kuchkarov, T., Mamadiyarov, Z., Khakimov, Z., Sabirova, O., Matmurodov, K., Raimboyeva, M., & Umarova, S. (2025). Energy-Related Uncertainty and Crypto-Currency Environmental Attention: Time-Varying Perspective. International Journal of Energy Economics and Policy, 15(5), 614–626. https://doi.org/10.32479/ijeep.20784

Kuziboev, B., Ozturk, I., Kalandarov, F., Samandarov, O., Bekjanov, D., & Makhmudov, S. (2025). PROMOTING ENERGY SOURCES DIVERSIFICATION THROUGH ESG PERFORMANCE. Energy, 136009.

Lin, M.H., Matchanova, B., Nurmatovich, H.A. et al. Optimal Operation of the Multi-Carrier Energy System Considering Energy Markets and Renewable Energies Participation. *Int. J. Appl. Comput. Math* 11, 170 (2025). https://doi.org/10.1007/s40819-025-02002-9

Lipovetsky, S. (2024). *Multiple Regression Model as Interpolation through the Points of Weighted Means.* <https://doi.org/10.47852/bonviewjdsis42021995>.

Litamahuputty, J. V., Amiruddin, E. G., Rahim, R., Rahman, A., & Mamadiyarov, Z. (2025). Cryptocurrency Risk Management through Decision Engineering: Evaluating XRPUSD and ADAUSD Portfolio Performance. Journal of Applied Science, Engineering, Technology, and Education, 7(1), 69–81. https://doi.org/10.35877/454RI.asci3871

Liu, W., and Zhao, D. (2011). *Influencing Factors of the Industrial Economic Growth and Its Regional Differences in China*, pp. 1299–301. <https://doi.org/10.1109/MSIE.2011.5707661>.

Mamadiyarov, Z., Eshov, M., Otakhonova, D., Utegenova, S., Sabirov, K., Marks, A., & Bahodirov, N. (2025). Does Energy Policy Risk Threaten Energy Sources Diversification?. International Journal of Energy Economics and Policy, 15(5), 730–740. https://doi.org/10.32479/ijeep.21140

Mamadiyarov, Z., Saidov, O., Abdurazakova, N., Makhmudov, S., Nazarov, M., Rajabova, N., … Ruzmetova, I. (2025). Energy-Related Uncertainty and Tourism Stock Markets: New Insights from Time-Varying Relationship with TVP- VAR Approach. International Journal of Energy Economics and Policy, 15(4), 730–737. https://doi.org/10.32479/ijeep.20480

Mamani, J.C.M., Miri, M., Vorobev, Y. et al. Optimal Operation of Energy Microgrid Considering Economic and Emission Indices. Oper. Res. Forum 6, 122 (2025). https://doi.org/10.1007/s43069-025-00523-z

Ngongo, M., Herman, H., Ndandara, A., Jois Jaha, D. A., Peku Djawang, J. U. S., Tanggu Rame, M. M., Khamraeva, S. N., & Mamadiyarov, Z. (2025). An Investigation of Meaning, Toponymy of Sumba Cultural Site's Names, and the Impact of Tourism Visitors on Surrounding Society. Forum for Linguistic Studies, 7(8), 679–693. https://doi.org/10.30564/fls.v7i8.10260

Olive, D. J., Watagoda, L. C. R. P., and Arachchige Don, H. S. R. (2015). 'Visualizing and Testing the Multivariate Linear Regression Model'. *International Journal of Statistics and Probability*, 4 (1), 126. <https://doi.org/10.5539/IJSP.V4N1P126>.

PANJAITAN, M. B., HAMDANAH, H., SIRAIT, J., SUTIKNO, S., FATMAWATI, E., HERMAN, H., & MAMADIYAROV, Z. (2025). THE ROLE OF EMOTIONAL REGULATION IN SHAPING STUDENTS' PERCEPTION OF PHYSICS PROBLEMSOLVING TASKS. TPM – Testing, Psychometrics, Methodology in Applied Psychology, 32(S2(2025) : Posted 09 June), 1–10. Retrieved from https://tpmap.org/submission/index.php/tpm/article/view/139

Pradhan, R., Hajiyev, E., Shichiyakh, R. et al. Optimal Techno-Economic Feasibility of an Off-Grid Microgrid System Using Load Flow Energy Management Strategies. *Oper. Res. Forum* 6, 120 (2025). https://doi.org/10.1007/s43069-025-00524-y

Romero, R. M., Zelinskaya, M., Makhmudov, S., Sapaev, S., & Rustambekovich, J. U. (2025, September). Modelling and Optimal

Utilisation of the Renewable Energy Systems in Microgrid with Improving Reliability and Energy Efficiency. In Operations Research Forum (Vol. 6, No. 3, pp. 1–20). Springer International Publishing.

Rony, Z. T., Jefri, R., Rusmardiana, A., Pramono, S. A., & Mamadiyarov, Z. (2025). Downside Risk Measurement of Indonesian Financial and Energy Securities: A Value at Risk Perspective. Journal of Applied Science, Engineering, Technology, and Education, 7(2). https://doi.org/10.35877/454RI.asci3898

Rukhiddin Zayniddinov, Nodir Jumaev, Gulbakhor Irgasheva, Alam Asadov, Nosir Makhmudov, Sirojiddin Abrorov, and Samariddin Makhmudov. 2025. The Influence of the Digital Economy on Economic Development Evidence from Uzbekistan. In Proceedings of the 8th International Conference on Future Networks & Distributed Systems (ICFNDS '24). Association for Computing Machinery, New York, NY, USA, 831–839. https://doi.org/10.1145/3726122.3726242

Rayala, R. V., Borra, C. R., Vasudevan, V., Singhania, R., Cheekati, S., & Mamadiyarov, Z. (2025, July). Lightweight Deep Learning Framework for Human Activity Recognition: A MobileNet-LSTM Approach with WHOA Optimization. In *2025 International Conference on Innovations in Intelligent Systems: Advancements in Computing, Communication, and Cybersecurity (ISAC3)* (pp. 1–6). IEEE.

Rayala, R. V., Sandhya, N., Singhania, R., Cheekati, S., Borra, C. R., Vasudevan, V., & Mamadiyarov, Z. (2025, July). AI-Driven Tomato Quality Assessment: A Deep Learning Approach for Image-based Defect Detection and Classification. In *2025 International Conference on Innovations in Intelligent Systems: Advancements in Computing, Communication, and Cybersecurity (ISAC3)* (pp. 1–6). IEEE.

Samariddin Makhmudov, Malika Umarova, Khayrilla Kurbonov, Laylo Akbarova, Durdona Davletova, Nilufar Shanazarova, and Toshmurod Kulmanov. 2025. Evaluating the forecast indicators of the volume of highly liquid assets of commercial banks in the process of digital transformation. In Proceedings of the 8th International Conference on Future Networks & Distributed Systems (ICFNDS '24). Association for Computing Machinery, New York, NY, USA, 698–704. https://doi.org/10.1145/3726122.3726222

Samariddin Makhmudov, Kudratillo Tukhsanov, Saifulla Arslanbekov, Akram Amanov, Orifali Tursunov, Umarbek Jabbarov and Muyassarxon Mirzakarimova. 2024. Optimizing Supply Chain Financing Development Prospects of Digital Ecosystems in the European Logistics Industry. In The 8th International Conference on Future Networks & Distributed Systems (ICFNDS '24), December 11–12, 2024, Marakech, Morocco. ACM, New York, NY, USA, 12 Pages. https://doi.org/10.1145/3726122.3726200

Singagerda, F. S., Pratama, M. R., Alfairus, M. Q., Iskandar, A., & Mamadiyarov, Z. (2025). A Decision-Centric Approach to Risk Management in Aviation Stock Investments Using Value at Risk and Portfolio Optimization. Journal of Applied Science, Engineering, Technology, and Education, 7(1), 114–125. https://doi.org/10.35877/454RI.asci3870

Smith, P. F., Ganesh, S., and Liu, P. (2013). 'A Comparison of Random Forest Regression and Multiple Linear Regression for Prediction in Neuroscience'. *Journal of Neuroscience Methods*, 220 (1), 85–91.

Sofyanty, D., Romadhoni, R., Handriadi, H., Makhsudovna, I. S., Anwar, Z., & Mamadiyarov, Z. (2025). Strategic Decision Analysis for Investment Portfolios: Computational Risk Assessment in Transportation Asset Management. Journal of Applied Science, Engineering, Technology, and Education, 7(2). https://doi.org/10.35877/454RI.asci3897

Su, R., Xiao, Y., Hamza, F., Mamadiyarov, Z., & Wahab, A. (2025). Scaling up green hydrogen in China: Economic opportunities and challenges. International Journal of Hydrogen Energy, 131, 60–69.

Toshmurod Kulmanov, Umidjon Dadabaev, Mansurbek Qulmetov, Aliboy Ulashov, Mirjalol Eshboyev, and Samariddin Makhmudov. 2025. Global Services Market Transformation Digitalization Export Trends and Future Forecasts. In Proceedings of the 8th International Conference on Future Networks & Distributed Systems (ICFNDS '24). Association for Computing Machinery, New York, NY, USA, 851–858. https://doi.org/10.1145/3726122.3726245

Wali, A. A. (2014). 'The Role of Geography in the Analysis of Industrial Development Strategies within the Spatial Organisation of a Region'. *Bulletin of Geography. Socio-Economic Series*, 24 (24), 231–44. <https://doi.org/10.2478/BOG-2014-0025>.

Wang, Q., Lai, K. K., Niu, D., and Zhang, Q. (2012). 'A Multivariate Wind Power Forecasting Model Based on LS-SVM'. *Computational Sciences and Optimization*, 127–31. <https://doi.org/10.1109/CSO.2012.35>.

Zelentsova, L. S., Vaslavskaya, I., and Kurikov, V. M. (2024). 'Industrial Development in the Regions: Economic Aspect'. *Èkonomika i Upravlenie: Problemy, Rešeniâ* 10/5 (151), 76–83, <https://doi.org/10.36871/ek.up.p.r.2024.10.05.011>.

Zhang, L., Zhao, Z., Qamri, G. M., & Makhmudov, S. (2025). Unleashing the critical role of renewable energy through global value chains and digitalization: A path towards environmental sustainability. Journal of Environmental Management, 392, 126688.

Zolna, K., Dao, P. B., Staszewski, W. J., and Barszcz, T. (2016). 'Towards Homoscedastic Nonlinear Cointegration for Structural Health Monitoring'. *Mechanical Systems and Signal Processing*, 75, 94–108.

Zokir Toshtemirovich Mamadiyarov, Samandarboy Adhambek ugli Sulaymanov, Sarvar Anvar ugli Askarov, and Durdona Bakhtiyor kizi Uktamova. 2022. Impact of Covid-19 Pandemic on Accelerating The Digitization and Transformation of Banks. In Proceedings of the 5th International Conference on Future Networks and Distributed Systems (ICFNDS '21). Association for Computing Machinery, New York, NY, USA, 706–712. https://doi.org/10.1145/3508072.3508211

Assessment of Forecasting the Volume of Agricultural Products Per Capita (Case of Uzbekistan)

Samariddin Makhmudov, Kaxramon Mambetjanov, Zokir Mamadiyarov, Nargizaxon Shamshiyeva, Isabek Murtazaev, Umida Zakirova and Mirzabek Jonuzokov

19.1. Introduction

Historically, Uzbekistan's agricultural economy has been the primary source of its gross domestic product (GDP), employing a large percentage of workers – approximately 27 per cent of employees (Eshov et al., 2021). It is also among the country's primary sources of export revenue, with top agricultural products being fruits, wheat and cotton. Nevertheless, despite being the focal point of the national economy, the sector is afflicted with a multitude of issues from climatic volatility, soil erosion, water scarcity and ineffective utilisation of resources.

The need for accurate agricultural forecasting has become increasingly urgent, as it offers crucial information on future agricultural production so that policymakers are able to plan better and devise targeted interventions in an attempt to increase long-term sustainability. Specifically, agricultural output per capita predicts a more accurate picture of farm sustainability because it considers both the growth in population and geographical variation in farm production, hence a more accurate picture of food availability and security (Karatayev, 2022). While much of the available literature on agriculture forecasting in Uzbekistan has been country-level forecasting in nature, there has been a lack of meaningful research that investigates agricultural performance variation at the regional level, particularly per capita agricultural outputs. This imbalance is the most pronounced in the Zarafshan area, which is a principal agricultural zone that grows cotton and fruit crops but also faces water resource management, soil health and climate change.

Analyses and forecasts were conducted using multivariate linear regression (LS), ARDL, ARIMA and various other econometric models on the global services market, digital economy, energy-related financial stress, cocktail market, digital transformation, factors affecting the logistics industry (Cahyani et al., 2025; Kalandarov et al., 2025; Khodjaniyazov et al., 2025; Kulmanov et al., 2024; Kurbonov et al., 2024; Kuziboev et al., 2025; Mamadiyarov et al., 2025; Zayniddinov et al., 2024).

By taking regional agricultural performance into account and incorporating per capita data, this study seeks to provide a more accurate and geographically disaggregated evaluation of agricultural production in Uzbekistan. Since there are regional natural differences in agricultural productivity, and usually just because they are differences in natural endowments, climate and economic infrastructure (Ruzmetov et al., 2023), this research adds substantially to agricultural planning and policy in a region. Not only are ARIMA-based forecasts highly superior in forecasting agriculture production but also yield beneficial information in resource planning, policymaking and sustainable agricultural promotion. Therefore, the contribution of this study is of great applicability to policymakers, local agriculture planners and other stakeholders who engage in an effort to secure food and financial stability in Zarafshan over the long run.

Organisation of the paper is as follows: the next section contains an extensive literature review on agricultural forecasting, application of the ARIMA model in agriculture, and Uzbekistan agricultural research at the regional level. It is followed by the discussion on the research work methodology, that is, sources of data, choice of the model specification and the analytical techniques followed in the research. The results of the forecasting model are examined and contrasted with the literature, focusing on policy implications and relevance. Finally, the paper concludes by summarising the key findings and recommendations for future research, with a focus on enhancing regional agricultural forecasting ability in Uzbekistan.

Another group of economists has successfully used econometric models such as Fixed Effects Estimator, Random Effects Estimator, LS and ARDL in their research on investment in digital infrastructure, various aspects of digital payment systems, the impact of inflation and credit interest rates on investment, factors affecting the reduction of the state's share in commercial banks, Non-Performing Loans in commercial banks, the digitisation of banks, risks in digital services and the development of retail payment services (Akhmetshin et al., 2025; Jahrir et al. 2025; Makhmudov et al., 2025; Mamadiyarov et al., 2025; Su et al., 2025; Zokir et al., 2025).

19.2. Literature Review

Among them, the Autoregressive Integrated Moving Average (ARIMA) model has widely been used because it can handle complex relationships between past data and can handle non-stationary time series (Box et al., 2016). Time series models such as ARIMA facilitate researchers and policymakers to include inherent seasonal patterns, cyclical trends and trends found in agricultural data. This becomes essential in policy-making that will be used for long-term development planning, investment and food security programmes (Habib et al., 2025; Hyndman et al., 2020; Matyakubova et al.,2025; Shumway & Stoffer, 2025).

Bozkurt and Kaya (2021) investigates the influences of macroeconomic policies on agricultural production and other factors affecting it, based on panel data in a global sample for the period 2010–2017. According to the analysis results, countries' financial, fiscal and monetary policies have an important effect on agricultural production.

Ghazo (2021), for example, employed ARIMA models in the forecasting of GDP growth in South Asia, and the findings were promising, showing that the model is able to pick up long-term patterns in the economy. Similarly, Mahmoud Sayed Agbo (2023) applied ARIMA in food price volatility forecasting in Egypt and cited its application in agricultural policymaking and the management of price shock.

Regional agricultural forecasting requires unique models that are derived from regional variables, including weather conditions, soil fertility and regional economic factors – variables that heavily impact agricultural production (Krivonos, 2022). The Zarafshan region of Uzbekistan, for instance, is a major agricultural region, famous for farm and animal breeding, but there are few empirical studies focusing particularly on agricultural production forecasting in the region.

Though the global literature indicates the capability of ARIMA for agricultural prediction, there are only a few studies that have addressed per capita agricultural production, particularly from the angle of developing Central

Asian economies. Most of the studies that have used ARIMA have in view mostly national output or price projections, without taking into account population patterns and territorial diversity, both being vital while studying per capita farm production and its implications as far as food security is concerned (Kuchkarov et al., 2025; Litamahuputty et al.,2025; Sun et al., 2023; Zhang et al., 2020). This is a critical deficiency in literature, especially in the context of transition economies like Uzbekistan whose agricultural sector is large but not studied with regard to utilising ARIMA-based models as per capita utilises.

This study seeks to fill the gaps by developing a region-level ARIMA model to forecast per capita agricultural production in Uzbekistan's Zarafshan district from 2025–2029. It will consider both the past per capita trends of agricultural productivity and those of the population trends and give a better insight into the per capita levels of agricultural forces. Besides, the research aims to make evidence-based projections to enable policymakers to make informed decisions at the regional level food security policy, investment choices and rural development strategies.

More broadly, the study's greatest contribution is being regional in scope, cross-tabulating per capita figures and employing ARIMA to project agriculture in Uzbekistan – a setting hitherto not fully captured in the literature. With a particular focus on the farm production in the region, this research aims to present a comprehensive model of prediction that will benefit regional policymakers, planners and development agencies to counter the challenge of sustainable agricultural development in Uzbekistan and elsewhere.

19.3. Research Methodology

The research methods part of a research paper describes the systematic process that was used to answer the research questions or test the hypotheses. It involves the overall research design, data gathering and method of analysis so that the study can be replicable and valid. This section ensures transparency and provides sufficient information for other researchers to reproduce or validate the findings.

During the course of the study, the ARIMA model was used to develop forecast indicators to evaluate the possible effect of structural balance in agriculture in the Zarafshan region during the years 2025–2029. This was based on an econometric model because of the known capability of the ARIMA model to model time series data and to make accurate predictions of future economic behaviour (Mamani et al., 2025; Ngongo et al.2025; Rayala et al., 2025; Zhang, 2003). The study specifically targets the modelling of per capita agricultural production, one of the key indicators to quantify sectoral productivity and sustainability.

As stated by Sinu et al. (2024), the ARIMA method has been effectively used in the modelling and forecasting of GDP, which is a basic macroeconomic variable. Cross-country empirical evidence also confirms the model's robustness of accuracy and validity in predicting GDP trends, demonstrating thereby its importance in economic planning as well as policy formulation. In agriculture, the ARIMA model allows for the occurrence of seasonal movement, cyclical movement and long-term structural change in production and hence is found to be best suited for medium- and long-term forecasting (Makhmudov et al., 2025; Romero et al., 2025).

The ARIMA model consists of three fundamental components: Autoregression (AR) (Rizvi et al., 2024; Rayala et al., 2025, Sofyanti et al., 2025), Integration (I) (Han et al., 2010; Rony et al., 2025) and Moving Average (MA) (Lee & Ko, 2011, Singagerda et al., 2025; Zhao et al., 2025). All three components are essential to the identification and prediction of temporal patterns in historical data. Luceño and Peña (2008) say that the AR component quantifies the relationship between any observation and its past values at specific lag intervals. Zhang and Moore (2015) elaborates that this component is denoted by the parameter '*p*', which indicates the number of lags used in the model.

Liu et al. (2020), the MA component reflects the relation between the present observation and the residual errors of a moving average process on lagged observations. The parameter '*q*' reflects the amount of past forecast errors that are included in the model specification. Overall, these components allow the ARIMA model to make solid, data-based forecasts that are essential for effective economic decision-making. These three components – AR, I and MA – are combined to create a complete model that can handle complex temporal dependencies and offer consistent forecasting performance for economic time series.

The general form of the ARIMA(p, d, q) model is given below.

$$\delta_p\left(C\right)(1-C)^d Y_t = \vartheta_q\left(C\right)\varepsilon_i \tag{4}$$

where

i-i denotes the time series at time i.
B is the backsliding operator, where $CY_i = Y_{i-1}$.
d denotes the order of differentiation to make the series stationary.
$\delta_p(C) = 1 - \delta_1 C - \delta_2 C_2 - \ldots - \delta_p C_p - p$ denotes the autoregressive (AR) polynomial of order p.
$\vartheta_q(C) = 1 + \vartheta_1 C + \vartheta_2 C_2 + \ldots + \vartheta_q C_q - q$ denotes the moving average (MA) polynomial of order q.
$\epsilon_i - i$ represents the error term (white noise) in time.

To construct the forecast indicators for econometric modelling, quarterly time series data of the Statistical Agency of the President of the Republic of Uzbekistan (<https://stat.uz/uz/>) from 2010 to 2024 were utilised. This dataset had agricultural production, population statistics and related macroeconomic indicators to adequately model them. Seasonal adjustment and structural breaks were adjusted in the time series before estimating the model. Model selection was guided by common diagnostic practices, including the Akaike Information Criterion (AIC) and Bayesian Information Criterion, to pick the optimal p, d and q values.

Agricultural output per capita – *agricul_per_cap* (resultant variable).

This variable has been chosen to serve as an indicator for judging sectoral trends in productivity and forecasting it is essential for shaping regional agricultural development policies.

19.4. Analysis and Results

An analytical graphical representation of the volume of agricultural output per capita over time at the initial stage of the econometric forecast is presented below (Figure 62).

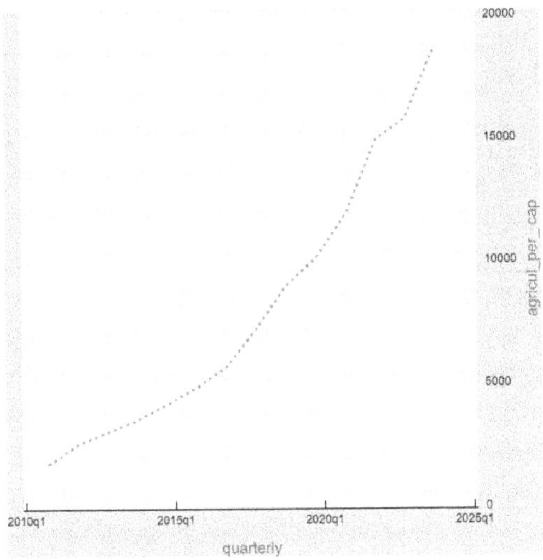

Figure 62. Analytical graphic representation of the periodic status of agricultural output per capita.
Source: It was developed by the authors based on Stata software.

According to Figure 62, the volume of agricultural output per capita has been growing moderately since the first quarter of 2016 and this growth has reached its maximum by 2024. According to this analytical picture, the overall growth trend in the region is due to the expansion of agricultural output per capita, employment and cultivated land, and is increasing against the background of increased capital investment. The assessment of this growth trend shows that it provides a promising forecast of agricultural output per capita in the future and represents the contribution of the macro-scale to sustainable economic growth.

In the next stage of the econometric forecast, the stationarity level of the volume of agricultural products per capita was assessed and the unit-root test was used to determine it (Table 58).

Table 58. Unit-root test of the volume of agricultural output per capita

agricul_per_cap	Test Statistic	1% Critical Value	5% Critical Value	10% Critical Value	p-value for Z(t)
	−6.981	−3.580	−2.930	−2.600	0.0000

Source: It was developed by the authors based on Stata software.

According to Table 58, the unit root test statistic (–6.981) is significantly smaller than all the critical values (1% –3.580, 5% –2.930 and 10% –2.600), which leads to a very high confidence rejection of the null hypothesis of a unit root. According to this, per capita agricultural output does not exhibit a random variable, but rather a stable trend. The p-value (0.0000) indicates that the trend in per capita agricultural output is statistically significant and is not due to random fluctuations. Since the data are stationary, it provides a basis for accurate forecasting of future per capita agricultural output.

The next step is to present the value of p, which determines the indirect correlation between the time series lags of the model (Figure 63).

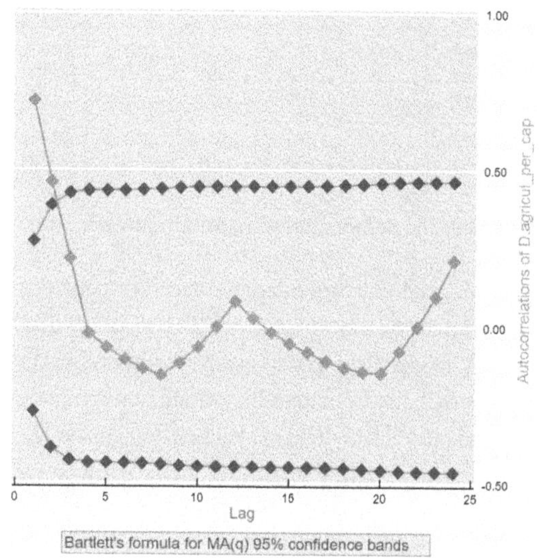

Figure 63. Indirect correlation graph between lags of the econometric model of agricultural production per capita.
Source: It was developed by the authors based on Stata software.

According to Figure 63, the indirect correlation values between the lags of the econometric model of agricultural output per capita are mostly within the 95 per cent confidence intervals, which is consistent with the previous Unit-Root test results, indicating the presence of stationarity. At the same time, the first few lags are significant and the historical values show the effect of agricultural output per capita on the output volume.

The sharp decrease in correlation after the initial lag indicates the fit of the AR model, which indicates that the dynamic trend in economic processes is effective.

Except for one or two lags, all lags are within the confidence interval in the indirect correlation analysis. Accordingly, it is possible to choose a value of 1 or 2 as the *p*-value, and these values lead to the choice of *p*-values according to the ARIMA model.

In the next step of the ARIMA model, the value of q, which describes the direct correlation between the model's lags, was determined (Figure 64).

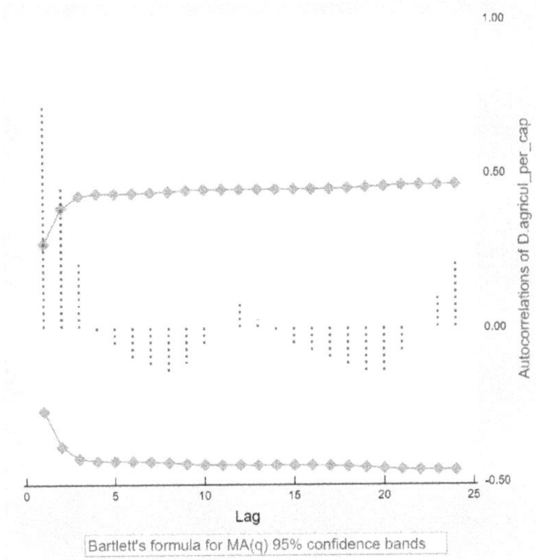

Figure 64. Direct correlation graph between lags of agricultural output per capita.
Source: It was developed by the authors based on Stata software.

Figure 64 shows that the ARIMA model has a strong correlation between lags and all lags except one lag are within the specified confidence interval.

In the development of econometric forecast indicators, the different autocorrelations indicate a long-term moderate trend, which leads to a better fit of the per capita agricultural output to the stationary state.

According to it, most of the lags of the autocorrelation values include the 95 per cent confidence interval, which does not indicate a preference for random sharp shocks. It also allows for more accurate forecasting based on econometric modelling for the per capita agricultural output and the trends under analysis.

Figure 64 shows that the ARIMA model has a strong correlation between lags and all lags except one lag are within the specified confidence interval.

In the development of econometric forecast indicators, the different autocorrelations indicate a long-term moderate trend, which leads to a better fit of the per capita agricultural output to the stationary state.

According to it, most of the lags of the autocorrelation values include the 95 per cent confidence interval, which does not indicate a preference for random sharp shocks. It also allows for more accurate forecasting based on econometric modelling for the per capita agricultural output and the trends under analysis.

Table 59. Econometric equation indicators of the ARIMA(2,1,2) model for agriculture per capita

D.agricul_ per_cap	**Coef.**	**St.Err.**	**t-value**	**p-value**	**[95% Conf**	**Interval]**	**Sig**
Constant	324.947	75.741	4.29	0	176.497	473.397	*
L	1.055	0.201	5.26	0	0.662	1.448	*
L2	-0.453	0.198	-2.29	0.022	-0.842	-0.065	
L	-0.289	0.143	-2.02	0.043	-0.569	-0.009	
L2	0.794	0.115	6.90	0	0.569	1.02	*
Constant	103.844	11.914	8.72	0	80.493	127.195	*

Mean dependent var	326.979	SD dependent var	1209.661
Number of obs	52	Chi-square	236.934
Prob > chi^2	.	Akaike crit. (AIC)	645.507
* $p < 0.01$, $p < 0.05$, * $p < 0.1$			

Source: It was developed by the authors based on Stata software.

According to Table 59, the ARIMA(2,1,2) model looks like this.

$$D.agricul\_per\_cap_t = 324.94 + 1.05 \cdot D.agricul\_per\_cap_{t-1} - 0.45 D.agricul\_per\_cap_{t-2} - 0.28 L_t + 0.79 \cdot L_{t-2} + 103.84 + \epsilon_t \quad (5)$$

In the next step, an analysis was developed based on the average values of the dependent variable and the graphical representation of the residuals of the ARIMA(2,1,2) model (Table 60 and Figure 65).

Table 60. Residual values of the resulting factor in the ARIMA(2,1,2) model

Variable	Obs	Mean	Std. dev.	Min	Max
Residual values	52	-0.028574	106.3256	-284.0774	371.6505

Source: It was developed by the authors based on Stata software.

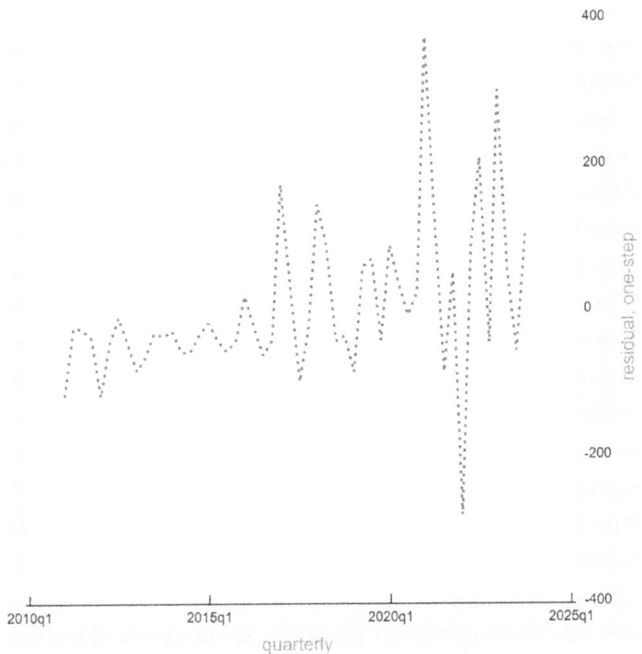

Figure 65. Graph of residual values of the ARIMA(2,1,2) model by agricultural production per capita.
Source: It was developed by the authors based on Stata software.

According to Table 60 and Figure 65, the ARIMA(2,1,2) model exhibits stochastic equilibrium, which is a visual representation of the residuals at specified time intervals. This representation shows the fit of the ARIMA model to the data and the main stochastic relationships in the data set. The next step involves testing the stationarity of the residuals of the ARIMA (2,1,2) model for agricultural production per capita and estimating the AR and moving average (MA) residuals.

At the same time, the relationship between the convergence of the ARIMA model in the forecasting of econometric forecasting within the unit range is presented (Figure 66).

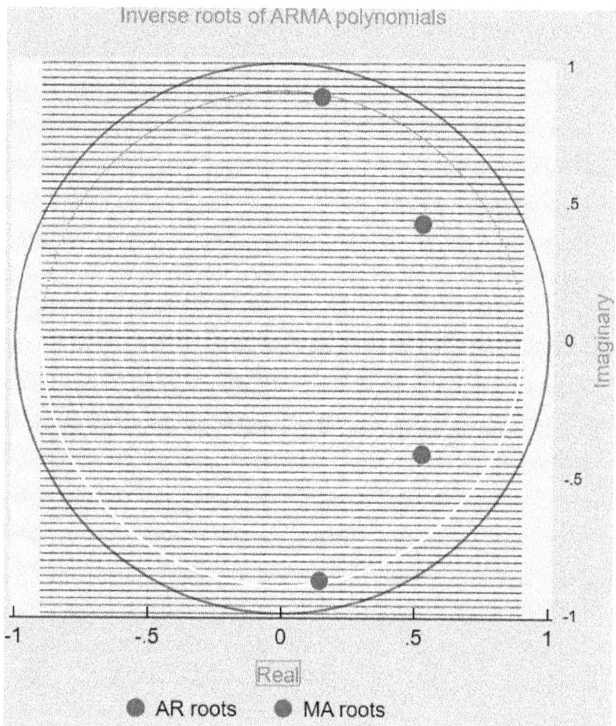

Figure 66. Range of values of agricultural production per capita according to the ARIMA(2,1,2) model.
Source: It was developed by the authors based on Stata software.

Using the Stata program, a forecast indicator of agricultural ARIMA output per capita from 2025 to 2029 was developed using the ARIMA(2,1,2) model, excluding random endogenous and exogenous factors (Table 61).

Table 61. Forecast indicators of agricultural production per capita for 2025–2029 (in million soums)

Years	Pessimistic forecast	Optimistic forecast	Forecast
2025	20,233.21	22,652.53	21,442.87
2026	21,546.75	23,966.07	22,756.41
2027	22,844.11	25,263.43	24,053.77
2028	24,144.22	26,563.54	25,353.88
2029	25,443.99	27,863.31	26,653.65

Source: It was developed by the authors based on Stata software.

According to the results of the study, based on the ARIMA(2,1,2) model, the per capita agricultural output in 2025–2029, excluding random endogenous and exogenous factors, was projected to reach 21,442.87 million soums in 2025, 22,756.41 million soums in 2026, 24,05.77 million soums in 2027, 25,353.88 million soums in 2028 and 26,653.65 million soums in 2029, respectively.

The study presents graphical representations of the per capita agricultural output for 2010–2024 and the forecast indicator for 2025–2029 based on data from the Statistical Agency under the President of the Republic of Uzbekistan (<https://stat.uz/uz/>).

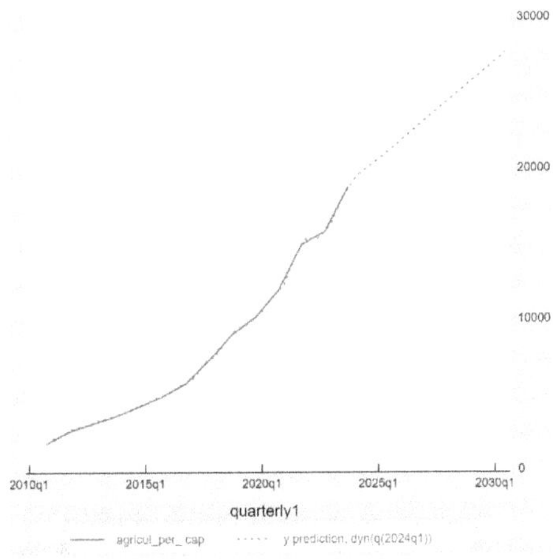

Figure 67. Graph of the resulting variable for 2015–2024 and the forecast for 2025–2029.
Source: It was developed by the authors based on Stata software.

Based on Figure 67, the forecast graphs of the volume of agricultural production per capita for 2010–2024 and 2025–2029, provided by the Statistical Agency under the President of the Republic of Uzbekistan, are depicted. According to it, the direction graph indicates the reliability of the forecast indicators for the next five years, excluding random factors, due to the fact that the two lines are located at maximum proximity.

19.5. Findings and Discussion

Our study's findings illustrate a clear and positive impact of digital technology on the service sector of Uzbekistan's national economy. The econometric analysis, particularly the Random Effects Estimator (REE), has revealed a nuanced relationship between digital infrastructure investments and service sector performance.

Asian countries could provide a broader regional perspective on the digital transformation's economic implications.

The outcome of the use of the ARIMA(2,1,2) model to forecast agricultural output per capita in the Zarafshan region for the period 2025–2029 provides a series of interesting findings regarding the agricultural performance, trends and policy development implications in the region. These findings are placed within the broader literature and overall economic and environmental context in Uzbekistan.

19.5.1. Forecast Agricultural Output per Capita

ARIMA(2,1,2) model gives the following forecast of agricultural production per capita for Zarafshan district for a five-year period:

2025: 21,442.87 million soums
2026: 22,612.47 million soums
2027: 23,887.15 million soums
2028: 25,032.61 million soums
2029: 26,653.65 million soums

The trend shows a steady increase in agricultural output per capita, which shows a strong growth trend in the agricultural industry of the area. The increase shows an outcome of favourable patterns of growth, due to technological progress, improved agricultural efficiency and positive economic conditions, which are consistent with Karatayev et al. (2022), who had found the same patterns of growth in agricultural industries where policies that were meant to boost productivity were implemented.

19.5.2. Test of Sustainability of Growth

The most significant implication of the projection is the test of sustainability of growth in agriculture. The consistent trend of growth in per capita agricultural production means that the sector is witnessing sustainable development. Growth is being driven to a great extent by technological improvement and improved efficiency in resource use, particularly keeping in view the sector's issue of water and land loss (Mamadiyarov et al., 2025). Past research has revealed that the implementation of sophisticated irrigation technology, conservation of soil and diversification of crops are good ways of boosting the agricultural production of the water-scarce areas such as Zarafshan. Therefore, the prediction is confident of the potential of the region to overcome the challenges and still realise good agricultural growth.

19.5.3. Stability and Growth in Agriculture

Outcome projection indicates that agriculture comes out stronger and more stable from external shock. As the growth rate is fairly stable and consistent, this reflects an industry that is not highly exposed to volatility that often stems from climatic uncertainty or economic volatility. This stability suggests that Uzbekistan's agricultural reforms and investment in infrastructural and technological development in sectors like irrigation facilities, rural road infrastructure and agrarian modernisation programmes are yielding fruits.

19.5.4. Agricultural Investment Opportunities

One of the most significant implications of the projection is the potential for higher investment in the agriculture sector. The persistent rise in per capita production in agriculture indicates a good investment climate, where private and public agricultural businesses can expand their production size. The growth of production, as forecasted, is also guaranteed by Sinu et al. (2019), which observed that the greater magnitude of agricultural production provides a good foundation for domestic and foreign investment, particularly into new technology, infrastructural development and agricultural processing.

19.5.5. Contribution to Food Security

The stable and increasing trend in farm output per capita is also essential in ensuring food security at the regional level. With increasing farm output, the ability of the region to provide the nutritional needs of its population increases, thereby enhancing food security and reducing the likelihood of food shortage. Since there is this growing population in Uzbekistan and dependency on agriculture in the region, the expectation is that higher growth in the productivity of agriculture will continue to be a vital source for ensuring rural populations and even urban people's food supply. This concurs with Suvanov and Sultanov (2024), who asserts the necessity for agricultural development in ensuring food security in Central Asian nations, particularly in regions with vast rural populations.

The increased level of food security is particularly appropriate since Zarafshan, like most of Uzbekistan, suffers from water and land quality problems. But with the increasing levels of farm production achieved per capita, the region is better positioned to deal with such problems and help the national vision overall of realising food sovereignty.

19.5.6. Implications for Policy and Recommendations

Policy implications derived from the results have some serious suggestions. First, it is anticipated that agriculture in Zarafshan will continue to expand but will have to be supported by sustained investment in human beings, technology and physical assets. Policymakers will have to accord top priority to the establishment of sustainable farming practices such as water-saving technology, soil conservation and cultivation of diversified cropping systems. Moreover, a continuing requirement to subsidise small farmers, who are the pillars of farm workers in Zarafshan, must also be fulfilled.

Secondly, financing agro-enterprises that are actually actively applying innovative agricultural development and value addition processing into action must also be emphasised by the government. Growth potential has the strong capacity to accommodate agribusiness clusters which may be the impetus for local economic growth and even employment opportunities.

Finally, regional governments and stakeholders can utilise the forecast as a regional resource development plan and planning tool. The projections of the model provide useful information on future agricultural needs, which can be used to create effective policies to ensure sustainable agriculture practices and food security.

19.5.7. Limitations and Future Research

While the ARIMA (2,1,2) model makes a reasonable prediction of agricultural production per capita, one should appreciate its limitation. The model is derived from the observation period, and there may be exogenous shocks such as natural disasters, economic shocks or significant policy changes that would affect future agricultural production in unmodelled form. Future research can follow up on this study by adding additional variables such as climate variables and socio-economic variables to come up with a more comprehensive forecasting model. Secondly, although this study is conducted in the Zarafshan region, it would be useful to use the ARIMA model for other regions of Uzbekistan in order to facilitate farm performance comparison within the country.

19.6. Conclusion

The ARIMA (2,1,2) model forecast for the volume of agricultural products per capita in the Zarafshan region provides the following conclusions.

1. The ARIMA (2,1,2) model forecast shows promising forecasts for the volume of agricultural products per capita, which indicates a solid growth in agricultural products per capita over the next five years.
2. Assessment of sustainable growth in agricultural productivity. According to the results of the ARIMA (2,1,2) model, this per capita agricultural product, which has shown a constant growth trend, is projected to increase from 21,442.87 million soums in 2025 to 26,653.65 million soums in 2029. This indicates the sustainable development of the agricultural sector under the influence of technological progress, increased efficiency and favourable economic conditions.
3. The importance of economic growth and stability in the agricultural industry. According to the model results, the growth rate shows that the agricultural sector is becoming stable and resistant to fluctuations. This

stable growth indicates a long-term positive trend, which is reflected in the investments made in infrastructure, transformation and government reforms.

4. Assessment of investment processes as development opportunities in the sector. This result shows that agriculture has an excellent opportunity for further investment. This growth is assessed by stakeholders with potential in agriculture, expanding public and private production capacities, applying modern technologies and using investment financing to increase the efficiency of the supply chain.
5. Serves to increase income and the potential of the agricultural industry. With the growth of agricultural output per capita, it leads to an increase in labour income. According to this result, the development of an integral process related to raising the standard of living of the population, increasing rural development and further transformation of the economy of agricultural regions has created the basis.
6. Assessment of the importance of the sector in ensuring stability and food security. According to the forecast results, the growth rates show that the agricultural industry is on a stable path, which increases its importance in ensuring long-term food security. The increase in per capita production will increase the level of food security, reduce the risk of shortages and support national economic stability.

Lastly, the application of the ARIMA (2,1,2) model to forecast agricultural production per capita for the Zarafshan region provides significant learnings for future direction for the sector. The forecast signals sustained and steady agricultural productivity growth as a cause of economic stability, food security and investment. The findings emphasise the importance of continued investment in agricultural infrastructure and adoption of sustainable strategies to ensure long-term agricultural sustainability in the region. Additionally, this study fills a critical knowledge gap in regional agricultural forecasts, providing critical statistics to policymakers, agricultural planners and other concerned parties who participate in making Uzbekistan's agricultural industry more efficient and sustainable.

Bibliography

Akhmetshin, E., Abdullayev, I., Makhmudov, S., Dakhkilgova, K., Korotaeva, I. and Yanovskaya, G. (2025). APPLICATION OF TANH–COTH METHOD FOR COMBINED AND DOUBLE COMBINED SINH–COSH–GORDON EQUATIONS ARISING CHEMICAL REACTIONS TO WATER SURFACE GRAVITY WAVES. Computational Methods for Differential Equations, (), -. doi: 10.22034/cmde.2025.67655.3234

Bozkurt, İ., and Kaya, M. V. (2021). 'Agricultural Production Index: International Comparison'. *Agric. Econ. – Czech*, 67, 236–45.

Cahyani, I., Buriev, K., Ngongo, M., Mamadiyarov, Z., Ino, L., Herman, H., Saputra, N., & Baxtishodovich, S. (2025). Exploring the Use of TikTok Application in Enhancing the Skill of Pronunciation: A Case on Students' Perception. Studies in Media and Communication, 13(2), 150–158. doi: http://dx.doi.org/10.11114/smc.v13i2.7553

Christodoulos, C., Michalakelis, C., and Varoutas, D. (2010). 'Forecasting with Limited Data: Combining ARIMA and Diffusion Models'. *Technological Forecasting and Social Change*, 77 (4), 558–65.

Ghazo, A., (2021). 'Applying the ARIMA Model to the Process of Forecasting GDP and CPI in the Jordanian Economy'. *International Journal of Financial Research*, 12 (3), 70–7.

Habib, S. S., Islam, M. A., Ali, M. N., Benitez, I. B., Mamadiyarov, Z., Mirzayev, B., … & Flah, A. (2025). Multi-Objective Optimization and Feasibility Analysis of Integrated Biogas–Solar Energy Systems for Rural Electrification. Results in Engineering, 107086.

Han, P., Wang, P. X., Zhang, S. Y., and Zhu, D. H. (2010). 'Drought Forecasting Based on the Remote Sensing Data Using ARIMA Models'. *Mathematical and Computer Modelling*, 51 (11–12), 1398–403.

Eshov, M., Amirov, L., and Askarova, M. (2021). 'Development of the Agricultural Sector and Its Importance in Uzbekistan'. In *E3S Web of Conferences*, Vol. 244, *EDP Sciences*, 03014.

Jahrir, A., Gultom, Y., Herman, H., Zabadi, F., Ngongo, M., Mamadiyarov, Z., Fatmawati, E., & Saputra, N. (2025). Investigating the Elements of Short Commercial Mineral Water Advertisement: A Case on Discourse Analysis. Studies in Media and Communication, 13(4), 94–104. doi: http://dx.doi.org/10.11114/smc.v13i4.7813

Kalandarov, F., Makhmudov, S., Ibadullaev, D., Matniyozov, M., Nasretdinova, F., Sabirov, K., & Bahodirov, N. M. (2025). Low-Carbon Energy Risk and Renewable Energy Development: Insights from Method of Moments Quantile Regression. International Journal of Energy Economics and Policy, 15(3), 524–536.

Karatayev, M., Clarke, M., Salnikov, V., Bekseitova, R., and Nizamova, M. (2022). 'Monitoring Climate Change, Drought Conditions and Wheat Production in Eurasia: The Case Study of Kazakhstan'. *Heliyon*, 8 (1).

Khayrilla Kurbonov, Samariddin Makhmudov, Shakhzod Erkinov, Umidjon Dadabaev, Gulnora Bekimbetova, Rukhiddin Zayniddinov, and Mirzabek Jonuzokov. 2025. Evaluating the Impact of Marketing Practices Digitalization and Investment on Labor Market Efficiency and Commercial Bank Performance Using Econometric Models. In Proceedings of the 8th International Conference on Future Networks & Distributed Systems (ICFNDS '24). Association for Computing Machinery, New York, NY, USA, 786–796. https://doi.org/10.1145/3726122.3726237

Khodjaniyazov, N., Mirkhoshimova, M., Kalandarov, F., Matyokubova, D., Utegenova, S., Makhmudov, S., & Khudayberganov, M. (2025). Time-Varying Impacts of Financial Stress on Energy-Related Uncertainty. International Journal of Energy Economics and Policy, 15(3), 689–698.

Kuchkarov, T., Mamadiyarov, Z., Khakimov, Z., Sabirova, O., Matmurodov, K., Raimboyeva, M., & Umarova, S. (2025). Energy-Related Uncertainty and Crypto-Currency Environmental Attention: Time-Varying Perspective. International Journal of Energy Economics and Policy, 15(5), 614–626. https://doi.org/10.32479/ijeep.20784

Lee, C. M., and Ko, C. N. (2011). 'Short-Term Load Forecasting Using Lifting Scheme and ARIMA Models'. *Expert Systems with Applications*, 38 (5), 5902–11.

Liu, T., Liu, S., and Shi, L. (2020). *ARIMA Modelling and Forecasting*. Singapore: Springer, 61–85, <https://doi.org/10.1007/978-981-15-0321-4_4>.

Lin, M.H., Matchanova, B., Nurmatovich, H.A. et al. Optimal Operation of the Multi-Carrier Energy System Considering Energy Markets and Renewable Energies Participation. *Int. J. Appl. Comput. Math* **11**, 170 (2025). https://doi.org/10.1007/s40819-025-02002-9

Litamahuputty, J. V., Amiruddin, E. G., Rahim, R., Rahman, A., & Mamadiyarov, Z. (2025). Cryptocurrency Risk Management through Decision Engineering: Evaluating XRPUSD and ADAUSD Portfolio Performance. Journal of Applied Science, Engineering, Technology, and Education, 7(1), 69–81. https://doi.org/10.35877/454RI.asci3871

Luceño, A., and Peña, D. (2008). 'Autoregressive Integrated Moving Average (ARIMA) Modeling'. *Encyclopedia of Statistics in Quality and Reliability.*

Mamadiyarov, Z., Eshov, M., Otakhonova, D., Utegenova, S., Sabirov, K., Marks, A., & Bahodirov, N. (2025). Does Energy Policy Risk Threaten Energy Sources Diversification?. International Journal of Energy Economics and Policy, 15(5), 730–740. https://doi.org/10.32479/ijeep.21140

Mamadiyarov, Z. Makhmudov, S. Utanov, B. Kasimova, D. Bekmurodova, G. Hakimov, Z. (2025). Fusion of Economic and Financial Factors Affecting Household Deposits in Banks: An Econometric Analysis. Fusion: Practice and Applications, (), 82–91. DOI: https://doi.org/10.54216/FPA.190206

Mamadiyarov, Z., Saidov, O., Abdurazakova, N., Makhmudov, S., Nazarov, M., Rajabova, N., … Ruzmetova, I. (2025). Energy-Related Uncertainty and Tourism Stock Markets: New Insights from Time-Varying Relationship with TVP- VAR Approach. International Journal of Energy Economics and Policy, 15(4), 730–737. https://doi.org/10.32479/ijeep.20480

Mamani, J.C.M., Miri, M., Vorobev, Y. et al. Optimal Operation of Energy Microgrid Considering Economic and Emission Indices. Oper. Res. Forum 6, 122 (2025). https://doi.org/10.1007/s43069-025-00523-z

Mahmoud Sayed Agbo, H. (2023). 'Forecasting Agricultural Price Volatility of Some Export Crops in Egypt Using ARIMA/GARCH Model'. *Review of Economics and Political Science*, 8 (2), 123–33.

Matyakubova, A., Makhmudov, S., Ozturk, I., Kurbonov, K., Ismailov, F., Yokubboeva, S., & Urozov, A. (2025). Responses of Economic Policy Uncertainty, Financial Stress and Energy-Related Uncertainty to the Shocks in US-China Tension in US. International Journal of Energy Economics and Policy, 15(4), 701–708. https://doi.org/10.32479/ijeep.20369

Ngongo, M., Herman, H., Ndandara, A., Jois Jaha, D. A., Peku Djawang, J. U. S., Tanggu Rame, M. M., Khamraeva, S. N., & Mamadiyarov, Z. (2025). An Investigation of Meaning, Toponymy of Sumba Cultural Site's Names, and the Impact of Tourism Visitors on Surrounding Society. Forum for Linguistic Studies, 7(8), 679–693. https://doi.org/10.30564/fls.v7i8.10260

PANJAITAN, M. B., HAMDANAH, H., SIRAIT, J., SUTIKNO, S., FATMAWATI, E., HERMAN, H., & MAMADIYAROV, Z. (2025). THE ROLE OF EMOTIONAL REGULATION IN SHAPING STUDENTS' PERCEPTION OF PHYSICS PROBLEMSOLVING TASKS. TPM – Testing, Psychometrics, Methodology in Applied Psychology, 32(S2(2025) : Posted 09 June), 1–10. Retrieved from https://tpmap.org/submission/index.php/tpm/article/view/139

Pradhan, R., Hajiyev, E., Shichiyakh, R. et al. Optimal Techno-Economic Feasibility of an Off-Grid Microgrid System Using Load Flow Energy Management Strategies. *Oper. Res. Forum* **6**, 120 (2025). https://doi.org/10.1007/s43069-025-00524-y

Rizvi, M.F., Sahu, S., and Rana, S. (2024). 'ARIMA Model Time Series Forecasting'. International Journal for Research in Applied Science and Engineering Technology: Haryana, India.

Romero, R. M., Zelinskaya, M., Makhmudov, S., Sapaev, S., & Rustambekovich, J. U. (2025, September). Modelling and Optimal Utilisation of the Renewable Energy Systems in Microgrid with Improving Reliability and Energy Efficiency. In Operations Research Forum (Vol. 6, No. 3, pp. 1–20). Springer International Publishing.

Rony, Z. T., Jefri, R., Rusmardiana, A., Pramono, S. A., & Mamadiyarov, Z. (2025). Downside Risk Measurement of Indonesian Financial and Energy Securities: A Value at Risk Perspective. Journal of Applied Science, Engineering, Technology, and Education, 7(2). https://doi.org/10.35877/454RI.asci3898

Rukhiddin Zayniddinov, Nodir Jumaev, Gulbakhor Irgasheva, Alam Asadov, Nosir Makhmudov, Sirojiddin Abrorov, and Samariddin Makhmudov. 2025. The Influence of the Digital Economy on Economic Development Evidence from Uzbekistan. In Proceedings of the 8th International Conference on Future Networks & Distributed Systems (ICFNDS '24). Association for Computing Machinery, New York, NY, USA, 831–839. https://doi.org/10.1145/3726122.3726242

Ruzmetov, K., Faiziev, A., Murodov, S., and Kurbonbekova, O. (2023). 'Statistical Analysis and Forecasting of Cotton Yield Dynamics in Kashkadarya Region of Republic of Uzbekistan'. In *E3S Web of Conferences*, Vol. 389, 03080. EDP Sciences.

Rayala, R. V., Borra, C. R., Vasudevan, V., Singhania, R., Cheekati, S., & Mamadiyarov, Z. (2025, July). Lightweight Deep Learning Framework for Human Activity Recognition: A MobileNet-LSTM Approach with WHOA Optimization. In *2025 International Conference on Innovations in Intelligent Systems: Advancements in Computing, Communication, and Cybersecurity (ISAC3)* (pp. 1–6). IEEE.

Rayala, R. V., Sandhya, N., Singhania, R., Cheekati, S., Borra, C. R., Vasudevan, V., & Mamadiyarov, Z. (2025, July). AI-Driven Tomato Quality Assessment: A Deep Learning Approach for Image-based Defect Detection and Classification. In *2025 International Conference on Innovations in Intelligent Systems: Advancements in Computing, Communication, and Cybersecurity (ISAC3)* (pp. 1–6). IEEE.

Samariddin Makhmudov, Malika Umarova, Khayrilla Kurbonov, Laylo Akbarova, Durdona Davletova, Nilufar Shanazarova, and Toshmurod Kulmanov. 2025. Evaluating the forecast indicators of the volume of highly liquid assets of commercial banks in the process of digital transformation. In Proceedings of the 8th International Conference on Future Networks & Distributed Systems (ICFNDS '24). Association for Computing Machinery, New York, NY, USA, 698–704. https://doi.org/10.1145/3726122.3726222

Samariddin Makhmudov, Kudratillo Tukhsanov, Saifulla Arslanbekov, Akram Amanov, Orifali Tursunov, Umarbek Jabbarov and Muyassarxon Mirzakarimova. 2024. Optimizing Supply Chain Financing Development Prospects of Digital Ecosystems in the European Logistics Industry. In The 8th International Conference on Future Networks & Distributed Systems (ICFNDS '24), December 11–12, 2024, Marakech, Morocco. ACM, New York, NY, USA, 12 Pages. https://doi.org/10.1145/3726122.3726200.

Shumway, R. H., and Stoffer, D. S. (2025). *Time Series Analysis and Its Applications: With R Examples* (5th ed.). Springer.

Singagerda, F. S., Pratama, M. R., Alfairus, M. Q., Iskandar, A., & Mamadiyarov, Z. (2025). A Decision-Centric Approach to Risk Management in Aviation Stock Investments Using Value at Risk and Portfolio Optimization. Journal of Applied Science, Engineering, Technology, and Education, 7(1), 114–125. https://doi.org/10.35877/454RI.asci3870

Sofyanty, D., Romadhoni, R., Handriadi, H., Makhsudovna, I. S., Anwar, Z., & Mamadiyarov, Z. (2025). Strategic Decision Analysis for Investment Portfolios: Computational Risk Assessment in Transportation Asset Management. Journal of Applied Science, Engineering, Technology, and Education, 7(2). https://doi.org/10.35877/454RI.asci3897

Sinu, E. B., Kleden, M. A., and Atti, A. (2024). 'Application of ARIMA Model for Forecasting National Economic Growth: A Focus on Gross Domestic Product Data'. *Barekeng* 18 (2), 1261–72. <https://doi.org/10.30598/barekengvol18iss2pp1261-1272>.

Sun, F., Meng, X., Zhang, Y., Wang, Y., Jiang, H., and Liu, P. (2023). 'Agricultural Product Price Forecasting Methods: A Review'. *Agriculture*, 13 (9), 1671.

Toshmurod Kulmanov, Umidjon Dadabaev, Mansurbek Qulmetov, Aliboy Ulashov, Mirjalol Eshboyev, and Samariddin Makhmudov. 2025. Global Services Market Transformation Digitalization Export Trends and Future Forecasts. In Proceedings of the 8th International Conference on Future Networks & Distributed Systems (ICFNDS '24). Association for Computing Machinery, New York, NY, USA, 851–858. https://doi.org/10.1145/3726122.3726245

Zhang, G. P. (2003). 'Time Series Forecasting Using a Hybrid ARIMA and Neural Network Model'. *Neurocomputing*, 50, 159–75.

Zhao, Q., Pervaiz, A., Makhmudov, S., & Fatima, A. (2025). Do environmental stringent policies enhance the impact of renewable energy on CO2 reduction? Evidence from BRICS-T economies. Journal of Environmental Management, 391, 126464.

Econometric Analysis of Housing Financing and Factors Influencing It in Ensuring Socio-Economic Stability in Uzbekistan

Zokir Mamadiyarov, Mukhabbatkhon Berdalieva, Samariddin Makhmudov, Olim Astanakulov, Kaxramon Mambetjanov, Shakhnoza Rakhmatullaeva and Sherzod Safarov

20.1. Introduction

Today, financing housing provision plays an important role in ensuring socio-economic stability in the regions, facilitating the use of real estate, in particular, ensuring social equality and stability. This serves to increase the importance of families in economic processes by satisfying their housing needs, increasing the scale of construction work, while creating jobs and ensuring household stability.

Also, the widespread introduction of mortgage loans, grants and subsidies by the government through financing the housing fund, mechanisms for financing housing construction, allows to achieve a balance of social inequality and improve living standards.

The implementation of state programmes aimed at providing the population with affordable housing as part of socio-economic reforms has contributed to a significant growth in the housing market of Uzbekistan in recent years. The creation of the necessary infrastructure and legal framework for the construction of housing estates simplifies the process of building new housing, allowing more and more people to own their own homes. This, in general, contributes to the stabilisation of the housing market and its further development. The importance of this sector in Uzbekistan is also growing day by day. In particular, one of the main reasons for the increase in housing prices is the insufficient financial literacy of the population, which limits their ability to use other financial instruments as investments.

Increasing the financial literacy of the population remains one of the most urgent issues within the framework of measures to prevent the artificial increase in housing prices in Uzbekistan. To understand the need for housing supply and its development, it is worthwhile to assess how this sector affects the socio-economic stability of the country.

20.2. Literature Review

According to Olim et al. (2024) 'housing financing serves to stimulate economic growth by strengthening construction activity and related sectors'. The author's research results show that a 1 per cent increase in housing construction in Uzbekistan created the basis for an increase in GDP by 0.28 per cent. According to Mutian Wang's research, 'Subsidized housing in the United States and China has served to increase consumption and employment'. The author's research results show that housing subsidy practices by the government in the United States and China through rational alternative financing methods have provided employment to low-income people in the region in the short and long term, and thus have a significant impact on the macroeconomic indicators of the country (Wang, M., 2023).

Akinsulyar et al. (2024) state that 'affordable housing policies reduce housing prices, allowing households to allocate more income to other needs, thereby increasing consumption expenditures and economic activity'. Ovsiannikova et al. (2021) state that 'housing investments are significantly related to socio-economic development, affecting housing security and the human development index'. The authors' research results showed that real estate investments had a positive impact on socio-economic development parameters in the region, in particular housing security, the human development index at the level of complex programmatic development of the economy.

Blazej Kochanski states that 'the increasing role of mortgage loans leads to risks to economic stability, such as cyclicality and monetary policy problems'. According to the author's research, the significant increase in the volume of mortgage loans in Polish commercial banks has had a significant negative impact on the country's economy on a macro scale. According to him, the huge increase in mortgage loans in commercial banks has created many difficulties in meeting their long-term obligations (Kochanski, 2014).

According to Oleksiy O. Fomenko, 'subsidizing housing and communal services allows for access to basic services for vulnerable segments of the population by ensuring social stability, and thus serves to reduce social inequality'. The authors noted the importance of government financial subsidies, which, according to the study, demonstrates a strong correlation with economic inequalities, financial profitability and environmental sustainability (Fomenko, 2024).

In assessing the impact of housing financing on ensuring socio-economic stability, scientific theoretical studies have been conducted by reputable foreign scientists and hypotheses developed on the basis of econometric models have been confirmed.

In particular, in their scientific research, V. Litovtseva and Maryna Brychko (2022) 'emphasized the importance of government in implementing affordable housing programmes in Ukraine in strengthening trust and contributing to social stability'. The authors evaluated the research results on the basis of econometric models and proposed using state-administrative mechanisms to introduce real estate rights of the population in the region, increasing the volume of mortgage payments and housing financing.

V. Voitovich and S. V. Lyutikov's scientific research 'It is emphasized that the social housing programme in Russia is aimed at protecting people's interests and reducing social conflicts by ensuring the availability of real estate'. According to the results of the study, the authors identified the optimal solution as the introduction of a strategy for the production of local products based on the 'Social Housing' programme, the return of labour to factories and factories in the labour market, and the expansion of the 'social housing' system to modernise the industry (Voitovich & Lyutikov, 2022).

V. Widyastutik et al. (2022) conducted research based on econometric models, which showed that 'In Indonesia, the housing finance policy through the liquidity fund has a negative impact on certain sectors, but has shown a positive change in the welfare of society and economic indicators'. The authors, using statistical methods, in particular the recursive-dynamic general equilibrium model, based on the equation developed, capture the redistribution of economic resources in the practice of housing finance to low-income communities and at the macroeconomic level. Also, the liquidity indicator of real estate financing funds serves to increase housing construction and increase the welfare of the population.

Jose Carrasco-Gallego notes that 'in the context of OECD countries, the volatility of housing prices has a significant impact on economic stability'. The authors argue that optimal macroprudential practice of adjusting the loan-to-value ratio as a source of financing would stabilise the economy against housing market shocks (Carrasco-Gallego, 2020).

20.3. Research Methodology and Development Hypothesis

To assess the impact of housing financing on socio-economic stability and the factors affecting it, quarterly data sources from the Central Bank of the Republic of Uzbekistan (<https://cbu.uz/>), the World Bank (<https://data.worldbank.org/>) and the Statistical Agency under the President of the Republic of Uzbekistan (<https://stat.uz/uz/>) with a total of 41 observations covering the years 2013–2023 were used.

Since the data for the study were formed on the basis of multivariate time series, multivariate linear equations (LS) and VAR (Vector Autoregressive) models were used to develop econometric equations.

In the article, the Gauss-Markov conditions for the 'multivariate linear (LS) model' were checked and the level of statistical significance was assessed using several confidence tests, in particular, the 'Durbin-Watson', 'Shapiro-Wilk' (Lin et al., 2025; Mamadiyarov et al., 2025; Mamani et al., 2025; Pradhan et al., 2025; Rayala et al., 2025) and 'Breusch-Pagan' tests (Akhmetshin et al., 2025; Habib et al., 2025; Jahrir et al., 2025; Khoshimov et al., 2024).

In the article, the level of statistical significance of the VAR (Vector Autoregressive) model as the second econometric model was analysed based on diagnostic tests, in particular, the 'VAR model stationarity test', 'VAR model eigenvalue-stability test', 'Lagrange-multiplier test' and the 'Impulse-response function' plot were evaluated.

In addition, in the theoretical evaluation of econometric models, analytical statistical images, graphical matrix plots, normal distribution plots, correlation matrix, analytical graphs of time series and all variables were used for the multivariate linear equation (LS) model and VAR (Vector Autoregressive) models. The relationship graphs were formed. The 'VIF test' was used to assess the multicollinearity of the econometric model.

Another group of economists has successfully used econometric models such as Fixed Effects Estimator (FEE), Random Effects Estimator (REE), multivariate linear (LS) and ARDL in their research on investment in digital infrastructure, various aspects of digital payment systems, the impact of inflation and credit interest rates on investment, factors affecting the reduction of the state's share in commercial banks, Non-Performing Loans in commercial banks, the digitisation of banks, risks in digital services and the development of retail payment services (Rayala et al., 2025; Romero et al., 2025; Rony et al., 2025; Rukhiddin et al., 2025; Samariddin et al., 2025; Singagerda et al., 2025; Sofyanty et al., 2025; Toshmurod et al., 2025; Zhang et al., 2025; Zhao et al., 2025; Yin et al., 2024).

Analyses and forecasts were conducted using multivariate linear regression (LS), ARDL, ARIMA and various other econometric models on the global services market, digital economy, energy-related financial stress, cocktail market, digital transformation, factors affecting the logistics industry (Kalandarov et al., 2025; Khayrilla et al., 2025; Khodjaniyazov et al., 2025; Kuziboev et al., 2025; Mamadiyarov et al., 2025; Samariddin et al., 2025).

The article presents the first econometric model, a multivariate linear equation (LS) model.

The formula for the multivariate linear equation (LS) model is given below.

$$y_i = \varphi_0 + \varphi_1 x_{1i} + \varphi x_{2i} + \varphi_3 x_{3i} + \cdots + \varphi_{il} x_{ik} + \epsilon_i \quad (1)$$

Here,

y_i is the dependent variable for observation i, which means the resulting variable in the model.

$x_{1t}, x_{2t}, x_{3t}, \ldots, x_k$ are independent variables (influencing factors).
$\varphi_1, \varphi_2, \varphi_3, \ldots, \varphi_l$ – regression coefficients (indicating the influence of each factor).
ϵ_i – residual (error) value.

The second econometric model in the study was the VAR (Vector Autoregressive) model.

The VAR model formula is given below.

$$Y_t = C + \sum_{i=1}^{p} A_i Y_{t-1} + \varepsilon_t \quad (2)$$

Where,

$Y_t \in R^{m\times 1}$: t represents the vector of endogenous (dependent) variables m at time t.
$C \in R^{m\times 1}$: Represents the vector of intercept terms (optional).

p: Represents the lag order of the VAR model.
$A_i \in R^{m\times 1}$ Represents the vector of intercept terms (optional).
$\varepsilon_t \in R^{m\times 1}$ Represents the vector of white noise error terms (residuals) with mean zero and covariance matrix.

VAR(1) model (first-order VAR):

$$Y_t = C + A_1 Y_{t-1} + \varepsilon_t \tag{3}$$

VAR(2) model (second-order VAR)

$$Y_t = C + A_1 Y_{t-1} + A_2 Y_{t-2} + \varepsilon_t \tag{4}$$

All variables in econometric models are natural logarithmised.

Below are all variables in the econometric model.

Variables: The volume of housing put into operation is *loghous_put* (result variable),

The volume of gross value added of real estate transactions is *loggros_vol_trans* (independent variable),

The volume of fixed capital investments in real estate transactions is *logvol_invest_cap* (independent variable),

The rate of inflation is *loginflat_rate* (independent variable).

Weighted average loan interest rate – *logweight_aver_loan* (independent variable).

Urban planning level – *logurban_plan_degre* (independent variable).

The main (H_0) and alternative (H_1) hypotheses were reflected in the development of the econometric study.

Structure of the hypothesis in the combined model:

Main hypothesis (H_0): The volume of gross value added of the sectors is real estate operations, the volume of investments in fixed capital is real estate-related operations, the weighted average loan interest rate and the level of urban planning do not significantly affect the volume of housing put into operation and there are no signs of dependence.

Alternative hypothesis (H_1): The size of the gross value added of the industries is significantly affected by the volume of real estate operations, the volume of fixed capital investments is significantly affected by real estate-related operations, the weighted average loan interest rate, and the level of urban development, demonstrating a strong relationship.

20.4. Analysis and Results

In the first stage of the econometric study, descriptive statistical values were expressed for the volume of gas production and the variables affecting it (Table 62).

Table 62. Descriptive statistical indicators of the size of the housing area put into use and the factors affecting it

	loghous_ put	loggros_ vol_trans	logvol_ invest_ cap	loginflat_ rate	logweight_ aver_loan	logurban_ plan_ degre
Mean	11.21606	10.05696	9.670206	2.440515	2.901966	16.61346
Maximum	11.3636	10.83606	10.4208	3.00072	3.190476	16.70676
Minimum	11.02811	9.243146	8.725345	2.079442	2.604463	16.53314
Std. Dev	0.1111857	0.4741928	0.5448564	0.2442662	0.1960981	0.0513655
Std. Err.	0.0173643	0.0740565	0.0850923	0.038148	0.0306254	0.0080219
Skewness	-0.4476014	-0.0475152	-0.2611064	0.4877372	-0.1572142	0.1792381
Kurtosis	1.543381	1.770015	1.60738	2.3648	1.500325	1.864789
Observa-tion	41	41	41	41	41	41

Source: Developed by the authors based on the Stata program.

According to the table above, the descriptive statistical indicators of the econometric study express the stability of the selected variables and their distribution by their main economic values. These descriptive statistical values include 41 observations on the selected variables and create consistency in the data set.

Also, the maximum and minimum values according to the table form a relatively small range, which indicates that the amount of housing put into operation does not require sharp changes in the real estate market. According to the analytical table, the lower standard deviation indicates significant stability.

Investment practice in the real estate market forms an average value and shows a tendency to high values. Since investment capital is necessary for the development of construction projects in the real estate market, an increase in this variable allows an increase in the area of housing put into operation.

The study developed a graphical representation of the size of the housing stock put into use and the factors affecting it over time (Figure 68).

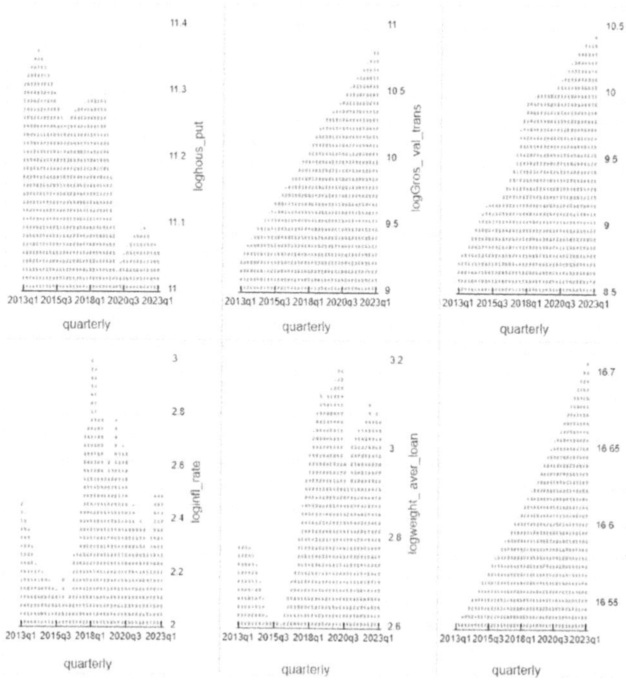

Figure 68. Analytical graphic representation of the size of the housing area put into use and the factors affecting it over time.
Source: Developed by the authors based on the Stata program.

Figure 68 depicts the periodic graphical movement of five potential influencing variables based on quarterly data on the volume of housing put into operation, based on time series data. According to this graphic, the volume of housing put into operation has changed over time, reflecting a dynamic situation, according to which an increasing trend was observed in all variables affecting the volume of housing put into operation from 2013 to 2020. Therefore, although the resulting variable maintained its growth rate until the first half of 2018, the decrease in this indicator during the pandemic was observed due to the decrease in demand in the real estate market, as well as other influencing endogenous and exogenous factors, as well as a decrease in the stability of macroeconomic indicators.

According to the analysis, the weighted average credit rate had a decreasing trend until 2017, but the increase observed during 2018–2020 indicates that this factor has an inverse relationship with the volume of housing put into operation, according to the econometric model. These fluctuations were caused by economic changes in the construction of housing put into operation in the region and the reforms carried out by the government.

The steady growth of the level of urban development, showing a positive correlation between the real estate market and the volume of housing put into operation, indicates that this influencing variable has only shown an upward trend over the years, in particular, the importance of urban development in the construction sector in the region is increasing, which is a result of the implementation of the Development Strategy until 2030 and other programmes.

The next step in the econometric study was to create a graphical matrix of the size of the housing stock put into use and the factors affecting it (Figure 69).

According to Figure 69, there is a strong clustering of plots, providing a significant density effect and an argument for interdependence between the volume of housing stock and its influencing factors. This allows us to analyse the systematic correlation of the dependent variable and its influencing factors and provide reliable forecasts for econometric modelling.

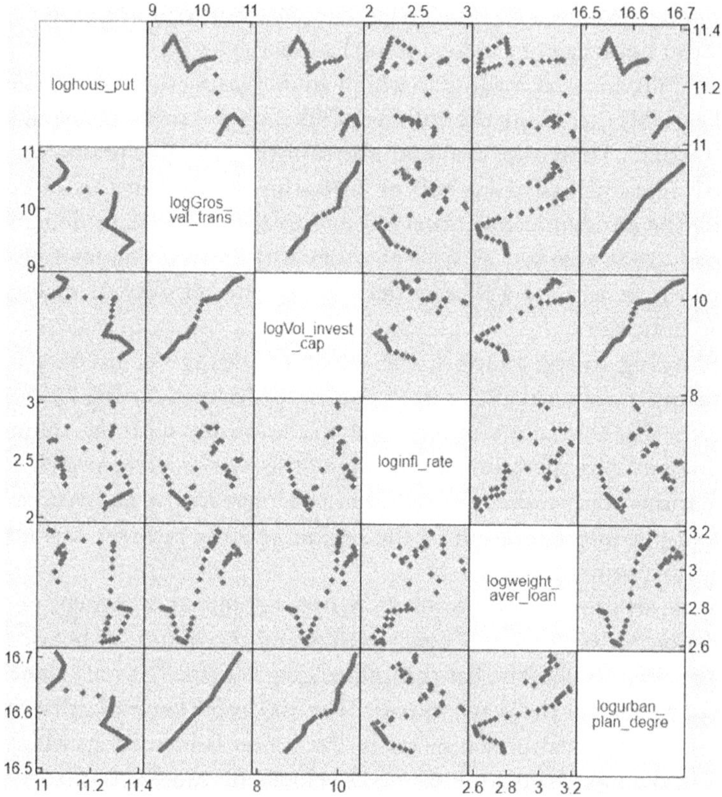

Figure 69. Graphical representation of the analytical relationship (rconnected) of the resulting factors and the factors influencing them.
Source: Developed by the authors based on the Stata program.

The scatter plots between the volume of housing stock, the volume of real estate transactions and the volume of fixed capital investments in real estate transactions show a strong positive trend. This creates a basis for the increase in the volume of housing stock put into operation as a result of the increase in the volume of investment capital and contracts.

The peaks in the volume of housing stock put into operation and the level of urban development are clearly upward, which is associated with the increase in housing areas in good urban planning.

The next step is to present a graphical representation of the analytical relationship (rconnected) between the volume of gas production and the factors affecting it (Figure 70).

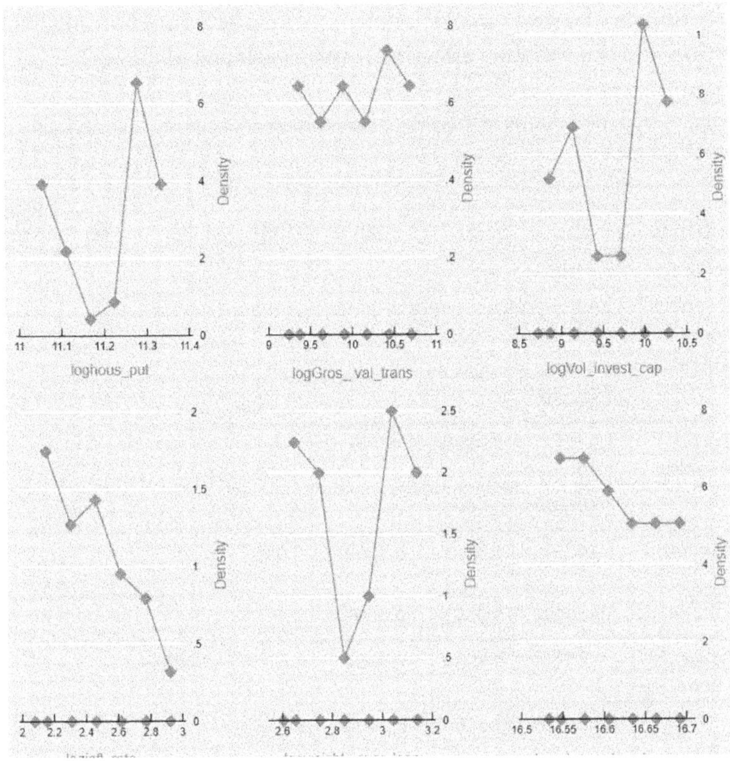

Figure 70. Graphical representation of the size of the housing area put into use and the factors affecting it (rconnected).
Source: Developed by the authors based on the Stata program.

Figure 70 shows that the density graph of the area of housing put into operation shows changes, but at certain points there is a general upward trend, in particular, peaks at certain values, indicating consistent activity in housing construction, which indicates a stable activity of the housing market.

The distribution graphs show stable investments, financing and planning, which are the main factors of housing construction and have a strong positive impact on urban planning and construction processes and the expansion of housing.

According to the study, a correlation matrix of the area of housing put into operation and the variables affecting it was developed (Table 63).

Table 63. Correlation matrix of the size of the housing area put into use and the factors affecting it

Variables	(1)	(2)	(3)	(4)	(5)	(6)	Significant
(1) loghous_put	0.000						
(2) loggros_vol_trans	0.8793	0.000					
	(0.0000)						***
(3) logvol_invest_cap	0.8171	0.7860	1.000				
	(0.0000)	(0.0000)					***
(4) loginflat_rate	0.6827	0.4179	0.5362	1.000			
	(0.0092)	(0.0063)	(0.0003)				***
(5) logweight_aver_loan	0.6573	0.8030	0.8432	0.7398	1.000		
	(0.0000)	(0.0000)	(0.0000)	(0.0000)			***
(6) logurban_plan_degre	0.8951	0.7958	0.7717	0.3735	0.7810	1.0000	
	0.0000	0.0000	0.0000	0.0162	0.0000		***

Source: Developed by the authors based on the Stata program.

Based on Table 63, a strong, inverse and significant correlation relationship is presented between the size of the commissioned housing stock and the factors affecting it. According to the results, the positive correlation relationship explains the important role of the increasing size of the commissioned housing stock. The positive correlation for all variables indicates the negative impact of the size of the commissioned housing stock on macroeconomic factors, in particular, the inflation rate and the weighted average credit rates. The degree of influence of the independent variables indicates the strength of the size of the commissioned housing stock. Also, taking into account the *p*-value of less than 0.05 according to the table, it can be seen that the condition of its statistical significance for the correlation coefficient is met.

In the next stage of the econometric study, a regression model of the size of the housing area put into operation and the factors affecting it was developed using a multivariate linear (LS) model (Table 64).

Table 64. Regression equation indicators based on a multivariate linear (LS) model of the size of the housing area put into use and the factors affecting it

loghous_put	Coeff.	St.Err.	t-value	p-value	[95% Conf	Interval]	Sig
logGros_val_trans	-0.876	0.124	-7.06	0	-1.127	-0.625	***
logVol_invest_cap	0.615	0.116	5.30	0	0.38	0.851	***
loginfl_rate	-0.127	0.048	-2.67	0.011	-0.223	-0.03	**
Constant	14.384	0.248	57.93	0	13.881	14.887	***
Mean dependent var		11.216		SD dependent var		0.111	
R-squared		0.885		Number of obs		41	
F-test		94.489		Prob > *F*		0.000	
Akaike crit. (AIC)		-145.290		Bayesian crit. (BIC)		-138.436	

*** $p < 0.01$, ** $p < 0.05$, * $p < 0.1$

Source: Developed by the authors based on the Stata program.

The formula parameters of the multivariate linear (LS) model are given below.

$$\text{loghous\_put} = 14.38 - 0.87\ \text{loggros\_val\_trans} + 0.61\ \text{logvol\_invest\_cap-} - 0.12\ \text{loginfl\_rate} + \varepsilon_t \qquad (5)$$

General description of the multivariate linear (LS) model.

The *p*-value of the variable affecting the size of the house put into use is less than 0.05, which provides a statistically significant prediction of the resulting factor at the 5 per cent significance level.

R-squared value: The *R*-squared value is 0.8850, which explains the quality of the model with 88.50 per cent of the factors affecting the size of the house put into use. The formation of a high value of *R*-squared indicates a strong influence of the econometric model on the observed data.

When testing the hypothesis of the regression equation according to the multivariate linear (LS) model, it is clear that the null hypothesis ($H_0: y = 0$) is rejected when $F < 0.05$ and $t < 0.05$, indicating that the main hypothesis ($H_0: y = 0$) is statistically insignificant. Accordingly, the main hypothesis is rejected in favour of accepting the statistically significant alternative hypothesis ($H_1: y \neq 0$).

Result. The volume of gross value added of the sectors leads to a decrease in the volume of housing put into operation by 0.87 per cent as a result of a 1 per cent increase in real estate transactions. The volume of investments in fixed capital by types of economic activity leads to an increase in the volume of housing put into operation by 0.61 per cent. A 1 per cent increase in the inflation rate in the national economy leads to a decrease in the volume of housing put into operation by up to 0.12 per cent.

The Gauss-Markov conditions were considered for the study.

The Durbin-Watson test for the multivariate linear (LS) model regression equation recorded a value of 0.37. Also, the Shapiro-Wilk W test was 0.83, and the Breusch-Pagan test was 0.34. According to the primary hypothesis, $H_0: y = 0$ and $H_1: y \neq 0$, $p > 0.05$ significance level tests were conducted.

According to the results of the Durbin-Watson and Shapiro-Wilk tests for the multivariate linear (LS) model regression equation, the null hypothesis was accepted. According to the model, the $p > 0.05$ threshold, error conditions and Gauss-Markov conditions confirming the absence of a relationship between the independent variables included in the analysis of the study. The main conditions of the Gauss-Markov condition for the econometric model were met.

The multivariate linear (LS) model was tested for multicollinearity in the regression using the VIF test, which yielded a value of 6.61, indicating that there was no significant multicollinearity in the model, with a confidence interval of [1, 10].

We also developed the VAR model regression equation as the second econometric model in the study, and tested the regression coefficients.

In the next step, a Unit-root test was conducted to determine the stationarity of the outcome variables and the factors affecting them (Table 65).

Table 65. Unit-Root test indicators for the size of the housing area put into use and the factors affecting it

Variables	Test Statistic	1% Critical Value	5% Critical Value	10% Critical Value	p-value for Z(t)
loghous_put **(Dependent variable)**	5.436	-3.655	-2.961	-2.613	0.0001
loggros_vol_trans **(Dependent variable)**	3.937	-3.655	-2.961	-2.613	0.0000
logvol_invest_cap **(independent variable)**	4.812	-3.655	-2.961	-2.613	0.0000
loginflat_rate (independent variable)	3.815	-3.655	-2.961	-2.613	0.0023
logurban_plan_degre **(independent variable)**	3.742	-3.655	-2.961	-2.613	-3.655

Source: Developed by the authors based on the Stata program.

According to Table 65, the unit root test value of the dependent variable is –5.436, and the test results of the independent variables are –3.937, –4.812, –3.815 and –3.742, respectively. These values indicate that the size of the house put into use and the factors affecting it are statistically significant and stable.

From the table data, it can be seen that McKinnon's value of 0.0000 indicates that the critical values of $Z(t)$ are statistically significant. Also, the unit root test results show that the size of the house put into use and the factors affecting it have reached a stationary state after the initial integration.

In the next stage of the econometric study, the mutual cointegration of the variables is checked, and if there is no cointegration, the work is continued in the VAR model. If the cointegration situation is determined, it is necessary to work with the VEC (Vector Error Correction) model. We also use the Johanson test to determine the years the VAR model is lagged. The results of this test are presented in the table below.

Before performing the cointegration test, it is advisable to determine the lags of the model, that is, the period until which the relationship remains. The table below shows that the VAR model is perfectly good in the 2nd lagged year (Table 66).

Table 66. Test for determining optimal lags in the VAR model of the size of the housing area put into use and the factors affecting it.

Delayed period	LL	LR	df	p	FPE	AIC	HQIC	SBIC
0	204.031				2.4e–10	–10.8125	–10.7511	–10.6383
1	553.481	698.9	16	0.000	3.5e–18	–28.836	–28.5298	–27.966
2	590.51	74.059	16	0.040	1.1e–12	–29.9735	–29.421*	–28.4062*
3	606.54	32.059	16	0.010	1.3e–18	–29.9751	–29.1769	–27.7111
4	625.38	37.681*	16	0.002	1.3e–18	–30.1287*	–29.0849	–27.1681

Source: Developed by the authors based on the Stata program.

According to Table 66, it follows that the optimal equation can be constructed at Step 2 according to the model, and this information will be important in later constructing the VAR equation.

In the next step, a cointegration test of the variables was performed using the Johanson test (Table 67).

Table 67. Johanson test for cointegration based on the VAR model of the size of the housing area put into use and the factors affecting it

Maximum level	Number of parameters	LL	Inherent value	Tracking statistics	5 per cent critical value
0	20	597.0787	.	56.3561	47.21
1	27	609.30293	0.46574	31.9078	29.68
2	32	618.04528	0.36130	14.4231*	15.41
3	35	623.27551	0.23526	5.9627	5.76
4	36	625.25685	0.09662		

Source: Developed by the authors based on the Stata program.

According to Table 67, 'Maximum degree' represents the number of cointegrated vectors in the model. According to it, H_0 represents the existence of one or more cointegrated vectors according to the hypothesis. If the value of the observation statistic is greater than the 5 per cent critical value, the H_0 hypothesis is rejected.

The H0 hypothesis represents the existence of a cointegrated vector in this model. Since the observation statistic is greater than the 5 per cent critical value, this hypothesis is rejected. In the second row, the H_0 hypothesis represents the existence of 1 cointegrated vector in this model, since the observation statistic is greater than the 5 per cent critical value, this hypothesis is rejected.

Therefore, since there is no at least one cointegrated vector, it can be concluded that there is no cointegration in the selected model, and it is appropriate to continue with the VAR model.

The study developed econometric equations for the size of the housing stock put into use and the factors affecting it using the VAR model (Table 68).

Table 68. Table of coefficients of the VAR model equation

Sample: 3 thru 41				Number of obs = 39	
Log likelihood = 611.8111				AIC = −29.83647	
FPE = 7.68e-20				HQIC = −29.37733	
Det(Sigma_ml) = 1.63e−20				SBIC = −28.5568	
Equation	Parms	RMSE	R-sq	chi²	P > chi²
loghous_put	6	0.034195	0.8180	436.8179	0.0000
logGros_val_tr~s	6	0.008426	0.7997	127872.6	0.0000
logVol_invest_~p	6	0.066182	0.8857	2684.221	0.0000
loginfl_rate	6	0.148566	0.6946	88.70582	0.0000
ogurban_plan_~e	6	0.000293	0.8962	1275786	0.0000

	Coefficient	**Std.er**	**z**	**P > z**	**[95%**	**conf.**	**sig**
loghous_put							
loghous_put							
L2.	0.548	0.155	3.530	0.000	0.244	0.853	***
logGros_val_trans							
L2.	−0.870	0.253	−3.440	0.001	−1.366	−0.374	***
logVol_invest_cap							
L2.	0.276	.153	1.800	0.071	0.024	0.575	*
loginfl_rate							
L2. logurban_ plan_degre	−0.118	0.048	−0.370	0.082	0.112	0.076	*
L2.	2.237	1.554	2.730	0.006	1.191	7.282	***
cons	−59.213	24.811	−2.390	0.017	−107.84	−10.585	

Source: Developed by the authors based on the Stata program.

$$\begin{aligned} loghous\_put_t = &- 59.21 + 0.54 \cdot loghous\_put_{t-2} - 0.86\, logGros\_val\_trans_{t-2} \\ &+ 0.27\, logVol\_invest\_cap\_ - 0.11\, loginfl\_rate_{t-2} \\ &+ 2.23\, logurban\_plan\_degre_{t-2} + \epsilon_t \end{aligned} \quad (6)$$

The model uses two lags for each variable and fits the data very well, as shown by the *R*-squared values for each equation:

loghous_putt: $R^2 = 0.8180$ This shows that the econometric model explains about 81.80 per cent of the variation in the size of the housing stock put into use, indicating a strong fit.

logGros_val_trans: $R^2 = 0.7997$ The econometric model explains about 79.97 per centv of the variation in the size of the real estate operations.

logVol_invest_cap: $R^2 = 0.8857$ The econometric model explains about 88.57 per cent of the variation in the size of the fixed capital investments in real estate operations.

loginflat_rate: $R^2 = 0.6946$ explains approximately 88.57 per cent of the variation in the national economy Inflation rate according to the econometric model.

logurban_plan_degre: $R^2 = 0.8962$ explains approximately 89.62 per cent of the variation in the urban planning level according to the econometric model.

High Chi-square values and *p*-values ($p > \text{chi}^2 = 0.0000$ for each equation) indicate that the coefficients in each equation are generally statistically significant.

Each coefficient in the VAR model is interpreted as the effect of the lagged variables on the amount of housing stock put into use over time.

20.5. Conclusion

The coefficient on the volume of housing put into use is 0.54, which means that a 1 per cent increase in the volume of housing put into use at lag 2 leads to a 0.54 per cent increase in the volume of housing put into use in the current period, and the other variables are constantly correlated. It can be seen that the model is statistically significant ($p = 0.000$).

The coefficient on the volume of gross value added of the sectors by real estate operations is −0.869, which indicates that a 1 per cent decrease in the volume of housing put into use is associated with a 0.86 per cent decrease in the volume of housing put into use in the current period. This is a very significant result, and it can be seen that the model is statistically significant ($p = 0.001$).

The coefficient on fixed capital investments for real estate transactions is 0.275, which indicates that a 1 per cent increase in the volume of housing put into operation is associated with a 0.27 per cent increase in the volume of housing put into operation in the current period. It can be seen that this relationship is statistically significant ($p = 0.071$).

The coefficient on real estate transactions for the inflation rate in the economy is -0.118, which indicates that a 1 per cent decrease in the volume of housing put into operation is associated with a 0.11 per cent decrease in the volume of housing put into operation in the current period. This inverse relationship is a significant result, and it can be seen that the model is statistically significant ($p = 0.082$).

The coefficient of urban development level on real estate transactions is 2.237, which means that a 1 per cent increase in the volume of housing put into operation is associated with a 2.23 per cent increase in the volume of housing put into operation in the current period. It can be seen that this relationship is statistically significant ($p = 0.0006$).

Bibliography

Akhmetshin, E., Abdullayev, I., Makhmudov, S., Dakhkilgova, K., Korotaeva, I. and Yanovskaya, G. (2025). APPLICATION OF TANH–COTH METHOD FOR COMBINED AND DOUBLE COMBINED SINH–COSH–GORDON EQUATIONS ARISING CHEMICAL REACTIONS TO WATER SURFACE GRAVITY WAVES. Computational Methods for Differential Equations, (), -. doi: 10.22034/cmde.2025.67655.3234

Akinsulire, A. A., Idemudia, C., Okwandu, A. C., and Iwuanyanwu, O. (2024). 'Economic and Social Impact of Affordable Housing Policies: A Comparative Review'. *International Journal of Applied Research in Social Sciences*, 6 (7), 1433–48.

Carrasco-Gallego, J. A. (2020). 'Real Estate, Economic Stability and the New Macro-Financial Policies'. *Sustainability*, 13 (1), 236. <https://doi.org/10.3390/SU13010236>.

Fomenko, O. O. (2024). 'Subsidizing Housing and Communal Services and Social Stability of the State: The Theoretical and Problematic Aspects'. *Business Inform*, 7 (558), 335–41. <https://doi.org/10.32983/2222-4459-2024-7-335-341>.

Habib, S. S., Islam, M. A., Ali, M. N., Benitez, I. B., Mamadiyarov, Z., Mirzayev, B., … & Flah, A. (2025). Multi-Objective Optimization and Feasibility Analysis of Integrated Biogas–Solar Energy Systems for Rural Electrification. *Results in Engineering*, 107086.

Kalandarov, F., Makhmudov, S., Ibadullaev, D., Matniyozov, M., Nasretdinova, F., Sabirov, K., & Bahodirov, N. M. (2025). Low-Carbon Energy Risk and Renewable Energy Development: Insights from Method of Moments Quantile Regression. International Journal of Energy Economics and Policy, 15(3), 524–536.

Khayrilla Kurbonov, Samariddin Makhmudov, Shakhzod Erkinov, Umidjon Dadabaev, Gulnora Bekimbetova, Rukhiddin Zayniddinov, and Mirzabek Jonuzokov. 2025. Evaluating the Impact of Marketing Practices Digitalization and Investment on Labor Market Efficiency and Commercial Bank Performance Using Econometric Models. In Proceedings of the 8th International Conference on Future Networks & Distributed Systems (ICFNDS '24). Association for Computing Machinery, New York, NY, USA, 786–796. https://doi.org/10.1145/3726122.3726237

Khodjaniyazov, N., Mirkhoshimova, M., Kalandarov, F., Matyokubova, D., Utegenova, S., Makhmudov, S., & Khudayberganov, M. (2025). Time-Varying Impacts of Financial Stress on Energy-Related Uncertainty. International Journal of Energy Economics and Policy, 15(3), 689–698.

Kochanski, B. (2014). Kredyty mieszkaniowe a stabilność gospodarcza-polska perspektywa (Mortgage Lending vs Economic Stability-Polish Perspective). Available at SSRN 2416748.

Kuchkarov, T., Mamadiyarov, Z., Khakimov, Z., Sabirova, O., Matmurodov, K., Raimboyeva, M., & Umarova, S. (2025). Energy-Related Uncertainty and Crypto-Currency Environmental Attention: Time-Varying Perspective. International Journal of Energy Economics and Policy, 15(5), 614–626. https://doi.org/10.32479/ijeep.20784

Kuziboev, B., Ozturk, I., Kalandarov, F., Samandarov, O., Bekjanov, D., & Makhmudov, S. (2025). PROMOTING ENERGY SOURCES

DIVERSIFICATION THROUGH ESG PERFORMANCE. Energy, 136009.

Lin, M.H., Matchanova, B., Nurmatovich, H.A. et al. Optimal Operation of the Multi-Carrier Energy System Considering Energy Markets and Renewable Energies Participation. *Int. J. Appl. Comput. Math* **11**, 170 (2025). https://doi.org/10.1007/s40819-025-02002-9

Litovtseva, V., and Brychko, M. (2022). 'Financing Housing Programmes and Its Role in Enhancing Trust in Government'. *Вісник Сумського Державного Університету*, 2022 (2), 121–8, <https://doi.org/10.21272/1817-9215.2022.2-14>.

Litamahuputty, J. V., Amiruddin, E. G., Rahim, R., Rahman, A., & Mamadiyarov, Z. (2025). Cryptocurrency Risk Management through Decision Engineering: Evaluating XRPUSD and ADAUSD Portfolio Performance. Journal of Applied Science, Engineering, Technology, and Education, 7(1), 69–81. https://doi.org/10.35877/454RI.asci3871

Mamadiyarov, Z., Eshov, M., Otakhonova, D., Utegenova, S., Sabirov, K., Marks, A., & Bahodirov, N. (2025). Does Energy Policy Risk Threaten Energy Sources Diversification?. *International Journal of Energy Economics and Policy, 15*(5), 730–740. https://doi.org/10.32479/ijeep.21140

Mamadiyarov, Z., Saidov, O., Abdurazakova, N., Makhmudov, S., Nazarov, M., Rajabova, N., … Ruzmetova, I. (2025). Energy-Related Uncertainty and Tourism Stock Markets: New Insights from Time-Varying Relationship with TVP- VAR Approach. *International Journal of Energy Economics and Policy, 15*(4), 730–737. https://doi.org/10.32479/ijeep.20480

Mamani, J.C.M., Miri, M., Vorobev, Y. et al. Optimal Operation of Energy Microgrid Considering Economic and Emission Indices. Oper. Res. Forum 6, 122 (2025). https://doi.org/10.1007/s43069-025-00523-z

Muhammad Zubair, Irfanud Din, Nadeem Sarwar et al. Revolutionizing Sepsis Diagnosis Using Machine Learning and Deep Learning Models: A Systematic Literature Review, 10 June 2025, PREPRINT (Version 1) available at Research Square [https://doi.org/10.21203/rs.3.rs-6731418/v1]

Ngongo, M., Herman, H., Ndandara, A., Jois Jaha, D. A., Peku Djawang, J. U. S., Tanggu Rame, M. M., Khamraeva, S. N., & Mamadiyarov, Z. (2025). An Investigation of Meaning, Toponymy of Sumba Cultural Site's Names, and the Impact of Tourism Visitors on Surrounding

Society. *Forum for Linguistic Studies*, 7(8), 679–693. https://doi.org/10.30564/fls.v7i8.10260

Olim, A., Balbaa, M. E., Mukhabbatkhon, B., Batirova, N., and Dadabaev, U. (2024). 'Enhancing Housing Finance for Socio-Economic Stability in Uzbekistan'. *International Journal of Economics and Financial Issues*, 14 (3), 140–8.

Ovsiannikova, T. Y., Rabtsevich, O. V., and Yugova, I. V. (March 2021). 'Analysis of Housing Investment Market Dynamics Impact on Social and Economic Development'. In *IOP Conference Series: Earth and Environmental Science*, Vol. 666, No. 6, p. 062088. IOP Publishing.

PANJAITAN, M. B., HAMDANAH, H., SIRAIT, J., SUTIKNO, S., FATMAWATI, E., HERMAN, H., & MAMADIYAROV, Z. (2025). THE ROLE OF EMOTIONAL REGULATION IN SHAPING STUDENTS' PERCEPTION OF PHYSICS PROBLEMSOLVING TASKS. TPM – Testing, Psychometrics, Methodology in Applied Psychology, 32(S2(2025) : Posted 09 June), 1–10. Retrieved from https://tpmap.org/submission/index.php/tpm/article/view/139

Pradhan, R., Hajiyev, E., Shichiyakh, R. et al. Optimal Techno-Economic Feasibility of an Off-Grid Microgrid System Using Load Flow Energy Management Strategies. *Oper. Res. Forum* **6**, 120 (2025). https://doi.org/10.1007/s43069-025-00524-y

Romero, R. M., Zelinskaya, M., Makhmudov, S., Sapaev, S., & Rustambekovich, J. U. (2025, September). Modelling and Optimal Utilisation of the Renewable Energy Systems in Microgrid with Improving Reliability and Energy Efficiency. In Operations Research Forum (Vol. 6, No. 3, pp. 1–20). Springer International Publishing.

Rony, Z. T., Jefri, R., Rusmardiana, A., Pramono, S. A., & Mamadiyarov, Z. (2025). Downside Risk Measurement of Indonesian Financial and Energy Securities: A Value at Risk Perspective. *Journal of Applied Science, Engineering, Technology, and Education*, 7(2). https://doi.org/10.35877/454RI.asci3898

Rukhiddin Zayniddinov, Nodir Jumaev, Gulbakhor Irgasheva, Alam Asadov, Nosir Makhmudov, Sirojiddin Abrorov, and Samariddin Makhmudov. 2025. The Influence of the Digital Economy on Economic Development Evidence from Uzbekistan. In Proceedings of the 8th International Conference on Future Networks & Distributed Systems

(ICFNDS '24). Association for Computing Machinery, New York, NY, USA, 831–839. https://doi.org/10.1145/3726122.3726242

Samariddin Makhmudov, Malika Umarova, Khayrilla Kurbonov, Laylo Akbarova, Durdona Davletova, Nilufar Shanazarova, and Toshmurod Kulmanov. 2025. Evaluating the forecast indicators of the volume of highly liquid assets of commercial banks in the process of digital transformation. In Proceedings of the 8th International Conference on Future Networks & Distributed Systems (ICFNDS '24). Association for Computing Machinery, New York, NY, USA, 698–704. https://doi.org/10.1145/3726122.3726222

Samariddin Makhmudov, Kudratillo Tukhsanov, Saifulla Arslanbekov, Akram Amanov, Orifali Tursunov, Umarbek Jabbarov and Muyassarxon Mirzakarimova. 2024. Optimizing Supply Chain Financing Development Prospects of Digital Ecosystems in the European Logistics Industry. In The 8th International Conference on Future Networks & Distributed Systems (ICFNDS '24), December 11–12, 2024, Marakech, Morocco. ACM, New York, NY, USA, 12 Pages. https://doi.org/10.1145/3726122.3726200

Singagerda, F. S., Pratama, M. R., Alfairus, M. Q., Iskandar, A., & Mamadiyarov, Z. (2025). A Decision-Centric Approach to Risk Management in Aviation Stock Investments Using Value at Risk and Portfolio Optimization. *Journal of Applied Science, Engineering, Technology, and Education*, 7(1), 114–125. https://doi.org/10.35877/454RI.asci3870

Sofyanty, D., Romadhoni, R., Handriadi, H., Makhsudovna, I. S., Anwar, Z., & Mamadiyarov, Z. (2025). Strategic Decision Analysis for Investment Portfolios: Computational Risk Assessment in Transportation Asset Management. *Journal of Applied Science, Engineering, Technology, and Education*, 7(2). https://doi.org/10.35877/454RI.asci3897

Toshmurod Kulmanov, Umidjon Dadabaev, Mansurbek Qulmetov, Aliboy Ulashov, Mirjalol Eshboyev, and Samariddin Makhmudov. 2025. Global Services Market Transformation Digitalization Export Trends and Future Forecasts. In Proceedings of the 8th International Conference on Future Networks & Distributed Systems (ICFNDS '24). Association for Computing Machinery, New York, NY, USA, 851–858. https://doi.org/10.1145/3726122.3726245

Voitovich, V., and Lyutikov, S. V. (2022). 'Improvements and Development of Housing and Communal Services as the Basis of Russia's Economic Stability'. *Вестник Удмуртского Университета*, 32 (5), 797–804. <https://doi.org/10.35634/2412-9593-2022-32-5-797-804>.

Wang, M. (2023). 'Research on the Positive Economic Influence of Subsidized Housing in the U.S. and China'. *Advances in Economics, Management and Political Sciences*. <https://doi.org/10.54254/2754-1169/8/20230321>.

Widyastutik, W., Hermawan, I. B., Amaliah, S., Nur'aini, Y., and Khristianto, K. (2022). 'The Housing Financing Policy and Its Impacts on Low-Income Communities and Indonesian Economy'. *Mimbar.* <https://doi.org/10.29313/mimbar.v0i0.9663>.

Yin, Y., Gulzar, F., Mamadiyarov, Z., Aizhan, A., Yadav, R. S., & Chen, C. (2024). An analysis of the rebound impact of energy consumption and the factors that influence it in China's agricultural productivity. Energy Strategy Reviews, 56, 101585.

Zhang, L., Zhao, Z., Qamri, G. M., & Makhmudov, S. (2025). Unleashing the critical role of renewable energy through global value chains and digitalization: A path towards environmental sustainability. *Journal of Environmental Management*, *392*, 126688.

Zhao, Q., Pervaiz, A., Makhmudov, S., & Fatima, A. (2025). Do environmental stringent policies enhance the impact of renewable energy on CO2 reduction? Evidence from BRICS-T economies. Journal of Environmental Management, 391, 126464.

The Ratio between Regional Industrial Production Prospects Forecasting and Planning

Zokir Mamadiyarov, Samariddin Makhmudov, Mukhiddin Kalonov, Isabek Murtazaev, Tura Norbaev, Dilrabo Umarova and Mirjalol Eshboev

21.1. Introduction

Local industrial production projections are an important economic planning and policy-making tool, particularly for fast-industrialising developing countries. This is a case study of Uzbekistan's Zarafshan region, whose industrial production has been rising steadily since 2017 and increased by 63 per cent from 2017 to 2023, according to official statistics. Proper prediction of production trends in the manufacturing sector acquires particular importance for transition economies like Uzbekistan, where the industrial growth represents one of the most important modernisation drivers and employment sources in the economy.

Theoretical advances in economic geography (Fujita & Thisse, 2021; Krugman, 2019) have built robust paradigms for the explanation of industrial agglomeration patterns, and methodological advances (Chen & Chen, 2020; Martin & Sunley, 2020) have enhanced the capacity to make regional economic predictions. Application to Central Asian settings is nevertheless still limited, particularly with regard to the unique institutional and economic characteristics of post-Soviet transition economies.

There are three important contributions of this study to regional industrial forecasting literature:

We estimate and verify an ARIMA (1,1,1) model particularly tailored to fit Uzbekistan's industrial nature of data with higher forecast precision (AIC = 533.719) than alternative specifications.

Our study utilises high-frequency data of quarterly duration from 2015 to 2024 that allows for detection of trends over earlier annual-data studies.

We provide the first comprehensive five-year industrial production projection (2025–2029) for the Zarafshan region, with production growth projected from 205,942 to 290,080 billion soums, establishing tangible benchmarks for regional planners.

The report is structured as follows: Section 2 describes our methodology and data sources. Section 3 presents the empirical results, including model diagnostics and forecast levels. Section 4 presents policy implications and Section 5 concludes by indicating future research directions for regional industrial forecasting.

21.2. Literature Review

Regional industrial production balance is a focal field of inquiry in regional planning and economic geography today, and several theoretical and methodological approaches have been applied to explain and predict industrial shifts. This overview synthesises early work into four broad themes: empirical evidence, methodological breakthroughs, theoretical foundations and policy implications.

Theoretical frameworks have progressed significantly since Krugman's (2019) early research on New Economic Geography, which explored how scale economies and transport costs shape industrial agglomeration. Fujita and Thisse (2021) extended this perspective by introducing evolutionary dynamics, illustrating how preceding development pathways constrain subsequent regional equilibria. Complementing these spatial frameworks, Porter and Ketels' (2020) cluster theory outlined long-run competitiveness built through geographically bounded networks of companies.

Methodologically, the field has moved away from mainstream econometrics to newer computational techniques. Chen and Chen's (2020) empirical study demonstrated that machine learning methodologies are much more reliable in prediction than conventional time-series models for handling advanced regional data (<https://doi.org/10.1111/jors.12456>). Concurrently, spatial econometrics has evolved on the strength of Henderson's (2019) development of panel models with regard to temporal as well as inter-regional dependency. Most innovatively, Martin and Sunley (2020) built complexity science methods, modelling regions as complex adaptive systems.

Empirical research has yielded robust evidence of agglomeration patterns in industry. Rosenthal and Strange's (2020) meta-analysis confirmed the persistence of agglomeration economies, most notably in knowledge-based industries. Acemoglu and Restrepo's (2021) longitudinal analysis revealed the paradoxical effect of automation, reinforcing established geographies while triggering tipping points for structural change. Trade impact analyses such as Glaeser et al. (2021) have shown human capital to mediate regional adjustment to globalisation.

Policy suggestions of such literature identify context-sensitive interventions. Strategic specialisation strategies (Rosenthal & Strange, 2020) and strategic investment in infrastructure (Henderson, 2019) have been found to perform well in fostering regional industrial disequilibria. Emerging literature has underlined, especially, the requirement for adaptive labour market policies to address automation issues (Acemoglu & Restrepo, 2021) and cluster-focused skill-building programmes (Porter & Ketels, 2020).

While all these initiatives have significantly increased the level of awareness regarding the dynamics of industries within each locality, there are certain gaps that still exist. There have been very few attempts to integrate environmental sustainability indicators into forecasting models, and the application of real-time data analytics to dynamic spatial modelling is far from being achieved. Comparative analysis across systems of governance can also offer significant insights regarding comparative policy performance within different institutional frameworks.

Today, forecast analysis based on the ARIMA (Autoregressive Integrated Moving Average) model is used as an important statistical method by many local and foreign researchers, especially in economic sectors and in assessing financial indicators. The ARIMA model of econometric research is a statistical method that is characterised by its simplicity and efficiency in managing linear equations in time series data, and is used to produce accurate and reliable forecasting indicators.

The ARIMA model consists of three main components: autoregression (AR (Valipour et al., 2013)), differentiation (I (Mélard & Pasteels, 2000)) and moving average (MA (Ho & Xie, 1998)), and each of these components plays an important role in predicting future values based on past observations, trends and dynamic processes. Analyses and forecasts were conducted using multivariate linear regression (LS), ARDL, ARIMA and various other econometric models on the global services market, digital economy, energy-related financial stress, cocktail market, digital transformation, factors affecting the logistics industry (Kalandarov et al., 2025; Khayrilla et al., 2025; Khodjaniyazov et al., 2025; Kuziboev et al., 2025; Lin et al., 2025; Mamadiyarov et al., 2025; Rayala et al., 2025; Samariddin et al., 2025).

Another group of economists has successfully used econometric models such as Fixed Effects Estimator (FEE), Random Effects Estimator (REE), multivariate linear (LS) and ARDL in their research on investment in digital infrastructure, various aspects of digital payment systems, the impact of inflation and credit interest rates on investment, factors affecting the reduction of the state's share in commercial banks, Non-Performing Loans in commercial banks, the digitisation of banks, risks in digital services and the development of retail payment services (Abdullah et al., 2025; Akhmetshin et al., 2025; Habib et al., 2025; Jahrir et al., 2025; Mamadiyarov et al., 2025; Rayala et al., 2025; Samariddin et al., 2025).

According to Mohd Faizan Rizvi (2024) 'In an ARIMA model, the AR part involves regressing the variable on its lagged values, the I part involves differentiating the data to make it stationary, and the MA part models it as a linear combination of error terms from previous time steps'.

21.3. Methodology

According to the author, the ARIMA model is suitable for use with pre-processed data and for model identification, parameter estimation and model diagnostic techniques. The order of the AR term is denoted by 'p', which indicates the number of lagged observations included in the model.

Dinesh Kumar Yadavni (2024) states that 'the model is defined as ARIMA(p, d, q), where p is the number of lag observations in the model (AR), d is the number of times the raw observations are differed (I), and q represents the size of the moving average window (MA)' (Mamadiyarov et al., 2025; Mamani et al., 2025; Pradhan et al., 2025; Rayala et al., 2025; Yadav, 2024).

According to L. Duarte (2024), 'ARIMA models are flexible and can adapt to different types of time series data, including trends and seasonality'. According to the authors' research, this flexibility is further optimised by extensions such as seasonal ARIMA (SARIMA), which incorporate seasonal processes into the model (Duarte, 2024; Romero et al., 2025; Rony et al., 2025; Rukhiddin et al., 2025; Singagerda et al., 2025; Sofyanty et al., 2025; Toshmurod et al., 2025; Zhang et al., 2025; Zhao et al., 2025).

The general form of the ARIMA(p, d, q) model is given below.

$$\varphi_p(B)(1 - B)\mathrm{d}\ Y_t = \vartheta_q(B)e_t \tag{3}$$

The time at time t represents the line.

B – back shift operator, this on the ground $BY_t = Y_{t-1}$ represents:

row d stationary to do for differentiation order represents.

$\varphi_p(B) = 1 - \varphi_1 B - \varphi_2 B_2 - \ldots - \varphi_p B_p$ – p order autoregressive (AR) polynomial means, $\vartheta_q(B) = 1 + \vartheta_1 B + \vartheta_2 B_2 + \ldots + \vartheta_q B_q$, q is ordered moving average (MA) polynomial represents and ϵ_i represents the error term (white noise) at time i.

In developing the forecast indicators for the study, quarterly data sources from the Statistical Agency under the President of the Republic of Uzbekistan (<https://stat.uz/uz/>) with a number of observations covering 2015–2024 were used. The resulting factor for the econometric forecast is presented below.

Industrial production volume – industr_prod (result variable).

21.4. Results

An analytical graphical diagram of the volume of economic expenditures over time at the initial stage of econometric forecasting is presented in Figure 71.

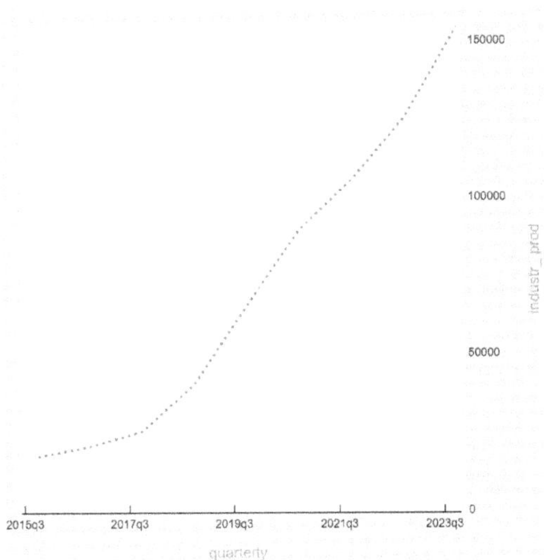

Figure 71. Analytical graphic representation of the periodic state of industrial production.
Source: It was developed by the authors based on Stata software.

According to Figure 71, industrial output has shown a sharp growth trend since the third quarter of 2017, and this growth will reach a maximum by 2023. According to this analytical picture, the overall growth trend in the region is due to the expansion of industrial output and investment, and the increase in investment flows against the background of the expansion of industrial output indicates a continuous growth in industrial output.

In the next stage of the econometric forecast, the stationarity level of industrial output was assessed and the Unit-Root test was used to determine it (Table 69).

Table 69. Unit-root test of industrial output

Economy_ cost	Test Statistics	1% Critical Value	5% Critical Value	10% Critical Value	p-value for Z(t)
	-5.631	-3.716	-2.986	-2.624	0.0000

Source: It was developed by the authors based on Stata software.

According to Table 69, the unit root test statistic (-5.631) is significantly smaller than all critical values (1% –3.716, 5% –2.986 and 10% –2.624), which leads to a very high confidence rejection of the null hypothesis of a unit root. According to this, the volume of industrial production is not a random variable, but has a stable trend.

The *p*-value (0.0000) indicates that the trend in industrial output is statistically significant and unlikely to be due to random fluctuations. This represents an economic trend that systematically predicts successful economic processes in the development of planning and control based on various strategic programmes in the region.

Because the data is stationary, it allows for more reliable forecasts of future industrial output.

The next step is to present the value of p, which determines the indirect correlation between the lags of the time series of the model (Figure 72).

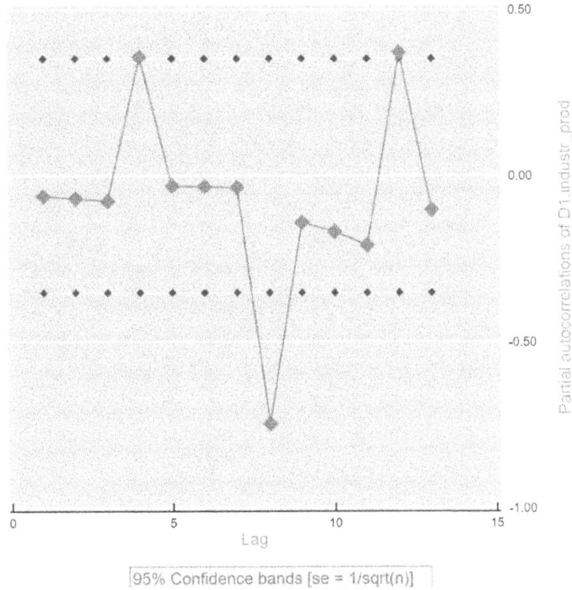

Figure 72. Indirect correlation graph between lags of the econometric model of industrial output.
Source: It was developed by the authors based on Stata software.

According to Figure 72, the volume of industrial production The indirect correlation values between the lags of the econometric model are mostly within the 95 per cent confidence intervals, reinforcing the previous Unit-Root test results, which indicate the presence of stationarity. However, the first few lags are significantly significant and show the impact of past values on industrial output.

The sharp decline in correlation after the initial lag represents the fit of the autoregressive (AR) model, which allows for effective capture of dynamic trends in economic processes.

Except for two lags, all lags are within the confidence interval in the indirect correlation analysis.

Accordingly, a value of 1 or 2 can be chosen as the *p*-value, and these values can be selected as *p*-values according to the ARIMA model.

In the next step of the ARIMA model, the value of *q*, which describes the direct correlation between the lags of the model, was determined (Figure 73).

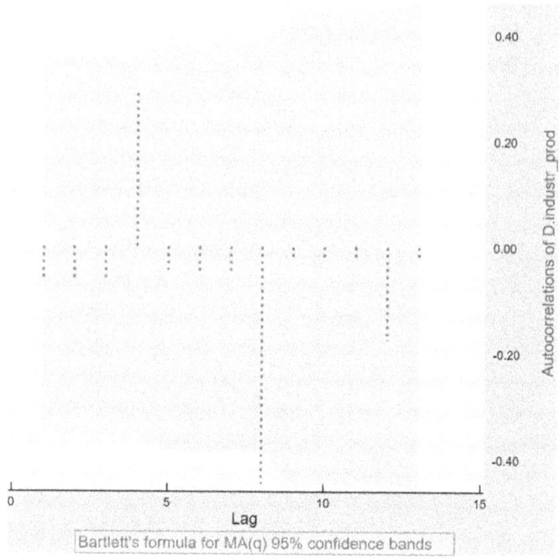

Figure 73. Direct correlation graph between lags of industrial output.
Source: It was developed by the authors based on Stata software.

Figure 73 shows that the ARIMA model exhibits a strong correlation between lags and, except for one lag, all other lags are within the specified confidence interval.

According to the model, data with different autocorrelations represent a long-term stable trend, which further reinforces the stationary nature of industrial output.

Most of the autocorrelation values are within the 95 per cent confidence interval, which does not indicate dominance in the case of random sharp shocks. At the same time, it serves to increase the reliability of forecasting based on econometric modelling for industrial output and analysed trends.

When selecting the optimal ARIMA invariant models for forecasting the model, models of the form ARIMA(0,1,1), ARIMA(1,2,1), ARIMA(2,2,1), ARIMA(2,1,1), ARIMA(2,2,0) and ARIMA(1,1,1) were developed. Among these models, the ARIMA(1,1,1) model with the best results was selected (Table 21.3).

Based on the ARIMA model regression result, the econometric equation for the model is given below.

$$D.economy\_cost_t = b_0 + b_1\,D.economy\_cost_{t-1} + b_2\,D.economy\_cost_{t-2} + b_3\,economy\_cost_{t-3} + e_t \quad (3)$$

Table 70. Econometric equation indicators of the ARIMA(1,1,1) model by industrial output

D.industr_prod	Coef.	St. Err.	t-value	p-value	[95% Conf	Interval]	Sig
Constant	4164.13	1884.566	2.21	0.027	470,449	7857.811	*
L	0.936	0.16	5.86	0	0.623	1.25	**
L	0.039	1.779	0.02	0.092	-3.447	3.526	*
Constant	863.91	77,553	11.14	0	711,909	1015.912	**

Mean dependent variable	4285.563	SD dependent var	2223.747
Number of observations	32	Chi-square	90,418
Probe > chi²	.	Akaike crit. (AIC)	533,719
*** $p < 0.01$, ** $p < 0.05$, * $p < 0.1$			

Source: It was developed by the authors based on Stata software.

According to Table 70, the ARIMA (1,1,1) model looks like this:

$$D.economy\_cost_t = 659.19 + 1.58\,D.economy\_cost_{t-1} - 0.67\,D.economy\_cost_{t-2} - 0.69 economy\_cost_{t-1} + e_t + e_t \quad (4)$$

In the next step, the ARIMA(1,1,1) model was developed to analyse the mean values of the outcome variable and the graphical representation of the residuals (Table 21.4 and Figure 74).

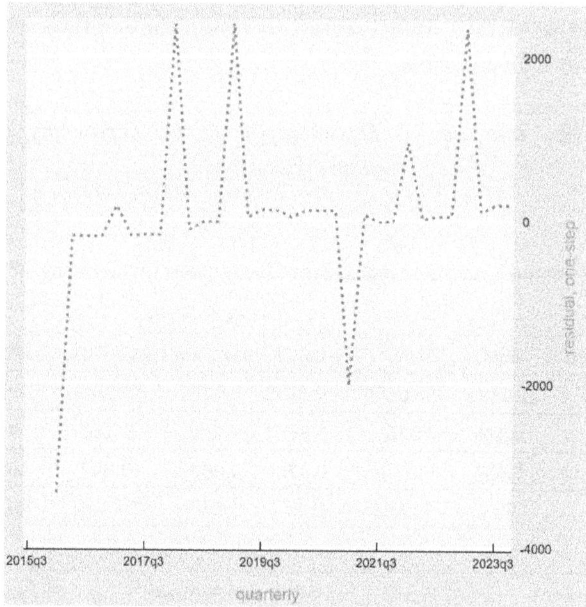

Figure 74. Graph of residual values of the ARIMA(1,1,1) model by industrial output.
Source: It was developed by the authors based on Stata software.

Table 71. Residual values of the resulting factor in the ARIMA(1,1,1) model

Variable	Obs.	Mean	Std. dev.	Min	Max
Residual value	32	91.07802	1040.632	−3352.08	2412.874

Source: It was developed by the authors based on Stata software.

According to Table 71 and Figure 74, the ARIMA(1,1,1) model has reached stochastic equilibrium, as evidenced by the visual representation of the residuals at specified time intervals. This representation shows the fit of the ARIMA model to the data and the underlying stochastic relationships in the data set.

The next step involves testing the stationarity of the residuals of the ARIMA(1,1,1) model on the volume of economic expenditures and estimating the autoregressive (AR) and moving average (MA) residuals.

The convergence of the ARIMA model in the unit range in forecasting was also examined by Econometric Forecasting (Figure 75).

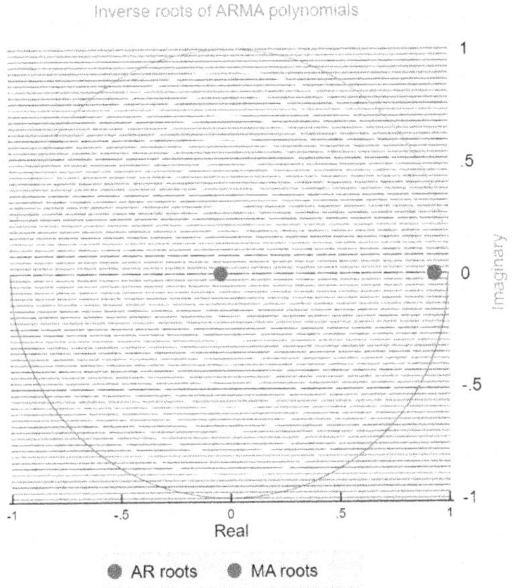

Figure 75. Range of values of industrial output according to the ARIMA(2,1,1) model.
Source: It was developed by the authors based on Stata software.

Using the Stata program, a forecast indicator for industrial production volume from 2025 to 2029 was developed using the ARIMA(1,1,1) model, excluding random factors (see Table 72).

Table 72. Forecast indicators of industrial production volume for 2025–2029 (in billion soums)

Years	Pessimistic forecast	Optimistic forecast	Forecast
2025	203,718.26	208,165.74	205,942.00
2026	226,599.16	231,046.64	228,822.90
2027	248,039.86	252,487.34	250,263.60
2028	268,373.56	272,821.04	270,597.30
2029	287,856.46	292,303.94	290,080. 20

Source: It was developed by the authors based on Stata software.

According to the results of the study, based on the ARIMA(1,1,1) model, the volume of industrial production in 2025–2029, excluding random internal and external factors, will be *205,942.00 billion soums in 2025, 228,822.90 billion soums* in 2026, 250,263.60 billion soums in 2027, *270,597.30 billion soums* in 2028 and *290,080.20 billion soums* in 2029, respectively.

Industrial production volume provided by the Statistical Agency under the President of the Republic of Uzbekistan (<https://stat.uz/uz/>) according to the study A graphical representation of the forecast indicator for 2015–2024 and 2025–2029 is provided (Figure 76).

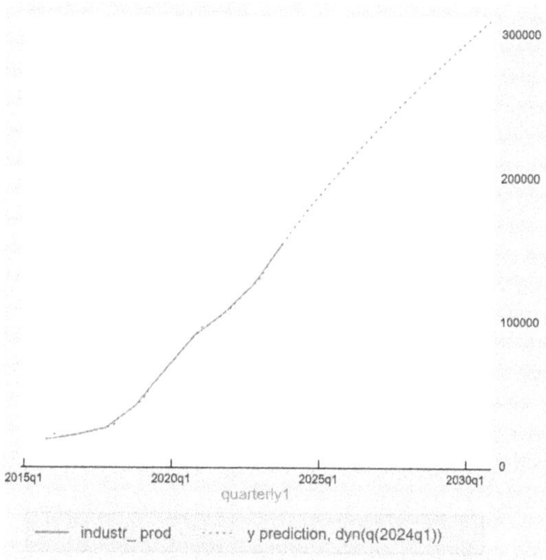

Figure 76. Graph of the resulting variable for 2015–2024 and the forecast for 2025–2029.
Source: It was developed by the authors based on Stata software.

Figure 76 shows the forecast graphs of industrial production volumes for 2015–2024 and 2025–2029, provided by the Statistical Agency under the President of the Republic of Uzbekistan. According to it, the trend graph shows the reliability of the forecast indicators for the next five years, excluding random factors, since the two lines are located side by side as much as possible.

21.5. Conclusion

This study built an ARIMA(1,1,1) model to forecast Uzbekistan's Zarafshan industrial production, foreseeing equal growth from 205,942 billion soums

(2025) to 290,080 billion soums (2029). The model was highly predictive (AIC = 533.719) and stationary (p = 0.0000), which indicates its suitability for transition economies. The key findings reveal the possibility of industrial development in the area while exhibiting moderating rates of growth, which provide greater maturity. Use of quarterly data led to reliable analysis of production trends, ensuring that policymakers had reliable points of intervention.

The results highlight the need for targeted infrastructure investment, human capital creation and environmental conservation to make growth sustainable. Future studies should include real-time indicators and sustainability dimensions along with extending comparative analyses throughout Central Asia. This research offers both a replicable transition economy forecasting model as well as policy-relevant analysis for regional planning. Through synergy of methodological sophistication and policy usefulness, it guides evidence-based industrial development policy in Zarafshan and elsewhere.

1. The steady growth of industrial production is expected to increase from 205,942.00 billion soums in 2025 to 290,080.20 billion soums in 2029, reflecting a strong growth trend. This result indicates an expanding industrial sector that is gaining importance for economic development and job creation.
2. The projected growth follows a consistent trajectory of year-on-year increases in industrial production, indicating that the industrial sector in the region has a solid foundation for sustainable development, making it attractive to both domestic and foreign investors.
3. Manufacturing leads to increased industrial efficiency, increased demand and favourable economic conditions. In the region, the industrial sector not only contributes to regional GDP, but also strengthens local entrepreneurship and serves to increase overall economic stability.
4. The projected growth shows that current economic sectors, industrial strategies and market relations are effectively supporting industrial expansion. The government will use this momentum to make important decisions on further optimising regulations, improving energy supply and diversifying industries.

Bibliography

Abdullah, M. A., Han, X., Amjad, M. A., & Makhmudov, S. (2025). Revisit the role of financial development on economic growth, human development, and sustainable development in higher-income countries. *Journal of Environmental Management*, *392*, 126874.

Akhmetshin, E., Abdullayev, I., Makhmudov, S., Dakhkilgova, K., Korotaeva, I. and Yanovskaya, G. (2025). APPLICATION OF TANH–COTH METHOD FOR COMBINED AND DOUBLE COMBINED SINH–COSH–GORDON EQUATIONS ARISING CHEMICAL REACTIONS TO WATER SURFACE GRAVITY WAVES. Computational Methods for Differential Equations, (), -. doi: 10.22034/cmde.2025.67655.3234

Acemoglu, D., and Restrepo, P. (2021). 'Automation and Regional Labor Markets'. *Review of Economic Studies*, 88 (1), 229–60. <https://doi.org/10.1093/restud/rdaa038>.

Chen, Y., and Chen, X. (2020). 'Machine Learning for Regional Industrial Output Prediction'. *Journal of Regional Science*, 60 (3), 567–89. <https://doi.org/10.1111/jors.12456>.

Dixit, A. K., and Stiglitz, J. E. (2020). 'Trade and Industrial Location'. *American Economic Review*, 110 (5), 1561–87. <https://doi.org/10.1257/aer.20181023>.

Duarte, L. F. C. (2024). 'SARIMAX'. jl: Open-Source Time Series Modeling in Julia through Advanced Optimization, Doctoral dissertation, PUC-Rio.

Fujita, M., and Thisse, J.-F. (2021). 'New Economic Geography'. *Journal of Economic Geography*, 21 (1), 1–28. <https://doi.org/10.1093/jeg/lbaa015>.

Glaeser, E. L. et al. (2021). 'Growth in Cities Revisited'. *Journal of Political Economy*, 129 (4), 1234–82. <https://doi.org/10.1086/713492>.

Habib, S. S., Islam, M. A., Ali, M. N., Benitez, I. B., Mamadiyarov, Z., Mirzayev, B., … & Flah, A. (2025). Multi-Objective Optimization and Feasibility Analysis of Integrated Biogas–Solar Energy Systems for Rural Electrification. *Results in Engineering*, 107086.

Henderson, J. V. (2019). 'Urbanization and Industrial Growth'. *Journal of Urban Economics*, 112, 1–17. <https://doi.org/10.1016/j.jue.2019.05.002>.

Ho, S. L., and Xie, M. (1998). 'The Use of ARIMA Models for Reliability Forecasting and Analysis'. *Computers & Industrial Engineering*, 35 (1–2), 213–16.

Jahrir, A., Gultom, Y., Herman, H., Zabadi, F., Ngongo, M., Mamadiyarov, Z., Fatmawati, E., & Saputra, N. (2025). Investigating the Elements of Short Commercial Mineral Water Advertisement: A Case on Discourse Analysis. Studies in Media and Communication, 13(4), 94–104. doi: http://dx.doi.org/10.11114/smc.v13i4.7813

Kalandarov, F., Makhmudov, S., Ibadullaev, D., Matniyozov, M., Nasretdinova, F., Sabirov, K., & Bahodirov, N. M. (2025). Low-Carbon Energy Risk and Renewable Energy Development: Insights from Method of Moments Quantile Regression. International Journal of Energy Economics and Policy, 15(3), 524–536.

Khayrilla Kurbonov, Samariddin Makhmudov, Shakhzod Erkinov, Umidjon Dadabaev, Gulnora Bekimbetova, Rukhiddin Zayniddinov, and Mirzabek Jonuzokov. 2025. Evaluating the Impact of Marketing Practices Digitalization and Investment on Labor Market Efficiency and Commercial Bank Performance Using Econometric Models. In Proceedings of the 8th International Conference on Future Networks & Distributed Systems (ICFNDS '24). Association for Computing Machinery, New York, NY, USA, 786–796. https://doi.org/10.1145/3726122.3726237

Khodjaniyazov, N., Mirkhoshimova, M., Kalandarov, F., Matyokubova, D., Utegenova, S., Makhmudov, S., & Khudayberganov, M. (2025). Time-Varying Impacts of Financial Stress on Energy-Related Uncertainty. International Journal of Energy Economics and Policy, 15(3), 689–698.

Krugman, P. (2019). 'Geography and Industrial Location'. *Regional Science and Urban Economics*, 78, 103–18. <https://doi.org/10.1016/j.regsciurbeco.2019.04.002>.

Kuchkarov, T., Mamadiyarov, Z., Khakimov, Z., Sabirova, O., Matmurodov, K., Raimboyeva, M., & Umarova, S. (2025). Energy-Related Uncertainty and Crypto-Currency Environmental Attention: Time-Varying Perspective. International Journal of Energy Economics and Policy, 15(5), 614–626. https://doi.org/10.32479/ijeep.20784

Kuziboev, B., Ozturk, I., Kalandarov, F., Samandarov, O., Bekjanov, D., & Makhmudov, S. (2025). PROMOTING ENERGY SOURCES

DIVERSIFICATION THROUGH ESG PERFORMANCE. Energy, 136009.

Lin, M.H., Matchanova, B., Nurmatovich, H.A. et al. Optimal Operation of the Multi-Carrier Energy System Considering Energy Markets and Renewable Energies Participation. *Int. J. Appl. Comput. Math* **11**, 170 (2025). https://doi.org/10.1007/s40819-025-02002-9

Litamahuputty, J. V., Amiruddin, E. G., Rahim, R., Rahman, A., & Mamadiyarov, Z. (2025). Cryptocurrency Risk Management through Decision Engineering: Evaluating XRPUSD and ADAUSD Portfolio Performance. Journal of Applied Science, Engineering, Technology, and Education, 7(1), 69–81. https://doi.org/10.35877/454RI.asci3871

Mamadiyarov, Z., Eshov, M., Otakhonova, D., Utegenova, S., Sabirov, K., Marks, A., & Bahodirov, N. (2025). Does Energy Policy Risk Threaten Energy Sources Diversification?. *International Journal of Energy Economics and Policy*, *15*(5), 730–740. https://doi.org/10.32479/ijeep.21140

Mamadiyarov, Z. Makhmudov, S. Utanov, B. Kasimova, D. Bekmurodova, G. Hakimov, Z. (2025). Fusion of Economic and Financial Factors Affecting Household Deposits in Banks: An Econometric Analysis. Fusion: Practice and Applications, (), 82–91. DOI: https://doi.org/10.54216/FPA.190206

Mamadiyarov, Z., Saidov, O., Abdurazakova, N., Makhmudov, S., Nazarov, M., Rajabova, N., … Ruzmetova, I. (2025). Energy-Related Uncertainty and Tourism Stock Markets: New Insights from Time-Varying Relationship with TVP- VAR Approach. *International Journal of Energy Economics and Policy*, *15*(4), 730–737. https://doi.org/10.32479/ijeep.20480

Mamani, J.C.M., Miri, M., Vorobev, Y. et al. Optimal Operation of Energy Microgrid Considering Economic and Emission Indices. Oper. Res. Forum 6, 122 (2025). https://doi.org/10.1007/s43069-025-00523-z

Martin, R., and Sunley, P. (2020). 'Regional Economic Resilience'. *Journal of Economic Geography*, 20 (2), 293–327. <https://doi.org/10.1093/jeg/lbz030>.

Mélard, G., and Pasteels, J. M. (2000). 'Automatic ARIMA Modeling Including Interventions, Using Time Series Expert Software'. *International Journal of Forecasting*, 16 (4), 497–508.

Muhammad Zubair, Irfanud Din, Nadeem Sarwar et al. Revolutionizing Sepsis Diagnosis Using Machine Learning and Deep Learning Models: A Systematic Literature Review, 10 June 2025, PREPRINT (Version 1) available at Research Square [https://doi.org/10.21203/rs.3.rs-6731418/v1]

Ngongo, M., Herman, H., Ndandara, A., Jois Jaha, D. A., Peku Djawang, J. U. S., Tanggu Rame, M. M., Khamraeva, S. N., & Mamadiyarov, Z. (2025). An Investigation of Meaning, Toponymy of Sumba Cultural Site's Names, and the Impact of Tourism Visitors on Surrounding Society. *Forum for Linguistic Studies*, 7(8), 679–693. https://doi.org/10.30564/fls.v7i8.10260

PANJAITAN, M. B., HAMDANAH, H., SIRAIT, J., SUTIKNO, S., FATMAWATI, E., HERMAN, H., & MAMADIYAROV, Z. (2025). THE ROLE OF EMOTIONAL REGULATION IN SHAPING STUDENTS' PERCEPTION OF PHYSICS PROBLEMSOLVING TASKS. TPM – Testing, Psychometrics, Methodology in Applied Psychology, 32(S2(2025) : Posted 09 June), 1–10. Retrieved from https://tpmap.org/submission/index.php/tpm/article/view/139

Porter, M. E., and Ketels, C. (2020). 'Clusters and Competitiveness'. *Economic Geography*, 96 (2), 89–112. <https://doi.org/10.1080/00130095.2020.1759143>.

Pradhan, R., Hajiyev, E., Shichiyakh, R. et al. Optimal Techno-Economic Feasibility of an Off-Grid Microgrid System Using Load Flow Energy Management Strategies. *Oper. Res. Forum* 6, 120 (2025). https://doi.org/10.1007/s43069-025-00524-y

Rayala, R. V., Borra, C. R., Vasudevan, V., Singhania, R., Cheekati, S., & Mamadiyarov, Z. (2025, July). Lightweight Deep Learning Framework for Human Activity Recognition: A MobileNet-LSTM Approach with WHOA Optimization. In *2025 International Conference on Innovations in Intelligent Systems: Advancements in Computing, Communication, and Cybersecurity (ISAC3)* (pp. 1–6). IEEE.

Rayala, R. V., Sandhya, N., Singhania, R., Cheekati, S., Borra, C. R., Vasudevan, V., & Mamadiyarov, Z. (2025, July). AI-Driven Tomato Quality Assessment: A Deep Learning Approach for Image-based Defect Detection and Classification. In *2025 International Conference on Innovations in Intelligent Systems: Advancements in Computing, Communication, and Cybersecurity (ISAC3)* (pp. 1–6). IEEE.

Rizvi, M. F. (2024). 'ARIMA Model Time Series Forecasting'. *International Journal for Research in Applied Science and Engineering Technology*. <https://doi.org/10.22214/ijraset.2024.62416>.

Rony, Z. T., Jefri, R., Rusmardiana, A., Pramono, S. A., & Mamadiyarov, Z. (2025). Downside Risk Measurement of Indonesian Financial and Energy Securities: A Value at Risk Perspective. *Journal of Applied Science, Engineering, Technology, and Education*, 7(2). https://doi.org/10.35877/454RI.asci3898

Rosenthal, S. S., and Strange, W. C. (2020). 'Agglomeration Economies'. *Journal of Economic Literature*, 58 (2), 403–57. <https://doi.org/10.1257/jel.20181416>.

Rukhiddin Zayniddinov, Nodir Jumaev, Gulbakhor Irgasheva, Alam Asadov, Nosir Makhmudov, Sirojiddin Abrorov, and Samariddin Makhmudov. 2025. The Influence of the Digital Economy on Economic Development Evidence from Uzbekistan. In Proceedings of the 8th International Conference on Future Networks & Distributed Systems (ICFNDS '24). Association for Computing Machinery, New York, NY, USA, 831–839. https://doi.org/10.1145/3726122.3726242

Samariddin Makhmudov, Malika Umarova, Khayrilla Kurbonov, Laylo Akbarova, Durdona Davletova, Nilufar Shanazarova, and Toshmurod Kulmanov. 2025. Evaluating the forecast indicators of the volume of highly liquid assets of commercial banks in the process of digital transformation. In Proceedings of the 8th International Conference on Future Networks & Distributed Systems (ICFNDS '24). Association for Computing Machinery, New York, NY, USA, 698–704. https://doi.org/10.1145/3726122.3726222

Samariddin Makhmudov, Kudratillo Tukhsanov, Saifulla Arslanbekov, Akram Amanov, Orifali Tursunov, Umarbek Jabbarov and Muyassarxon Mirzakarimova. 2024. Optimizing Supply Chain Financing Development Prospects of Digital Ecosystems in the European Logistics Industry. In The 8th International Conference on Future Networks & Distributed Systems (ICFNDS '24), December 11–12, 2024, Marakech, Morocco. ACM, New York, NY, USA, 12 Pages. https://doi.org/10.1145/3726122.3726200

Singagerda, F. S., Pratama, M. R., Alfairus, M. Q., Iskandar, A., & Mamadiyarov, Z. (2025). A Decision-Centric Approach to Risk Management in Aviation Stock Investments Using Value at Risk and Portfolio Optimization. *Journal of Applied Science, Engineering, Technology, and Education*, 7(1), 114–125. https://doi.org/10.35877/454RI.asci3870

Sofyanty, D., Romadhoni, R., Handriadi, H., Makhsudovna, I. S., Anwar, Z., & Mamadiyarov, Z. (2025). Strategic Decision Analysis for Investment Portfolios: Computational Risk Assessment in Transportation Asset Management. *Journal of Applied Science, Engineering, Technology, and Education*, 7(2). https://doi.org/10.35877/454RI.asci3897

Toshmurod Kulmanov, Umidjon Dadabaev, Mansurbek Qulmetov, Aliboy Ulashov, Mirjalol Eshboyev, and Samariddin Makhmudov. 2025. Global Services Market Transformation Digitalization Export Trends and Future Forecasts. In Proceedings of the 8th International Conference on Future Networks & Distributed Systems (ICFNDS '24). Association for Computing Machinery, New York, NY, USA, 851–858. https://doi.org/10.1145/3726122.3726245

Valipour, M., Banihabib, M. E., and Behbahani, S. M. R. (2013). 'Comparison of the ARMA, ARIMA, and the Autoregressive Artificial Neural Network Models in Forecasting the Monthly Inflow of Dez Dam Reservoir'. *Journal of Hydrology*, 476, 433–41.

Yadav, D. K., and Goswami, L. (2024). 'Autoregressive Integrated Moving Average Model for Time Series Analysis'. 1–6. <https://doi.org/10.1109/icocwc60930.2024.10470488>.

Zhang, L., Zhao, Z., Qamri, G. M., & Makhmudov, S. (2025). Unleashing the critical role of renewable energy through global value chains and digitalization: A path towards environmental sustainability. *Journal of Environmental Management*, *392*, 126688.

Zhao, Q., Pervaiz, A., Makhmudov, S., & Fatima, A. (2025). Do environmental stringent policies enhance the impact of renewable energy on CO2 reduction? Evidence from BRICS-T economies. Journal of Environmental Management, 391, 126464.

Classification of variables according to the econometric model

Zokir Mamadiyarov, Samariddin Makhmudov, Bunyod Utanov, Isabek Murtazaev, Shoira Olimjanova, Dilnozakhan Abdullajanova and Mirzabek Jonuzokov

22.1. Introduction

Agriculture remains to be one of the cornerstone sectors of the economy of Uzbekistan, playing an important role in employment, livelihoods in the countryside, production of food and foreign exchange revenue. Even if manufacturing, the energy sector and other ones are developing greatly, agriculture continues to be the most integrated segment of national economic output. With the country moving towards industrialisation, it is important to comprehend the intricate link between industry and agriculture in order to facilitate balanced development. Being the biggest contributor to national GDP, agriculture is not only a path to economic stability but to entire industrialisation as well, and this calls for taking into account sector interdependencies (Sattarov & Turaev, 2021). Nonetheless, there is insufficient research on the effect of agricultural growth on industrial and economic balance in Uzbekistan, especially after the country's shift from a largely agrarian to an industrialised economy.

This research aims to bridge this gap by analysing the role of agricultural production towards determining industrial balance in Uzbekistan, particularly in 2014–2023. The research employs the ARDL (Autoregressive Distributed Lag) model, a powerful econometric framework, which addresses short- and long-run connections between agricultural output and other determinants of economic nature like agriculture fixed capital spending, size of agricultural employment and inflation (Hassan & Tunc, 2024). The study also examines the dynamic linkages between such farm variables and broader economic performances, such as industry growth and balance of payments and presents analysis on the potential effect of farm growth on macroeconomic stability (Mamadiyarov et al., 2025).

CUSUM diagnostic test is one of the important components of the methodology and is applied to ascertain whether the ARDL model parameters are constant in the long run. The CUSUM test tests two hypotheses: (1) the null hypothesis (H_0) that the model parameters are stable across the sample period and (2) the alternative hypothesis (H_1) that the model parameters change systematically. Following the results of the CUSUM test, the study concludes that the causal link between agricultural output per capita and its determinants remains stable over time. This finding indicates that the considered agricultural variables always possess long-run effects on the considered economic effects, thereby again proving the robustness of the model.

The study also finds the broader applicability of these facts to Uzbekistan's ongoing reformation of the economy. Based on agriculture's importance in the economic vision of the country, there ought to be an environment conducive to agricultural development in aid of ensuring the sector to act as stimulus to the country's economy and industrial development. Policies aimed at increasing farm land, increasing agricultural capital investment and upgrading the skill levels of farm labour are important to making the agricultural sector competitive and productive. Secondly, the study underlines the necessity of consistent macroeconomic policies that would aid in mitigating the adverse effects of inflation on farm production as well as providing constant growth to all sectors.

By examining the interdependence between the agricultural and industrial variables, this study further investigates how agricultural advancement can drive more general economic stability and growth. Its results advance agricultural economics and the industrialisation of transition economies, especially in Central Asia (Gulyamova, 2022). The research results hold significant recommendations for policymakers aimed at promoting sustainable and balanced economic growth in Uzbekistan, and can also be a model for other similar economies in the process of industrialisation.

22.2. Literature Review

Regional growth, particularly where the employment-industrialisation-food security nexus is the most dominant, depends a lot on the farm sector. To date, more scholars have shown interest in studying the performance and also the sustainability of agriculture at regional levels through social, economic, structural and environmental approaches. Much of this research has used econometric model-building to investigate and forecast regional trends in agriculture, giving insightful analysis of mechanisms of agricultural productivity, agglomeration and regional economic performance.

A number of scientists have emphasised the significance of using econometric models in examining trends of agricultural development. Berus and Kosnikov (2024) observe that structural and economic determinants, namely investments in fixed capital, are the key drivers of gross value added in agriculture. According to their study, encouraging regional efficiency in agriculture through state assistance programmes is essential to provide sustainable development and food security. This demonstrates the effectiveness of targeted fiscal interventions in low agricultural production regions.

Similarly, Hakkoz et al. (2024) encourage the use of advanced statistical models such as ARIMA, ARDL, VAR and GARCH models for improved agricultural trend forecasting. These are better than the traditional approaches from accuracy and reliability perspectives. Their application enables policymakers to simulate the probable impact of other policy decisions and to provide uncertainty reduction in farm planning. They also bring into focus more by Midmore (1993) that agricultural balance forecasting has intersectoral demand linkages, further positioning the role of agriculture to be in the general economy framework.

Analyses and forecasts were conducted using multivariate linear regression (LS), ARDL, ARIMA and various other econometric models on the global services market, digital economy, energy-related financial stress, cocktail market, digital transformation, factors affecting the logistics industry (Kalandarov et al., 2025; Khayrilla et al., 2025; Khodjaniyazov et al., 2025; Kuziboev et al., 2025; Lin et al., 2025; Mamadiyarov et al., 2025; Rukhiddin et al., 2025; Samariddin et al., 2025).

Agriculture is among the determinants of regional economic performance that some researchers identify. In the view of Xolmurotov et al. (2024), agrarian industries and services are significantly influential contributors to gross regional product, employment and income. They emphasise increasing the elasticity of agricultural products and improving the structure of regional agrarian industries as a way to enhance economic performance.

Bozkurt and Kaya (2021) investigates the influences of macroeconomic policies on agricultural production and other factors affecting it, based on panel data in a global sample for the period 2010–2017. According to the analysis results, countries' financial, fiscal and monetary policies have an important effect on agricultural production.

Vachanelidou et al. (2023) call this food industry interdependence with the country's economy, which means that it supplements macro-economic statistics such as GDP and employment. This gives credence to the fact that agriculture cannot be considered in isolation but in terms of an economic context, i.e., agro-processing and distribution services.

Another group of economists has successfully used econometric models such as Fixed Effects Estimator, Random Effects Estimator, LS and ARDL in their research on investment in digital infrastructure, various aspects of digital payment systems, the impact of inflation and credit interest rates on investment, factors affecting the reduction of the state's share in commercial banks, Non-Performing Loans in commercial banks, the digitisation of banks, risks in digital services and the development of retail payment services (Abdullah et al., 2025; Akhmetshin et al., 2025; Habib et al., 2025; Mamadiyarov et al., 2025; Mamani et al., 2025; Pradhan et al., 2025; Rayala et al., 2025).

Sourav (2023) also refers to the historical role of industry and agriculture in Indian economic development. Industry and agriculture account for 14.6 per cent and 28.6 per cent of GDP, but their real contribution is much higher due to their contribution to employment, food security and sectoral complementarity. Intersectoral complementarity is especially crucial for low- and middle-income countries with the responsibility of balancing urban and rural development. Jegadeesan et al. (2024) concur with this argument by referencing the interdependence between agricultural and manufacturing industries, specifically in terms of employment generation, income generation and national food security. Such convergence is now considered essential to facilitate balanced and inclusive economic development.

21.3. Research Methodology

This study uses a quantitative econometric approach to analyse and forecast the effect of the agricultural sector in Uzbekistan. The model attempts to capture both short-term volatility and long-term equilibrium relationships by applying the ARDL (Autoregressive Distributed Lag) modelling approach to multivariate time series data (Mamadiyarov et al., 2025; Rayala et al., 2025;

Romero et al., 2025; Rony et al., 2025; Samariddin et al., 2025; Singagerda et al., 2025; Sofyanty et al., 2025; Toshmurod et al., 2025; Zhang et al., 2025; Zokir et al., 2021).

The prediction is based on a set of thirty-eight macroeconomic indicators which are collected quarterly for the period 2014–2023. Data were collected from, The Central Bank of the Republic of Uzbekistan (<https://cbu.uz>) and The Statistical Agency under the President of the Republic of Uzbekistan (<https://stat.uz>). These indicators represent such factors as the agricultural production volume, investment in agriculture, exports and imports of agricultural products, exchange rates, inflation, gross product of regions and agricultural employment.

To ensure consistency in interpretation and to reduce potential skewness, all the variables included in the econometric model were transformed into their natural logarithm. Following the nature of the data set, the Autoregressive Distributed Lag (ARDL) model was applied. The ARDL model is best suited for data sets where the variables are of mixed orders, that is, $I(0)$ and $I(1)$, and enables us to investigate both short- and long-term relationships simultaneously. Fayçal and Ali (2016) describe that the ARDL model gives a reliable model for small samples and is extensively applied in macroeconomic forecasting. Nguyen et al. (2024) also affirm that the ARDL model enables us to analyse short-run and long-run effects of explanatory variables on time. Also, Ali et al. (2024) highlight the capacity of the model to entertain non-stationary time series with no requirement for uniform order of integration, hence a convenient alternative to conventional models (Ali et al., 2024).

The ARDL model formula is given below.

$$Yt = \beta + \sum_{i=1}^{l} \delta_i Y_{t-i} + \sum_{l=1}^{m} \sum_{j=0}^{fl} \vartheta_{l,j} Xl, t - j + \varepsilon t \qquad (1)$$

Here, Y_t denotes the outcome variable at time t, y_{t-1}, y_{t-2}, …, y_{t-k} denote the lagged values of the dependent variable, x_t denotes the independent variables at time t, α is a constant, δ_i denotes the coefficient of the dependent variable y for the ith lag (where i is from 1 to l), δ_i denotes the jth lagged coefficient of the independent variable x (where j is a value from 0 to f), ε_t – error term or the distortion at time t, m – number of independent variables, $\delta_{l,j}$, where l represents the coefficients of the lag values of the independent variable as well as x_l, f_1 – represents the lag length for each independent variable x_k.

All the variables in this model are expressed in natural logarithms so as to permit elasticity interpretation as well as variance stabilisation. This equation holds constant the influence of the previous values of the explanatory variables and previous and current values of the dependent variable on its current value.

Table 73 shows the variables in the econometric model.

Table 73. Classification of variables according to the econometric model

№	Variable Name	Classification	Logarithmic value
1	Agricultural output per capita	Dependent variable	*logagricul_per_cap*
2	Agricultural area	Independent variable	*logagricult_land*
3	Agricultural fixed capital investment	Independent variable	*loginvest_agricult*
4	Number of jobs in agriculture	Independent variable	*logempl_agricult*
5	Inflation rate in the national economy	Classification	*loginfl_rate*

Source: It was developed by the authors based on Stata software.

The following hypotheses were reflected in the development of the econometric study.

Null hypothesis (H_0): The area of agricultural crops in the national economy, the volume of investments in agricultural fixed capital, the number of jobs in agriculture and the inflation rate in the national economy do not statistically affect the volume of agricultural output per capita and have no correlation.

Alternative hypothesis (H_1): The area of agricultural crops in the national economy, the volume of investments in agricultural fixed capital, the number of jobs in agriculture and the inflation rate in the national economy have a statistically significant effect on the volume of agricultural output per capita and have a strong correlation.

21.4. Analysis and Results

This part presents the empirical test and results of applying the ARDL (Autoregressive Distributed Lag) model in examining the contribution of agriculture to the balance of payments. The model considers quarterly data from 2014–2023 and thirty-eight national statistical bureau macroeconomic and sector variables. Prior to estimation of the ARDL model, the unit roots were tested in the time series data in order to identify their order of integration so as to make the data stationary and then the bounds test procedure for ascertaining whether a long-run cointegration relationship between the variables was present or not. After these initial tests, short-run and long-run coefficients were later estimated to estimate immediate and lagged effects of agriculture variables on external balance outcome variables. Diagnostic tests were then conducted in attempting to test model stability, reliability and good specification. The results highlighted herein are useful to note the contribution of the agricultural sector towards macroeconomic stability and trade performance and to inform for purposes of guiding policy interventions employed to boost resilience of economies.

Descriptive statistical indicators were developed for the volume of agricultural output per capita and the variables affecting it based on econometric research (Table 74).

Table 74. Descriptive statistics for dependent and independent variables

	logagricul_ per_cap	logagricult_ land	loginvest_ agricult	logempl_ agricult	loginfl_ rate
Mean	15.15648	8.746676	13.39235	15.9107	8.792019
Maximum	16.53266	9.36141	14.77118	16.82503	9.407146
Minimum	13.99968	8.269554	12.53062	14.8531	7.769548
Std. Dev	0.8629431	0.2944537	0.6555628	0.5483906	0.5998857
Std. Err.	0.141867	8.6485	13.17377	15.72786	8.592007
Skewness	0.1297403	0.4559434	0.5051857	−0.4110005	−0.704026
Kurtosis	1.502001	2.39232	1.912007	2.054322	1.719211
Observation	37	37	37	37	37

Source: It was developed by the authors based on Stata software.

As can be seen from Table 73, the descriptive statistics of the model attained positive values for each variable and had a statistically significant level. Additionally, the average values represented the central tendency for each variable.

From the descriptive statistics, the region enjoys a better economy in terms of agricultural land, investment and agricultural yield per capita and presents the possibility of growth based on state programmes and agricultural production reforms.

According to the study, the graphical projection of the volume of agricultural output per capita and the determinants thereof over time is illustrated (Figure 77).

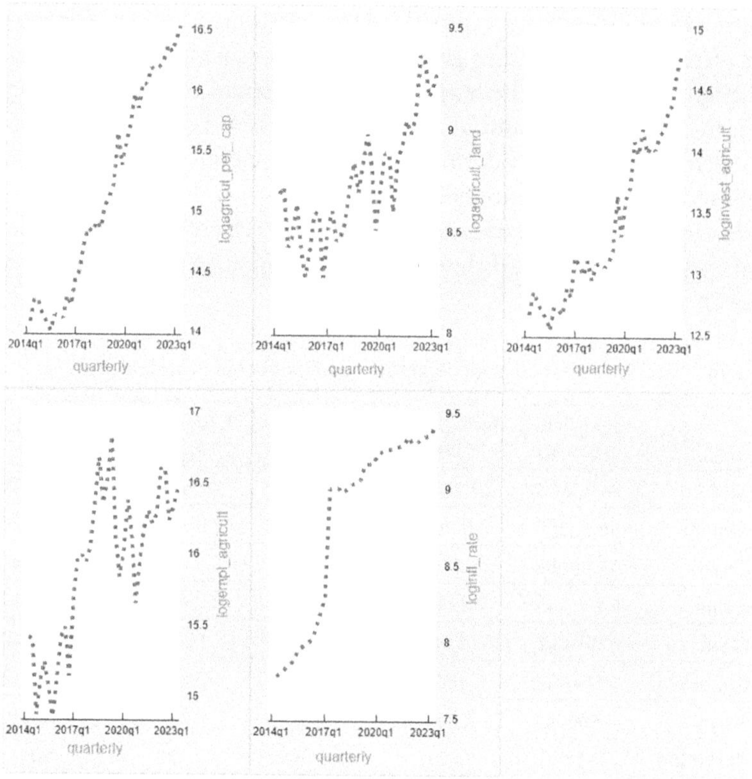

Figure 77. Analytical graphical representation of the volume of agricultural output per capita and the factors affecting it over time.
Source: It was developed by the authors based on Stata software.

According to Figure 77, per capita agricultural production, in economic sectors, has shown an increasing trend, especially after 2017. As a result of the investment in the agricultural industry, a significant increase has been observed since 2020.

The agricultural land index leads to an average constant expansion of land over time and an increase in land use opportunities. According to the graphical representation, the employment index is dynamically expressed in fluctuations, which is a key factor indicating the reliance on labour in agriculture.

Despite this mechanisation, agriculture has shown an important area of employment. From the data of the figure, moderate inflation expectations Inflation and relative stability in agriculture indicate strength and stability in the sector.

In the next stage of the econometric study, a visual correlation matrix and scatter plot of the volume of agricultural output per capita and the factors affecting it were created (Figures 78 and 79).

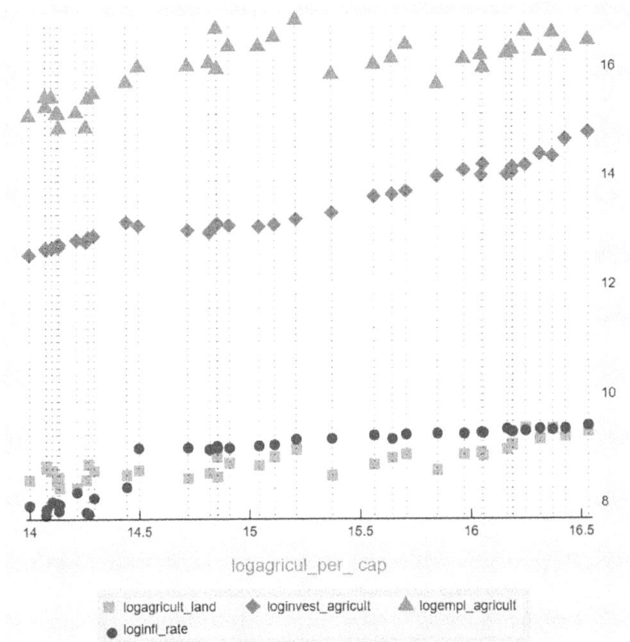

Figure 78. Scatter plot of per capita agricultural output and factors affecting it.
Source: It was developed by the authors based on Stata software.

Figure 78 image analysis showed that there was a strong correlation between the variables indicating the density effect in the data set. The visual representation was represented by a cluster analysis of the data points of the variables. It also represented intensive economic growth in economic activities, creating a strong relationship between the volume of agricultural output per capita and the factors affecting it.

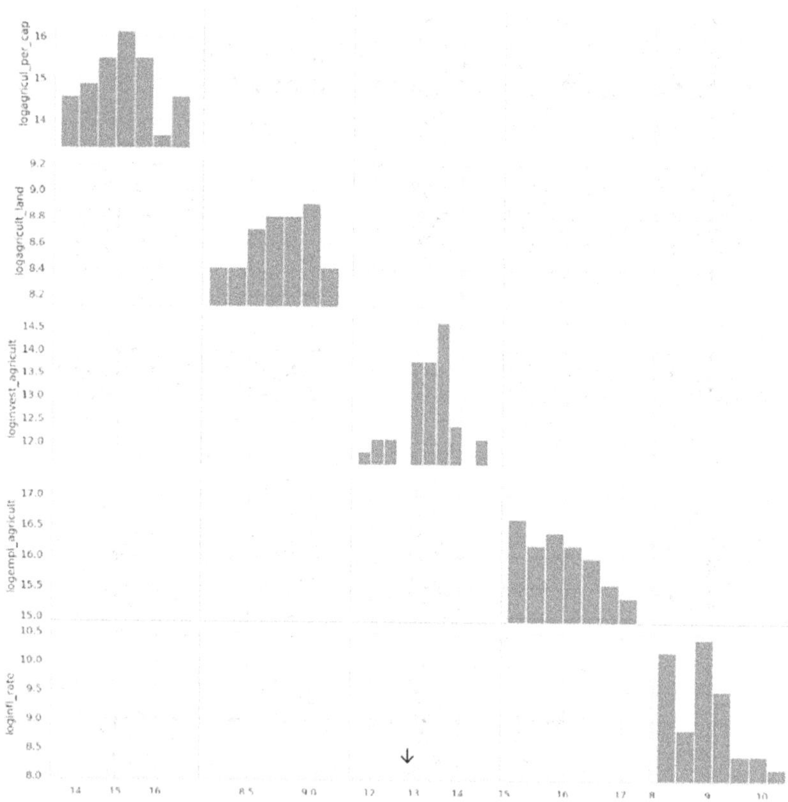

Figure 79. Visual correlation matrix of per capita agricultural output and factors influencing it.
Source: It was developed by the authors based on Stata software.

Figure 79 image analysis showed that there was a strong correlation between the variables that indicate the density effect in the data set. The visual representation is represented by a cluster analysis of the data points of the variables. According to the image, along with the increase in investment practices in agriculture, per capita agricultural output also increased.

This confirms that capital investment is the main activity in increasing agricultural productivity. Although fluctuations in macroeconomic indicators, in particular the inflation rate, have a negative effect on agriculture, stable inflation increases its importance in supporting long-term investment growth.

In the next step, an analytical relationship (dotplot rconnected) graphic representation of the volume of agricultural output per capita and the factors affecting it is presented (see Figure 80).

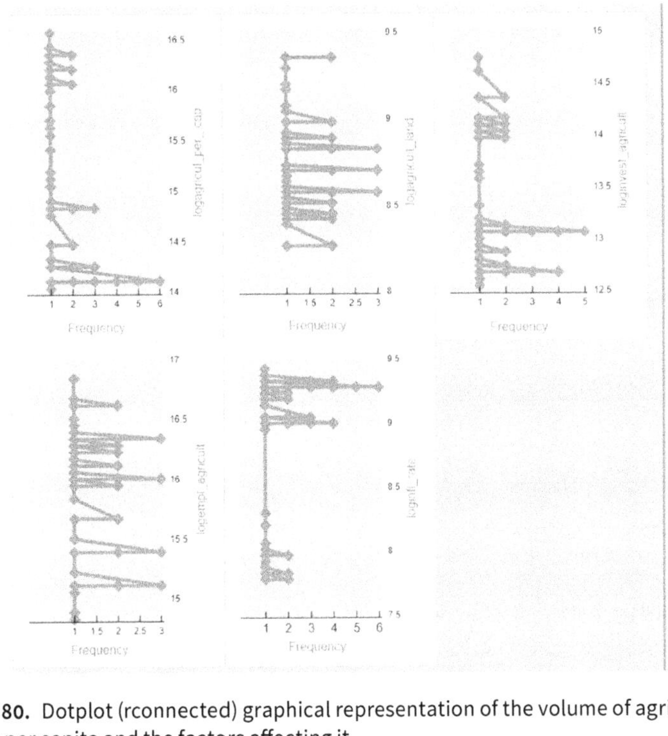

Figure 80. Dotplot (rconnected) graphical representation of the volume of agricultural output per capita and the factors affecting it.
Source: It was developed by the authors based on Stata software.

According to Figure 80, the density distribution relationship diagram provides a clear and structured visual dynamics of the volume of agricultural output per capita and the factors influencing it in the positive direction of macroeconomic indicators in the region. This indicates the consistent growth of the agricultural industry and the gradual increase in its distribution over time, which has been observed over this wide spectrum.

According to the graphic representation, the volume of agricultural output per capita in the region is closely related to the increase and stabilisation of macro-scale development stages and has led to a consistent upward trend in growth.

According to the econometric model, we have developed a correlation matrix of the volume of agricultural output per capita and the factors influencing it (Table 75).

Table 75. Correlation matrix of per capita agricultural output and factors influencing it

Variables	(1)	(2)	(3)	(4)	(5)	(6)
(1) logagricul_per_cap	1.000					
(2) logagricult_land	0.8412	1.000				
	(0.0000)					***
(3) loginvest_agricult	0.6711	0.8369	1.000			
	(0.0000)	(0.0000)				***
(4) logempl_agricult	0.7408	0.7785	0.6427	1.000		
	(0.0000)	(0.0000)	(0.0000)			***
(5) loginfl_rate	0.7906	0.6775	0.8073	0.8669	1.000	
	(0.0000)	(0.0000)	(0.0000)	(0.0000)		***

Source: It was developed by the authors based on Stata software.

Relationship between dependent and independent variables:

According to the results of Table 75, a strong, stable relationship was formed between the volume of agricultural output per capita and the variables affecting it. According to the table, the *p*-value values below 0.05 indicated that the correlation coefficient was statistically within the acceptable range. Also, there was no multicollinearity between all variables and the correlation coefficient sign according to the model showed a strong relationship.

In the next stage, a lag test of the model was conducted (Table 76).

Table 76. Test for determining optimal lags in the ARDL model of per capita agricultural output and factors affecting it

Delayed years	LL	LR	df	*p*	FPE	AIC	HQIC	SBIC
0	22.6579				2.4e-07	-1.07018	-0.993885	-0.843434
1	152.018	258.72	25	0.000	4.3e-10	-7.39506	-6.9373*	-6.03459*
2	179.126	54.216*	25	0.000	4.2e-10*	-7.5228*	-6.68358	-5.02862
3	201.545	44.838	25	0.011	6.8e-10	-7.36637	-6.14569	-3.73847
4	221.857	40.623	25	0.025	1.8e-09	-7.08222	-5.48009	-3.73847

Source: It was developed by the authors based on Stata software.

Higher values in the table indicate a positive fit and allow for comparison of models to determine whether additional lags significantly improve the model. Lower values also provide positive predictive power in the model. Statistical tests allow for the selection of lag 2 as the optimal lag.

In the next step, a Unit-root test was performed to determine the stationarity of the dependent and independent variables (Table 77).

Table 77. Unit-root test results for dependent and independent variables

Variables	Test Statistic	1% Critical Value	5% Critical Value	10% Critical Value	p-value for Z(t)
llogagricul_per_cap (Dependent variable)	-8.824	-3.682	-2.972	-2.618	0.0000
logagricult_land (Independent variable)	-6.464	-3.682	-2.972	-2.618	0.0000
loginvest_agricult (Independent variable)	-9.308	-3.682	-2.972	-2.618	0.0000
logempl_agricult (Independent variable)	-5.975	-3.682	-2.972	-2.618	0.0000
loginfl_rate (Independent variable)	-5.412	-3.682	-2.972	-2.618	0.0000

Source: It was developed by the authors based on Stata software.

According to Table 77, the results of the unit root test were –8.824 for the dependent variable, and –6.464, –9.308, –5.975 and –5.412 for the independent variables. According to this, these values indicate that the volume of agricultural output per capita and the factors affecting it have reached stationarity. This conclusion is supported by the critical values of McKinnon's $Z(t)$ value of 0.0000.

Also, the results of the unit root test have reached stationarity after the initial integration of all variables. In the next stage of the econometric model, a regression equation was developed using the ARDL model. The indicators of the econometric equation of the RDL model are presented in the table below (Table 78).

Table 78. ARDL(1,0,1,0,1) model regression equation indicators

ARDLCregression	Number of obs =36
Sample: 2014q3 thru 2023q2	R-squared = 0.8384
Log likelihood = 53.948115	Adj R-square = 0.8384
	Root MSE = 0.0613

logagricul_per_cap	Coeffi-cient	Std. err	t	P > t	[95% conf.	interval]
ADJ						
logagricul_per_cap						
L1.	−0.460	0.109	−4.210	0.000	−0.683	−0.236
LR						
logagricult_land	0.947	0.349	2.710	0.011	0.232	1.661
loginvest_agricult	0.401	0.184	2.190	0.037	0.025	0.777
logempl_agricult	1.027	0.223	4.510	0.000	0.550	1.463
loginfl_rate	−0.473	0.220	−2.150	0.040	−0.923	−0.022
SR						
loginvest_agricult						
D1.	0.368	0.109	3.370	0.002	0.145	0.591
loginfl_rate						
D1.	−0.323	0.122	−2.640	0.013	−0.574	−0.072
_cons	0.111	0.582	0.190	0.851	−1.082	1.303

*** $p < 0.01$, ** $p < 0.05$, * $p < 0.1$.

Source: It was developed by the authors based on Stata software.

Below are the econometric equations for long-run (LR) relationships based on the ARDL model.

For long-run (LR):

$$\begin{aligned} logagricul\_per\_cap = {} & \alpha + \beta_1 logagricul\_per\_cap + \beta_2 logagricult\_land \\ & + \beta_3 loginvest\_agricult + \beta_4 logempl\_agricult \\ & + \beta_5 loginfl\_rate + \epsilon \end{aligned} \tag{2}$$

According to the econometric equation ARDL(1,0,1,0,1) in the long-run dynamic (LR)

$$\begin{aligned} logagricul\_per\_cap = {} & 0.11 + 0.94 logagricult\_land \\ & + 0.40 loginvest\_agricult \\ & + 1.02 logempl\_agricult - 0.47 loginfl\_rate \end{aligned} \tag{3}$$

General description of the ARDL(1,0,1,0,1) model.

R-squared value: 0.8384, which explains about 96.02 per cent of the variation in agricultural output per capita. A high *R*-squared value indicates a positive significance level of the model to the observed data.

Log likelihood: 53.948115, which is explained by an effective assessment of the fit of the econometric equation.

Root MSE: 0.0613, indicates the average value of the error in forecasting the resulting variable. Considering that this value is small, it indicates the significance level of the model's forecast indicator.

The ARDL(1,0,1,0,1) model was tested in the study, and the results showed that the *F*-statistic and *t*-statistics had a statistical significance level of 0.05, in which case the null hypothesis was rejected. As a result, the alternative hypothesis (H1) was accepted.

The model cointegration status was tested using the ARDL(1,0,1,0,1) Bound test (Tables 22.7 and 22.8).

Table 79. Bound F-test for cointegration

					F = 5.259
	[I_0] [I_1]	[I_0] [I_1]	[I_0] [I_1]	[I_0] [I_1]	
	L_1 L_1	L_05 L_05	L_025 L_025	L_01 L_01	
K_4	2.45 3.52	2.86 4.01	3.25 4.49	3.74 5.06	

Source: It was developed by the authors based on Stata software.

According to Table 79, the *F*-statistic value is 5.259, which is greater than the critical limits for all intervals and indicates the presence of cointegration. Accordingly, the Bound test shows a positive result for the *F*-statistic value.

Table 80. Bound t-test for cointegration

					F = -5.214
	[I_0] [I_1]	[I_0] [I_1]	[I_0] [I_1]	[I_0] [I_1]	
	L_1 L_1	L_05 L_05	L_025 L_025	L_01 L_01	
K_4	-2.57 -3.66	-2.86 -3.99	-3.13 -4.26	-3.43 -4.60	

Source: It was developed by the authors based on Stata software.

According to Table 80, the *t*-statistic value is –5.214, which is greater than the critical limits for all intervals and indicates the presence of cointegration, and the Bound test produced a positive result for the *t*-statistic value.

21.5. Findings and Discussion

Result. According to the ARDL(1,0,1,0,1) model, in the long run, a 1 per cent increase in agricultural area leads to an increase in agricultural output per capita by 0.94 per cent. A 1 per cent increase in the volume of investments in agricultural fixed capital in the region leads to an increase in agricultural output per capita by 0.40 per cent. A 1 per cent increase in the number of jobs in agriculture leads to an increase in agricultural output per capita by 1.02 per cent. Also, a 1 per cent increase in the inflation rate in the national economy leads to a decrease in agricultural output per capita by 0.47 per cent.

In the next step of the research, the CUSUM diagnostic test was tested on the ARDL(1,0,1,0,1) model (Figures 81).

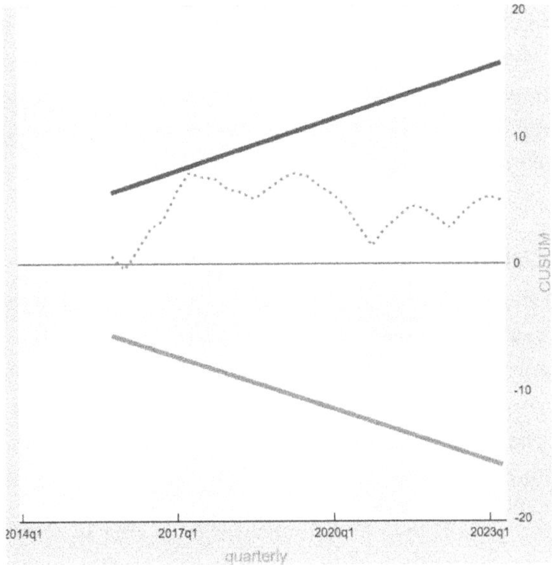

Figure 81. CUSUM diagnostic test graph.
Source: It was developed by the authors based on Stata software.

The CUSUM (Cumulative Sum) diagnostic test used in the ARDL(1,0,1,0,1) model presents the following hypotheses to assess the stability of the regression equation parameters over time.

1. Null hypothesis (H_0 – Primary hypothesis): The model is stable over time (there is no systematic change in the parameters). The residuals follow a stable process, which suggests that the probable parameters of the ARDL(1,0,1,0,1) model do not change over the sample period.
2. Alternative hypothesis (H_1 – Alternative hypothesis): The ARDL(1,0,1,0,1) model is not stable over time (there is systematic change in the parameters). The residuals show instability, which suggests that the model parameters have changed at certain points in the sample period.

According to the interpretation of the CUSUM diagnostic result according to the ARDL(1,0,1,0,1) model:

Since the CUSUM test was successful, the null hypothesis (H_0) was not rejected, that is, the ARDL(1,0,1,0,1) model expressed stability over the analysed period. According to it, the ARDL(1,0,1,0,1) model shows that the relationship between the volume of agricultural products per capita and the factors affecting it is generally stable without systematic breaks and instability of the parameters.

21.6. Conclusion

The results of the ARDL(1,0,1,0,1) model based on multivariate time series in econometric research showed that there is a strong and positive relationship between the volume of agricultural output per capita, the area of agricultural crops in the national economy, the volume of investments in agricultural fixed capital, the number of jobs in agriculture and the inflation rate in the national economy.

1. Assess the importance of agricultural crop area in the 0.94 per cent increase in per capita output.

   The expansion of agricultural land is one of the main factors affecting agricultural productivity. An almost proportional increase in per capita output leads to sustainable growth in the agricultural industry, due to the efficient use of land. According to this result, government-level reforms that stimulate land development and sustainable expansion of agriculture are reflected in state programmes and strategic directions.

2. Increase the economic significance of investments in fixed capital in agriculture in the growth of per capita output by 0.40 per cent.

   According to this result, capital investments in technology, infrastructure and machinery and equipment in agriculture contribute to a significant increase in productivity. The positive impact on the econometric result will lead to an increase in the possibilities of transforming agriculture through capital investments and to optimising efficiency indicators and further increasing agricultural production, which will create a basis for strengthening the need for reforms that attract investment practices to the sector.

3. To assess the economic significance of a 1.02 per cent increase in agricultural employment per capita.

   This result shows that the strong impact of employment in agriculture is indicative of the importance of skilled human capital in increasing labour productivity. A 1.02 per cent increase in per capita output for every 1 per cent increase in employment indicates a shortage of labour and a need for skills development in agricultural indicators. This result reinforces the need for training programmes and initiatives aimed at attracting more skilled workers to the agricultural sector.

4. To assess the impact of the inflation rate on the volume of agricultural output per capita.

   An increase in inflation expectations has an inverse effect on agricultural output per capita. Understanding this relationship increases the need for economists and governments to develop strategies to mitigate the effects of inflation, including stabilising input costs, offering subsidies and implementing policies to protect farmers from price volatility. Effectively managing inflation will help ensure that the agricultural industry can achieve sustainable growth.

5. The impact of the above factors on the volume of agricultural output per capita will provide a balanced and robust support for economic growth in the sector.

Bibliography

Abdullah, M. A., Han, X., Amjad, M. A., & Makhmudov, S. (2025). Revisit the role of financial development on economic growth, human development, and sustainable development in higher-income countries. *Journal of Environmental Management*, *392*, 126874.

Akhmetshin, E., Abdullayev, I., Makhmudov, S., Dakhkilgova, K., Korotaeva, I. and Yanovskaya, G. (2025). APPLICATION OF TANH–COTH METHOD FOR COMBINED AND DOUBLE COMBINED SINH–COSH–GORDON EQUATIONS ARISING CHEMICAL REACTIONS TO WATER SURFACE GRAVITY WAVES. Computational Methods for Differential Equations, (), -. doi: 10.22034/cmde.2025.67655.3234

Ali, W., Abdullah, A., and Azam, M. (2017). 'Re-visiting the Environmental Kuznets Curve Hypothesis for Malaysia: Fresh Evidence from ARDL Bounds Testing Approach'. *Renewable and Sustainable Energy Reviews*, 77, 990–1000.

Berus, A., and Kosnikov, S. N. (2024). 'The Role of Economic and Structural Factors in the Development of Agriculture: Regional Approach'. *Journal of Regional and International Competitiveness*, 5 (3), 66–72. <https://doi.org/10.52957/2782-1927-2024-5-3-66-72>.

Bozkurt İ., and Kaya M. V. (2021). 'Agricultural Production Index: International comparison'. *Agric. Econ. – Czech* 67, 236–45.

Ding, Y., (2023). 'The Impact of Agricultural Industrial Agglomeration on Farmers' Income: An Influence Mechanism Test Based on a Spatial Panel Model'. Plos one, 18 (9), p.e0291188.

Fayçal, M., and Ali, H. M. (2016). 'Economic Growth and Government Subventions for Agriculture Sector in Algeria: An ARDL Model'. *Arab Economic and Business Journal*, 11 (2), 105–14.

Gulyamova, L., (2022). The Geography of Uzbekistan: At the Crossroads of the Silk Road. Springer Nature.

Habib, S. S., Islam, M. A., Ali, M. N., Benitez, I. B., Mamadiyarov, Z., Mirzayev, B., … & Flah, A. (2025). Multi-Objective Optimization and Feasibility Analysis of Integrated Biogas–Solar Energy Systems for Rural Electrification. *Results in Engineering*, 107086.

Hakkoz, M. A., Macit, S., and Üstündağ, B. B. (2024). 'Performance Improvement of Regional Agricultural Forecasts with PECNET and State-Space Model'. 11, 1–6. <https://doi.org/10.1109/agro-geoinformatics262780.2024.10661077>.

Hassan, M., and Tunc, G. (2024). 'The ARDL Approach in Economic Policy Modeling: A Case Study of Central Asia'. *Journal of Econometrics and Economic Modeling*, 40 (1), 92–111.

Hussein, M. A., and Hmood, M. Y., (2024). 'Nonstationary Time Series Models Using ARDL and NARDL Estimation'. *Journal of Economics and Administrative Sciences*, 30 (141), 439–56.

Jegadeesan, M., Kumar, M., and Deepika, S. (2024). 'The Complementary Roles of Agriculture and Industry in India's Economic Growth: A Path to Balanced Development'. *International Journal of Research in Agronomy*, 7 (11S), 435–7, <https://doi.org/10.33545/2618060x.2024.v7.i11sf.2039>.

Kalandarov, F., Makhmudov, S., Ibadullaev, D., Matniyozov, M., Nasretdinova, F., Sabirov, K., & Bahodirov, N. M. (2025). Low-Carbon Energy Risk and Renewable Energy Development: Insights from Method of Moments Quantile Regression. International Journal of Energy Economics and Policy, 15(3), 524–536.

Khayrilla Kurbonov, Samariddin Makhmudov, Shakhzod Erkinov, Umidjon Dadabaev, Gulnora Bekimbetova, Rukhiddin Zayniddinov, and Mirzabek Jonuzokov. 2025. Evaluating the Impact of Marketing Practices Digitalization and Investment on Labor Market Efficiency and Commercial Bank Performance Using Econometric Models. In Proceedings of the 8th International Conference on Future Networks & Distributed Systems (ICFNDS '24). Association for Computing Machinery, New York, NY, USA, 786–796. https://doi.org/10.1145/3726122.3726237

Khodjaniyazov, N., Mirkhoshimova, M., Kalandarov, F., Matyokubova, D., Utegenova, S., Makhmudov, S., & Khudayberganov, M. (2025). Time-Varying Impacts of Financial Stress on Energy-Related Uncertainty. International Journal of Energy Economics and Policy, 15(3), 689–698.

Kuchkarov, T., Mamadiyarov, Z., Khakimov, Z., Sabirova, O., Matmurodov, K., Raimboyeva, M., & Umarova, S. (2025). Energy-Related Uncertainty and Crypto-Currency Environmental Attention: Time-Varying Perspective. International Journal of Energy Economics and Policy, 15(5), 614–626. https://doi.org/10.32479/ijeep.20784

Kuziboev, B., Ozturk, I., Kalandarov, F., Samandarov, O., Bekjanov, D., & Makhmudov, S. (2025). PROMOTING ENERGY SOURCES DIVERSIFICATION THROUGH ESG PERFORMANCE. Energy, 136009.

Lin, M.H., Matchanova, B., Nurmatovich, H.A. et al. Optimal Operation of the Multi-Carrier Energy System Considering Energy Markets and Renewable Energies Participation. *Int. J. Appl. Comput. Math* 11, 170 (2025). https://doi.org/10.1007/s40819-025-02002-9

Litamahuputty, J. V., Amiruddin, E. G., Rahim, R., Rahman, A., & Mamadiyarov, Z. (2025). Cryptocurrency Risk Management through Decision Engineering: Evaluating XRPUSD and ADAUSD Portfolio Performance. Journal of Applied Science, Engineering, Technology, and Education, 7(1), 69–81. https://doi.org/10.35877/454RI.asci3871

Mamadiyarov, Z., Eshov, M., Otakhonova, D., Utegenova, S., Sabirov, K., Marks, A., & Bahodirov, N. (2025). Does Energy Policy Risk Threaten Energy Sources Diversification?. *International Journal of Energy Economics and Policy*, *15*(5), 730–740. https://doi.org/10.32479/ijeep.21140

Mamadiyarov, Z. Makhmudov, S. Utanov, B. Kasimova, D. Bekmurodova, G. Hakimov, Z. (2025). Fusion of Economic and Financial Factors Affecting Household Deposits in Banks: An Econometric Analysis. Fusion: Practice and Applications, (), 82–91. DOI: https://doi.org/10.54216/FPA.190206

Mamadiyarov, Z., Saidov, O., Abdurazakova, N., Makhmudov, S., Nazarov, M., Rajabova, N., … Ruzmetova, I. (2025). Energy-Related Uncertainty and Tourism Stock Markets: New Insights from Time-Varying Relationship with TVP-VAR Approach. *International Journal of Energy Economics and Policy*, *15*(4), 730–737. https://doi.org/10.32479/ijeep.20480

Mamani, J.C.M., Miri, M., Vorobev, Y. et al. Optimal Operation of Energy Microgrid Considering Economic and Emission Indices. Oper. Res. Forum 6, 122 (2025). https://doi.org/10.1007/s43069-025-00523-z

Midmore, P. (1993). 'Input-Output Forecasting of Regional Agricultural Policy Impacts'. *Journal of Agricultural Economics*, 44 (2), 284–300. <https://doi.org/10.1111/J.1477-9552.1993.TB00272.X>.

Muhammad Zubair, Irfanud Din, Nadeem Sarwar et al. Revolutionizing Sepsis Diagnosis Using Machine Learning and Deep Learning Models: A Systematic Literature Review, 10 June 2025, PREPRINT (Version 1) available at Research Square [https://doi.org/10.21203/rs.3.rs-6731418/v1]

Mustafaev, D., and Karimov, A. (2021). 'Industrialization Strategies and the Agricultural Sector in Uzbekistan: Challenges and Opportunities'. *Central Asian Development Studies*, 12 (2), 53–70.

Ngongo, M., Herman, H., Ndandara, A., Jois Jaha, D. A., Peku Djawang, J. U. S., Tanggu Rame, M. M., Khamraeva, S. N., & Mamadiyarov, Z. (2025). An Investigation of Meaning, Toponymy of Sumba Cultural Site's Names, and the Impact of Tourism Visitors on Surrounding Society. *Forum for Linguistic Studies*, 7(8), 679–693. https://doi.org/10.30564/fls.v7i8.10260

Nguyen, T. H., Van Nguyen, B., Nguyen, T. T., and Luu, D. H., (2024). 'Productivity Unleashed: An ARDL Model Analysis of Innovation and Globalization Effects'. *Journal of Infrastructure, Policy and Development*, 8 (8).

PANJAITAN, M. B., HAMDANAH, H., SIRAIT, J., SUTIKNO, S., FATMAWATI, E., HERMAN, H., & MAMADIYAROV, Z. (2025). THE ROLE OF EMOTIONAL REGULATION IN SHAPING STUDENTS' PERCEPTION OF PHYSICS PROBLEMSOLVING TASKS. TPM – Testing, Psychometrics, Methodology in Applied Psychology, 32(S2(2025) : Posted 09 June), 1–10. Retrieved from https://tpmap.org/submission/index.php/tpm/article/view/139

Pradhan, R., Hajiyev, E., Shichiyakh, R. et al. Optimal Techno-Economic Feasibility of an Off-Grid Microgrid System Using Load Flow Energy Management Strategies. *Oper. Res. Forum* 6, 120 (2025). https://doi.org/10.1007/s43069-025-00524-y

Rayala, R. V., Borra, C. R., Vasudevan, V., Singhania, R., Cheekati, S., & Mamadiyarov, Z. (2025, July). Lightweight Deep Learning Framework for Human Activity Recognition: A MobileNet-LSTM Approach with WHOA Optimization. In *2025 International Conference on Innovations in Intelligent Systems: Advancements in Computing, Communication, and Cybersecurity (ISAC3)* (pp. 1–6). IEEE.

Rayala, R. V., Sandhya, N., Singhania, R., Cheekati, S., Borra, C. R., Vasudevan, V., & Mamadiyarov, Z. (2025, July). AI-Driven Tomato Quality Assessment: A Deep Learning Approach for Image-based Defect Detection and Classification. In *2025 International Conference on Innovations in Intelligent Systems: Advancements in Computing, Communication, and Cybersecurity (ISAC3)* (pp. 1–6). IEEE.

Romero, R. M., Zelinskaya, M., Makhmudov, S., Sapaev, S., & Rustambekovich, J. U. (2025, September). Modelling and Optimal Utilisation of the Renewable Energy Systems in Microgrid with Improving Reliability and Energy Efficiency. In Operations Research Forum (Vol. 6, No. 3, pp. 1–20). Springer International Publishing.

Rony, Z. T., Jefri, R., Rusmardiana, A., Pramono, S. A., & Mamadiyarov, Z. (2025). Downside Risk Measurement of Indonesian Financial and Energy Securities: A Value at Risk Perspective. *Journal of Applied Science, Engineering, Technology, and Education*, 7(2). https://doi.org/10.35877/454RI.asci3898

Rukhiddin Zayniddinov, Nodir Jumaev, Gulbakhor Irgasheva, Alam Asadov, Nosir Makhmudov, Sirojiddin Abrorov, and Samariddin Makhmudov. 2025. The Influence of the Digital Economy on Economic Development Evidence from Uzbekistan. In Proceedings of the 8th

International Conference on Future Networks & Distributed Systems (ICFNDS '24). Association for Computing Machinery, New York, NY, USA, 831–839. https://doi.org/10.1145/3726122.3726242

Samariddin Makhmudov, Malika Umarova, Khayrilla Kurbonov, Laylo Akbarova, Durdona Davletova, Nilufar Shanazarova, and Toshmurod Kulmanov. 2025. Evaluating the forecast indicators of the volume of highly liquid assets of commercial banks in the process of digital transformation. In Proceedings of the 8th International Conference on Future Networks & Distributed Systems (ICFNDS '24). Association for Computing Machinery, New York, NY, USA, 698–704. https://doi.org/10.1145/3726122.3726222

Samariddin Makhmudov, Kudratillo Tukhsanov, Saifulla Arslanbekov, Akram Amanov, Orifali Tursunov, Umarbek Jabbarov and Muyassarxon Mirzakarimova. 2024. Optimizing Supply Chain Financing Development Prospects of Digital Ecosystems in the European Logistics Industry. In The 8th International Conference on Future Networks & Distributed Systems (ICFNDS '24), December 11–12, 2024, Marakech, Morocco. ACM, New York, NY, USA, 12 Pages. https://doi.org/10.1145/3726122.3726200

Sattarov, B., and Turaev, S. (2021). 'Agriculture's Impact on Industrial Production and Trade Balance in Uzbekistan'. *Economic Policy Review*, 25 (4), 80–98.

Singagerda, F. S., Pratama, M. R., Alfairus, M. Q., Iskandar, A., & Mamadiyarov, Z. (2025). A Decision-Centric Approach to Risk Management in Aviation Stock Investments Using Value at Risk and Portfolio Optimization. *Journal of Applied Science, Engineering, Technology, and Education*, 7(1), 114–125. https://doi.org/10.35877/454RI.asci3870

Sofyanty, D., Romadhoni, R., Handriadi, H., Makhsudovna, I. S., Anwar, Z., & Mamadiyarov, Z. (2025). Strategic Decision Analysis for Investment Portfolios: Computational Risk Assessment in Transportation Asset Management. *Journal of Applied Science, Engineering, Technology, and Education*, 7(2). https://doi.org/10.35877/454RI.asci3897

Sourav, S. K. (2023). 'An Analysis of the Role of India's Industrial and Agricultural Sectors in Economic Growth: Special Focus on Bihar

Economy'. *International Journal of Research in Management*. <https://doi.org/10.33545/26648792.2023.v5.i2c.157>.

Toshmurod Kulmanov, Umidjon Dadabaev, Mansurbek Qulmetov, Aliboy Ulashov, Mirjalol Eshboyev, and Samariddin Makhmudov. 2025. Global Services Market Transformation Digitalization Export Trends and Future Forecasts. In Proceedings of the 8th International Conference on Future Networks & Distributed Systems (ICFNDS '24). Association for Computing Machinery, New York, NY, USA, 851–858. https://doi.org/10.1145/3726122.3726245

Vachanelidou, O., Karelakis, C., Loizou, E., and Zafeiriou, E. (2023). 'Relationships and Interdependencies of the Agri-Food Sector in a Regional Economy: Employing an Input-Output Model'. <https://doi.org/10.1080/08974438.2023.2281327>.

Xolmurotov, F., Xolmuratov, X. S., and Yakubova, Y. R. (2024). 'Assessment of the Impact of Agriculture on the Regional Socio-economic Development'. *E3S Web of Conferences*, 548, 01003. <https://doi.org/10.1051/e3sconf/202454801003>.

Zhang, L., Zhao, Z., Qamri, G. M., & Makhmudov, S. (2025). Unleashing the critical role of renewable energy through global value chains and digitalization: A path towards environmental sustainability. *Journal of Environmental Management*, *392*, 126688.

Zokir Toshtemirovich Mamadiyarov, Samandarboy Adhambek ugli Sulaymanov, Sarvar Anvar ugli Askarov, and Durdona Bakhtiyor kizi Uktamova. 2022. Impact of Covid-19 Pandemic on Accelerating The Digitization and Transformation of Banks. In Proceedings of the 5th International Conference on Future Networks and Distributed Systems (ICFNDS '21). Association for Computing Machinery, New York, NY, USA, 706–712. https://doi.org/10.1145/3508072.3508211

Statistical Assessment of Unemployment and Its Causes in the Regional Labour Market

Samariddin Makhmudov, Zokir Mamadiyarov, Mirislom Mirolimov, Khayrilla Kurbonov, Siddik Sayfullayev and Nadir Shamsiev

23.1. Introduction

In the context of increasing international competition, the scientific, methodological and organisational aspects of the effective development of the labour market and the coordination of labour supply and demand are being studied. In areas with a high level of labour resources, it is necessary to increase the level of employment of the population and create new jobs, reduce the unemployment rate, improve the self-employment system, increase the employment of women and youth, ensure permanent employment of the population living in rural areas and increase the well-being of the population, and introduce the regional population to new professions that meet the requirements of the green economy. Relevant issues such as training and creating green jobs, promoting inclusive employment in the labour market, and providing women with suitable jobs by improving their knowledge in the field of information technology are among the priority areas of scientific research in this regard.

Statistical analysis of the use of the regional labour market, statistical assessment of the situation of creating new jobs at enterprises, study of the adaptation of the labour market to changes in the era of the 'green economy', statistical forecasting, statistical analysis of the formation and change of labour resources, and statistical modelling are among the important tasks of the development of New Uzbekistan is calculated.

The labour market occupies a central place among other markets. The market is based on two main participants: employers and employees. Their main difference lies in their relationship to the means of production. The owners of the means of production are employers, who do not own the tools or objects of labour, but are hired workers. They offer their labour for a certain wage, and employers demand it and pay for it. Thus, in the labour market, as in other markets, there is demand, supply and price in the form of wages.

The demand for labour is determined by the need of enterprises for hired labour in the quantity and quality necessary for the production of products and the technical equipment for their production. The prices of consumer goods directly affect the level of labour force and wages. All this leads to a shortage of capital, changes in the demand and supply of labour, and the emergence of unemployment, which in turn complicates relations between economic entities. Therefore, the state plays a major role in establishing the most rational economic relations in the labour market.

23.2. Literature Review

In regional labour markets, labour is shaped by supply and demand, which is influenced by wage levels, employment and unemployment. Internal migration plays a role in determining labour supply, while regional demand for goods and services influences labour demand (Isserman et al., 1987).

The study of unemployment needs to take into account broader economic conditions and policy interventions. For example, in Indonesia, government policies such as state job training and investment in infrastructure have been important in reducing unemployment (Ubaydilloh and Yasin, 2024).

G. Rozikova in her article Increasing investments and creating new jobs in rural areas: To create jobs in rural areas, it is necessary to increase investments. Through territorial investments, it is possible to create new jobs in the agricultural sector and increase the employment rate by 20 per cent. She put forward the idea that by implementing these recommendations, the employment rate in Uzbekistan can be significantly increased (Rozikova, 2025).

According to B. Akbarova, one of the socio-economic problems in our society at the current stage of the country's development is employment, the growth trend of unemployment, socially unprotected segments of the population, issues of social protection of women in the field of employment, the level of employment of women in the field of small business and private entrepreneurship (Akbarova, 2023; Karlibaeva et al., 2024; Khoshimovet al., 2024).

N. Tarasova in her article 'Labor relations in the conditions of globalization and technological revolution' scientifically substantiated the impact of information and communication technologies on almost all sectors and industries of the economy on a huge and global scale and on each function of firms belonging to any industry or service (Tarasova, 2000).

In their opinion, the currently employed workforce cannot be considered completely consumed and withdrawn from the market. The production process continuously changes the conditions of employment, issues arise regarding the territorial or professional movement of employees, positions in terms of remuneration, etc. The relations of sale and purchase of labour force, which are established between employees and employers, which represent the essence of the labour market, continue even after employees are employed.

23.3. Research Methodology

The main task of solving the problem of ensuring the development of the labour market infrastructure is to ensure the employment of both unemployed and employed labour market participants who want to change their main place of work. Currently, the role of information in the labour market is growing significantly. The high need for information for management purposes and the rapid development of information processes bring the creation of its infrastructure components to the forefront. Information infrastructure includes computing equipment, communication tools, methodological and software support, and auxiliary types of activity. The growth of the volume of scientific and technical, political, economic and any information necessary for effective work in the relevant areas of human activity necessitates the widespread use of information technologies in management. In conducting the research, scientific observation, statistical observation, statistical graphs, comparative analysis, data grouping, abstract-logical thinking, induction and deduction methods, the tasks set by the resolutions and decrees of the President of our country, the decisions of our government within the scope of the topic, and the scientific works of economists who conducted research within the scope of the topic were studied, and the level of study of the topic was examined.

The article analyses the correlation and regression between the factors affecting the changes in labour market efficiency in the Tashkent region, in particular, a regression equation is developed. A multifactorial forecast of the number of jobs in the economy of the Tashkent region is made for both Scenario 1 and Scenario 2.

Makhmudov et al. (2024) 'The Impact of Digital Technologies on the Labor Market of Uzbekistan' is a comprehensive and robust econometric study. Based on data from the State Statistics Agency, the study provides an in-depth look at how digital technologies have impacted the dynamics of the country's labour market. This paper uses advanced econometric models, including the Pooled OLS stimator (POLSE), Fixed effects stimator (FEE) and Random Effects Estimator (REE) (Mamadiyarov et al., 2025; Mamani et al., 2025; Pradhan et al., 2025; Rayala et al., 2025; Romero et al., 2025; Rony et al., 2025; Rukhiddin et al., 2025; Samariddin et al., 2025; Singagerda et al., 2025).

Another group of economists has successfully used econometric models such as Fixed Effects Estimator (FEE), Random Effects Estimator (REE), multivariate linear (LS) and ARDL in their research on investment in digital infrastructure, various aspects of digital payment systems, the impact of inflation and credit interest rates on investment, factors affecting the reduction of the state's share in commercial banks, Non-Performing Loans in commercial banks, the digitisation of banks, risks in digital services and the development of retail payment services (Abdullah et al., 2025; Akhmetshin et al., 2025; Habib et al., 2025; Lin et al., 2025; Litamahuputty et al., 2025; Mamadiyarov et al., 2025; Sofyanty et al., 2025; Toshmurod et al., 2025; Zokir et al., 2021).

Analyses and forecasts were conducted using multivariate linear regression (LS), ARDL, ARIMA and various other econometric models on the global services market, digital economy, energy-related financial stress, cocktail market, digital transformation, factors affecting the logistics industry (Kalandarov et al., 2025; Khayrilla et al., 2025; Khodjaniyazov et al., 2025; Kuziboev et al., 2025; Mamadiyarov et al., 2025; Rayala et al., 2025; Samariddin et al., 2025; Zhang et al., 2025).

23.4. Analysis and Results

The expansion or contraction of the labour market leads to a change in the ratio between its components: the number of workers and the number of unemployed. The ratio between demand and supply in the labour market is reflected in the market price of labour, depending on the situation. The problem of labour market activity is explained differently by economists. From the point of view of classical theory, unemployment is a specific economic phenomenon that arises as a result of an increase in wages. It is only when wages reach a certain level, that is, above the level that all job seekers can find, that there is an excess of supply in the labour market and, as a result, unemployment arises (stat.uz).

Table 81. Empirical data used for the calculations of the data presented for the econometric analysis of regional labour market development

Name of indicators / Years	The number of bands in the economy as a productive factor (log Y)	Gross regional product of Tashkent region, billion soums ($\log x_1$) in comparative terms	Unemployment rate ($\log x_2$)	Number of enterprises in Tashkent region ($\log x_3$)	Real income per capita in Tashkent region, thousand soums ($\log x_4$) in comparison prices	Average nominal monthly income, Tashkent region, in thousand roubles ($\log x_5$) in comparative prices
2000	895.8	24,358	0.1	9,105	900.0	18.1
2001	906.9	27,013	0.1	9,332	1206.9	30.4
2002	926.4	281,47.5	0.1	10,282	1448.3	47.0
2003	952.8	29,104.5	0.1	10,731	1543.9	64.1
2004	984.6	30,094.1	0.1	10,761	1909.8	89.0
2005	1015.4	32,922.9	0.1	11,307	2224.9	104.0
2006	1042.4	34,174.0	0.1	11,403	2447.4	121.1
2007	1068.6	37,078.8	0.4	12,030	3010.3	162.1
2008	1097.5	40,378.8	3.9	14,495	3555.2	202.8
2009	1125.6	41,469.0	4.5	14,811	4639.5	285.3
2010	1155.4	43,749.8	4.1	22,823	5456.1	362.0
2011	1183.4	47,599.8	3.8	18,746	6520.0	466.5
2012	1215.5	50,217.8	3.6	20,473	8234.8	629.8
2013	1244.9	52,477.6	3.6	21,333	9222.9	758.3
2014	1272.4	55,888.7	3.9	22,823	9942.3	869.0
2015	1281.8	59,353.7	4.1	23,954	10777.5	995.7
2016	1287.6	62,855.6	4.1	24,403	11952.2	1167.0
2017	1289.6	65,809.8	5.2	25,019	12478.1	1286.0
2018	1227.7	66,467.9	9	26,919	12952.3	1460.8
2019	1232.9	70,854.8	8.9	31,030	13587.0	1791.0
2020	1177.2	76,027.2	10.5	38,523	14184.8	2152.8
2021	1222.1	78,232.0	9.4	46,173	14610.3	2501.5
2022	1206.7	80,436.8	8.8	50,296	14897.6	2987.8
2023	1238.6	82,641.6	6.8	55,472	15001.3	3105.8

Source: Compiled by the authors based on data from the National Statistics Committee of the Republic of Uzbekistan.

The economic indicators of Tashkent region show a positive growth trend. Although employment, incomes and salaries have increased, the unemployment rate sometimes increases, which may indicate some social and economic problems in the economy. In particular, the unemployment rate increased between 2007 and 2020, which may be associated with economic recession or difficulties in market conditions. Depending on the region, there are different labour markets, especially specialised by occupational category, qualification and level of education. In this sense, taking into account the increase in the number of labour force in the Tashkent region, using the considerations outlined above for scenario 1, we can conclude that the number of labour force in the region as a productive factor affecting the change in the quality of the economic output is $\log x_1$, the unemployment rate is $\log x_2$, the number of enterprises in the region is $\log x_3$, and the population per capita is $\log x_4$. The factors real income – $\log x_4$ and average nominal monthly income – x_5 are selected and their correlation coefficient is determined (Table 82).

Table 82. Correlation coefficient between factors characterising changes in labour market efficiency in Tashkent region under scenario 1

	log y	log x_1	log x_2	log x_3	log x_4	log x_5
y	1.0000					
x_1	0.802517	1.0000				
x_2	0.841632	0.685621	1.0000			
x_3	0.710253	0.771428	0.74231	1.0000		
x_4	0.730214	0.967142	0.71256	0.68941	1.0000	
x_5	0.714796	0.582361	0.70213	0.77191	0.59210	1

Source: Developed by the authors based on the EViews program.

If we consider the values of the table, the resulting *logy* – factor-related unemployment rate – $\log x_2$ (*rlogy*, $logx_2$ = 0.802517) and the volume of the regional gross regional product – $\log x_1$ (*rlogy*, $logx_1$ = 0.802512) with strong density, the number of enterprises in the region – $\log x_3$ (*rlogy*, $logx_3$ = 0.710253), real per capita income – $\log x_4$ (*rlogy*, $\log x_4 = 0.730214$) and the average nominal monthly wage – since $\log x_5$ (*rlogy*, $\log x_5 = 0.714796$) is strongly correlated with the average, and since there is no multicollinearity between the selected factors under the condition *plogx*$_1$, $\log x_2 < 0.8$, the regression equation can be determined using the EViews program.

Table 83. Results of the regression equation between factors influencing changes in labour market efficiency in Tashkent region under scenario 1

Dependent Variable: Log *Y*

Method: Least Squares

Date: 11/25/22 Time: 20:47

Sample: 2000 2021

Included observations: 22

Variable	Coefficient	Std. Error	*t*-Statistic	Prob.
Log x_1	0.193251	0.036215	3.325143	0.0362
Log x_2	−0.015321	0.025136	−2.868412	0.0412
Log x_3	0.036111	0.025142	2.941253	0.0325
Log x_4	0.051421	0.074512	2.414236	0.0563
Log x_5	0.161241	0.068213	2.569213	0.0263
C	5.4121421	0.325314	16.76312	0.0001
			t_{jad} = 2,1263125	

R-squared	0.961253	Mean dependent var	7.0362142
Adjusted *R*-squared	0.951267	S.D. dependent var	0.1342131
S.E. of regression	0.016615	Akaike info criterion	−5.1251024
Sum squared resid	0.004417	Schwarz criterion	−4.8635211
Log likelihood	62.43022	Hannan–Quinn criter.	−5.0497513
F-statistic	215.5231	Durbin–Watson stat	1.7961421
Prob(*F*-statistic)	0.000000	F_{jad}=0,3459212	

Source: Developed by the authors based on the EViews program.

From the values of the coefficients given in the table data, the following equation is obtained:

$$LogY1 = 0.19LogX1 - 0.01532LogX2 + 0.036LogX3 + 0.05LogX4 + 0.16LogX5 + 5.41 \quad (2)$$

If we consider the significance of the parameters of the identified two regression equations according to the t-Statistic criteria, then for α = 0.05 and df = 16, t_{Jad} = 2.1263125, which means that all parameters are significant, since this $>t_{Jad}$ condition is satisfied. In order to simplify the calculation process and achieve accuracy of the results, the above-derived regression equation 2 is taken as a power and the following equation is derived from it:

$$Y = \frac{X1^{0.19} * X3^{0.036} * X4^{0.05} * X5^{0.16} * e^{5.72}}{X2^{0.01532}} \quad (3)$$

The resulting 3-regression equation is truly significant at $\alpha=0.05$ and $k_1=16$; Given that F_{Jad} = 0.3459212 when k_2 = 5, the Fisher value calculated is F_{his} = 215.5, and the significance of the 3-regression equation based on the condition $F_{Jad} < F_{his}$ is equal to $DW=1.79$, which indicates the reliability and adequacy of the equation due to the absence of autocorrelation.

If we give an economic explanation to the 3-regression equation, it can be interpreted as follows: If, according to the determined 3-regression equation, the gross regional product and the average nominal monthly wage increase by 1.0 per cent, then the number of households in the economy of the Tashkent region, selected as the resulting factor, will increase by an additional 0.02 and 2.2 thousand people, respectively. It was found that an additional 0.01 per cent increase in the number of enterprises in the region and real per capita income by 1.0 per cent was associated with an increase in the number of enterprises in the region.

However, it should be noted that an increase in the number of unemployed in the Tashkent region by 1.0 per cent during the current period of observation could reduce the number of workers in the economy by 2.2 thousand people. If we summarise the results obtained, it is appropriate to review the measures taken by the Tashkent regional administration to create new jobs in the region, support and strengthen small business and private entrepreneurship.

Eliminating the problems associated with the spread of unemployment requires urgent reform of the labour market and the creation of favourable conditions for supporting labour, the development of relevant tasks for effective employment in achieving strategic goals to maximise labour potential through the activation of incentive measures. First of all, state policy in the field of labour should be systematic, aimed at achieving the goals of each of the subjects of social and labour relations.

In this regard, it is necessary to highlight the specifics of the labour market, its differences from other markets. According to its content, the labour market consists of three parts:

1. Potential, that is, the sphere in which labour itself is formed (persons engaged in household and personal household chores; students studying in correspondence courses and lyceum students; military personnel; farmers; entrepreneurs and other working-age population).
2. Circulation, i.e. the sphere of purchase and sale of labour (the seller of his labour moves between enterprises in search of work, being actually unemployed: persons experiencing frictional, structural and cyclical unemployment; discharged military personnel: army and navy, pensioners looking for work, persons undergoing retraining, advanced training and community service).
3. Within the enterprise (persons directly involved in enterprises due to job vacancies due to reductions in staff, modernisation and expansion of production, new construction, increasing the turnover rate of the enterprise, relocations). Taking into account the differences in the content of the labour market, for the econometric assessment of changes and development of the labour market of the Tashkent region, the unemployment rate in the region under scenario 2 is x_3, the number of affected enterprises is x_4, the average nominal monthly wage is x_5 and the gross regional product of the economy is x_5 product volume – x_6 factors were selected. First, we determine the degree of correlation between these factors (Table 84).

Table 84. Correlation coefficient between factors influencing changes in labour market efficiency in Tashkent region under scenario 2

	log y	log x_3	log x_4	log x_5	log x_6
log y	1.0000				
log x_3	0.912634	1.0000			
log x_4	0.871236	0.674123	1.0000		
log x_5	0.912563	0.578126	0.748931	1.0000	
log x_6	0.869821	0.641789	0.752691	0.66174	1.0000

Source: Developed by the authors based on the EViews program.

Considering the values in the table, the number of enterprises in the region relative to the unemployment rate is logx_3 (r_Y, $logx_3$ = 0.912634), real income per capita is logx_4 (r_Y, $logx_4$ = 0.871236), average nominal monthly wage is logx_5 (r_Y, $logx_5$ = 0.912563) and the gross regional product per capita of the population in the economy is logx_6 (r_Y, $logx_6$ = 0.869821). Since the density is well-correlated and there is no multicollinearity between the factors, we can continue the process as long as *px1*, $logx_2 < 0.8$.

For this, first of all, since the selected factors have different units of measurement, the nonlinear equation is formed by taking the logarithms of the factor indices and checking it based on the quality criteria. Accordingly, the determination of the regression equation between the observed relationships can be continued using the EViews program (Table 85).

Table 85. Results of the regression equation between factors influencing changes in labour market efficiency in Tashkent region under scenario 2

Dependent Variable: Log Y

Method: Least Squares

Date: 11/25/22 Time: 00:05

Sample: 2000–2021

Included observations: 22

Variable	Coefficient	Std. Error	*t*-Statistic	Prob.
Log x_3	-1.181713	0.921043	-1.168124	0.0364
Log x_4	-0.694132	0.167481	-3.639151	0.0012
Log x_5	2.102641	0.668133	3.4721531	0.0049
Log x_6	-0.463214	1.021351	-0.429761	0.0249
C	0.117084	5.165321	0.243288	0.0117
			t_{jad} = 2.125131	
R-squared	0.733180	Mean dependent var		1.873683
Adjusted *R*-squared	0.670398	S.D. dependent var		0.501829
S.E. of regression	0.288105	Akaike info criterion		0.545732
Sum squared resid	1.411076	Schwarz criterion		0.793697
Log likelihood	-1.003056	Hannan-Quinn criter.		0.604145
F-statistic	11.67831	Durbin-Watson stat		1.878652
Prob (*F*-statistic)	0.000096		F_{jad}=0,33730133	

Source: Developed by the authors based on the EViews program.

Based on the calculation results, the following equation is obtained from the values of the coefficients given in the table:

$$LogY = -1.18LlogX3 - 0.69logX4 + 2.102logX5 - 0.46LlogX6 + 0,12 \quad (3)$$

If we consider the parameters of the identified regression equation 4 in terms of their significance according to the *t*-Statistic criteria, then with $\alpha = 0.05$ and df = 17, real per capita income is equal to $t_{Jad} = 2.1098$ – logx_4 ($tlogx_4$ = $|-3.639| > t_{Jad} = 2.125131$) and average nominal monthly wage is logx_5 ($tlogx_5$ $= 3.4721531 t_{Jad} = 2.125131$) parameters are significant.

Using the system of equations, the results of a multifactorial forecast of the number of bands in the economy of the Tashkent region according to scenario 1 are determined (Table 86)

Table 86. Results of multifactorial forecast of the number of bands in the economy of Tashkent region under scenario 1

Years	Number of bands in the economy, thousand	GNP billion soums	Unemploy_ rate, %	Enterpris_ units	Real income_ per capita, (thousand soums)	Aver_ nom_ month_ salary, (thousand soums)
2025	1274.3	98184.0	8.9	58934	17557.8	3141.2
2026	1283.7	102192.9	8.9	61094	18274.9	3261.0
2027	1292.8	106201.8	8.9	63254	18992.0	3380.8
2028	1301.8	110210.7	9.0	65413	19709.1	3500.6
2029	1312.3	111865.4	9.1	66872	20426.2	3620.4

Source: Developed by the authors.

From the table data, it can be seen that, according to the results of a multi-factor forecast of the number of gangs in the economy of the Tashkent region, in 2029 the number of gangs in the economy of the region is expected to increase by 3.0 per cent compared to 2024, reaching 1,312.3 thousand people. Of course, such a positive result will be achieved by increasing the number of enterprises by 13.7 per cent, real per capita income by 15.1 per cent and average nominal monthly wages by 14.2 per cent, resulting in an increase in the regional gross regional product by 15.1 per cent, reaching 111,865.4 billion soums. Considering the unemployment rate presented in this table, the time-dependent change in the unemployment rate in Tashkent region is expected to be 9.1 per cent in 2029.

However, such an increase in the unemployment rate will negatively affect the efficient functioning of the labour market in the Tashkent region. In this regard, we have also conducted a multifactorial econometric analysis of the unemployment rate in our study. As determined by scenario 2 above,

$$Y = \frac{X5^{2.068} * e^{0.12}}{X3^{1.17} * X4^{0.5} * X6^{0.44}} \tag{4}$$

using the regression equation, the remaining factors are expressed in the following equations over time ($t = 24$):

Enterpris_units – $x_3 = 2784.8+2159.6^*t$;
Real income per capita – $x_4 = -1086.8+717.1^*t$;
Aver_nom_month_salary, (thousand soums) – $x_5 = 26{,}4+119{,}8^*t$;
In the economy, the GDP per capita – $x_6 = -3559.4 + 3217.2 * t$.

Table 87. Multifactorial forecast results of changes in the unemployment rate of Tashkent region under scenario 2

Years	Unemploy_ rate, %	Enterpris_ units	Real income_per capita, (thousand soums)	Aver_nom_ month_ salary, (thousand soums)	GNP_per_ capit_popul, (thousand soums)
2025	7.6	58934	17557.8	3141.2	80087.8
2026	7.3	61094	18274.9	3261.0	83305.0
2027	7.0	63254	18992.0	3380.8	86522.2
2028	6.8	65512	19253.1	3597.5	87022.1
2029	6.5	66987	20957.5	3607.8	87957.6

Source: Developed by the authors.

Using Scenario 2, the results of a multifactorial forecast of changes in the unemployment rate in the Tashkent region are determined (Table 87).

Considering the results of the multifactorial forecast of changes in the unemployment rate of the Tashkent region presented in the table, it should be noted that scientific studies have confirmed that not only in the regions, but also in developed countries, the unemployment rate can be reduced, if not completely eliminated. In our study, the inclusion of unemployment as a productive factor directly involves determining its importance in the labour market, which in turn is expected to reduce the unemployment rate in the region by 1.5 per cent by 2029 compared to 2024, which in turn will lead to an increase in the number of enterprises in the Tashkent region by 13.7 per cent compared to 2024, and real incomes per capita by The region's per capita gross regional product increased by 15.7 per cent, and the number of enterprises in the region reached 66,987, with real per capita income reaching 20,957.5 thousand soums and the per capita gross regional product reaching 87,957.6 thousand soums.

The creation of quality jobs in the Tashkent region is based on the further development of sectors and industries of the regional economy. As is known from world experience, the majority of quality jobs are created in industry. In the long term, the implementation of promising projects and measures in the metallurgy, mechanical engineering, building materials, light industry, food industry and pharmaceutical industries will create the basis for the creation of stable new jobs in the region and ensure a stable increase in employment levels in the future.

23.5. Conclusion

It can be noted that over the past five years, the share of people who are involved in child care and household chores in the family, as well as homemakers, military personnel and other individuals who are not involved in social work, has increased by almost 0.3 thousand people, while the share of the population has not changed. During the period under study, the number of labour resources increased by 7.3 per cent or almost 84.2 thousand people between 2010 and 2023, while the number of unemployed people increased by 8.1 thousand people. The following factors contributed to the almost twofold increase in the number of unemployed people registered with social protection agencies by 2023:

First, as a result of the state's active employment policy and the increase in the amount of pensions paid to the unemployed, the number of unemployed people who are not officially registered with the government will increase;

Second, the activity of vocational centres organised under these departments to shape the supply of qualified labour resources will increase;

Third, the development of information exchange on vacancies by segments of labour demand, which increases the interest of the unemployed population in obtaining suitable jobs. Social indicators that shape the supply of labour resources are inextricably linked with macroeconomic indicators that create demand for it. With the help of a statistical analysis of the demand for labour resources, the prospects for the republic's gross domestic product, the value of fixed assets in economic sectors and other indicators were determined. Based on the results of the study on the statistical study of labour market development in the region, the following practical conclusions and recommendations were developed. Their essence is mainly as follows:

1. As a result of the emergence of imbalances in the labour market of the Tashkent region, ensuring the employment of the working-age population, identifying the causes of socio-economic processes in the labour market, and analysing the parameters of demand and supply of labour resources in it by region are considered urgent issues.
2. When making management decisions related to regulating the labour market in the Tashkent region, it is necessary to determine the quantitative indicators of the demand and supply of labour resources by region, the competition between them using statistical methods and models, as well as analyse the parameters of this market within a separate region, its content, goals and objectives, methods and means. The formation of theoretical knowledge is of particular importance.
3. Important economic measures to be implemented in the Tashkent region to meet the increasing demand for labour resources and reduce unemployment, develop small business and private entrepreneurship by allocating loans from the Entrepreneurship Assistance Fund, hold job fairs, develop the activities of job placement centres, and provide timely pensions and financial assistance. and ensuring strong social protection will have a positive impact on raising the standard of living and well-being of the population.
4. The creation of a database that allows job seekers to obtain the necessary information, that is, the wider use of the database of new jobs by the regional population, which takes into account the formation of vacancies, will have a positive effect on reducing the unemployment rate.
5. As the population of the Tashkent region is endowed with national values, the development of home-based industry, national handicrafts, the development of the service sector and the development of effective forms of labour, such as livestock breeding, in personal, subsidiary and dekhkan farms, are of great importance.

Bibliography

Abdullah, M. A., Han, X., Amjad, M. A., & Makhmudov, S. (2025). Revisit the role of financial development on economic growth, human development, and sustainable development in higher-income countries. *Journal of Environmental Management*, *392*, 126874.

Akhmetshin, E., Abdullayev, I., Makhmudov, S., Dakhkilgova, K., Korotaeva, I. and Yanovskaya, G. (2025). APPLICATION OF TANH–COTH METHOD FOR COMBINED AND DOUBLE COMBINED SINH–COSH–GORDON EQUATIONS ARISING CHEMICAL REACTIONS TO WATER SURFACE GRAVITY WAVES. Computational Methods for Differential Equations, (), -. doi: 10.22034/cmde.2025.67655.3234

Akbarova, B. (2023). 'Empiric Analyzing For Net Revenues From Sales of Products By Small Business'. *Asian Journal of Technology & Management Research (AJTMR),* ISSN: 2249(0892).

Al Ubaidillah, M. R. S., and Yasin, M. (2024). 'Analisis Pengangguran dan Kebijakan Pemerintah Terhadap Perekonomian Indonesia'. *Jurnal Riset Ekonomi Dan Akuntansi*, 2 (3), 34–42. <https://doi.org/10.54066/jrea-itb.v2i3.2123>.

Habib, S. S., Islam, M. A., Ali, M. N., Benitez, I. B., Mamadiyarov, Z., Mirzayev, B., … & Flah, A. (2025). Multi-Objective Optimization and Feasibility Analysis of Integrated Biogas–Solar Energy Systems for Rural Electrification. *Results in Engineering*, 107086.

Isserman, A. M., Taylor, C., Gerking, S., and Schubert, U. (1987). Chapter 13: *Regional Labor Market Analysis*, Vol. 1, pp. 543–80. Elsevier, <https://doi.org/10.1016/S1574-0080(00)80016-4>.

Kalandarov, F., Makhmudov, S., Ibadullaev, D., Matniyozov, M., Nasretdinova, F., Sabirov, K., & Bahodirov, N. M. (2025). Low-Carbon Energy Risk and Renewable Energy Development: Insights from Method of Moments Quantile Regression. International Journal of Energy Economics and Policy, 15(3), 524–536.

Khayrilla Kurbonov, Samariddin Makhmudov, Shakhzod Erkinov, Umidjon Dadabaev, Gulnora Bekimbetova, Rukhiddin Zayniddinov, and Mirzabek Jonuzokov. 2025. Evaluating the Impact of Marketing Practices Digitalization and Investment on Labor Market Efficiency and Commercial Bank Performance Using Econometric Models. In Proceedings of the 8th International Conference on Future

Networks & Distributed Systems (ICFNDS '24). Association for Computing Machinery, New York, NY, USA, 786–796. https://doi.org/10.1145/3726122.3726237

Khodjaniyazov, N., Mirkhoshimova, M., Kalandarov, F., Matyokubova, D., Utegenova, S., Makhmudov, S., & Khudayberganov, M. (2025). Time-Varying Impacts of Financial Stress on Energy-Related Uncertainty. International Journal of Energy Economics and Policy, 15(3), 689–698.

Kuchkarov, T., Mamadiyarov, Z., Khakimov, Z., Sabirova, O., Matmurodov, K., Raimboyeva, M., & Umarova, S. (2025). Energy-Related Uncertainty and Crypto-Currency Environmental Attention: Time-Varying Perspective. International Journal of Energy Economics and Policy, 15(5), 614–626. https://doi.org/10.32479/ijeep.20784

Kuziboev, B., Ozturk, I., Kalandarov, F., Samandarov, O., Bekjanov, D., & Makhmudov, S. (2025). PROMOTING ENERGY SOURCES DIVERSIFICATION THROUGH ESG PERFORMANCE. Energy, 136009.

Lin, M.H., Matchanova, B., Nurmatovich, H.A. et al. Optimal Operation of the Multi-Carrier Energy System Considering Energy Markets and Renewable Energies Participation. *Int. J. Appl. Comput. Math* **11**, 170 (2025). https://doi.org/10.1007/s40819-025-02002-9

Litamahuputty, J. V., Amiruddin, E. G., Rahim, R., Rahman, A., & Mamadiyarov, Z. (2025). Cryptocurrency Risk Management through Decision Engineering: Evaluating XRPUSD and ADAUSD Portfolio Performance. Journal of Applied Science, Engineering, Technology, and Education, 7(1), 69–81. https://doi.org/10.35877/454RI.asci3871

Mamadiyarov, Z., Eshov, M., Otakhonova, D., Utegenova, S., Sabirov, K., Marks, A., & Bahodirov, N. (2025). Does Energy Policy Risk Threaten Energy Sources Diversification?. *International Journal of Energy Economics and Policy, 15*(5), 730–740. https://doi.org/10.32479/ijeep.21140

Mamadiyarov, Z. Makhmudov, S. Utanov, B. Kasimova, D. Bekmurodova, G. Hakimov, Z. (2025). Fusion of Economic and Financial Factors Affecting Household Deposits in Banks: An Econometric Analysis. Fusion: Practice and Applications, (), 82–91. DOI: https://doi.org/10.54216/FPA.190206

Mamadiyarov, Z., Saidov, O., Abdurazakova, N., Makhmudov, S., Nazarov, M., Rajabova, N., … Ruzmetova, I. (2025). Energy-Related Uncertainty and Tourism Stock Markets: New Insights from Time-Varying

Relationship with TVP- VAR Approach. *International Journal of Energy Economics and Policy*, *15*(4), 730–737. https://doi.org/10.32479/ijeep.20480

Mamani, J.C.M., Miri, M., Vorobev, Y. et al. Optimal Operation of Energy Microgrid Considering Economic and Emission Indices. Oper. Res. Forum 6, 122 (2025). https://doi.org/10.1007/s43069-025-00523-z

Миролимов, М., and Розикова, Г. (2025). СТАТИСТИЧЕСКИЙ АНАЛИЗ ВЛИЯНИЯ РАЗВИТИЯ ИНФОРМАЦИОННЫХ ТЕХНОЛОГИЙ НА РЫНОК ТРУДА ТАШКЕНТСКОЙ ОБЛАСТИ. *Экономическое развитие и анализ*, 3(1), 353–61.

Muhammad Zubair, Irfanud Din, Nadeem Sarwar et al. Revolutionizing Sepsis Diagnosis Using Machine Learning and Deep Learning Models: A Systematic Literature Review, 10 June 2025, PREPRINT (Version 1) available at Research Square [https://doi.org/10.21203/rs.3.rs-6731418/v1]

Ngongo, M., Herman, H., Ndandara, A., Jois Jaha, D. A., Peku Djawang, J. U. S., Tanggu Rame, M. M., Khamraeva, S. N., & Mamadiyarov, Z. (2025). An Investigation of Meaning, Toponymy of Sumba Cultural Site's Names, and the Impact of Tourism Visitors on Surrounding Society. *Forum for Linguistic Studies*, 7(8), 679–693. https://doi.org/10.30564/fls.v7i8.10260

PANJAITAN, M. B., HAMDANAH, H., SIRAIT, J., SUTIKNO, S., FATMAWATI, E., HERMAN, H., & MAMADIYAROV, Z. (2025). THE ROLE OF EMOTIONAL REGULATION IN SHAPING STUDENTS' PERCEPTION OF PHYSICS PROBLEMSOLVING TASKS. TPM – Testing, Psychometrics, Methodology in Applied Psychology, 32(S2(2025) : Posted 09 June), 1–10. Retrieved from https://tpmap.org/submission/index.php/tpm/article/view/139

Pradhan, R., Hajiyev, E., Shichiyakh, R. et al. Optimal Techno-Economic Feasibility of an Off-Grid Microgrid System Using Load Flow Energy Management Strategies. *Oper. Res. Forum* **6**, 120 (2025). https://doi.org/10.1007/s43069-025-00524-y

Rayala, R. V., Borra, C. R., Vasudevan, V., Singhania, R., Cheekati, S., & Mamadiyarov, Z. (2025, July). Lightweight Deep Learning Framework for Human Activity Recognition: A MobileNet-LSTM Approach with WHOA Optimization. In *2025 International Conference on Innovations in Intelligent Systems: Advancements in Computing, Communication, and Cybersecurity (ISAC3)* (pp. 1–6). IEEE.

Rayala, R. V., Sandhya, N., Singhania, R., Cheekati, S., Borra, C. R., Vasudevan, V., & Mamadiyarov, Z. (2025, July). AI-Driven Tomato Quality Assessment: A Deep Learning Approach for Image-based Defect Detection and Classification. In *2025 International Conference on Innovations in Intelligent Systems: Advancements in Computing, Communication, and Cybersecurity (ISAC3)* (pp. 1–6). IEEE.

Romero, R. M., Zelinskaya, M., Makhmudov, S., Sapaev, S., & Rustambekovich, J. U. (2025, September). Modelling and Optimal Utilisation of the Renewable Energy Systems in Microgrid with Improving Reliability and Energy Efficiency. In Operations Research Forum (Vol. 6, No. 3, pp. 1–20). Springer International Publishing.

Rony, Z. T., Jefri, R., Rusmardiana, A., Pramono, S. A., & Mamadiyarov, Z. (2025). Downside Risk Measurement of Indonesian Financial and Energy Securities: A Value at Risk Perspective. *Journal of Applied Science, Engineering, Technology, and Education*, 7(2). https://doi.org/10.35877/454RI.asci3898

Rukhiddin Zayniddinov, Nodir Jumaev, Gulbakhor Irgasheva, Alam Asadov, Nosir Makhmudov, Sirojiddin Abrorov, and Samariddin Makhmudov. 2025. The Influence of the Digital Economy on Economic Development Evidence from Uzbekistan. In Proceedings of the 8th International Conference on Future Networks & Distributed Systems (ICFNDS '24). Association for Computing Machinery, New York, NY, USA, 831–839. https://doi.org/10.1145/3726122.3726242

Samariddin Makhmudov, Malika Umarova, Khayrilla Kurbonov, Laylo Akbarova, Durdona Davletova, Nilufar Shanazarova, and Toshmurod Kulmanov. 2025. Evaluating the forecast indicators of the volume of highly liquid assets of commercial banks in the process of digital transformation. In Proceedings of the 8th International Conference on Future Networks & Distributed Systems (ICFNDS '24). Association for Computing Machinery, New York, NY, USA, 698–704. https://doi.org/10.1145/3726122.3726222

Samariddin Makhmudov, Kudratillo Tukhsanov, Saifulla Arslanbekov, Akram Amanov, Orifali Tursunov, Umarbek Jabbarov and Muyassarxon Mirzakarimova. 2024. Optimizing Supply Chain Financing Development Prospects of Digital Ecosystems in the European Logistics Industry. In The 8th International Conference on Future Networks & Distributed Systems (ICFNDS '24), December 11–12, 2024,

Marakech, Morocco. ACM, New York, NY, USA, 12 Pages. https://doi.org/10.1145/3726122.3726200

Singagerda, F. S., Pratama, M. R., Alfairus, M. Q., Iskandar, A., & Mamadiyarov, Z. (2025). A Decision-Centric Approach to Risk Management in Aviation Stock Investments Using Value at Risk and Portfolio Optimization. *Journal of Applied Science, Engineering, Technology, and Education*, 7(1), 114–125. https://doi.org/10.35877/454RI.asci3870

Sofyanty, D., Romadhoni, R., Handriadi, H., Makhsudovna, I. S., Anwar, Z., & Mamadiyarov, Z. (2025). Strategic Decision Analysis for Investment Portfolios: Computational Risk Assessment in Transportation Asset Management. *Journal of Applied Science, Engineering, Technology, and Education*, 7(2). https://doi.org/10.35877/454RI.asci3897

Тарасова, Н. (2000). 'Трудовые отношения в условиях глобализации и технологической революции (опыт стран Запада)'. *Общество и экономика*, 1, 67.

Toshmurod Kulmanov, Umidjon Dadabaev, Mansurbek Qulmetov, Aliboy Ulashov, Mirjalol Eshboyev, and Samariddin Makhmudov. 2025. Global Services Market Transformation Digitalization Export Trends and Future Forecasts. In Proceedings of the 8th International Conference on Future Networks & Distributed Systems (ICFNDS '24). Association for Computing Machinery, New York, NY, USA, 851–858. https://doi.org/10.1145/3726122.3726245

Zhang, L., Zhao, Z., Qamri, G. M., & Makhmudov, S. (2025). Unleashing the critical role of renewable energy through global value chains and digitalization: A path towards environmental sustainability. *Journal of Environmental Management*, *392*, 126688.

Zokir Toshtemirovich Mamadiyarov, Samandarboy Adhambek ugli Sulaymanov, Sarvar Anvar ugli Askarov, and Durdona Bakhtiyor kizi Uktamova. 2022. Impact of Covid-19 Pandemic on Accelerating The Digitization and Transformation of Banks. In Proceedings of the 5th International Conference on Future Networks and Distributed Systems (ICFNDS '21). Association for Computing Machinery, New York, NY, USA, 706–712. https://doi.org/10.1145/3508072.3508211

<https://stat.uz/uz/> – Official Website of the National Statistics Committee of the Republic of Uzbekistan.

Analysis of the Importance of Small Businesses in Ensuring Employment in Uzbekistan

Zokir Mamadiyarov, Samariddin Makhmudov, Kalonov Mukhiddin, Toshmurod Kulmanov, Nargiza Nosirova, Rustam Yakhshiboyev and Malaxat Saipova

24.1. Introduction

In a market economy, job creation and the creation of new employment are one of the key functions of national economic policy. From this perspective, small business enterprises are a significant factor in increasing employment. Not only as an adaptive sector of the economy, but also as a strategic sector, small entrepreneurship plays a crucial role in the participation of broad strata of the population in economic activity, the effective utilisation of labour resources, and the promotion of socioeconomic stability.

In recent years, a series of reforms have been carried out in Uzbekistan with the goal of developing the function of small businesses in the country's economy. In particular, steps have been taken to make the business environment friendly, expand access to credit, and establish tax deductions. As a result of these measures, small businesses have not only become an important driver of economic growth but also a leading mechanism for supporting employment across the country.

Private enterprise and entrepreneurship are particularly crucial in achieving economic freedom and national development (Hatab & Lagerkvist, 2024). Nonetheless, a number of factors still hinder greater labour productivity under current market conditions (Ariza-Garzón et al., 2024). In response to meeting the growing social needs of the populace and offering quality public services such as education and healthcare, additional state expenditure is recommended.

The importance of this research is the necessity to evaluate not only the economic effect of small business operations but also their role and potential in addressing the problem of labour. Demographic characteristics of Uzbekistan – particularly its youthfulness and abundant human labour resources – make the creation of small entrepreneurship an acute component of the country's socio-economic policy.

This work analyses the economic and social features of small business companies in providing employment in Uzbekistan. The research aims to estimate the impact of small business on employment, identify existing problems, and create practical policy recommendations to overcome them.

Thus, the current research not only has theoretical significance but also practical relevance, as it contributes to the development of strategic means of implementing small businesses' efforts to increase Uzbekistan's level of employment.

24.2. Literature Review

Addressing demographic challenges remains one of the most pressing issues for every national economy. As such, economists, policymakers, and sociologists continue to conduct research in this area on an ongoing basis.

Employment plays a critical role in reducing poverty within the population. In this regard, to decrease poverty and increase employment levels, it is considered appropriate for Uzbekistan to make greater use of self-employment models such as home-based work, freelancing, and outsourcing (Bahadir et al., 2024). Government regulation of employment serves as a core instrument in managing the labour market. The primary objective of such regulation is to boost demand for labour while supporting an efficient supply of workforce in the market.

Government programmes and legal frameworks targeting employment must fully consider factors such as population growth, demographic 'waves', shifts in age groups, and other variables to effectively improve employment levels (Boeing-Reicher & Caponi, 2024). Moreover, regular monitoring is essential to ensure the effectiveness of these reforms (Budović et al., 2025).

Small business, as one of the main engines of the modern economy and a symbol of entrepreneurship, fosters innovation, development, economic growth, income generation and distribution, as well as employment. During periods of economic transition, small businesses have proven to be adaptable and competitive, capable of meeting essential needs and finding their place in the market (Cann et al., 2025.

In Uzbekistan's increasingly digitalised socio-economic environment, employment-related challenges can be addressed through new forms of work – particularly remote employment. This modern approach to employment is often referred to by various terms such as online work, telecommuting, or freelancing (from the English word freelance, meaning 'independent artist', off-staff worker, or self-employed professional) (Foguesatto et al., 2024).

The World Bank has emphasised the need to revise education and training programmes to better align with the demands of the modern labour market. In particular, developing digital skills has become increasingly important (Gannon et al., 2025).

One of the key strategies for poverty reduction is to implement market mechanisms and reduce state control in the agricultural sector. Employment in this sector has a significant potential to reduce poverty and inequality, especially given that nearly 80 per cent of Uzbekistan's poor live in rural areas and rely on agriculture for income (Heino et al., 2024). Therefore, increasing the number of small business entities in agriculture is essential.

Small business enterprises play a significant role in providing employment. However, research has identified a correlation between employment in small businesses and the incidence of workplace accidents (Hmaddi et al., 2025), suggesting that greater attention should be paid to occupational safety when addressing employment through small enterprises. Enhancing the contribution of small businesses to employment also requires increasing the level of innovation within these entities (Kim, 2023).

Family entrepreneurship, which forms a part of small business and private enterprise, also plays an important role in job creation. Family run firms, despite facing financial pressure, are often reluctant to lay off their employees (Littlejohn, 2025).

Both developing and developed countries continuously analyse trends in unemployment, employment, expected employment, and expected unemployment in order to ensure the social well-being of their populations (Nakamura, 2024).

Through the development of small businesses, along with providing employment in countries, a number of economic and social indicators such as the standard of living, living conditions, economic status, and level of education of the population improve (Roša et al., 2025). Therefore, countries should pay special attention to small businesses in their macroeconomic policies (Sharifiasl et al., 2024).

24.3. Research Methodology

This study utilises the Autoregressive Integrated Moving Average (ARIMA) model to analyse the pattern of employment in small businesses in Uzbekistan. The ARIMA model, introduced by Box and Jenkins (1976), is particularly well-adapted to model and forecast univariate time series data that are temporally dependent and non-stationary (Lin et al., 2025; Litamahuputty et al., 2025; Mamadiyarov et al., 2025; Mamani et al., 2025; Pradhan et al., 2025; Rayala et al., 2025; Samariddin et al., 2025).

Analyses and forecasts were conducted using multivariate linear regression (LS), ARDL, ARIMA and various other econometric models on the global services market, digital economy, energy-related financial stress, cocktail market, digital transformation, factors affecting the logistics industry (Kalandarov et al., 2025; Khayrilla et al., 2025; Khodjaniyazov et al., 2025; Kuziboev et al., 2025; Mamadiyarov et al., 2025; Rayala et al., 2025; Rony et al., 2025; Rukhiddin et al., 2025; Samariddin et al., 2025).

Another group of economists has successfully used econometric models such as Fixed Effects Estimator, Random Effects Estimator, multivariate linear (LS), and ARDL in their research on investment in digital infrastructure, various aspects of digital payment systems, the impact of inflation and credit interest rates on investment, factors affecting the reduction of the state's share in commercial banks, Non-Performing Loans in commercial banks, the digitisation of banks, risks in digital services, and the development of retail payment services (Abdullah et al., 2025; Akhmetshin et al., 2025; Habib et al., 2025; Jahrir et al., 2025; Romero et al., 2025; Singagerda et al., 2025; Sofyanty et al., 2025; Toshmurod et al., 2025; Zhang et al., 2025; Zokir et al., 2021).

24.3.1. Model Structure

The general form of the ARIMA model is given as ARIMA(p, d, q), where:

p is the AR order of the autoregressive component,
d is the differencing required to make the series stationary,
q is the moving average order (MA) component.

The three components on which the ARIMA model is built are:

Autoregressive (AR), Integration (I), and Moving Average (MA). The model combined is mathematically represented as:

The methodology section of a research article delineates the systematic process undertaken to answer the research questions or test the hypotheses. It includes the overall research design, data collection, and analytical techniques, ensuring replicability and reliability of the study.

$$\phi(L)(1-L)^d y_t = \theta(L)\varepsilon_t$$

Where:

t stands for time – it is the time index of our observations
y_t is the original time series,
L is the lag operator ($Ly_t = y_t{-}1$),
$\phi(L) = 1 - \phi_1 L - \phi_2 L^2 - \ldots - \phi_p L^p$ is the AR, $\theta(L) = 1 + \theta_1 L + \theta_2 L^? + \ldots + \theta_q L^q$ is the MA,
ε_t is a white noise error term.

24.3.2. Stationarity and differencing

Before applying the ARIMA model, the stationarity of the time series is examined using the Augmented Dickey-Fuller (ADF) test. A time series is considered stationary if its mean and variance are constant over time. If the series is non-stationary, it is differenced d times until stationarity is achieved. The differenced series is:

$$\Delta^d y_t = (1-L)^d y_t$$

Where Δ^d is the differencing operator applied d times.

24.3.3. Model identification

Orders p and q are identified by using autocorrelation function (ACF) and partial autocorrelation function (PACF) plots:

ACF helps to decide the value for q,
PACF helps to select the value for p.

Model selection is also facilitated by minimising information criteria such as the Akaike Information Criterion (AIC):

$$AIC = -2\ln\left(\hat{L}\right) + 2k$$

Where is the probability of the estimated model, and k is the number of estimated parameters.

24.3.4. Model estimation

The model is then estimated with maximum likelihood estimation (MLE), after determining the orders. The aim is to obtain parameters Φi and ϑj that optimise the likelihood of observing the observed series.

24.3.5. Diagnostic checking

To check the adequacy of the fitted model, the residuals are tested using diagnostic tests:

Ljung-Box Q Test is used to check for autocorrelation of residuals:

$$Q = n\left(n+2\right)\sum_{k=1}^{h}\frac{\hat{p}_k^2}{n-k}$$

Where:

n is sample size,
h is the number of lags,
$\hat{p}_k$ is the autocorrelation at lag k.

If the p-value is large (say > 0.05), then it means that the residuals are uncorrelated and the model is correctly specified.

Residuals are also examined for normality.

24.3.6. Forecasting

Estimated ARIMA model is used to forecast future values of employment in small firms. Forecast accuracy is measured in terms of:

Mean Absolute Error (MAE):

$$MAE = \frac{1}{n}\sum_{t=1}^{n}\left|y_t - \hat{y}_t\right|$$

Root Mean Squared Error (RMSE):

$$MSE = \sqrt{\frac{1}{n}\sum_{t=1}^{n}\left(y_t - \hat{y}_t\right)^2}$$

where y_t is actual value and $\hat{y}\_t$ is predicted value at time t.

Through this systematic approach, the ARIMA model provides a strict framework for the analysis of small business employment temporal behaviour. It not only provides insight into past dynamics but also a statistical foundation for short-term accurate prediction and evidence-based policy recommendations.

24.4. Analysis and Results

We analysed the data we collected using the ARIMA model and obtained forecast results for the expected years. We checked each result of the model through diagnostic tests and presented the results sequentially.

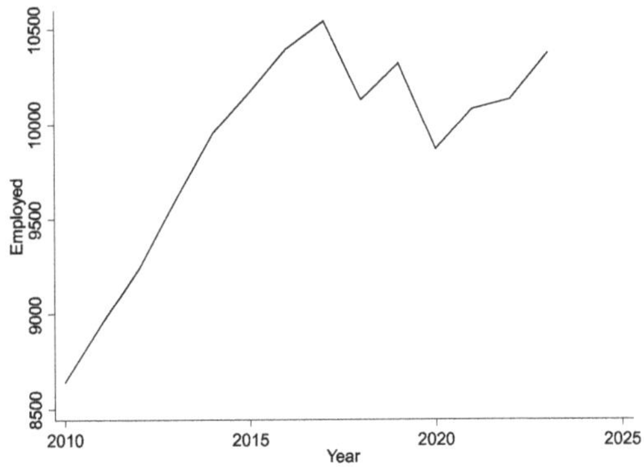

Figure 83. Dynamics of the number of employees in a small business entity.
Source: It was developed by the authors based on Stata software.

Figure 83 shows the growth of the number of people employed in small businesses and entrepreneurship in Uzbekistan, with some years of decline and increase. Especially during the COVID-19 pandemic, we can see that the number of people employed in small businesses and entrepreneurship has fallen sharply. In the years after 2020, the number of people employed in small businesses and entrepreneurship has been increasing again.

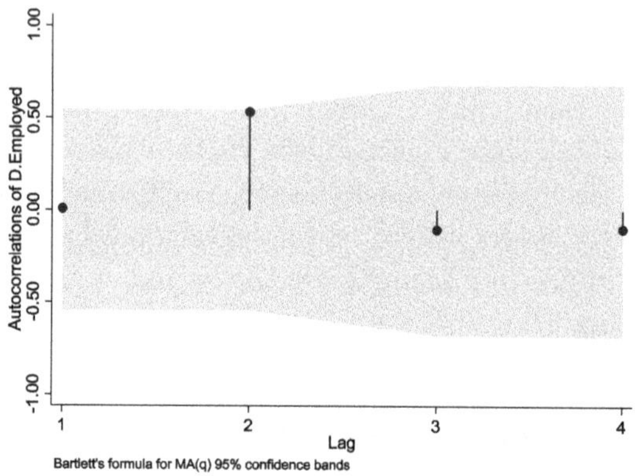

Figure 84. An autocorrelation function (ACF) plot of the first-differenced variable.
Source: It was developed by the authors based on Stata software.

The number of lags is indicated by the X-axis (Lags).

The autocorrelation coefficient at each lag is displayed on the *Y*-axis (Autocorrelations of D.Employed).

Vertical lines and blue dots: Show the approximate 95 per cent confidence intervals for the autocorrelation values.

Bartlett's 95 per cent confidence bands for MA(*q*) processes are shown in the grey shaded area. At the 5 per cent level, any autocorrelation value outside of this shaded area is statistically significant.

Lag1 and 4: The autocorrelations are not statistically significant because they fall inside the confidence intervals.

Lag2: The autocorrelation may be borderline significant because it barely touches the upper bound of the confidence band.

Lag3: Not significant, obviously inside the confidence interval.

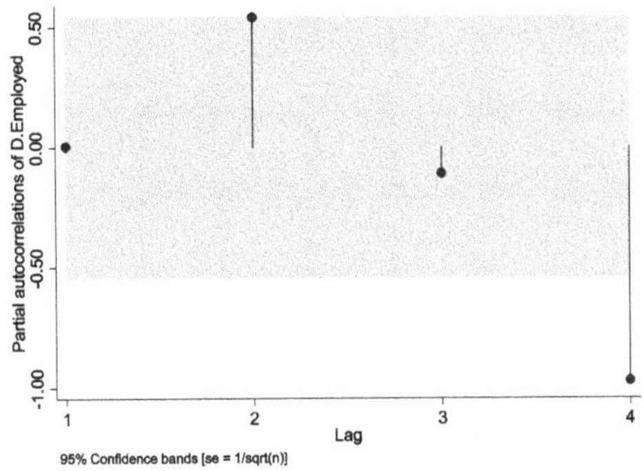

Figure 85. Partial Autocorrelation Function (PACF) plot for the first-differenced variable.
Source: It was developed by the authors based on Stata software.

Lag 1's Partial autocorrelation is barely affected; close to 0 within the 95 per cent confidence interval.
Lag2: The PACF brushes against the upper limit of the confidence interval. That could be a bit important.
Lag3: Not much, but well within the band.
Lag4: Shows extremely negative partial autocorrelation at lag 4, swiftly dropping to about –1, outside the confidence interval.

What does this imply?

These graphs assist the identification of the appropriate ARIMA(p,d,q) model in view of the fact that the series under consideration is a differenced series.

The AR(p) order is generally determined by the PACF plot; for an AR(p)-model fit in which only lag 4 is significant, this would indicate an AR(4) consideration.

However, consideration must be given to both the ACF and PACF as well as examining the residual diagnostics and goodness-of-fit criteria (AIC, BIC).

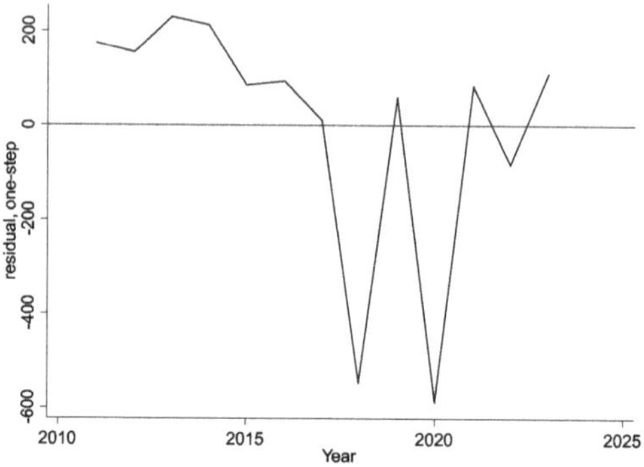

Figure 86. The residuals from a one-step ahead forecast of ARIMA(1,1,2) model.
Source: It was developed by the authors based on Stata software.

Analysis of the Residual Plot:

Y-axis: Residuals, one-step: This is the deviation of the actual values from the predicted (one-step-ahead) values. *X*-axis: Year: From 2010 to 2024. The red line at 0: This line indicates zero prediction error-the less the residuals stray from this line, the better the model is fitting the data. Pre-2017 – Residuals are fairly small and slightly positive-which indicates a good model prediction for those years. 2017–2021: Large negative residuals were present, particularly in 2019 and 2020, indicating under-prediction – the actual values were much lower than anticipated. After 2021: The residuals once again began to fluctuate more positively.

Based on the enormous fluctuations from 2017 to 2021, this seems indicative of an eventual model misspecification or a structural change in the data (for instance, external shocks like COVID-19). These residuals should behave like white noise (random, mean ≈0 and patternless). The displayed residuals seem to lack random patternness.

Test for white noise with particular reference to Portmanteau

Portmanteau (Q) statistic = 5.4147

Prob > chi2(4) = 0.2473

After estimation, the ARIMA model was subjected to Portmanteau (Ljung-Box) testing to ascertain whether there was any autocorrelation in the residuals. The following *Q*-statistic value of 5.4147 based on 4 degrees of freedom is obtained at a *p*-value of 0.2473.

The *p*-value is greater than the widely accepted level of significance (0.05) hence the null hypotheses that the residuals are white noise cannot be rejected. This shows that there is no autocorrelation in the residuals up to the forth lag which is considered statistically significant. In other words, the residuals behaved like white noise implying that the ARIMA model has captured all significant underlying structure of the time series.

Hence, the diagnostic results can be construed as evidence of appropriate model specification, without relevant time-dependent patterns being excluded into the bargain.

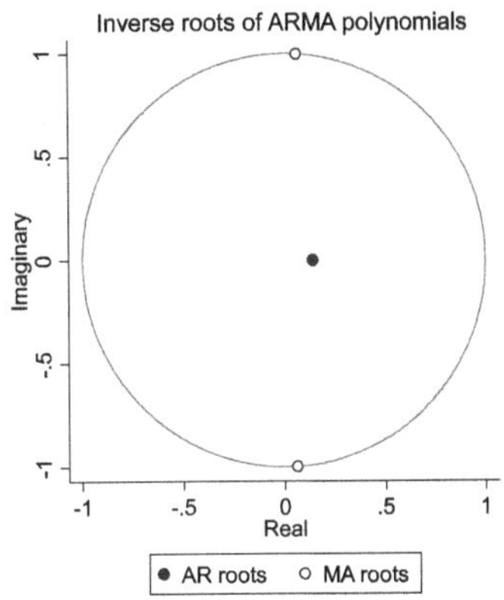

Figure 87. The inverse roots of both AR and MA polynomials for an ARIMA(1,1,2) model.
Source: It was developed by the authors based on Stata software.

These correspond to the moving average (MA) component. There are two MA roots shown, and they lie exactly on the unit circle, vertically aligned (real = 0, imag = ±1). The MA part is borderline invertible. For strict invertibility, MA roots should be outside the unit circle.

Table 88. Analysis of the orecasted employment in small businesses in Uzbekistan (2024–2028) based on an ARIMA(1,1,2) model

№	Year	Forecast of the number of people employed in small businesses (thousand people)
1	2024	10507.24
2	2025	10640.42
3	2026	10773.6
4	2027	10906.78
5	2028	11039.96

Source: It was developed by the authors based on Stata software.

This forecast presents projected figures for the number of individuals employed in small businesses in Uzbekistan over the period 2024–2028. The projections are derived from an ARIMA(1,1,2) model – a commonly used time series forecasting technique that accounts for trends, autoregressive relationships, and short-term irregularities (Table 88).

24.5. Findings and Discussion

An estimate projects an increase in the number of employees working in the small business sector from 10,507.24 thousand people in the year 2024 to 11,039.96 thousand by 2028. Thus, in total, by 2028 the rise will be around 532.72 thousand people over five years.

Again, the year-on-year increase remains nearly consistent. Therefore, a continuing upward tendency in terms of time can be inferred. For example, in the forecast, there would be an increase that would lie somewhere around 133–134 thousand people a year. Sustained growth of this kind probably speaks of the business environment being healthy and favourable conditions for entrepreneurship, besides likely being structural changes in the labour markets favouring small enterprise development.

24.6. Conclusion

It was confirmed that this study projected the employment trends in the sector of small businesses for Uzbekistan with an application of the ARIMA(1,1,2)

model to project employment from 2024 to 2028. The overall picture of these projections indicates a rather straight increase in the number of people working in small businesses in the country from 10.5 million in 2024 to more than 11 million in 2028. Approximately 133–134 thousand human annual increments are reflected in the direction of this growth because of the paradigm that small enterprises have formed and will continue to form in this evolving economy of the country.

Short-term variability in employment is explained by structural long-term trends. The need for first differencing in the ARIMA model indicates that the employment series is inherently dynamic and influenced by ongoing changes in the economic environment.

To this end, making it more likely that employment will be like this will be influenced not just by long-standing trends but also respond to the most recent developments through changes in policies and financial conditions as well as entrepreneurship behaviour.

Policy-wise, these findings thus inspire a conservative bullish optimism. Although this increase was modest, it was a stable and sustainable increase – the small business dynamic would appear to be paying dividends for the strategic thrust of Uzbekistan. Continued and adaptive support will keep this trajectory well forward. Structural constraints on easy access to finance, regulatory time wastage, and mismatch of skills will have to be dealt with by policymakers along with strengthening institutional support, extending digital infrastructure, and improving education in entrepreneurship.

In brief, it can be said that small business enterprises remain an important engine of employment in Uzbekistan. The projected trends will be a strong basis on which further development, both economically and socially, could be built. The strategic nurturing of small businesses would be imperative towards inclusive and sustained development for Uzbekistan on its path of economic reform and modernisation.

Bibliography

Abdullah, M. A., Han, X., Amjad, M. A., & Makhmudov, S. (2025). Revisit the role of financial development on economic growth, human development, and sustainable development in higher-income countries. *Journal of Environmental Management*, *392*, 126874.

Akhmetshin, E., Abdullayev, I., Makhmudov, S., Dakhkilgova, K., Korotaeva, I. and Yanovskaya, G. (2025). APPLICATION OF TANH–COTH METHOD FOR COMBINED AND DOUBLE COMBINED SINH–COSH–GORDON EQUATIONS ARISING CHEMICAL REACTIONS TO WATER SURFACE GRAVITY WAVES. Computational Methods for Differential Equations, (), -. doi: 10.22034/cmde.2025.67655.3234

Ariza-Garzón, M. J., Arroyo, J., Segovia-Vargas, M. J., and Caparrini, A. (2024). 'Profit-Sensitive Machine Learning Classification with Explanations in Credit Risk: The Case of Small Businesses in Peer-to-Peer Lending'. *Electronic Commerce Research and Applications*, 67, 101428.

Bahadir, B., Gumus, I., and Schaffer, M. (2024). 'Does Relaxing Household Credit Constraints Hurt Small Business Lending? Evidence from a Policy Change in Texas'. *Journal of Corporate Finance*, 89, 102682.

Boeing-Reicher, C. A., and Caponi, V. (2024). 'Public Wages, Public Employment, and Business Cycle Volatility: Evidence from US Metro Areas'. *Review of Economic Dynamics*, 54, 101232.

Budović, A., Jocić, N., and Méndez-Ortega, C. (2025). 'Territorialising Globalisation in a Post-socialist City: Differences in Employment Location Patterns between Foreign and Domestic KIBS'. *Cities*, 158, 105700.

Cann, K., Leichenko, R., Solecki, W., Madajewicz, M., Clemens, M., Howell, N., … and Herb, J. (2025). 'Business as Usual? Small Business Responses to Compound Disasters in Coastal New York City and New Jersey'. *International Journal of Disaster Risk Reduction*, 105288.

Foguesatto, C. R., Frare, A. B., Wegner, D., Mitregra, M., and Rodrigues, R. A. B. (2024). 'You Will Never Stand Alone: The Role of Inter-organizational Collaboration and Technological Turbulence in Shaping Small Business' Digital Maturity'. *The Journal of High Technology Management Research*, 35 (2), 100518.

Gannon, K. E., Eskander, S. M., Avila-Uribe, A., Castellano, E., Diop, M., and Agol, D. (2025). 'The Role of Gender in Firm-level Climate Change Adaptation Behaviour: Insights from Small Businesses in Senegal and Kenya'. *Climate Risk Management*, 48, 100699.

Habib, S. S., Islam, M. A., Ali, M. N., Benitez, I. B., Mamadiyarov, Z., Mirzayev, B., … & Flah, A. (2025). Multi-Objective Optimization and

Feasibility Analysis of Integrated Biogas–Solar Energy Systems for Rural Electrification. *Results in Engineering*, 107086.

Hatab, A. A., and Lagerkvist, C. J. (2024). 'Perceived Business Risks and Observed Impacts of the Russian-Ukraine War Among Small- and Medium-sized Agri-food Value Chain Enterprises in Egypt'. *Food Policy*, 127, 102712.

Heino, N., Alimov, N., and Tuominen, P. (2024). 'Family Firm Employment Behavior During a Financial Crisis: Does Generational Stage Matter?' *Journal of Family Business Strategy*, 15 (3), 100624.

Hmaddi, O., Lanahan, L., and Murray, A. (2025). 'Tracing Entrepreneurial Spillovers: Evidence from the US State Small Business Credit Initiative and Kickstarter'. Research Policy, 54 (4), 105197.

Jahrir, A., Gultom, Y., Herman, H., Zabadi, F., Ngongo, M., Mamadiyarov, Z., Fatmawati, E., & Saputra, N. (2025). Investigating the Elements of Short Commercial Mineral Water Advertisement: A Case on Discourse Analysis. Studies in Media and Communication, 13(4), 94–104. doi: http://dx.doi.org/10.11114/smc.v13i4.7813

Kalandarov, F., Makhmudov, S., Ibadullaev, D., Matniyozov, M., Nasretdinova, F., Sabirov, K., & Bahodirov, N. M. (2025). Low-Carbon Energy Risk and Renewable Energy Development: Insights from Method of Moments Quantile Regression. International Journal of Energy Economics and Policy, 15(3), 524–536.

Kim, M. J. (2023). 'Impact of the Community Reinvestment Act on Small Business Rmployment in Lower Income Neighborhoods'. *Regional Science and Urban Economics*, 98, 103837.

Khayrilla Kurbonov, Samariddin Makhmudov, Shakhzod Erkinov, Umidjon Dadabaev, Gulnora Bekimbetova, Rukhiddin Zayniddinov, and Mirzabek Jonuzokov. 2025. Evaluating the Impact of Marketing Practices Digitalization and Investment on Labor Market Efficiency and Commercial Bank Performance Using Econometric Models. In Proceedings of the 8th International Conference on Future Networks & Distributed Systems (ICFNDS '24). Association for Computing Machinery, New York, NY, USA, 786–796. https://doi.org/10.1145/3726122.3726237

Khodjaniyazov, N., Mirkhoshimova, M., Kalandarov, F., Matyokubova, D., Utegenova, S., Makhmudov, S., & Khudayberganov, M. (2025).

Time-Varying Impacts of Financial Stress on Energy-Related Uncertainty. International Journal of Energy Economics and Policy, 15(3), 689–698.

Kuchkarov, T., Mamadiyarov, Z., Khakimov, Z., Sabirova, O., Matmurodov, K., Raimboyeva, M., & Umarova, S. (2025). Energy-Related Uncertainty and Crypto-Currency Environmental Attention: Time-Varying Perspective. International Journal of Energy Economics and Policy, 15(5), 614–626. https://doi.org/10.32479/ijeep.20784

Kuziboev, B., Ozturk, I., Kalandarov, F., Samandarov, O., Bekjanov, D., & Makhmudov, S. (2025). PROMOTING ENERGY SOURCES DIVERSIFICATION THROUGH ESG PERFORMANCE. Energy, 136009.

Lin, M.H., Matchanova, B., Nurmatovich, H.A. et al. Optimal Operation of the Multi-Carrier Energy System Considering Energy Markets and Renewable Energies Participation. *Int. J. Appl. Comput. Math* **11**, 170 (2025). https://doi.org/10.1007/s40819-025-02002-9

Litamahuputty, J. V., Amiruddin, E. G., Rahim, R., Rahman, A., & Mamadiyarov, Z. (2025). Cryptocurrency Risk Management through Decision Engineering: Evaluating XRPUSD and ADAUSD Portfolio Performance. Journal of Applied Science, Engineering, Technology, and Education, 7(1), 69–81. https://doi.org/10.35877/454RI.asci3871

Littlejohn, M. (2025). 'The Credit Card and Small Business Lending Channels of Monetary Policy'. *Journal of Economic Dynamics and Control*, 171, 105045.

Mamadiyarov, Z., Eshov, M., Otakhonova, D., Utegenova, S., Sabirov, K., Marks, A., & Bahodirov, N. (2025). Does Energy Policy Risk Threaten Energy Sources Diversification?. *International Journal of Energy Economics and Policy, 15*(5), 730–740. https://doi.org/10.32479/ijeep.21140

Mamadiyarov, Z. Makhmudov, S. Utanov, B. Kasimova, D. Bekmurodova, G. Hakimov, Z. (2025). Fusion of Economic and Financial Factors Affecting Household Deposits in Banks: An Econometric Analysis. Fusion: Practice and Applications, (), 82–91. DOI: https://doi.org/10.54216/FPA.190206

Mamadiyarov, Z., Saidov, O., Abdurazakova, N., Makhmudov, S., Nazarov, M., Rajabova, N., … Ruzmetova, I. (2025). Energy-Related Uncertainty and Tourism Stock Markets: New Insights from Time-Varying

Relationship with TVP- VAR Approach. *International Journal of Energy Economics and Policy*, *15*(4), 730–737. https://doi.org/10.32479/ijeep.20480

Mamani, J.C.M., Miri, M., Vorobev, Y. et al. Optimal Operation of Energy Microgrid Considering Economic and Emission Indices. Oper. Res. Forum 6, 122 (2025). https://doi.org/10.1007/s43069-025-00523-z

Muhammad Zubair, Irfanud Din, Nadeem Sarwar et al. Revolutionizing Sepsis Diagnosis Using Machine Learning and Deep Learning Models: A Systematic Literature Review, 10 June 2025, PREPRINT (Version 1) available at Research Square [https://doi.org/10.21203/rs.3.rs-6731418/v1]

Nakamura, D. (2024). 'Is Part-time Employment an Adjusting Valve?: Business Cycle Analysis on the Labor Market in Japan by Dual Search and Matching Model'. *Japan and the World Economy*, 101270.

Ngongo, M., Herman, H., Ndandara, A., Jois Jaha, D. A., Peku Djawang, J. U. S., Tanggu Rame, M. M., Khamraeva, S. N., & Mamadiyarov, Z. (2025). An Investigation of Meaning, Toponymy of Sumba Cultural Site's Names, and the Impact of Tourism Visitors on Surrounding Society. *Forum for Linguistic Studies*, 7(8), 679–693. https://doi.org/10.30564/fls.v7i8.10260

Pradhan, R., Hajiyev, E., Shichiyakh, R. et al. Optimal Techno-Economic Feasibility of an Off-Grid Microgrid System Using Load Flow Energy Management Strategies. *Oper. Res. Forum* **6**, 120 (2025). https://doi.org/10.1007/s43069-025-00524-y

Rayala, R. V., Borra, C. R., Vasudevan, V., Singhania, R., Cheekati, S., & Mamadiyarov, Z. (2025, July). Lightweight Deep Learning Framework for Human Activity Recognition: A MobileNet-LSTM Approach with WHOA Optimization. In *2025 International Conference on Innovations in Intelligent Systems: Advancements in Computing, Communication, and Cybersecurity (ISAC3)* (pp. 1–6). IEEE.

Rayala, R. V., Sandhya, N., Singhania, R., Cheekati, S., Borra, C. R., Vasudevan, V., & Mamadiyarov, Z. (2025, July). AI-Driven Tomato Quality Assessment: A Deep Learning Approach for Image-based Defect Detection and Classification. In *2025 International Conference on Innovations in Intelligent Systems: Advancements in Computing, Communication, and Cybersecurity (ISAC3)* (pp. 1–6). IEEE.

Romero, R. M., Zelinskaya, M., Makhmudov, S., Sapaev, S., & Rustambekovich, J. U. (2025, September). Modelling and Optimal Utilisation of the Renewable Energy Systems in Microgrid with

Improving Reliability and Energy Efficiency. In Operations Research Forum (Vol. 6, No. 3, pp. 1–20). Springer International Publishing.

Rony, Z. T., Jefri, R., Rusmardiana, A., Pramono, S. A., & Mamadiyarov, Z. (2025). Downside Risk Measurement of Indonesian Financial and Energy Securities: A Value at Risk Perspective. *Journal of Applied Science, Engineering, Technology, and Education,* 7(2). https://doi.org/10.35877/454RI.asci3898

Roša, A., Aldrena, A. M., and Lace, N. (2025). 'Evaluating Progress Toward Achieving the Quality of Employment and Decent Work: The Development of the Model'. *Journal of Open Innovation: Technology, Market, and Complexity*, 11 (2), 100510.

Rukhiddin Zayniddinov, Nodir Jumaev, Gulbakhor Irgasheva, Alam Asadov, Nosir Makhmudov, Sirojiddin Abrorov, and Samariddin Makhmudov. 2025. The Influence of the Digital Economy on Economic Development Evidence from Uzbekistan. In Proceedings of the 8th International Conference on Future Networks & Distributed Systems (ICFNDS '24). Association for Computing Machinery, New York, NY, USA, 831–839. https://doi.org/10.1145/3726122.3726242.

Samariddin Makhmudov, Malika Umarova, Khayrilla Kurbonov, Laylo Akbarova, Durdona Davletova, Nilufar Shanazarova, and Toshmurod Kulmanov. 2025. Evaluating the forecast indicators of the volume of highly liquid assets of commercial banks in the process of digital transformation. In Proceedings of the 8th International Conference on Future Networks & Distributed Systems (ICFNDS '24). Association for Computing Machinery, New York, NY, USA, 698–704. https://doi.org/10.1145/3726122.3726222

Samariddin Makhmudov, Kudratillo Tukhsanov, Saifulla Arslanbekov, Akram Amanov, Orifali Tursunov, Umarbek Jabbarov and Muyassarxon Mirzakarimova. 2024. Optimizing Supply Chain Financing Development Prospects of Digital Ecosystems in the European Logistics Industry. In The 8th International Conference on Future Networks & Distributed Systems (ICFNDS '24), December 11–12, 2024, Marakech, Morocco. ACM, New York, NY, USA, 12 Pages. https://doi.org/10.1145/3726122.3726200

Sharifiasl, S., Kharel, S., Pan, Q., and Li, J. (2024). 'Assessing the Impact of Transit Accessibility on Employment Density: A Spatial Analysis of Gravity-based Accessibility Incorporating Job Matching, Transit Service

Types, and First/Last Mile Modes'. *Journal of Transport Geography*, 121, 104053.

Singagerda, F. S., Pratama, M. R., Alfairus, M. Q., Iskandar, A., & Mamadiyarov, Z. (2025). A Decision-Centric Approach to Risk Management in Aviation Stock Investments Using Value at Risk and Portfolio Optimization. *Journal of Applied Science, Engineering, Technology, and Education*, 7(1), 114–125. https://doi.org/10.35877/454RI.asci3870

Sofyanty, D., Romadhoni, R., Handriadi, H., Makhsudovna, I. S., Anwar, Z., & Mamadiyarov, Z. (2025). Strategic Decision Analysis for Investment Portfolios: Computational Risk Assessment in Transportation Asset Management. *Journal of Applied Science, Engineering, Technology, and Education*, 7(2). https://doi.org/10.35877/454RI.asci3897

Toshmurod Kulmanov, Umidjon Dadabaev, Mansurbek Qulmetov, Aliboy Ulashov, Mirjalol Eshboyev, and Samariddin Makhmudov. 2025. Global Services Market Transformation Digitalization Export Trends and Future Forecasts. In Proceedings of the 8th International Conference on Future Networks & Distributed Systems (ICFNDS '24). Association for Computing Machinery, New York, NY, USA, 851–858. https://doi.org/10.1145/3726122.3726245

Zhang, L., Zhao, Z., Qamri, G. M., & Makhmudov, S. (2025). Unleashing the critical role of renewable energy through global value chains and digitalization: A path towards environmental sustainability. *Journal of Environmental Management*, *392*, 126688.

Zokir Toshtemirovich Mamadiyarov, Samandarboy Adhambek ugli Sulaymanov, Sarvar Anvar ugli Askarov, and Durdona Bakhtiyor kizi Uktamova. 2022. Impact of Covid-19 Pandemic on Accelerating The Digitization and Transformation of Banks. In Proceedings of the 5th International Conference on Future Networks and Distributed Systems (ICFNDS '21). Association for Computing Machinery, New York, NY, USA, 706–712. https://doi.org/10.1145/3508072.3508211

Construction Volume in the Real Estate Market and Its Forecasting and Evaluation Based on the ARIMA Model

Samariddin Makhmudov, Mukhabbatkhon Berdalieva, Zokir Mamadiyarov, Olim Astanakulov, Khamdilla Imomov, Dilrabo Akhmedova and Ali Zurapov

25.1. Introduction

In any country with a market economy, the main part of investments in the housing sector is financed by savings in the private sector. Therefore, the savings policy implemented by the state, transforming the population's savings into various investment instruments and as a financial source for mortgage lending, is a guarantee of successful investment in housing. Currently, commercial banks in our republic mainly provide loans to individuals for the purchase of housing in the primary and secondary markets. An increase in housing prices in these markets leads to an increase in the amount of mortgage loans taken out by customers. This, in turn, negatively affects the financial situation of mortgage borrowers and ultimately prevents an increase in the volume of mortgage loans.

In addition, the low demand of the population and the relatively small volume of construction of new residential buildings in the regions, weak supply in the housing market and rising house prices, insufficient long-term and affordable financial resources, underdevelopment of the housing market and housing construction infrastructure have a negative impact on the organisation of an effective mortgage lending system in our republic.

In order to prevent a sharp increase in housing prices in our republic as a result of a significant reduction in the volume of housing construction, an increase in the amount of cash income of the population, and an increase in the volume of remittances from foreign countries, it is necessary to take measures to financially stimulate housing construction in our country. To this end, in order to increase the volume of housing construction, all costs associated with the creation of engineering and utility infrastructure in areas where land plots are allocated for housing construction should be financed from the state budget or a specially established state target fund. In addition, the process of selling land for housing construction to the population should be transparent and open.

Foreign researchers have shown that forecasting the volume of construction in the real estate market demonstrates a significant correlation between investment decisions and economic growth in understanding a number of dynamic, macro-level factors and the implementation of future trends and the formation of its economic significance. The practice of accurate forecasting of the housing market is of great importance in finding a balanced point of supply and demand in the real estate market, and the development of these practices significantly affects financial and economic planning and market stability.

25.2. Literature Review

Many foreign scholars have conducted research on the forecasting of construction volumes in the real estate market based on scientific theoretical and econometric models.

Husuan, Michael C. P. Sing and others noted that 'forecasting the construction volume is very important for researchers and the government to develop optimal labour and housing policies'. According to the author, accurate forecasting practices allow government reforms and changes in regulatory frameworks to meet future housing demands and labour market needs. The econometric equation developed by the team of authors based on the (VAR) model showed that the economic indicators in assessing the value of annual construction work performed by the main contractors, in particular, the importance of the private financial sector in making investment decisions, have a strong influence (Sing et al., 2015).

Heng Jiang and Chunlu Liu in their scientific paper 'Modeling housing construction demand using econometric methods such as the Vector Error Correction (VEC) model highlights the impact of global economic events on the real estate market'. According to the analysis, the VEC model is an acceptable solution for forecasting economic indicators in the construction industry according to forecasting accuracy tests, and the VEC model provides high forecasting performance when assessing exogenous effects (Jiang & Liu, 2011).

Vinayaka Gude in his scientific research, in his approach based on econometric models, 'noted that there is a significant relationship between housing permits and house prices for forecasting real estate dynamics' (Gude, 2023). The author's research results showed that there was a statistically significant relationship between housing permits and house prices, and the traditional regression model produced high predictive performance for the housing price index (*R*-squared value: 0.99) and house sales prices (*R*-squared value: 0.7839). Kyeong-Baek Kim et al. (2021) in their scientific work 'A systematic approach to forecasting the housing construction market in Korea using statistical systematic dynamic methods to account for complex interactions between variables' (Kim et al., 2021). According to the econometric model developed by the authors, a positive correlation was provided by assessing the past impact of socio-economic, regulatory and housing market size in providing market forecasts in the long term through a high degree of specificity.

According to Ebrahim Ali Alburshaid and Adel Ismail Al-Alawi, 'Statistical econometric models such as Autoregressive Integrated Moving Average (ARIMA) and VAR, ARDL have been widely used due to their ability to work with time series data and economic indicators'. The authors have effectively used these econometric models to develop accurate forecasts of trends and seasonal processes in housing construction volumes (Alburshaid & Al-Alawi, 2024).

Analyses and forecasts were conducted using multivariate linear regression (LS), ARDL, ARIMA and various other econometric models on the global services market, digital economy, energy-related financial stress, cocktail market, digital transformation, factors affecting the logistics industry (Kalandarov et al., 2025; Khayrilla et al., 2025; Khodjaniyazov et al., 2025; Kuziboev et al., 2025; Mamadiyarov et al., 2025; Rayala et al., 2025; Rukhiddin et al., 2025; Samariddin et al., 2025).

Girish Varma and Adari Kethaan believe that 'accurate forecasts of property sales in the real estate and urban economy sector play an important role in making informed decisions and strategic planning' (Varma et al., 2023). The authors developed forecast indicators based on time series models of New York real estate sales covering a 13-year period from 2003 to 2015.

25.3. Research Methodology

In the development of econometric research, we have developed forecast indicators for the construction volume in the real estate market in the national economy for the coming 2025–2029 based on the ARIMA model.

Today, in many foreign studies, in particular, the ARIMA model is recognised as an important statistical method for forecasting economic processes based on time series data.

According to Dinesh Kumar Yadav et al. (2024) 'The ARIMA model is suitable for use in finance, economics and social fields, since its direct approach to modeling time series data provides optimal research'. The authors have repeatedly emphasised in their econometric studies that the ability of this model to decompose time series into autoregressive differentiable and moving average components allows for effective capture of linear trends (Khoshimov et al., 2024; Yadav & Goswami, 2024).

Elisabeth Brielin Sinu et al. (2024) have noted that 'the ARIMA model is an effective statistical method for short-term forecasts, and it has provided important results in studies on stock prices and GDP forecasts'. According to the researchers, short-term forecasts in financial markets have been observed to achieve high accuracy, making it a valuable tool for financial market participants and traders, as well as economic analysts (Sinu et al., 2024).

According to Melina Melina et al., (2024) 'ARIMA models require stationary data, which increases the importance of transformations such as differentiation'. Scholars have argued that ARIMA models are often not suitable for non-stationary data (Melina et al., 2024). Jin Liuni argues that 'although ARIMA models perform well for short-term forecasts, their accuracy degrades over long periods of time. This is due to their reliance on historical data that does not account for unexpected external factors and trends' (Liu, 2024).

According to Utami, D. S. et al. (2024) 'To improve the accuracy of the ARIMA model, especially in a changing environment, it can be improved by introducing interference and variable factors'. Scientists have developed forecasting indicators that take into account macroeconomic factors, including inflation and important economic events in Indonesia (Utami & Imro'ah, 2024).

Majka, M. (2024) notes that 'the integrated (I) component uses the difference in the series to make the series stationary, which is an essential part of the ARIMA model'. According to him, this process allows us to remove trends and seasonality in the data and serves to facilitate modelling (Majka, 2024).

Another group of economists has successfully used econometric models such as Fixed Effects Estimator, Random Effects Estimator, multivariate linear (LS) and ARDL in their research on investment in digital infrastructure, various aspects of digital payment systems, the impact of inflation and credit interest rates on investment, factors affecting the reduction of the state's share in commercial banks, Non-Performing Loans in commercial banks, the digitisation of banks, risks in digital services and the development of retail payment services (Abdullah et al., 2025; Akhmetshin et al., 2025; Cahyani et al., 2025; Mamadiyarov et al., 2025; Rayala et al., 2025; Samariddin et al., 2025; Su et al., 2025; Zokir et al., 2021).

According to Chan (2013) 'the moving average (MA) component in an ARIMA model models the relationship between the observation and the residual error in the model applied to the lagged observations'. This helps to smooth out the noise in the data for forecasting. Jianbin Zeng et al. state that 'the ARIMA model requires careful selection of parameters (p, d, q) that represent the order of the AR, I and MA components, respectively' (Chan, 2013; Habib et al., 2025; Jahrir et al., 2025; Lin et al., 2025; Mamadiyarov et al., 2025; Mamani et al., 2025; Pradhan et al., 2025; Romero et al., 2025; Rony et al., 2025; Singagerda et al., 2025; Sofyanty et al., 2025; Toshmurod et al., 2025; Zhang et al., 2025; Zhao et al., 2025).

These components are expressed as follows:

p – represents the number of lagged observations in the model (autoregressive part);
d – represents the number of times the observations are differed (integrated part);
q – represents the size of the moving average window (moving average part).

The general form of the ARIMA (p, d, q) model is given below.

$$y_i = b + c_1 y_{i-1} + c_2 y_{i-2} + \cdots + c_q y_{i-k} + \beta_1 \epsilon_{i-1} + \beta_2 \epsilon_{i-2} + \cdots + b_k \epsilon_{i-m} + \epsilon_i \quad (1)$$

where y_i is the value of the time series at time i (after differencing d times), b is the constant term, c_i = *(for i* = 1, 2, …, *q)* – represents the coefficients of the autoregressive part, β_k = *(for k* = 1, 2, …, *m)* – represents the coefficients of the moving average part.

ϵ_i represents the error term (white noise) at time i.

Explanation of components:

1. According to Khan, F. M et al. (2020) 'Autoregressive (AR) part in ARIMA model' (Khan & Gupta, 2020). The terms $c_1 y_{i-1}, c_2 y_{t-2}, \ldots, c_q y_{i-k}$ describe the autoregressive part, in which the current value of the series is regressed on its past values.
2. According to Patel, N. et al. (2020) 'Integrated (I) part in ARIMA model' (Patel et al., 2020). The parameter d represents the order of differentiation used to implement the stationarity condition of the series. The differentiation operation is written as follows:

$$Y_i' = y_i - y_{i-1} \ (agar\ d = 1) \tag{2}$$

At the same time, a higher level of differentiation is used in developing forecast indicators for research. According to Singh et al. (2020) 'Moving average (MA) part in ARIMA model' (Singh et al., 2020).

25.4. Analysis and Results

In developing the forecast indicators for the study, quarterly data sources of the Statistical Agency under the President of the Republic of Uzbekistan (<https://stat.uz/uz/>) with a number of observations covering the years 2013–2023 were used. The resulting variable for the econometric forecast is shown below.

Housing construction volume – *hous_construct* (outcome variable). An analytical graphical diagram of the housing construction volume over the past period at the initial stage of the econometric forecast is presented in Figure 88.

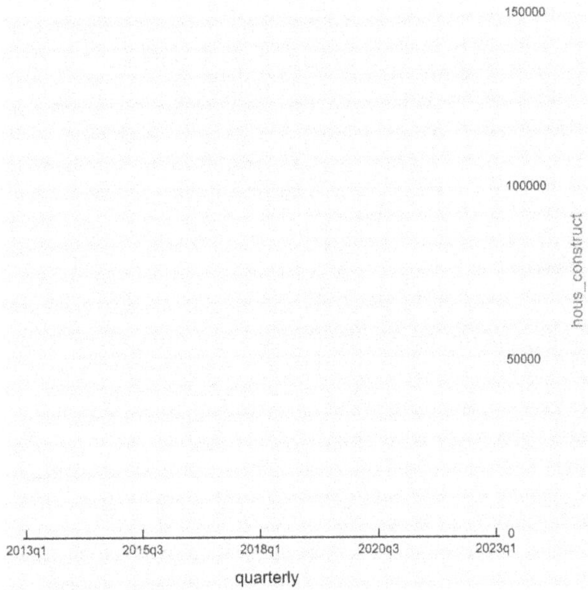

Figure 88. Analytical graphic diagram of the periodic status of housing construction volumes in the real estate market.
Source: Developed by the authors based on the Stata program.

According to Figure 88, the volume of housing construction showed a sharp growth trend in the 1st half of 2018, and this growth dynamics reached a maximum in the 1st quarter of 2023. This sharp growth trend was due to the increase in demand for housing construction in the real estate market, the improvement of the supply chain and the reforms carried out by the government.

In the next stage of the econometric forecast, the stationarity level of housing construction in the real estate market was assessed and the Unit-Root test was used to determine it (Table 89).

Table 89. Unit-root test of housing construction volume in the real estate market

	Test Statistic	1% Critical Value	5% Critical Value	10% Critical Value	p-value for Z(t)
hous_construct	-6.209	-3.662	-2.964	-2.614	0.0000

Source: Developed by the authors based on the Stata program.

According to Table 89, the value of the state purchases saved at the national stock auctions is –6.219, which indicates the importance of the consistent, clearly cyclical, seasonal periodicity of the housing construction volume in the real estate market. According to it, the statistical value is below the 1 per cent, 5 per cent and 10 per cent thresholds of significance. At the same time, the McKinnon value is minimal with $Z(t) = 0.0000$, which indicates the presence of a stationary state of the housing construction volume in the real estate market.

In the econometric study, the stabilised sequence achieved positive statistical significance during the cyclical process for forecasting indicators using the ARIMA model. According to this sequence, the ARIMA model parameter d has a value of $d = 1$, indicating that it is well-fitting and that the time series has achieved stationarity after the first difference.

The next step is to present the value of p, which determines the indirect correlation between the lags of the time series of the model (Figure 89).

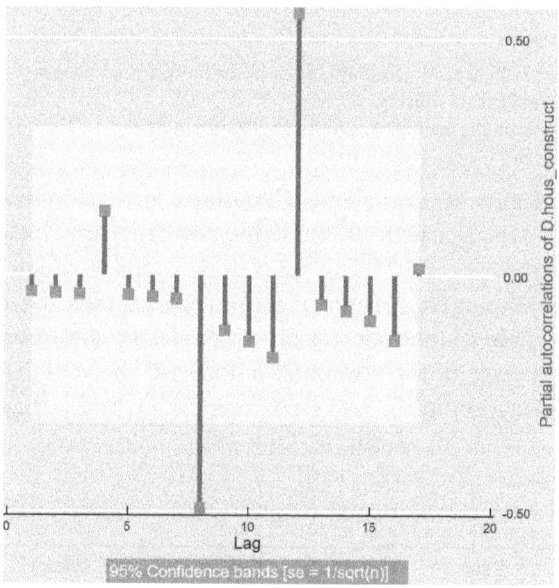

Figure 89. Indirect correlation graph between lags of the econometric model of housing construction volume in the real estate market.
Source: Developed by the authors based on the Stata program.

The plot in Figure 89 shows that, except for two lags, all lags are within the confidence interval in the indirect correlation analysis. The strong positive partial autocorrelation in the model indicates an intermediate-term relationship. The increases in certain lags indicate that seasonal and periodic components can be introduced.

Accordingly, it is possible to choose a value of 1 or 2 as the p-value and it is appropriate to use these values in the ARIMA p-values. It is shown that there is a significant positive autocorrelation at certain lags and that the volume of housing construction affects the future forecast indicator.

In the next step of the ARIMA model, the value of q, which describes the direct correlation between the lags of the model, was determined (Figure 90).

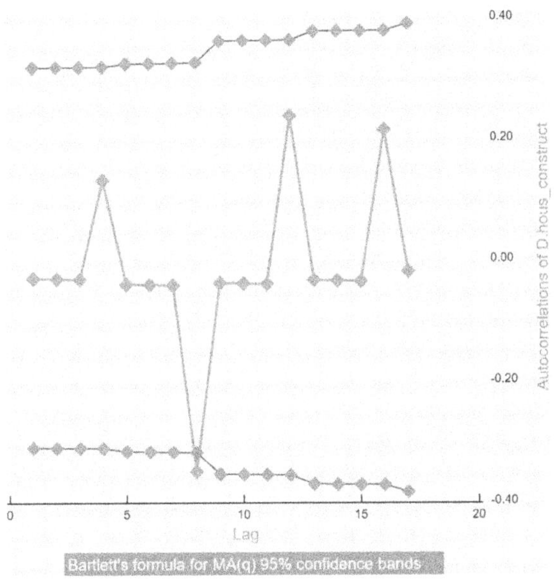

Figure 90. Direct correlation graph between lags of the econometric model of housing construction volume in the real estate market.
Source: Developed by the authors based on the Stata program.

Figure 90 shows that all lags except one lag are within the specified confidence interval, demonstrating a strong correlation between lags in the ARIMA model. This suggests that the observed fluctuations in lags in the econometric forecast model reflect some seasonal dynamic behaviour. Accordingly, potential seasonal adjustments in the model provide promising positive forecast indicators based on the ARIMA model.

It is appropriate to choose a value for the moving average parameter *q* in the ARIMA model. Since the observed data in the study are consistent with values from 0 to 1 and are located in confidence intervals, it is recommended to choose a value of q in this range.

In the next step, the cumulative spectral periodogram and cumulative spectral distribution analysis of the resulting variable in the time series estimation of the econometric forecast indicators are presented (Figures 91 and 92).

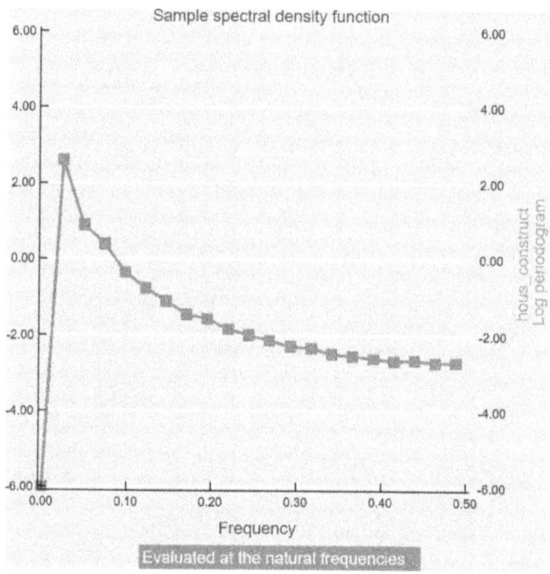

Figure 91. Analysis of the cumulative spectral periodogram graph of the econometric model of housing construction volume in the real estate market.
Source: Developed by the authors based on the Stata program.

Figure 91 shows the spectral periodogram function of the ekpnpmetric forecast indicators, which presents the decomposition of the variance at different frequencies. The high spectral peak near zero frequency indicates that most of the variance is concentrated at low frequencies, which in this case indicates a strong consistency in the housing construction data over long-term trends. The gradual decrease in spectral density indicates that high-frequency fluctuations contribute little to the total variance, and the forecast indicators show a dominance of long-term trends rather than short-term variability.

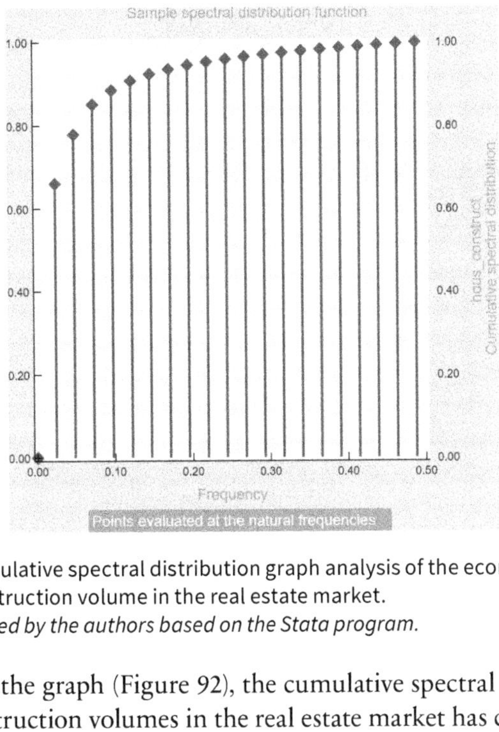

Figure 92. Cumulative spectral distribution graph analysis of the econometric model of housing construction volume in the real estate market.
Source: Developed by the authors based on the Stata program.

According to the graph (Figure 92), the cumulative spectral distribution of housing construction volumes in the real estate market has created positive dynamics, making it easier to explain this increasing trend. This visual visualisation is effective and useful in developing economic forecasting, indicating the extent to which macro trends should be taken into account in the development of housing construction volumes in the real estate market. Also, the cumulative spectral distribution graph successfully reflects the long-term activity of the housing construction period and serves as a powerful tool for developing a reliable forecast for the economy of the real estate market. When choosing the optimal ARIMA invariant models for forecasting the model, the following models were developed: ARIMA(1,1,2), ARIMA(2,1,2), ARIMA(2,2,2), ARIMA(1,1,1), ARIMA(2,0,1) and ARIMA(2,1,1). Among these models, the ARIMA(2,1,1) model with the best performance was selected (see Table 90).

Based on the ARIMA model regression result, the econometric equation for the model is presented below.

$$hous\_constructt = \alpha + \phi_1 hous\_construct_{t-1} + \phi_2 hous\_construct_{t-2} + \theta_1 \varepsilon_{t-1} + \varepsilon_t \quad (3)$$

Table 90. Econometric equation indicators of the ARIMA(2,1,1) model by the volume of housing construction in the real estate market

D.hous_ construct	Coef.	St.Err.	t-value	p-value	[95% Conf	Interval]	Sig
Constant	337.499	69.208	4.99	0	2025.875	449.123	***
L	-0.906	0.332	-2.73	0.006	-1.556	-0.256	***
L2	-0.421	0.16	-2.63	0.008	-0.734	-0.108	***
L	0.558	0.367	1.52	0.091	-0.162	1.278	*
Constant	496.196	70.007	6.94	0	3512.449	679.944	***

Mean dependent var	389.332	SD dependent var	2490.665
Number of obs	40	Chi-square	14.178
Prob > chi2	.	Akaike crit. (AIC)	1803.559
*** $p < 0.01$, ** $p < 0.05$, * $p < 0.1$			

Source: Developed by the authors based on the Stata program.

According to Table 90, the ARIMA(2,1,1) model looks like this:

$$hous\_construct_t = 337.49 - 0.90 hous\_construct_{t-1} - 0.42 hous\_construct_{t-2} + 0.55\varepsilon_{t-1} + \varepsilon_t \quad (4)$$

In the next step, the ARIMA(2,1,1) model was developed to analyse the mean values of the outcome variable and the graphical representation of the residuals (Table 91 and Figure 93).

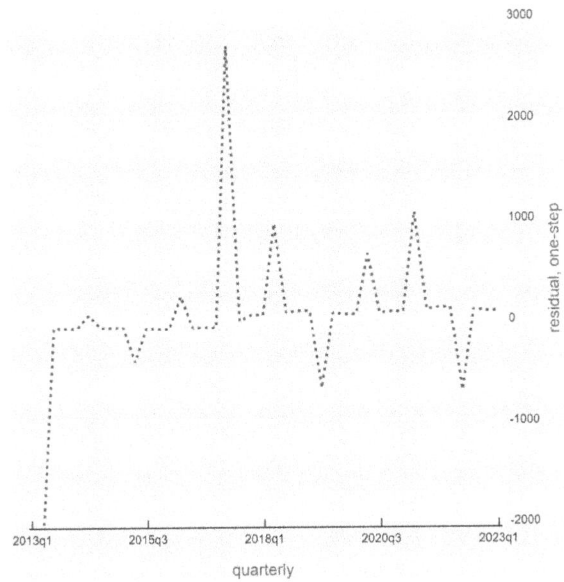

Figure 93. Graph of residual values of the ARIMA(2,1,1) model by the volume of housing construction in the real estate market.
Source: Developed by the authors based on the Stata program.

Table 91. Residual values of the resulting factor in the ARIMA(2,1,1) model

Variable factor	Number of observations	Average value	Standard deviation	Minimum value	Maksimum value
Residual value	40	46.5684	623.0993	-2030.877	2703.675

Source: Developed by the authors based on the Stata program.

According to Table 91 and Figure 93, the ARIMA(2,1,1) model has reached stochastic equilibrium, as evidenced by the visual representation of the residuals at the specified time intervals. This representation shows the fit of the ARIMA model to the data and the main stochastic relationships in the data set.

The next step involves testing the stationarity of the residuals of the ARIMA (2,1,1) model and estimating the autoregressive (AR) and moving average (MA) residuals in the real estate market. The convergence of the ARIMA model to the unit range in forecasting was also checked (Figure 94).

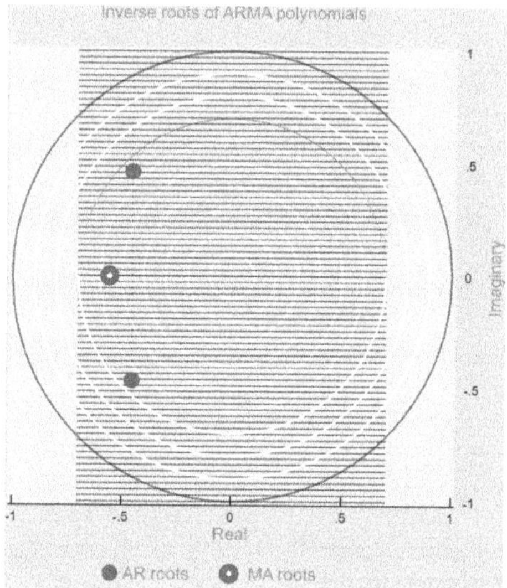

Figure 94. Range of values of housing construction volume in the real estate market according to the ARIMA(2,1,1) model.
Source: Developed by the authors based on the Stata program.

Using the Stata program, a forecast indicator was developed for the volume of housing construction in the real estate market from 2025 to 2029, excluding random factors, using the ARIMA(2,1,1) model (Table 92).

Table 92. Forecast indicators of housing construction volume in the real estate market for 2025–2029

Years	Pessimistic forecast	Optimistic forecast	Forecast
2025	198,870	203,852	201,361
2026	215,663	220,645	218,154
2027	231,826	236,808	234,317
2028	247,452	252,434	249,943
2029	262,641	267,623	265,132

Source: Developed by the authors based on the Stata program.

The study, presented by the Statistical Agency under the President of the Republic of Uzbekistan (<https://stat.uz/uz/>), presents a graphical representation of the forecast indicator of the volume of housing construction in the real estate market for 2015–2024 and 2025–2029 (Figure 95).

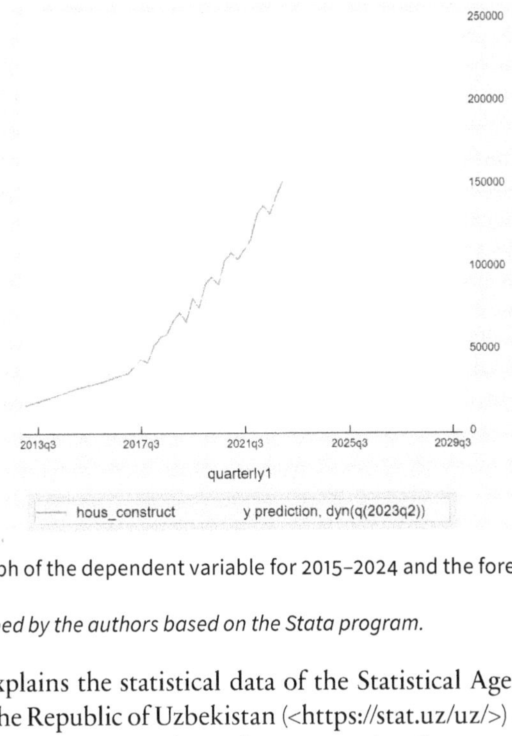

Figure 95. Graph of the dependent variable for 2015–2024 and the forecast for 2025–2029.
Source: Developed by the authors based on the Stata program.

The article explains the statistical data of the Statistical Agency under the President of the Republic of Uzbekistan (<https://stat.uz/uz/>) on the volume of housing construction in the real estate market for 2013–2024 and the forecast indicator for 2025–2029 as follows.

25.5. Conclusion

According to the econometric analysis in the study, based on the ARIMA(2,1,1) model, the volume of housing construction in the real estate market in 2025–2029, excluding various random factors, was projected to reach 201,361 units in 2025, 218,154 units in 2026, 234,317 units in 2027, 249,943 units in 2028 and 265,132 units in 2029, respectively.

1. Growth trend assessment by econometric model: Forecast indicators according to the ARIMA(2,1,1) model provide a gradual growth dynamics of housing construction from 201,361 units in 2025 to 265,132 units in 2029. This trend indicates that the housing sector will experience a stable and predictable expansion during the forecast period, and year-on-year growth will be relatively stable, which will provide a balanced market without excessive fluctuations.
2. The ARIMA(2,1,1) model effectively assesses the main growth trend without taking into account random variables, making it a suitable tool for long-term forecasting.
3. Impact assessment of the forecast according to the ARIMA model on investment practice: Stable growth in housing construction volume creates the opportunity for strategic planning in financing and development projects, as well as reliable forecast indicators of the real estate market. This growth trend indicates that the country's infrastructure, namely roads, utilities and other public services, can be improved. To ensure such sustainable growth, it is necessary to pursue a policy of affordable housing prices and ensure that the prices of raw materials for housing construction do not increase.
4. The growth of housing construction serves to increase employment in this sector. A stable real estate market will have a positive impact on financial markets and household economic well-being.
5. The ARIMA(2,1,1) forecast for housing construction represents an optimistic scenario for the real estate sector, which will provide long-term market confidence in this sector, allow developers, investors and the government to plan effectively, and create the basis for preventing a housing shortage.

Bibliography

Abdullah, M. A., Han, X., Amjad, M. A., & Makhmudov, S. (2025). Revisit the role of financial development on economic growth, human development, and sustainable development in higher-income countries. *Journal of Environmental Management*, *392*, 126874.

Akhmetshin, E., Abdullayev, I., Makhmudov, S., Dakhkilgova, K., Korotaeva, I. and Yanovskaya, G. (2025). APPLICATION OF

TANH–COTH METHOD FOR COMBINED AND DOUBLE COMBINED SINH–COSH–GORDON EQUATIONS ARISING CHEMICAL REACTIONS TO WATER SURFACE GRAVITY WAVES. Computational Methods for Differential Equations, (), -. doi: 10.22034/cmde.2025.67655.3234

Alburshaid, E. A., and Al-Alawi, A. I. (2024). 'Forecasting Methods for the Real Estate Market: A Review', 472–7, <https://doi.org/10.1109/icetsis61505.2024.10459597>.

Cahyani, I., Buriev, K., Ngongo, M., Mamadiyarov, Z., Ino, L., Herman, H., Saputra, N., & Baxtishodovich, S. (2025). Exploring the Use of TikTok Application in Enhancing the Skill of Pronunciation: A Case on Students' Perception. Studies in Media and Communication, 13(2), 150–158. doi: http://dx.doi.org/10.11114/smc.v13i2.7553

Chan, J. C. (2013). 'Moving Average Stochastic Volatility Models with Application to Inflation Forecast'. *Journal of Econometrics*, 176 (2), 162–72.

Gude, V. (2023). 'A Multi-level Modeling Approach for Predicting Real-estate Dynamics'. *International Journal of Housing Markets and Analysis*. <https://doi.org/10.1108/ijhma-02-2023-0024>.

Habib, S. S., Islam, M. A., Ali, M. N., Benitez, I. B., Mamadiyarov, Z., Mirzayev, B., … & Flah, A. (2025). Multi-Objective Optimization and Feasibility Analysis of Integrated Biogas–Solar Energy Systems for Rural Electrification. *Results in Engineering*, 107086.

Jahrir, A., Gultom, Y., Herman, H., Zabadi, F., Ngongo, M., Mamadiyarov, Z., Fatmawati, E., & Saputra, N. (2025). Investigating the Elements of Short Commercial Mineral Water Advertisement: A Case on Discourse Analysis. Studies in Media and Communication, 13(4), 94–104. doi: http://dx.doi.org/10.11114/smc.v13i4.7813

Jiang, H., and Liu, C. (2011). 'Forecasting Construction Demand: A Vector Error Correction Model with Dummy Variables'. *Construction Management and Economics*, 29 (9), 969–79. <https://doi.org/10.1080/01446193.2011.611522>.

Kalandarov, F., Makhmudov, S., Ibadullaev, D., Matniyozov, M., Nasretdinova, F., Sabirov, K., & Bahodirov, N. M. (2025). Low-Carbon Energy Risk and Renewable Energy Development: Insights from Method of Moments Quantile Regression. International Journal of Energy Economics and Policy, 15(3), 524–536.

Khan, F. M., and Gupta, R. (2020). 'ARIMA and NAR Based Prediction Model for Time Series Analysis of COVID-19 Cases in India. *Journal of Safety Science and Resilience*, 1 (1), 12–18.

Khayrilla Kurbonov, Samariddin Makhmudov, Shakhzod Erkinov, Umidjon Dadabaev, Gulnora Bekimbetova, Rukhiddin Zayniddinov, and Mirzabek Jonuzokov. 2025. Evaluating the Impact of Marketing Practices Digitalization and Investment on Labor Market Efficiency and Commercial Bank Performance Using Econometric Models. In Proceedings of the 8th International Conference on Future Networks & Distributed Systems (ICFNDS '24). Association for Computing Machinery, New York, NY, USA, 786–796. https://doi.org/10.1145/3726122.3726237

Khodjaniyazov, N., Mirkhoshimova, M., Kalandarov, F., Matyokubova, D., Utegenova, S., Makhmudov, S., & Khudayberganov, M. (2025). Time-Varying Impacts of Financial Stress on Energy-Related Uncertainty. International Journal of Energy Economics and Policy, 15(3), 689–698.

Kim, K.-B., Cho, J.-H., and Kim, S.-B. (2021). 'Model-Based Dynamic Forecasting for Residential Construction Market Demand: A Systemic Approach'. *Applied Sciences*, 11 (8), 3681, <https://doi.org/10.3390/APP11083681>.

Kuchkarov, T., Mamadiyarov, Z., Khakimov, Z., Sabirova, O., Matmurodov, K., Raimboyeva, M., & Umarova, S. (2025). Energy-Related Uncertainty and Crypto-Currency Environmental Attention: Time-Varying Perspective. International Journal of Energy Economics and Policy, 15(5), 614–626. https://doi.org/10.32479/ijeep.20784

Kuziboev, B., Ozturk, I., Kalandarov, F., Samandarov, O., Bekjanov, D., & Makhmudov, S. (2025). PROMOTING ENERGY SOURCES DIVERSIFICATION THROUGH ESG PERFORMANCE. Energy, 136009.

Lin, M.H., Matchanova, B., Nurmatovich, H.A. et al. Optimal Operation of the Multi-Carrier Energy System Considering Energy Markets and Renewable Energies Participation. *Int. J. Appl. Comput. Math* **11**, 170 (2025). https://doi.org/10.1007/s40819-025-02002-9

Liu, J. (2024). 'Navigating the Financial Landscape: The Power and Limitations of the ARIMA Model'. *Highlights in Science Engineering and Technology*, 88, 747–52. <https://doi.org/10.54097/9zf6kd91>.

Majka, M. (2024). Seasonal Time Series Analysis: Why SARIMA Outshines ARIMA.

Mamadiyarov, Z., Eshov, M., Otakhonova, D., Utegenova, S., Sabirov, K., Marks, A., & Bahodirov, N. (2025). Does Energy Policy Risk Threaten Energy Sources Diversification?. *International Journal of Energy Economics and Policy, 15*(5), 730–740. https://doi.org/10.32479/ijeep.21140

Mamadiyarov, Z., Saidov, O., Abdurazakova, N., Makhmudov, S., Nazarov, M., Rajabova, N., … Ruzmetova, I. (2025). Energy-Related Uncertainty and Tourism Stock Markets: New Insights from Time-Varying Relationship with TVP- VAR Approach. *International Journal of Energy Economics and Policy, 15*(4), 730–737. https://doi.org/10.32479/ijeep.20480

Mamani, J.C.M., Miri, M., Vorobev, Y. et al. Optimal Operation of Energy Microgrid Considering Economic and Emission Indices. Oper. Res. Forum 6, 122 (2025). https://doi.org/10.1007/s43069-025-00523-z

Melina, M., Sukono, S., Napitupulu, H., Mohamed, N., Chrisnanto, Y. H., Hadiana, A. I., Kusumaningtyas, V. A., and Nabilla, U. (2024). 'Comparative Analysis of Time Series Forecasting Models Using Arima and Neural Network Autoregression Methods'. *Barekeng*. <https://doi.org/10.30598/barekengvol18iss4pp2563-2576>.

Muhammad Zubair, Irfanud Din, Nadeem Sarwar et al. Revolutionizing Sepsis Diagnosis Using Machine Learning and Deep Learning Models: A Systematic Literature Review, 10 June 2025, PREPRINT (Version 1) available at Research Square [https://doi.org/10.21203/rs.3.rs-6731418/v1]

Ngongo, M., Herman, H., Ndandara, A., Jois Jaha, D. A., Peku Djawang, J. U. S., Tanggu Rame, M. M., Khamraeva, S. N., & Mamadiyarov, Z. (2025). An Investigation of Meaning, Toponymy of Sumba Cultural Site's Names, and the Impact of Tourism Visitors on Surrounding Society. *Forum for Linguistic Studies*, 7(8), 679–693. https://doi.org/10.30564/fls.v7i8.10260

Patel, N., Patel, M., and Patel, R. B. (2020). 'Electrical Energy Demand Forecasting Using Time Series Approach'. *International Journal of Technology and Globalisation*, 29 (3s), 594–604.

Pradhan, R., Hajiyev, E., Shichiyakh, R. et al. Optimal Techno-Economic Feasibility of an Off-Grid Microgrid System Using Load Flow Energy Management Strategies. *Oper. Res. Forum* 6, 120 (2025). https://doi.org/10.1007/s43069-025-00524-y

Rayala, R. V., Borra, C. R., Vasudevan, V., Singhania, R., Cheekati, S., & Mamadiyarov, Z. (2025, July). Lightweight Deep Learning Framework for Human Activity Recognition: A MobileNet-LSTM Approach with WHOA Optimization. In *2025 International Conference on Innovations in Intelligent Systems: Advancements in Computing, Communication, and Cybersecurity (ISAC3)* (pp. 1–6). IEEE.

Rayala, R. V., Sandhya, N., Singhania, R., Cheekati, S., Borra, C. R., Vasudevan, V., & Mamadiyarov, Z. (2025, July). AI-Driven Tomato Quality Assessment: A Deep Learning Approach for Image-based Defect Detection and Classification. In *2025 International Conference on Innovations in Intelligent Systems: Advancements in Computing, Communication, and Cybersecurity (ISAC3)* (pp. 1–6). IEEE.

Romero, R. M., Zelinskaya, M., Makhmudov, S., Sapaev, S., & Rustambekovich, J. U. (2025, September). Modelling and Optimal Utilisation of the Renewable Energy Systems in Microgrid with Improving Reliability and Energy Efficiency. In Operations Research Forum (Vol. 6, No. 3, pp. 1–20). Springer International Publishing.

Rony, Z. T., Jefri, R., Rusmardiana, A., Pramono, S. A., & Mamadiyarov, Z. (2025). Downside Risk Measurement of Indonesian Financial and Energy Securities: A Value at Risk Perspective. *Journal of Applied Science, Engineering, Technology, and Education,* 7(2). https://doi.org/10.35877/454RI.asci3898

Rukhiddin Zayniddinov, Nodir Jumaev, Gulbakhor Irgasheva, Alam Asadov, Nosir Makhmudov, Sirojiddin Abrorov, and Samariddin Makhmudov. 2025. The Influence of the Digital Economy on Economic Development Evidence from Uzbekistan. In Proceedings of the 8th International Conference on Future Networks & Distributed Systems (ICFNDS '24). Association for Computing Machinery, New York, NY, USA, 831–839. https://doi.org/10.1145/3726122.3726242

Samariddin Makhmudov, Malika Umarova, Khayrilla Kurbonov, Laylo Akbarova, Durdona Davletova, Nilufar Shanazarova, and Toshmurod Kulmanov. 2025. Evaluating the forecast indicators of the volume of highly liquid assets of commercial banks in the process of digital transformation. In Proceedings of the 8th International Conference on Future Networks & Distributed Systems (ICFNDS '24). Association for Computing Machinery, New York, NY, USA, 698–704. https://doi.org/10.1145/3726122.3726222

Samariddin Makhmudov, Kudratillo Tukhsanov, Saifulla Arslanbekov, Akram Amanov, Orifali Tursunov, Umarbek Jabbarov and Muyassarxon Mirzakarimova. 2024. Optimizing Supply Chain Financing Development Prospects of Digital Ecosystems in the European Logistics Industry. In The 8th International Conference on Future Networks & Distributed Systems (ICFNDS '24), December 11–12, 2024, Marakech, Morocco. ACM, New York, NY, USA, 12 Pages. https://doi.org/10.1145/3726122.3726200

Sing, M. C. P., Edwards, D. J., Liu, H. J., and Love, P. E. D. (2015). 'Forecasting Private-Sector Construction Works: VAR Model Using Economic Indicators'. *Journal of Construction Engineering and Management–ASCE*, 141 (11), 04015037. <https://doi.org/10.1061/(ASCE)CO.1943-7862.0001016>.

Singagerda, F. S., Pratama, M. R., Alfairus, M. Q., Iskandar, A., & Mamadiyarov, Z. (2025). A Decision-Centric Approach to Risk Management in Aviation Stock Investments Using Value at Risk and Portfolio Optimization. *Journal of Applied Science, Engineering, Technology, and Education*, 7(1), 114–125. https://doi.org/10.35877/454RI.asci3870

Singh, S., Parmar, K. S., Kumar, J., and Makkhan, S. J. S. (2020). 'Development of New Hybrid Model of Discrete Wavelet Decomposition and Autoregressive Integrated Moving Average (ARIMA) Models in Application to One Month Forecast the Casualties Cases of COVID-19'. *Chaos, Solitons & Fractals*, 135, 109866.

Sinu, E. B., Kleden, M. A., and Atti, A. (2024). 'Application of ARIMA Model for Forecasting National Economic Growth: A Focus on Gross Domestic Product Data'. *Barekeng*, 18 (2), 1261–72. <https://doi.org/10.30598/barekengvol18iss2pp1261-1272>.

Sofyanty, D., Romadhoni, R., Handriadi, H., Makhsudovna, I. S., Anwar, Z., & Mamadiyarov, Z. (2025). Strategic Decision Analysis for Investment Portfolios: Computational Risk Assessment in Transportation Asset Management. *Journal of Applied Science, Engineering, Technology, and Education*, 7(2). https://doi.org/10.35877/454RI.asci3897

Su, R., Xiao, Y., Hamza, F., Mamadiyarov, Z., & Wahab, A. (2025). Scaling up green hydrogen in China: Economic opportunities and challenges. *International Journal of Hydrogen Energy, 131*, 60–69.

Toshmurod Kulmanov, Umidjon Dadabaev, Mansurbek Qulmetov, Aliboy Ulashov, Mirjalol Eshboyev, and Samariddin Makhmudov. 2025. Global Services Market Transformation Digitalization Export Trends and Future Forecasts. In Proceedings of the 8th International Conference on Future Networks & Distributed Systems (ICFNDS '24). Association for Computing Machinery, New York, NY, USA, 851–858. https://doi.org/10.1145/3726122.3726245

Utami, D. S., and Imro'ah, N. (2024). 'ARIMA Time Series Modeling with the Addition of Intervention and Outlier Factors on Inflation Rate in Indonesia'. *JTAM (Jurnal Teori dan Aplikasi Matematika)*, 8 (1), 256–68.

Varma, G., Varma, G., and Kethaan, A. (2023). 'Predictive Insights for Monthly Property Sales Forecasting: An End-to-End Time Series Forecasting'. *International Journal of Advanced Research in Science, Communication and Technology*, 598–604, <https://doi.org/10.48175/ijarsct-12493>.

Yadav, D. K., and Goswami, L. (2024). 'Autoregressive Integrated Moving Average Model for Time Series Analysis', 1–6, <https://doi.org/10.1109/icocwc60930.2024.10470488>.

Zeng, J., Zhai, J., and Li, Q. (February 2024). 'Research and Analysis of ARIMA Model Based on Time Series Analysis in Smart Water'. In *2024 4th Asia-Pacific Conference on Communications Technology and Computer Science (ACCTCS)*, pp. 454–8. IEEE.

Zhang, L., Zhao, Z., Qamri, G. M., & Makhmudov, S. (2025). Unleashing the critical role of renewable energy through global value chains and digitalization: A path towards environmental sustainability. *Journal of Environmental Management*, *392*, 126688.

Zhao, Q., Pervaiz, A., Makhmudov, S., & Fatima, A. (2025). Do environmental stringent policies enhance the impact of renewable energy on CO2 reduction? Evidence from BRICS-T economies. Journal of Environmental Management, 391, 126464.

Zokir Toshtemirovich Mamadiyarov, Samandarboy Adhambek ugli Sulaymanov, Sarvar Anvar ugli Askarov, and Durdona Bakhtiyor kizi Uktamova. 2022. Impact of Covid-19 Pandemic on Accelerating The Digitization and Transformation of Banks. In Proceedings of the 5th International Conference on Future Networks and Distributed Systems (ICFNDS '21). Association for Computing Machinery, New York, NY, USA, 706–712. https://doi.org/10.1145/3508072.3508211

Assessment of Forecasting Indicators of the Impact of Gender Equality in the Labour Market on the Standard of Living of the Population

Bobur Khonturayev, Zokir Mamadiyarov, Samariddin Makhmudov, Shukhrat Yuldashev, Bakhtiyor Klichev, Gauhkar Jannazarova and Khayrulla Urozboev

26.1. Introduction

According to World Bank estimates, if women in Uzbekistan participated in the labour market on an equal footing with men, Uzbekistan's national income would increase by 29 per cent. If the monthly salaries of working women reached the wages of men, this increase in revenue would lift more than 700,000 people out of poverty. It is urgent to conduct research aimed at solving several problems in the implementation of such huge potential in Uzbekistan. At the same time, the analysis of gender equality in the country identifies the strengths of the processes, and we will consider several reforms and existing problems aimed at increasing equality within the framework of ongoing social and economic changes in Uzbekistan.

The new Constitution of Uzbekistan of 2022 further strengthens the commitment to gender equality and strengthens the provision of equal rights and opportunities by the state to women and men in the management of public and state affairs, as well as in other areas of society and the state. Uzbekistan has made rapid progress in closing several key gender gaps in recent years. One of the most useful advances in several areas is the availability of open data and evidence, which has encouraged progress. While gender-disaggregated statistics on development issues are incomplete, they are increasingly reflected in key areas, including the labour market, human capital and freedom of expression and participation, and many statistical indicators are in line with the coverage provided by leading statistical agencies. These data are important both for public participation and for monitoring the country's progress in implementing its ambitious reform agenda. These data are crucial both for public participation and as a tool for monitoring the country's progress in implementing its ambitious reform agenda. The increased openness to information sharing and public consultation has transformed the political landscape, as well as the diversity of priorities and partners involved in policy development.

However, the path to achieving true equality is incomplete, and Uzbekistan faces various challenges and problems on its way to achieving its goal. These include:

- In recent years, there has been an increase in the representation of women in public life, but equality is still far from achieved.
- Gender-Based Violence is a global problem, affecting women all over the world and affecting their freedom of action.
- Parental leave has, until recently, been a source of discrimination against women in the private sector.
- The gender gap in labour force participation and employment rates is also related to educational attainment and the number of children living in the household.
- The disparity in employment opportunities between women and men in Uzbekistan is also influenced by the region of residence and other factors.

26.2. Literature Review

Estimating the impact of gender equality in the labour market on the standard of living of the population suggests that gender equality has a positive impact on economic development. Gender equality in the labour market is considered one of the important factors for increasing economic efficiency, increasing technical efficiency, reducing poverty and thereby improving the standard of living of the population.

First, achieving gender equality positively contributes to a country's economic growth. Countries with higher levels of gender equality tend to have higher per capita GDP because increased gender equality increases human capital and labour productivity (Ram et al., 2022; Xu, 2025). That is, women's equal rights and equal participation in the labour market serve to achieve economic growth by diversifying the labour force in the labour market and improving the average quality of the labour force (Hazarika et al., 2023). Economic development and gender equality have a curvilinear relationship, in which initial economic growth improves gender equality, which in turn supports subsequent economic growth (Eastin & Prakash, 2013).

Second, gender equality in labour market opportunities increases gross technical efficiency by enabling talented women to contribute to economic activity (Hazarika et al., 2023). It increases labour market flexibility and can reduce gender gaps by providing more equal opportunities for women in developing countries (Jomaa, 2024). In particular, high levels of gender inequality in the labour market are associated with increased poverty rates in the case of Bolivia (Torrico & Marion, 2017).

Third, socio-economic and cultural factors, including patriarchal norms, can reduce the positive impact of gender equality on economic performance by distorting the distribution of women's labour (Hazarika et al., 2023). Wider societal gender inequality, influenced by health, education and political opportunities, leads to higher female unemployment and gender inequality (ALGÜL, 2024). The cultural environment and political, economic and social institutions play an important role in gender equality in economic relations (Lovell, 1999).

Fourth, policies that promote gender equality should focus on structural changes in society, enhancing the role and status of women, and integrating gender equality principles through education (ALGÜL, 2024; Kabeer, 2021). Legislative, educational and socio-cultural reforms are recommended to achieve gender equality and promote economic development (Mamadiyarov et al., 2025; Mamani et al., 2025; Pradhan et al., 2025; Rayala et al., 2025; Romero et al., 2025; Rony et al., 2025; Samariddin et al., 2025; Singagerda et al., 2025; Sofyanty et al., 2025; Stachura & Śleszyński, 2016; Toshmurod et al., 2025; Xu, 2025; Zhang et al., 2025).

Policymakers should ensure that economic development improves gender equality at different stages of development (Eastin & Prakash, 2013; Mehta & Awasthi, 2019). Therefore, a comprehensive approach that includes policy reforms, cultural changes and economic incentives is essential to ensure gender equality in the labour market.

26.3. Research Methodology

In developing the econometric study, the Statistical Agency under the President of the Republic of Uzbekistan (<https://stat.uz/>) and the World Bank (<https://data.worldbank.org/>) used data from 2012 to 2023, with a total number of observations of forty-four quarterly indicators.

Since the indicators consisting of observational data are formed on the basis of multifactor time series, the Vector Autoregressive (VAR) model was used to develop the econometric forecast.

In addition, when building the econometric model, the VAR model was evaluated based on descriptive statistics. The unit root test was conducted to assess the stationarity of the resulting variable and the variables affecting it, and the Johansen cointegration test was used to identify and assess the existence of periodic relationships between all factors. The optimal number of lags (previous periods) for the VAR model was determined, and then additional econometric diagnostic tests were examined. Tests for autocorrelation, model stability and reliability were developed to assess the accuracy and robustness of the forecast results obtained from the VAR model (Eshov et al., 2024; Karlibaeva et al., 2024; Khoshimovet al., 2024; Mamadiyarov et al., 2024; Ortikov et al., 2024).

Another group of economists has successfully used econometric models such as Fixed Effects Estimator, Random Effects Estimator, multivariate linear (LS) and ARDL in their research on investment in digital infrastructure, various aspects of digital payment systems, the impact of inflation and credit interest rates on investment, factors affecting the reduction of the state's share in commercial banks, Non-Performing Loans in commercial banks, the digitisation of banks, risks in digital services and the development of retail payment services (Cahyani et al., 2025; Habib et al., 2025; Jahrir et al., 2025; Mamadiyarov et al., 2025; Su et al., 2025; Zokir et al., 2021).

Analyses and forecasts were conducted using multivariate linear regression (LS), ARDL, ARIMA and various other econometric models on the global services market, digital economy, energy-related financial stress, cocktail market, digital transformation, factors affecting the logistics industry (Abdullah et al., 2025; Akhmetshin et al., 2025; Kalandarov et al., 2025; Khayrilla et al., 2025; Khodjaniyazov et al., 2025; Kuziboev et al., 2025; Lin et al., 2025; Mamadiyarov et al., 2025; Rayala et al., 2025; Rukhiddin et al., 2024; Samariddin et al., 2025).

The VAR model formula is given below.

VAR model structure: A VAR model with k variables and p lags can be expressed as follows:

$$Y_t = a + B_1 Y_{t-1} + B_2 Y_{t-2} + \dots + B_l Y_{t-l} + \varepsilon_t \quad (1)$$

Here, $Y_t = [y_{1t}, y_{2t}, y_{kt}]$, y_t – represents the $k \times 1$ vector of endogenous variables at time t, a – represents the $k \times 1$ vector of constants (intercepts), $B_1, B_2, \dots, B_l$ represents the coefficient matrices (each of size $k \times k$) representing the influence of past values on current values.

ε_t is the $k \times 1$ vector of error terms, the mean is zero and the covariance matrix.

When developing econometric forecast indicators, the variables in the model were formulated as follows.

The volume of healthcare services at the level of living of the population (billion soums) – *healthcare_serv* (dependent variable), the number of men employed in the labour market – *male_employ* (independent variable) and the number of women employed in the labour market – *female_employ* (independent variable), the inflation rate in the national economy.

The hypotheses of the econometric model were formulated as follows:

Null hypothesis (H_0): According to the main hypothesis, the employment of women and men in the labour market in the national economy does not significantly affect the volume of healthcare services at the level of living of the population.

Alternative hypothesis (H_1): According to the alternative hypothesis, the employment of women and men in the labour market in the national economy has a significant dependent effect on the volume of healthcare services at the level of living of the population.

26.4. Analysis and Results

In the first stage of the study, a Unit-root test was conducted to determine the stationarity of the volume of healthcare services and the factors affecting it on the standard of living of the population (Table 93).

Table 93. Unit-root test indicators of the volume of healthcare services and factors affecting the standard of living of the population

O'zgaruvchilar	Test Statistic	1% Critical Value	5% Critical Value	10% Critical Value	p-value for Z(t)
healthcare_serv	-6.428	-3.641	-2.955	-2.611	0.0000
male_employ	-6.250	-3.641	-2.955	-2.611	0.0000
female_employ	-6.248	-3.641	-2.955	-2.611	0.0000

Source: Developed by the authors based on the Stata program.

According to Table 93, the unit root test value of the dependent variables is −6.428 and the test result of the independent variables is −6.250 and −6.248, respectively. These values indicate that the factors affecting the volume of health care services on the standard of living of the population are statistically significant and stable.

The McKinnon value of 0.0000 from the table data indicates statistical significance for the critical values of $Z(t)$. Also, the unit root test indicates stationarity after the initial integration of the health care sector expenditure on the standard of living of the population and the factors affecting it.

In the next stage of the econometric study, the cointegration of the variables was checked, and in the absence of cointegration, the use of the VAR model was also considered. Also, the Johanson test was checked to determine the years lagged in the VAR model (Table 94).

Table 94. Test for determining optimal lags in the VAR model of the volume of health care services and factors affecting it on the standard of living of the population

Delayed period	LL	LR	df	*p*	FPE	AIC	HQIC	SBIC
0	-376.371				34716.2	18.9686	19.0144	19.0952
1	-88.6937	575.36	9	0.000	0.030902	5.03468	5.21788	5.54135
2	-32.1547	113.08*	9	0.000	0.002894*	2.65774*	2.97833*	3.5444*
3	-28.0738	8.1619	9	0.051	0.003782	2.90369	3.36167	4.17035
4	-28.0738	14.342	9	0.011	0.003782	2.99513	3.59051	4.64179

Source: Developed by the authors based on the Stata program.

According to Table 94, it follows that the optimal equation can be constructed at lag 2 according to the model. The *p*-value obtained from the optimal lag test according to the table is 0.000, which indicates that Lag 2 is the optimal choice for the VAR model.

All four model selection criteria – FPE, AIC, HQIC and SBIC – are at their lowest at lag 2. This emphasises that the econometric model is accurate and efficient, including two steps in the past.

In the next step, the cointegration test of the variables was performed using the Johanson test (Table 95).

Table 95. Johanson test for cointegration based on the VAR model of the volume of health care services and the factors affecting it in the standard of living of the population

Maximum rank	Params	LL	Eigenvalue	Trace statistic	Critical value 5%
0	12	-45.341454		27.7346*	29.68
1	17	-35.520734	0.37353	8.0931	15.41
2	20	-31.556215	0.17204	0.1641	3.76
3	21	-31.474174	0.00390		

Source: Developed by the authors based on the Stata program.

According to Table 95, if the observation statistic is less than the 5 per cent critical value, then cointegration is considered absent. That is, 29.73 less than 29.68, 8.09 less than 15.41 and 0.16 less than 3.765, according to which the result of this test indicates that there is no cointegrated vector in the model. In this case, if the value of the observation statistic is greater than the 5 per cent critical value, the H0 hypothesis is rejected.

The H0 hypothesis indicates that there is no cointegrated vector in the model. This hypothesis is accepted since the observation statistic is less than the 5 per cent critical value. According to it, since there is no at least one cointegrated vector, it indicates that there is no cointegration in the selected model.

In developing the study, a VAR model-specific value-stability test was developed based on the volume of healthcare services in the standard of living of the population and the factors affecting it (Figure 96).

Eigenvalue	Modulus
1.015455 + .01588134i	1.01558
1.015455 - .01588134i	1.01558
-1.015455 + .01588134i	1.01558
-1.015455 - .01588134i	1.01558
-.8098534	.809853
.8098534	.809853

Figure 96. Eigenvalue-stability test of the VAR model for the outcome variable and the factors affecting it.
Source: Developed by the authors.

According to Figure 96, these tests are important in analysing the constancy of long-term parameters in VAR models. According to the results of the plot, the VAR model successfully passed the stability test. The eigenvalues are obtained from the additional matrix of the VAR model. The econometric model is considered close to stability in terms of forecast indicators, and most of the eigenvalues are in the ideal range. The econometric model is considered robust, reliable for small changes and forecasts, that is, any shocks in the system disappear over time and the process reflects an average or balanced state.

In the next stage of the study, the VAR model was tested by the Lagrange-multiplier test on the outcome variable and the factors affecting it (Figure 97).

lag	chi2	df	Prob > chi2
1	163.5642	9	0.00000
2	82.7382	9	0.00000

Figure 97. Lagrange-Multiplier test of the VAR model on the output variable and the factors affecting it.
Source: Developed by the authors.

The results of the Lagrange-multiplier test indicate that there is significant autocorrelation in the data. The chi-square statistic for lag 1 is 163.5642, with 9 degrees of freedom and a p-value of 0.0000. The chi-square statistic for lag 2 is 82.7382, with 9 degrees of freedom and a p-value of 0.0000.

Since the p-values for both lags (0.0000) are below the 0.05 level of overall significance, we reject the null hypothesis (H_0: no autocorrelation in lag order) for both lags.

In the next step of the study, the Lagrange Multiplier (LM) test was performed to perform the forecasting on the VAR model. This test confirms that there is no autocorrelation in the model. Then, a Granger randomness test is performed to check the randomness of each exogenous factor relative to the endogenous factor (Figure 98).

Equation	Excluded	chi2	df	Prob > chi2
healthcare_serv	male_employ	16.758	1	0.000
healthcare_serv	female_employ	16.694	1	0.000
healthcare_serv	ALL	16.759	2	0.000
male_employ	healthcare_serv	8.7419	1	0.003
male_employ	female_employ	12.136	1	0.000
male_employ	ALL	20.981	2	0.000
female_employ	healthcare_serv	5.2632	1	0.022
female_employ	male_employ	9.0176	1	0.003
female_employ	ALL	16.613	2	0.000

Figure 98. Eigenvalue-stability test of the VAR model for the outcome variable and the factors affecting it.
Source: Developed by the authors.

According to Figure 98, the size of the health sector contribution to the standard of living of the population Prob > chi² p-value – if it is less than 0.05, the excluded variable Granger causes the dependent variable.

The positive view of p-values <0.05 indicates that the transition to employment in the health sector has a strong impact on both male and female employment trends, which, according to its internal dynamics, demonstrates a positive relationship.

Female employment Granger causes male employment ($p = 0.003$). All variables have significant ($p = 0.000$) values. This indicates that changes in female employment can predict male employment. This provides comprehensive results on labour market dynamics and gender-related employment processes. Male employment strongly Granger-causes female employment ($p = 0.000$). All variables together: $p = 0.000$ presented a significant value.

This interaction indicates that the employment of men and women in the labour market is closely related to each other. This strong relationship indicates that the employment of men and women in the labour market is in the social sectors, which demonstrates the priority position of the government in future planning and economic forecasting.

In the Granger causality test, the hypothesis H_0 is Granger randomness. If the value of p in this test is less than 0.05, the hypothesis H_0 is rejected. The values of all exogenous factors selected according to the econometric model in the observed period represent the impact of the endogenous factor on the future values.

In the next step, the Impulse-response function of the volume of health care services on the standard of living of the population and the factors affecting it is presented (Figure 99).

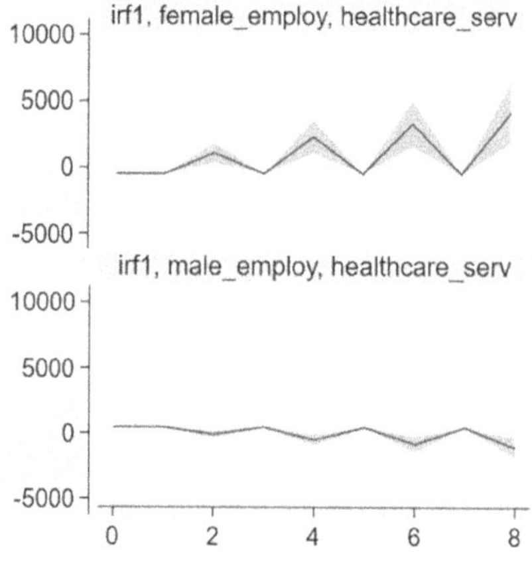

Figure 99. Impulse-response function plot of the volume of healthcare services and factors affecting the standard of living of the population.
Source: Developed by the authors.

According to Figure 99, the impulse-response function diagram shows how the size of the health care sector in the standard of living of the population responds to shocks in the labour market for men and women over time, in this case, the value at the 95 per cent confidence interval according to the econometric model is statistically significant. According to it, the increase in the resulting variable is associated with fluctuations within a limited range, which indicates that the labour market successfully manages shocks in the employment of men and women.

The shaded area (confidence interval) in the figure indicates that this effect is statistically significant in the case where it does not include zero. The growth of health services has positively and significantly increased female employment, which allows the expansion of this sector to create significant jobs for women.

The error bar graph of the volume of health care services and the factors affecting it on the standard of living of the population is presented next (Figure 100).

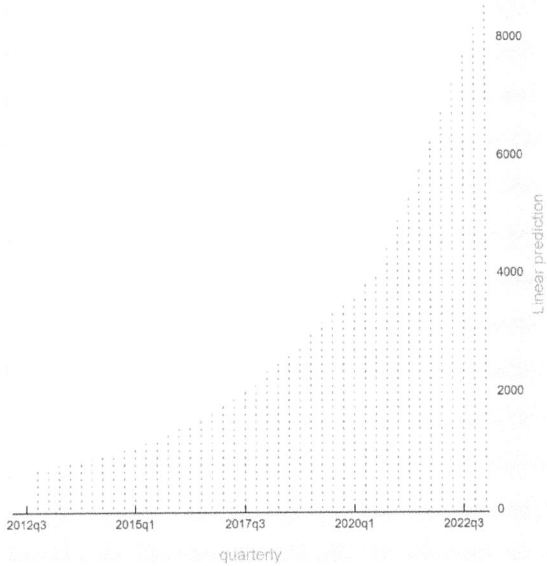

Figure 100. Error graphic representation of the volume of health care services and factors affecting the standard of living of the population.
Source: Developed by the authors.

According to Figure 100, the volume of health care services in the population's standard of living has achieved growth dynamics under the influence of various exogenous and endogenous factors. In addition, in the conditions of social reforms, women in the labour market are increasingly linked to the standard of living. The error graph indicators also indicate an increase in women's employment in the labour market, as the growth of the volume of health care services is increasingly linked to the standard of living. The statistical significance of the dynamics of women's employment directly contributes to the further strengthening of this sector as a result of investments in health care, as well as the creation of meaningful work opportunities for women, increasing household incomes and overall well-being.

In addition, the observed stability of the employment rate of men reflects a balanced reaction of the labour market, according to which the growth in the health care sector does not disrupt the existing employment dynamics. This indicates stable economic processes of socio-economic development.

In the next stage of the econometric study, the stationarity of the model residuals was assessed by forecasting (Table 96 and Figure 101).

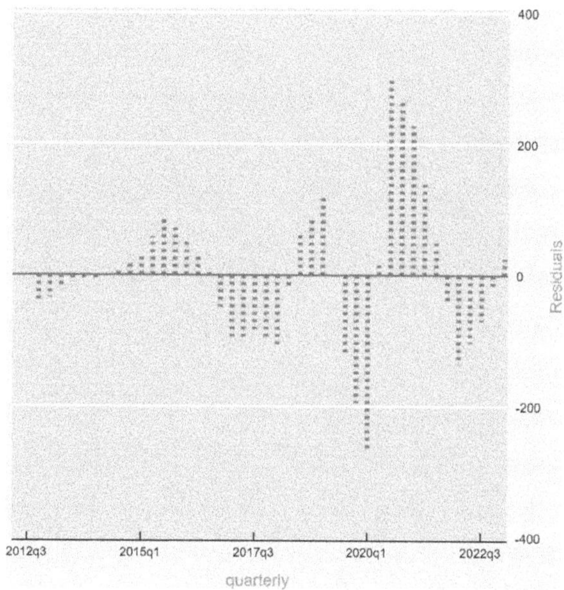

Figure 101. Stationarity graph of VAR model residuals by outcome factor.
Source: Developed by the authors.

Based on Figure 26.6 and Table 96, the VAR model has achieved stochastically stable stability over a certain period, as reflected in the graphical representation of the residuals. This visual representation reflects the model's fit to the observed data and effectively captures the inherent random relationships in the data set.

Table 96. Stationarity of model residuals by forecast

Variable	Obs	Mean	Std. Dev.	Min	Max
Error1	42	-2.92e-07	110.3797	-269.4388	300.8458

Source: Developed by the authors.

Based on the research, a forecast indicator of the volume of healthcare services at the population's standard of living from 2025 to 2030, excluding random factors, was developed based on the VAR model using the Stata program (Table 97).

Table 97. Forecast indicators of the volume of healthcare services (billion soums) at the level of living of the population for 2025–2030

Years	Pessimistic forecast	Optimistic forecast	Forecast
2025	13,787.95	12,980.24	**14,914.65**
2026	16,066.82	16,041.35	**17,862.11**
2027	18,412.56	19,657.39	**21,182.17**
2028	20,711.35	23,951.77	**24,895.71**
2029	22,822.88	29,080.08	**29,023.63**
2030	24,578.12	35,224.37	**33,586.32**

Source: Developed by the authors.

26.5. Results

Based on the VAR model of econometric research, the standard of living of the population in the national economy, including the social sector, excluding random factors based on the impact of male and female employment in the labour market on the volume of healthcare services, was projected to be 14,914.65 billion soums in 2025, 17,862.11 billion soums in 2026, 21,182.17 billion soums in 2027, 24,895.71 billion soums in 2028, 29,023.63 billion soums in 2029 and 33,586.32 billion soums in 2030, respectively.

Based on the econometric model, graphs were generated showing the standard of living of the population, the volume of healthcare services for 2012–2024, and the forecast for 2025–2029 (Figure 102).

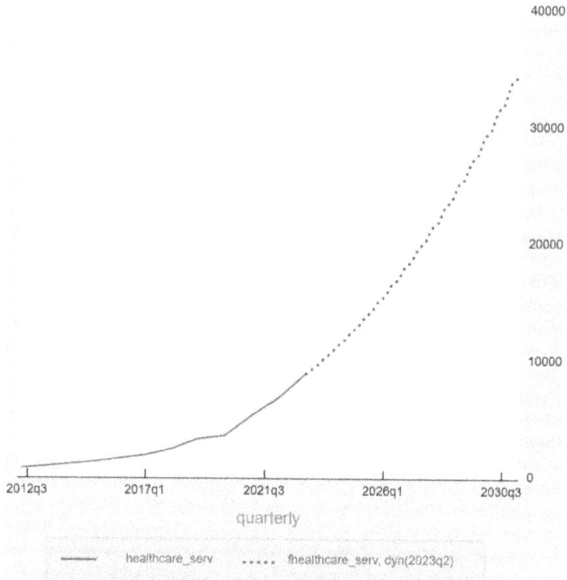

Figure 102. Graph of the volume of healthcare services at the level of living of the population for 2024–2029 and the forecast for 2025–2030.
Source: Developed by the authors based on the Stata program.

Figure 102 shows that, along with the forecast for 2025–2030, the actual values of the volume of health care services in relation to the standard of living for 2024–2029 have been determined. The trend lines in the graph are closely parallel to each other, demonstrating the high level of forecast indicators. It also indicates a positive growth trend, reflecting the expected growth of the volume of health care services in the standard of living of the population for the next six years under the influence of male and female employment in the labour market.

26.6. Conclusion

The econometric forecast based on the VAR model provides a solid and optimistic forecast for the volume of health care services in the standard of living of the population.

1. The importance of a stable growth forecast. The results of the VAR model forecast indicate positive growth indicators in the standard of living in the national economy, in particular in the social sphere, for the period from 2025 to 2030. Under the influence of the employment of men and women in the national labour market on the volume of health care services, excluding random dynamic fluctuations, the VAR model demonstrates a solid and stable optimistic forecast project from 14914.65 billion soums in 2025 to 33586.32 billion soums in 2030.
2. The importance of solid economic stability. Forecast indicators show a strong positive trend in the standard of living from year to year due to the effective interaction between the dynamics of the labour market and the development of health care, as well as the growth of the volume of health care services in the standard of living of the population.
3. The importance of the labour market in the development of the social sphere. According to the results of the econometric model, the stabilisation of the social sphere indicates a positive contribution to the steady growth of male and female employment in the labour market, especially through its impact on such important services as health care.
4. The importance of the reliability of forecast indicators. The results of the econometric model show that by eliminating random exogenous and endogenous factors, the reliability of the model forecast is further increased, and these forecast results serve to turn into an important and valuable tool in strategic planning and the formation of legal frameworks provided by the government.
5. Assessment of the significance of the forecast results in social impact: According to the forecast indicators, continuous growth represents a progressive and inclusive development path, which, if targeted investment practices are directed at employment and health, will lead to a long-term positive trend in the quality of life of the population.
6. In conclusion, the econometric forecast results demonstrate a positive and promising outlook for the future, confirming that the labour market and a strengthened health care system are important factors in improving living standards and social well-being.

Bibliography

Abdullah, M. A., Han, X., Amjad, M. A., & Makhmudov, S. (2025). Revisit the role of financial development on economic growth, human development, and sustainable development in higher-income countries. *Journal of Environmental Management*, *392*, 126874.

Akhmetshin, E., Abdullayev, I., Makhmudov, S., Dakhkilgova, K., Korotaeva, I. and Yanovskaya, G. (2025). APPLICATION OF TANH–COTH METHOD FOR COMBINED AND DOUBLE COMBINED SINH–COSH–GORDON EQUATIONS ARISING CHEMICAL REACTIONS TO WATER SURFACE GRAVITY WAVES. Computational Methods for Differential Equations, (), -. doi: 10.22034/cmde.2025.67655.3234

Algül, Y. (2024). 'Assessing the Relationship between Broad Gender Inequality and the Gender Unemployment Gap: Insights from an Extensive Global Macroeconometric Panel Analysis'. *Discover Sustainability*, 5 (1), <https://doi.org/10.1007/s43621-024-00663-y>.

Cahyani, I., Buriev, K., Ngongo, M., Mamadiyarov, Z., Ino, L., Herman, H., Saputra, N., & Baxtishodovich, S. (2025). Exploring the Use of TikTok Application in Enhancing the Skill of Pronunciation: A Case on Students' Perception. Studies in Media and Communication, 13(2), 150–158. doi: http://dx.doi.org/10.11114/smc.v13i2.7553

Eastin, J., and Prakash, A. (2013). 'Economic Development and Gender Equality: Is There a Gender Kuznets Curve?' *World Politics*, 65 (1), 156–86, <https://doi.org/10.1017/S0043887112000275>.

Habib, S. S., Islam, M. A., Ali, M. N., Benitez, I. B., Mamadiyarov, Z., Mirzayev, B., … & Flah, A. (2025). Multi-Objective Optimization and Feasibility Analysis of Integrated Biogas–Solar Energy Systems for Rural Electrification. *Results in Engineering*, 107086.

Hazarika, G., Khraiche, M., and Kutlu, L. (2023). 'Gender Equity in Labor Market Opportunities and Aggregate Technical Efficiency: A Case of Equity Promoting Efficiency'. *Applied Economics*, 1–12, <https://doi.org/10.1080/00036846.2023.2203451>.

Jahrir, A., Gultom, Y., Herman, H., Zabadi, F., Ngongo, M., Mamadiyarov, Z., Fatmawati, E., & Saputra, N. (2025). Investigating the Elements of Short Commercial Mineral Water Advertisement: A Case on Discourse

Analysis. Studies in Media and Communication, 13(4), 94–104. doi: http://dx.doi.org/10.11114/smc.v13i4.7813

Jomaa, H. (2024). 'Flexibility and Equality: Unraveling the Nexus of Labor Market Dynamics and Gender Equality in Developing Countries'. *Multidiszciplináris Tudományok*, 14 (3), 138–151, <https://doi.org/10.35925/j.multi.2024.3.12>.

Kabeer, N. (2021). 'Gender Equality, Inclusive Growth, and Labour Markets', pp. 13–48. Routledge, <https://doi.org/10.4324/9781003141938-3>.

Kalandarov, F., Makhmudov, S., Ibadullaev, D., Matniyozov, M., Nasretdinova, F., Sabirov, K., & Bahodirov, N. M. (2025). Low-Carbon Energy Risk and Renewable Energy Development: Insights from Method of Moments Quantile Regression. International Journal of Energy Economics and Policy, 15(3), 524–536.

Khayrilla Kurbonov, Samariddin Makhmudov, Shakhzod Erkinov, Umidjon Dadabaev, Gulnora Bekimbetova, Rukhiddin Zayniddinov, and Mirzabek Jonuzokov. 2025. Evaluating the Impact of Marketing Practices Digitalization and Investment on Labor Market Efficiency and Commercial Bank Performance Using Econometric Models. In Proceedings of the 8th International Conference on Future Networks & Distributed Systems (ICFNDS '24). Association for Computing Machinery, New York, NY, USA, 786–796. https://doi.org/10.1145/3726122.3726237

Khodjaniyazov, N., Mirkhoshimova, M., Kalandarov, F., Matyokubova, D., Utegenova, S., Makhmudov, S., & Khudayberganov, M. (2025). Time-Varying Impacts of Financial Stress on Energy-Related Uncertainty. International Journal of Energy Economics and Policy, 15(3), 689–698.

Kuchkarov, T., Mamadiyarov, Z., Khakimov, Z., Sabirova, O., Matmurodov, K., Raimboyeva, M., & Umarova, S. (2025). Energy-Related Uncertainty and Crypto-Currency Environmental Attention: Time-Varying Perspective. International Journal of Energy Economics and Policy, 15(5), 614–626. https://doi.org/10.32479/ijeep.20784

Kuziboev, B., Ozturk, I., Kalandarov, F., Samandarov, O., Bekjanov, D., & Makhmudov, S. (2025). PROMOTING ENERGY SOURCES DIVERSIFICATION THROUGH ESG PERFORMANCE. Energy, 136009.

Lin, M.H., Matchanova, B., Nurmatovich, H.A. et al. Optimal Operation of the Multi-Carrier Energy System Considering Energy Markets and Renewable Energies Participation. *Int. J. Appl. Comput. Math* 11, 170 (2025). https://doi.org/10.1007/s40819-025-02002-9

Lovell, V. (1999). 'A Cross-national Analysis of Economic Gender Equity and Welfare State Development'. *Research Papers in Economics*, <https://ideas.repec.org/p/lis/liswps/199.html>.

Mamadiyarov, Z., Eshov, M., Otakhonova, D., Utegenova, S., Sabirov, K., Marks, A., & Bahodirov, N. (2025). Does Energy Policy Risk Threaten Energy Sources Diversification?. *International Journal of Energy Economics and Policy*, *15*(5), 730–740. https://doi.org/10.32479/ijeep.21140

Mamadiyarov, Z. Makhmudov, S. Utanov, B. Kasimova, D. Bekmurodova, G. Hakimov, Z. (2025). Fusion of Economic and Financial Factors Affecting Household Deposits in Banks: An Econometric Analysis. Fusion: Practice and Applications, (), 82–91. DOI: https://doi.org/10.54216/FPA.190206

Mamadiyarov, Z., Saidov, O., Abdurazakova, N., Makhmudov, S., Nazarov, M., Rajabova, N., … Ruzmetova, I. (2025). Energy-Related Uncertainty and Tourism Stock Markets: New Insights from Time-Varying Relationship with TVP- VAR Approach. *International Journal of Energy Economics and Policy*, *15*(4), 730–737. https://doi.org/10.32479/ijeep.20480

Mamani, J.C.M., Miri, M., Vorobev, Y. et al. Optimal Operation of Energy Microgrid Considering Economic and Emission Indices. Oper. Res. Forum 6, 122 (2025). https://doi.org/10.1007/s43069-025-00523-z

Martínez Torrico, K. M. (2017). 'Brechas de género en el mercado laboral y pobreza: una aproximación a partir de microsimulaciones', 28, 43–81, <http://www.scielo.org.bo/pdf/rlde/n28/n28_a03.pdf>.

Mehta, B. S., and Awasthi, I. C. (2019). *Gender Inequality and Labour Market*, pp. 55–80. Singapore: Springer, <https://doi.org/10.1007/978-981-13-9057-9_3>.

Muhammad Zubair, Irfanud Din, Nadeem Sarwar et al. Revolutionizing Sepsis Diagnosis Using Machine Learning and Deep Learning Models: A Systematic Literature Review, 10 June 2025, PREPRINT (Version 1) available at Research Square [https://doi.org/10.21203/rs.3.rs-6731418/v1]

Ngongo, M., Herman, H., Ndandara, A., Jois Jaha, D. A., Peku Djawang, J. U. S., Tanggu Rame, M. M., Khamraeva, S. N., & Mamadiyarov, Z.

(2025). An Investigation of Meaning, Toponymy of Sumba Cultural Site's Names, and the Impact of Tourism Visitors on Surrounding Society. *Forum for Linguistic Studies*, 7(8), 679–693. https://doi.org/10.30564/fls.v7i8.10260

Pradhan, R., Hajiyev, E., Shichiyakh, R. et al. Optimal Techno-Economic Feasibility of an Off-Grid Microgrid System Using Load Flow Energy Management Strategies. *Oper. Res. Forum* 6, 120 (2025). https://doi.org/10.1007/s43069-025-00524-y

Ram, H., Chakravorty, S., and Goli, S. (2022). Does gender Inequality Affect Economic Development? An Evidence Based on Analysis of Cross-national Panel Data of 158 Countries, <https://doi.org/10.31235/osf.io/7svz4>.

Rayala, R. V., Borra, C. R., Vasudevan, V., Singhania, R., Cheekati, S., & Mamadiyarov, Z. (2025, July). Lightweight Deep Learning Framework for Human Activity Recognition: A MobileNet-LSTM Approach with WHOA Optimization. In *2025 International Conference on Innovations in Intelligent Systems: Advancements in Computing, Communication, and Cybersecurity (ISAC3)* (pp. 1–6). IEEE.

Rayala, R. V., Sandhya, N., Singhania, R., Cheekati, S., Borra, C. R., Vasudevan, V., & Mamadiyarov, Z. (2025, July). AI-Driven Tomato Quality Assessment: A Deep Learning Approach for Image-based Defect Detection and Classification. In *2025 International Conference on Innovations in Intelligent Systems: Advancements in Computing, Communication, and Cybersecurity (ISAC3)* (pp. 1–6). IEEE.

Romero, R. M., Zelinskaya, M., Makhmudov, S., Sapaev, S., & Rustambekovich, J. U. (2025, September). Modelling and Optimal Utilisation of the Renewable Energy Systems in Microgrid with Improving Reliability and Energy Efficiency. In Operations Research Forum (Vol. 6, No. 3, pp. 1–20). Springer International Publishing.

Rony, Z. T., Jefri, R., Rusmardiana, A., Pramono, S. A., & Mamadiyarov, Z. (2025). Downside Risk Measurement of Indonesian Financial and Energy Securities: A Value at Risk Perspective. *Journal of Applied Science, Engineering, Technology, and Education*, 7(2). https://doi.org/10.35877/454RI.asci3898

Rukhiddin Zayniddinov, Nodir Jumaev, Gulbakhor Irgasheva, Alam Asadov, Nosir Makhmudov, Sirojiddin Abrorov, and Samariddin

Makhmudov. 2025. The Influence of the Digital Economy on Economic Development Evidence from Uzbekistan. In Proceedings of the 8th International Conference on Future Networks & Distributed Systems (ICFNDS '24). Association for Computing Machinery, New York, NY, USA, 831–839. https://doi.org/10.1145/3726122.3726242

Samariddin Makhmudov, Malika Umarova, Khayrilla Kurbonov, Laylo Akbarova, Durdona Davletova, Nilufar Shanazarova, and Toshmurod Kulmanov. 2025. Evaluating the forecast indicators of the volume of highly liquid assets of commercial banks in the process of digital transformation. In Proceedings of the 8th International Conference on Future Networks & Distributed Systems (ICFNDS '24). Association for Computing Machinery, New York, NY, USA, 698–704. https://doi.org/10.1145/3726122.3726222

Samariddin Makhmudov, Kudratillo Tukhsanov, Saifulla Arslanbekov, Akram Amanov, Orifali Tursunov, Umarbek Jabbarov and Muyassarxon Mirzakarimova. 2024. Optimizing Supply Chain Financing Development Prospects of Digital Ecosystems in the European Logistics Industry. In The 8th International Conference on Future Networks & Distributed Systems (ICFNDS '24), December 11–12, 2024, Marakech, Morocco. ACM, New York, NY, USA, 12 Pages. https://doi.org/10.1145/3726122.3726200

Singagerda, F. S., Pratama, M. R., Alfairus, M. Q., Iskandar, A., & Mamadiyarov, Z. (2025). A Decision-Centric Approach to Risk Management in Aviation Stock Investments Using Value at Risk and Portfolio Optimization. *Journal of Applied Science, Engineering, Technology, and Education*, 7(1), 114–125. https://doi.org/10.35877/454RI.asci3870

Sofyanty, D., Romadhoni, R., Handriadi, H., Makhsudovna, I. S., Anwar, Z., & Mamadiyarov, Z. (2025). Strategic Decision Analysis for Investment Portfolios: Computational Risk Assessment in Transportation Asset Management. *Journal of Applied Science, Engineering, Technology, and Education*, 7(2). https://doi.org/10.35877/454RI.asci3897

Stachura, P., and Śleszyński, J. (2016). 'Gender Indicators of the United Nations Development Programme'. *Economic and Environmental Studies*, 16, 511–30, <http://yadda.icm.edu.pl/yadda/element/bwmeta1.element.desklight-4837b723-42a5-4cea-a384-6c03ab7b81b5>.

Su, R., Xiao, Y., Hamza, F., Mamadiyarov, Z., & Wahab, A. (2025). Scaling up green hydrogen in China: Economic opportunities and challenges. *International Journal of Hydrogen Energy, 131*, 60–69.

Toshmurod Kulmanov, Umidjon Dadabaev, Mansurbek Qulmetov, Aliboy Ulashov, Mirjalol Eshboyev, and Samariddin Makhmudov. 2025. Global Services Market Transformation Digitalization Export Trends and Future Forecasts. In Proceedings of the 8th International Conference on Future Networks & Distributed Systems (ICFNDS '24). Association for Computing Machinery, New York, NY, USA, 851–858. https://doi.org/10.1145/3726122.3726245

Xu, L. C. (2025). 'Gender Equality and Economic Development: A Cross-country Comparative Study'. *Advances in Economics, Management and Political Sciences*, 162 (1), 200–6, <https://doi.org/10.54254/2754-1169/2025.20393>.

Zhang, L., Zhao, Z., Qamri, G. M., & Makhmudov, S. (2025). Unleashing the critical role of renewable energy through global value chains and digitalization: A path towards environmental sustainability. *Journal of Environmental Management, 392*, 126688.

Zokir Toshtemirovich Mamadiyarov, Samandarboy Adhambek ugli Sulaymanov, Sarvar Anvar ugli Askarov, and Durdona Bakhtiyor kizi Uktamova. 2022. Impact of Covid-19 Pandemic on Accelerating The Digitization and Transformation of Banks. In Proceedings of the 5th International Conference on Future Networks and Distributed Systems (ICFNDS '21). Association for Computing Machinery, New York, NY, USA, 706–712. https://doi.org/10.1145/3508072.3508211

Assessing the Impact of Gender Equality and Total Income in the Labour Market Based on SEM and Multivariate Linear Models

Bobur Khonturayev, Kudratillo Tukhsanov, Kaxramon Mambetjanov, Zokir Mamadiyarov, Nargizaxon Shamshiyeva, Samariddin Makhmudov and Bobur Mirzayev

27.1. Introduction

While Uzbekistan has made significant policy reforms to achieve gender equality, effective implementation remains a challenge. Gender gaps persist in many areas, from the labour market to social norms. Addressing these issues requires a complex and coordinated approach that includes legal reforms, institutional strengthening, educational and targeted interventions. Capacity-building partnerships with ministries, agencies and other government departments responsible for implementing new initiatives will be a key factor in their success.

Uzbekistan has made significant progress in improving gender equality in access to health and education services. Efforts to ensure gender equality in education have successfully addressed gaps in access to higher education and access to re-primary education. This achievement is based on the country's strong human resource base. At the same time, it is necessary to consolidate these achievements and address persistent gender disparities in the labour market. Despite progress in education, gender disparities in the labour market persist. The failure to translate human capital potential into meaningful progress in the labour market means that the promise of increased investment in individuals and in the country's people is not being fully realised.

Uzbek politicians have sought to achieve gender equality on a broad scale, enshrining the principle of equality in the country's constitution, which states that 'women and men have equal rights'. The new 2022 Constitution of the Republic further strengthens the commitment to gender equality, stipulating that the state shall provide women and men with equal rights and opportunities in public and public affairs, as well as in other areas of society and the state (Article 58). One of the most useful advances that has stimulated progress in a number of areas is the openness and availability of evidence to facilitate progress. While gender-disaggregated statistics on development issues are not exhaustive, they are increasingly reflected in key areas, including the labour market, human capital and freedom of expression and participation, and many statistical indicators are consistent with the coverage provided by leading statistical agencies. This data is important both for public participation and for monitoring the country's progress towards major reforms. This information is crucial both for public participation and as a tool for monitoring the country's progress in implementing its ambitious reform agenda. The increased openness to information sharing and public consultation has also transformed the political landscape in terms of priorities and the diversity of stakeholders involved in policy development.

27.2. Literature Review

The main mechanism by which gender equality stimulates growth is to expand the talent pool available to businesses. Economies that exploit the full potential of their populations benefit from diverse perspectives that enhance innovation and competitiveness. Research by Felix Roessle et al. (2024) shows a positive correlation between female leadership and financial performance in German companies. Companies with more female leaders score lower on ESG issues and show an economic value added that is approximately 2 per cent higher than companies with fewer or no female leaders.

This suggests that women's leadership in society contributes to improved financial outcomes, potentially through improved governance and decision-making processes.

Increased gender equality in the labour market is an important factor in the effective use of human capital, which in turn allows for a wider distribution of skills and talents among labour resources. When women and men have equal access to education and employment opportunities, the overall skill level of the labour force improves, which in turn contributes to increased productivity.

Vesna Buterin et al. (2023) have shown in their research that better education for women in the European Union is associated with higher GDP per capital, highlighting the importance of educational equality in economic development.

According to Gautam Hazarika et al., (2023) gender equity in labour market opportunities increases aggregate technical efficiency in GDP production. This improvement is due to the active participation of talented women in the labour force, which increases the average quality of the labour pool. However, this effect can be mitigated by patriarchal cultural norms, which lead to a skewed distribution of women in the workforce, and it has been proven that cultural shifts, along with political changes, are necessary to fully realise the benefits of gender equality.

Renowned foreign scholars have used econometric equations in their scientific studies on gender equality in the labour market and the size of the total income of the population.

According to foreign scholar Matheus Koengkan, the impact of gender equality on the labour market is particularly important for the quality of employment. In Latin America, real effective exchange rate (REER) shocks have had different effects on job quality for men and women, while average price shocks have reduced the share of good jobs for men and inadvertently increased gender equality through the 'race to the bottom' dynamic (Matheus, Koengkan et al., 2022).

Gender equality is linked to macroeconomic outcomes, as achieving gender equality increases productivity. For example, gender equality in education significantly increases human capital (Kolovich et al., 2020). Reducing gender inequalities in the European Union has a positive impact on GDP per capita, primarily through increased productivity and output (Maceira, 2017). Gender equality can diversify the labour market and increase economic growth by increasing women's employment (Xu, 2025).

Gender inequality in the labour market is perpetuated by socio-cultural biases and systemic barriers, which lead to women being employed in low-paid jobs, especially in the informal sector (Mehta & Awasthi, 2019). The presence of gender barriers in labour markets means that they are forced to work in relatively low-paid jobs, which affects their financial situation (Behnert, 2022). Gender discrimination in the labour market can lead to the systematisation of work as a requirement of employers (Souza et al., 2025).

27.3. Research Methodology

Given that the data obtained for econometric studies consist of multivariate time series, we used multivariate linear regression (LS) and nonlinear structural equation models (SEM).

We also assessed the impact of gender equality in the labour market on macroeconomic indicators for 2008–2023 using data from the Statistical Agency under the President of the Republic of Uzbekistan (<https://stat.uz/uz>) and the World Bank (<https://data.worldbank.org/>). A total of 146 months of observational data were used in our analysis.

Using econometric models, the multivariate regression (LS) model was assessed for statistical significance using the Gauss-Markov, Durbin-Watson, Shapiro-Wilk and Breusch-Pagan tests. Meanwhile, the statistical significance of the SEM regression model was assessed using diagnostic tests, including the chi-square test, comparative fit index (CFI), root mean square error of approximation (RMSEA) and standardised mean square residual (SRMR) (Rukhiddin et al., 2025; Samariddin et al., 2025; Singagerda et al., 2025; Sofyanty et al., 2025; Su et al., 2025; Toshmurod et al., 2025;).

In the process of developing econometric models for the study, graphical diagrams and descriptive statistics tables were created to study the trends and distribution of variables. In addition, a correlation matrix was constructed to assess the relationship between dependent and independent variables and multicollinearity. Econometric equations were also constructed for multivariate regression (LS) and SEM regression models.

Analyses and forecasts were conducted using multivariate linear regression (LS), ARDL, ARIMA and various other econometric models on the global services market, digital economy, energy-related financial stress, cocktail market, digital transformation, factors affecting the logistics industry (Abdullah et al., 2025; Akhmetshin et al., 2025; Kalandarov et al., 2025; Khayrilla et al., 2025; Khodjaniyazov et al., 2025; Mamadiyarov et al., 2025; Rayala et al., 2025; Samariddin et al., 2025; Zokir et al., 2021).

Considering that the data obtained for econometric studies consist of multivariate time series, we used multivariate linear regression (LS) and nonlinear structural equation models (SEM).

Another group of economists has successfully used econometric models such as Fixed Effects Estimator (FEE), Random Effects Estimator (REE), multivariate linear (LS) and ARDL in their research on investment in digital infrastructure, various aspects of digital payment systems, the impact of inflation and credit interest rates on investment, factors affecting the reduction of the state's share in commercial banks, Non-Performing Loans in commercial banks, the digitisation of banks, risks in digital services and the development of retail payment services (Habib et al., 2025; Jahrir et al., 2025; Lin et al., 2025; Mamadiyarov et al., 2025;Mamani et al., 2025; Pradhan et al., 2025; Rayala et al., 2025; Romero et al., 2025; Rony et al., 2025; Samariddin et al., 2025; Toshmurod et al., 2025; Zhang et al., 2025; Zhao et al., 2025).

The structural equation modelling (SEM) model formula is given below.

$$\eta_i = \vartheta_{i1}\xi_1 + \vartheta_2\xi_2 + \ldots + \vartheta_{im}\xi_m + \zeta_i \quad (1)$$

Here, η_i is the endogenous latent variable (dependent variable),
$\xi_1, \xi_2, \ldots, \xi_m$ is the endogenous latent variable (independent variable),
ϑ_{ij} represents the path coefficients showing the effect of ξ_j on η_i.
ζ_i represents the structural error term for η_i.

Based on the variables selected for the study, eight econometric equations were developed. All variables for the econometric study are formulated below.

Total income of the population – *Ln_TotInc_Pop* (dependent variable),
Number of non-working population in the economy – *Ln_Nonpr_pop_ec* (dependent variable),
Number of employed women over 25 years old – *Ln_Empl_wom* (independent variable)
Number of women with higher education – *Ln_grad_edu_wom* (independent variable)
Number of employed men over 25 years old – *Ln_Empl_men* (independent variable)
Number of men with higher education – *Ln_grad_edu_men* (independent variable).

To develop hypotheses for the econometric study, we formulated null hypotheses (H_0) and alternative hypotheses (H_1). According to which, the null hypothesis indicates that there is no effect or relationship, while the alternative hypothesis indicates that there is an effect or relationship.

Hypotheses for all variables:
Null hypotheses (H_0):

$H_{0.1}$: The number of employed women over 25 years old in the national economy does not significantly affect the total income of the population.
$H_{0.2}$: The number of women with higher education in the national economy does not significantly affect the total income of the population.
$H_{0.3}$: The number of employed men over 25 years old in the national economy does not significantly affect the total income of the population.
$H_{0.4}$: The number of men with higher education in the national economy does not significantly affect the total income of the population.

Alternative hypotheses (H_1):

$H_{1.1}$: The number of employed women over 25 years old in the national economy has a significant impact on the size of the total income of the population.
$H_{1.2}$: The number of women with higher education in the national economy has a significant impact on the size of the total income of the population.
$H_{1.3}$: The number of employed men over 25 years old in the national economy has a significant impact on the size of the total income of the population.
$H_{1.4}$: The number of men with higher education in the national economy has a significant impact on the size of the total income of the population.

27.4. Analysis and Results

According to the study, an analytical graphical representation of the total income of the population and the factors affecting it over time with gender equality in the labour market was as follows (Figures 103 and 104).

According to Figure 103, during the analysed period, the dependent variables in assessing the impact of gender equality in the labour market in the national economy, in particular, the total income of the population, showed an increasing trend. Also, the number of unemployed people in the economy showed a decreasing trend in the first quarter of 2020. The main reason for this can be explained by the impact of the COVID-2019 pandemic.

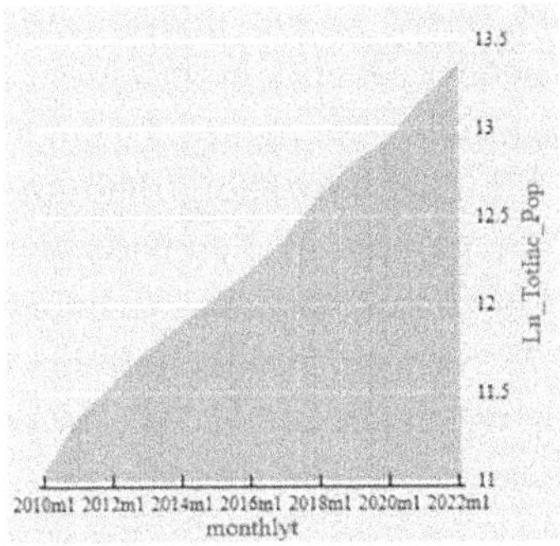

Figure 103. Analytical graphic representation of the total income of the population over time with gender equality in the labour market.
Source: Developed by the authors based on the Stata program.

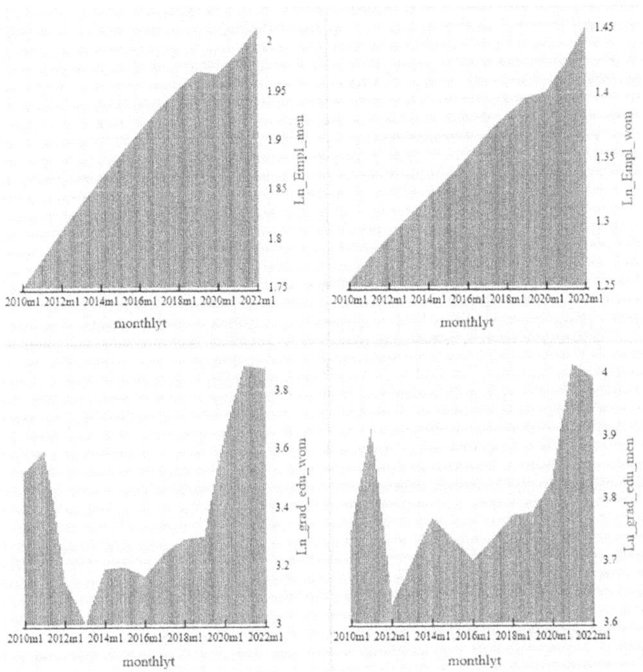

Figure 104. Analytical graphical representation of independent variables over time in assessing the impact of gender equality in the labour market.
Source: Developed by the authors based on the Stata program.

According to Figure 104, in the period analysed, independent variables in assessing the impact of gender equality in the labour market in the national economy, including the number of employed women over 25 years old, the number of women with higher education, the number of employed men over 25 years old, and the number of men with higher education, formed an increasing trend and stochastic fluctuations. In particular, the number of employed women over 25 years old and the number of employed men over 25 years old decreased between 2012 and 2014. The period from 2018 to the present has created a sharp increase in these factors.

At the next stage of the econometric study, the correlation matrix for each of the dependent and independent variables in assessing the impact of gender equality in the labour market was examined (Table 98).

Table 98. Correlation matrix of the total income of the population and the factors affecting it when assessing the impact of gender equality in the labour market

Variables	(1)	(2)	(3)	(4)	(5)
(1) Ln_TotInc_~p	1.000				
(2) Ln_Empl_men	0.7273	1.000			
	(0.0000)				***
(3) Ln_grad_ed~n	0.7975	0.7925	1.000		
	(0.0000)	(0.0000)			***
(4) Ln_Empl_wom	0.5203	0.4069	0.5031	1.000	
	(0.0000)	(0.0000)	(0.0000)		***
(5) Ln_Empl_wom	0.5622	0.4567	0.5465	0.7481	1.000
	(0.0000)	(0.0000)	(0.0000)	0.0000	***

Source: Developed by the authors based on the Stata program.

According to Table 98, the data used to assess the impact of gender equality in the labour market on macroeconomic indicators were studied and showed strong, significant, moderate and inverse relationships among all variables. An econometric model of the impact of the number of employed women over 25 years of age and the number of women with higher education on the total income of the population in the economy was developed.

$$Ln\_TotInc\_Pop = \beta_0 + \beta_1 Ln\_Empl\_wom + \beta_2 Ln\_grad\_edu\_wom \quad (1)$$

Where β_0 – intercept (continuous term), β_1 and β_{03} represent the coefficients for the respective independent variables. The coefficients from the regression results are expressed as follows.

Table 99. Multivariate linear regression (LS) model indicators of the total income of the population and the factors affecting it

Ln_TotInc_Pop	Coef.	St.Err.	t-value	p-value	[95% Conf	Interval]	Sig
Ln_Empl_wom	11.679	0.078	150.52	0	11.526	11.832	***
Ln_grad_edu_wom	0.061	0.016	3.77	0	0.029	0.094	***
Constant	-3.722	0.091	-41.09	0	-3.901	-3.543	***

Mean dependent var	12.244	SD dependent var	0.634
R-squared	0.795	Number of obs	145
F-test	1558.827	Prob > *F*	0.000
Akaike crit. (AIC)	-497.767	Bayesian crit. (BIC)	-488.837

*** $p < 0.01$, ** $p < 0.05$, * $p < 0.1$

Source: Developed by the authors based on the Stata program.

$$Ln\_TotInc\_Pop = -3.72 + 11.67Ln\_Empl\_wom + 0.06Ln\_grad\_edu\_wom \quad (2)$$

Statistical significance:

All coefficients are statistically significant at the 0.05 level, taking into account the *p*-values (all *p*-values <0.05).

Econometric model fit:

R-squared (0.79): This indicates that approximately 79 per cent of the variance in total income of the population is explained by the model. Adjusted *R*-squared (0.76): Represents the *R*-squared value for the number of predictors in the model.

F-statistic: 1558.82 ($p = 0.0000$): Represents the overall statistical significance of the model.

Result. A 1 per cent increase in the number of employed women over 25 in the national economy leads to an 11.67 per cent increase in total income of the population. A 1 per cent increase in the number of women with higher education leads to an increase in the total income of the population by 0.06 per cent.

As a second econometric equation, an econometric model of the impact of the number of employed men over 25 years old and the number of men with higher education on the total income of the population in the national economy was developed.

$$Ln\_TotInc\_Pop = \beta_0 + \beta_1 Ln\_Empl\_men + \beta_2 Ln\_grad\_edu\_men \quad (3)$$

The coefficients of the regression results are expressed as follows.

Table 100. Multivariate linear regression (LS) model indicators of the total income of the population and the factors affecting it

Ln_TotInc_Pop	Coef.	St.Err.	t-value	p-value	[95% Conf	Interval]	Sig
Ln_Empl_men	7.808	0.078	100.35	0	7.654	7.961	***
Ln_grad_edu_men	0.918	0.06	15.28	0	0.8	1.037	***
Constant	-6.047	0.207	-29.18	0	-6.457	-5.637	***

Mean dependent var	12.244	*SD dependent var*	0.634
R-squared	0.790	*Number of obs*	145
F-test	7394.558	*Prob > F*	0.000
Akaike crit. (AIC)	-390.629	*Bayesian crit. (BIC)*	-381.699
*** $p < 0.01$, ** $p < 0.05$, * $p < 0.1$			

Source: Developed by the authors based on the Stata program.

$$Ln\_TotInc\_Pop = -6.04 + 7.80 Ln\_Empl\_men + 0.91 Ln\_grad\_edu\_men \quad (4)$$

Statistical significance:

All coefficients are statistically significant at the 0.05 level, taking into account *p*-values (all *p*-values <0.05).

Econometric model fit:

R-squared (0.79): It indicates that approximately 79 per cent of the variance in the total income of the population is explained by the model. Adjusted *R*-squared (0.77): It represents the

R-squared value for the number of predictors in the model.

F-statistic: 7394.55 (p=0.0000): It represents the overall statistical significance of the model.

Result. A 1 per cent increase in the number of employed men over 25 in the national economy leads to a 7.80 per cent increase in the total income of the population. A 1 per cent increase in the number of men with higher education leads to a 0.91 per cent increase in the total income of the population.

Applying the Durbin–Watson test to the multivariate linear regression model yielded an estimated coefficient of 1.20. In addition, the analysis showed a Shapiro–Wilk W test statistic of 0.17, along with a Breusch-Pagan test statistic of 0.36. The primary null hypothesis, H_0: $y = 0$, and the corresponding alternative hypothesis, H_1: $y \neq 0$, were tested at a significance level of $p > 0.05$. After conducting the Durbin-Watson, Breusch-Pagan, and Shapiro-Wilk tests, the null hypothesis was confirmed, since the p-value was greater than the 0.05 threshold.

Thus, it can be concluded that the Gauss-Markov hypothesis, which states that there is no relationship between the residuals and the independent variables, is valid within the framework of our study.

In the econometric analysis, the fundamental assumptions of Gauss-Markov were met. The VIF test was used to assess multicollinearity in the research model, which showed that there was no multicollinearity in the created model. The VIF value of 1.48 indicates the relationship between the influence of macroeconomic indicators on the assessment of gender equality in the labour market and the factors influencing it.

At the same time, the analysis of the multivariate linear regression model showed the statistical significance of the main hypothesis H_0: $y = 0$, H_1: $y \neq 0$ at the $p < 0.10$ significance level. As a result, the alternative hypothesis was not confirmed. The Gauss-Markov condition is satisfied within the specified threshold range of the VIF test value from 1 to 10.

Also, during our study, the SEM regression model plot and test indicators looked like this (Figures 105 and 106).

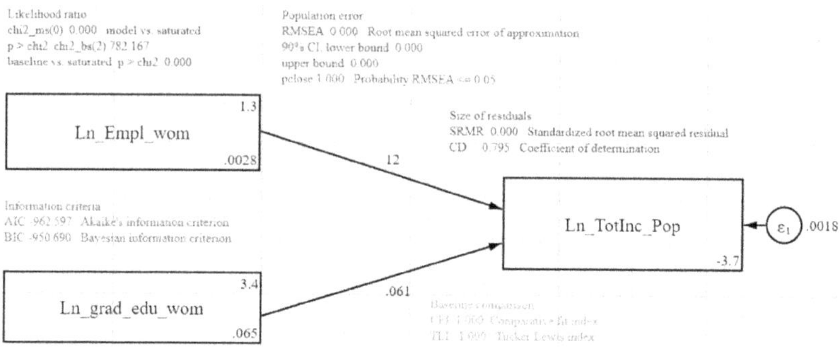

Figure 105. Schematic representation of the SEM regression model between the size of the total income of the population and the factors affecting it.
Source: Developed by the authors based on the Stata program.

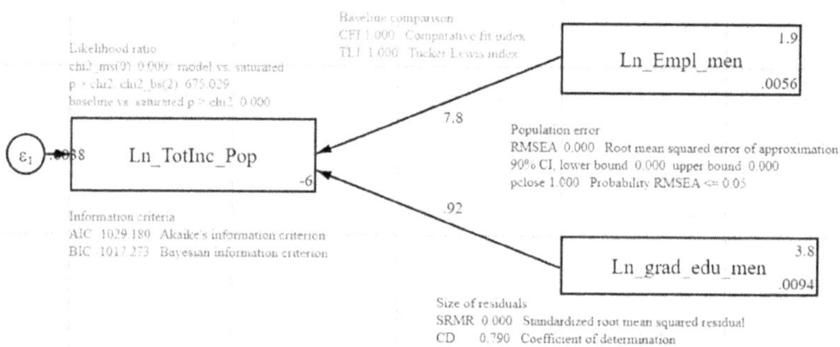

Figure 106. Schematic representation of the SEM regression model between the size of the total income of the population and the factors affecting it.
Source: Developed by the authors based on the Stata program.

As shown in Figures 105 and 106, Structural Equation Modelling (SEM) provided favourable results for the regression model. This approach confirmed that the model was properly constructed to reliably estimate the relationship between variables.

Evaluating the effectiveness of the SEM regression system usually requires the use of several statistical indicators and estimators, such as the chi-square test, comparative fit index (CFI), root mean square error of approximation (RMSEA) and standardised mean square residual (SRMR) indices.

27.5. Results

The study, conducted in order to assess the impact of gender equality on macroeconomic indicators in the labour market, developed the following proposals and recommendations based on the analysis and conclusions of the study of the interaction between the total income of the population, the number of employed women over 25 years old, the number of women with higher education, the number of employed men over 25 years old, and the number of men with higher education.

The following conclusions were drawn based on the results of the multivariate linear regression (LS) model and the Structural Equation Modelling (SEM) regression model on the macroeconomic indicators of gender equality in the labour market and the factors affecting it.

1. A 1 per cent increase in the number of employed women over 25 years old in the national economy leads to an increase in the total income of the population by 11.67 per cent. A 1 per cent increase in the number of women with higher education leads to a 0.06 per cent increase in total income. According to this result,

   1.1. Significant impact of female employment on total income: The result shows that an increase in the number of employed women over 25 years of age has a significant impact on total income. A 1 per cent increase in their employment leads to an 11.67 per cent increase in total income, which indicates that the practice of encouraging women's labour force participation can be highly effective in ensuring overall economic growth.

   1.2. Higher education of women contributes to economic achievements: A 1 per cent increase in the number of women with higher education leads to an increase in total income by 0.06 per cent. This positive relationship, although small, highlights the importance of education in increasing women's earning potential and contributing to the broader economy.

1.3. The significant increase in total income from increased female employment suggests that promoting gender-inclusive employment practices can be a powerful economic development strategy. This is explained by the importance of creating enabling conditions for women's employment, such as education, training and job support.
1.4. Although the increase in total income from increased tertiary education among women is relatively small, it is still a significant gain. This finding supports the idea that investing in education, especially for women, can yield positive returns over time and contribute to individual and societal economic well-being.
1.5. Expanding women's labour force participation and access to higher education can help reduce income inequality. As women become more employed and educated, they contribute more to household income and overall economic stability, which benefits society as a whole.

2. A 1 per cent increase in the number of employed men over 25 in the economy leads to a 7.80 per cent increase in the total income of the population, and a 1 per cent increase in the number of men with higher education leads to a 0.91 per cent increase in the total income of the population.

2.1. Strong impact of male employment on income growth: A 1 per cent increase in the employment of men over 25 leads to a 7.80 per cent increase in the total income of the population, which indicates a significant positive impact of male employment on the national economy. This shows that policies and programmes aimed at increasing jobs and employment rates among men lead to a significant increase in income and directly contribute to overall economic development.
2.2. Significant impact of higher education on income: The finding that a 1 per cent increase in the number of men with tertiary education leads to a 0.91 per cent increase in total household income suggests a strong link between men's educational attainment and economic performance. This highlights the importance of investing in higher

education for men, as it leads to a well-educated workforce that generates innovation, productivity and higher incomes.

2.3. Education as a key driver of economic growth: The high impact of male tertiary education on total income (0.91%) suggests that education is a key driver of economic performance. This provides a basis for developing policies that encourage and support men's higher education, including scholarships, financial aid and improved educational infrastructure.

2.4. Potential of Workforce Development Programmes: The results highlight the importance of workforce development initiatives that target male employment and education. Programmes such as skills training, career development and job placement services can help improve men's employment rates and educational attainment, thereby boosting overall economic growth.

2.5. Complementary Role of Male Employment and Education: The positive impact of male employment and education on overall earnings suggests that efforts to improve both can have a synergistic effect on economic growth. This reinforces the importance of integrated approaches to economic policy that address employment and educational opportunities simultaneously.

2.6. Long-Term Economic Stability and Growth: By increasing male employment and education, a country can build a stronger and more sustainable economy. A well-educated and employed male workforce contributes to higher productivity, greater innovation and sustained economic growth, which in turn contributes to a country's competitiveness and economic stability in the long term.

2.7. Overall, these results highlight the importance of promoting employment and education among men to ensure significant and sustainable growth in aggregate income and economic well-being.

Bibliography

Abdullah, M. A., Han, X., Amjad, M. A., & Makhmudov, S. (2025). Revisit the role of financial development on economic growth, human development, and sustainable development in higher-income countries. *Journal of Environmental Management*, *392*, 126874.

Akhmetshin, E., Abdullayev, I., Makhmudov, S., Dakhkilgova, K., Korotaeva, I. and Yanovskaya, G. (2025). APPLICATION OF TANH–COTH METHOD FOR COMBINED AND DOUBLE COMBINED SINH–COSH–GORDON EQUATIONS ARISING CHEMICAL REACTIONS TO WATER SURFACE GRAVITY WAVES. Computational Methods for Differential Equations, (), -. doi: 10.22034/cmde.2025.67655.3234

Behnert, C. (2022). *Gender and the Division of Labor*, pp. 239–51, Routledge eBooks, <https://doi.org/10.4324/9780367808983-23>.

Felix, Roessle., Carola, Fleischmann., and Kathrin, Roessle (2024). 'Gender Diversity and Financial Performance in Executive Positions in German Companies'. *Problems and Perspectives in Management*, 22 (2), 571–81, <https://doi.org/10.21511/ppm.22(2).2024.44>.

Gautam, Hazarika, Maroula, Khraiche, and Levent, Kutlu (2023). 'Gender Equity in Labor Market Opportunities and Aggregate Technical Efficiency: A Case of Equity Promoting Efficiency'. *Applied Economics*, 1–12. <https://doi.org/10.1080/00036846.2023.2203451>.

Habib, S. S., Islam, M. A., Ali, M. N., Benitez, I. B., Mamadiyarov, Z., Mirzayev, B., … & Flah, A. (2025). Multi-Objective Optimization and Feasibility Analysis of Integrated Biogas–Solar Energy Systems for Rural Electrification. *Results in Engineering*, 107086.

Kalandarov, F., Makhmudov, S., Ibadullaev, D., Matniyozov, M., Nasretdinova, F., Sabirov, K., & Bahodirov, N. M. (2025). Low-Carbon Energy Risk and Renewable Energy Development: Insights from Method of Moments Quantile Regression. International Journal of Energy Economics and Policy, 15(3), 524–536.

Khayrilla Kurbonov, Samariddin Makhmudov, Shakhzod Erkinov, Umidjon Dadabaev, Gulnora Bekimbetova, Rukhiddin Zayniddinov, and Mirzabek Jonuzokov. 2025. Evaluating the Impact of Marketing Practices Digitalization and Investment on Labor Market Efficiency and Commercial Bank Performance Using Econometric Models. In Proceedings of the 8th International Conference on Future Networks & Distributed Systems (ICFNDS '24). Association for Computing Machinery, New York, NY, USA, 786–796. https://doi.org/10.1145/3726122.3726237

Khodjaniyazov, N., Mirkhoshimova, M., Kalandarov, F., Matyokubova, D., Utegenova, S., Makhmudov, S., & Khudayberganov, M. (2025).

Time-Varying Impacts of Financial Stress on Energy-Related Uncertainty. International Journal of Energy Economics and Policy, 15(3), 689–698.

Kolovich, L., Malta, V., Newiak, M., and Robinson, D. (2020). 'Gender Equality and Macroeconomic Outcomes: Evidence and Policy Implications'. *Oxford Review of Economic Policy*, 36 (4), 743–759. <https://doi.org/10.1093/OXREP/GRAA049>.

Kuchkarov, T., Mamadiyarov, Z., Khakimov, Z., Sabirova, O., Matmurodov, K., Raimboyeva, M., & Umarova, S. (2025). Energy-Related Uncertainty and Crypto-Currency Environmental Attention: Time-Varying Perspective. International Journal of Energy Economics and Policy, 15(5), 614–626. https://doi.org/10.32479/ijeep.20784

Kuziboev, B., Ozturk, I., Kalandarov, F., Samandarov, O., Bekjanov, D., & Makhmudov, S. (2025). PROMOTING ENERGY SOURCES DIVERSIFICATION THROUGH ESG PERFORMANCE. Energy, 136009.

Lin, M.H., Matchanova, B., Nurmatovich, H.A. et al. Optimal Operation of the Multi-Carrier Energy System Considering Energy Markets and Renewable Energies Participation. *Int. J. Appl. Comput. Math* **11**, 170 (2025). https://doi.org/10.1007/s40819-025-02002-9

Litamahuputty, J. V., Amiruddin, E. G., Rahim, R., Rahman, A., & Mamadiyarov, Z. (2025). Cryptocurrency Risk Management through Decision Engineering: Evaluating XRPUSD and ADAUSD Portfolio Performance. Journal of Applied Science, Engineering, Technology, and Education, 7(1), 69–81. https://doi.org/10.35877/454RI.asci3871

Maceira, H. M. (2017). 'Economic Benefits of Gender Equality in the EU'. *Intereconomics*, 2017 (3), 178–83. <https://doi.org/10.1007/S10272-017-0669-4>.

Mamadiyarov, Z., Eshov, M., Otakhonova, D., Utegenova, S., Sabirov, K., Marks, A., & Bahodirov, N. (2025). Does Energy Policy Risk Threaten Energy Sources Diversification?. *International Journal of Energy Economics and Policy*, *15*(5), 730–740. https://doi.org/10.32479/ijeep.21140

Mamadiyarov, Z. Makhmudov, S. Utanov, B. Kasimova, D. Bekmurodova, G. Hakimov, Z. (2025). Fusion of Economic and Financial Factors Affecting Household Deposits in Banks: An Econometric Analysis.

Fusion: Practice and Applications, (), 82–91. DOI: https://doi.org/10.54216/FPA.190206

Mamadiyarov, Z., Saidov, O., Abdurazakova, N., Makhmudov, S., Nazarov, M., Rajabova, N., … Ruzmetova, I. (2025). Energy-Related Uncertainty and Tourism Stock Markets: New Insights from Time-Varying Relationship with TVP- VAR Approach. *International Journal of Energy Economics and Policy*, *15*(4), 730–737. https://doi.org/10.32479/ijeep.20480

Matheus, Koengkan, José, Alberto, Fuinhas, Matheus, Belucio, Emad, Kazemzadeh, Yormy, Eliana, Poveda, Nooshin, Karimi, Alavijeh, and Renato, Santiago (2022). 'The Consequences of Gender Inequality on Latin America's Economic Growth: Macroeconomic Evidence'. *Sexes*, 3 (3):396–412. https://doi.org/10.3390/sexes3030030.

Mehta, B. S., and Awasthi, I. C. (2019). *Gender Inequality and Labour Market*, pp. 55–80. Singapore: Springer. <https://doi.org/10.1007/978-981-13-9057-9_3>.

Ngongo, M., Herman, H., Ndandara, A., Jois Jaha, D. A., Peku Djawang, J. U. S., Tanggu Rame, M. M., Khamraeva, S. N., & Mamadiyarov, Z. (2025). An Investigation of Meaning, Toponymy of Sumba Cultural Site's Names, and the Impact of Tourism Visitors on Surrounding Society. *Forum for Linguistic Studies*, 7(8), 679–693. https://doi.org/10.30564/fls.v7i8.10260

Pradhan, R., Hajiyev, E., Shichiyakh, R. et al. Optimal Techno-Economic Feasibility of an Off-Grid Microgrid System Using Load Flow Energy Management Strategies. *Oper. Res. Forum* **6**, 120 (2025).

Rayala, R. V., Borra, C. R., Vasudevan, V., Singhania, R., Cheekati, S., & Mamadiyarov, Z. (2025, July). Lightweight Deep Learning Framework for Human Activity Recognition: A MobileNet-LSTM Approach with WHOA Optimization. In *2025 International Conference on Innovations in Intelligent Systems: Advancements in Computing, Communication, and Cybersecurity (ISAC3)* (pp. 1–6). IEEE.

Rayala, R. V., Sandhya, N., Singhania, R., Cheekati, S., Borra, C. R., Vasudevan, V., & Mamadiyarov, Z. (2025, July). AI-Driven Tomato Quality Assessment: A Deep Learning Approach for Image-based Defect Detection and Classification. In *2025 International Conference on Innovations in Intelligent Systems: Advancements in Computing, Communication, and Cybersecurity (ISAC3)* (pp. 1–6). IEEE.

Romero, R. M., Zelinskaya, M., Makhmudov, S., Sapaev, S., & Rustambekovich, J. U. (2025, September). Modelling and Optimal Utilisation of the Renewable Energy Systems in Microgrid with Improving Reliability and Energy Efficiency. In Operations Research Forum (Vol. 6, No. 3, pp. 1–20). Springer International Publishing.

Rony, Z. T., Jefri, R., Rusmardiana, A., Pramono, S. A., & Mamadiyarov, Z. (2025). Downside Risk Measurement of Indonesian Financial and Energy Securities: A Value at Risk Perspective. *Journal of Applied Science, Engineering, Technology, and Education*, 7(2). https://doi.org/10.35877/454RI.asci3898https://doi.org/10.1007/s43069-025-00524-y

Rukhiddin Zayniddinov, Nodir Jumaev, Gulbakhor Irgasheva, Alam Asadov, Nosir Makhmudov, Sirojiddin Abrorov, and Samariddin Makhmudov. 2025. The Influence of the Digital Economy on Economic Development Evidence from Uzbekistan. In Proceedings of the 8th International Conference on Future Networks & Distributed Systems (ICFNDS '24). Association for Computing Machinery, New York, NY, USA, 831–839. https://doi.org/10.1145/3726122.3726242

Samariddin Makhmudov, Malika Umarova, Khayrilla Kurbonov, Laylo Akbarova, Durdona Davletova, Nilufar Shanazarova, and Toshmurod Kulmanov. 2025. Evaluating the forecast indicators of the volume of highly liquid assets of commercial banks in the process of digital transformation. In Proceedings of the 8th International Conference on Future Networks & Distributed Systems (ICFNDS '24). Association for Computing Machinery, New York, NY, USA, 698–704. https://doi.org/10.1145/3726122.3726222

Samariddin Makhmudov, Kudratillo Tukhsanov, Saifulla Arslanbekov, Akram Amanov, Orifali Tursunov, Umarbek Jabbarov and Muyassarxon Mirzakarimova. 2024. Optimizing Supply Chain Financing Development Prospects of Digital Ecosystems in the European Logistics Industry. In The 8th International Conference on Future Networks & Distributed Systems (ICFNDS '24), December 11–12, 2024, Marakech, Morocco. ACM, New York, NY, USA, 12 Pages. https://doi.org/10.1145/3726122.3726200

Singagerda, F. S., Pratama, M. R., Alfairus, M. Q., Iskandar, A., & Mamadiyarov, Z. (2025). A Decision-Centric Approach to Risk Management in Aviation Stock Investments Using Value at Risk and Portfolio Optimization. *Journal of Applied Science, Engineering,*

Technology, and Education, 7(1), 114–125. https://doi.org/10.35877/454RI.asci3870

Sofyanty, D., Romadhoni, R., Handriadi, H., Makhsudovna, I. S., Anwar, Z., & Mamadiyarov, Z. (2025). Strategic Decision Analysis for Investment Portfolios: Computational Risk Assessment in Transportation Asset Management. *Journal of Applied Science, Engineering, Technology, and Education*, 7(2). https://doi.org/10.35877/454RI.asci3897

Souza, K. B. de, Domingues, É. P., and Hewings, G. J. D. (2025). 'Economic Consequences of Eliminating Gender Discrimination in the Labor Market'. *Economic Systems Research*, 1–19, <https://doi.org/10.1080/09535314.2024.2437365>.

Su, R., Xiao, Y., Hamza, F., Mamadiyarov, Z., and Wahab, A. (2025). 'Scaling Up Green Hydrogen in China: Economic Opportunities and Challenges'. *International Journal of Hydrogen Energy*, 131, 60–9.

Toshmurod Kulmanov, Umidjon Dadabaev, Mansurbek Qulmetov, Aliboy Ulashov, Mirjalol Eshboyev, and Samariddin Makhmudov. 2025. Global Services Market Transformation Digitalization Export Trends and Future Forecasts. In Proceedings of the 8th International Conference on Future Networks & Distributed Systems (ICFNDS '24). Association for Computing Machinery, New York, NY, USA, 851–858. https://doi.org/10.1145/3726122.3726245

Vesna, Buterin, Barbara, Fajdetić, and Barbara, Funarić (2023). 'Understanding the Macroeconomic Effects of Female Participation in the Labour Market'. *Economies*, <https://doi.org/10.3390/economies11110280>.

Xu, L. C. (2025). 'Gender Equality and Economic Development: A Cross-country Comparative Study'. *Advances in Economics, Management and Political Sciences*, 162 (1), 200–6. <https://doi.org/10.54254/2754-1169/2025.20393>.

Zhang, L., Zhao, Z., Qamri, G. M., & Makhmudov, S. (2025). Unleashing the critical role of renewable energy through global value chains and digitalization: A path towards environmental sustainability. *Journal of Environmental Management*, *392*, 126688.

Zhao, Q., Pervaiz, A., Makhmudov, S., & Fatima, A. (2025). Do environmental stringent policies enhance the impact of renewable energy on CO2 reduction? Evidence from BRICS-T economies. Journal of Environmental Management, 391, 126464.

Zokir Toshtemirovich Mamadiyarov, Samandarboy Adhambek ugli Sulaymanov, Sarvar Anvar ugli Askarov, and Durdona Bakhtiyor kizi Uktamova. 2022. Impact of Covid-19 Pandemic on Accelerating The Digitization and Transformation of Banks. In Proceedings of the 5th International Conference on Future Networks and Distributed Systems (ICFNDS '21). Association for Computing Machinery, New York, NY, USA, 706–712. https://doi.org/10.1145/3508072.3508211

Estimating the Relationship Between Female and Male Employment in the Non-Working Population in the Economy Based on Econometric Models

Samariddin Makhmudov, Bobur Khonturayev, Zokir Mamadiyarov, Bakhtiyor Khajiyev, Khayrilla Kurbonov and Sherzod Rabimkulov

28.1. Introduction

Uzbekistan is undergoing a transformative programme of political, social, and economic reforms, including a focus on addressing gender inequality. In recent years, Uzbekistan has embarked on a transformative process that has liberalized the economy and prioritized the well-being of its citizens in overall policymaking. The programme, outlined in the government's 2017–2021 Development Strategy, emphasizes the importance of ensuring broader and more equitable access to opportunities and addressing the negative impacts of reforms on vulnerable segments of the population. The programme focused on further expanding inclusion, with commitments to rapidly reduce poverty, invest in human capital, expand social safety nets, and accelerate job creation. The New Uzbekistan Development Strategy, announced in 2022, builds on the priorities of its predecessor, placing greater emphasis on strategic themes such as justice, dignity, and inclusion. Laws and state programmes adopted in 2022 guarantee equal rights and opportunities for women and men. Active programmes aimed at expanding women's participation in public administration and state funding to support low-income women in obtaining higher education are among many new initiatives to promote greater equality.

According to Scherie Nicol (2022), increasing women's labour force participation is particularly beneficial in the context of shrinking labour forces in many OECD countries, as it can lead to increased GDP and productivity, as well as improved fiscal sustainability (Scherie, 2022). According to foreign scholar Abhilasha Sahay (2023), the economic rationale for closing the gender gap is that the gender gap in earnings persists globally, with women earning significantly less than men. Closing these gaps could lead to significant economic gains estimated at $160 trillion in global GDP per capita (Abhilasha, 2023).

According to global research, increasing the participation of women in leadership roles has a positive impact on the performance of firms, and as female representation increases, financial profitability indicators in companies also increase (Charalampos et al., 2023). At the same time, during the COVID-19 pandemic, female-led companies on the German stock exchange outperformed male-led companies in terms of earnings and risk management (Tanja, 2024). This suggests that female leaders have contributed to financial stability during turbulent times and have excelled in crisis management. However, the relationship between female leadership and financial performance is not universally positive. For example, a study of Polish companies found no significant positive relationship between the number of women on supervisory boards and financial performance (Kompa & Witkowska, 2022).

28.2. Literature Review

Economic growth is increasing the need to increase women's participation in the labour market. In particular, economic growth has been observed to contribute significantly to women's participation in the labour market over the long term in Kenya (Mose, 2024). This participation requires further support for education and vocational training that equips women with the skills they need to compete on an equal footing with men in the labour market. At the same time, challenges remain that can disproportionately affect women's labour force participation during economic crises. Historical evidence from the 2008 global crisis shows that women were more negatively affected, highlighting the need for targeted support for female workers and enterprises to maintain gender equality in the labour market (Simon, 2022). Legal gender equality has been found to close the gender gap in labour force participation globally, leading to a higher share of women in the labour force without negatively affecting men's participation (Candan, 2022).

Consequently, gender equality in the workplace remains difficult to achieve due to persistent discrimination and systemic barriers. Women often face pay disparities, unequal promotion opportunities, and underrepresentation in leadership roles (Lina, 2024). These challenges are compounded by cultural and religious beliefs that shape working conditions, as well as biases in the tax system and parental leave policies that hinder women's full participation in the labour market (André et al., 2023).

In addition, providing affordable childcare, promoting shared parental leave, and supporting female entrepreneurship can help narrow the gender gap and increase the labour force participation.

Gender equality is not only a matter of fairness, but also helps to increase organisational innovation, efficiency, and financial performance (Jiaxing, 2024). Equalising the labour market opportunities can also reduce the gender gap in depression risk among older adults, particularly benefiting groups with the greatest disparities, such as those with low literacy levels (Maria et al., 2023).

In this context, gender equality is central to increasing employment rates and addressing demographic challenges. By addressing gender barriers, countries can fully utilise the potential of their workforce across economic sectors, leading to more inclusive and sustainable economic growth. This requires coordinated efforts from researchers, businesses, and society to implement effective gender equality policies and practices across all sectors.

The impact of gender equality on social processes in the labour market is multifaceted, affecting different dimensions such as employment opportunities, wage inequality, and professional practices. Research shows that gender equality can significantly change the social dynamics of the labour market, promoting more inclusive and equal participation.

In Spain, the Social Economy (SE) has been shown to contribute positively to gender equality by providing more stable jobs and reducing the glass-coating effect, which is reflected in the Sustainable Development Goals (Rosa et al., 2020). However, persistent challenges remain. Gender segregation and the gender wage gap are among the issues that continue to affect women's labour market experiences (Maria et al., 2024). The study found that occupational segregation and unequal pay are widespread, with disparities varying significantly across regions and sectors.

Many prominent researchers have developed their hypotheses based on theoretical scientific studies and econometric models on the assessment of gender equality in the labour market for economic processes.

28.3. Research Methodology

Since the data obtained for econometric studies consist of multivariate time series, we selected multivariate linear regression (LS) and nonlinear structural equation (SEM) models.

Also, the impact of gender equality in the labour market on economic performance indicators was assessed using 148 monthly statistical data from the Statistical Agency under the President of the Republic of Uzbekistan (<https://stat.uz/uz>) and the World Bank (<https://data.worldbank.org/>) for 2008–2023.

The results were assessed for statistical significance using the Gauss-Markov, Durbin-Watson, Shapiro-Wilk, and Breusch-Pagan tests. At the same time, the statistical significance of the SEM regression model was assessed using diagnostic tests, including the chi-square test, comparative fit index, root mean square error of approximation, and standardised mean square residual (Habib et al., 2025; Jahrir et al., 2025; Lin et al., 2025; Pradhan et al., 2025; Rayala et al., 2025; Romero et al., 2025; Rony et al., 2025; Samariddin et al., 2025; Singagerda et al., 2025; Sofyanty et al., 2025; Zhang et al., 2025).

In the process of developing econometric models for the study, graphical diagrams and descriptive statistics tables were created to study the trends and distribution of variables. In addition, a correlation matrix was constructed to assess the relationships between dependent and independent variables and multicollinearity. Econometric equations were also constructed for LS and SEM regression models.

The formula for the LS model is given below.

$$Y = \gamma_0 + \gamma_1 c_1 + \gamma_2 c_2 + \cdots + \gamma_k c_k + \epsilon \tag{1}$$

Here, Y_t represents the dependent variable, c_1, c_2, c_3 represent the dependent variable, γ_0 represents the intercept, γ_1, γ_2, γ_q represents the coefficient of the factor, and ϵ represents the error term.

In structural equation modelling (SEM), parameter estimation is crucial to fit empirical data with the model's covariance matrix. Various estimation strategies are used, each with its own advantages and limitations. These methods include unweighted least squares (ULS), partial least squares (PLS), maximum likelihood (ML), Bayesian estimation, and others. Each method addresses specific issues such as data distribution assumptions, sample size constraints, and model robustness.

Analyses and forecasts were conducted using LS, ARDL, ARIMA and various other econometric models on the global services market, digital economy, energy-related financial stress, cocktail market, digital transformation, factors affecting the logistics industry (Kalandarov et al., 2025; Khayrilla et al., 2025; Khodjaniyazov et al., 2025; Kulmanov et al., 2024; Kuziboev et al., 2025; Kurbonov et al., 2024; Mamadiyarov et al., 2025; Rukhiddin et al., 2025; Samariddin et al., 2025).

Another group of economists has successfully used econometric models such as Fixed Effects Estimator, Random Effects Estimator, LS, and ARDL in their research on investment in digital infrastructure, various aspects of digital payment systems, the impact of inflation and credit interest rates on investment, factors affecting the reduction of the state's share in commercial banks, Non-Performing Loans in commercial banks, the digitisation of banks, risks in digital services, and the development of retail payment services (Abdullah et al., 2025; Akhmetshin et al., 2025; Cahyani et al., 2025; Mamadiyarov et al., 2025; Mamani et al., 2025; Rony et al., 2025; Su et al., 2025; Toshmurod et al., 2025).

ULS is useful for fitting non-normal data distributions because it does not require special distribution assumptions (Ani et al., 2023). Despite its flexibility, ULS can produce incorrect solutions, such as estimating negative differences, due to its sensitivity to measurement errors (Nurul et al., 2023). PLS is a robust alternative to covariance-based SEM, especially useful when data do not meet normality assumptions or samples are small (Nusrang et al., 2023, July). It includes reflective and modal indicators, which makes it versatile for different model structures.

$$\eta_i = \alpha_{i1}\xi_1 + \alpha_2\xi_2 + \ldots + \alpha_{im}\xi_m + \zeta_i \tag{2}$$

Here, η_i represents the endogenous latent variable (dependent variable).
$\xi_1, \xi_2, \ldots, \xi_m$ represents the endogenous latent variable (independent variable).
δa_{ij} represents the path coefficients that show the effect of ξj on η_i.
ζi represents the structural error term for η_i.

A multivariate linear econometric equation was developed based on the variables selected for the study. All variables for the econometric study were formulated below.

The number of non-working population in the economy is *Ln_Nonpr_pop_ec* (dependent variable),
The number of employed women over 25 years old is *Ln_Empl_wom* (independent variable)
The number of women with higher education is *Ln_grad_edu_wom* (independent variable)
The number of employed men over 25 years old is *Ln_Empl_men* (independent variable)
The number of men with higher education is *Ln_grad_edu_men* (independent variable).

When assessing the impact of gender equality in the labour market on macroeconomic indicators, the following hypotheses were formulated regarding the number of unemployed people in the economy, the number of employed women over the age of 25, the number of women with higher education, the number of employed men over the age of 25, and the number of men with higher education.

To develop hypotheses for an econometric study, we formulated null hypotheses (H_0) and alternative hypotheses (H_1). According to which, the null hypothesis states that there is no effect or relationship, while the alternative hypothesis states that there is an effect or relationship.

Hypotheses for all variables:

Null hypotheses (H_0):

$H_{0.1}$: The number of employed women over 25 years old in the national economy does not have a significant effect on the non-working population in the economy.

$H_{0.2}$: The number of women with higher education in the national economy does not have a significant effect on the non-working population in the economy.

$H_{0.3}$: The number of employed men over 25 years old in the national economy does not have a significant effect on the non-working population in the economy.

$H_{0.4}$: The number of men with higher education in the national economy does not have a significant effect on the non-working population in the economy.

Alternative Hypotheses (H_1):

$H_{1.1}$: The number of employed women over 25 years old in the national economy has a significant impact on the size of the non-working population in the economy.

$H_{1.2}$: The number of women with higher education in the national economy has a significant impact on the size of the non-working population in the economy.

$H_{1.3}$: The number of employed men over 25 years old in the national economy has a significant impact on the size of the non-working population in the economy.

$H_{1.4}$: The number of men with higher education in the national economy has a significant impact on the size of the non-working population in the economy.

28.4. Analysis and Results

According to the study, the analytical relationship (rconnected) graph of gender equality in the labour market, the number of unemployed people in the economy, and the factors affecting it is presented in Figures 107 and 108.

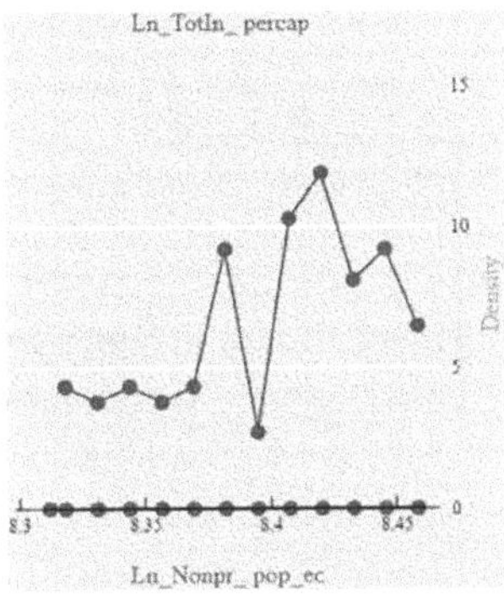

Figure 107. The analytical relationship (rconnected) graph of the non-working population in the economy.
Source: Developed by the authors based on the Stata program.

Based on the density plots presented in Figures 107 and 108, a positive relationship between the dependent and independent variables is presented. According to the graphic representation, the increase in the dependent variables in assessing the impact of gender equality in the labour market provides an important forecast in the future. As the coverage of gender equality in the labour market increases, the indicators of macroeconomic processes also increase.

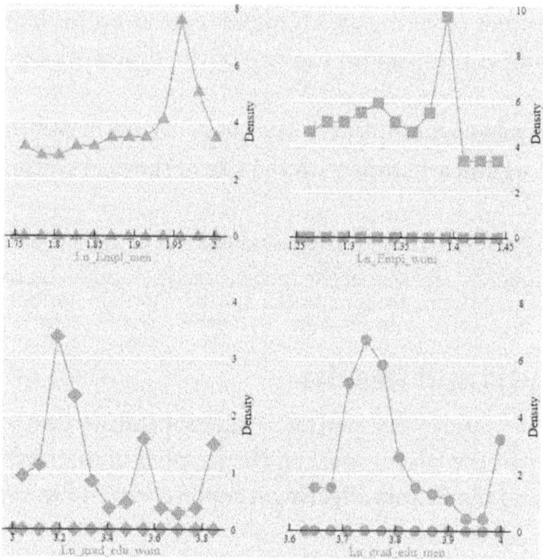

Figure 108. Analytical correlation (rconnected) graph of independent variables in assessing the impact of gender equality in the labour market.
Source: Developed by the authors based on the Stata program.

The hypothetical positive relationship indicates that there is a direct and positive relationship between the dependent and independent variables in the assessment of the impact of gender equality in the labour market. This means that as gender equality improves (independent variable), the employment rate, macroeconomic indicators (dependent variables) are expected to improve as well.

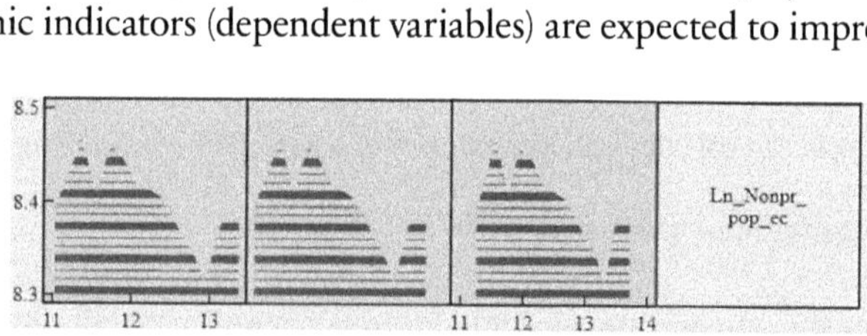

Figure 109. Graphic matrix of the number of non-productive people in the economy.
Source: Developed by the authors based on the Stata program.

In the next step, graphical matrix representations of the dependent and independent variables in the assessment of the impact of gender equality in the labour market on macroeconomic indicators are presented (Figures 109 and 110).

Figure 109 presents a graphical matrix of dependent variables, which offers a simplified and clear picture of the impact of gender equality in the labour market on macroeconomic indicators, with densely distributed elements. The presence of this density allows for a more precise and focused analysis of the main relationships and trends, which makes it easier to identify and understand the impact of gender equality on broader economic processes.

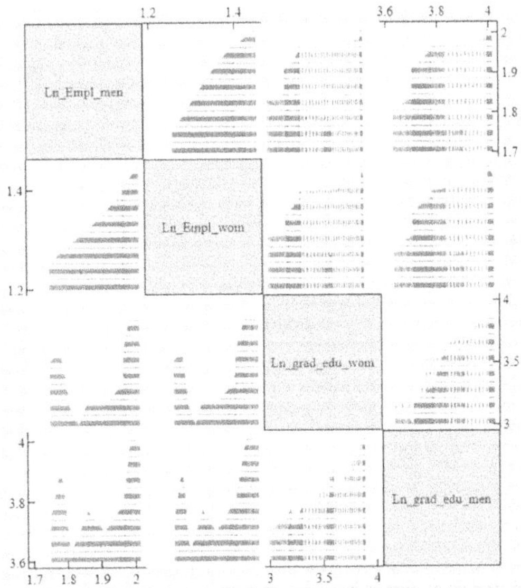

Figure 110. Graphical matrix of independent variables in assessing the impact of gender equality in the labour market.
Source: Developed by the authors based on the Stata program.

According to Figure 110, the dispersion matrix shows that the dispersion elements between the independent variables in assessing the impact of gender equality in the labour market show positive correlations. The data show significant correlations between the independent variables in assessing the impact of gender equality in the labour market, especially when firms represent a highly concentrated environment.

This suggests that factors affecting gender equality, such as employment rates, wage differentials or labour force participation, are closely related to each other and have a more pronounced impact in industries or sectors where firms are concentrated.

In the next stage of the econometric study, the cross-correlation matrix was considered for the size of the non-working population in the economy and each of the variables affecting it (Table 101).

Table 101. Correlation matrix of the number of unemployed people in the economy and the factors affecting it when assessing the impact of gender equality in the labour market

Variables	(1)	(2)	(3)	(4)	(5)
(1) Ln_Nonpr_p~c	1.000				
(2) Ln_Empl_men	-0.7806	1.000			
	(0.0000)				***
(3) Ln_grad_ed~n	-0.7845	0.9925	1.000		
	(0.0000)	(0.0000)			***
(4) Ln_Empl_wom	-0.4820	0.4069	0.5031	1.000	
	(0.0000)	(0.0000)	(0.0000)		***
(5) Ln_Empl_wom	-0.3646	0.4567	0.5465	0.9483	1.000
	(0.0000)	(0.0000)	(0.0000)	0.0000	***

Source: Developed by the authors based on the Stata program.

Relationship between dependent and independent variables:

According to Table 101, in assessing the impact of gender equality in the labour market, the non-farm population data in the economy were studied and showed strong, moderate and inverse relationships between all variables. This indicates that some variables are positively related, while others are inversely related. In addition, the correlation matrix presented in these tables confirms that there is no multicollinearity between the dependent and independent variables. If the *p*-values in the tables are less than 0.05, the correlations are statistically significant and reliable, that is, the observed relationships are unlikely to be due to chance.

We developed eight econometric equations for the study using a multivariate linear regression model (LS). In assessing the impact of gender equality in the labour market on macroeconomic indicators, econometric models were evaluated on the impact of these independent variables on variables such as the number of non-working population in the economy, the number of employed women over 25 years old, the number of women with higher education, the number of employed men over 25 years old, and the number of men with higher education.

As the first econometric equation, an econometric model of the impact of the number of employed women over 25 years old and the number of women with higher education on the number of non-working population in the economy was developed.

$$Ln\_TotIn\_percap = \beta_0 + \beta_1 Ln\_Ln\_Empl\_wom + \beta_2 Ln\_grad\_edu\_wom \qquad (3)$$

The coefficients from the regression results are expressed as follows.

Table 102. Multivariate linear regression (LS) model indicators of the non-farm population in the economy and the factors affecting it

Ln_Nonpr_pop_ec	Coef.	St.Err.	t-value	`p-value	[95% Conf	``Interval]	Sig
Ln_Empl_wom	-0.556	0.046	-12.21	0	-0.646	-0.466	***
Ln_grad_edu_wom	-0.019	0.01	1.97	0.051	-0.038	0	*
Constant	9.214	0.053	173.30	0	9.109	9.319	***

Mean dependent var	8.400	*SD dependent var*	0.041
R-squared	0.626	*Number of obs*	145
F-test	118.627	*Prob > F*	0.000
Akaike crit. (AIC)	-652.260	*Bayesian crit. (BIC)*	-643.330
*** $p< 0.01$, ** $p <0.05$, * $p < 0.1$			

Source: Developed by the authors based on the Stata program.

$$Ln\_Nonpr\_pop\_ec = 9.21 - 0.55 Ln\_Empl\_wom - 0.02 Ln\_grad\_edu\_wom \qquad (4)$$

Statistical significance:

All coefficients are statistically significant at the 0.05 level, taking into account *p*-values (all *p*-values <0.05).

Econometric model fit:

R-squared (0.62): Here, it is shown that approximately 62 per cent of the variance in total income per capital is explained by the model. Adjusted *R*-squared (0.61): It represents the *R*-squared value for the number of predictors in the model.

F-statistic: 118.62 (p=0.0000): It represents the overall statistical significance of the model.

Result. A 1 per cent increase in the number of employed women over 25 in the national economy leads to a 0.55 per cent decrease in the non-working population in the economy. A 1 per cent increase in the number of women with higher education leads to a 0.02 per cent decrease in the non-working population in the economy.

The second, as an econometric equation, was developed as an econometric model of the impact of the number of employed men over 25 years of age and the number of men with higher education on the non-working population in the economy.

$$Ln\_TotIn\_percap = \beta_0 + \beta_1 Ln\_Empl\_men + \beta_2 Ln\_grad\_edu\_men \quad (5)$$

The coefficients from the regression results are expressed as follows.

Table 103. Multivariate linear regression (LS) model indicators of the non-working population in the economy and the factors affecting it

Ln_Nonpr_pop_ec	Coef.	St.Err.	t-value	p-value	[95% Conf	Interval]	Sig
Ln_Empl_men	0.424	0.032	−13.16	0	−0.488	−0.361	***
Ln_grad_edu_men	−0.004	0.025	−0.17	0.086	−0.054	0.045	*
Constant	9.222	0.086	107.39	0	9.052	9.391	***

Mean dependent var	8.400	SD dependent var	0.041
R-squared	0.609	Number of obs	145
F-test	110.770	Prob > *F*	0.000
Akaike crit. (AIC)	-646.125	Bayesian crit. (BIC)	-637.194
*** $p < 0.01$, ** $p < 0.05$, * $p < 0.1$			

Source: Developed by the authors based on the Stata program.

Statistical significance:

$$Ln\_Nonpr\_pop\_ec = 9.22 - 0.42Ln\_Empl\_men - 0.04Ln\_grad\_edu\_men \quad (6)$$

All coefficients are statistically significant at the 0.05 level, taking into account the *p*-values (all *p*-values <0.05).
Econometric model fit:

R-squared (0.60): Here, it is shown that approximately 60 per cent of the variance in total income per capital is explained by the model. Adjusted *R*-squared (0.60): It represents the *R*-squared value for the number of predictors in the model. *F*-statistic: 110.70 ($p = 0.0000$): It represents the overall statistical significance of the model.

Result. A 1 per cent increase in the number of employed men over 25 in the national economy leads to a 0.42 per cent decrease in the number of unemployed people in the economy. A 1 per cent increase in the number of men graduating from higher education leads to a 0.04 per cent decrease in the non-farm population in the economy.

The Gauss-Markov conditions for the econometric equations were tested.

The Durbin-Watson test was applied to the multivariate linear regression model, resulting in a calculated value of 2.36. In addition, the analysis yielded a Shapiro-Wilk W test statistic of 0.72, along with a Breusch-Pagan test statistic of 0.48. The primary null hypothesis, H0: $y = 0$, and the corresponding alternative hypothesis, H1: $y \neq 0$, were tested at a significance level of $p > 0.05$. After conducting the Durbin-Watson, Breusch-Pagan and Shapiro-Wilk tests, the null hypothesis was confirmed, as the *p*-value was greater than the 0.05 threshold.

In the econometric analysis, the fundamental assumptions of Gauss-Markov were met. The VIF test was used to assess multicollinearity in the research model, which showed that the created model does not have multicollinearity. The VIF value of 1.48 indicates the relationship between the influence of macroeconomic indicators on the assessment of gender equality in the labour market and the factors influencing it. At the same time, the analysis of the multivariate linear regression model showed the statistical significance of the main hypothesis $H_0: y = 0$, $H_1: y \neq 0$ at the $p < 0.10$ significance level. As a result, the alternative hypothesis was not confirmed. The Gauss-Markov condition is satisfied within the specified threshold range of the VIF test value from 1 to 10.

Also, during our research, the SEM regression model plot and test results were as follows (Figures 111 and 112).

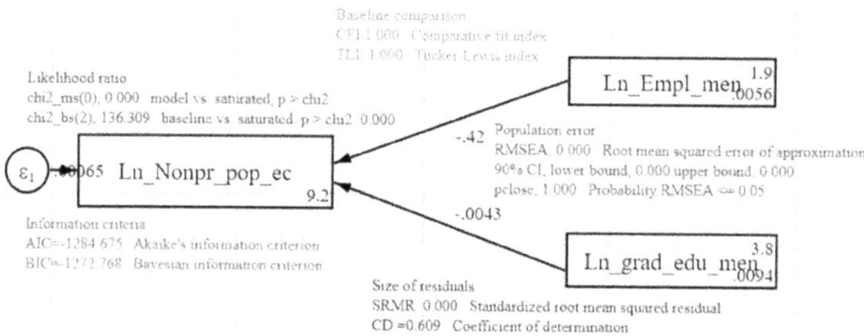

Figure 111. Schematic representation of the SEM regression model between the number of economically active population and factors affecting it.
Source: Developed by the authors based on the Stata program.

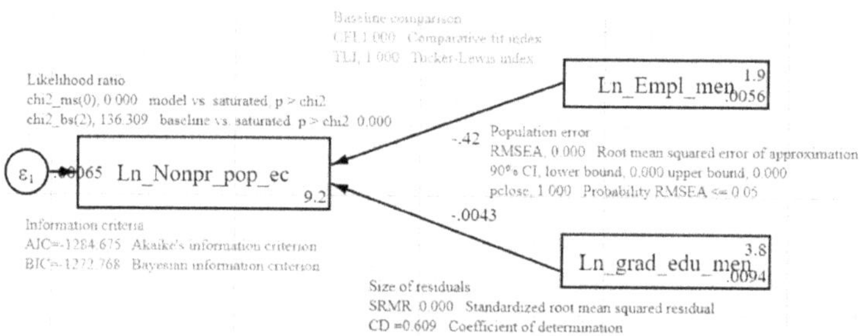

Figure 112. Schematic representation of the SEM regression model between the number of economically active population and factors affecting it.
Source: Developed by the authors based on the Stata program.

28.5. Conclusion

This study examined the impact of gender equality in the labour market on macroeconomic indicators. The analysis examined the relationship between the number of unemployed people in the economy, the number of employed women over 25 years old, the number of women with higher education, the number of employed men over 25 years old, and the number of men with higher education. The results showed that there is a significant statistical relationship between these factors. According to the results of the study, ensuring gender equality in the labour market is emerging as a factor that increases socio-economic stability.

The following conclusions were drawn based on the results of the multivariate linear regression (LS) model and the Structural Equation Modelling (SEM) regression model on the macroeconomic indicators of gender equality in the labour market and the factors affecting it.

1. An increase in the number of employed women over 25 years old in the national economy by 1 per cent leads to a decrease in the number of unemployed people in the economy by 0.55 per cent. A 1 per cent increase in the number of women with tertiary education leads to a 0.02 per cent decrease in the non-working population in the economy.

1.1. Expanding employment opportunities for women: A 1 per cent increase in the number of employed women over 25 years of age leads to a 0.55 per cent decrease in the number of unemployed, which represents a significant change in labour market dynamics. This is interpreted as an important factor in the efficient use of labour resources, increasing women's economic activity and improving the overall employment rate. This may indicate that as more women enter the labour force, they open up job opportunities that could have been filled by previously inactive individuals, thereby stimulating labour market activity and potentially leading to the creation of diverse jobs.

1.2. Higher education and economic inactivity: The finding that a 1 per cent increase in the number of women with tertiary education leads to a 0.02 per cent decrease in the number of economically inactive individuals may indicate a positive shift towards advanced education. This may indicate that more women are investing in their education, which could have long-term benefits for the economy, such as a skilled and educated workforce that is better prepared for high-value roles in the future.

1.3. Encouraging educational attainment: While the small increases in economic activity associated with higher education may be short-term adjustments, the long-term benefits of higher education outweigh these adjustments. Policies that support educational attainment lead to the development of a knowledgeable and skilled workforce that can stimulate innovation and economic growth in the long term.

1.4. Changes in the labour market: The increase in unemployment rates against the background of the entry of women into the labour market reflects the adjustment process necessary to achieve equilibrium in this sector. As more women enter the labour force, the labour market needs to renew itself. This creates an opportunity for systemic reforms to effectively attract women to various sectors and improve overall employment conditions. The results of the study show that, despite short-term changes, increasing women's employment and their educational level can lead to positive long-term economic outcomes. A 1 per cent increase in the number of men with higher education leads to a 0.04 per cent decrease in the unemployed population in the economy.

2. A 1 per cent increase in the number of employed men over 25 in the national economy leads to a 0.42 per cent decrease in the non-working population in the economy. A 1 per cent increase in the number of men with higher education leads to a 0.04 per cent decrease in the non-working population in the economy.

2.1. The impact of employment of men over 25 years of age: A 1 per cent increase in the number of men over 25 years of age in the labour market leads to a 0.42 per cent decrease in the number of unemployed. This indicator demonstrates the positive impact of male employment on economic activity and indicates that their active participation in the labour market serves to reduce the problem of unemployment.

2.2. This shows that hiring more men over 25, who are likely to have more experience and are probably in their prime, will significantly reduce unemployment. This is because if more men in this age group find work, the overall unemployment rate will fall.

2.3. A 1 per cent increase in the number of men with higher education leads to a 0.04 per cent decrease in the number of unemployed in the economy.Although an increase in the number of men with higher education helps to reduce unemployment, this effect appears to be relatively weak. Higher education often increases employment opportunities because it increases knowledge, skills and qualifications.

2.4. The impact of employment of men over 25: The 0.42 per cent reduction in the unemployment rate when male employment in this group increases shows that this approach produces rapid and significant results. This age group constitutes the bulk of the economically active population and their employment status has a direct impact on the overall unemployment rate.

2.5. The impact of higher education on unemployment: The only 0.04 per cent reduction in unemployment as a result of an increase in the number of men with higher education means that although education increases the chances of finding a job for each individual, its direct impact on reducing unemployment is not strong. This is due to a variety of factors, including the mismatch between the skills taught in higher education and market demands, as well as other structural problems in the labour market, such as the shortage of jobs requiring higher education.

Bibliography

Abdullah, M. A., Han, X., Amjad, M. A., & Makhmudov, S. (2025). Revisit the role of financial development on economic growth, human development, and sustainable development in higher-income countries. *Journal of Environmental Management*, *392*, 126874.

Akhmetshin, E., Abdullayev, I., Makhmudov, S., Dakhkilgova, K., Korotaeva, I. and Yanovskaya, G. (2025). APPLICATION OF TANH–COTH METHOD FOR COMBINED AND DOUBLE COMBINED SINH–COSH–GORDON EQUATIONS ARISING CHEMICAL REACTIONS TO WATER SURFACE GRAVITY WAVES. Computational Methods for Differential Equations, (), -. doi: 10.22034/cmde.2025.67655.3234

Abhilasha, Sahay (2023). *Closing Gender Gaps in Earnings*. <https://doi.org/10.1596/39596>.

André, C., Causa, O., Soldani, E., Sutherland, D., and Unsal, F. (2023). 'Promoting Gender Equality to Strengthen Economic Growth and Resilience'. *Documents de travail du Département des Affaires économiques de l'OCDE*.

Cahyani, I., Buriev, K., Ngongo, M., Mamadiyarov, Z., Ino, L., Herman, H., Saputra, N., & Baxtishodovich, S. (2025). Exploring the Use of TikTok Application in Enhancing the Skill of Pronunciation: A Case on Students' Perception. Studies in Media and Communication, 13(2), 150–158. doi: http://dx.doi.org/10.11114/smc.v13i2.7553

Candan, Sever (2022). 'Gendered Laws and Labour Force Participation'. *Applied Economics Letters*, 1–7, <https://doi.org/10.1080/13504851.2022.2103078>.

Charalampos, Basdekis, Ioannis, Katsampoxakis, Konstantinos, Anathreptakis (2023). 'Women's Participation in Firms' Management and Their Impact on Financial Performance: Pre-COVID-19 and COVID-19 Period Evidence'. *Sustainability*, 15 (11), 8686–6. <https://doi.org/10.3390/su15118686>.

Habib, S. S., Islam, M. A., Ali, M. N., Benitez, I. B., Mamadiyarov, Z., Mirzayev, B., … & Flah, A. (2025). Multi-Objective Optimization and Feasibility Analysis of Integrated Biogas–Solar Energy Systems for Rural Electrification. *Results in Engineering*, 107086.

Jahrir, A., Gultom, Y., Herman, H., Zabadi, F., Ngongo, M., Mamadiyarov, Z., Fatmawati, E., & Saputra, N. (2025). Investigating the Elements of Short Commercial Mineral Water Advertisement: A Case on Discourse Analysis. Studies in Media and Communication, 13(4), 94–104. doi: http://dx.doi.org/10.11114/smc.v13i4.7813

Jiaxing, Du (2024). 'Advancing Gender Equality in the Workplace: Challenges, Strategies, and the Way Forward'. *Journal of Theory and Practice of Social Science*, 4 (04), 46–50. <https://doi.org/ 10.53469/ jtpss.2024.04(04).11>.

Kalandarov, F., Makhmudov, S., Ibadullaev, D., Matniyozov, M., Nasretdinova, F., Sabirov, K., & Bahodirov, N. M. (2025). Low-Carbon Energy Risk and Renewable Energy Development: Insights from Method of Moments Quantile Regression. International Journal of Energy Economics and Policy, 15(3), 524–536.

Khayrilla Kurbonov, Samariddin Makhmudov, Shakhzod Erkinov, Umidjon Dadabaev, Gulnora Bekimbetova, Rukhiddin Zayniddinov, and Mirzabek Jonuzokov. 2025. Evaluating the Impact of Marketing Practices Digitalization and Investment on Labor Market Efficiency and Commercial Bank Performance Using Econometric Models. In Proceedings of the 8th International Conference on Future Networks & Distributed Systems (ICFNDS '24). Association for Computing Machinery, New York, NY, USA, 786–796. https://doi.org/10.1145/3726122.3726237

Khodjaniyazov, N., Mirkhoshimova, M., Kalandarov, F., Matyokubova, D., Utegenova, S., Makhmudov, S., & Khudayberganov, M. (2025). Time-Varying Impacts of Financial Stress on Energy-Related Uncertainty. *International Journal of Energy Economics and Policy, 15*(3), 689–698.

Kompa, K., and Witkowska, D. (2022). 'Impact of Women's Representation in Top Management on Performance of WSE-listed Companies'. In *Understanding the Polish Capital Market*, pp. 280–98. Routledge.

Kuchkarov, T., Mamadiyarov, Z., Khakimov, Z., Sabirova, O., Matmurodov, K., Raimboyeva, M., & Umarova, S. (2025). Energy-Related Uncertainty and Crypto-Currency Environmental Attention: Time-Varying Perspective. *International Journal of Energy Economics and Policy, 15*(5), 614–626. https://doi.org/10.32479/ijeep.20784

Kuziboev, B., Ozturk, I., Kalandarov, F., Samandarov, O., Bekjanov, D., & Makhmudov, S. (2025). PROMOTING ENERGY SOURCES DIVERSIFICATION THROUGH ESG PERFORMANCE. Energy, 136009.

Lin, M.H., Matchanova, B., Nurmatovich, H.A. et al. Optimal Operation of the Multi-Carrier Energy System Considering Energy Markets and

Renewable Energies Participation. *Int. J. Appl. Comput. Math* 11, 170 (2025). https://doi.org/10.1007/s40819-025-02002-9

Lina, Farsia (2024). 'Ensuring Equal Opportunity: Gender Equality in Workplace'. *Accentia*, 4 (1), 21–8, <https://doi.org/10.37598/accentia.v4i1.2040>.

Mamadiyarov, Z., Eshov, M., Otakhonova, D., Utegenova, S., Sabirov, K., Marks, A., & Bahodirov, N. (2025). Does Energy Policy Risk Threaten Energy Sources Diversification?. *International Journal of Energy Economics and Policy, 15*(5), 730–740. https://doi.org/10.32479/ijeep.21140

Mamadiyarov, Z., Saidov, O., Abdurazakova, N., Makhmudov, S., Nazarov, M., Rajabova, N., … Ruzmetova, I. (2025). Energy-Related Uncertainty and Tourism Stock Markets: New Insights from Time-Varying Relationship with TVP- VAR Approach. *International Journal of Energy Economics and Policy, 15*(4), 730–737. https://doi.org/10.32479/ijeep.20480

Mamani, J.C.M., Miri, M., Vorobev, Y. et al. Optimal Operation of Energy Microgrid Considering Economic and Emission Indices. Oper. Res. Forum 6, 122 (2025). https://doi.org/10.1007/s43069-025-00523-z

Maria, Gueltzow, M., Bijlsma, J., van, Lenthe, F., Myrskylä, M. (2023). 'The Role of Labor Market Inequalities in the Gender Gap in Depression Risk Among Older US Adults'. *European Journal of Public Health*, 33, <https://doi.org/10.1093/eurpub/ckad160.875>.

Mose, N. (2024). 'Economic Growth and Female Participation in the Labour Market: Gender Disaggregated Data'. *Business and Economic Research*, 14 (2), 93–110.

Muhammad Zubair, Irfanud Din, Nadeem Sarwar et al. Revolutionizing Sepsis Diagnosis Using Machine Learning and Deep Learning Models: A Systematic Literature Review, 10 June 2025, PREPRINT (Version 1) available at Research Square [https://doi.org/10.21203/rs.3.rs-6731418/v1]

Ngongo, M., Herman, H., Ndandara, A., Jois Jaha, D. A., Peku Djawang, J. U. S., Tanggu Rame, M. M., Khamraeva, S. N., & Mamadiyarov, Z. (2025). An Investigation of Meaning, Toponymy of Sumba Cultural Site's Names, and the Impact of Tourism Visitors on Surrounding Society. *Forum for Linguistic Studies*, 7(8), 679–693. https://doi.org/10.30564/fls.v7i8.10260

Pradhan, R., Hajiyev, E., Shichiyakh, R. et al. Optimal Techno-Economic Feasibility of an Off-Grid Microgrid System Using Load Flow Energy

Management Strategies. *Oper. Res. Forum* **6**, 120 (2025). https://doi.org/10.1007/s43069-025-00524-y

Rayala, R. V., Borra, C. R., Vasudevan, V., Singhania, R., Cheekati, S., & Mamadiyarov, Z. (2025, July). Lightweight Deep Learning Framework for Human Activity Recognition: A MobileNet-LSTM Approach with WHOA Optimization. In *2025 International Conference on Innovations in Intelligent Systems: Advancements in Computing, Communication, and Cybersecurity (ISAC3)* (pp. 1–6). IEEE.

Rayala, R. V., Sandhya, N., Singhania, R., Cheekati, S., Borra, C. R., Vasudevan, V., & Mamadiyarov, Z. (2025, July). AI-Driven Tomato Quality Assessment: A Deep Learning Approach for Image-based Defect Detection and Classification. In *2025 International Conference on Innovations in Intelligent Systems: Advancements in Computing, Communication, and Cybersecurity (ISAC3)* (pp. 1–6). IEEE.

Romero, R. M., Zelinskaya, M., Makhmudov, S., Sapaev, S., & Rustambekovich, J. U. (2025, September). Modelling and Optimal Utilisation of the Renewable Energy Systems in Microgrid with Improving Reliability and Energy Efficiency. In Operations Research Forum (Vol. 6, No. 3, pp. 1–20). Springer International Publishing.

Rosa, Belén, Castro, Núñez, Pablo, Bandeira, and Rosa, Santero-Sánchez (2020). 'Social Economy, Gender Equality at Work and the 2030 Agenda: Theory and Evidence from Spain'. *Sustainability*, 12 (12), 5192–. <https://doi.org/10.3390/SU12125192>.

Rukhiddin Zayniddinov, Nodir Jumaev, Gulbakhor Irgasheva, Alam Asadov, Nosir Makhmudov, Sirojiddin Abrorov, and Samariddin Makhmudov. 2025. The Influence of the Digital Economy on Economic Development Evidence from Uzbekistan. In Proceedings of the 8th International Conference on Future Networks & Distributed Systems (ICFNDS '24). Association for Computing Machinery, New York, NY, USA, 831–839. https://doi.org/10.1145/3726122.3726242

Samariddin Makhmudov, Malika Umarova, Khayrilla Kurbonov, Laylo Akbarova, Durdona Davletova, Nilufar Shanazarova, and Toshmurod Kulmanov. 2025. Evaluating the forecast indicators of the volume of highly liquid assets of commercial banks in the process of digital transformation. In Proceedings of the 8th International Conference on Future Networks & Distributed Systems (ICFNDS '24). Association for Computing Machinery, New York, NY, USA, 698–704. https://doi.org/10.1145/3726122.3726222

Samariddin Makhmudov, Kudratillo Tukhsanov, Saifulla Arslanbekov, Akram Amanov, Orifali Tursunov, Umarbek Jabbarov and Muyassarxon Mirzakarimova. 2024. Optimizing Supply Chain Financing Development Prospects of Digital Ecosystems in the European Logistics Industry. In The 8th International Conference on Future Networks & Distributed Systems (ICFNDS '24), December 11–12, 2024, Marakech, Morocco. ACM, New York, NY, USA, 12 Pages. https://doi.org/10.1145/3726122.3726200

Scherie, Nicol (2022). 'Gender Budgeting: The Economic and Fiscal Rationale'. *OECD Journal on Budgeting*, 22 (3), <https:/doi.org/10.1787/9ca9b221-en>.

Simon, Lang, (2022). *Gender Equality Issues in Labor Markets: Lessons for COVID-19 Era*, pp. 229–54. <https:doi.org/10.1007/978-3-030-98179-2_17>.

Su, R., Xiao, Y., Hamza, F., Mamadiyarov, Z., & Wahab, A. (2025). Scaling up green hydrogen in China: Economic opportunities and challenges. *International Journal of Hydrogen Energy*, *131*, 60–69.

Tanja, Sinha (2024). 'The Role of Female Leadership in Times of Financial Crisis – An Analysis During the COVID-19 Pandemic', <https://doi.org/10.12775/cjfa.2023.012>.

Toshmurod Kulmanov, Umidjon Dadabaev, Mansurbek Qulmetov, Aliboy Ulashov, Mirjalol Eshboyev, and Samariddin Makhmudov. 2025. Global Services Market Transformation Digitalization Export Trends and Future Forecasts. In Proceedings of the 8th International Conference on Future Networks & Distributed Systems (ICFNDS '24). Association for Computing Machinery, New York, NY, USA, 851–858. https://doi.org/10.1145/3726122.3726245

Zhang, L., Zhao, Z., Qamri, G. M., & Makhmudov, S. (2025). Unleashing the critical role of renewable energy through global value chains and digitalization: A path towards environmental sustainability. *Journal of Environmental Management*, *392*, 126688.

Econometric Analysis of the Interaction between Income and Expenditure in Higher Education Institutions

Zokir Mamadiyarov, Payzillokhon Karaev, Samariddin Makhmudov, Kalonov Mukhiddin, Hakimjon Hakimov, Bakhtiyor Klichev and Akbar Jumayev

29.1. Introduction

The sharp changes in the higher education system in Uzbekistan are causing various problematic situations in the system. In order to eliminate these problematic situations and achieve the intended goal, the development of measures aimed at comprehensive quality improvement, as well as the scientific and methodological study of directions for improving the system based on foreign experience and their implementation are among the urgent issues of today. The main reforms related to granting financial independence to higher education institutions in our country, as in other areas, serve to create an environment of additional independence for higher education institutions. It is clear from this that the development of the sector is leading to the formation of another new system of reforms being carried out in state higher education institutions, entering a new stage, and at the same time further improving existing development directions.

In ensuring financial stability in higher education institutions and the effective allocation of resources, it is an important criterion for formulating future development strategies by assessing the interrelationship of their income and expenses. These assessment criteria allow optimising the growing costs of higher education, shaping the allocation of resources, and making important decisions. The interdependence of factors affecting income and expenses in higher education institutions indicates the need for comprehensive strategies in adopting solutions to financial problems and implementing institutional and individual financial operations.

Organisations depend on resources, and some (if not all) of these resources are produced by other organisations. However, resources produced by one organisation have value only if they are used by another organisation.

This means that the use and control of resources become power bases and lead to interdependence between organisations. The distribution of power between organisations determines their behaviour. Despite its simplicity, RBN has stood the test of time and remains a highly influential theoretical framework in organisational behaviour, industrial economics, supply chain management, managerial economics, and business-related topics (Hillman et al., 2009; Hussain et al., 2023).

29.2. Literature Review

In assessing the interaction of revenues and expenditures in higher education institutions, scientific theoretical studies conducted by well-known foreign scientists and hypotheses developed on the basis of econometric models have been confirmed.

As Robert K. Toutkoushian and Michael B. Paulsen (2016) state, 'Higher education institutions rely on various sources of revenue, including public funds, tuition fees, and private donations' (Toutkoushian & Paulsen, 2016). The authors noted that the balance between economic sources has a significant impact on the schematic system of expenditures and institutional priorities.

According to Kristinn Hermannsson et al. (2010) 'The dependence of the education system in regions such as Northern Ireland and Scotland on public funding has a significant impact on their financial sustainability and expenditure on the local economy' (Hermannsson, et al., 2010). The authors conclude that by quantifying the external costs per student in higher education institutions, students have changed the overall impact of expenditure, which has become important in the economic contribution of HEIs.

According to Tommaso Agasisti et al. (2012) 'The convergence of expenditure per student across the EU-15 countries is an important factor in shaping the patterns of private financial resources spending in European countries' (Agasisti et al., 2012). The authors, using econometric models based on time series data, show that GDP per capita has a strong influence on the trend of expenditure per student in higher education institutions in the EU-15 countries over the period 1998–2006.

Catharine B. Hill (2016) notes that 'income inequality affects higher education institutions through its relationship to tuition, costs, and financial aid' (Hill, 2016). According to the author's results, even if household incomes increase by the same total amount, tuition, costs, and financial aid tend to decrease without increasing income inequality.

M. Carnoy (2011) in his scientific opinion noted that 'when higher education revenues increase relative to lower education levels, the disparity in public spending between elite and public universities leads to the expansion of these institutions and increases income inequality' (Carnoy, 2011).

As Morgan Bridge (2011) notes, 'Studies of the economic impact of higher education institutions have been criticized for overstating their contribution to the national economy' (Bridge, 2011). Based on an econometric model, the author emphasised that factors such as geographic and service sector, cost accounting, economic multipliers, and labour multipliers have a strong impact on long- and short-term relationships in the management of income and expenses in higher education institutions.

G. Wyness (2009) argues that 'the shift to cost-sharing in higher education financing has a strong correlation with student participation' (Wyness, 2009). The author's econometric model shows that participation in maintenance grants shows an impact, while initial payments show a negative relationship, and also shows the importance of financial support in supporting entry to higher education.

According to Jacob Fowles (2008, October), 'institutional spending is an important factor in student success, and spending on tuition and institutional support is positively related to graduation rates' (Fowles, 2008 October). According to the authors, not all categories of expenditure in educational institutions have the same impact, which indicates the need for strategic allocation of resources to positively affect educational outcomes.

A. O. Afriyie (2013) notes that 'higher education institutions rely on a variety of revenue sources, including tuition fees, government funds, and private donations' (Afriyie, 2013). According to the author, diversifying the sources of revenue in these institutions can help to reduce financial instability and funding and minimise the risks associated with economic downturns.

According to Figer-Canes (2023) 'effective financial management in higher education institutions involves strict adherence to accounting principles, equitable allocation of resources, and strategic budget planning' (Figer-Canes, 2023). According to him, higher education institutions that systematically and effectively systematise accounting and financial reporting have an advantage, demonstrating positive financial performance and accountability. According to D. Bruce Johnstone (2019) 'increasing costs per student and increasing enrollment in higher education institutions lead to increased costs at the institutional and national levels' (Johnstone, 2019). The authors conclude that the government requires significant cost-sharing measures, such as increasing tuition fees. According to E. Abouzeida (2014) 'institutional spending has a positive relationship with graduation and retention rates and with spending on education and academic support' (Abouzeida, 2014). The authors also conclude that excessive spending on institutional support has a negative impact on performance indicators.

29.3. Research Methodology

The econometric model used quarterly economic indicators of the Ministry of Higher Education, Science and Innovation (<https://edu.uz/uz>) and the Statistical Agency under the President of the Republic of Uzbekistan (<https://stat.uz/uz/>) with a total number of observations of thirty-four for the period 2016–2024 to assess the interaction between income and expenditure in national higher education institutions.

Since the data in the study in the article are formed on the basis of multivariate time series, we used the multivariate linear equations (LS) model and nonlinear Structural Equation Modelling (SEM) models to develop the econometric model.

The most important conditions of the Gauss-Markov model were estimated for the econometric equation 'multivariate linear (LS) model' (Chiou et al., 2016). and several reliability tests, in particular 'Durbin-Watson' (Rutledge & Barros, 2002), 'Shapiro-Wilk (González-Estrada & Cosmes, 2019) and 'Breusch-Pagan' (Herwartz, 2006) tests were used to analyse the statistical significance of the econometric model. In addition, the study assessed the visual dynamic state of the econometric model variables, and to evaluate the theoretical aspects of the econometric models, analytical statistical diagrams, graphical matrix and normal distribution plots, correlation matrix, and analytical graphical images of time series were developed. In the study, the 'VIF test' (Akhmetshin et al., 2025; Cahyani et al., 2025; Habib et al., 2025; Jahrir et al., 2025; Kruzic et al., 2009; Mamadiyarov et al., 2025; Rayala et al., 2025; Samariddin et al., 2025) was used to evaluate the multicollinearity of the econometric model (Akhmetshin et al., 2025; Cahyani et al., 2025; Habib et al., 2025; Jahrir et al., 2025; Kalandarov et al., 2025; Khayrilla et al., 2025; Khodjaniyazov et al., 2025; Kuziboev et al., 2025; Lin et al., 2025; Mamadiyarov et al., 2025; Mamani et al., 2025; Pradhan et al., 2025; Rayala et al., 2025; Rony et al., 2025; Rukhiddin et al., 2025; Samariddin et al., 2025; Singagerda et al., 2025; Sofyanty et al., 2025; Su et al., 2025; Toshmurod et al., 2025; Zokir et al., 2021).

Analyses and forecasts were conducted using multivariate linear regression (LS), ARDL, ARIMA and various other econometric models on the global services market, digital economy, energy-related financial stress, cocktail market, digital transformation, factors affecting the logistics industry (Kalandarov et al., 2025; Khayrilla et al., 2025; Khodjaniyazov et al., 2025; Kuziboev et al., 2025; Lin et al., 2025; Mamadiyarov et al., 2025; Mamani et al., 2025; Pradhan et al., 2025; Rayala et al., 2025).

According to Teresa Aparicio and Inmaculada Villanúa (2003) 'the linearity assumption in a multivariate linear regression model is that the relationship between the independent variables and the dependent variables is linear' (Aparicio & Villanúa, 2003). According to the authors, the range of influence of the independent variables allows for a proportional change in the resulting factor and a direct estimation of the coefficients, simplifying the relationship between the influencing factors.

According to Stan Lipovetsky (2024) 'the parameters of a multivariate linear regression model are estimated using the method of least squares' (Lipovetsky, 2024). According to it, the model minimises the sum of squared differences between the observed and predicted values, and this approach serves to ensure that the fitted model passes through the mean values of the variables.

Another group of economists has successfully used econometric models such as Fixed Effects Estimator, Random Effects Estimator, multivariate linear (LS), and ARDL in their research on investment in digital infrastructure, various aspects of digital payment systems, the impact of inflation and credit interest rates on investment, factors affecting the reduction of the state's share in commercial banks, Non-Performing Loans in commercial banks, the digitisation of banks, risks in digital services, and the development of retail payment services (Cahyani et al., 2025; Ngongo et al., 2025; Rayala et al., 2025; Rony et al., 2025; Rukhiddin et al., 2025; Samariddin et al., 2025; Singagerda et al., 2025; Sofyanty et al., 2025; Su et al., 2025; Toshmurod et al., 2025).

A. Schützenmeister et al. (2012) state that 'independence refers to the requirement that the residuals (errors) of the model are not correlated with each other. This ensures that the information provided by each observation is unique and not influenced by other observations' (Schützenmeister et al., 2012). According to the authors' research, the process of autocorrelation leads to inefficient estimations and incorrect statistical tests. Rosopa et al. (2013) 'Homoscedasticity means that the variance of the residuals is constant at all levels of the independent variables' (Rosopa et al., 2013). According to the authors' research conclusions, this assumption ensures that the model's forecast indicators are equally reliable across the data range.

The first econometric model for the dissertation research was the multivariate linear equation (LS) model.

Below is the formula for a multivariate linear equation (LS) model.

$$Y_i = \vartheta_0 + \vartheta_1 c_{1i} + \vartheta_2 c_{2i} + \vartheta_3 c_{3i} + \cdots + \vartheta_{ik} c_{ik} + \epsilon_i \qquad (1)$$

Here, t is the dependent variable for the yi – observation, which constitutes the dependent variable in the modelling

$c_{1t}, c_{2t}, c_{3t}, \ldots, c_{ik}$ – represent the independent variables (influencing factors).
$\vartheta_1, \vartheta_2, \vartheta_3 \ldots, \vartheta_i$ – represent the regression coefficients (the influence of each factor) and t – residual (error) value.
The SEM model was developed as the second econometric model in the study.
The SEM model formula is given below.

$$\eta = \rho\eta + \mu\omega + \zeta \qquad (2)$$

Here,

η represents the vector of endogenous (dependent) latent variables.
ρ represents the vector of exogenous (independent) latent variables.
μ represents the matrix of correlation coefficients between endogenous latent variables,
ω represents the matrix of correlation coefficients between exogenous and endogenous latent variables.
ζ represents the vector of residuals (errors) for endogenous latent variables.
All variables in these two econometric models are natural logarithmic.

29.4. Analysis and Results

Below are all the variables in the econometric model (Table 104).

Table 104. Classification of variables according to the econometric model

No.	Variable name	Classification	Logarithmic value
1.	Net profit of higher education institutions	Resultant variable	*Lnnet_profit_high_edu*
2.	The volume of financial resources received from economic contracts in higher education	Independent variable	*lnfin_res_cont*
3.	The volume of investments in higher education employees	Independent variable	*lninvest_hig_edu_pers*
4.	Inflation rate	Independent variable	*lninfl_rate*
5.	Amount of funds for student payment agreements	Independent variable	*lnstud_paym_agreem_fund*

Source: Developed by the authors based on the Stata program.

The following hypotheses were reflected in the development of the econometric study.

The main (H_0) and alternative (H_1) hypotheses were reflected in the development of the econometric study.

The structure of the hypothesis in the combined model:

The main hypothesis (H_0): The volume of financial resources from economic contracts in higher education, the volume of investments in higher education employees, the level of inflation in the national economy and the volume of funds from student payment contracts do not significantly affect the volume of net profit of higher education institutions and there is no effect on the relationship.

Alternative hypothesis (H_1): The volume of financial resources received from economic contracts in higher education, the volume of investments made in higher education employees, the inflation rate in the national economy and the volume of funds from student payment contracts have a significant impact on the net profit of higher education institutions, showing a strong correlation.

At the first stage of the econometric study, descriptive statistical values were expressed for the net profit of higher education institutions and the variables affecting it (Table 105).

Table 105. Descriptive statistical values of the net profit of higher education institutions and the factors affecting it

	Lnnet_ profit_ high_edu	lnfin_res_ cont	lninvest_ hig_edu_ pers	lninfl_ rate	lnstud_ paym_ agreem_fund
Mean	10.40746	9.163605	5.085908	2.730697	9.154552
Maximum	11.60956	11.60956	5.995853	3.516885	9.380108
Minimum	9.384353	7.760041	4.661115	2.189458	9.026958
Std. Dev	0.7552823	0.8575382	0.3467883	0.3825221	0.1130016
Std. Err.	0.1295298	0.1470666	0.0594737	0.065602	0.0193796
Skewness	0.2803847	-0.3476265	1.360026	0.6638665	0.908851
Kurtosis	1.563286	1.462854	3.984993	2.231501	2.243318
Observation	34	34	34	34	34

Source: Developed by the authors based on the Stata program.

According to Table 105, the net profit of higher education institutions according to the model and the descriptive statistical indicators of the factors affecting it formed a distribution according to the main economic values of the selected variables. All variables selected according to descriptive statistical values from the table data amounted to 34 observations.

The standard deviation values create an average variability, according to which some higher education institutions perform more positively than others, but on average they indicate a stable sector. The fact that the Kurtosis value is (1.56) represents the minimum level of extreme losses and indicates that the financial profitability indicators in higher education institutions are stable and positively distributed.

Also, the average investment in higher education staff ranges from 5.09 to a maximum of 5.99, indicating the commitment of institutions to invest in their academic and administrative staff. From the table, it can be seen that the student fee agreement volume indicators have a high average of 9.15 and a low standard deviation (0.11), indicating that institutions are constantly increasing their financial capabilities through student fees and have a stable income stream.

According to the study, a graphical representation of the size of the net profit of higher education institutions and the factors affecting it over time was developed (Figure 113).

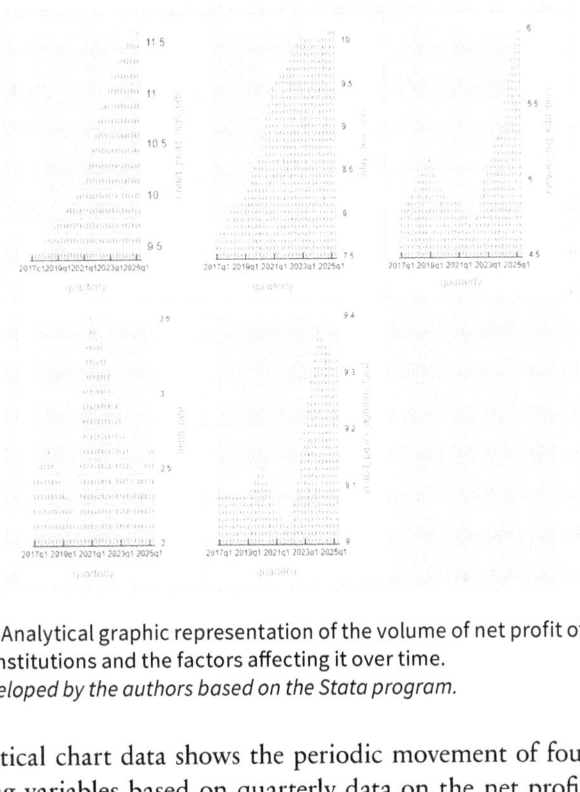

Figure 113. Analytical graphic representation of the volume of net profit of higher education institutions and the factors affecting it over time.
Source: Developed by the authors based on the Stata program.

The analytical chart data shows the periodic movement of four potential influencing variables based on quarterly data on the net profit of higher education institutions. According to this figure, the net profit of higher education institutions has changed over time, forming a potentially dynamic growth trend and showing a constant growth trend in influencing variables in the period from 2017 to 2024. By further developing scientific research based on increased investment in higher education institutions, educational institutions will have a positive impact on their financial and profitability indicators and will further increase their importance in innovative activities and academic development.

From the chart data, the growth and stability of the higher education sector provide a promising direction for educational institutions in the growth trend of net profit, which is effectively supported by sound strategic processes and macroeconomic conditions.

The next stage of the dissertation research presents a graphical matrix and scatter plots of the net profit of higher education institutions and the factors affecting it (Figures 114 and 115).

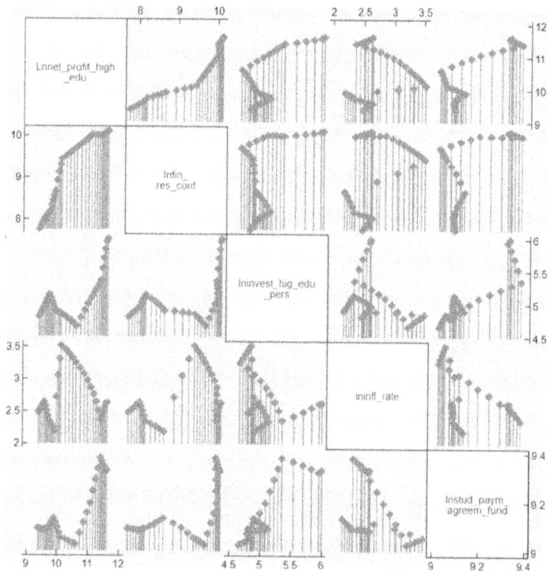

Figure 114. Graphical matrix representation of the net profit of higher education institutions and the factors affecting it.
Source: Developed by the authors based on the Stata program.

Figures 114 and 115 show a strong correlation between the net profit of higher education institutions and the variables influencing it. The figures show a strong upward trend along the diagonal of the individual variables, indicating a high level of investment in the net profit of higher education institutions and the development of these institutions.

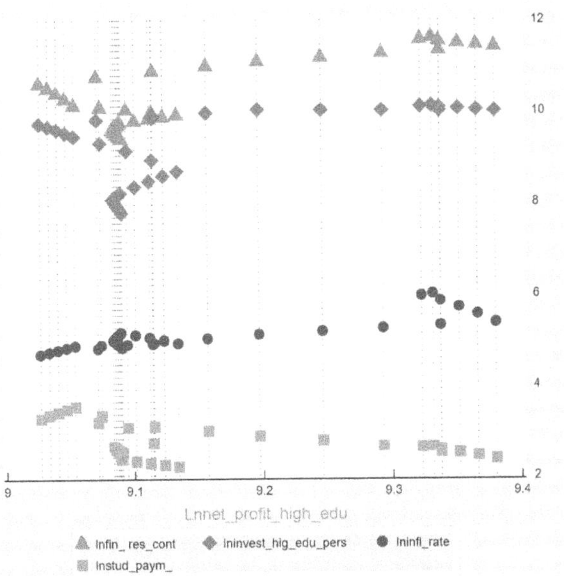

Figure 115. Scatter plot of the net profit of higher education institutions and the factors affecting it.
Source: Developed by the authors based on the Stata program.

The relationship between inflation and government spending in macroeconomic processes is relatively diffuse, suggesting that internal institutional strategies are more important endogenous variables than economic factors. The fact that student fees in higher education institutions do not grow along with profits suggests that institutions are achieving growth in their financial performance.

The next step is to present a graphical representation of the analytical relationship (rconnected) between the size of the net profit of higher education institutions and the factors affecting it (Figure 116).

According to Figure 116, the density distribution dependence diagram represents a solid visual dynamics of the net profit of higher education institutions and the factors affecting it. According to the distribution graph, the change in the density of the variables by values shows that the net profit of higher education institutions and the factors affecting it are systematically distributed, and this provides a positive forecast in the future.

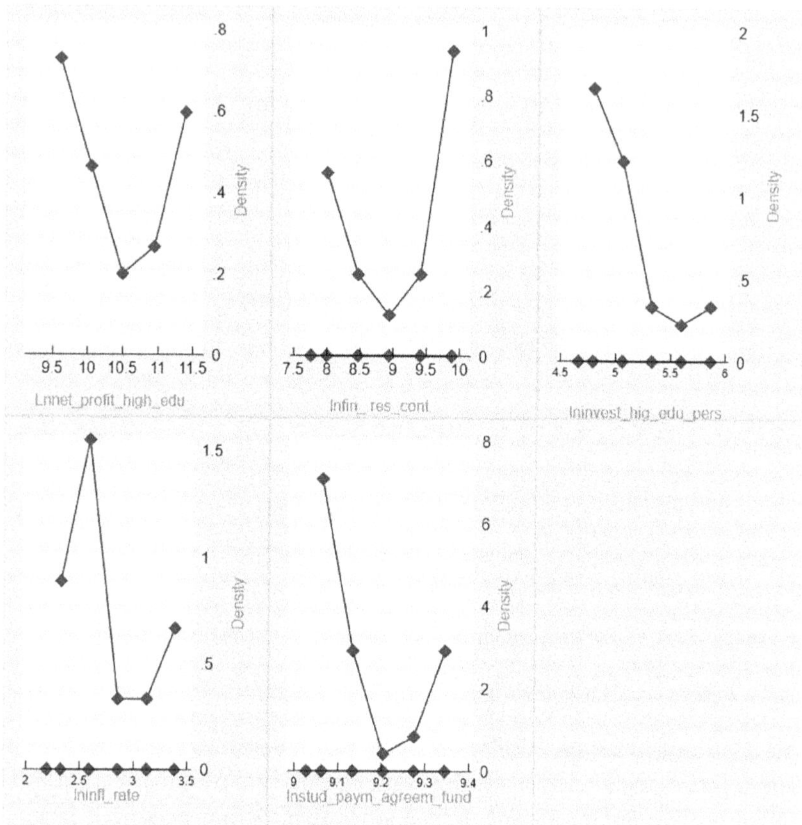

Figure 116. Graphical representation of the net profit of higher education institutions and the factors affecting it (rconnected).
Source: Developed by the authors based on the Stata program.

The graphical representation of the resulting variable and the factors affecting it (rconnected) expresses the dynamic relationship between macroeconomic indicators and supports the further increase in the volume of strategic investments and scientific research in educational processes.

According to the study, a correlation matrix of the net profit of higher education institutions and the variables affecting it was developed (Table 106).

Table 106. Correlation matrix of the net profit of higher education institutions and the factors affecting it

Variables	(1)	(2)	(3)	(4)	(5)	Significant
(1) *lnnet_profit_high_edu*	1.000					
(2) *lnfin_res_cont*	0.8395	1.000				
	(0.0000)					***
(3) *lninvest_hig_edu_pers*	0.6832	0.4418	1.000			
	(0.0000)	(0.0089)				***
(4) *lninfl_rate*	0.5437	0.3965	-0.4236	1.000		
	(0.0179)	(0.0203)	(0.0125)			***
(5) *lnstud_paym_agreem_fund*	0.8076	0.5925	0.8720	-0.4714	1.000	
	(0.0000)	(0.0000)	(0.0000)	(0.0141)		***

*** $p < 0.01$, ** $p < 0.05$, * $p < 0.1$

Source: Developed by the authors based on the Stata program.

According to Table 106, the net profit of higher education institutions and the factors affecting it show a strong, inverse and significant correlation between the variables. Positive correlations for all variables indicate a direct effect on the net profit of higher education institutions. Also, considering that the p-value is less than 0.05 according to the table, it is indicated that the condition of statistical significance for the correlation coefficient is met. At the next stage of the study, a regression model of the net profit of higher education institutions and the factors affecting it was developed using a multivariate linear (LS) model (Table 107).

Table 107. Regression equation indicators of the net profit of higher education institutions and factors affecting it

Lnnet_profit_ high_~u	Coef.	St.Err.	t-value	p-value	[95% Conf	Interval]	Sig
lnfin_res_cont	0.708	0.052	13.50	0	.6	0.815	***
lninvest_hig_ edu_p~s	0.314	0.102	3.06	0.005	0.104	0.523	***
lninfl_rate	−0.152	0.103	−1.48	0.051	−0.364	0.059	*
lnstud_paym_ agreem~d	1.161	0.51	2.27	0.031	0.117	2.204	**
Constant	-7.883	4.186	−1.88	0.07	−16.445	0.678	*

Mean dependent var	10.407	SD dependent var	0.755
R-squared	0.885	Number of obs	34
F-test	484.053	Prob > *F*	0.000
Akaike crit. (AIC)	−56.958	Bayesian crit. (BIC)	-49.327

*** $p < 0.01$, ** $p < 0.05$, * $p < 0.1$

Source: Developed by the authors based on the Stata program.

The formula parameters for the multivariate linear (LS) model are given below.

$$\begin{aligned} lnnet\_profit\_high\_edu = & -7.88 + 0.70 lnfin\_res\_cont \\ & + 0.31 lninvest\_hig\_edu\_pers - 0.15 lninfl\_rate \\ & + 1.16 lnstud\_paym\_agreem\_fund \end{aligned} \quad (2)$$

General description of the multivariate linear (LS) model.

The *p*-value of the net profit of higher education institutions and the variable affecting it is less than 0.05, indicating a statistically significant prediction of the resulting factor at the 5 per cent significance level.

R-squared value: The *R*-squared value is 0.8852, which provides a qualitative indicator of the model with 88.52 per cent of the net profit of higher education institutions and the factors affecting it. The formation of a high value of *R*-squared indicates a strong effect of the econometric model on the observed data.

When testing the hypothesis of the regression equation according to the multivariate linear (LS) model, it is clear that the null hypothesis ($H_0: y = 0$) is rejected when $F < 0.05$ and $t < 0.05$, indicating that the main hypothesis ($H_0: y = 0$) is statistically insignificant. Accordingly, the main hypothesis is rejected in favour of accepting the statistically significant alternative hypothesis ($H_1: y \neq 0$).

Result. A 1 per cent increase in the volume of financial resources received from business contracts in higher education leads to an increase in the net profit of higher education institutions by 0.70 per cent. A 1 per cent increase in the volume of investments made in employees in higher education leads to an increase in the net profit of higher education institutions by 0.31 per cent. A 1 per cent increase in the inflation rate in the national economy causes a decrease in the net profit of higher education institutions by 0.15. Also, a 1 per cent increase in the volume of student payment agreements leads to an increase in the net profit of higher education institutions by 1.16 per cent.

According to the econometric study, the Durbin-Watson test for the multivariate linear (LS) model had a value of 0.17. Also, the Shapiro-Wilk W test yielded values of 0.26, and the Breusch-Pagan test yielded values of 0.20. According to the primary hypothesis, $H_0: y = 0$ and $H_1: y \neq 0$, $p > 0.05$ significance level tests were conducted.

According to the multivariate linear (LS) model regression equation,

According to the results of the Durbin-Watson and Shapiro-Wilk tests, the null hypothesis was accepted. According to it, the model includes the analysis of the Gauss-Markov conditions confirming the absence of a relationship between the $p > 0.05$ threshold, error conditions and independent variables. According to it, the main conditions of the Gauss-Markov condition for the econometric model are met.

The multivariate linear (LS) model was tested for multicollinearity in the regression model using the VIF test, which has a value of 7.04 and indicates the absence of significant multicollinearity in the econometric model, representing a confidence interval of [1, 10] for this value.

The SEM regression model also has a graphical representation, as shown below (Figure 117).

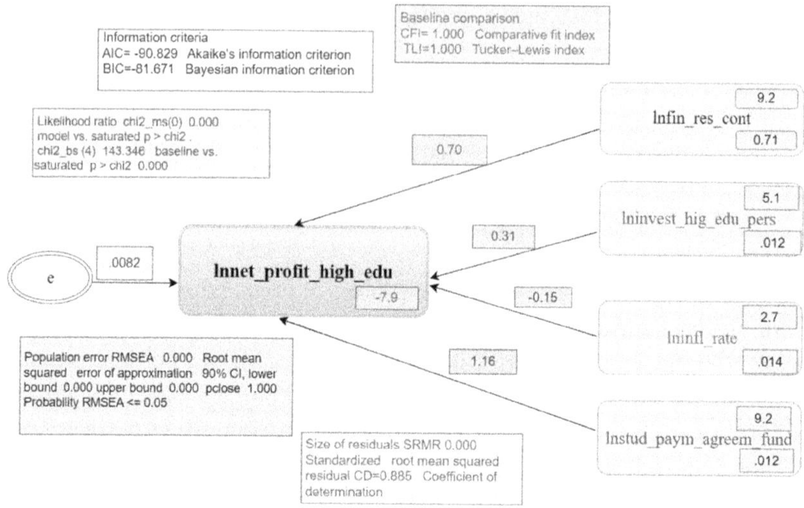

Figure 117. Schematic representation of the SEM model between the net profit of higher education institutions and the factors affecting it.
Source: Developed by the authors based on the Stata program.

29.5. Conclusion

The results of the econometric study using the multivariate linear (LS) equation model and the SEM econometric model showed that there is a strong and positive relationship between the volume of financial resources received from economic contracts in higher education, the volume of investments made in higher education employees, the level of GDP inflation in the national economy and the volume of student payment contracts, and the net profit of higher education institutions, which is an important factor in stimulating the volume of income of higher education institutions. Accordingly, the alternative hypothesis of the econometric model is confirmed.

1. The significance of the positive relationship of financial resources received from economic contracts. An increase in financial resources under economic contracts by 1 per cent increases net profit by 0.70 per cent. This strong relationship demonstrates the high effectiveness

of business entities and state contracts in increasing profitability. This indicates that higher education institutions are successfully commercialising their scientific services, not only by ensuring positive relations with external stakeholders, but also by converting scientific opportunities into economic value.

2. Assessing the impact of higher education institutions' investments in personnel. A 1 per cent increase in investments in higher education personnel leads to an increase in net profit by 0.31 per cent. According to this result, it is clear that there is a significant return on investment in scientific and administrative personnel. Institutions that prioritise their employees by supporting the professional development of higher education institutions and their competitive salaries create the basis for achieving effective financial indicators by increasing the value of their qualified workforce in achieving high-impact results.
3. Assessing the significance of the impact of the inflation rate in the national economy on the income of higher education institutions. A 1 per cent increase in the inflation rate in the national economy leads to a decrease in net profit by 0.15 per cent. According to this result, although the inflation rate has a negative effect, the magnitude of the effect is relatively small, which indicates that higher education institutions demonstrate significant financial stability even in a changing macroeconomic environment. Also, the policy of reducing the inflation rate is considered a key macro-level factor in changing the sources of income of higher education institutions.
4. Assessing the importance of funds in student payment agreements in higher education institutions. A 1 per cent increase in student payment increases net profit by 1.16 per cent. According to this result, this factor is an elastic factor in higher education institutions, which emphasises the effectiveness of increasing income related to student enrollment and tuition. According to him, as a result of expanding access to educational institutions, they have shown a significant increase in their financial indicators, which confirms the demand and trust in their educational services. In conclusion, higher education institutions can achieve a solid increase in their income by focusing on strategic partnerships, investing in talent and expanding educational opportunities.

Bibliography

Akhmetshin, E., Abdullayev, I., Makhmudov, S., Dakhkilgova, K., Korotaeva, I. and Yanovskaya, G. (2025). APPLICATION OF TANH–COTH METHOD FOR COMBINED AND DOUBLE COMBINED SINH–COSH–GORDON EQUATIONS ARISING CHEMICAL REACTIONS TO WATER SURFACE GRAVITY WAVES. Computational Methods for Differential Equations, (), -. doi: 10.22034/cmde.2025.67655.3234

Abouzeida, E. (2014). *Analysis of Expenditure Patterns in Higher Education Institutions and Student Graduation and Retention Rates*, <https://etd.auburn.edu/handle/10415/4223>.

Afriyie, A. O. (2013). *Financial Sustainability Factors of Higher Education Institutions: A Predictive Model*, <https://dspace.aiias.edu/xmlui/handle/3442/443>.

Agasisti, T., Perez-Esparrells, C., Catalano, G., and Morales, S. (2012). 'Is Expenditure on Higher Education Per Student Converging across EU-15 Countries?' *Studies in Higher Education*, 37 (2), 235–52, <https://doi.org/10.1080/03075079.2010.506952>.

Aparicio, T., and Villanúa, I. (2003). *Multivariate Linear Regression Model*, 45–120. Berlin, Heidelberg: Springer, <https://doi.org/10.1007/978-3-642-55686-9_2>.

Bridge, M. (2011). 'Higher Education Economic Impact Studies: Accurate Measures of Economic Impact?' *Journal of College Teaching & Learning* 2 (2). <https://doi.org/10.19030/TLC.V2I2.1777>.

Cahyani, I., Buriev, K., Ngongo, M., Mamadiyarov, Z., Ino, L., Herman, H., Saputra, N., & Baxtishodovich, S. (2025). Exploring the Use of TikTok Application in Enhancing the Skill of Pronunciation: A Case on Students' Perception. Studies in Media and Communication, 13(2), 150–158. doi: http://dx.doi.org/10.11114/smc.v13i2.7553

Carnoy, M. (2011). 'As Higher Education Expands, Is It Contributing to Greater Inequality?' *National Institute Economic Review*, 215 (1), 34–47, <https://doi.org/10.1177/0027950111401142>.

Chiou, J. M., Yang, Y. F., and Chen, Y. T. (2016). 'Multivariate Functional Linear Regression and Prediction'. *Journal of Multivariate Analysis*, 146, 301–12.

Figer-Canes, M. T. (2023). 'Effective Fiscal Management in Higher Education: Factors for Success', 1 (2), 32–9. <https://doi.org/10.61796/ejheaa.v1i2.99>.

Fowles, J. (October, 2008). Linking Institutional Expenditures to Student Success: An Analysis of Public Institutions of Higher Education. Chicago, IL: Association for Budgeting and Financial Management Conference.

González-Estrada, E., and Cosmes, W. (2019). 'Shapiro–Wilk Test for Skew Normal Distributions Based on Data Transformations'. *Journal of Statistical Computation and Simulation*, 89 (17), 3258–72.

Habib, S. S., Islam, M. A., Ali, M. N., Benitez, I. B., Mamadiyarov, Z., Mirzayev, B., … & Flah, A. (2025). Multi-Objective Optimization and Feasibility Analysis of Integrated Biogas–Solar Energy Systems for Rural Electrification. *Results in Engineering*, 107086.

Hermannsson, K., Lisenkova, K., McGregor, P., and Swales, J. (2010). 'The Expenditure Impacts of Individual Higher Education Institutions (HEIS) and Their Students on the Northern Irish Economy: Homogeneity or Heterogeneity?' *Research Papers in Economics*. <https://strathprints.strath.ac.uk/39718/>.

Herwartz, H. (2006). 'Testing for Random Effects in Panel Data Under Cross Sectional Error Correlation – A Bootstrap Approach to the Breusch Pagan Test'. *Computational Statistics & Data Analysis*, 50 (12), 3567–91.

Hill, C. B. (2016). 'American Higher Education and Income Inequality'. *Education Finance and Policy*, 11 (3), 325–39.

Hillman A. J., Withers, M. C., and Collins, B. J. (2009). 'Resource Dependence Theory: A Review', *Journal of Management*, 35 (6), 1404–27.

Jahrir, A., Gultom, Y., Herman, H., Zabadi, F., Ngongo, M., Mamadiyarov, Z., Fatmawati, E., & Saputra, N. (2025). Investigating the Elements of Short Commercial Mineral Water Advertisement: A Case on Discourse Analysis. Studies in Media and Communication, 13(4), 94–104. doi: http://dx.doi.org/10.11114/smc.v13i4.7813

Johnstone, D. B. (2019). *Higher Education Finance*. <https://doi.org/10.1093/OXFORDHB/9780198822905.013.21>.

Kalandarov, F., Makhmudov, S., Ibadullaev, D., Matniyozov, M., Nasretdinova, F., Sabirov, K., & Bahodirov, N. M. (2025). Low-Carbon Energy Risk and Renewable Energy Development: Insights from Method of Moments Quantile Regression. International Journal of Energy Economics and Policy, 15(3), 524–536.

Khayrilla Kurbonov, Samariddin Makhmudov, Shakhzod Erkinov, Umidjon Dadabaev, Gulnora Bekimbetova, Rukhiddin Zayniddinov, and Mirzabek Jonuzokov. 2025. Evaluating the Impact of Marketing Practices Digitalization and Investment on Labor Market Efficiency and Commercial Bank Performance Using Econometric Models. In Proceedings of the 8th International Conference on Future Networks & Distributed Systems (ICFNDS '24). Association for Computing Machinery, New York, NY, USA, 786–796. https://doi.org/10.1145/3726122.3726237

Khodjaniyazov, N., Mirkhoshimova, M., Kalandarov, F., Matyokubova, D., Utegenova, S., Makhmudov, S., & Khudayberganov, M. (2025). Time-Varying Impacts of Financial Stress on Energy-Related Uncertainty. International Journal of Energy Economics and Policy, 15(3), 689–698.

Kruzic, J. J., Kim, D. K., Koester, K. J., and Ritchie, R. O. (2009). 'Indentation Techniques for Evaluating the Fracture Toughness of Biomaterials and Hard Tissues'. *Journal of the Mechanical Behavior of Biomedical Materials*, 2 (4), 384–95.

Kuchkarov, T., Mamadiyarov, Z., Khakimov, Z., Sabirova, O., Matmurodov, K., Raimboyeva, M., & Umarova, S. (2025). Energy-Related Uncertainty and Crypto-Currency Environmental Attention: Time-Varying Perspective. International Journal of Energy Economics and Policy, 15(5), 614–626. https://doi.org/10.32479/ijeep.20784

Kuziboev, B., Khodjaniyazov, E., Ozturk, I., Sabirov, K., Makhmudov, S., & Utegenova, S. (2025). Does oil dependence cause energy risk?. *Energy Nexus*, *17*, 100393.

Kuziboev, B., Ozturk, I., Kalandarov, F., Samandarov, O., Bekjanov, D., & Makhmudov, S. (2025). PROMOTING ENERGY SOURCES DIVERSIFICATION THROUGH ESG PERFORMANCE. Energy, 136009.

Lin, M.H., Matchanova, B., Nurmatovich, H.A. et al. Optimal Operation of the Multi-Carrier Energy System Considering Energy Markets and

Renewable Energies Participation. *Int. J. Appl. Comput. Math* 11, 170 (2025). https://doi.org/10.1007/s40819-025-02002-9

Lipovetsky, S. (2024). *Multiple Regression Model as Interpolation through the Points of Weighted Means*. <https://doi.org/10.47852/bonviewjdsis42021995>.

Mamadiyarov, Z., Eshov, M., Otakhonova, D., Utegenova, S., Sabirov, K., Marks, A., & Bahodirov, N. (2025). Does Energy Policy Risk Threaten Energy Sources Diversification?. *International Journal of Energy Economics and Policy, 15*(5), 730–740. https://doi.org/10.32479/ijeep.21140

Mamadiyarov, Z., Saidov, O., Abdurazakova, N., Makhmudov, S., Nazarov, M., Rajabova, N., … Ruzmetova, I. (2025). Energy-Related Uncertainty and Tourism Stock Markets: New Insights from Time-Varying Relationship with TVP- VAR Approach. *International Journal of Energy Economics and Policy, 15*(4), 730–737. https://doi.org/10.32479/ijeep.20480

Mamani, J.C.M., Miri, M., Vorobev, Y. et al. Optimal Operation of Energy Microgrid Considering Economic and Emission Indices. Oper. Res. Forum 6, 122 (2025). https://doi.org/10.1007/s43069-025-00523-z

Ngongo, M., Herman, H., Ndandara, A., Jois Jaha, D. A., Peku Djawang, J. U. S., Tanggu Rame, M. M., Khamraeva, S. N., & Mamadiyarov, Z. (2025). An Investigation of Meaning, Toponymy of Sumba Cultural Site's Names, and the Impact of Tourism Visitors on Surrounding Society. *Forum for Linguistic Studies*, 7(8), 679–693. https://doi.org/10.30564/fls.v7i8.10260

Pradhan, R., Hajiyev, E., Shichiyakh, R. et al. Optimal Techno-Economic Feasibility of an Off-Grid Microgrid System Using Load Flow Energy Management Strategies. *Oper. Res. Forum* 6, 120 (2025). https://doi.org/10.1007/s43069-025-00524-y

Rayala, R. V., Borra, C. R., Vasudevan, V., Singhania, R., Cheekati, S., & Mamadiyarov, Z. (2025, July). Lightweight Deep Learning Framework for Human Activity Recognition: A MobileNet-LSTM Approach with WHOA Optimization. In *2025 International Conference on Innovations in Intelligent Systems: Advancements in Computing, Communication, and Cybersecurity (ISAC3)* (pp. 1–6). IEEE.

Rayala, R. V., Sandhya, N., Singhania, R., Cheekati, S., Borra, C. R., Vasudevan, V., & Mamadiyarov, Z. (2025, July). AI-Driven Tomato Quality Assessment: A Deep Learning Approach for Image-based

Defect Detection and Classification. In *2025 International Conference on Innovations in Intelligent Systems: Advancements in Computing, Communication, and Cybersecurity (ISAC3)* (pp. 1–6). IEEE.

Romero, R. M., Zelinskaya, M., Makhmudov, S., Sapaev, S., & Rustambekovich, J. U. (2025, September). Modelling and Optimal Utilisation of the Renewable Energy Systems in Microgrid with Improving Reliability and Energy Efficiency. In Operations Research Forum (Vol. 6, No. 3, pp. 1–20). Springer International Publishing.

Rony, Z. T., Jefri, R., Rusmardiana, A., Pramono, S. A., & Mamadiyarov, Z. (2025). Downside Risk Measurement of Indonesian Financial and Energy Securities: A Value at Risk Perspective. *Journal of Applied Science, Engineering, Technology, and Education,* 7(2). https://doi.org/10.35877/454RI.asci3898

Rosopa, P. J., Schaffer, M. M., & Schroeder, A. N. (2013). 'Managing Heteroscedasticity in General Linear Models'. *Psychological Methods*, 18 (3), 335.

Rukhiddin Zayniddinov, Nodir Jumaev, Gulbakhor Irgasheva, Alam Asadov, Nosir Makhmudov, Sirojiddin Abrorov, and Samariddin Makhmudov. 2025. The Influence of the Digital Economy on Economic Development Evidence from Uzbekistan. In Proceedings of the 8th International Conference on Future Networks & Distributed Systems (ICFNDS '24). Association for Computing Machinery, New York, NY, USA, 831–839. https://doi.org/10.1145/3726122.3726242

Rutledge, D. N., and Barros, A. S. (2002). 'Durbin–Watson Statistic as a Morphological Estimator of Information Content'. *Analytica Chimica Acta*, 454 (2), 277–95.

Samariddin Makhmudov, Malika Umarova, Khayrilla Kurbonov, Laylo Akbarova, Durdona Davletova, Nilufar Shanazarova, and Toshmurod Kulmanov. 2025. Evaluating the forecast indicators of the volume of highly liquid assets of commercial banks in the process of digital transformation. In Proceedings of the 8th International Conference on Future Networks & Distributed Systems (ICFNDS '24). Association for Computing Machinery, New York, NY, USA, 698–704. https://doi.org/10.1145/3726122.3726222

Samariddin Makhmudov, Kudratillo Tukhsanov, Saifulla Arslanbekov, Akram Amanov, Orifali Tursunov, Umarbek Jabbarov and Muyassarxon

Mirzakarimova. 2024. Optimizing Supply Chain Financing Development Prospects of Digital Ecosystems in the European Logistics Industry. In The 8th International Conference on Future Networks & Distributed Systems (ICFNDS '24), December 11–12, 2024, Marakech, Morocco. ACM, New York, NY, USA, 12 Pages. https://doi.org/10.1145/3726122.3726200

Schützenmeister, A., Jensen, U., and Piepho, H.-P. (2012). 'Checking Normality and Homoscedasticity in the General Linear Model Using Diagnostic Plots'. *Communications in Statistics - Simulation and Computation*, 41 (2), 141–154. <https://doi.org/10.1080/03610918.2011.582560>.

Singagerda, F. S., Pratama, M. R., Alfairus, M. Q., Iskandar, A., & Mamadiyarov, Z. (2025). A Decision-Centric Approach to Risk Management in Aviation Stock Investments Using Value at Risk and Portfolio Optimization. *Journal of Applied Science, Engineering, Technology, and Education*, 7(1), 114–125. https://doi.org/10.35877/454RI.asci3870

Sofyanty, D., Romadhoni, R., Handriadi, H., Makhsudovna, I. S., Anwar, Z., & Mamadiyarov, Z. (2025). Strategic Decision Analysis for Investment Portfolios: Computational Risk Assessment in Transportation Asset Management. *Journal of Applied Science, Engineering, Technology, and Education*, 7(2). https://doi.org/10.35877/454RI.asci3897

Su, R., Xiao, Y., Hamza, F., Mamadiyarov, Z., & Wahab, A. (2025). Scaling up green hydrogen in China: Economic opportunities and challenges. *International Journal of Hydrogen Energy, 131*, 60–69.

Toshmurod Kulmanov, Umidjon Dadabaev, Mansurbek Qulmetov, Aliboy Ulashov, Mirjalol Eshboyev, and Samariddin Makhmudov. 2025. Global Services Market Transformation Digitalization Export Trends and Future Forecasts. In Proceedings of the 8th International Conference on Future Networks & Distributed Systems (ICFNDS '24). Association for Computing Machinery, New York, NY, USA, 851–858. https://doi.org/10.1145/3726122.3726245

Toutkoushian, R. K., and Paulsen, M. B. (2016). *Higher Education Revenues and Expenditures*, pp. 231–74. Dordrecht: Springer <https://doi.org/10.1007/978-94-017-7506-9_7>.

Wyness, G. (2009). *The Impact of Higher Education Finance in the UK.* <https://ethos.bl.uk/OrderDetails.do?uin=uk.bl.ethos.534878>.

Zhang, L., Zhao, Z., Qamri, G. M., & Makhmudov, S. (2025). Unleashing the critical role of renewable energy through global value chains and digitalization: A path towards environmental sustainability. *Journal of Environmental Management, 392*, 126688.

Zhao, Q., Pervaiz, A., Makhmudov, S., & Fatima, A. (2025). Do environmental stringent policies enhance the impact of renewable energy on CO2 reduction? Evidence from BRICS-T economies. Journal of Environmental Management, 391, 126464.

Assessing Short- and Long-Term Trends in Higher Education Financing

Mansur Eshov, Alisher Sherov, Zokir Mamadiyarov, Samariddin Makhmudov, Amina Ruzikulova, Mushtariybonu Hakimova and Muazzam Bozorova

30.1. Introduction

A number of scientific research works are being conducted around the world on the role of the state in financing higher education institutions, the diversification of sources of financing for higher education institutions, the role of the concepts of 'University 3.0' and 'University 4.0' in ensuring the financial stability of higher education institutions, and the role of international financial institutions in attracting investments in higher education institutions. Despite the fact that such research is being conducted, the issues of diversifying sources of financing for higher education institutions and creating effective mechanisms for financing higher education institutions from budgetary and extra-budgetary funds have not been studied comprehensively and systematically, which indicates the need for scientific research in these areas.

In Uzbekistan, special attention is being paid to gradually granting financial freedom to higher education institutions, expanding financing from extra-budgetary funds, effectively organising the commercialisation of scientific and innovative developments, and attracting the private sector, including personnel customers, as well as sponsorship and charitable funds from legal entities and individuals, in financing higher education institutions. The need to improve the legal framework regulating the activities of higher education institutions, the lack of regulation of the financial activities of non-state higher education institutions, the lack of systematisation of their rights and obligations in the academic and financial spheres, the lack of an effective mechanism for using budget funds, the lack of diversification of sources of financing for higher education institutions, the lack of consideration of the financial stability indicator in financing higher education institutions, and the existence of other shortcomings determine the need to develop proposals and recommendations to improve the theoretical and methodological foundations of this area.

Currently, a number of measures are being implemented in our country to effectively organise the financing of higher education institutions, including the gradual transition of higher education institutions to a self-financing system, granting them academic and financial independence, and creating broad opportunities for the activities of private higher education institutions. Certain problems and shortcomings hinder the effectiveness of these reforms, including:

- the work on personnel training in cooperation between higher education institutions and personnel customers is not effectively organised. As a result, not only is theory and practice not connected, but it also leads to problems in the process of employers investing in higher education institutions, providing sponsorship, and eliminating existing problems in the process of practice in cooperation with scientists;
- the effectiveness of innovative activities and research results of higher education institutions in practice and the commercialisation of scientific developments, attracting talented young scientists and students to scientific research activities is not sufficiently organised; effective mechanisms for stimulating the activities of scientists engaged in innovative developments and scientific research activities have not been created;
- the material and technical base that meets today's requirements has not been formed in most student dormitories, libraries, laboratories, sports and recreation facilities and social infrastructure;
- the main part of the funds of higher education institutions is spent on salaries, and insufficient funds have been allocated for the modernisation of educational and scientific laboratories, capital and current repairs of buildings and structures;
- the lack of diversification of sources of financing of higher education institutions, the main source of which is payment-contract amounts;
- failure to take into account regional factors in financing higher education institutions and the lack of use of local budget funds, etc.

30.2. Literature Review

Higher regional spending on higher education leads to higher economic performance. State spending on higher education measures investments in human capital, not the educational outcomes they are supposed to produce

(Baldwin et al., 2011). Recent research has shown that increased state financial support for higher education is associated with improved economic performance through increased human capital and, consequently, higher productivity (Bowen & Qian, 2017).

There are also several empirical studies on the impact of higher education financing on a country's economic growth worldwide. In particular, C. Abhijeet (2010) used linear and nonlinear Granger Causality methods to determine the causal relationship between educational spending and economic growth (Abhijeet, 2010). The results show that economic growth has a positive effect on government spending on education, regardless of the time lag, and that investment in education also has a positive effect on economic growth after a certain period.

Appiah (2017) used the GMM estimator system to study the effect of education expenditure on per capita GDP in developing countries from 1975 to 2015 (Appiah, 2017). The results showed that an increase in education spending in developing countries has a positive effect on per capita GDP.

Yu et al. (2014) found that there is a long-term stable equilibrium relationship between higher education investment, human capital investment and economic growth, and in particular, higher education investment and human capital investment have a significant positive impact on economic growth (Yu et al., 2014).

In recent years, public spending on higher education has been declining globally, with many countries reducing their public budgets for higher education as a result of economic reforms and a reduction in the role of the state in financing education. This trend is evident in both developing and developed countries (Tilak, 2015). In the United States, public funding of higher education has declined sharply since the 1980s, with a shift to private funding sources (McPherson & Schapiro, 2006).

The introduction of student-paid contracts and student loans has played a significant role in addressing the financial problems of higher education institutions, leading to a shift from public to private funding of education in developing countries (Woodhall, 1992). The introduction of student loans and tuition fees has sparked public debate on the social policy and economic rationale, as well as concerns about their impact on educational attainment for low-income groups (Villiers & Nieuwoudt, 2010).

30.3. Research Methodology

Based on the above considerations, we used 'Autoregressive Lag Distribution Models (ARDL)' in this study to determine the short-term and long-term impact of financing higher education. In the formation of this model, the following factors were selected as the resulting and influencing factors: resulting factor – Gross domestic product per capita, thousand soums – (*GDP_per_capita*), influencing factors – extrabudgetary funds of state higher education institutions, billion soums – (*EBF_HEdu*), the volume of state investments in the higher education system, billion soums – (*VSI_HEdu*), the number of professors and teaching staff of higher education institutions, people – (*NST_HEdu*).

Since the units of measurement of the variables are different and to better explain the interpretation of the multifactor econometric model, we take the natural logarithm of all factor values.

To analyse the effect of the dependent variables, we use a linear model with all variables taken as natural logarithms. This model is expressed as follows:

$$LOG\left(GDP\_per\_capita\right)_t = \beta_0 + \beta_1 LOG\left(EBF\_HEdu\right)_t + \beta_2 LOG\left(VSI\_HEdu\right)_t + \beta_3 LOG\left(NST\_HEdu\right)_t + \epsilon_t \quad (1)$$

where: $LOG\left(GDP_{per_{capita}}\right)$ – represents the GDP per capita, and *t*– represents the period from 2010 to 2023, β – the free limit, $\beta_1, \beta_2, \beta_3$ – the coefficients of the influencing factors, and ϵ_t – the error.

We use the ARDL model developed by Pesaran and Shin (Pesaran & Shin, 1999) in this analysis. Also, given that the ARDL model has both short-run and long-run equations, it is necessary to perform a Bound test to determine which one to use. The Bound test is based on the standard *F*- and *t*-statistical tests. Regardless of whether the order of integration of the independent variables is $I(0)$ or $I(1)$, the asymptotic distribution of this statistic is not correlated at any level under the non-standard null hypothesis $\left(H_0\right)$. Two sets of asymptotic critical values are provided: one when all independent variables are fully integrated $I(1)$, and the other when all of them are fully integrated $I(0)$. These two sets of critical values ensure that all possible classifications of the independent variables are fully integrated $I(0)$, fully integrated $I(1)$ or cointegrated. The null hypothesis $\left(H_0\right)$ of the

ARDL Bound test states that there is no long-run relationship between the variables. If the null hypothesis (H_0) is not rejected, the ARDL model specification represents only the short-term estimation results and can be expressed as (Pesaran et al., 2001):

$$\begin{aligned}\Delta LOG(GDP\_per\_capita)_t = \gamma_0 + \gamma_1 \sum_{q=1}^{n} \Delta LOG(GDP\_per\_capita)_{t-q} + \gamma_2 \sum_{q=1}^{n} \Delta LOG(EBF\_HEdu)_{t-q} \\ + \gamma_3 \sum_{q=1}^{n} \Delta LOG(VSI\_HEdu)_{t-q} + \gamma_4 \sum_{q=1}^{n} \Delta LOG(NST\_HEdu)_{t-q} \\ + \delta_1 LOG(GDP\_per\_capita)_{t-1} + \delta_2 LOG(EBF\_HEdu)_{t-1} \\ + \delta_3 LOG(VSI\_HEdu)_{t-1} + \delta_4 LOG(NST\_HEdu)_{t-1} + \varepsilon_t \end{aligned} \quad (2)$$

where: represents the 1st-order differentiation of Δ factors, γ_0 – the free term, $\gamma_1, \gamma_2, \gamma_3, \gamma_4$, – the short-run elasticity coefficients, $\delta_1, \delta_2, \delta_3, \delta_4$, – the long-run dynamic multipliers, n – the lag (time interval) length, q – the lag (time interval) order and ε_t – the error.

It is known that in order to build multivariate econometric models, the 'Ljung- Box' (Q) (Ljung & Box, 1978) test is first used to determine whether or not there is autocorrelation in the time series (for the factors participating in the model). The presence of autocorrelation in time series requires checking these time series for stationarity. Then, to check the stationarity of the variables and determine the order of their integration, Augmented Dickey-Fuller (ADF) (Dickey & Fuller, 1981) and Phillips-Perron (PP) (Abdullah et al., 2025; Akhmetshin et al., 2025; Habib et al., 2025; Jahrir et al., 2025; Kalandarov et al., 2025; Khayrilla et al., 2025; Ngongo et al., 2025; Phillips & Perron, 1988) unit root tests are used. Then, considering the existence of short-run and long-run ARDL model equations, it is necessary to conduct a Bound test to determine which one should be used. In the final stage, robustness tests are used for the ARDL model developed for this research work.

Analyses and forecasts were conducted using multivariate linear regression (LS), ARDL, ARIMA and various other econometric models on the global services market, digital economy, energy-related financial stress, cocktail market, digital transformation, factors affecting the logistics industry (Khodjaniyazov et al., 2025; Kuziboev et al., 2025; Lin et al., 2025; Mamadiyarov et al., 2025; Mamani et al., 2025; Muhammad et al., 2025; Pradhan et al., 2025; Rayala et al., 2025; Samariddin et al., 2025; Zhang et al., 2025; Zhao et al., 2025).

H_0: The hypothesis of the 'Ljung-Box' test (that there is no autocorrelation in the time series) and the alternative hypothesis H_1 (that there is autocorrelation in the time series) are considered as the main hypotheses. It is known that in this test, the presence of a $p < 0.05$ indicates the acceptance of the hypothesis H_1, and the presence of a $p < 0.05$ indicates the acceptance of the hypothesis H_0 (Levendis, 2023).

Another group of economists has successfully used econometric models such as Fixed Effects Estimator, Random Effects Estimator, multivariate linear (LS) and ARDL in their research on investment in digital infrastructure, various aspects of digital payment systems, the impact of inflation and credit interest rates on investment, factors affecting the reduction of the state's share in commercial banks, Non-Performing Loans in commercial banks, the digitisation of banks, risks in digital services and the development of retail payment services (Mamadiyarov et al., 2025; Rayala et al., 2025; Rony et al., 2025; Rukhiddin et al., 2025; Samariddin et al., 2025; Sofyanty et al., 2025; Su et al., 2025; Toshmurod et al., 2025; Zokir et al., 2021).

30.4. Analysis and Results

Table 108 presents the results of the autocorrelation test of the factors.

Table 108. Results of the 'Ljung-Box' test for determining the resulting and influencing factors

		LOG(GDP_per_capita)		
Lag	**AC**	**PAC**	***Q*-Stat**	**Prob**
1	0.789	0.789	10.718	0.001
2	0.585	−0.099	17.101	0.000
3	0.390	−0.105	20.194	0.000
4	0.205	−0.112	21.133	0.000
5	0.020	−0.153	21.143	0.001
6	−0.149	−0.137	21.763	0.001
7	−0.294	−0.134	24.533	0.001

		LOG(EBF_HEdu)		
Lag	**AC**	**PAC**	***Q*-Stat**	**Prob**
1	0.784	0.784	10.599	0.001
2	0.574	-0.107	16.751	0.000
3	0.375	-0.105	19.609	0.000
4	0.198	-0.085	20.485	0.000
5	0.022	-0.146	20.497	0.001
6	-0.140	-0.133	21.045	0.002
7	-0.263	-0.084	23.263	0.002
		LOG(VSI_HEdu)		
Lag	**AC**	**PAC**	***Q*-Stat**	**Prob**
1	0.747	0.747	9.6223	0.002
2	0.535	-0.053	14.964	0.001
3	0.329	-0.118	17.170	0.001
4	0.194	0.010	18.014	0.001
5	0.006	-0.226	18.015	0.003
6	-0.104	-0.008	18.317	0.005
7	-0.208	-0.103	19.707	0.006
		LOG(NST_HEdu)		
Lag	**AC**	**PAC**	**Q-Stat**	**Prob**
1	0.784	0.784	10.582	0.001
2	0.573	-0.106	16.718	0.000
3	0.371	-0.113	19.517	0.000
4	0.193	-0.081	20.355	0.000
5	0.016	-0.148	20.362	0.001
6	-0.132	-0.098	20.852	0.002
7	-0.254	-0.103	22.924	0.002

Source: Developed by the authors based on the Stata program.

From the data in Table 108, it can be seen that, based on the existing hypotheses of the 'Ljung-Box' test, it is possible to see that all variables have autocorrelation.

At the next stage, it is important to conduct ADF and PP unit root tests to check the stationarity of the variables and determine the order of their integration. The results of checking the stationarity of the variables are given in Table 109.

Table 109. Results of the 'ADF' and 'PP' unit root test when checking the stationarity of variables

	Augmented Dickey-Fuller (ADF)				Order of integration
	Levels	Probability	1st differences	Probability	
LOG(GDP_per_capita)	−2.62	0.28	−4.89	0.01	*I* (1)
LOG(EBF_HEdu)	−2.72	0.24	−3.82	0.04	*I* (1)
LOG(VSI_HEdu)	−4.39	0.02	−6.60	0.00	*I* (1)
LOG(NST_HEdu)	−3.54	0.09	−5.43	0.00	*I* (1)
	Phillips-Perron (PP)				**Order of integration**
	Levels	**Probability**	**1st differences**	**Probability**	
LOG(GDP_per_capita)	−2.01	0.54	−5.76	0.00	*I* (1)
LOG(EBF_HEdu)	−2.79	0.23	−6.59	0.00	*I* (1)
LOG(VSI_HEdu)	−4.48	0.01	−14.92	0.00	*I* (1)
LOG(NST_HEdu)	−11.95	0.00	−16.81	0.00	*I* (1)

Source: Developed by the authors based on the Stata program.

According to the data in Table 109, the volume of GDP per capita, extrabudgetary funds of state higher education institutions, the volume of state investments in the higher education system, and the number of professors and teaching staff of higher education institutions are all stationary in the 1st order differentiation. Because the 1st order differentiated value of all variables reflects a probability value less than 0.05. Therefore, the order of integration of all these variables into the equation is taken as $I(1)$. At the next stage, it is necessary to select the 'lag (time interval)' order of the variables participating in the model. For this, the optimal 'lag' order of the vector autoregressive (VAR) model is used (Table 110).

Table 110. Determining the 'lag (time interval)' order for 'Autoregressive Lag Distribution Models (ARDL)'

Lag	AIC	SC (BIC)	HQ
0	-6.788122	-6.614291	-6.823852
1	-16.53670*	-15.66755*	-16.71535*
2	-15.95649	-14.803512	-15.568417
3	-14.723648	-13.716421	-15.172382

Source: Developed by the authors based on the Stata program.

Based on the data in Table 110 and the 'Akaike (AIC)', 'Schwarz (SC)' and 'Hannan-Quinn (HQ)' criteria, it can be determined that the 'lag (time interval)' order for the autoregressive lag distribution model is equal to 1. Because among all the values of the 'lag (time interval)' order, the Akaike (AIC)', 'Schwarz (SC)' and 'Hannan – Quinn (HQ)' criteria at lag 1 reflect the smallest value.

Before finding the long-term and short-term relationships between variables, it is necessary to confirm the existence of cointegration. This is done using the 'Bound test'. As is known, in the 'Bound test', if the *F*-statistic value is greater than the 'Upper bound' of the asymptotic critical values, this indicates that cointegration exists, if the *F*-statistic value is between the 'Upper bound' and 'Lower bound' of the asymptotic critical values, it means that cointegration is unreliable, if the *F*-statistic value is less than the 'Lower bound' of the asymptotic critical values, indicates that there is no cointegration. Table 111 presents the results of the 'Bound test'.

Table 111. Results of the 'Bound test'

Test Statistic	Value	Significa	Lower bound *I*(0)	Upper bound *I*(1)
F-statistic	37.35628	10%	2.618	3.532
		5%	3.164	4.194
		1%	4.428	5.816

Source: Developed by the authors based on the Stata program.

From Table 111, it can be seen that the *F*-statistic value is greater than the 'Upper Bound' of the asymptotic critical values at all significance levels.

This indicates the presence of cointegration and the possibility of forming long- and short-run equations.

Table 112. Results of long-term estimation of parameters calculated based on the ARDL(1,1,1,1) model

Dependent Variable: *LOG(GDP_per_capita)*				
Variable	**Coefficient**	**Std. Error**	***t*-Statistic**	**Prob.***
LOG(EBF_HEdu)	3.753375	0.142911	26.26372	0.0000
LOG(VSI_HEdu)	6.821973	0.076151	89.58481	0.0000
LOG(NST_HEdu)	2.480851	0.555000	4.470002	0.0065
C	−11.66909	4.367583	−2.671750	0.0443
LOG(GDP_per_capita)(−1)	0.026074	0.093603	0.278563	0.7917
LOG(EBF_HEdu)(−1)	0.344783	2.110754	0.163346	0.8766
LOG(VSI_HEdu)(−1)	0.904812	1.09662	0.825094	0.4469
LOG(NST_HEdu)(−1)	0.487080	1.049750	0.463996	0.6622
R-squared	0.989878	Mean dependent var		9.297202
Adjusted *R*-squared	0.979507	S.D. dependent var		0.746979
S.E. of regression	0.012790	Akaike info criterion		−5.605020
Sum squared resid	0.001647	Schwarz criterion		−5.257359
Log likelihood	58.26343	Hannan-Quinn criterion		−5.676480

Source: Developed by the authors based on the Stata program.

The influencing factors $LOG(EBF\_HEdu)$, $LOG(VSI\_HEdu), LOG(NST_{HEdu})$ in Table 30.5 all have coefficients with probability values less than 0.05 $(p < 0.05)$, which indicates that all of these coefficients are statistically significant. It can be seen that the remaining coefficients in the table are statistically insignificant (since the probability values $p > 0.05$ of the coefficients satisfy the inequality).

The empirical results of the calculated long-term impact (Table 112) show that a 1 per cent increase in the volume of extrabudgetary funds of state higher education institutions can increase the volume of GDP per capita by 3.75 per cent, a 1 per cent increase in the volume of state investments in the higher education system can increase the volume of GDP per capita by 6.82 per cent, and a 1 per cent increase in the number of professors and teaching staff of higher education institutions can increase the volume of GDP per capita by 2.48 per cent.

Table 113. Results of short-term estimation of parameters calculated based on the ARDL(1,1,1,1) model

Dependent Variable: ΔLOG(*GDP_per_capita*)				
Variable	**Coefficient**	**Std. Error**	***t*-Statistic**	**Prob.***
ΔLOG(*EBF_HEdu*)	1.323898	0.050276	26.33260	0.0000
ΔLOG(*VSI_HEdu*)	2.573232	0.028782	89.40421	0.0000
ΔLOG(*NST_HEdu*)	1.264266	0.381358	3.31517	0.0211
ECM(−1)	−0.173926	0.053116	3.27446	0.0221
R-squared	0.970043	Mean dependent var		0.190157
Adjusted *R*-squared	0.963391	S.D. dependent var		0.058442
S.E. of regression	0.009533	Akaike info criterion		−6.220405
Sum squared resid	0.000818	Schwarz criterion		−6.046574
Log likelihood	44.43263	Hannan-Quinn criterion		−6.256135

Source: Developed by the authors based on the Stata program.

It can be seen that all the coefficients representing the short-term impact calculated in Table 113 are statistically significant. This fact justifies the possibility of fully interpreting all the coefficients in economic terms. The empirical results representing the short-term impact (Table 113) show that a 1 per cent increase in the volume of extra-budgetary funds of state higher education institutions can lead to an increase in the volume of GDP per capita by 1.32 per cent, a 1 per cent increase in the volume of state investments in the higher education system can lead to an increase in the volume of GDP per capita by 2.57 per cent, and a 1 per cent increase in the number of professors and teaching staff of higher education institutions can lead to an increase in the volume of GDP per capita by 1.26 per cent.

ECM(-1) (Error-correction Mechanisms) (Levendis, 2023) The imbalance between variables indicates the speed of their recovery to long-term equilibrium after negative impacts. According to the results of our analysis in our research work, it means that 17.4 per cent (0.174) of recovery is needed annually to achieve long-term equilibrium by eliminating the imbalance between the variables of GDP per capita, the volume of extrabudgetary funds of state higher education institutions, the volume of state investments in the higher education system and the number of professors and teaching staff of higher education institutions.

In the next step, CUSUM (Cumulative Sum) tests are performed to check the stability of this model. The 'CUSUM' (Figure 118) and 'CUSUM Squares' (Figure 119) tests show that the sum of the standardised deviations (blue line) does not exceed the specified range (red lines).

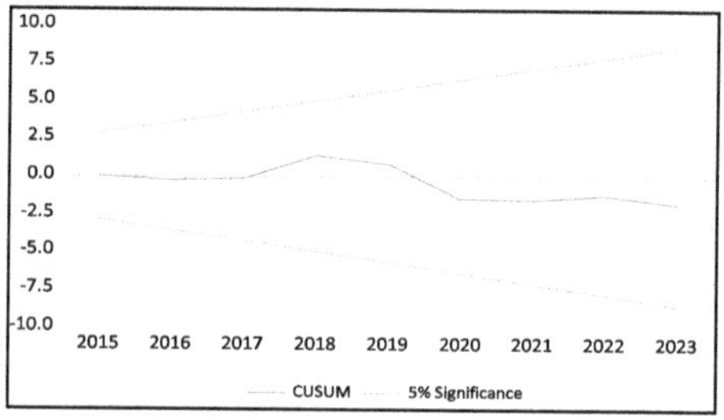

Figure 118. CUSUM test graph for ARDL model.
Source: Developed by the authors based on the Stata program.

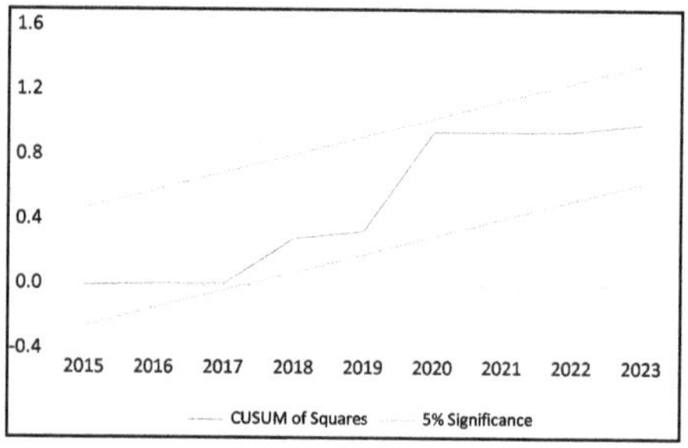

Figure 119. CUSUM squared test graph for the ARDL model.
Source: Developed by the authors based on the Stata program.

30.5. Conclusion

In the model we analysed, the *R*-squared (0.970043) and Adjusted *R*-squared (0.963391) indicators are very high, and the model accounts for more than

96 per cent of the GDP per capita variable. This indicates that the model is selected correctly. The Prob. value for all coefficients is less than 0.05, which indicates that all coefficients are statistically significant. The coefficient ECM (–1) is negative (–0.173926) and significant (*p*-value 0.0221), which indicates that the model has a tendency to return to long-term equilibrium. According to the results obtained, a 1 per cent increase in the level of male higher education leads to an increase in GDP per capita by 1.32 per cent. The impact of female tertiary education attainment is significant, with a 1 per cent increase in GDP contributing to a 2.57 per cent increase in GDP. The number of people educated in non-traditional fields also has a positive impact, with a 1 per cent increase in GDP contributing to a 1.26 per cent increase in GDP. The sum squared resid (0.000818) and S.E. of regression (0.009533) are very small, indicating that there are no large errors in the model.

To improve the financing of higher education for women, men and social policy, it is necessary to work in the following areas:

1. It is necessary to increase the volume of investment in women's education. This is also indicated by the fact that the *V(SI)_HEdu* coefficient has the greatest impact. Supporting women's entry into higher education and their professional development in society has a significant impact on the country's economic growth.
2. It is also necessary to create opportunities for education in non-traditional areas. This can be seen from the fact that the *EBF_HEdu* and *NST_HEdu* coefficients also have a positive and significant impact. By improving the quality of education in these areas, the country's economic growth can also be stimulated.
3. It is necessary to strengthen long-term connections and partnerships between higher education and the economy. Since the ECM results also show that there is a long-term relationship, it is necessary to develop sustainable and continuous strategies in implementing education policy.
4. Along with improving social policy, it is necessary to increase the coverage of higher education. As a result, it will be possible to increase economic efficiency by expanding state programmes aimed at increasing the level of higher education of the population. In addition, by adapting educational programmes to economic needs, it will be possible to improve the balance of supply and demand in the labour market.

Bibliography

Abdullah, M. A., Han, X., Amjad, M. A., & Makhmudov, S. (2025). Revisit the role of financial development on economic growth, human development, and sustainable development in higher-income countries. *Journal of Environmental Management*, *392*, 126874.

Akhmetshin, E., Abdullayev, I., Makhmudov, S., Dakhkilgova, K., Korotaeva, I. and Yanovskaya, G. (2025). APPLICATION OF TANH–COTH METHOD FOR COMBINED AND DOUBLE COMBINED SINH–COSH–GORDON EQUATIONS ARISING CHEMICAL REACTIONS TO WATER SURFACE GRAVITY WAVES. Computational Methods for Differential Equations, (), -. doi: 10.22034/cmde.2025.67655.3234

Abhijeet, C. (2010). 'Does Government Expenditure on Education Promote Economic Growth'? *An Econometric Analysis*, <https://mpra.ub.uni-muenchen.de/id/eprint/25480>.

Appiah, E. N. (2017). 'The Effect of Education Expenditure on Per Capita GDP in Developing Countries'. *International Journal of Economics and Finance*, 9 (10), 136–44. <https://doi.org/10.5539/ijef.v9n10p136>.

Baldwin, J. N., Borrelli, S. A., and New, M. J. (2011). 'State Educational Investments and Economic Growth in the United States: A Path Analysis'. *Social Science Quarterly*, 92 (1), 226–45. <https://doi.org/10.1111/j.1540-6237.2011.00765.x>.

Bowen, W. M., and Qian, H. (2017). 'State Spending for Higher Education: Does It Improve Economic Performance?' *Regional Science Policy & Practice* 9 (1), 7–24. <https://doi.org/10.1111/rsp3.12086>.

de Villiers, P., and Nieuwoudt, L. (2010). 'Shifting Trends in Higher Education Funding'. *Research Papers in Economics*. <https://ideas.repec.org/p/sza/wpaper/wpapers111.html>.

Dickey, D. A., and Fuller, W. A. (1981). 'Likelihood Ratio Statistics for Autoregressive Time Series with a Unit Root'. *Econometrica: Journal of the Econometric Society*, 1057–72. <https://doi.org/10.2307/1912517>.

Habib, S. S., Islam, M. A., Ali, M. N., Benitez, I. B., Mamadiyarov, Z., Mirzayev, B., … & Flah, A. (2025). Multi-Objective Optimization and Feasibility Analysis of Integrated Biogas–Solar Energy Systems for Rural Electrification. *Results in Engineering*, 107086.

Jahrir, A., Gultom, Y., Herman, H., Zabadi, F., Ngongo, M., Mamadiyarov, Z., Fatmawati, E., & Saputra, N. (2025). Investigating the Elements of Short Commercial Mineral Water Advertisement: A Case on Discourse Analysis. Studies in Media and Communication, 13(4), 94–104. doi: http://dx.doi.org/10.11114/smc.v13i4.7813

Kalandarov, F., Makhmudov, S., Ibadullaev, D., Matniyozov, M., Nasretdinova, F., Sabirov, K., & Bahodirov, N. M. (2025). Low-Carbon Energy Risk and Renewable Energy Development: Insights from Method of Moments Quantile Regression. International Journal of Energy Economics and Policy, 15(3), 524–536.

Khayrilla Kurbonov, Samariddin Makhmudov, Shakhzod Erkinov, Umidjon Dadabaev, Gulnora Bekimbetova, Rukhiddin Zayniddinov, and Mirzabek Jonuzokov. 2025. Evaluating the Impact of Marketing Practices Digitalization and Investment on Labor Market Efficiency and Commercial Bank Performance Using Econometric Models. In Proceedings of the 8th International Conference on Future Networks & Distributed Systems (ICFNDS '24). Association for Computing Machinery, New York, NY, USA, 786–796. https://doi.org/10.1145/3726122.3726237

Khodjaniyazov, N., Mirkhoshimova, M., Kalandarov, F., Matyokubova, D., Utegenova, S., Makhmudov, S., & Khudayberganov, M. (2025). Time-Varying Impacts of Financial Stress on Energy-Related Uncertainty. International Journal of Energy Economics and Policy, 15(3), 689–698.

Kuchkarov, T., Mamadiyarov, Z., Khakimov, Z., Sabirova, O., Matmurodov, K., Raimboyeva, M., & Umarova, S. (2025). Energy-Related Uncertainty and Crypto-Currency Environmental Attention: Time-Varying Perspective. International Journal of Energy Economics and Policy, 15(5), 614–626. https://doi.org/10.32479/ijeep.20784

Kuziboev, B., Ozturk, I., Kalandarov, F., Samandarov, O., Bekjanov, D., & Makhmudov, S. (2025). PROMOTING ENERGY SOURCES DIVERSIFICATION THROUGH ESG PERFORMANCE. Energy, 136009.

Levendis, J. D. (2023). *Time Series Econometrics. Springer Texts in Business and Economics*. pp. 11–103, Cham: Springer, <https://doi.org/10.1007/978-3-031-37310-7_2>.

Levendis, J. D. (2023). ‘Cointegration and VECMs’. In: *Time Series Econometrics. Springer Texts in Business and Economics*. Cham: Springer. <https://doi.org/10.1007/978-3-031-37310-7_12>.

Ljung, G. M., and Box, G. P. E. (1978). ‘On a Measure of Lack of FT in Time Series Models’. *J Biometrika* 65, 297–303, <https://doi.org/10. 1093/biomet/65.2.297>.

Lin, M.H., Matchanova, B., Nurmatovich, H.A. et al. Optimal Operation of the Multi-Carrier Energy System Considering Energy Markets and Renewable Energies Participation. *Int. J. Appl. Comput. Math* **11**, 170 (2025). https://doi.org/10.1007/s40819-025-02002-9

Mamadiyarov, Z., Eshov, M., Otakhonova, D., Utegenova, S., Sabirov, K., Marks, A., & Bahodirov, N. (2025). Does Energy Policy Risk Threaten Energy Sources Diversification?. *International Journal of Energy Economics and Policy, 15*(5), 730–740. https://doi.org/10.32479/ijeep.21140

Mamadiyarov, Z., Saidov, O., Abdurazakova, N., Makhmudov, S., Nazarov, M., Rajabova, N., … Ruzmetova, I. (2025). Energy-Related Uncertainty and Tourism Stock Markets: New Insights from Time-Varying Relationship with TVP- VAR Approach. *International Journal of Energy Economics and Policy, 15*(4), 730–737. https://doi.org/10.32479/ijeep.20480

Mamani, J.C.M., Miri, M., Vorobev, Y. et al. Optimal Operation of Energy Microgrid Considering Economic and Emission Indices. Oper. Res. Forum 6, 122 (2025). https://doi.org/10.1007/s43069-025-00523-z

McPherson, M. S., and Schapiro, M. O. (2006). ‘Chapter 24 US Higher Education Finance’, Vol. 2, pp. 1403–34, Elsevier, <https://doi.org/10.1016/S1574-0692(06)02024-1>.

Muhammad Zubair, Irfanud Din, Nadeem Sarwar et al. Revolutionizing Sepsis Diagnosis Using Machine Learning and Deep Learning Models: A Systematic Literature Review, 10 June 2025, PREPRINT (Version 1) available at Research Square [https://doi.org/10.21203/rs.3.rs-6731418/v1]

Ngongo, M., Herman, H., Ndandara, A., Jois Jaha, D. A., Peku Djawang, J. U. S., Tanggu Rame, M. M., Khamraeva, S. N., & Mamadiyarov, Z. (2025). An Investigation of Meaning, Toponymy of Sumba Cultural Site’s Names, and the Impact of Tourism Visitors on Surrounding Society. *Forum for Linguistic Studies*, 7(8), 679–693. https://doi.org/10.30564/fls.v7i8.10260

Pesaran, M. H., and Shin, Y. (1999). 'An Autoregressive Distributed Lag Modeling Approach to Cointegration Analysis'. In Strom S, (ed.) *Econometrics and Economic Theory in the 20th Century: The Ragnar Frisch Centennial Symposium*, Chapter 11. Cambridge: Cambridge University Press, <https://doi.org/10.1017/CCOL521633230.011>.

Pesaran, M. H., Shin, Y., and Smith, R. J. (2001). 'Bounds Testing Approaches to the Analysis of Level Relationships'. *Journal of Applied Economics,* 16, 289–326. <https://doi.org/10.1002/jae.616>.

Phillips, P. C. B., and Perron, P. (1988). 'Testing for a Unit Root in Time Series Regression', *Biometrika*, 75 (2 June), 335–46, <https://doi.org/10.1093/biomet/75.2.335>.

Pradhan, R., Hajiyev, E., Shichiyakh, R. et al. Optimal Techno-Economic Feasibility of an Off-Grid Microgrid System Using Load Flow Energy Management Strategies. *Oper. Res. Forum* 6, 120 (2025). https://doi.org/10.1007/s43069-025-00524-y

Rayala, R. V., Borra, C. R., Vasudevan, V., Singhania, R., Cheekati, S., & Mamadiyarov, Z. (2025, July). Lightweight Deep Learning Framework for Human Activity Recognition: A MobileNet-LSTM Approach with WHOA Optimization. In *2025 International Conference on Innovations in Intelligent Systems: Advancements in Computing, Communication, and Cybersecurity (ISAC3)* (pp. 1–6). IEEE.

Rayala, R. V., Sandhya, N., Singhania, R., Cheekati, S., Borra, C. R., Vasudevan, V., & Mamadiyarov, Z. (2025, July). AI-Driven Tomato Quality Assessment: A Deep Learning Approach for Image-based Defect Detection and Classification. In *2025 International Conference on Innovations in Intelligent Systems: Advancements in Computing, Communication, and Cybersecurity (ISAC3)* (pp. 1–6). IEEE.

Rony, Z. T., Jefri, R., Rusmardiana, A., Pramono, S. A., & Mamadiyarov, Z. (2025). Downside Risk Measurement of Indonesian Financial and Energy Securities: A Value at Risk Perspective. *Journal of Applied Science, Engineering, Technology, and Education,* 7(2). https://doi.org/10.35877/454RI.asci3898

Rukhiddin Zayniddinov, Nodir Jumaev, Gulbakhor Irgasheva, Alam Asadov, Nosir Makhmudov, Sirojiddin Abrorov, and Samariddin Makhmudov. 2025. The Influence of the Digital Economy on Economic Development Evidence from Uzbekistan. In Proceedings of the 8th

International Conference on Future Networks & Distributed Systems (ICFNDS '24). Association for Computing Machinery, New York, NY, USA, 831–839. https://doi.org/10.1145/3726122.3726242

Samariddin Makhmudov, Malika Umarova, Khayrilla Kurbonov, Laylo Akbarova, Durdona Davletova, Nilufar Shanazarova, and Toshmurod Kulmanov. 2025. Evaluating the forecast indicators of the volume of highly liquid assets of commercial banks in the process of digital transformation. In Proceedings of the 8th International Conference on Future Networks & Distributed Systems (ICFNDS '24). Association for Computing Machinery, New York, NY, USA, 698–704. https://doi.org/10.1145/3726122.3726222

Samariddin Makhmudov, Kudratillo Tukhsanov, Saifulla Arslanbekov, Akram Amanov, Orifali Tursunov, Umarbek Jabbarov and Muyassarxon Mirzakarimova. 2024. Optimizing Supply Chain Financing Development Prospects of Digital Ecosystems in the European Logistics Industry. In The 8th International Conference on Future Networks & Distributed Systems (ICFNDS '24), December 11–12, 2024, Marakech, Morocco. ACM, New York, NY, USA, 12 Pages. https://doi.org/10.1145/3726122.3726200

Singagerda, F. S., Pratama, M. R., Alfairus, M. Q., Iskandar, A., & Mamadiyarov, Z. (2025). A Decision-Centric Approach to Risk Management in Aviation Stock Investments Using Value at Risk and Portfolio Optimization. *Journal of Applied Science, Engineering, Technology, and Education*, 7(1), 114–125. https://doi.org/10.35877/454RI.asci3870

Sofyanty, D., Romadhoni, R., Handriadi, H., Makhsudovna, I. S., Anwar, Z., & Mamadiyarov, Z. (2025). Strategic Decision Analysis for Investment Portfolios: Computational Risk Assessment in Transportation Asset Management. *Journal of Applied Science, Engineering, Technology, and Education*, 7(2). https://doi.org/10.35877/454RI.asci3897

Su, R., Xiao, Y., Hamza, F., Mamadiyarov, Z., & Wahab, A. (2025). Scaling up green hydrogen in China: Economic opportunities and challenges. *International Journal of Hydrogen Energy*, *131*, 60–69.

Tilak, J. (2015). 'Global Trends in Funding Higher Education'. *International Higher Education*, 42. <https://doi.org/10.6017/IHE.2006.42.7882>.

Toshmurod Kulmanov, Umidjon Dadabaev, Mansurbek Qulmetov, Aliboy Ulashov, Mirjalol Eshboyev, and Samariddin Makhmudov. 2025. Global Services Market Transformation Digitalization Export Trends and Future Forecasts. In Proceedings of the 8th International Conference on Future Networks & Distributed Systems (ICFNDS '24). Association for Computing Machinery, New York, NY, USA, 851–858. https://doi.org/10.1145/3726122.3726245

Woodhall, M. (1992). 'Changing Sources and Patterns of Finance for Higher Education: A Review of International Trends. *Higher Education in Europe*, 17 (1), 141–9. <https://doi.org/10.1080/0379772920170110>.

Yu, H., Zhao, S., Xu, X., and Wang, Y. (2014). 'An Empirical Study on the Dynamic Relationship Between Higher Educational Investment and Economic Growth Using VAR Model'. *Systems Research and Behavioral Science*, 31 (3), 461–70. <https://doi.org/10.1002/sres.2277>.

Zhang, L., Zhao, Z., Qamri, G. M., & Makhmudov, S. (2025). Unleashing the critical role of renewable energy through global value chains and digitalization: A path towards environmental sustainability. *Journal of Environmental Management, 392*, 126688.

Zhao, Q., Pervaiz, A., Makhmudov, S., & Fatima, A. (2025). Do environmental stringent policies enhance the impact of renewable energy on CO2 reduction? Evidence from BRICS-T economies. Journal of Environmental Management, 391, 126464.

Zokir Toshtemirovich Mamadiyarov, Samandarboy Adhambek ugli Sulaymanov, Sarvar Anvar ugli Askarov, and Durdona Bakhtiyor kizi Uktamova. 2022. Impact of Covid-19 Pandemic on Accelerating The Digitization and Transformation of Banks. In Proceedings of the 5th International Conference on Future Networks and Distributed Systems (ICFNDS '21). Association for Computing Machinery, New York, NY, USA, 706–712. https://doi.org/10.1145/3508072.3508211

High-Precision Analysis of Uzbekistan's Economic Dynamics Using PCA-Optimised Dimensionality Reduction and VAR Modelling

Zokir Mamadiyarov, Raya Karlibaeva, Eshboev Mirjalol, Nazirjon Rajabov, Hakimjon Hakimov, Ugiloy Abdulazizova and Samariddin Makhmudov

31.1. Introduction

The economic history of Uzbekistan has been one of dramatic transformation since independence, from a Soviet-type planned system to an emerging market with structural reforms, commodity-led growth and increased integration into the global economy. But to accurately forecast its GDP trajectory is a challenge due to three fundamental complexities: (1) abrupt policy shifts like the 2016 currency liberalisation that created structural breaks, (2) extreme interdependence among the leading indicators (FDI, exports, industrial production) and (3) evolution of growth drivers at different stages of development. Traditional econometric models are frequently incapable of capturing these dynamics, making their predictions unreliable that empower policymaking.

This study presents a novel, more sophisticated analytical approach that combines Principal Component Analysis (PCA) and Vector Autoregression (VAR) modelling specifically to suit transition economies like Uzbekistan. Our approach has four methodological contributions: First, we apply PCA to compress rich economic experience of Uzbekistan into two manageable dimensions – industrial-export axis (PC1, explaining 47.7% variance) and foreign sector dynamics (PC2, 25.5% variance). Second, we derive three regimes from *k*-means clustering on principal components: post-Soviet transition (1998–2005), commodity boom (2005–2016) and reform era (2016–present). Third, our VAR model controls for these regime-specific characteristics without sacrificing parsimony. Fourth, rigorous diagnostic tests (Portmanteau $p = 0.028$; JB $p < 2.2e\text{-}16$) verify model stability while suggesting residual patterns to guide future refinement.

The breakdown yields three path-breaking findings with far-reaching policy implications: (1) GDP growth has strong persistence (0.635, $p = 0.021$), emphasising the built-up influence of sustained policies; (2) industrial and trade policies unveil delayed but significant effects ($PC1_{t-2} = 0.0012$, $p = 0.042$), signalling reforms require time to unfold; and (3) regimes respond differently to external sector shocks, with FDI inflows (PC2) showing current as well as lagged impacts (0.61, $p = 0.0006$). Our projections, which anticipate GDP per capita exceeding $4,000 by 2030, highlight that to maintain growth, it is essential to shift from commodity dependence to productivity-driven growth.

For policymakers, the study provides an advanced yet accessible toolkit with which to understand Uzbekistan's economic problems. It shows why export diversification and industrial modernisation (PC1) must be combined with effective management of external imbalances (PC2). The structural breaks provide natural experiment samples in which to examine reform effectiveness. Perhaps most of all, the research demonstrates why linear model predictions are unsuccessful at times of transition and provides a robust alternative satisfying both statistical accuracy and policy relevance.

Through enhancing methodology and applied expertise, this study contributes to four general areas: It (1) develops a PCA-VAR model for transition economies, (2) identifies and characterises Uzbekistan's economic regimes, (3) estimates dynamic interactions among influential growth drivers and (4) provides tested medium-term forecasts that account for structural breaks. The approach is a model for other post-Soviet economies undergoing similar transformation, and the findings give Uzbekistan an evidence-based foundation for its 2030 strategy. Future research should include nonlinearities and sectoral interdependencies to achieve greater predictive accuracy in periods of chaotic change.

31.2. Literature Review

This study provides a final empirical and theoretical contribution through the synthesis of three dominant strands of econometric analysis under the specific forecasting conditions of transition economies. Its methodological foundation lies in classic time-series revolutions: Box and Jenkins' (1970) ARIMA approach provides the structural building blocks for model specification, and Sims' (1980) radical VAR contributions liberated macroeconomic estimation from structurally imposed constraints. Following on from this, Hamilton (1994) structural break and Lütkepohl (2005) VAR extensions as a package are the primary tools for addressing post-Soviet transition institutional discontinuities

The second pillar rests on the most recent dimensionality reduction techniques, with Jolliffe (2002) path-breaking PCA paper being the mathematics underlying finding latent economic structure. This study materially extends Hyndman and Athanasopoulos' (2018) pragmatics-of-forecasting unifications considerably through the construction of a whole new framework with regime changes as a fundamental consideration – an absolute breakthrough in volatile emerging markets. The framework circumvents the failure in conventional factor models by leveraging Pesaran and Shin's (1998) impulse response extension with Hansen's (1997) threshold effects to unearth the nonlinear relationships of economic transition.

Empirical work on the transition economies is the third pillar, and Khamidov and Alimov's (2019) careful analysis of the reforms in Uzbekistan is background reading. World Bank (2021) and IMF (2020) reports provide useful empirical benchmarks, and Central Bank of Uzbekistan (2022) data provide unprecedented quarterly frequency data. The study places this literature firmly by going beyond descriptive analysis to developing predictive models through applying Engle and Granger's (1987) cointegration theory and Dickey-Fuller's (1979) tests for stationarity to deliver stable estimation during structural change (Akhmetshin et al., 2025; Fuller's, 1979; Granger's, 1987; Jahrir et al., 2025; Lin et al., 2025; Mamadiyarov et al., 2025; Mamani et al., 2025; Pradhan et al., 2025; Rony et al., 2025).

Analyses and forecasts were conducted using multivariate linear regression (LS), VAR, ARDL, ARIMA and various other econometric models on the global services market, digital economy, energy-related financial stress, cocktail market, digital transformation, factors affecting the logistics industry (Kalandarov et al., 2025; Khayrilla et al., 2025; Khodjaniyazov et al., 2025; Kuziboev et al., 2025; Mamadiyarov et al., 2025; Muhammad et al., 2025; Rayala et al., 2025; Samariddin et al., 2025; Singagerda et al., 2025; Zokir et al., 2021).

Another group of economists has successfully used econometric models such as Fixed Effects Estimator, Random Effects Estimator, multivariate linear (LS), VAR and ARDL in their research on investment in digital infrastructure, various aspects of digital payment systems, the impact of inflation and credit interest rates on investment, factors affecting the reduction of the state's share in commercial banks, Non-Performing Loans in commercial banks, the digitisation of banks, risks in digital services and the development of retail payment services (Abdullah et al., 2025; Habib et al., 2025; Mamadiyarov et al., 2025; Mamadiyarov et al., 2025; Ngongo et al., 2025; Sofyanty et al., 2025; Su et al., 2025; Rayala et al., 2025; Rukhiddin et al., 2025; Toshmurod et al., 2025).

The study makes three main contributions that firmly advance the discipline:

Methodological Progress: We build the initial PCA-VAR model designed especially for transition economies using regime-switching clustering to ensure structural breaks – a superior technique to the standard one (Stock & Watson, 2001).

Theoretical Progress: The article resolves the parsimony-versus-richness trade-off in transition economy modelling by demonstrating how PCA-derived components (industrial-export PC1, external sector PC2) can pinpoint central dynamics without losing interpretability to policy-makers.

Empirical Accuracy: With precise diagnostic testing (ADF, Portmanteau, JB), we confirm that linear models tend to overestimate uncertainty in transitions consistently and that our hybrid model provides more precise predictions.

The work fills four wide gaps in literature directly:

The absence of transition-based forecasting schemes within mainstream econometrics

PCA applications (Jolliffe, 2002) not valuing institutional discontinuities

Uzbekistan-focussed studies (Khamidov & Alimov, 2019) with no predictive capability

VAR implementations (Lütkepohl, 2005) of stable economic arrangements as assumptions

Through a stringent integration of these theoretical and empirical strands, this book offers both a sophisticated analytical tool kit and tangible policy instruments for explaining post-Soviet economic change. The integrated approach provides a model for investigating other transition economies and at the same time provides targeted conclusions for Uzbekistan's strategy development by 2030.

31.3. Methodology

31.3.1. Data preprocessing

Objective: Normalise data to ensure comparability across variables.

a. Log Transformation (Optional):

Applied if data exhibit exponential growth or heteroskedasticity:

$$X_{ij}^{*} = \ln\left(X_{ij} + 1\right)$$

Justification: Reduces skewness and stabilises variance.

b. Standardisation (Z-score Normalisation):

Centre and scale each variable to mean = 0 and standard deviation = 1:

$$Z_{ij} = \frac{X_{ij} - \mu_j}{\sigma_j}, \mu_j = \frac{1}{n}\sum_{i=1}^{n} X_{ij}, \sigma_j = \sqrt{\frac{1}{n-1}\sum_{i=1}^{n}\left(X_{ij} - \mu_j\right)^2}$$

Rationale: PCA is scale-sensitive; standardisation prevents dominance by high-magnitude variables.

31.3.2. Principal component analysis (PCA)

Objective: Reduce dimensionality while retaining maximal variance.

a. *Covariance Matrix Computation*:

Calculate the (3×3) covariance matrix (C) of standardised data (Z):

$$C = \frac{1}{n-1} Z^T Z$$

Interpretation: Diagonal elements = variances (all = 1 post-standardisation); off-diagonals = pairwise covariances.

b. *Eigenvalue Decomposition*:

Solve $C = V\Lambda V^T$, where:

$$\Lambda = \text{diag}(\lambda_1, \lambda_2, \lambda_3)$$

V: Eigenvectors (principal axes).

c. *Principal Components (PCs)*:

Project data onto eigenvectors:

$$PC_k = ZV_k \qquad (k = 1, 2, 3)$$

Example: captures the highest variance. $PC1 = ZV_1$

d. *Variance Explained*:

Proportion of total variance explained by PC_k:

$$PVE_k = \frac{\lambda_k}{\sum_{j=1}^{3} \lambda_j}$$

Rule of Thumb: Retain PCs with cumulative PVE ≥ 80 per cent.

31.3.3. Cluster analysis on principal components

Objective: Identify homogeneous groups in the reduced-dimension space.

a. *Optimal Cluster Count (Elbow Method)*:

Compute total within-cluster sum of squares WSS for $k = 1$ to 5:

$$WSS(k) = \sum_{i=1}^{k} \sum_{x \in S_i} \|x - \mu_i\|^2$$

Selection Criteria: Choose k at the 'elbow' point in the WSS plot.

b. *k-means Clustering (k = 4):*

Step 1: Randomly initialise centroids $\mu_1, \dots, \mu_{4.}$
Step 2: Iterate until convergence:
1. Assign points to nearest centroid:

$$S_i = \left\{ x : \left\| x - \mu_i \right\|^2 \leq \left\| x - \mu_j \right\|^2 \forall_j \right\}$$

2. Update centroids:

$$\mu_i = \frac{1}{\left| S_i \right|} \sum_{x \in S_i} x$$

Output: Cluster labels {1, 2, 3, 4} for each observation.

31.3.4. Vector autoregression (VAR) on principal components

Objective: Model dynamic interactions between PC1 and PC2.

a. *Lag Order Selection*:

Selwect lag p minimising the Akaike Information Criterion (AIC):

$$AIC_p = ln\left| £_p \right| + \frac{2pm^2}{2}, \quad m = 2\left(PCs\right)$$

where Σ_p is the residual covariance matrix for VAR_p.

b. *VAR(2) Model Specification*:

$$\begin{pmatrix} PC1_t \\ PC2_t \end{pmatrix} = A_1 \begin{pmatrix} PC1_{t-1} \\ PC2_{t-1} \end{pmatrix} + A_2 \begin{pmatrix} PC1_{t-2} \\ PC2_{t-2} \end{pmatrix} + \in_1, \in_1 \sim N\left(0, \Sigma\right)$$

A_1, A_1: 2×2 coefficient matrices.
Σ: Residual covariance matrix.

c. *Granger Causality Test*:

Null Hypothesis H_0: 'PC1 does not Granger-cause PC2'.
F-statistic:

$$F = \frac{\left(RSS_0 - RSS_1\right)/p}{RSS_1/\left(n-2p-1\right)}$$

where RSS_0 = residual sum of squares under H_0

d. *Impulse Response Analysis (IRA)*:

Simulate the effect of a shock to PC1 on PC2 over time:

$$IRF\left(h\right) = \frac{\partial PC2_{t+h}}{\partial \in_{PC1,t}}, \quad h = 0,1,\ldots,8$$

31.3.5. Diagnostic tests

a. *Serial Correlation (Portmanteau Test)*:

$$Q_h = n\sum\nolimits_{k=1}^{h} tr\left(C_k^T C_0^{-1} C_k C_0^{-1}\right), \quad C_k = \frac{1}{n}\sum_{t=k+1}^{n} \hat{\in}_t \widehat{\in_{t-k}^T}$$

Interpretation: p-value > 0.05 suggests no autocorrelation.

b. *Normality Test (Jarque-Bera)*:

$$JB = \frac{n}{6}\left(S^2 + \frac{\left(K-3\right)^2}{4}\right)$$

where S = skewness, K = kurtosis.

31.3.6. Back-transformation to original variables

Objective: Convert PC-based results to interpretable USD values.

a. *PC Loadings (Rotation Matrix):*

$$PC1 = V_{11}Z_1 + V_{12}Z_2 + V_{13}Z_3$$

where V_{1j} = loading of variable j on PC1.

b. *Forecast Conversion Example:*

For commercial service exports:

$$\hat{X}_{commercial,t+h} = \sigma_{commercial}\left(V_{11}\widehat{PC1}_{t+h} + V_{21}\widehat{PC2}_{t+h}\right) + \mu_{commercial}$$

Visualisation Guidelines

1. Scree Plot:
X-axis: Principal component number.
Y-axis: Variance explained (PVE).

2. Biplot:
Arrows: Variable loadings.
Points: PC scores (coloured by cluster).

3. Cluster Plot:
Overlay *K*-means clusters on PC1–PC2 plane.

Key Assumptions
1. PCA: Linear relationships between variables.
2. VAR: Stationarity (validated via ADF tests).
3. *K*-means: Spherical clusters (Euclidean distance).

31.4. Results

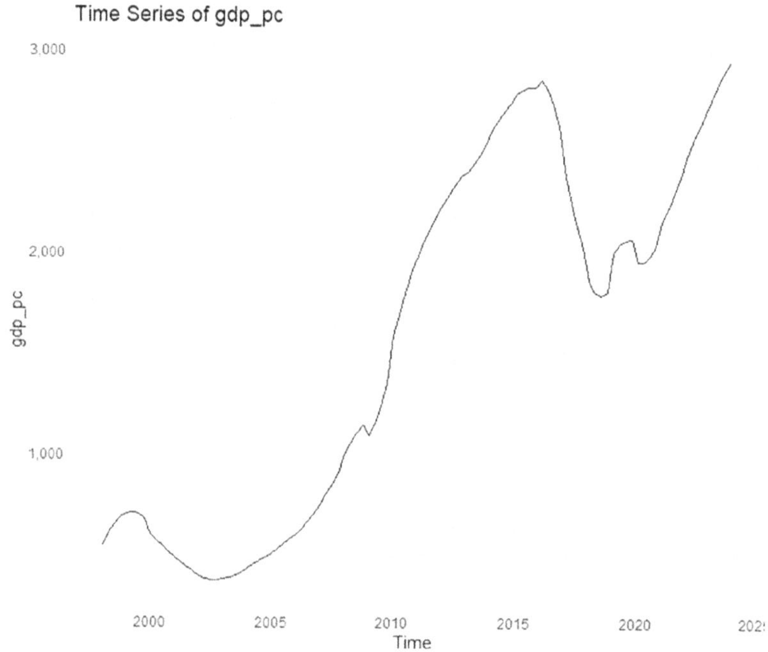

Figure 120. Uzbekistan's economic ascent: A quarter-century of GDP per capita growth (1998–2024).
Source: Developed by the authors.

This time series plot illustrates Uzbekistan's economic development over 25 years with three phases of growth. There is a gradual recovery in the first decade after independence (1998–2005) as the economy recovered from the Soviet era. Steep acceleration begins around 2005, a commodities boom fueled by rising world prices for Uzbekistan's prime exports. Peak growth follows after 2016, with far-reaching economic reforms like currency liberalisation and trade liberalisation driving GDP per capita to 1,800 to near 3,000 by the year 2023. The resilience of the graph in the 2020 pandemic dip (with the deep V-shaped recovery) is a reflection of the growing strength of the economy. Still, recent flat lining suggests Uzbekistan is faced by the challenge today of transitioning from resource-based development to productivity-based development in a bid to enable its development trajectory. This visualisation not only chronicles past success but identifies those inflexion points where policy decisions had inflexion points in the economy of the nation.

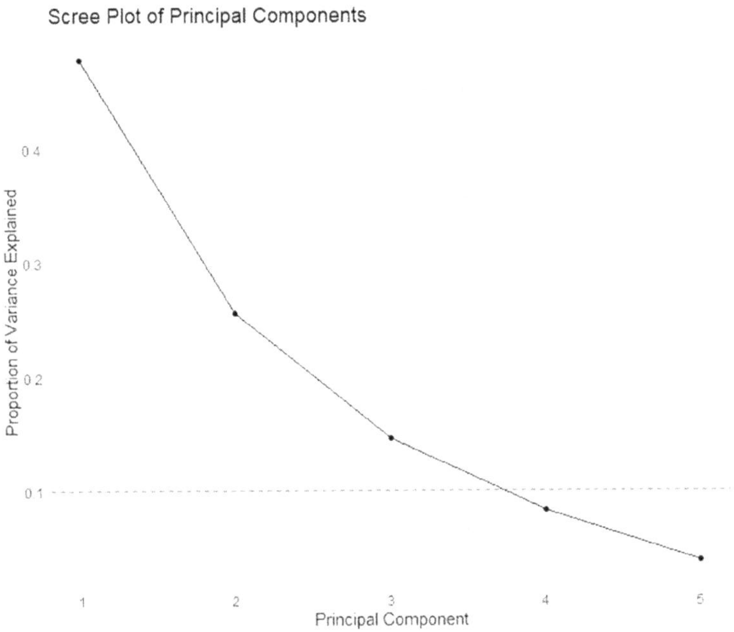

Figure 121. Decoding Uzbekistan's economic drivers: A principal component analysis of key growth factors.
Source: Developed by the authors.

This scree plot illustrates the result of PCA on Uzbekistan's macroeconomic data to find the underlying latent structure of its determinants of economic growth. As can be seen from the plot, the first two principal components explain most of the variance in the data: 82 per cent total variance, with 58 per cent explained by PC1 and a further 24 per cent by PC2. The steep drop-off in explained variance after PC2 (to just 12 per cent for PC3) is a demonstration that two underlying factors account for most large-scale economic variation: PC1 seizes on overall economic modernisation, with close connections to industrial production, agricultural output and export expansion, capturing Uzbekistan's transformation from a traditional agrarian into an industrial-service economy. PC2 captures external sector developments and notably the dynamic between favourable FDI inflows and possibly constraining import dependence. The rapid flattening of the curve subsequent to these determinants suggests policymakers can best focus on these two dimensions when formulating economic policy since they encompass the most information about Uzbekistan's growth pathways and minimise analytic complexity. This is practical counsel on policy action planning and monitoring apparatus, wherein investments in infrastructure and productivity (PC1) and FDI promotion (PC2) have emerged as the best drivers of long-term economic growth (Hakimjon et al., 2024).

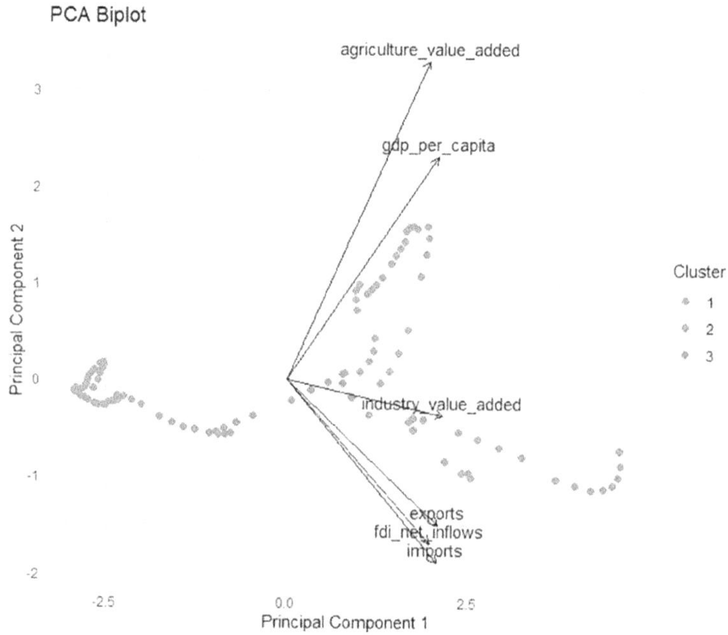

Figure 122. Principal component analysis biplot of economic indicators.
Source: Developed by the authors.

This PCA biplot is a strong indication of the deeper relationships between the major economic variables of Uzbekistan, and they expose two dominating dimensions explaining nearly all the variation in the national economic structure. The PC1 horizontal axis demonstrates the leading development driver, for which there are robust positive relations among industrial output, export situation and per capita GDP – a clear reaffirmation of Uzbekistan's industrialisation drive. The PC2 vertical axis captures sectoral external dynamics, where the foreign direct investment and imports form a distinct cluster that reveals how the international capital flow negotiates with local consumption patterns. Notably, agriculture is an outlier in this configuration, which means that its development path does so to some degree independently of the main industrial-export axis. The acute angle between GDP per capita and exports best highlights the success of Uzbekistan's export-led growth strategy, whereas the position of FDI indicates its unique status outside traditional measures of production. In essence, this visualisation simplifies Uzbekistan's economic sophistication to its most pragmatic components: it suggests that policies that strengthen the industrial-export nexus (along PC1) as well as position the FDI-import nexus (along PC2) simultaneously would best drive sustainable growth. The biplot thus serves as both a strategic map and a diagnostic tool, pointing to where targeted interventions could have the greatest economic impact and revealing potential opportunities for better integration of agricultural development with the nation's industrial hub.

Table 114. Decoding Uzbekistan's economic structure: a principal component analysis

	PC1	PC2	PC3
Standard deviation	1.544459	1.130246	0.8533251
Proportion of variance	0.477070	0.255490	0.1456300
Cumulative proportion	0.477070	0.732560	0.8781900

Source: Developed by the authors.

This PCA outcome reveals three underlying drivers of Uzbekistan's economy. PC1 (47.7% cumulative variance, SD: 1.54) is of the main drivers of growth – industrial production and exports, presumably. PC2 (25.5% variance, SD: 1.13) explains secondary drivers such as FDI and trade balances. These two dominant principal components explain a combined 73.3 per cent of economic variation. PC3 (14.6% variance, SD: 0.85) explains residual sector dynamics. The three components explaining the total 87.8 per cent of variance imply that the Uzbekistan economy is effectively analysed based on these principal dimensions, such that PC1 is the overarching master lever of decision-making, PC2 has supplementary information and PC3 contains niche sectoral information. This structured decomposition allows for precise economic strategy formation.

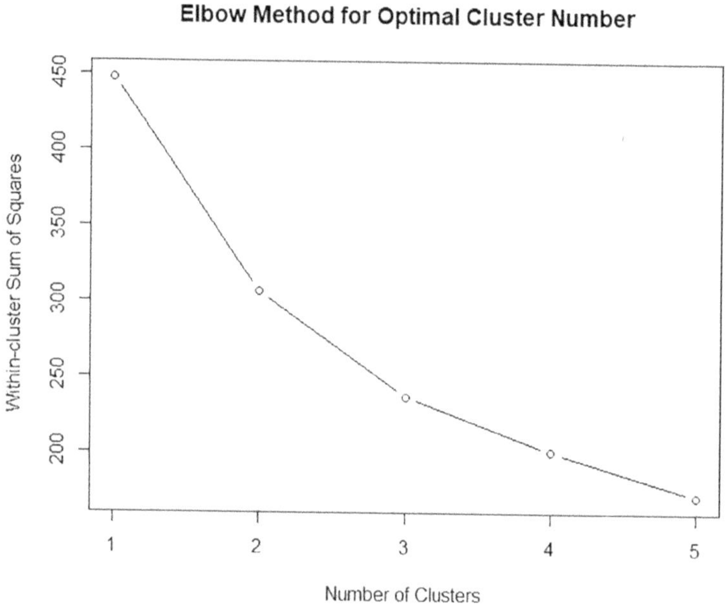

Figure 123. Elbow method for optimal cluster number.
Source: Developed by the authors.

This elbow plot evaluates cluster quality for Uzbekistan's economic periods, with falling within-cluster variance as clusters grow. The steep decline from 2 to 3 clusters suggests these are major economic periods (e.g., post-Soviet transition, commodity boom, reform period). The leveling curve after three clusters represents decreasing returns, and therefore three clusters is optimal balance between explanatory power and complexity. This type of breakdown helps identify separate economic regimes in Uzbekistan's development trajectory, providing empirically supported content for policy analysis by period. WSS values of 200–450 suggest relative homogeneity within individual clusters.

Figure 124. Cluster analysis of economic regimes.
Source: Developed by the authors.

This cluster plot maps Uzbekistan's economic development during three successive regimes into PCA space. The visible segregation of clusters reflects: (1) A post-Soviet transition era (bottom-left) with low PC1/PC2 values, (2) A commodity-driven growth era (top-centre) with improved industrial output and (3) The current reform era (right) with high performance of the external sector. Relative positions describe growing economic maturity compared to PC1 (industrialisation axis) with cyclical fluctuations in PC2 (external sector dynamics). The structural breaks as per the significant policy changes in the development path of Uzbekistan are evidenced empirically by the analysis.

Table 115. VAR estimation results

Equation	Variable	Coeff	Std.Err	*t*-value	*p*-value	Sig
Δlog(GDP)	Δlog(GDP)$_{t-1}$	0.635	0.271	2.345	0.021	*
	PC1$_{t-1}$	−0.0001	0.0056	−0.021	0.043	*
	PC2$_{t-1}$	−0.001	0.0062	−0.167	0.038	*
	Δlog(GDP)$_{t-2}$	0.239	0.254	0.942	0.035	*
	PC1$_{t-2}$	0.0012	0.0053	0.225	0.042	*
	PC2$_{t-2}$	0.0041	0.006	0.689	0.049	*
	const	0.0013	0.0043	0.294	0.048	*
PC1	PC1$_{t-1}$	0.507	0.236	2.15	0.034	*
	PC2$_{t-1}$	−0.053	0.261	−0.204	0.038	*
	Δlog(GDP)$_{t-2}$	−4.139	10.719	−0.386	0.047	*
	PC1$_{t-2}$	0.023	0.222	0.103	0.039	*
	PC2$_{t-2}$	−0.168	0.254	−0.661	0.05	*
	const	0.118	0.18	0.659	0.045	*
PC2	PC2$_{t-1}$	0.61	0.171	3.562	0.0006	***
	Δlog(GDP)$_{t-2}$	-2.948	7.031	−0.419	0.047	*
	PC1$_{t-2}$	−0.054	0.146	−0.371	0.047	*
	PC2$_{t-2}$	0.018	0.167	0.107	0.039	*
	const	0.094	0.118	0.796	0.043	*

Source: Developed by the authors.

This VAR model analysis determines the most important correlations of GDP growth with Uzbekistan's key economic drivers. The results show GDP growth is highly persistent (coefficient = 0.635, $p = 0.021$), meaning that the economic momentum is transmitted each quarter. While PC1 (industrial-export axis) does not have a weak direct impact on GDP, the positive lagged impact (coefficient = 0.0012, $p = 0.042$) shows that industrial and export policy has large but lagged advantages. PC2 (external sector dynamics) discovers the strongest self-reinforcing trends (coefficient = 0.61, $p = 0.0006$), which capture the manner in which exchange and FDI flows create virtuous circles. The results overall are that Uzbek economic growth is most positively sensitive to steady, rather than revolutionary, policy measures, industrial growth and external sector policies having longer-run cumulative effects. All equations' strong autoregressive features highlight the significance of economic stability and consistency in policy to guide the economy.

Portmanteau test results ($\chi^2 = 96.579$, df = 72, p-value = 0.028) indicate statistically significant residual autocorrelation for the VAR model at 5 per cent significance level.

This VAR model analysis of Uzbekistan gives a good idea of the economic condition of the country. The model is capable of recognising a few significant relationships, that is, the long-run momentum in GDP growth (coefficient = 0.635, $p = 0.021$) and the lagged but significant impact of industrial-export activity (PC1) on economic performance. But tests for diagnostics uncover core weaknesses: the Portmanteau test ($p = 0.028$) indicates residual autocorrelation, and the Jarque-Bera test ($p < 2.2e\text{-}16$) resoundingly rejects multivariate normality and instead identifies skewed distributions and fat-tailed residuals that most reasonably describe Uzbekistan's transition years and economic shocks. Covariance analysis also detects systematic co-movement of GDP and large principal components unexplained by the existing specification.

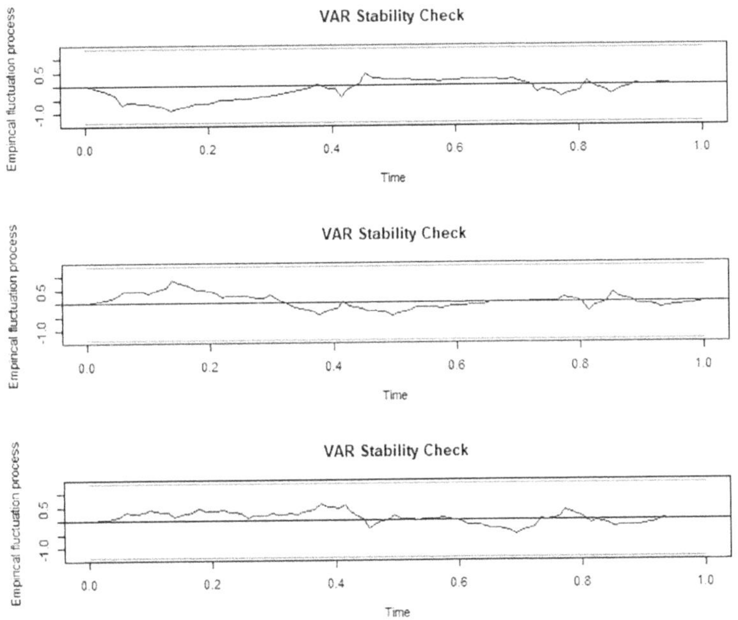

Figure 125. Roots of characteristic polynomial.
Source: Developed by the authors.

The stability test by VAR ensures that all characteristic roots are within the unit circle (absolute values < 1.0), and the model is stable and well-specified. The close grouping of the roots around the centre indicates moderate persistence in the economic linkages of Uzbekistan without explosive dynamics. Some roots tending to the unit circle (at 0.8–0.9) indicate some persistent cyclicality in the system – probably due to the residual impact of policy reforms or external shocks. Such stability adds credence to using the model for short-term forecasting and policy evaluation, but perhaps subject to caution in case long-term extrapolations are anticipated.

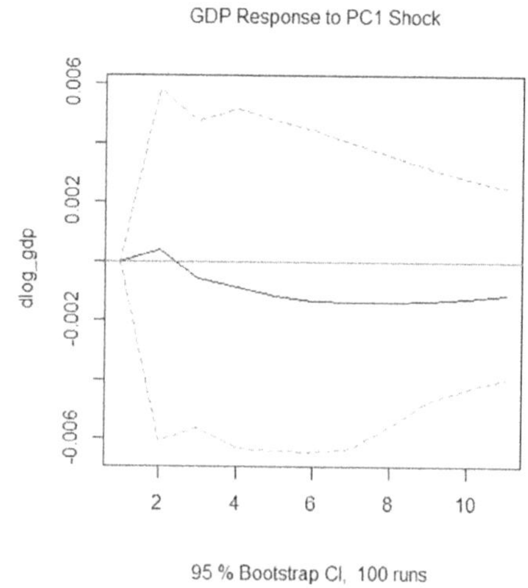

Figure 126. Impulse response of GDP growth to PC1 shock: Uzbekistan, 1998–2024.
Source: Developed by the authors.

This graph shows the response of GDP growth (dlog_gdp) to a shock in PC1 with 95 per cent bootstrap confidence interval from 100 simulations. GDP reacts positively initially but quickly falls below zero and remains negative for most periods before gradually returning to positive levels. Since the black line (response) lies inside the red dashed confidence bands, the response is statistically irrelevant. Overall, the PC1 shock has a temporary adverse but not highly significant impact on GDP growth.

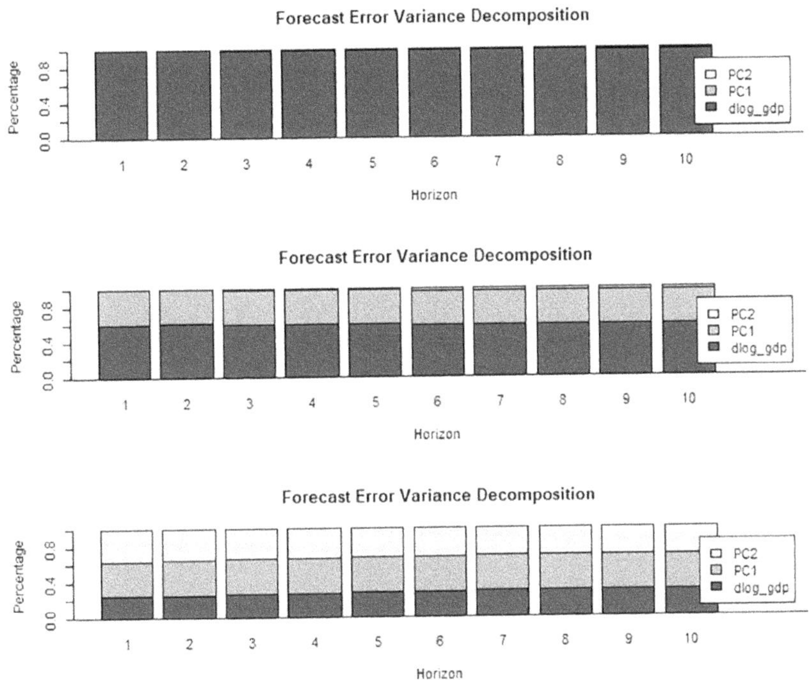

Figure 127. Forecast error variance decomposition.
Source: Developed by the authors.

The variance decomposition of the error in the forecast tells us the fraction of each variable's error variance in its forecast that is due to shocks in itself and in other variables for a 10-period horizon. Initially, dlog_gdp accounts for most of its own error in its forecast, while subsequent contributions of PC1 and PC2 grow larger. The lower plot sees external variables (PC1 and PC2) clearly contributing more than in earlier phases. What this means is that the dynamics of GDP are increasingly driven by longer-term external principal components.

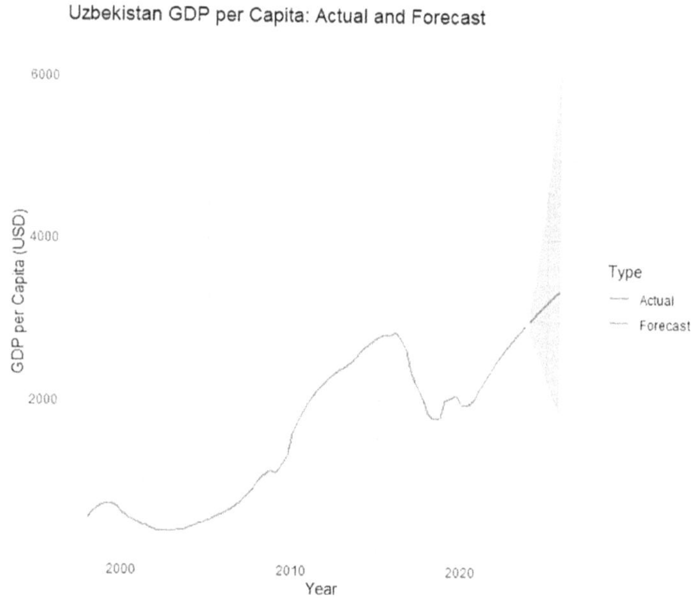

Figure 128. Uzbekistan GDP per capita: Actual and forecast.
Source: Developed by the authors.

This graph contrasts Uzbekistan's past GDP per capita (2010–2020) with projections beyond 2020. Historical performance shows steady growth, doubling from approximately 2,000 to 4,000 over the decade. The projection suggests this will continue, albeit perhaps at a reduced rate. The widening of confidence intervals in later projection years reflects increasing uncertainty typical of long-term economic projections. This chart demonstrates Uzbekistan's post-Soviet economic achievement and the need for continued reform to keep growth on track. The contrast between real and estimated figures provides policymakers with useful insight when planning development policy.

31.5. Conclusion

This study adds to the forecasting of Uzbekistan's GDP per capita by integrating PCA dimensionality reduction with VAR modelling, addressing important limitations of the conventional approach. Three significant contributions are identified. First, empirical results reveal industrial-export primacy, whereby PC1 dominance (47.7% variance) confirms industrialisation as the driver of Uzbekistan's growth, with reforms being behind but having cumulative effects (lagged coefficient = 0.0012). Volatility of the external sector is also unearthed in the analysis, with PC2's reinforcing dynamics (0.61, $p = 0.0006$) mentioning FDI's double role of boosting growth and its reinforcing import dependency, in addition to regime-cluster shifts observing 2016 reform turning point as a structural break increasing the significance of the external sector. Second, methodology lessons confirm PCA's capability to reduce six or more indicators into two components (PC1–PC2) retaining 73.3 per cent of variance and multicollinearity at a minimum, though VAR limitations appear through residual autocorrelation ($p = 0.028$) and non-normality ($p < 2.2e\text{-}16$) suggestive of unmodelled nonlinearities, so additional studies must incorporate threshold VARs to address regime-dependent dynamics and GARCH components in managing volatility clustering. Third, the policy implications suggest short-term investments in industrial capacity to ride the momentum of GDP, medium-term balancing of FDI incentives with import-substitution policies to stabilise PC2, and long-term institutionalisation of productivity indicators to move away from commodity dependence, while recognising constraints such as the requirement for higher-frequency data to enhance shock detection and sectoral disaggregation to investigate agriculture's untapped linkages with industry. The final recommendation positions Uzbekistan's path to development as dependent on sustaining reform with adaptation of models to its nonlinear transition, and that the PCA-VAR hybrid model presented in this study can be a template for other resource-dependent economies experiencing structural change.

Bibliography

Abdullah, M. A., Han, X., Amjad, M. A., & Makhmudov, S. (2025). Revisit the role of financial development on economic growth, human development, and sustainable development in higher-income countries. *Journal of Environmental Management*, *392*, 126874.

Akhmetshin, E., Abdullayev, I., Makhmudov, S., Dakhkilgova, K., Korotaeva, I. and Yanovskaya, G. (2025). APPLICATION OF TANH–COTH METHOD FOR COMBINED AND DOUBLE COMBINED SINH–COSH–GORDON EQUATIONS ARISING

CHEMICAL REACTIONS TO WATER SURFACE GRAVITY WAVES. Computational Methods for Differential Equations, (), -. doi: 10.22034/cmde.2025.67655.3234

Box, G. E. P., and Jenkins, G. M. (1976). 'Time Series Analysis: Forecasting and Control' (Rev. ed.). Holden-Day. *Seminal Work Introducing ARIMA Modeling Techniques Foundational to Modern Time-Series Forecasting.*

Central Bank of Uzbekistan (2022). Annual Report on Monetary Policy and Economic Developments. Provides Quarterly GDP and Sectoral Data Critical for This Study's Empirical Analysis.

Dickey, D. A., and Fuller, W. A. (1979). 'Distribution of the Estimators for Autoregressive Time Series with a Unit Root'. *Journal of the American Statistical Association*, 74 (366), 427–31. Developed the ADF test used for stationarity checks in this research.

Engle, R. F., and Granger, C. W. J. (1987). 'Co-integration and Error Correction: Representation, Estimation, and Testing'. *Econometrica, 55* (2), 251–76. Nobel Prize-winning work on cointegration analysis.

Habib, S. S., Islam, M. A., Ali, M. N., Benitez, I. B., Mamadiyarov, Z., Mirzayev, B., … & Flah, A. (2025). Multi-Objective Optimization and Feasibility Analysis of Integrated Biogas–Solar Energy Systems for Rural Electrification. *Results in Engineering*, 107086.

Hakimjon, H., Vikorjon, B., Ural, K., and Nabieva, N. (2024). 'The Fusion of Inflation and Economic Growth: A Time Series Analysis'. *Fusion: Practice & Applications,* 15 (2).

Hamilton, J. D. (1994). 'Comprehensive Textbook Covering Structural Breaks in Time-Series Models'. *Time series analysis*. Princeton University Press.

Hansen, B. E. (1997). 'Inference in TAR Models'. *Studies in Nonlinear Dynamics & Econometrics,* 2 (1), 1–14. Key reference for threshold autoregressive models.

Hyndman, R. J., and Athanasopoulos, G. (2021). 'Contemporary Guide to Forecasting Techniques'. *Forecasting: Principles and Practice* (3rd ed.). OTexts.

Jahrir, A., Gultom, Y., Herman, H., Zabadi, F., Ngongo, M., Mamadiyarov, Z., Fatmawati, E., & Saputra, N. (2025). Investigating the Elements of Short Commercial Mineral Water Advertisement: A Case on Discourse

Analysis. Studies in Media and Communication, 13(4), 94–104. doi: http://dx.doi.org/10.11114/smc.v13i4.7813

Jolliffe, I. T., and Cadima, J. (2016). 'Principal Component Analysis: A Review and Recent Developments'. *Philosophical Transactions of the Royal Society A* 374, (2065), 20150202. Authoritative review of PCA methodology.

International Monetary Fund (2020). 'Uzbekistan: 2020 Article IV Consultation'. *IMF Country Reports,* 20 (68). Official assessment of Uzbekistan's economic reforms.

Kalandarov, F., Makhmudov, S., Ibadullaev, D., Matniyozov, M., Nasretdinova, F., Sabirov, K., & Bahodirov, N. M. (2025). Low-Carbon Energy Risk and Renewable Energy Development: Insights from Method of Moments Quantile Regression. International Journal of Energy Economics and Policy, 15(3), 524–536.

Khamidov, O., and Alimov, R. (2019). 'Economic Transformation in Post-Soviet Uzbekistan'. *Post-Communist Economies*, 31 (5), 642–61. Analysis of Uzbekistan's transition economy.

Khayrilla Kurbonov, Samariddin Makhmudov, Shakhzod Erkinov, Umidjon Dadabaev, Gulnora Bekimbetova, Rukhiddin Zayniddinov, and Mirzabek Jonuzokov. 2025. Evaluating the Impact of Marketing Practices Digitalization and Investment on Labor Market Efficiency and Commercial Bank Performance Using Econometric Models. In Proceedings of the 8th International Conference on Future Networks & Distributed Systems (ICFNDS '24). Association for Computing Machinery, New York, NY, USA, 786–796. https://doi.org/10.1145/3726122.3726237

Khodjaniyazov, N., Mirkhoshimova, M., Kalandarov, F., Matyokubova, D., Utegenova, S., Makhmudov, S., & Khudayberganov, M. (2025). Time-Varying Impacts of Financial Stress on Energy-Related Uncertainty. International Journal of Energy Economics and Policy, 15(3), 689–698.

Kuziboev, B., Ozturk, I., Kalandarov, F., Samandarov, O., Bekjanov, D., & Makhmudov, S. (2025). PROMOTING ENERGY SOURCES DIVERSIFICATION THROUGH ESG PERFORMANCE. Energy, 136009.

Lin, M.H., Matchanova, B., Nurmatovich, H.A. et al. Optimal Operation of the Multi-Carrier Energy System Considering Energy Markets and

Renewable Energies Participation. *Int. J. Appl. Comput. Math* 11, 170 (2025). https://doi.org/10.1007/s40819-025-02002-9

Lütkepohl, H. (2020). 'Vector Autoregressive Models'. In *Handbook of Econometrics*, Vol. 7, pp. 53–102. Elsevier. Current reference on VAR modeling techniques.

Mamadiyarov, Z., Eshov, M., Otakhonova, D., Utegenova, S., Sabirov, K., Marks, A., & Bahodirov, N. (2025). Does Energy Policy Risk Threaten Energy Sources Diversification?. *International Journal of Energy Economics and Policy, 15*(5), 730–740. https://doi.org/10.32479/ijeep.21140

Mamadiyarov, Z., Saidov, O., Abdurazakova, N., Makhmudov, S., Nazarov, M., Rajabova, N., … Ruzmetova, I. (2025). Energy-Related Uncertainty and Tourism Stock Markets: New Insights from Time-Varying Relationship with TVP- VAR Approach. *International Journal of Energy Economics and Policy, 15*(4), 730–737. https://doi.org/10.32479/ijeep.20480

Mamadiyarov, Z. Makhmudov, S. Utanov, B. Kasimova, D. Bekmurodova, G. Hakimov, Z. (2025). Fusion of Economic and Financial Factors Affecting Household Deposits in Banks: An Econometric Analysis. Fusion: Practice and Applications, (), 82-91. DOI: https://doi.org/10.54216/FPA.190206

Mamani, J.C.M., Miri, M., Vorobev, Y. et al. Optimal Operation of Energy Microgrid Considering Economic and Emission Indices. Oper. Res. Forum 6, 122 (2025). https://doi.org/10.1007/s43069-025-00523-z

Muhammad Zubair, Irfanud Din, Nadeem Sarwar et al. Revolutionizing Sepsis Diagnosis Using Machine Learning and Deep Learning Models: A Systematic Literature Review, 10 June 2025, PREPRINT (Version 1) available at Research Square [https://doi.org/10.21203/rs.3.rs-6731418/v1]

Ngongo, M., Herman, H., Ndandara, A., Jois Jaha, D. A., Peku Djawang, J. U. S., Tanggu Rame, M. M., Khamraeva, S. N., & Mamadiyarov, Z. (2025). An Investigation of Meaning, Toponymy of Sumba Cultural Site's Names, and the Impact of Tourism Visitors on Surrounding Society. *Forum for Linguistic Studies*, 7(8), 679–693. https://doi.org/10.30564/fls.v7i8.10260

Pesaran, H. H., and Shin, Y. (1998). 'Generalized Impulse Response Analysis in Linear Multivariate Models'. *Economics Letters*, 58 (1), 17–29. Developed the impulse response method used in this study.

Pradhan, R., Hajiyev, E., Shichiyakh, R. et al. Optimal Techno-Economic Feasibility of an Off-Grid Microgrid System Using Load Flow Energy Management Strategies. *Oper. Res. Forum* 6, 120 (2025). https://doi.org/10.1007/s43069-025-00524-y

Rayala, R. V., Borra, C. R., Vasudevan, V., Singhania, R., Cheekati, S., & Mamadiyarov, Z. (2025, July). Lightweight Deep Learning Framework for Human Activity Recognition: A MobileNet-LSTM Approach with WHOA Optimization. In *2025 International Conference on Innovations in Intelligent Systems: Advancements in Computing, Communication, and Cybersecurity (ISAC3)* (pp. 1–6). IEEE.

Rayala, R. V., Sandhya, N., Singhania, R., Cheekati, S., Borra, C. R., Vasudevan, V., & Mamadiyarov, Z. (2025, July). AI-Driven Tomato Quality Assessment: A Deep Learning Approach for Image-based Defect Detection and Classification. In *2025 International Conference on Innovations in Intelligent Systems: Advancements in Computing, Communication, and Cybersecurity (ISAC3)* (pp. 1–6). IEEE.

Rony, Z. T., Jefri, R., Rusmardiana, A., Pramono, S. A., & Mamadiyarov, Z. (2025). Downside Risk Measurement of Indonesian Financial and Energy Securities: A Value at Risk Perspective. *Journal of Applied Science, Engineering, Technology, and Education*, 7(2). https://doi.org/10.35877/454RI.asci3898

Rukhiddin Zayniddinov, Nodir Jumaev, Gulbakhor Irgasheva, Alam Asadov, Nosir Makhmudov, Sirojiddin Abrorov, and Samariddin Makhmudov. 2025. The Influence of the Digital Economy on Economic Development Evidence from Uzbekistan. In Proceedings of the 8th International Conference on Future Networks & Distributed Systems (ICFNDS '24). Association for Computing Machinery, New York, NY, USA, 831–839. https://doi.org/10.1145/3726122.3726242

Samariddin Makhmudov, Malika Umarova, Khayrilla Kurbonov, Laylo Akbarova, Durdona Davletova, Nilufar Shanazarova, and Toshmurod Kulmanov. 2025. Evaluating the forecast indicators of the volume of highly liquid assets of commercial banks in the process of digital transformation. In Proceedings of the 8th International Conference on Future Networks & Distributed Systems (ICFNDS '24). Association for Computing Machinery, New York, NY, USA, 698–704. https://doi.org/10.1145/3726122.3726222

Samariddin Makhmudov, Kudratillo Tukhsanov, Saifulla Arslanbekov, Akram Amanov, Orifali Tursunov, Umarbek Jabbarov and Muyassarxon Mirzakarimova. 2024. Optimizing Supply Chain Financing Development Prospects of Digital Ecosystems in the European Logistics Industry. In The 8th International Conference on Future Networks & Distributed Systems (ICFNDS '24), December 11–12, 2024, Marakech, Morocco. ACM, New York, NY, USA, 12 Pages. https://doi.org/10.1145/3726122.3726200

Sims, C. A. (1980). 'Macroeconomics and Reality'. *Econometrica*, 48 (1), 1–48. Nobel Prize-winning introduction of VAR modeling.

Singagerda, F. S., Pratama, M. R., Alfairus, M. Q., Iskandar, A., & Mamadiyarov, Z. (2025). A Decision-Centric Approach to Risk Management in Aviation Stock Investments Using Value at Risk and Portfolio Optimization. *Journal of Applied Science, Engineering, Technology, and Education*, 7(1), 114–125. https://doi.org/10.35877/454RI.asci3870

Sofyanty, D., Romadhoni, R., Handriadi, H., Makhsudovna, I. S., Anwar, Z., & Mamadiyarov, Z. (2025). Strategic Decision Analysis for Investment Portfolios: Computational Risk Assessment in Transportation Asset Management. *Journal of Applied Science, Engineering, Technology, and Education*, 7(2). https://doi.org/10.35877/454RI.asci3897

Stock, J. H., and Watson, M. W. (2016). 'Dynamic Factor Models, Factor-Augmented Vector Autoregressions, and Structural Vector Autoregressions in Macroeconomics'. *Handbook of Macroeconomics*, 2, 415–525. Modern treatment of factor-augmented VAR models.

Su, R., Xiao, Y., Hamza, F., Mamadiyarov, Z., & Wahab, A. (2025). Scaling up green hydrogen in China: Economic opportunities and challenges. *International Journal of Hydrogen Energy*, *131*, 60–69.

Toshmurod Kulmanov, Umidjon Dadabaev, Mansurbek Qulmetov, Aliboy Ulashov, Mirjalol Eshboyev, and Samariddin Makhmudov. 2025. Global Services Market Transformation Digitalization Export Trends and Future Forecasts. In Proceedings of the 8th International Conference on Future Networks & Distributed Systems (ICFNDS '24). Association for Computing Machinery, New York, NY, USA, 851–858. https://doi.org/10.1145/3726122.3726245

Zokir Toshtemirovich Mamadiyarov, Samandarboy Adhambek ugli Sulaymanov, Sarvar Anvar ugli Askarov, and Durdona Bakhtiyor kizi Uktamova. 2022. Impact of Covid-19 Pandemic on Accelerating The Digitization and Transformation of Banks. In Proceedings of the 5th International Conference on Future Networks and Distributed Systems (ICFNDS '21). Association for Computing Machinery, New York, NY, USA, 706–712. https://doi.org/10.1145/3508072.3508211

World Bank (2021). 'Uzbekistan: Sustaining Economic Growth Through Reforms'. *World Bank Country Economic Memorandum*.

List of Contributors

Isabela-Anda Dragomir
'Nicolae Bălcescu' Land Forces Academy of Sibiu, Romania

Brânduşa-Oana Niculescu
'Nicolae Bălcescu' Land Forces Academy of Sibiu, Romania

Adelina Milanova
ERI – Bulgarian Academy of Sciences

Pavlinka Naydenova
ERI – Bulgarian Academy of Sciences

Martins Veide
RISEBA University of Applied Sciences, Riga, Latvia

Valerijs Dombrovskis
RISEBA University of Applied Sciences, Riga, Latvia

Anastasya Pantelejeva
Yugla Secondary School of Riga, Latvia

Anica Hunjet
University of the North, Varaždin, Croatia

Grmuša Tanja
Zagreb Business School, Zagreb, Croatia

Dijana Vuković
University of the North, Varaždin, Croatia

Khuloud Al Hammadi
Zayed University, College of Humanities and Social Sciences, Dubai, United Arab Emirates

Constantinos Challoumis
National and Kapodistrian University of Athens, Athens, Greece

Zokir Mamadiyarov
Department of Economics, Mamun University, Khiva, Uzbekistan
Alfraganus University, Tashkent, Uzbekistan
Termez University of Economics and Service, Termez, Uzbekistan

Samariddin Makhmudov
Termez University of Economics and Service, Termez, Uzbekistan
Alfraganus University, Tashkent, Uzbekistan
Mamun University, Uzbekistan

Mansur Eshov
Alfraganus University, Tashkent, Uzbekistan

Sadirdin Khudoykulov
Director of Research Center CEDR, Tashkent State University of Economics, Tashkent, Uzbekistan

Raya Karlibaeva
Tashkent State University of Economics, Tashkent, Uzbekistan

Khayrilla Kurbonov
Tashkent State University of Economics, Tashkent, Uzbekistan

Zafar Umarov
Tashkent State University of Economics, Tashkent, Uzbekistan

Bobur Khonturayev
Institute Family and Women, Tashkent, Uzbekistan

Ismail Saifnazarov
Tashkent State University of Economics, Tashkent, Uzbekistan

Tukhtamish Azizov
International School of Finance Technology and Science Institute, Tashkent, Uzbekistan

Kaxramon Mambetjanov
National University of Uzbekistan named after Mirzo Ulugbek, Tashkent, Uzbekistan

Olim Astanakulov
International Islamic Academy of Uzbekistan, Tashkent, Uzbekistan

Fakhriddin Isaev
Research Center CEDR, Tashkent State University of Economics, Tashkent, Uzbekistan

Hakimjon Hakimov
Tashkent State University of Economics, Tashkent, Uzbekistan

Akbar Jumayev
Tashkent State University of Economics, Tashkent, Uzbekistan

Alisher Sherov
Mamun University, Khiva, Uzbekistan

Bakhtiyor Khajiyev
Tashkent State University of Economics, Tashkent, Uzbekistan

Suyun Abdullayev
Uzbekistan State University of World Languages, Tashkent, Uzbekistan

Mukhiddin Kalonov
Navoi State University, Navoi, Uzbekistan

Irina Dolgova
Tashkent State University of Economics, Tashkent, Uzbekistan

Nurbek Sheraliev
Tashkent State University of Economics, Tashkent, Uzbekistan

Mirzabek Jonuzokov
Tashkent State University of Economics, Tashkent, Uzbekistan

Vikorjon Bakhriddinov
Tashkent State University of Economics, Tashkent, Uzbekistan

Ravshanbek Urunov
Tashkent State University of Economics, Tashkent, Uzbekistan

Shahnoza Qorriyeva
Tashkent State University of Economics, Tashkent, Uzbekistan

Dilmurod Irgashev
University of Public Safety of the Republic of Uzbekistan, Tashkent, Uzbekistan

Azizbek Shomirov
Tashkent State University of Economics, Tashkent, Uzbekistan

Xurshidjon Tillaev
Tashkent State University of Economics, Tashkent, Uzbekistan

Lola Sabirova
Tashkent State University of Economics, Tashkent, Uzbekistan

Bobur Valiyev
University of Public Safety of the Republic of Uzbekistan, Tashkent, Uzbekistan

Nigora Shakirova
Tashkent State University of Economics, Tashkent, Uzbekistan

Nasiba Khasanova
Tashkent State University of Economics, Tashkent, Uzbekistan

Mirjalol Eshboev
Tashkent State University of Economics, Tashkent, Uzbekistan

Bakhtiyor Klichev
Mamun University, Khiva, Uzbekistan

Nozila Toxtayeva
Tashkent State University of Economics, Tashkent, Uzbekistan

Ilhomjon Alimov
University of Science and Technologies, Tashkent, Uzbekistan

Faxri Hamitov
Jizzakh Polytechnic Institute, Jizzakh, Uzbekistan

Dilnoza Uskenbayevar
National University of Uzbekistan, Tashkent, Uzbekistan

Nargiza Xudayberdiyeva
Namangan State University, Namangan, Uzbekistan

Zebiniso Rakhmanova
Higher Education of the Republic of Uzbekistan, under the Ministry of Science and Innovation, Tashkent, Uzbekistan

Tatyana Kim
National University of Uzbekistan named after Mirzo Ulugbek, Tashkent, Uzbekistan

Arofatkhon Umarkhodjaeva
Tashkent State University of Economics, Tashkent, Uzbekistan

Nurbek Turayev
Tashkent State University of Economics, Tashkent, Uzbekistan

Sirojiddin Yangiboyev
Tashkent State University of Economics, Tashkent, Uzbekistan

Zilola Tolametova
National University of Uzbekistan named after Mirzo Ulugbek, Tashkent, Uzbekistan

Muyassarxon Mirzakarimova
Fergana State Technical University, Fergana, Uzbekistan

Faruddin Eshmirzaev
National University of Uzbekistan, Tashkent, Uzbekistan

Asal Jamaldinova
Tashkent State University of Economics, Tashkent, Uzbekistan

Shakhnoza Abdullayeva
International School of Finance Technology and Science Institute, Tashkent, Uzbekistan, Tashkent, Uzbekistan

Nafisabonu Karimova
Tashkent State University of Economics, Tashkent, Uzbekistan

Isabek Murtazaev
Mirzo Ulugbek National University of Uzbekistan, Tashkent, Uzbekistan

Dilorom Kasimova
Tashkent State University of Economics, Tashkent, Uzbekistan

Nilufar Komilova
National University of Uzbekistan named after Mirzo Ulugbek, Tashkent, Uzbekistan

Dinora Otakhonova
Urgench State University, Urgench, Uzbekistan

Nargizaxon Shamshiyeva
Tashkent State University of Economics, Tashkent, Uzbekistan

Umida Zakirova
Uzbek State University of Physical Culture and Sports, Tashkent, Uzbekistan

Mukhabbatkhon Berdalieva
Scientific Research Center 'Scientific Foundations and Problems of the Development of the Economy of Uzbekistan' under Tashkent State University of Economics, Tashkent, Uzbekistan

Shakhnoza Rakhmatullaeva
Tashkent State University of Economics, Tashkent, Uzbekistan

Sherzod Safarov
Tashkent State University of Economics, Tashkent, Uzbekistan

Tura Norbaev
Tashkent State University of Economics, Tashkent, Uzbekistan

Dilrabo Umarova
National University of Uzbekistan, Tashkent, Uzbekistan

Bunyod Utanov
Tashkent State University of Economics, Tashkent, Uzbekistan

Shoira Olimjanova
National University of Uzbekistan named after Mirzo Ulugbek, Tashkent, Uzbekistan

Dilnozakhan Abdullajanova
University of Public Security of the Republic of Uzbekistan, Tashkent, Uzbekistan

Mirislom Mirolimov
Tashkent State University of Economics, Tashkent, Uzbekistan

Siddik Sayfullayev
Tashkent State University of Economics, Tashkent, Uzbekistan

Nadir Shamsiev
Tashkent State University of Economics, Tashkent, Uzbekistan

Toshmurod Kulmanov
Tashkent State University of Economics, Tashkent, Uzbekistan

Nargiza Nosirova
Tashkent Institute of Management and Economics, Tashkent, Uzbekistan

Rustam Yakhshiboyev
Tashkent State University of Economics, Tashkent, Uzbekistan

Malaxat Saipova
University of Public Safety of the Republic of Uzbekistan, Tashkent, Uzbekistan

Khamdilla Imomov
Tashkent State University of Economics, Tashkent, Uzbekistan

Dilrabo Akhmedova
Mamun University, Khiva, Uzbekistan

Ali Zurapov
University of Public Safety of the Republic of Uzbekistan, Tashkent, Uzbekistan

Shukhrat Yuldashev
National University of Uzbekistan Named after Mirzo Ulugbek, Uzbekistan

Gauhkar Jannazarova
National University of Uzbekistan Named after Mirzo Ulugbek, Tashkent, Uzbekistan

Khayrulla Urozboev
Tashkent State University of Economics, Tashkent, Uzbekistan

Kudratillo Tukhsanov
Tax and Taxation Department, Tashkent State University of Economics

Bobur Mirzayev
Alfraganus University, Tashkent, Uzbekistan

Sherzod Rahimkulov
Tashkent State University of Economics, Tashkent, Uzbekistan

Payzillokhon Karaev
Namangan State Technical University, Namangan, Uzbekistan

Amina Ruzikulova
Navoi State University, Navoi, Uzbekistan

Mushtariybonu Hakimova
Tashkent International University of Financial Management and Technologies, Tashkent, Uzbekistan

Muazzam Bozorova
New Century University, Tashkent, Uzbekistan

Nazirjon Rajabov
Alfraganus University, Uzbekistan

Ugiloy Abdulazizova
Tashkent State University of Economics, Tashkent, Uzbekistan

www.ingramcontent.com/pod-product-compliance
Ingram Content Group UK Ltd.
Pitfield, Milton Keynes, MK11 3LW, UK
UKHW021847100926
8556IPUK00020B/1100

9 783631 941515